Endorsement Statement from Pearson

In order to ensure that this resource offers high-quality support for the associated Pearson qualification, it has been through a review process by the awarding body. This process confirms that this resource fully covers the teaching and learning content of the specification or part of a specification at which it is aimed. It also confirms that it demonstrates an appropriate balance between the development of subject skills, knowledge and understanding, in addition to preparation for assessment.

Endorsement does not cover any guidance on assessment activities or processes (e.g. practice questions or advice on how to answer assessment questions), included in the resource nor does it prescribe any particular approach to the teaching or delivery of a related course.

While the publishers have made every attempt to ensure that advice on the qualification and its assessment is accurate, the official specification and associated assessment guidance materials are the only authoritative source of information and should always be referred to for definitive guidance.

Pearson examiners have not contributed to any sections in this resource relevant to examination papers for which they have responsibility.

Examiners will not use endorsed resources as a source of material for any assessment set by Pearson.

Endorsement of a resource does not mean that the resource is required to achieve this Pearson qualification, nor does it mean that it is the only suitable material available to support the qualification, and any resource lists produced by the awarding body shall include this and other appropriate resources.

ESSENTIALS OF GLOBAL POLITICS

PEARSON EDEXCEL A-LEVEL

Vicki Sutton, Joanna Wilcox,
Laurie Huggett-Wilde

BLOOMSBURY ACADEMIC
LONDON · NEW YORK · OXFORD · NEW DELHI · SYDNEY

BLOOMSBURY ACADEMIC
Bloomsbury Publishing Plc, 50 Bedford Square, London, WC1B 3DP, UK
Bloomsbury Publishing Inc, 1359 Broadway, New York, NY 10018, USA
Bloomsbury Publishing Ireland, 29 Earlsfort Terrace, Dublin 2, D02 AY28, Ireland

BLOOMSBURY, BLOOMSBURY ACADEMIC and the Diana logo
are trademarks of Bloomsbury Publishing Plc

First published in Great Britain 2026

Copyright © Vicki Sutton, Joanna Wilcox, Laurie Huggett-Wilde, 2026

Vicki Sutton, Joanna Wilcox and Laurie Huggett-Wilde have asserted their right under the
Copyright, Designs and Patents Act, 1988, to be identified as Authors of this work.

Cover design: Eleanor Rose
Cover image © gmast3r / Getty Images

All rights reserved. No part of this publication may be: i) reproduced or transmitted in any form, electronic or mechanical, including photocopying, recording or by means of any information storage or retrieval system without prior permission in writing from the publishers; or ii) used or reproduced in any way for the training, development or operation of artificial intelligence (AI) technologies, including generative AI technologies. The rights holders expressly reserve this publication from the text and data mining exception as per Article 4(3) of the Digital Single Market Directive (EU) 2019/790.

Bloomsbury Publishing Plc does not have any control over, or responsibility for, any third-party websites referred to or in this book. All internet addresses given in this book were correct at the time of going to press. The author and publisher regret any inconvenience caused if addresses have changed or sites have ceased to exist, but can accept no responsibility for any such changes.

A catalogue record for this book is available from the British Library.

Library of Congress Cataloging-in-Publication Data

Names: Wilcox, Joanna author | Sutton, Vicki author | Hugget-Wilde, Laurie author
Title: Essentials of global politics : for Edexcel A-level politics / Joanna Wilcox, Vicki Sutton, Laurie Hugget-Wilde.
Description: London ; New York : Bloomsbury Academic, 2026. | Series: Essentials of... for Edexcel A-level politics | Includes bibliographical references and index. | Summary: "Designed to align perfectly with the new Edexcel Politics A-Level specification, this new essential textbook offers students everything they need to succeed in their Global Politics exam in component 3 of the A-level course. It covers all of the core topics in global politics, from the impact of globalisation to the different areas of global governance, and shows students how to apply the relevant IR theories and perspectives to these topics"– Provided by publisher.
Identifiers: LCCN 2025029828 (print) | LCCN 2025029829 (ebook) | ISBN 9781350353572 paperback | ISBN 9781350353565 hardback | ISBN 9781350353541 pdf | ISBN 9781350353558 epub
Subjects: LCSH: World politics–Study and teaching (Secondary)–Great Britain | World politics–Examinations–Study guides | International relations–Study and teaching (Secondary)–Great Britain | International relations–Examinations–Study guides
Classification: LCC JZ1310 .W55 2026 (print) | LCC JZ1310 (ebook) | DDC 327.101076–dc23/eng/20260112
LC record available at https://lccn.loc.gov/2025029828
LC ebook record available at https://lccn.loc.gov/2025029829

ISBN: HB: 978-1-350-35356-5
PB: 978-1-350-35357-2
ePDF: 978-1-350-35354-1
eBook: 978-1-350-35355-8

Series: Essentials of ... for Edexcel A-Level Politics

Typeset by Integra Software Services Pvt. Ltd.
Printed and bound in Great Britain
by Bell & Bain Ltd, Glasgow
For product safety related questions contact productsafety@bloomsbury.com.

To find out more about our authors and books visit
www.bloomsbury.com and sign up for our newsletters.

Brief Contents

1	Comparative Theories	2
2	The State and Globalisation	36
3	Power and Developments	74
4	Political Global Governance	106
5	Economic Global Governance	148
6	Human Rights Global Governance	188
7	Environmental Global Governance	224
8	Analysing and Evaluating Global Governance	260
9	Regionalism and the European Union	292
10	Exam Focus	332
	Index	363

Contents

Specification Table	ix
Key Topic Debates	xii
About the Authors	xiii
Tour of the Book	xiv
Digital Resources	xvi
Acknowledgements	xvii

1 Comparative Theories — 2

The main ideas of realism	4
The main ideas of liberalism	13
Comparative analysis of realism and liberalism	20
Anarchical society and the society of states theory	26
Realist and liberal explanations of developments in global politics post-2000	29

2 The State and Globalisation — 36

The nation-state and state sovereignty	38
What is globalisation?	41
Types of globalisation	43
The impact of globalisation	56
Globalisation and contemporary global issues	59

3 Power and Developments — 74

Power	76
Classification of state power within global politics	84
Polarity	84

4 Political Global Governance — 106

The United Nations (UN)	108
NATO	137

5 Economic Global Governance — 148

Introducing economic global governance — 150
Poverty and development — 154
Economic global governance institutions — 161
Analysing and evaluating economic global governance — 177

6 Human Rights Global Governance — 188

Human rights — 190
International law — 191
Sources of authority in international human rights law — 192
International courts and tribunals — 196

7 Environmental Global Governance — 224

The climate crisis — 226
Competing views on environmental issues — 227
Environmental global governance — 233
International conferences and agreements — 239
Obstacles to meaningful progress on international cooperation — 248

8 Analysing and Evaluating Global Governance — 260

Analysing global governance — 262
Evaluating global governance — 269

9 Regionalism and the European Union — 292

Regionalism — 294
The relationship between regionalism and globalisation — 299
Development of regional organisations excluding the EU — 301
The European Union (EU) — 306
Political integration — 310
Economic integration — 314
Security integration — 316
Federalism and the EU — 318
The process of 'widening' the EU — 320
Is the EU a significant global actor? — 323

10 Exam Focus — 332

The exam — 332
Introduction to the Assessment Objectives (AOs) — 334
Synopticity in global politics — 335
Breadth of questions — 335

Showing balance in your answers	336
Assessment objectives in detail	337
Levels-based mark schemes	345
Section A questions	346
Section B question	348
Section C question	349
Putting it all together	353
Final thought	363
Index	364

Specification Table

Specification	Book Contents
Component III: Global and Comparative Politics	
1 The state and globalisation	
1.1 The state: nation-state and of national sovereignty	Chapter 2 page 38
1.1.1 Characteristics of a nation-state and of national sovereignty	Chapter 2 pages 39–41
1.2 Globalisation	Chapter 2 pages 41–42
1.2.1 The process of globalisation	Chapter 2 pages 43
1.2.2 Its impact on the state system	Chapter 2
1.3 Debates about the impact of globalisation, including its advantages and disadvantages	Chapter 2 pages 55–56
1.4 The ways and extent to which globalisation addresses and resolves contemporary issues, such as poverty, conflict, human rights and the environment	Chapter 2 page 63
2 Global governance: political and economic	
2.1 Political	Chapter 4
2.1.1 The United Nations (UN)	Chapter 4 page 110
2.1.2 North Atlantic Treaty Organisation (NATO)	Chapter 4 page 135
2.2 Economic	Chapter 5
2.2.1 International Monetary Fund (IMF) and the World Bank	Chapter 5 page 156
2.2.3 Significance of how economic global governance deals with the issue of poverty	Chapter 5 pages 156–160
2.3 The ways and extent to which these institutions address and resolve contemporary global issues, such as those involving conflict, poverty, human rights and the environment	Chapter 5 pages 156–179
2.3.1 How the following prevents the IMF and World Bank from effectively addressing and resolving the issues above	Chapter 5 page 171
2.3.2 The role and significance of the global civil society and non-state actors, including non-governmental organisations (NGOs) in addressing and resolving the issues above	Chapter 4, 5, 8
3 Global governance: human rights and environmental	
3.1 Human rights	Chapter 6
3.1.1 Origins and development of international law and institutions	Chapter 6 pages 191–209
3.1.2 The key issues of these institutions in dealing with human rights	Chapter 6 pages 191–209
3.2 Environmental	Chapter 7

3.2.1 The role and significance of the United Nations Framework Convention on Climate Change (UNFCCC)	Chapter 7 pages 238–239
3.3 The ways and extent to which these institutions address and resolve contemporary global issues, such as those involving conflict, poverty, human rights and the environment	Chapters 6 and 7
3.3.1 How the following issues affect international law from effectively addressing and resolving the issues above: -Debate about the effectiveness and implications for state sovereignty and the extent to which international law is accepted and enforced -Performance of the international courts, including controversies	Chapter 6
3.3.2 How the following issues affect global environmental governance from effectively addressing and resolving the issues above: -Competing views about how to tackle environmental issues -Strengths and weaknesses of international agreements -Obstacles to international cooperation and agreement	Chapter 7
3.3.3 The role and significance of the global civil society and non-state actors, including non-governmental organisations (NGOs) in addressing and resolving the issues above	Chapter 6, 7, 8
4 Power and developments	
4.1 Different types of power	Chapter 3 pages 76–80
4.2 Differing significance of states in global affairs and how and why state power is classified	Chapter 3
4.3 Polarity	Chapter 3 pages 84–93
4.4 Different systems of government	Chapter 3 page 93
4.5 Development and spread of: liberal economies, rule of law, democracy	Chapter 3 pages 95–96
4.6 The ways and extent to which the changing relationships and actions of states in relation to power and developments address and resolve contemporary global issues, such as those involving conflict, poverty, human rights and the environment	Chapter 3
5 Regionalism and the EU	
5.1 Regionalism	Chapter 9 page 296
5.1.1 The different forms -Growth of regionalism and regionalism in different forms, including economic, security and political	Chapter 9 pages 297–299
5.1.2 Debates about and the reasons for and significance of regionalism	Chapter 9 page 299
5.2 Development of regional organisations, excluding the EU	Chapter 9 pages 303–304
5.3 Factors that have fostered European integration and the major developments through which this has occurred	Chapter 9 page 308

5.4 Significance of the EU as an international body/global actor, including the constraints and obstacles affecting: -Its political, economic, structural and military influence in global politics	Chapter 9
5.5 The ways and extent to which regionalism addresses and resolves contemporary global issues involving conflict, poverty, human rights and the environment	Chapter 9 page 131
6 Comparative theories	
6.1 Main ideas of realism	Chapter 6 page 192
6.2 Main ideas of liberalism	Chapter 6 page 192
6.3 Divisions between realism and liberalism	Chapter 6 page 193
6.4 Main ideas of the anarchical society and society of states theory	Chapter 6
6.5 An evaluation of the extent to which realism and liberalism explain recent developments (since 2000) in global politics	Chapter 6

Key Topic Debates

Has cultural globalisation led to cultural homogenisation?	55
Does globalisation undermine state sovereignty?	63
Does globalisation increase poverty and inequality?	66
Does globalisation resolve contemporary global issues?	70
Is hard power redundant in global politics?	83
Does the United States remain a global hegemon?	90
Are liberal democracies in decline?	102
Is the use of the veto justifiable?	122
Should the Security Council be reformed?	124
Can the UN effectively resolve conflict, reduce poverty, protect human rights and the environment?	137
Does political global governance fail to maintain peace and security?	144
Is economic global governance effective?	181
Has economic global governance reformed in response to crisis and criticism?	184
Are human rights more effectively protected by humanitarian intervention than by international courts and tribunals?	218
Is environmental global governance effective?	247
Is the slow rate of progress on climate action due primarily to global economic inequalities?	257
Has global civil society had a significant impact on global governance and international law?	277
Has global governance through the United Nations (UN) addressed human rights issues more successfully than environmental concerns?	281
Is global governance reducing poverty but failing to protect the environment?	283
Is global governance more concerned with economic issues rather than human rights issues?	285
Does regionalism protect states from globalisation, or does it promote it?	300
Is the EU federal?	320
Is the EU a significant global actor?	325
Does regionalism undermine state sovereignty?	327
Have regional organisations impacted positively on poverty, conflict, human rights and the environment?	329

About the Authors

VICKI SUTTON is currently a Housemistress and Head of Futures at St Leonards School in St Andrews, Scotland. She has over ten years' experience as a Head of Politics at Charterhouse and St George's College, Weybridge. In addition she has ten years' experience as a Senior Examiner for a large exam board. Global politics is her absolute passion and in addition to her extensive teaching experience she has a PhD in politics specialising in the state recognition practices of the United Kingdom in the Western Balkans.

JOANNA WILCOX has taught social sciences since 2003. Since completing a master's degree in Politics in 2015, she has taught Politics A Level at Brighton Hove and Sussex Sixth Form College. Joanna has co-authored two books for the Extended Project, presented politics revision workshops for Tutor2U, and written numerous articles on contemporary political events for student audiences. Her main interests are global governance, the politics of international development and the European Union.

LAURIE HUGGETT-WILDE is currently Director of Faculty at the College of Richard Collyer, a large Sixth Form College in south-east England. Prior to this he worked at Godalming College as Head of History and Politics for ten years, teaching global, US and British politics. Laurie has also written several articles for *Politics Review* across these topics. His love for global politics led him to complete a Masters in International Relations.

Tour of the Book

Chapter Previews
These give you a broad outline of what each chapter will cover, including a brief overview of ideas or events that will help you to understand the themes of the chapter.

Key Questions and Debates
A list of the key questions and debates addressed by the chapter. This is also a handy revision tool for checking you have understood everything covered within each topic – can you answer these questions after reading the chapter?

Specification Checklists
Useful checklists of the points from the Edexcel specification that will be covered by each chapter. The course and the exam are both built around these specification points.

Spec key term
These highlight and explain the key terms you need to know for a good understanding of global politics. You can find these in the margins.

Chapter Links
References to other sections of the book where important concepts are discussed, helping you to see links between topics.

Definitions
Definitions of the key terms named in the Pearson Edexcel specification. These are important to understand because they can be used in exam questions.

Exam Tips
Key advice on how to do well in specific aspects of your exam, and information about common mistakes or misunderstandings.

Case Studies
These examples illustrate key issues in global politics and enhance your understanding of them. The 'context' section gives you background of the issue, and the 'significance' section explains its meaning and relevance to the wider themes of the topic.

xiv

Tour of the Book

Exam Focus Chapter
A whole chapter devoted to exam skills, with detailed instructions on how to structure your essays and meet key A-Level requirements.

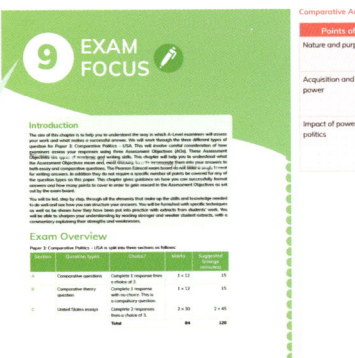

Comparative Analysis
These help you to compare two elements of the course content, or to compare the strengths and weaknesses of one element. These comparisons form the basis of answering 12-mark questions on the exam.

Milestones
A timeline of key events that relate to a specific topic or theme, which will help you to track how specific issues develop over time.

Key Debate Summaries
These summaries of each side of the debate can be used to gain a quick overview or to revise the main ideas. You will find one of these summary tables after each Key Debate.

Key Debates
A great deal of this book is organised around key debates in global politics, which often relate to the questions you could be asked in the exam. Debates typically include three or four areas of focus, with for and against points given for each. This design will help you to structure your essays.

Comparative Theories
These boxes highlight the different theoretical perspectives, such as realist and liberal perspectives, on different issues from the course. You will need to bring theory into your essays for some of the exam components, so these boxes will help you to link your arguments to those of key theorists.

Chapter Summaries
At the end of each chapter there is a bullet-point list summarising the key points covered by the chapter. This is helpful for quickly recapping all of the material covered by that topic.

Exam Style Questions
These questions are in the same style as the ones you will respond to in your exams. You can use them to practise your question interpretation and planning skills, as well as to practise drafting full answers. Not all of the possible exam questions will be included here, but you should get a good indication of the types of questions and topic areas you can expect to come up.

Further Resources
A list of books, articles and websites that will help you to explore the topic further.

Digital Resources

Teachers who use this book gain access to a password-protected selection of resources to enhance teaching and learning. Visit **https://bloomsbury.pub/essentials-of-global-politics** to find:

- **Annotated sample student essays:** Student answers with commentary from the authors, highlighting common strengths and weaknesses. Learn what examiners look for and how they apply assessment objectives. These samples will help you to write strong answers that meet the requirements of the examination board.
- **Interactive flashcards:** Test your understanding of all the key terms found in the book.
- **Critical thinking questions:** Stimulate deeper reflection on major issues in global politics.
- **Bonus case studies:** Gain insights on pivotal events and developments in global politics.
- **Revision guidance:** Expert tips from the authors to help you plan and organize your study effectively.

xvi

Acknowledgements

The publisher and authors wish to thank the organisations and people listed below for permission to reproduce material from their publications.

- Dr Diana Galeeva for Figure 1.4: The Kantian Triangle of Peace
- The Economist Intelligence Unit for Map 3.3: Democracy Index 2024
- European Parliament for Figure 9.2: How do the institutions of the European Union work together?
- The United Nations for Figure 4.6: The Sustainable Development Goals

1 COMPARATIVE THEORIES

Chapter Preview

International relations theories help us understand global politics by offering explanatory lenses. Realism, liberalism and anarchical society theory each provide unique perspectives.

Realism suggests that the most important actors in global politics are states, given that there is no world government to compel states to do anything (hence, global politics is anarchical). States are prone to conflict, which remains the normal state of affairs in global politics. States are deeply suspicious of one another and find cooperation very difficult, since states should only rely on themselves in order to survive in what is a very precarious situation.

Liberalism takes a more optimistic approach than realism. Whilst states remain important actors in their own right, liberalism accepts that there are many actors that make a difference in global politics, ranging from international and regional organisations through to civil society groups such as non-governmental organisations. Combined, all these actors play an important role in creating areas of global governance which guide behaviour in global politics. For liberalism, global politics has the potential to be cooperative and peaceful.

Incorporating aspects of both realism and liberalism, anarchical society theory accepts many of the propositions of each. Like realism, it acknowledges that global politics is indeed anarchical, and yet, like liberalism, accepts that through the multiple and overlapping array of relationships that exist in global politics, states can form a type of 'society' and avoid conflict between one another.

Key Questions and Debates

» What are the differences between realism and liberalism concerning:
  ○ Anarchy and the likelihood of global governance?
  ○ States and the impact of international organisations?
  ○ The inevitability of war and the likelihood of peace?
  ○ The importance of power in global politics?
  ○ Human nature?
» What are the areas of disagreement/agreement between realists and liberals concerning anarchical society and society of states theory?
» Do realism or liberalism best explain developments in global politics since 2000?

Specification Checklist

6.1 Main ideas of realism
» States as key actors in global politics and the balance of power (state sovereignty)
» International anarchy and its implications
» Inevitability of war
» The security dilemma

6.2 Main ideas of liberalism
» The significance of morality and optimism on human nature
» Possibility of harmony and balance
» Likelihood of global governance
» Impact and growth of international organisations

6.3 Divisions between realism and liberalism in relation to:
» Human nature and power
» Order and security and the likelihood of conflict
» Impact of international organisations and the significance of states

6.4 Main ideas of the anarchical society and society of states theory
» Acceptance that there is anarchy in the global system – absence of overarching authority
» States have an informal understanding that ensures a degree of cooperation – based on norms and rules that increase levels of trust and reciprocal behaviour

6.5 An evaluation of the extent to which realism and liberalism explain developments in global politics since 2000

Source: ELYAS /AFP via Getty Images

Component III: Global Politics

> **Exam Tip:**
> Realist and liberal viewpoints will be explored throughout this textbook in relation to different topics.

> **Spec key term**
> **Realism:** A theory of international relations which argues that global politics is characterised by war and conflict. This is because of human nature and the anarchical structure of the international system, which render states stuck in a perpetual game of power politics.

The main ideas of realism

Realism is a theory of international relations which suggests that global politics is characterised by war and conflict. Realists allege that they offer a timeless theory and that states are forever destined to fight. They draw upon a human history rich with examples of destructive wars and conflict, as well as a present where it is never difficult to find evidence of human brutality (see Photo 1.1).

Realists suggest they offer an explanatory theory of global politics that is 'realistic' based on their experience of the world around them. They reject explanations of global politics which are based on moralistic or idealistic thinking and claim to see the world as it really is.

The importance of states

For realists, states are the most important actors in global politics; realism is a state-centric theory. For this reason, realists are sceptical about the significance of international or regional organisations and non-state actors such as non-governmental organisations (e.g. Oxfam). Realists refer to the 'state system' or 'system of states' to describe the fact that global politics is composed of states; in this system, states have the most authority and answer to no higher actor. No other political actor can or should compel states to take actions that they would otherwise not have taken. This is because states are sovereign. In other words, all states have authority within their own borders to make and enforce whatever laws they see fit. This is why realists are not interested in the existence or protection of human rights or democratic rights within states. Neither are realists concerned about the type of government that exists within a state because this is irrelevant to its conduct or behaviour in global politics. According to realists, states behave the same way regardless of what type of state they are.

The importance of power

Realists acknowledge that in practice, states are not equally sovereign. They understand state power as measurable capabilities: military forces and hardware, natural resources and economic output. These capabilities can enhance national security and can be used to coerce other states,

> **Definition**
> **State:** A sovereign power within defined borders. According to the Montevideo Convention (1933), a state has a defined territory, a permanent population, a government and the ability to enter into international relations with other states.
>
> **State-centrism:** The idea that the sovereign state is the most important actor in and the only actor that matters to any explanations of global politics.

Photo 1.1 Myanmar has been embroiled in an internal armed conflict since 1948. This image shows displaced people suffering from the impacts of ongoing war in 2024. Persistent conflicts like this arguably support the realist theory that war is inevitable between and within states.

Source: Thierry Falise/LightRocket via Getty Images

Comparative Theories

for example through military threat or economic sanctions. This is known as **'hard power'**. For example, Russia invaded and occupied eastern Ukraine in 2022. Despite heavy fighting, Russia retained control of these areas. Its greater hard power capabilities allowed it to violate Ukrainian territorial sovereignty.

International anarchy and its implications

All realists agree that the international system is anarchic, meaning that there is no **world government** to compel states to take any particular action. This does not mean that **anarchy** necessarily creates disorder, but it is quite possible. Realists sometimes depict international anarchy using the **Billiard Ball Model**.

In the Billiard Ball Model, each individual state is represented by a billiard ball, which is protected by an outer shell (see Figure 1.1). This outer shell depicts its **sovereignty**. The space in between each billiard ball is empty, and this leaves the billiard balls free to crash into one another. This empty space represents international anarchy; there is nothing to prevent violent collisions between states because there is no higher authority above the state that can stop them. Because each state does not possess the same amount of power, in reality, the billiard balls are not the same size. This means that some collisions are more impactful than others and have greater repercussions on global politics. For example, since its recognition as an independent state in 2011, there have been frequent border clashes between Sudan and South Sudan. The impact of these border clashes is localised; it does not have a significant impact on the state system as a whole. On the other hand, Russia's invasion of Ukraine in February 2022 has had an enormous impact on the state system. Russia has significant power, and the implications of its invasion have not only affected Ukraine but also both states' networks of alliances. Returning to the Billiard Ball Model, the clashes between the 'balls' of Sudan and South Sudan have not affected other balls, but in the case of Russia's invasion of Ukraine, it has affected multiple 'balls' through the sheer force of the impact.

For realists, international anarchy has a number of implications:

1. Global politics is a **self-help** system, and states seek to acquire power to guarantee their **survival**.
2. States will sometimes seek to alter the **balance of power** in their favour to help ensure their survival.
3. States struggle to **cooperate**, especially to submit to higher sources of authority such as regional or international organisations.

We will now explore each of these implications of international anarchy.

Figure 1.1 The Billiard Ball Model

Source: iStock.com/babushka_p90

> **Definition**
> **Anarchy:** The idea that there is no world government and therefore no higher authority above the state.
>
> **Billiard Ball Model:** A model used by realists to show how war is probably under international anarchy.

> **Spec key term**
> **Hard power:** The ability of one actor (usually, but not necessarily, a state) to influence another through the use of threats or rewards, typically involving military or economic actions.
>
> **World government:** The idea of a common political authority with legislative and executive power over states.
>
> **Sovereignty:** Absolute and unlimited power and authority.

> **Exam Tip:** 'International anarchy' in global politics is different from 'anarchy' as studied in non-core political ideas, which is the idea that a society should be organised without a state government. International anarchy is organised entirely around sovereign states, with no power above them.

1 A self-help system

For realists, states all behave in identical ways; they are **egotistical**, and each state will pursue their **national interests**. According to realists, the primary goal of all states is to survive under international anarchy, which is a space of great uncertainty, fear and distrust because each state prioritises its own national interest to survive above the interests of other states. To do this, states must acquire hard power, such as by increasing the size of their armies and the quantity and sophistication of their military equipment. This relentless, competitive pursuit and acquisition of hard power is what realists term '**power politics**'. A consequence of international anarchy is that the states system is a self-help system, meaning that states can only rely on their own efforts to guarantee their survival and security. A state can only rely upon its own efforts to guarantee its own security. Realist theorist John Mearsheimer famously suggested that there is no global 911 (999) for states to call when their survival is threatened. He argues that 'in international politics, God helps those who help themselves', illustrating the importance of self-help.

States are inherently distrusting of other states and struggle to cooperate, especially over matters of security. This is because power in global politics is said to be **zero-sum**. Zero-sum means that power is finite, and by one state gaining power, another state is somewhere losing its power. In this sense, realists are concerned about **relative gains**. In order to cooperate, a state must be certain that it is benefiting more from cooperation than the state with whom it is cooperating. Hence, it must end up 'relatively' better off than the other state.

2 The balance of power

A further implication of international anarchy for realists is the **balance of power** (see Photo 1.3). This refers to the distribution of power in the international system. The dangers inherent under international anarchy lead states to invest in hard power resources to increase their overall chances of survival. Whilst realists accept that it is unwise to rely on other states for their security, they accept that it is sometimes necessary, especially for states which do not have access to lots of hard power. As a policy, the balance of power refers to efforts by states to actively increase their chances of survival vis-à-vis other states. States can do this by entering into **alliances** with other states.

Such behaviours were seen during the Cold War where the majority of states (with the exception of the Non-Aligned Movement) bandwagoned with either the United States or the Soviet Union, which were each attempting to balance the power of the other; this system of alliances created a **bipolar** balance of power because power in global politics was balanced between two rival poles. Realists are keen to emphasise that such alliances are only ever temporary at best, since states make calculations based on present circumstances as opposed to developing enduring relationships between one another based upon shared values or ideas.

States have two options when choosing who to enter into alliances with:

1. **Balancing** – some states might seek to balance the power of a rival state by forming alliances with a coalition of other states. See case study on the *Shanghai Cooperation Organisation*.
2. **Bandwagoning** – some states, especially those that are less powerful, may choose to bandwagon with a more powerful state, which may offer the weaker state protection in the form of a security umbrella. This has typically been seen in relation to nuclear weapons, with the United States offering protection under its nuclear umbrella to states in return for them forgoing their own development and acquisition of such weapons. The North Atlantic Treaty Organisation (NATO) represents an example of bandwagoning where the majority of members receive the protection of all its members, including the United States, in the event a member state is attacked.

The balance of power can also refer to the **polarity** of the international system. Realists undoubtedly prefer either a bipolar or **unipolar** system. In a bipolar system, the implications of international anarchy are easier to manage, since one pole only has the other pole to monitor. In such instances, survival is normally guaranteed through the idea of **mutually assured destruction**. In a unipolar system, one dominant power (the hegemon) is so strong that no other state can realistically challenge it, leading to a degree of stability and order which is enforced by the **hegemon**. In contrast, realists are fearful of the implications of multipolarity. This is because there are too many sources of power for states to monitor, and in such a system, it is far easier to make miscalculations. For further discussion of the balance of power, see Chapter 4.

Definition

Egoism: Or selfish behaviour whereby human beings and states prioritise their own interests above all others.

National interest: Refers to a state's strategic goals, often focused on survival. Realists believe that states will seek to achieve this through military and economic strength while liberals promote the national interest by emphasisng shared values like democracy and human rights.'

Power politics: The competitive pursuit and acquisition of power in global politics.

Zero-sum: When gains for one actor result in a loss for another.

Relative gains: States must gain more from cooperation than any other state. Realists are concerned about relative gains because they view power in global politics as zero-sum.

3 Cooperation in regional or international organisations

A final consequence of international anarchy for realists is that they are very sceptical about the possibilities for enduring cooperation in regional or international organisations. Because states are concerned about relative gains, cooperation is extremely difficult. However, realists do concede that cooperation can take place on a limited or temporary basis. This is usually because it enhances their overall security and chances of survival, or it is a low-stakes issue that does not threaten a state's overall power. By joining NATO, its member states increase their overall security. This is because Article 5 provides for collective security, whereby if a member state is attacked by a non-member state, NATO members are obliged to offer support. In this sense, the least powerful members of NATO are bandwagoning with its strongest members. In the case of NATO, European members have serious concerns about the willingness of the USA to to trigger Article 5 if Russia extends its military operations beyond Ukraine (see **Case Study: The Iran Nuclear Deal**). This example illustrates why, for realists, cooperation can never be relied upon as a replacement for self-help.

For realists, cooperation is at best limited because there is always the strong likelihood that states will break their agreements, and so they must always be prepared for this possibility. Realists sometimes draw upon **game theory**, in particular the Prisoner's Dilemma, to explain the fragility of cooperation. The Prisoner's Dilemma identifies why two states might be unable to cooperate on a given issue, even if it appears to be in their collective interests to do so. Imagine the scenario that State A and State B are looking to reach an agreement to avoid developing nuclear weapon (see Table 1.1). If both State A and State B cooperate, then both states will ensure their survival because neither risks being attacked by the other. If both State A and State B defect and develop the new weapon, while neither gains a decisive advantage over the other, the overall security environment deteriorates. An arms race ensues, resources are diverted, and the heightened risk of accidental escalation or miscalculation makes this a less desirable outcome than mutual cooperation, even if it avoids immediate vulnerability for either. However, if one state cooperates and the other defects, the state which cooperates is at a significant disadvantage to the state that defects, therefore threatening its survival. In game theory, regardless of what the other

Photo 1.2 This poster, by Polish artist Roman Cieslewicz, was published by the French left-wing magazine *Opus International* during the Cold War in 1968. It shows the United States and the Soviet Union (CCCP) as twin superheroes.

Source: David Pollack/Corbis Historical via Getty Images

> **Definition**
>
> **Balance of power:** The distribution of power in the international system. Realists distinguish between the balance of power as a policy and a consequence of anarchy. Depending on the number of dominant states in the system, the balance of power may be unipolar, bipolar or multipolar. See chapter 3: Power and Developments.
>
> **Alliance:** A treaty or agreement between two or more states agreeing to cooperate on issues of shared concern, such as security.
>
> **Polarity:** Refers to the distribution of power in the international system.
>
> **Bipolar:** A system where power is distributed across two dominant states.
>
> **Unipolar:** A system where there is one preponderant power or hegemon.

CASE STUDY: THE SHANGHAI COOPERATION ORGANISATION – AN EXERCISE IN BALANCING AND BANDWAGONING?

Context

In June 2001, the Shanghai Cooperation Organisation (SCO) was formed by Russia, China, the Kyrgyz Republic, Kazakhstan, Tajikistan and Uzbekistan. It is a permanent intergovernmental organisation which is headquartered in Beijing, China. The SCO has since expanded to include four additional new permanent members, including India (2017), Pakistan (2017), Iran (2023) and Belarus (2024). In addition to its permanent members, it has a number of observer states and dialogue states (which include Myanmar, Saudi Arabia and Turkey). It is not a collective security organisation like NATO, but it has at its core an aim to cooperate in a multitude of spheres, including military cooperation, intelligence-sharing, counterterrorism, tourism and trade, to mention just a few. The members of the SCO regularly participate in joint military exercises or so-called 'war-games' in their peace mission exercises. The SCO covers 40 per cent of the world's population and accounts for approximately 32 per cent of global GDP (gross domestic product).

Whilst some of the member states of the SCO (most notably former Soviet Republics) are keen to avoid confrontation with Western institutions such as NATO, for Russia and China, the SCO's formation and expansion are increasingly being viewed as a strategic balancing effort to counter Western influence in its geographical spheres of influence and globally. Russian President Vladimir Putin claimed in 2024 that the SCO is a pillar of a new **multipolar** world order and views it as a source of global stability.

The SCO was recently legitimised as a credible intergovernmental organisation when, in September 2023, the UN General Assembly agreed to set up a cooperation agreement between the two institutions.

Significance

The SCO is seen by many as an attempt by its members to balance the power of the United States and its allies, and to contribute towards arguments that global politics is no longer unipolar or dominated by a US hegemony. The reaction of NATO and some Western states to the organisation would indicate that they too view this as an organisation which rivals their own power. The 2023 General Assembly resolution was voted against by the United States, and a number of its NATO allies abstained, including the United Kingdom and all European Union (EU) member states.

While the SCO is often interpreted as a balancing organisation against US hegemony, for some states, it also represents an attempt to bandwagon, aligning with powerful non-Western poles for security or influence. It is interesting that Saudi Arabia applied for a Dialogue Partnership, given that its long-standing rival, Iran, is a permanent member of the SCO. This could well reflect Saudi attempts to protect its own position by bandwagoning with a non-Western bloc during a period of global power shifts as we arguably move from unipolarity to multipolarity. Some commentators suggest that Iran and Turkey have used their relationship with the SCO to signal to the United States and its European allies that they have alternative options. Whilst Turkey is itself a member of NATO, it is increasingly enjoying closer military, political and economic ties to Russia, and having all but abandoned its former ambition to join the EU, is now looking to carve out influence elsewhere. For Iran, increasingly under pressure from US and European sanctions since pulling out of the 2015 Iran Nuclear Deal, it is a way of signalling it is not internationally isolated. India plays a more interesting role within the SCO, since it does not enjoy friendly relations with China because of tension and conflict along their shared borders, but does enjoy strong relations with Russia, with both states cooperating in areas such as defence. However, India has also been traditionally more keen to court the attention of Western states. India may well play a crucial role in the balance of power in future years.

state does, defection is always the most rational choice for a state concerned about maximising its own security and chances of survival. This grim logic, characteristic of realist thought, is rooted in international anarchy, where self-help is paramount and trust is a dangerous luxury. The Prisoner's Dilemma explains why Israel was concerned about the 2015 Iran Nuclear Deal (see **Case Study: The Iran Nuclear Deal**).

Table 1.1 A Payoff Matrix for the Security Dilemma in International Relations

	State A Cooperates (Does NOT build a new weapon)	State B Defects (Does build a new weapon)
State A Cooperates (Does NOT build a new weapon)	Both: Secure, stable (2,2) Both states benefit equally from cooperation. Although defection is always possible at a later point in time.	State A: Vulnerable (0,3) State B is at a significant advantage to State A, increasing its overall security and reducing the security of State A.
State A Defects (Does build a new weapon)	State A: Advantage (3,0) State A is at a significant advantage compared to State B, increasing its overall security and reducing the security of State B.	Both: Insecure, Arms Race (1,1) Both states do not benefit from cooperation. Neither is at a disadvantage in relation to the other.

Key

Numerical Value	Description
3	Best Outcome (exploit other)
2	Second-Best Outcome (mutual cooperation)
1	Third-Best Outcome (mutual defection/arms race)
0	Worst Outcome (being exploited)

> **Definition**
>
> **Hegemon:** An unchallenged superpvower, which exists without competitors in the international system.
>
> **Multipolar:** A system where power is distributed across multiple sources.
>
> **Mutually Assured Destruction (MAD):** A defence strategy, where two nuclear states know that a nuclear attack will trigger immediate retaliation, resulting in total annihilation of both sides. MAD makes war irrational. It creates stability through fear of the consequences of war.

Whilst realists agree about the existence of international anarchy and some of its implications, they disagree about whether international anarchy is a cause of war in global politics: See the Security Dilemma, page 12–13.

The inevitability of war

Most realists agree that war is inevitable in global politics. Consequently, all realists support the idea that the key goal of states should be the acquisition of hard power in order to survive under international anarchy. However, realists disagree among themselves on the question of **why** war is inevitable. **Classical realists** argue that war is inevitable because of human nature. They argue that because human nature is competitive and selfish, states will behave in the same way, and this will lead to war between them. For **neo-realists** (sometimes known as **structural realists**), they argue that war is inevitable due to the logic of international anarchy. For neo-realists, this means the dangers of existing under international anarchy compel states to fight wars against each other.

Human nature and the inevitability of war

Realism, especially in its classical form, posits a profoundly pessimistic and sceptical view of human nature, arguing that human beings are inherently egotistical, selfish, competitive and power-seeking. Human beings are driven by *animus dominandi* (a lust for power). Human beings are incapable of altruistic behaviour. If human beings engage in moral behaviour, realists contend it is ultimately driven by self-interest and calculated for personal benefit. For realists, human nature is biologically fixed and is not affected by nurture. It is immutable and universal, meaning it is fixed and unchangeable

Classical realists contend that this inherent human predisposition towards self-interest, fear and a desire for power explains why war is an inevitable feature of international relations; in other words, human nature is the root cause of war. They draw upon a long and ancient tradition of thought, evident in the writings of figures such as Thucydides, Machiavelli and Hobbes, to underpin this argument. Importantly, these thinkers would not claim to be 'realist' thinkers. This is because they were writing many centuries before the international relations theory of realism was developed after the First World War.

- Greek Historian Thucydides (c. 431–404 BCE), writing about the Peloponnesian War which took place in the fifth century BCE, argued that human beings were motivated by their desire for 'fear, self-interest and honour'. In a famous encounter between the Athenians and the islanders of Melos, the Athenians urged the Melians to surrender or else the men would be killed and the women and children taken for slaves, arguing that 'The strong do as they will, and the weak suffer what they must.'
- Italian Philosopher Niccolò Machiavelli (1469–1527), in his book *The Prince*, had an extremely negative view of what he saw as the changeless nature of humans. He famously described human beings as being 'insatiable, arrogant, crafty and shifting, and above all else malignant, iniquitous, violent and savage'. Consequently, his advice was to rule with cunning, cruelty and manipulation where the circumstances required it.
- English Philosopher Thomas Hobbes (1588–1679), in his book *Leviathan*, examined the period of the English Civil War in the seventeenth century. Hobbes likened the Civil War to a 'state of nature', referring to a society with no political authority; the state of nature therefore resembled human beings in their 'natural' state prior to the emergence of the state. Hobbes argued that life in the so-called state of nature would be 'solitary, poor, nasty, brutish and short' because life would represent 'the war of all against all'. This was because there would be no greater power to prevent human violence.

Classical realists would explain contemporary events in global politics based on their views of human nature. For example, they would argue that Russian President Vladimir Putin decided to invade Ukraine in February 2022 because his actions were rooted in the inherent human desire for power, personal glory and dominance. They would see this as a manifestation of the animus dominandi, where Putin sought to expand his influence and punish the Ukrainian people for seeking a closer relationship with NATO and the European Union, which he perceived as a challenge to Russia's traditional sphere of influence and his own authority.

Classical realists believe war is inevitable because states are led by people, and human nature is fundamentally flawed. States are prone to competition and conflict just as individuals are, so the brutal anarchy of Hobbes' state of nature can also be seen at the international level. Classical realist Hans Morgenthau (1948) summarised this idea as 'the social world [is] but a projection of human nature onto the collective plain'.

Anarchy and the inevitability of war

The importance of human nature for the inevitability of war is contested by **neo-realists** (sometimes known as structural realists), most notably Kenneth Waltz (1979). For neo-realists, war is a direct consequence of international anarchy, which compels states to prioritise their survival through self-help, leading to security dilemmas and potential war. Therefore, international anarchy is a cause of war. For neo-realists, there are two key consequences of international anarchy. First, there is no higher authority to mediate conflict between states, and therefore disputes can quickly escalate into armed conflict. Second, states cannot rely on other states to come to their assistance if they are under attack because it is a self-help system.

Because of the risks presented by international anarchy, states rely on their own efforts to accumulate power. For Kenneth Waltz, it is the consequences of the unequal distribution of power under international anarchy that are responsible for war. Whilst all states are sovereign, they do not have equal amounts of power, which can be sought for defence or for aggressive expansion. Because it is a self-help system, each state must ensure its own survival by ensuring it has enough

Exam Tip:
The specification does not differentiate between classical and neo-realism, and so you cannot be penalised if you choose not to use this distinction in your essays. The two subsets of realism present a useful point of distinction to analyse realist views and can help when structuring your answers.

CASE STUDY: THE IRAN NUCLEAR DEAL

Context

The relationship between Iran and the United States (and its Western allies) was fractured following the 1979 Iranian Revolution, which saw damaging sanctions placed upon the new Iranian regime, costing it billions of dollars. Iran signed the Non-Proliferation Treaty (NPT) in 1968, agreeing to refrain from acquiring nuclear weapons. However, since then, it has been repeatedly accused of non-compliance. It has been accused of failing to cooperate with the International Atomic Energy Agency (IAEA), a condition of the NPT. It has also conducted undisclosed nuclear activities, with experts suggesting it has been seeking to develop its own nuclear weapons. Consequently, Iran has continued to be subject to international sanctions.

In 2015, the European Union and the UN Security Council (UNSC) Permanent Five member states were able to secure a deal with Iran. In this deal, Iran agreed to: (1) allow the IAEA inspectors to inspect its nuclear facilities; (2) reduce its enrichment of uranium grade to 3.67 per cent for energy purposes only (weapons-grade uranium is 90 per cent); and (3) give up 98 per cent of its enriched uranium supplies. In return, all sanctions on the Iranian regime would be lifted, and over $100 billion of assets would be unfrozen. Reactions to the deal were mixed. Upon becoming president in 2016, Donald Trump remained suspicious of Iran, with his former national security adviser, John Bolton, famously saying that Iran would 'lie, cheat and deceive'.

Despite Iran abiding by the terms of the deal, in May 2018, the United States abandoned the deal and reinstated full sanctions on Iran. The EU, while initially seeking to preserve the deal, later prevented the expiration of certain nuclear-related sanctions due to sunset in October 2023, effectively maintaining them given Iran's non-compliance. By doing this, the United States hoped to place pressure on the Iranian regime to halt its support of regional conflicts and development of ballistic missiles.

From 2019, the Iranian regime itself began to break the terms of the deal by enriching uranium grade beyond the 3.67 per cent agreed to 60 per cent (as of 2024). It has also restricted access to IAEA inspectors, who have now claimed that they are unable to verify that Iran's nuclear programme is exclusively peaceful.

Significance

The failure of the Iran Nuclear Deal is evidence of the difficulties in state-to-state cooperation highlighted by realism. First, the failure of the deal highlights the fact that defection from agreements helps increase overall security. Under its president, Donald Trump, the United States was not willing to risk Iranian defection whilst it chose the path of cooperation. Paradoxically, this decision ultimately led to the Iranian's breaking the terms of the deal, hence increasing the insecurity faced by all parties to the agreement. Realists emphasise that under international anarchy, cooperation is difficult because states are concerned about relative gains, and ultimately, the United States felt that it did not gain from the agreement and following the imposition of sanctions, the Iranian regime, too, felt that it did not gain from the agreement. Second, the failure of the nuclear deal shows the difficulties in enforcing international treaties and enforcing compliance. Neither the United States was obliged to continue its support of the agreement, nor was the Iranian regime obliged to continue upholding the agreement following the US decision to abandon it. Finally, it shows that the position of the dominant or hegemonic power is crucial in upholding international agreements. Despite EU support for the deal, Iran's distrust of the United States and fears for its own security meant that it was not willing to continue refraining from developing its nuclear weapons programme to secure themselves.

power. Because states are concerned about relative gains, they will constantly monitor and survey the military power of other states. This is incredibly difficult to ascertain, given that states both exaggerate and under exaggerate their power. Therefore, it is unclear how much power a state will need in order to survive under international anarchy. In some cases, states want to actively extend their power, not simply to survive, but to thrive by becoming the dominant power. The question of how much power a state should have is one that neo-realists disagree with. For **offensive neo-realists** such as John Mearsheimer (2001), states are 'power maximisers' and will seek the maximum amount of power possible. This is because, for offensive neo-realists, all states aspire to become a **hegemonic** power; therefore, survival is synonymous with hegemony. Consequently, for offensive

> **Exam Tip:** You are not expected to explain the logic of the Prisoner's Dilemma in the examination. However, you can use the concept to explain state behaviour in Section B answers. For example, 'The Prisoner's Dilemma is used by realists to explain why states find it difficult to co-operate, because in circumstances where they cannot be certain of another state's intention, defection is a more reliable national security strategy than co-operation.'

neo-realists, wars of conquest are viewed as acceptable means to extend a state's power and influence in global politics. On the other hand, **defensive neo-realists** such as Waltz (1979) believe states are 'security maximisers' and only want to have enough power to survive. This would mean having enough power to defend yourself if you were attacked.

The inherent ambiguity surrounding the accumulation of power poses significant challenges for all states within an anarchic international system. It creates an issue of interpretation, since it is impossible to know with accuracy why other states are acquiring military power; is it for offensive (power-maximising) or defensive (security-maximising) purposes? Because states cannot leave their survival to chance under international anarchy, they have to assume the worst of other states. Consequently, states end up embroiled in **arms races** where each state seeks a relative advantage over another. This leads to what neo-realists call the **security dilemma**.

The security dilemma

The security dilemma, originally coined by John H. Herz (1950), is a realist idea (particularly associated with neo-realism), which argues that as a state seeks to build its defensive military power, it unintentionally creates insecurity in other states who in turn begin rival attempts to increase their own military power (see Figure 1.2). This leads to an escalating arms race, and consequently, war becomes a highly probable outcome.

For neo-realists such as Mearsheimer (2001), this situation is intensified by international anarchy, and states are helpless to resist it in their quest for survival. Indeed, Mearsheimer suggests in his famous work *The Tragedy of Great Power Politics* that 'this situation is genuinely tragic'. It is tragic because states end up fated to fight in wars that diminish their overall security. Under international anarchy, states rely on their own self-help efforts to survive. There is no alternative to this because states do not trust one another and can never be certain of the intentions of others – are they a potential ally or a potential enemy? Consequently, each state in the international system seeks to increase its own military power. Given that it is impossible to know whether such moves are for defensive or offensive purposes, states must naturally assume the worst. States must interpret for themselves why another state is seeking to increase its power. This leads to increased arms build-ups as states view the actions of others through negative lenses. It also enhances the feeling of

> **Definition**
>
> **Arms race:** An arms race is a situation where two or more states engage in a competition to have the most hard power. This could involve acquiring the most power numerically or in terms of technological sophistication.

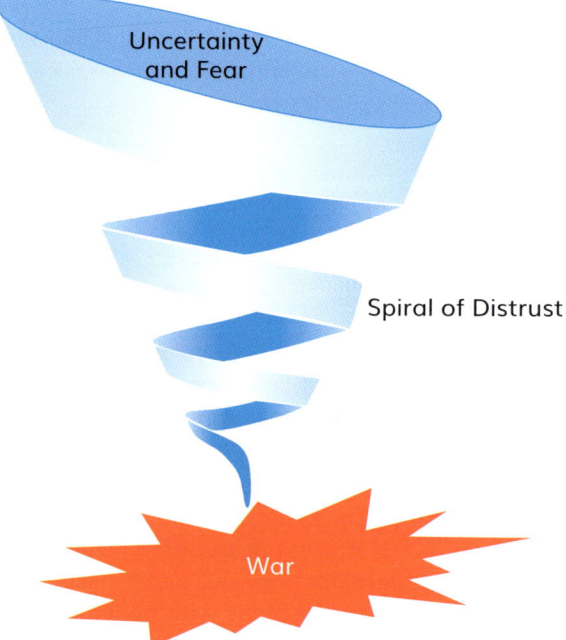

Figure 1.2 The Security Dilemma.

mutual hostility that exists in global politics because the build-up of arms leads to spiralling distrust. It is not hard to imagine how this situation can escalate into full-blown war between states. Booth and Wheeler refer to this as a 'security paradox' because in the case of defensive states who were merely trying to enhance the security of their state, they end up less secure because of the security dilemma.

Crucially, the security dilemma is not limited to the overt build-up of military power. Its dynamics can also be observed in the accumulation of economic or diplomatic (soft) power, which cumulatively impacts how a state views its own security situation. For instance, a state's aggressive pursuit of economic dominance or its successful expansion of diplomatic influence might be interpreted by rivals as a strategic threat, prompting countermeasures in those non-military domains. Economically, we see this in the relationship between the United States and China. Throughout both his terms in office, US President Donald Trump has frequently criticised China for its trade surplus, suggesting it achieves this through its heavy subsidisation of businesses and dumping of products on the global economy. This strategy, seen by realists as prioritising relative economic gains, undercuts competitors and forces them out of business, reinforcing a zero-sum view of international trade where one state's economic strength comes at the expense of another's. In turn, the United States has responded by introducing high tariffs on Chinese imports so that they no longer undercut US manufacturers. This illustrates how the security dilemma can play out in different spheres of global politics.

Overall, realism suggests that war is an inevitable feature of global politics, but realists disagree on the fundamental reasons why. The tension exists between classical realists, who argue that war is rooted in an immutable, inherently self-interested human nature, and neo-realists (or structural realists), who contend that conflict is a direct consequence of the anarchic structure of the international system. For neo-realists, this anarchy compels states to rely on self-help, often leading to a security dilemma where actions taken by one state to enhance its own security are perceived as threatening by others, thereby generating a cycle of countermeasures and escalating distrust that makes war a constant possibility.

The main ideas of liberalism

Liberalism is a theory of international relations which suggests that global politics, while still occasionally marked by conflict, possesses significant potential for peace and cooperation between states. Like realists, liberals agree that the state is an important actor in global politics, but they reject that it is the only important actor. Liberalism proposes a mixed-actor model of global politics whereby it is constituted by a range of actors, including states and regional and international organisations, as well as non-state actors such as non-governmental organisations. Whereas realists claim to be 'realistic', liberalism is often criticised for being at best too optimistic and at worst too idealistic.

In the following sections, we will examine the main ideas of liberalism, which include its ideas about human nature, the possibility of harmony and balance and the likelihood of **global governance**.

Human nature

Liberals, while acknowledging that human nature can at times be egotistical, fundamentally disagree with realists that this inherent self-interest inevitably leads to negative outcomes in global politics. For liberals, human nature is capable of rationalism. In this respect, it is rational for human beings to want to survive and flourish. However, whereas for realists this quest for survival is based on the narrow national interests of states alone, for liberals, this is based on mutual or **enlightened self-interests**. In this sense, liberals highlight how human beings are capable of altruistic and moral behaviour and in some cases enjoy helping fellow humankind when in difficulty. It is such ideas that feed liberalism's support for universal human rights and humanitarian intervention. Liberals recognise that the conditions for survival will only come about through creating the conditions for mutual cooperation between different international actors. Because human beings wish to survive, it would be irrational for them to expose themselves to the risk of violent death in war and conflict. Therefore, liberals prefer to settle their disputes through diplomatic strategies such as discussion and mediation. They are also happy to refer to higher authorities to do this on their behalf. Because human beings want to flourish, they want to develop a system of global governance to help regulate and improve upon areas of cooperation.

> **Spec key term**
>
> **Security dilemma:** A situation where the defensive actions taken by one state to increase its own security are unintentionally perceived as threatening by others, prompting countermeasures. This can lead to an arms race and potentially, war.
>
> **Liberalism:** A theory of international relations which argues that war and conflict in global politics is not inevitable and instead, global politics can be characterised by peace and harmony.
>
> **Global governance:** A complex, mostly 'intergovernmental' process where states work together to make decisions. States create and maintain the institutions, laws and norms of global governance to address issues they cannot solve alone. Non-state actors are sometimes involved.

> **Definition**
>
> **Enlightened self-interests:** Enlightened self-interest is the idea that states can achieve greater mutual benefit from co-operating with other states than they can by prioritising their own narrow self-interest at the expense of other states.

CASE STUDY: REALISM AND THE CHINA-INDIA BORDER DISPUTE

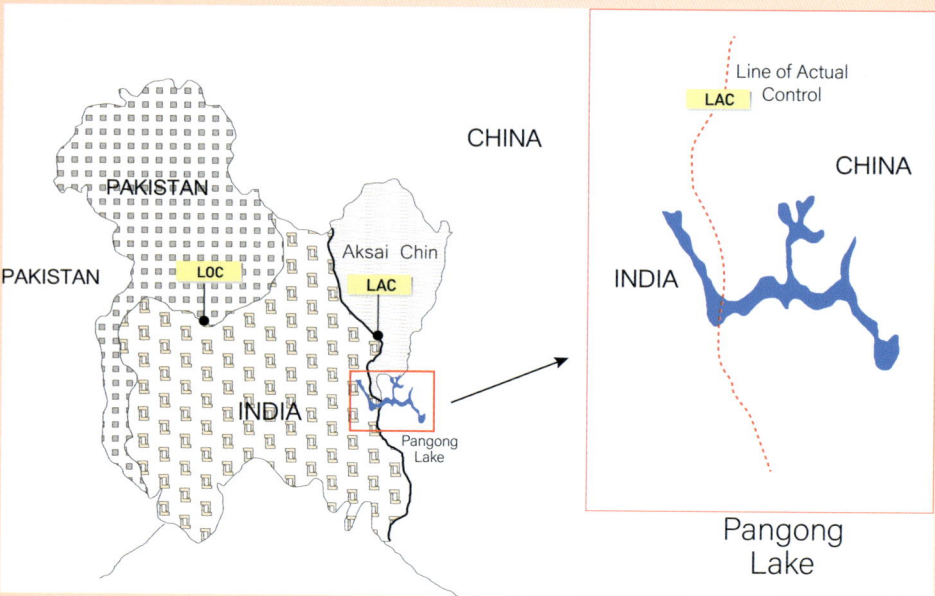

Map 1.1 India and China border dispute

Source: istock.com/Sajid Sk

Context

The 2,100-mile Himalayan border, known as the Line of Actual Control (LAC), is a constant source of tension between nuclear-armed rivals China and India (see Map 1.1). The border's unclear delineation, complicated by rivers, lakes and snow caps, fuels frequent disputes. Both sides fought a major war in 1962 over the contested border, which saw India defeated. Both sides reached an agreement in 1996 prohibiting firearms and explosives along the frontier to reduce the risk of future escalation.

Despite this, tensions flared dramatically in June 2020 with the Galwan Valley clashes, where soldiers fought in hand-to-hand combat with sticks and rocks, resulting in casualties on both sides (twenty Indian, four Chinese deaths). China blamed India for provocation, while India accused China of significant troop deployments and occupying vast swathes of its territory, triggered by India's construction of a strategic road to an air base in Ladakh. Both nations are now actively militarising the border, building infrastructure like roads and settlements, leading to mutual concerns about military build-ups. China interprets Indian construction as encroachment, responding with its own fortifications and troop increases.

De-escalation efforts, including military and diplomatic talks since June 2020, have yielded limited success. Hundreds of skirmishes occur annually. More serious incidents include January 2021 clashes causing injuries, and reciprocal accusations of gunfire in September 2021, marking a serious breach of the 1996 agreement. In December 2022, Indian forces removed Chinese soldiers from their side of the border. These ongoing confrontations underscore the deep-seated mistrust and the persistent challenge of managing the undefined Himalayan frontier.

Significance

This case study stands as a stark contemporary example of the security dilemma in action. Despite shared aspirations for regional stability, the inherent distrust stemming from an anarchic international system, coupled with the unique geographical challenges of the region, continually pushes both nuclear-armed states towards actions perceived as defensive, yet interpreted as threatening by the other, thereby fuelling a persistent cycle of insecurity and confrontation. The risk of escalation is serious, given that in a self-help system, each state must rely on its own efforts to ensure its security.

This case study also raises further issues about the escalation of cycles of distrust. Whilst not officially verified, it is suggested that new weapons technology is also being tested in this region. A Chinese academic, Jin Carong, claims that high-energy electromagnetic radiation technology (so-called microwave weapons) was used, which left Indian soldiers vomiting and unable to stand. Both sides deny that such weapons were used.

Finally, the case is significant because neither China nor India can afford to go to war against the other. China is one of India's biggest trading partners and the risk of war between the two would greatly damage its economy and increase its already high levels of poverty.

This ability of human beings to cooperate to achieve their shared goals is possible for liberals because they are not concerned about relative gains. Instead, liberals argue that cooperation between individuals leads to **absolute gains**. This means that everyone benefits from cooperation, and the question of who benefits the most is irrelevant. Liberals apply this idea to cooperation between all international actors, including states. So long as all states benefit from cooperation, it does not matter if a single state benefits from cooperation more than another.

Possibility of harmony and balance

Unlike realists, liberals believe in the possibility of harmony and balance in global politics. Liberals do not mean balance in the same way realists do in respect of the balance of power. Harmony and balance for liberals means a world where states and other international actors can achieve a state of relative peace, stability and cooperation through various means, including cooperation in intergovernmental organisations (IGOs) such as the UN. For liberals, peace and stability is not only desirable, it is achievable.

Liberals argue that global politics is characterised by a condition of **complex interdependence**. The theory of complex interdependence was first suggested by liberal scholars Robert Keohane and Joseph Nye (1977), and it is used to refer to the multitude of relationships that link international actors together, which combined, make the use of military force much less desirable because of the high costs it would inflict on these interconnections. Whilst the state is the key actor in global politics, it is also supported by a range of other international actors, including IGOs and regional organisations, and non-state actors, each important in their own right and capable of contributing to global governance. Moreover, in some circumstances, states are also willing to submit to a higher authority and give up some of their sovereignty. For example, in the case of the United Nations, states recognise the authority of the Security Council to issue legally binding resolutions concerning matters of international peace and security. Liberals propose that global politics represents a cobweb of complex relations. Whereas the Billiard Ball Model describes an empty space between states whereby states are free to crash into one another, the **Cobweb Model** depicts complex interdependence by showing that states are in fact suspended in a web of complex relations which prevent them from crashing into one another, resulting in war (see Figure 1.3).

> **Definition**
>
> **Absolute gains:** States find cooperation beneficial because all states are better off as a result; it does not matter if some states benefit more than others.

> **Spec key term**
>
> **Complex interdependence:** Refers to the complex range of relationships which connect states and international actors across a diverse range of issues, which makes the use of military force less desirable.

Figure 1.3 The Cobweb Model

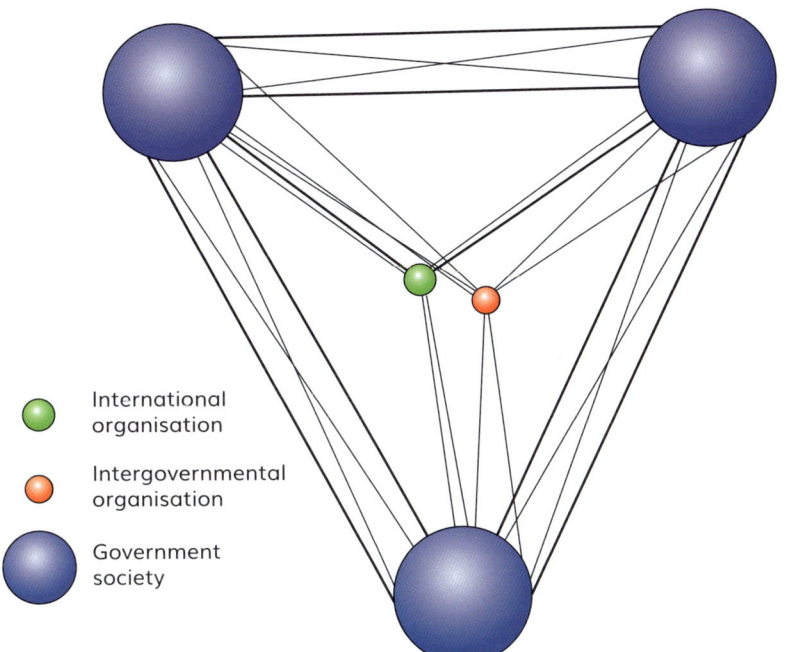

- International organisation
- Intergovernmental organisation
- Government society

Source: Based on Keohane and Nye's concept of complex interdependence

> **Definition**
>
> **The Cobweb Model:** A visual representation of liberal complex interdependence theory, which illustrates the dense network of relationships between states, contrasting with the realist view of states as independent actors.

Component III: Global Politics

Definition

International organisations: A broad term to encompass any organisation that operates internationally.

Intergovernmental organisations (IGOs): These are organisations whose members are sovereign states. They are normally established by treaty or formal agreements between states.

Kantian Triangle: The theory that peace emerges from three mutually reinforcing factors: international law and organisations, democracy, and international trade. Together, these can incentivise cooperation and reduce conflict among states.

Crucially, interdependence in one issue area often leads to spillover effects in other areas, leading to an ever-increasing depth and range of cooperation between states. This is easily seen in global politics today, whereby initial post-First World War cooperation between states was predominantly economically focused, we now see cooperation across contemporary global issues including conflict, poverty, human rights and the environment. The ways in which these contemporary issues are addressed in global politics is explored throughout this textbook.

Liberals focus on three main areas of cooperation which foster and develop complex interdependence between states, which include:

1. Impact and growth of international organisations and international law
2. Impact of democracy
3. Impact of international trade

Alone, each of these areas of cooperation helps contribute towards harmony and balance in global politics. However, combined, they offer powerful incentives for peace. The relationship between these three areas is shown in the **Kantian Triangle**. The Kantian Triangle shows how each of these areas of cooperation, when combined, creates powerful incentives for peace (see Figure 1.4). The Kantian Triangle is a contemporary adaptation of Immanuel Kant's theory of Perpetual Peace (1795).

1 Growth of international organisations and international law

Liberals place enormous importance on the impact of **international organisations** in global politics. International organisations can include a range of actors, including **intergovernmental organisations (IGOs)**, **regional organisations (ROs)** and **non-governmental organisations (NGOs)**. Their formation represents the pinnacle of cooperation occurring between international actors.

International organisations can be formed on either a formal or an informal basis. Formal organisations are established on an official basis through the establishment of a physical institution or building, and often have either a written constitution or a set of rules which bind all members. For example, the UN has its headquarters in New York City and is governed by the UN Charter. Informal organisations

Exam Tip: A common mistake is claiming liberals oppose war. In fact, liberals see war as a last resort. They support the use of force when justified under international law. It may be used in self-defence. It may be authorised by the UN Security Council for humanitarian purposes or to restore international peace.

Figure 1.4 The Kantian Triangle of Peace

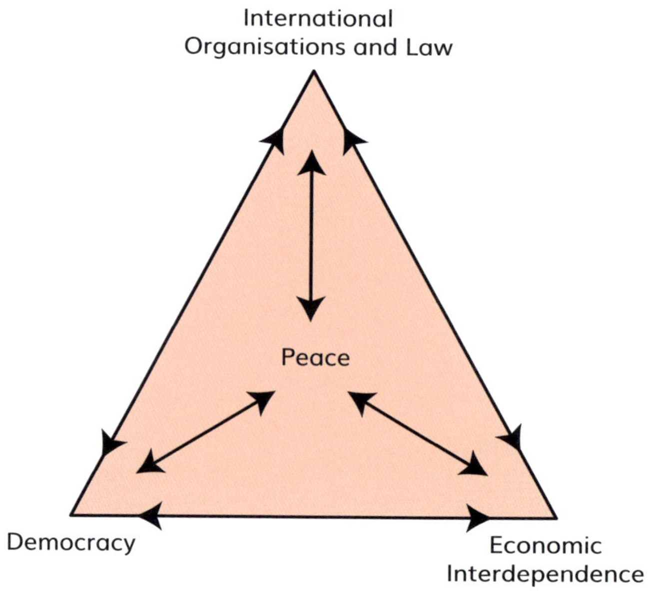

Source: Galeeva, D. (2018, 5 February). 'How national identity will shape the future of liberalism: The consequences of Brexit in the EU, and of the 2017 crisis in the GCC. Al-Mesbar Center'. Originally presented at the Gulf Research Meeting, Cambridge, 1–4 August 2017. Retrieved from https://mesbar.org/national-identity-will-shape-future-liberalism-consequences-brexit-eu-2017-crisis-gcc/

may not have a physical building or a formally agreed-upon set of rules guiding their operations. For example, the Group of Seven (G7) and Group of Twenty (G20) do not have official headquarters or an agreed set of rules Chapter 5.

Since the end of the Second World War, many international organisations have been established, with the UN being the most well known (see Table 1.2). All recognised states are members of multiple international organisations, suggesting that states view these organisations as legitimate tools of statecraft to pursue their national interests. For example, the UK is a member of hundreds of IGOs, including the UN, NATO, the Commonwealth and the G7.

The theory of **liberal institutionalism,** which sits within the Kantian Triangle, argues that international organisations (IOs) are indispensable architects of global harmony and balance, fundamentally transforming international anarchy into one more amenable to cooperation. Their appeal to states lies in a multifaceted range of advantages, ranging from short-to-long term.

In the short-to-medium term, IOs serve as vital platforms for states to achieve absolute gains. They significantly reduce transaction costs which refer to the costs of carrying out different activities. This is because they provide established frameworks, standardised procedures and dedicated secretariats for negotiation and implementation of decisions. This efficiency allows states to share resources, pool expertise and coordinate policies across diverse issue areas far more effectively than by acting unilaterally or through purely bilateral channels. For instance, organisations like Interpol exemplify this by facilitating the rapid sharing of critical intelligence on transnational threats like terrorism and organised crime, thereby enhancing the collective security of member states at a lower individual cost. Beyond resource sharing, IOs also increase transparency and predictability, making it easier for states to assess intentions, monitor compliance and build trust in repeated interactions.

While realists use the Prisoner's Dilemma to highlight the difficulty of cooperation due to mutual fear of defection, liberals argue that, in reality, states and international actors engage across numerous issue areas. This means the Prisoner's Dilemma is rarely a one-off event; instead, it is iterative, or played continually. This repeated interaction alters state calculations: they realise that cooperation is ultimately more beneficial than defection. States become wary of the 'shadow of the future', understanding that their current actions will impact future interactions. Consequently, states prioritise their reputations and adopt reciprocal strategies like 'tit-for-tat', where cooperation on one issue encourages cooperation from others on both current and future matters.

Looking to the medium-to-long term, the impact of IOs extends beyond mere efficiency gains to a more profound transformation of state behaviour and even their identity. By providing continual forums for dialogue and interaction – whether in formal sessions or informal corridors – IOs foster a process of socialisation among state representatives. Through repeated engagement, states begin to develop shared norms, values and understandings, gradually moving beyond narrow self-interest to recognise common interests and shared fates. This shared ideational framework cultivates mutual trust and generates shared expectations about appropriate behaviours, often evolving beyond the initial mandates of the institution. For example, the World Trade Organisation (WTO), initially focused on trade liberalisation, has fostered norms around fair trade practices that influence domestic policies. Similarly, the European Union demonstrates how extensive institutionalisation can ultimately lead

> **Exam Tip:**
> A common misconception by students in the exam is to attribute the Kantian Triangle to liberal philosopher Immanuel Kant. Whilst Kant's work laid the foundation for liberal ideas about peace, it was later liberal scholars such as Keohane and Nye (1977) and Bruce Russett and John Oneal (2001) who tested the links between the three components of the Kantian Triangle in their article 'Triangulating Peace: Democracy, Interdependence, and International Organisations'.

> **Definition**
> **Regional organisations (ROs):** A type of IGO whose membership is normally restricted to states or entities within a specific geographical area.
>
> **Liberal institutionalism:** The theory that international institutions, laws, and norms help states cooperate, reduce conflict, and manage anarchy by promoting transparency, trust, and mutually beneficial outcomes.

Table 1.2 **Estimated number of IGOs/NGOs**

Decade End	IGOs	NGOs
1940	40–50	800–900
1960	150–200	1,300–1,500
1980	300–250	9,000–10,000
2000	400–500	35,000–40,000
2020	600–700	50,000–60,000

Source: Union of International Associations.

> **Definition**
>
> **Non-governmental organisations (NGOs):** These are non-profit, private organisations that operate across borders. They normally offer expert knowledge and campaign or provide assistance on specific issues, for example, the protection of human rights (e.g. Human Rights Watch or Amnesty International) or environmental rights (e.g. Greenpeace or World Wildlife Fund).

to the formation of a 'security community' where war between members becomes unthinkable (see Chapter 4). This process ultimately helps to mitigate the security dilemma, as states come to see each other less as potential threats and more as reliable partners, reducing the incentive for competitive arms build-ups and fostering international harmony and balance.

International law performs a similar, indeed often intertwined, function for liberals as IOs. By establishing shared expectations about the reasonable conduct or behaviour of states, it provides a crucial layer of predictability under international anarchy. For example, it is clearly stipulated in international law that states cannot pursue wars of aggression, with war being permissible only in self-defence or by approval of the United Nations Security Council. Beyond the broader rules on the use of force, international law also clearly outlines rules regarding the development and use of specific weapons technology. For example, the Non-Proliferation Treaty commits non-nuclear weapons states not to acquire nuclear weapons. These principles significantly reduce the uncertainty of international anarchy, thereby helping to mitigate the security dilemma by providing a common understanding of legitimate and illegitimate uses of force and the types of force permitted. This allows for a greater degree of balance and harmony. States comply with international law most of the time not only because it helps to create certainty about the behaviour of would-be adversaries but also because adhering to these established rules reduces the transaction costs of their interactions and helps build a valuable reputation for trustworthiness in the international community. Moreover, international legal frameworks often provide avenues for dispute resolution, further encouraging peaceful interactions. For example, the International Court of Justice (ICJ) is the part of the UN which manages disputes between its member states (see Chapter 3).

2 Democracy

Unlike realists, liberals are concerned about what goes on within the state, and they believe that the type of government a state has can have an impact on state behaviour. Liberals have a preference for democratic systems of government whereby there are regular free and fair elections. They especially support the establishment of liberal democracy which is additionally characterised by constitutionalism, separation of powers and minority rights. The **Democratic Peace Theory** asserts that democracies do not fight wars against other democracies, which helps to foster harmony and balance in global politics. Democratic states have a shared identity which helps build cooperative and friendly relations between them. It would be inconceivable that a democracy wages a war of aggression against a fellow democracy. There are many examples to support the claim that democracies do not wage wars against democracies; for example, the United States and Canada share the longest undefended border in the world, and yet have never fought a war. Some liberals go as far as to say that all democracies are peaceful to all states irrespective of type of government, yet others assert they can be especially violent in their conduct towards non-democratic states such as authoritarian states. Democratic Peace Theory claims that democratic states are less inclined to engage in warfare for the following reasons:

- Democratic governments are held to account through regular, free and fair elections. If a government pursues aggressive policies that are not supported by the public, it risks losing power in the next general election.
- Democratic states have burgeoning civil society movements that help hold governments to account. They can organise protests and publish information about government behaviour. For example, in 2003, the 'Stop the War' protest in the UK against the Iraq War was one of the largest protests in UK history.
- In constitutional democracies, the decision to go to war is complex and requires approval and coordination from many different institutions of state, providing checks and balances to manage the use of force.
- Ethical foreign policies are an important source of **soft power** for democratic states.

> **Spec key term**
>
> **International law:** The law that governs states and other international actors. It is derived from both treaties and custom (i.e. the behaviour of states).
>
> **Soft power:** A term coined by Joseph Nye, refers to a state or actor achieving their goals through the use of attraction and influence (for example through their culture, political values or foreign policies) rather than coercion (hard power).

On the other hand, non-democratic states are less constrained in their external behaviour because their legitimacy often stems from non-democratic sources. Their legitimacy often derives from foreign policy successes or perceptions of power, frequently secured through successful wars or militarism (even short of direct conflict). Therefore, such states cannot be relied upon to maintain harmony and balance in the international system. It is for this very reason that democratic states often include conditionality in their relations with other states that sometimes include upholding democratic principles, rule of law and human rights protections. Democratic Peace Theory has been strongly debated. For example, India and Pakistan, both democracies, fought over Kashmir province in 1999. This evidence challenges the theory. In response, some proponents have refined the theory by adjusting their definition of democracy – for example, applying it only to liberal democracies. That would exclude Pakistan.

The impact of democratic and non-democratic states on global politics will be considered further in Chapter 3.

3 Trade

Balance and harmony are also achieved through trade between states. Liberals (specifically, or interdependence liberals) focus on the importance of the creation of a single global economy built upon the liberal principles of **free trade** and interdependence between states. In reality, the majority of trade in contemporary global politics is not 'free' and instead is characterised by **trade liberalisation**, referring to efforts taken to reduce barriers to trade in global politics. For example, the World Trade Organisation works towards its goal of building a global economy based on the principle of free trade, by helping to bring about trade liberalisation. For liberals, free trade is the ideal, but in their analysis, they accept that this is not realised in practice and therefore focus on the pacifying effects of trade liberalisation and deepening economic interdependence.

According to liberals, in a globalised economy, states specialise in producing what they have a comparative advantage in, rendering no state truly self-sufficient. This means states become reliant on one another for essential materials, goods and services they cannot provide themselves. Given the high costs involved, this interdependence compels states to reconsider aggressive militaristic policies. Such actions could, first, lead to economic sanctions being imposed on them, and second, result in the denial of access to vital resources. In democratic states, the impact of this is magnified: the government in question could lose legitimacy and risk losing power at the next general election. Conversely, in a non-democratic state, the loss of access to these required supplies could severely damage the state's legitimacy, which often hinges on successful outcomes. Some liberals take this further, suggesting that repeated trade between states fosters friendships and a shared identity, making the possibility of conflict seem unthinkable. Liberal economist Richard Cobden (1846) echoed this sentiment by claiming that trade would unite mankind in 'the bonds of eternal peace', emphasising the important role played by trade in establishing harmony and balance.

Likelihood of global governance

Liberals believe that complex interdependence, where states are deeply interconnected across various issue areas, creates the imperative for global governance. Global governance, in this context, refers to the multifaceted system of rules, norms, institutions and processes that shape the behaviour of political actors in the absence of a single world government. Far from being monolithic, global governance manifests in various forms – encompassing political, economic, human rights and environmental governance, for instance – each addressing distinct issue areas. Liberals fervently support global governance because it is seen as the primary mechanism for managing the inherent challenges and realising the mutual benefits of this interdependence. It provides the necessary frameworks to facilitate cooperation, mitigate the negative effects of international anarchy, and collectively address transnational problems (such as climate change, pandemics or financial crises) that no single state can solve alone. By establishing predictable norms and avenues for dispute resolution, global governance ultimately works to reduce the transaction costs of international interactions and foster a more stable and harmonious international system

Whilst the notion of world government was once popular amongst liberal theorists, this is now no longer the case. Liberals largely abandoned the idea of a literal world government due to deep-seated concerns about the potential for tyranny and the unprecedented concentration of power it would entail, which conflicts with core liberal values of individual liberty and limited government. Instead, they embraced the concept of global governance, viewing it as a more pragmatic and safer means to foster cooperation and manage shared challenges through decentralised rules, norms and institutions, without fully sacrificing national sovereignty or risking global authoritarianism.

> **Definition**
>
> **Free trade:** Refers to the removal of barriers to trade between trading partners; for example tariffs, quotas or subsidies.
>
> **Trade liberalisation:** Refers to the reduction of barriers to trade, as opposed to their outright removal.

> **Exam Tip:** Section B of the exam is a single compulsory 12 mark question on comparative theories. This part of the chapter addresses many practice questions. Notice that the content used in different questions overlaps significantly. The key to answering this question is in applying the theoretical knowledge you have learned in different ways to answer the specific question asked. Chapter 10 has more detail on exam technique.

Comparative analysis of realism and liberalism

Having looked at the theories of realism and liberalism, this section will now draw this together to analyse their key differences across different issue areas outlined in the Pearson Edexcel Politics Specification syllabus.

Please note that in Section B answers, it is important to illustrate some of your points with contemporary examples. This section does not integrate these and instead focuses on the key differences between the theories so that you understand them fully – see Chapter 10, Exam Focus Chapter for further guidance. When you write your own answers, you should incorporate examples from this chapter, the chapters throughout the textbook and your own wider knowledge to support your answers.

Comparative Analysis: The differences between realism and liberalism concerning the likelihood of conflict.

Realists – Human nature is responsible for conflict

» Human nature is egotistical and guided by non-rational appetites. Drawing upon an ancient tradition of political philosophy, realists argue that human beings are fundamentally self-interested and egoistic, driven by a desire for power or security, and prone to domination.

» States are governed by human beings, and it is therefore expected that they will behave in the same way as humans towards one another. They will look for opportunities to exploit others and maximise their own power or security relative to others.

Liberals – Human nature is rational and capable of morality

» Human nature is inherently rational, capable of morality and motivated to make progress. Given war's destructive nature, its pursuit is deemed irrational, making individuals and states more inclined towards peace.

» Furthermore, human beings are capable of moral or altruistic behaviour, fundamentally disagreeing with the notion of an innate will to dominate others. Instead, human nature generally prefers not to inflict pain and suffering on others, recognising a mutual self-interest in avoiding harm based on shared values and common interests.

Realists – The structure of the international system means that conflict is likely

» Conflict is likely because of international anarchy. It is a self-help system, and states have to rely on their own efforts to survive; there is no global 911 (999) to come to the aid of states in trouble.

» States' quest for power causes anxiety in other states, since it is unclear whether they are acquiring power for defensive or offensive purposes. This leads to increasing spirals of distrust and militarisation, with the eventual outcome being war, as epitomised by the security dilemma.

Liberals – The international system is characterised by complex interdependence, which helps promote peace between states

» States are bound together in a complex web of interdependence that makes conflict unlikely. This is depicted by the Kantian Triangle, which emphasises the role of the following:

  o Democracy – democracies are inherently peaceful in their conduct. The rising number of democracies in the twentieth and twenty-first centuries suggests that we can be optimistic about the possibilities for peace.

  o International organisations and law – create shared expectations about the behaviour of states and facilitate peaceful interactions.

  o Trade – trade interdependence makes war costly, since states rely upon one another to buy/sell materials, goods and services.

Realists – States struggle to cooperate because they are concerned about relative gains

» States are concerned about relative gains, meaning that they are only willing to cooperate if they benefit the most from the cooperation.

» Since states are inclined to cheat, it is imprudent to rely upon other states for their security.

Liberals – There are powerful and compelling reasons for states to cooperate because they emphasise absolute gains

» States prioritise achieving mutual benefits from cooperation, irrespective of who gains the most, as long as all benefit.

» The cross-border security issues facing the international community today require collective action by all international actors to solve, e.g. terrorism, climate change and pandemics.

Comparative Analysis Summary

Points of Contrast	Realism	Liberalism
Human nature and its implications for conflict	Human nature is responsible for conflict	Human nature is rational and capable of morality
The structure of the international system in promoting conflict	The structure of the international system means that conflict is likely	The international system is characterised by complex interdependence which helps promote peace between states
The ability of states to cooperate on security issues	States struggle to cooperate because they are focused on relative gains	There are powerful and compelling reasons for states to cooperate, driven by the pursuit of absolute gains

Comparative Analysis: The differences between realism and liberalism concerning human nature.

Realists – Human nature is egotistical

» Human nature is egotistic, self-interested and driven by a will to dominate. Realists draw upon an ancient tradition of philosophers to justify this view. For example, Machiavelli argues that human nature is 'insatiable, arrogant, crafty and shifting, and above all else malignant, iniquitous, violent and savage', indicating that human nature is unpleasant.

Liberals – Human nature is rational and moral

» Human nature is inherently rational, capable of morality and motivated to make progress. Given war's destructive nature, its pursuit is deemed irrational, making individuals and states more inclined towards peace.

» Furthermore, human beings are capable of moral or altruistic behaviour, fundamentally disagreeing with the notion of an innate will to dominate others. Instead, human nature generally prefers not to inflict pain and suffering on others, recognising a mutual self-interest in avoiding harm based on shared values and common interests.

Realists – For classical realists, human nature explains why war and conflict occurs between states

» States, being governed by human beings who are fundamentally egoistic and driven by a will to dominate, are therefore expected to mirror this inherent behaviour in their international relations. Consequently, states seek opportunities to exploit others and to maximise their own power and influence, mirroring humanity's insatiable desire for power after power. This innate competitiveness and suspicion, born from the very nature of humanity, fosters an atmosphere of distrust among states, which makes cooperation difficult. This ultimately leads to conflict.

» Neo-realists agree that human nature is driven by a will to dominate, but this is not the cause of conflict. Conflict is a consequence of international anarchy. It is a self-help system, and states have

> **Exam Tip:** Note the similar points made in the comparative analysis of human nature, compared to the analysis of the likelihood of conflict. This demonstrates how AO1 knowledge is reusable in different contexts.

to rely on their own efforts to survive; there is no global 911 (999) to come to the aid of states in trouble.

» States' quest for power causes anxiety in other states, since it is unclear whether they are acquiring power for defensive or offensive purposes. This leads to increasing spirals of distrust and militarisation, with the eventual outcome being war, as epitomised by the security dilemma.

Liberals – Argue that human rationality leads states to recognise the benefits of cooperation and therefore seek to engage with international organisations to achieve shared goals.

» It is rational and logical for states to work together within international organisations to resolve collective dilemmas such as climate change and human rights violations.

» Such cooperation promotes absolute gains, where all participating states benefit. Engagement within these bodies helps to both reduce the individual costs of addressing global issues and increase collective capabilities, thereby making solutions more attainable.

Realists – Human nature is fixed and unchanging.

» Human nature is fixed and has remained constant throughout human civilisation, explaining why there is evidence of organised violence between human beings since antiquity.

» Because of this, any efforts to alter the human condition to eliminate conflict are futile, as their true nature will always re-emerge.

Liberals – Human nature is not fixed and can change.

» Liberals argue that human nature is not fixed, but is fundamentally capable of learning, adapting and improving. This transformation occurs significantly through processes like education and socialisation with others.

» Human beings, utilising their shared rationality, can thereby overcome inherent egoism, fostering increasingly peaceful and cooperative behaviours. Consequently, many liberals envision human nature as continually evolving along a path of progression towards greater global harmony.

Comparative Analysis Summary

Points of Contrast	Realism	Liberalism
Characteristics of human nature	Human nature is egotistical and self-interested	Human nature is rational and moral
The outcomes of human nature for war and conflict	Human nature is responsible for war and conflict between states	Human nature means that states are naturally cooperative and form intergovernmental organisations
Capacity for change	Human nature is fixed	Human nature is not fixed

Comparative Analysis: The differences between realism and liberalism concerning power.

Nature and purpose of power

Realists – The acquisition of hard power is in the national interest of states.

» Power as capabilities: realists emphasise the importance of power as capabilities. This refers to the amount of power a state physically possesses and is usually quantifiable, i.e. it can be measured. Realists prioritise hard power, such as military power. This can include, for example, the size of a state's army or number of types of weapons it possesses.

» Realists favour the acquisition of military and economic power (power as capabilities), which enables them to use hard power such as military action or economic sanctions.

- » Realists view the acquisition of power as essential to survival. For classical realists, this is because it is human nature to want to dominate others. For neo-realists, this is because under international anarchy, states exist in a self-help system and rely on their own efforts to survive.

Liberals – Power is a tool for cooperation.
- » Liberals view power more broadly than realists and favour the acquisition of both hard and soft power.
- » Soft power enables states to achieve their goals through their ability to influence the behaviour of others through attraction and persuasion, rather than coercion.
- » Beyond soft power, liberals argue that even hard power can be a critical tool for cooperation. It can be utilised by states to build consensus, facilitate negotiations, establish or strengthen international institutions, and collectively address shared global challenges such as human rights through peacekeeping or humanitarian intervention.

Acquisition and distribution of power

Realists – States want to increase their relative power in global politics.
- » States are concerned about relative gains, comparing their capabilities to those of other states rather than merely focusing on absolute gains as do liberals.
- » To increase their chances of survival, states can choose from an array of strategies. They may engage in balancing, forming alliances with other states to counter the power of a stronger adversary or bandwagoning, aligning with the stronger power in the hope of sharing in its benefits or avoiding its wrath. However, given that states are distrusting of other states, such alliances are only temporary at best. The Prisoner's Dilemma illustrates that under international anarchy, defection always produces the best outcome for a state to increase its overall security.
- » The distribution of power in the international system is a determinant of the stability of the system. Realists prefer either hegemonic or bipolar systems to achieve this (see Chapter 3).

Liberals – The distribution of power in the system can be managed by states.
- » States are inclined to cooperate and pool their sovereignty to achieve collective goals because they favour absolute gains. This collaborative approach enables them to address key global challenges such as combating climate change, promoting human rights or preventing conflict.
- » Liberals favour multipolar systems, viewing them as more conducive to establishing harmony and balance. A system with multiple influential actors naturally encourages multilateralism and shared responsibility, aligning with the liberal preference for global governance.

Impact of power on global politics

Realists – The acquisition of power leads to competition and conflict.
- » Power is zero-sum, meaning that for each state that acquires power, another loses it.
- » States acquire power for different reasons – either because they are power maximisers (offensive realists) or security maximisers (defensive realists) – and this creates a fundamental dilemma of interpretation for other states. Under international anarchy, states are compelled to assume the worst about the acquisition of power by other states, assuming it is for offensive reasons. This distrust is precisely what leads to the security dilemma, a spiralling situation or tit-for-tat behaviour which can ultimately result in conflict.

Liberals – The acquisition of power can contribute to harmony and balance.
- » The acquisition of power is seen as positive-sum. This means that when one state gains power, it can lead to benefits for the entire international community, rather than being a zero-sum game where one's gain is another's loss.
- » This leads to harmony and balance because it creates shared incentives for cooperation and reduces distrust. In particular, it reduces the risk of a security dilemma because states are unlikely to view other states with distrust.

Comparative Analysis Summary

Points of contrast	Realism	Liberalism
Nature and purpose of power	States acquire hard power in order to survive	View the acquisition of power as an important tool for cooperation
Acquisition and distribution of power	States are concerned about relative power Prefer a unipolar or bipolar system	States favour absolute gains Prefer a multipolar system
Impact of power on global politics	Power is zero-sum The acquisition of power leads to competition and conflict	Power is positive-sum The acquisition of power can help establish harmony and balance in the international system

Comparative Analysis: The differences between realists and liberals concerning the significance of states and the impact of international organisations.

The significance of states

Realists – Sovereign states are the most significant actors in global politics.

» Realism is a state-centric theory which argues that states are the most significant actors in global politics.

» They argue that all states are sovereign and have authority within their own borders and the right to non-interference.

» All states, irrespective of how powerful they are, place survival as their key national interest. Under international anarchy.

Liberals – States operate amongst many actors which can have power over states. Sovereignty is not the sole domain of states.

» The international arena is not exclusively the domain of states. Instead, states must contend with a multitude of powerful actors – including IGOs, ROs, transnational corporations and NGOs – who exert considerable influence in global politics.

» Whilst states are sovereign, their sovereignty is not absolute. States sometimes choose to pool their sovereignty in supranational IGOs or ROs, such as the UN or EU. Additionally, it is increasingly viewed that state sovereignty is conditional on the protection of human rights. These ideas form the basis of humanitarian intervention and responsibility to protect (see Chapter 6).

The impact of the type of government in the state

Realists – The type of government within a state has no impact on its behaviour in global politics.

» Realists are often accused of treating states as black-boxes. In other words, they are not concerned by their inner workings. They are concerned about their behaviour and interactions at the international level. Here, they argue that all states operate in a self-help system with survival as their key national interest.

Liberals – The type of government that exists within a state has important consequences for its conduct in global politics.

» Liberals are concerned about the type of government that exists within a state and have a preference for democratic government.

» Liberals use the Democratic Peace Theory to explain why democracies are more peaceful than non-democracies. They suggest that democracies are inherently peaceful in their conduct because their behaviour is constrained by a range of factors, including their shared democratic norms and values, accountability to their public and institutional constraints which shape the process of deciding to use force. For liberals, the increased number of democracies in the twentieth and twenty-first centuries suggests that we can be optimistic about the possibilities for international peace.

» Increasingly, liberals are also interested in the promotion of good governance within states. This can include the upholding of the rule of law, respect for human rights and efficient and responsive public institutions (see Chapter 8).

The role of international organisations

Realists – Sceptical about the role of IOs in global politics.

» Realists are deeply sceptical of IOs and the possibilities for enduring cooperation within them, primarily due to the fundamental nature of the international system, which they view as anarchic. In such a system, states are driven by self-interest and a constant concern for survival, leading to a focus on relative gains.

» States view cooperation with suspicion and distrust. Whilst they accept that states can cooperate within IOs, they think this will only be temporary at best. The Prisoner's Dilemma illustrates how, under international anarchy, the most rational choice for a state is to defect from cooperative arrangements.

Liberals – Positive about the role of IOs in global politics.

» Liberals see IOs as critical in transforming international anarchy into a more harmonious environment. IOs form a key component of the Kantian Triangle, which demonstrates why peace is possible in global politics.

» Institutions help facilitate absolute gains between their members. All members benefit from reduced transaction costs, enabling them to tackle global issues more effectively.

» Institutions also foster repeated cooperation between states, which encourages them to prioritise their reputations and adopt reciprocal strategies whereby current cooperation can lead to future cooperation, making defection less likely.

» Institutions can help states to develop shared norms and identities, making conflict between them less likely.

» IOs are a vital part of global governance, helping to create rules guiding behaviour across different issue areas.

Comparative Analysis Summary

Points of Contrast	Realism	Liberalism
Significance of States	States are the most important actors in global politics	States are one of many different actors in global politics. State sovereignty is not absolute; it can be pooled, and it is conditional
Type of Government	Realists are not concerned about the type of government in a state; they treat the state as a black box	Liberals favour democratic systems of government
Role of International Organisations	Realists are sceptical about the role of IOs in global politics	Liberals are positive about the role of IOs as they can help create peace and harmony in the international system

Spec key term

Anarchical society (also known as society of states): Theory that the states of the world can be members of a society despite the anarchical nature of the international system.

Exam Tip:
There is confusion among students about anarchical society and society of states theory. Please remember that they are NOT different theories, they are the same theory which is sometimes referred to as either anarchical society or society of states. The specification also treats them as the same theory.

Anarchical society and the society of states theory

The Anarchical Society is the title of a book written in 1977 by Hedley Bull and is the founding text of the 'English School' of international relations theory. The English School proposes a more flexible understanding of international relations which combines some of the core arguments of realism and liberalism.

Realism and liberalism both explain the reasons why states might behave in predictable ways, which do not change over time. This means they are explanatory theories of state behaviour. However, Bull was not intending to produce an entire theory of international relations to rival realism or liberalism, but instead wanted to offer a historical exploration of the circumstances in which 'order' could be said to exist in global politics. Bull showed that in different historical periods, and in the policies of different states and their leaders, either realism or liberalism could better explain global politics than the other. He highlighted that there were elements of truth in both realist and liberal perspectives, showing that the question of how order is established in global politics may change over time. There are three broad elements to his argument.

1. States exist in an anarchical 'state of nature'.

Bull claims that 'the starting point of international relations is the **existence of states**, or independent political communities each of which possesses a government and asserts sovereignty in relation to a particular portion of the earth's surface and a particular segment of the human population'. In other words, accepting the **realist** view that sovereign states are the key actors in global politics.

Bull also accepts the **realist** proposition that there is international anarchy because there is no world government. However, he does not agree that the consequence of international anarchy is that states are destined for war. In fact, Bull's version of international anarchy looks very different from Hobbesian 'state of nature' analogy used by **realists** to explain why the international system is predisposed to war. **Realists** imagine a wild, ungoverned state of nature where states are out for

Photo 1.3 An observation deck at a Starbucks Coffee in South Korea with views of North Korea's Gaepung County. North Korea has significant restrictions on communication with the outside world. The socio-economic isolation of North Korea is one of the factors contributing to its classification as a 'rogue state'.

Source: Bloomberg via Getty Images

themselves, and life is a constant, brutal fight for survival. There is no trust, no rules and violence is always just around the corner. This is how realists see the international system, leading them to believe war is inevitable. Bull's understanding of anarchy is akin to the **Lockean** 'state of nature', a view shared by liberal philosophers. Liberal key thinker, John Locke, had a different view of the state of nature to Conservative thinker, Thomas Hobbes. Locke argued that life in the state of nature could be peaceful as individuals could cooperate with one another. In the **Lockean** state of nature, even without a formal government, individuals (or in this case, states) can still live together in a loosely connected society. They are guided by *natural law* (which is essentially common sense and rationality). While there's no higher power forcing them to cooperate, states can still form relationships, develop unwritten rules and find ways to avoid continual conflict. It is not perfect order, but it is not pure chaos either. So, for Bull, the absence of a world government does not mean a free-for-all. Instead, he believes states can create a sort of international society among themselves, where cooperation and order are possible through shared understanding and norms.

2. There may be an international society of states, not just an international state system.

A **system of states** (or international system) is formed when two or more states frequently interact and significantly affect each other's choices; they form an international system, functioning as if they are components of a single entity.

A **society of states** (or **international society**) exists when a collection of states realises they share certain interests and values, and consequently agree to a common set of rules for their interactions and participate in shared institutions. An international society is formed. Bull noted that these societies historically tended to share a common culture or civilisation. Yet, by the late twentieth century, he proposed that an international society would more likely be built on *cosmopolitanism*, a recognition of the equivalent worth of all human beings. Bull observed that global politics has seen times when order resembled a 'system of states' (states with contact and mutual impact) and other times when a more evolved 'society of states' emerged; for instance, Europe after the 1648 *Treaty of Westphalia*.

Unlike **realists** and **liberals**, who are both fixed on their ideas of international anarchy and complex interdependence, respectively, Bull acknowledged that the two types of order he identified can change over time. There might be a period where global politics resembles a system of states and another where it resembles a society of states. The two types of order can also co-exist (i.e. there may be some states which exist as a system of states and others that form a society of states), and there can be more than one international society at any one time. Importantly, a society of states always emerges from a system of states; in other words, the system comes before the society. Surprisingly, Bull did not give much attention to the question of how states transition from one type of order to the other.

3. Order is more likely in an international society of states.

Order in an **international system** of states operates according to the **realist** theory of international relations. In seeking to survive, states accumulate power, but since it is impossible to identify whether states are acquiring power to maximise their power or their security, it leads to the security dilemma, where war is a likely outcome.

Order in an **international society of states** is maintained by:

- **Common interests** – Despite having varied and often opposing goals, states often recognise certain **common interests** as essential for international stability. These interests typically stem from a collective desire to avoid unchecked violence, ensure the reliability of agreements and safeguard their national sovereignty.

- **Rules** – To maintain these common interests, states adhere to **prescribed rules of conduct**. These rules may encompass formal international law, prevailing moral standards, established custom or practice or practical operational guidelines.

- **Institutions** – To operationalise these rules, **institutions** are essential. These can be established organisations, such as the United Nations or the World Bank, international agreements and treaties, like the Non-Proliferation Treaty (1970) or importantly, practices such as diplomacy, international law, the balance of power and even war itself.

The overlap between **liberalism** and the society of states is clear. Because states have a shared common interest in survival and because they want to achieve absolute gains, states can agree to establish, follow and enforce a rules-based order.

> **Definition**
>
> **Natural law:** The existence of a set of laws that are universal and are discovered through human reason alone.
>
> **Cosmopolitanism:** The belief that all human beings are equal and of an equivalent worth. This links to the idea of universal human rights.
>
> **Treaty of Westphalia:** A treaty signed by European state in 1648. In it, they agreed that they each had an equal right to independence and should not interfere in each other's domestic affairs.

Table 1.3 Areas of Agreement and Disagreement between Anarchical Society/Society of States Theory and Realism/Liberalism

Anarchical Society theory	Realism	Liberalism
Global politics is characterised by anarchy and power politics between sovereign states.	**Realists agree because:** Anarchical society theory accepts realism's starting points of states as the primary actors in international anarchy and the importance of power in global politics. States use hard power as a means to achieve their own goals.	**Liberals generally agree** that global politics is anarchic because states are sovereign. States can use soft power to achieve their goals. Diplomacy is an important tool of statecraft that contributes to soft power.
Despite anarchy, order and stability are possible. However, international anarchy is enduring, whereas order and stability may be temporary. History shows periods of an anarchical system of autonomous states, interspersed with periods of an anarchical society of states.	**Defensive neorealists agree** that conflict is not inevitable. Kenneth Waltz argues that stability can be achieved through a balance of power between competing states. However, this balance can sometimes shift, producing instability.	**Liberals agree** with Anarchical society theory's optimism that order and cooperation are possible. The 'society of states' will form shared rules and norms. It is in states' own interests to follow these. States that ignore these can be isolated by others.
States create international organisations in which they co-operate according to shared norms and values, although sovereign states remain the key actors in these.	**Realists disagree** with the idea of an interconnected 'society of states' that pursues common interests. They believe that states only engage in international institutions if they can use them to achieve their own interests, so if they engage at all, it is likely to be temporary and unreliable.	**Liberals disagree** with the anarchical society theory's assumption that the sovereign state remains the primary actor in global politics; they also see IGOs as important. Liberals argue that states can pool sovereignty through supranational organisations and can make binding treaties which constrain their sovereignty.
Synoptic links	Realists believe that international anarchy resembles Hobbes' conception of the anarchic 'state of nature', in which conflict is inevitable. This is because, in the absence of a supranational authority, states pursue their own national interests, which do not coincide with those of other states. Realists are therefore sceptical about the role of shared values in state behaviour. The Anarchical Society theory challenges the Hobbesian view that anarchy inevitably leads to conflict.	Liberals believe that international anarchy has been transformed by complex interdependence, which incentivises co-operation, whilst the Anarchical Society theory suggests state behaviour is guided by shared norms and values of co-operation. These ideas both bear some resemblance to Locke's conception of the state of nature, in which a society or 'commonwealth' of rational, sovereign individuals can co-operate for the common good.

Section B questions on the anarchical society theory/society of states theory

Questions on this are likely to ask **how realists and liberals view this theory**. This is because the comparative element of comparative politics questions will always focus on realism and liberalism. To answer this question, use the structure below. Please note that unlike other Section B comparative questions, answers for this question do benefit from a brief introduction outlining the basic argument of anarchical society and society of states theory. A major weakness of pupil exam answers was that they had no awareness of the theory, and the analysis was either inaccurate or focused exclusively on realism and liberalism.

How to structure an answer on the Anarchical Society Theory

Introduction (a brief overview of anarchical society/society of states theory):	→ Hedley Bull coined the anarchical society/society of states theory, and it is associated with the English School of International Relations. → It suggests that states are the most important actors in international politics and that they exist under international anarchy. → Order in the system can change over time; at times it represents a system of states whereby states factor one another into their calculations and engage in temporary cooperation, or a society of states whereby states have shared interests, rules and institutions. → Anarchical society/society of states theory draws upon both realism and liberalism in different ways and shares many similarities and differences between the two theories.
Similarities between both realism and liberalism and anarchical society/society of states theory:	→ Areas of agreement between anarchical society/society of states theory and realism. → Areas of agreement between anarchical society/society of states theory and liberalism (see table 1.3).
Differences between both realism and liberalism and anarchical society/society of states theory:	→ Areas of disagreement between anarchical society/society of states theory and realism. → Areas of disagreement between anarchical society/society of states theory and liberalism.

Realist and liberal explanations of developments in global politics post-2000

Developments in global politics can be analysed through either a realist or liberal lens: the same event can look very different depending on which explanatory lens it is viewed from. Once you understand the key arguments of realists and liberals, it is possible to apply them to key developments in global politics. As you read through this textbook, you will need to think about the examples provided and whether you think realism or liberalism provides the best explanation for them (in some cases, this is done for you).

Table 1.4 applies realist and liberal explanations to some key developments in global politics post-2000.

Exam Tip:
It is good practice to stay informed about the most recent developments in global politics and analyse them using your knowledge of realism and liberalism. The use of these recent developments can help differentiate Level 4 from Level 3 answers (see Chapter 10).

Table 1.4 Key Developments in Global Politics Post-2000

Development and overview	Realist explanation	Liberal explanation
11 September 2000 (9/11) Terrorist Attack on the US On 11 September 2001, al-Qaeda terrorists hijacked four commercial airplanes. Two struck the World Trade Center, one hit the Pentagon and another crashed in Pennsylvania. Nearly 3,000 people died in these coordinated attacks. The events prompted the United States to launch the 'War on Terror', leading to military interventions in Afghanistan and later Iraq.	Realists would view 9/11 as an illustration of the vulnerability of states to non-state actors and the enduring importance of national security. The US response, particularly the subsequent 'War on Terror', is seen as a classic realist move to reassert its power and deterrence capability, eliminate a perceived threat and prevent future attacks through unilateral action when necessary.	Liberals would emphasise 9/11 as a devastating attack on democratic values and the liberal international order, highlighting the fragility of peace when violent non-state actors operate outside international norms and institutions. They would call for a comprehensive global response involving international law enforcement cooperation, intelligence sharing, and addressing the root causes of terrorism (e.g. poverty, political grievances, lack of democracy).
The Global Financial Crisis (2008) In 2008, a severe worldwide economic crisis erupted, primarily triggered by the collapse of the US housing market and complex financial products. This led to a credit crunch, banking failures (e.g. Lehman Brothers), stock market crashes and a global recession. Addressed by the G20, it necessitated massive government bailouts and significant international financial interventions to stabilise the world economy.	Realists would interpret the Global Financial Crisis as a demonstration of economic power competition and the inherent instability that arises when states prioritise narrow economic gains without sufficient attention to strategic stability. They might also point to the initial nationalistic responses (e.g. protectionist pressures, 'beggar-thy-neighbour' policies) as states prioritised their own domestic economies. The crisis revealed the danger of mutual vulnerabilities inherent in an interconnected globalised system. For realists, the ultimate solutions still resided within the actions of powerful states protecting their own economic interests, even if some cooperation was necessary to prevent systemic collapse.	Liberals would see the Global Financial Crisis as an example of global interdependence and the need for international institutions and cooperation to manage complex transnational problems. They would argue that the crisis was exacerbated by a lack of international financial regulation, insufficient oversight of global capital flows, and failures in multilateral coordination. Liberals would advocate for strengthening institutions like the IMF (International Monetary Fund) and the G20, increasing transparency, and developing globally agreed-upon regulatory frameworks to prevent future crises and ensure the stability and prosperity of the interconnected global economy through collective action.

Development and overview	Realist explanation	Liberal explanation
Brexit (UK's Withdrawal from the EU), 2016. In a 2016 referendum, the UK voted to leave the EU by a narrow 51 per cent majority. Following years of complex negotiations, the UK officially withdrew on 31 January 2020, ending its 47-year membership. This triggered significant changes to its trade, immigration and regulatory policies, impacting both the UK and the wider EU.	Realists interpret Brexit as a clear manifestation of the primacy of national interest and state sovereignty. The UK, perceiving a loss of control over its borders, laws and trade policy within the EU (a supranational institution), chose to reassert its autonomy and relative power on the global stage. Concerns about national security, regaining control over immigration and achieving greater economic self-sufficiency are seen as core drivers.	Liberals largely view Brexit as a significant setback for international cooperation, economic integration and the liberal international order. They see the weakening of a strong regional institution like the EU, which has historically promoted peace, extensive trade and shared democratic values among its members, as a significant step backwards. The decision is often viewed as irrational in purely economic terms, as it sacrifices the absolute gains derived from deep integration and frictionless trade. The subsequent social and economic challenges faced by the UK are often cited as evidence of the inherent benefits and stability that come from strong international cooperation and institutional ties.
Global Response to the Covid-19 Pandemic, 2020. Beginning in early 2020, the Covid-19 pandemic rapidly spread globally, causing immense health, economic and social disruption. While massive vaccine development occurred, the global response was often characterised by nationalistic policies, intense competition for resources and challenges to international coordination, despite widespread recognition of the virus's global nature.	Realists would emphasise the primacy of national interest and state-centric, self-help behaviour throughout the pandemic. They would point to rapid border closures, the intense competition for medical supplies and vaccine nationalism, where states prioritised their own populations (e.g. hoarding personal protective equipment, striking bilateral vaccine deals) over coordinated global collective action. International organisations like the WHO were often sidelined or struggled to effectively coordinate a truly global response due to a lack of genuine commitment from powerful states.	Liberals would highlight the initial widespread calls for global cooperation, the vital efforts of international organisations (e.g. the WHO), and the unprecedented scientific collaboration across borders to rapidly develop vaccines and treatments and share data. While acknowledging instances of nationalistic behaviour, liberals would argue that the pandemic underscored the absolute necessity of multilateralism and shared responsibility for transnational challenges.

Component III: Global Politics

> **Exam Tip:**
> In Section B, you could be asked to analyse realist and liberal views of developments in global politics since 2000. In this question, you could use one of two approaches:
>
> **Approach One:** Select two/three key developments and analyse realist and liberal interpretations of them (as per Table 1.4).
>
> **Approach Two:** Select two/three global issues explored in this textbook (e.g. conflict, environment, poverty and human rights) and analyse realist and liberal interpretations of them (using information from chapters in this textbook).

Development and overview	Realist explanation	Liberal explanation
Russia's Invasion of Ukraine, February 2022. On 24 February 2022, Russia launched a full-scale invasion of Ukraine, escalating the conflict that began in 2014 (see Chapter 3). Russian forces crossed borders from multiple directions, aiming for key cities like Kyiv. The invasion led to widespread destruction, millions of displaced persons, and a significant international response, including extensive sanctions against Russia and military aid to Ukraine.	Realists see this invasion primarily as a power struggle and a response to Russia's perceived security threats. Russia, a great power, viewed NATO expansion eastward and Ukraine's growing alignment with the West as an existential challenge to its sphere of influence and national security. Vladimir Putin's actions are interpreted as a classic attempt to restore Russia's relative power in its near abroad, to create a buffer zone and to challenge the US-led liberal international order.	Liberals fundamentally view this as a gross violation of international law, national sovereignty and democratic principles. They emphasise Russia's blatant disregard for international institutions like the UN Charter, human rights and the self-determination of the Ukrainian people. For liberals, the invasion highlights the fragility of peace when autocratic states reject the established rules-based order. They advocate for strong multilateral responses, diplomatic efforts, economic sanctions and robust support for democratic norms, believing that collective action and adherence to international law are essential to restore stability and deter future aggression.

Comparative Theories

 ## Chapter Summary

- ✓ Realism argues that global politics is characterised by international anarchy. It is a self-help system where sovereign states are the primary actors pursuing survival and power. It views the international order as inherently competitive and conflict-prone due to human nature and the absence of a world government.

- ✓ For realists, war is seen as inevitable due to the egoistic nature of humans (classical realism) or structural pressures of international anarchy (neo-realism), with peace only possible as a temporary balance of power. The security dilemma ensures that even defensive actions provoke distrust, leading to arms races and war.

- ✓ Liberalism views global politics as a cooperative arena where multiple actors (not just states) interact through institutions, laws and shared norms. It emphasises human rationality, moral progress and the potential for peace through mutual interests.

- ✓ Peace is seen as achievable through democracy, trade and international organisations, which create complex interdependence. War is not inevitable but results from either a deliberate choice (e.g. self-defence, humanitarian intervention) or from a breakdown in cooperation, poor governance or lack of institutional frameworks.

- ✓ Anarchical society theory and society of states theory acknowledge the realist notion of international anarchy but argues that states can form a 'society of states' governed by norms, rules and mutual interests. It blends realism's caution with liberalism's optimism.

- ✓ While recognising the absence of a world government, anarchical society theory and society of states theory suggests that war can be avoided through shared understandings and informal rules that foster predictable, cooperative behaviour among states.

 ## Exam Style Questions

- Analyse the differences between realists and liberals on their views of international anarchy and global governance. (12)
- Analyse the differences between realists and liberals on their views of developments in global politics since 2000. (12)
- Analyse the differences between realists and liberals on the impact and growth of international organisations. (12)
- Analyse the views between realists and liberals concerning the likelihood of conflict. (12)
- Analyse the differences between realism and liberalism concerning the anarchical society/society of states theory.

 ## Further Resources

https://www.youtube.com/watch?v=-WwCm889Vqo 'Balance of Power'. A useful video explaining balance of power and the strategies of balancing and bandwagoning.

https://www.youtube.com/watch?v=WSTpzOEk0VA 'Realism in International Relations explained in 60 seconds'. This is a useful introductory video explaining the key ideas of realism.

https://www.youtube.com/watch?v=oKfyvL2wQIA 'How Realism in International Relations Shapes the World'. This video goes into further depth about the key ideas of realism using real-world examples to illustrate them.

https://www.youtube.com/watch?v=Hl43BizGd5c 'Realism vs. Liberalism – Global Politics Theories Compared'. This video compares different explanations of global politics offered by realism and liberalism.

https://www.youtube.com/watch?v=lV9zxxNwMY4 'What is Liberalism in Global Politics'. This video goes into further depth about the key ideas of liberalism using real-world examples to illustrate them.

 Visit https://bloomsbury.pub/essentials-of-global-politics to access additional materials to support teaching and learning.

2 THE STATE AND GLOBALISATION

Chapter Preview

This chapter explores the 'nation-state' and 'state sovereignty'. This is the idea that nation-states are the primary actors in global politics, and that they have the right in international law to autonomous control of their own territories, without interference by other actors.

The sovereignty of the nation-state has been challenged by globalisation. Nation-states have become increasingly interconnected and interdependent through economic, cultural and political relations. Globalisation means that even local or national events can have global implications. Whilst globalisation itself is not new, globalisation as we know it today has escalated steadily from the Second World War onwards and rapidly intensified following the end of the Cold War in the 1990s.

In recent decades there has been a significant backlash against globalisation as some nation-states seek to reassert their sovereignty. This has been driven by many factors. First, the increasing volatility of the global economy, evidenced by the Global Financial Crisis (2008). Secondly, the rise of nationalism and identity politics, particularly in the wake of the 2016 US election in which Donald Trump became US president, and thirdly in the fallout from the Covid-19 pandemic (2020). Critically, the powerful nation-states that were once the major beneficiaries of globalisation are struggling to retain their top positions. The backlash against globalisation has resulted in what some have labelled 'the return of the nation-state', characterised by increased protectionist policies, a re-evaluation of international trade agreements, and, in some cases, a tightening of immigration and migration policies. Some commentators have called this process deglobalisation.

Key Questions and Debates
» What are the characteristics of the nation-state and state sovereignty?
» Which factors have driven the process of globalisation?
» What is the impact of globalisation on global politics?
» What are the different types of globalisation – economic, cultural and political?
» What impact does globalisation have on contemporary global issues?

Specification Checklist

1.1 The state: nation-state and national sovereignty
» Characteristics of a nation-state and of national sovereignty

1.2 Globalisation
» The process of globalisation: complex web of interconnectedness – the driving factors of globalisation are the interlinking of people (social), countries, institutions, culture, economics, technology and politics
» Its impact on the state system
» Widening and deepening interconnectedness and interdependence
» Challenge to state control over citizens in areas such as law, especially through the development of international law. How and why this has resulted in humanitarian and forcible intervention
» The debate between hyperglobalisers, globalisation sceptics and transformationalists, including the realist and liberal views

1.3 Debates about the impact of globalisation, including its advantages and disadvantages
» The impact of globalisation, and its implications for the nation-state and national sovereignty

1.4 The ways and extent to which globalisation addresses and resolves contemporary issues, such as poverty, conflict, human rights and the environment

Source: Sofia Cangiano / Unsplash

Component III: Global Politics

Spec key term

The nation-state: An autonomous political community, based within a shared territory bound together by shared citizenship and nationality.

State sovereignty: The idea that all states exercise authority within their borders and have the right to non-intervention in their external affairs.

The nation-state and state sovereignty

The 'nation-state' and the principle of 'state sovereignty' are the cornerstones of global politics but are themselves contested concepts and their meaning and relevance has changed (*and will continue to change*) over time.

The state

Although the specification does not define the 'state', you will understand the term as referring to the sovereign authority of government in components 1 and 2.

In international law, the criteria for what should be considered to be a 'state' were set out in the Montevideo Convention of 1933. This outlined that a state should have:

- A defined territory
- A permanent population
- An effective government
- The capacity to enter into relations with other states

These criteria raise more questions than they answer – for example, is a state still a state if it lacks an effective government or if the legitimacy of its government is disputed by its own people, resulting in civil war? And what does the 'capacity' to enter into relations with other states really mean? Therefore, in global politics, a different definition has become more meaningful: a **political entity** becomes a state when it is recognised by other states, conferring the right to full membership of the United Nations (UN).

There are currently 193 member states in the UN. South Sudan is the newest member, having joined in 2011. In addition, there are also two non-member observer states in the UN, the Holy See and Palestine, both of which can attend General Assembly debates and discussions but cannot vote on resolutions. Palestine's status in the UN has long been contested.

Chapter Link

The UN and its member states are dealt with in depth in **Chapter 4: Political Global Governance**, where there is a detailed explanation of the debate over Palestinian statehood.

Definition

Political entity or state-like-entity: A territory which meets the criteria for statehood but lacks formal recognition and is considered part of the territory of another state. For example, Somaliland is a political entity that is considered by most states to be a part of Somalia, so, whilst it is a state-like entity, it is not a recognised state.

Photo 2.1 Iraqi Kurds protest for Kurdistan independence at an event to urge people to vote in the independence referendum, September 2017.

Source: Safin Hamid /AFP via Getty Images

The nation-state

The 'nation-state' is an ideal form of state, which the specification defines as an 'autonomous political community held together by citizenship and nationality'. This definition requires some explanation.

A nation refers to a group of people who share a common identity and sense of belonging based on a shared language, religion, culture or race and ethnicity. The nation is sometimes understood as a 'political community' as this group seeks to prioritise its own national identity and interests. Nationality is subjective: a nation exists if a group of people identify itself as a nation. Most states, like the UK, have multiple nations living inside their borders (including England, Northern Ireland, Scotland and Wales), so there are many more nations than there are recognised states in global politics. There are also nations, such as the Kurds, who live in territory that has been divided between different states (see photo 2.2).

In contrast, the concept of 'citizenship' is a formal recognition of the individual by the state, regardless of their subjective national identity. It refers to a citizen's right to live in and enjoy rights conferred by a state. Hence, someone with a Scottish national identity is likely to be a British citizen with a British passport. Different states have different rules for citizenship based on birthplace and parentage, but they all have rules that confer citizenship to some people and not to others. Therefore, for ease of general use, the population of the 'nation-state' is often understood as the citizens recognised by a governing state, regardless of their own national identities.

The idea of an 'autonomous political community' implies self-rule by the nation or at least rule by their consent, often described as 'self-determination'. However, separatist struggles for national self-determination are very common: Somaliland, Palestine, Tibet and 'East Turkistan' (Chinese: Xinjiang) are a few examples. In these cases, the national political community is not autonomous. Furthermore, many so-called nation-states are ruled by unelected authoritarians: the populations of Iran or North Korea could also not accurately be described as 'autonomous political communities'. However, in general use, the term 'nation-state' tends to be applied to any state with its own sovereign government, able to function without outside interference, regardless of the consent of its people.

In sum, the term 'nation-state' is problematic, not only because the terms 'nation' and 'state' are themselves problematic, but because it is an ideal that tends not to stand up to contact with reality, and because in general use it is applied much more broadly than it should be.

For this reason, in this book, we tend to refer to the broader term 'state' rather than 'nation-state'. By 'state', we mean a territory with a sovereign government, recognised and accepted as a full UN member by other states.

> **Exam Tip:** Students who studied the Nationalism option in Component 2 may be familiar with the 'nation', 'state' and 'nation-state', but other students may not be. Do not worry – Component 3b *Global Politics* does not define the 'nation' or the 'state' and you do not have to differentiate between them. However, you should understand that the 'nation-state' is a problematic concept, and that national separatist struggles within states are a common cause of civil wars – which is particularly relevant to global politics.

State sovereignty

Closely linked to the concept of the state is the concept of state sovereignty. The origins of state sovereignty can be traced back to the Treaty of Westphalia in 1648, where it was agreed between European states that they each had an equal right to independence and should not interfere in each other's domestic affairs. Today, state sovereignty is understood as being a state's authority within its borders and the protection of its borders in international law.

The principle of state sovereignty is the cornerstone of international relations today and is a key principle outlined in the UN Charter. The UN Charter is the foundational treaty of the UN and outlines the key goals and principal organs of the organisation. By becoming member states of the UN, members agree to follow the terms of the UN Charter. Table 2.1 shows the key aspects of the UN Charter which relate to state sovereignty. See Chapter 4 for more detail on the UN Charter.

Sovereignty is often understood to have two distinct dimensions: internal and external (see Table 2.2). Internal sovereignty refers to a state having authority within its own borders. In this respect, a state has the political independence to govern as it sees fit, i.e. making laws and enforcing them. External sovereignty refers to the permanence or 'inviolability' of a state's borders. Because states have the right to external sovereignty, it is against international law for another state to pursue a war of aggression against a fellow state or to take territory from another state. The use of force against a fellow state is only permissible in self-defence (i.e. to defend against an attack) or if authorised by the UN Security Council (UNSC). External sovereignty also means that states should be free from outside interference in their domestic affairs, for example, freedom from interference by another state in their elections.

> **Exam Tip:** Whilst these are not terms in the specification, and you will not be asked questions on the distinction between internal or external sovereignty, they are useful themes. Stronger exam answers will normally make a distinction between internal and external sovereignty in their answers.

Chapter Link

The UN Charter and the powers of the UNSC to authorise states to enforce these principles of international law are discussed in greater depth in **Chapter 4: Political Global Governance**, and the Responsibility to Protect is a key feature of **Chapter 6: Human Rights Global Governance**.

Table 2.1 The UN Charter and State Sovereignty

Article	Text	What does this mean?
2 (1)	Establishes the 'sovereign equality' of all UN member states.	All member states are **equally** sovereign. No member state is more or less sovereign than another.
2 (4)	Prohibits the threat or use of force against the 'territorial integrity or political independence' of any state.	States are not allowed to threaten or use force against other states, either to challenge the authority of the state to make laws within its borders or to change its existing borders.
2 (7)	Upholds the principle of 'non-intervention' in the domestic affairs of states (unless permitted by the UN Security Council – see Chapter 4, p. X).	States should not interfere in the affairs of other states. Because states have authority within their borders, other states should avoid involving themselves in the business of running the state.

Table 2.2 Differences between Internal and External Sovereignty

	Internal sovereignty	External sovereignty
What is it?	A state has the authority to govern within its own borders as it sees fit. For example, the state can choose which political system to implement, and has the right to make and enforce laws.	A state is independent on the international stage; its borders are secure and it is independent from outside interference in its internal affairs.
Examples of when a state might **possess** this type of sovereignty.	All member states of the UN have the right to their internal sovereignty, recognised in Chapter 2(7) of the UN Charter. For example, the national government of the United Kingdom based in Westminster exercises control over all reserved matters affecting the UK.	All member states of the UN have the right to their external sovereignty, recognised in Chapter 2(4) of the UN Charter. For example, the United Kingdom is recognised within its external borders, by other states.
Examples of when a state might **lack** this type of sovereignty.	A failed state may no longer have its internal sovereignty. This is either because it does not control its own territory or does not exercise effective governance within its territory. For example, Somalia would fit into this category because it neither exercises control over its full territory, owing to part of its territory being a breakaway state, Somaliland, and some of its territory being occupied by the terrorist group, Al Shabab. It also does not have effective governance in the area under governmental control, with widespread poverty and corruption rife.	A state which commits gross human rights violations, such as crimes against humanity or genocide against its population, could lose its external sovereignty under the idea of humanitarian intervention (see Chapter 6). For example, in 1998, NATO launched airstrikes against the sovereign territory of Serbia due to the human rights violations it was committing against its ethnic Albanian population in Kosovo. Following this, the UN established an International Administration in Kosovo, exercising its authority to govern within Kosovo, removing Serbian authority within the territory.

State sovereignty is held in such high regard by states that any violations are met with condemnation. For example, when Russia invaded the sovereign state of Ukraine in 2022, it was met with condemnation as Russia had violated the territorial integrity (external sovereignty) of its neighbour. Similarly, when Russian agents poisoned a Russian dissident in Salisbury in 2018, this undermined the UK's external sovereignty.

However, in practice, state sovereignty is not absolute, and not all states are equally sovereign. Increasingly, it is held that with sovereignty comes responsibility, a notion sometimes referred to as 'sovereignty as responsibility'. This is the basis of the UN idea of the Responsibility to Protect – the idea that if a state is committing mass atrocity crimes (e.g. genocide, war crimes, ethnic cleansing or crimes against humanity) then the international community has a responsibility to help stop it, including the possibility of taking military action against the perpetrator state. A further challenge to the sovereign state is the process of globalisation, which we will look at in the following section.

What is globalisation?

If you walked down London's Oxford Street, you could have some Thai food for lunch, buy yourself a T-shirt designed in the United States, but produced in Pakistan, before getting out your Chinese phone to watch a South Korean drama on an American streaming service. The world has never been as interconnected as it currently is. **Globalisation** is the term used to describe the ever-widening and deepening connections across the world that have taken place following the Second World War and at a much more rapid intensity following the end of the Cold War. However, there is now considerable debate about whether globalisation is in decline, a trend called '**deglobalisation**' (See case study: The United States and the Deglobalisation Movement, page 53).

Globalisation is not a singular event. Instead, it should be understood as a process of widening and deepening connections between states, across multiple domains, including economics, culture and politics see table 2.3.

The world cannot be neatly divided into 'globalised' and 'non-globalised' areas: the degree of global interconnectedness and integration varies widely between states and in different regions of the world, and between the economic, cultural and political domains.

There are many different drivers of the processes of globalisation (and deglobalisation). See table 2.4. (remember that globalisation is not a one-way process – it can also retreat through deglobalisation):

> **Definition**
>
> **Globalisation:** A process whereby we see the emergence of a complex web of interconnectedness that means that the experiences of states and their citizens are increasingly shaped by global events.
>
> **Deglobalisation:** The process of declining interconnectedness and integration among states.

Table 2.3 Widening and Deepening Globalisation

Widening ↔	The concept of 'widening' in the context of globalisation refers to its **extent** or **reach**. This encompasses two key dimensions: firstly, its **spatial expansion**, meaning the increasing number of geographical locations, regions and countries becoming interconnected within global networks. Secondly, 'widening' also applies to the **proliferation across different types of globalisation**, such as economic, cultural and political integration. These various forms of globalisation are not static but are continually evolving, leading to new areas of interconnectedness and expanding the overall scope of globalisation.
Deepening ↕	The concept of 'deepening' globalisation refers to the **increasing intensity, significance and impact** of global interconnectedness across its various dimensions. This 'depth' can be understood in relation to the **growing volume of interactions**, encompassing trade, investment, communication and cultural exchange. Furthermore, deepening globalisation is often associated with a **complex and evolving relationship with state sovereignty**. This can manifest as a perceived **erosion or transformation of traditional state authority**, where the capacity of the state to exert exclusive control within its borders or regulate the cross-border flows of goods, people, services and ideas is increasingly challenged or mediated by transnational actors, global norms and interconnected systems.

> **Chapter Link**
>
> In global politics, distinctions are made between states based upon the level of power they can project internationally, thereby having influence over other states; for example there are superpowers, great powers and emerging powers. See **Chapter 3: Power and Developments** for more on these types.

Table 2.4 Drivers of Globalisation

Driver	Explanation
People (social)	People can drive globalisation in lots of different ways. They can drive globalisation through their behaviour as consumers with their demand for global goods and services such as fashion, food, music and social media. Increased opportunities for global travel and tourism also drive the process of globalisation helping to make the world more interconnected.
States	States can drive the process of globalisation through their policy decisions. Their economic policies can promote trade between states, and they can also make it easier for transnational corporations to operate within their borders. Economically, states can also join regional organisations or regional trading agreements, which can operate to make the world more interconnected (see **Chapter 9**). States can also join intergovernmental organisations, such as the World Trade Organisation, whose role is to break down barriers to trade between states. More broadly, state membership of IGOs helps to create more opportunities for interdependence between states across different issue areas. States can also develop their infrastructure to help increase the movement of goods, people and services, as well as to encourage global travel. Finally, states can introduce policies to support innovation in technology, which helps to drive forward globalisation.
Institutions	Institutions such as IGOs can help drive forward globalisation by creating increased opportunities for interdependence between states and other global actors by encouraging cooperation across different issue areas (widening) and increased intensity of cooperation within issues (deepening).
Culture	The emergence of global brands and popular culture, as well as social media, has played an important role in promoting globalisation. They have led to the emergence of a common global culture; however, the extent to which this is the case is the subject of controversy (see Key Debate, p53-55).
Economics	There are many economic drivers of globalisation which have helped to create greater interdependence. In particular, neoliberal economic policies have helped bring about increased trade agreements and the breaking down of barriers to trade through the development of free trade. Economic necessities have also led to the movement of labour across the world.
Technology	Technology has been a major driver of globalisation. Technological innovation has helped bring about greater levels of global trade, especially through facilitating financial transactions across the world. It has helped to foster connections between people from one part of the world to another. It has also enabled greater infrastructural projects, which help facilitate globalisation worldwide.
Politics	Politics is a major driver of globalisation because without the political desire to foster interdependence, it simply would not happen. If globalisation has happened, it is because politics has enabled it. Likewise, in some cases, politics is also a major driver in the process of retreating from globalisation.

Types of globalisation

Globalisation can be classified into three distinct yet interconnected types: **economic**, **cultural** and **political**. While many events or phenomena, such as the rise of transnational corporations (TNCs) and global social media platforms have ramifications across these three categories, analysing the impact of globalisation through these lenses can help to clarify the ways in which it has transformed global politics.

Economic globalisation

Economic globalisation refers to the emergence of a single global economy or market.

This manifests through several key processes, including:

1. **The increasing interconnectedness and integration of national economies.** This happens due to the cross-border flows of people, goods, capital and services, which deepens the interconnectedness of national economies. It is often driven by the desire to liberalise trade, meaning the removal of obstacles to movement such as travel visas, trade tariffs or variations in regulations between states.

2. **The role of transnational corporations (TNCs).** These powerful actors operate across national borders, shaping and facilitating the creation of a global marketplace that operates beyond the direct control of individual states.

We will now explore each of these aspects of economic globalisation in more detail, illustrating them with examples.

Increasing interconnectedness and integration of national economies

The interconnectedness of the global economy is driven by its capitalist economic system. Within this system, the key goal is to generate profit. To do this, businesses tend to establish operations where production costs are lower – for example, if there is easy access to raw materials, cheap and plentiful supply of labour or low regulations and corporation taxes. The pursuit of profit in a capitalist economy strongly incentivises specialisation and trade based on comparative advantage.

The theory of comparative advantage means that a state produces what it is able to produce most efficiently, which gives it an advantage over other producers elsewhere. Utilising comparative advantage further deepens global interconnectedness because of the necessity of extensive international trade to meet demand for goods and services produced in different places. Following the period of stagnation and inflation in the 1970s, neoliberalism came to dominate the global economy, which also helped to drive interdependence and integration. Neoliberalism views the global economy as a self-regulating system, independent from state control. It encourages free trade between states, foreign direct investment to drive economic growth and low taxation to allow the economy to thrive.

World trade increased steadily in the wake of the Second World War, which saw the establishment of the institutions of global economic governance. However, it was not until the 1990s that we witnessed the rapid acceleration of world trade. This was due to two main developments:

1. **The economic growth of China**

    Following economic reforms in the 1970s, the Chinese economy gradually opened itself up to international trade. Owing to its large population and plentiful supply of cheap labour, China was able to position itself as a major global manufacturing hub and is referred to as 'the World's Factory'. The growth of China led to a surge in both imports (of raw materials) and exports (manufactured goods), further driving global trade.

2. **The collapse of the Soviet Union**

    The dissolution of the Soviet Union in 1991 led to the opening of new markets with the newly formed Russian Federation and fifteen new states providing new opportunities for global trade.

Figure 2.1 shows the rapid growth in world trade from 1990 to the present day, demonstrating the level of economic interconnectedness in global politics today.

The extent of interconnectedness is most clearly evidenced by the impact of global economic crises. Figure 2.1 indicates that there have been two sudden decelerations in global trade. First, the world

> **Exam Tip:**
> Deglobalisation is not a term on the specification, so you will not be asked a specific question about it. However, it is important that you are aware that globalisation is a two-way process; if you have a question on the impact of globalisation, it is important to acknowledge recent trends towards deglobalisation.

> **Exam Tip:**
> Economic, cultural and political globalisation are named on the Pearson Edexcel specification, so you could be asked to compare their features, causes or impacts. In a 30-mark question, you could be asked to evaluate the impact of one or more of these types of globalisation.

Chapter Link

The theory of comparative advantage and the influence of neoliberal ideas on global financial institutions are explained in **Chapter 5: Economic Global Governance**.

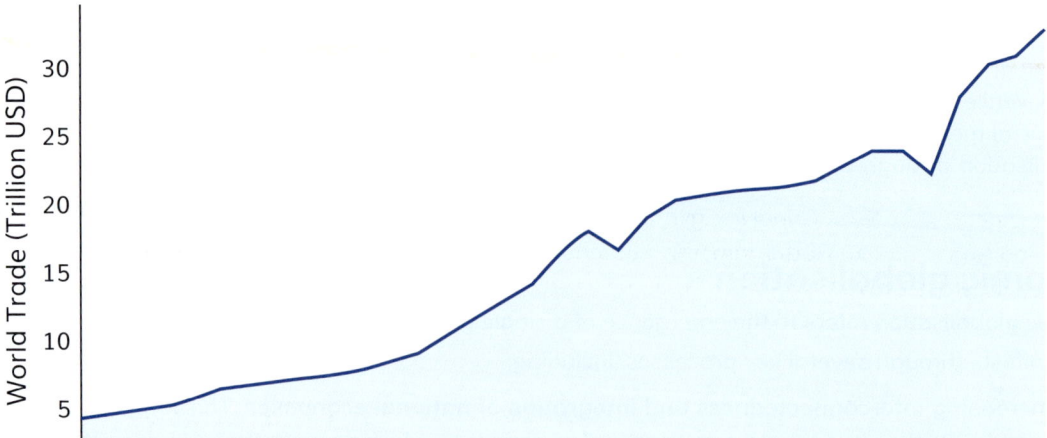

Figure 2.1 World trade (1990–2024)

Source: Graph created with data from the World Trade Organisation

economy shrank between 2007 and 2009 due to the **Global Financial Crisis (GFC)**. The Global Financial Crisis (GFC) began in the United States. The banking crisis resulted from widespread sales of high-risk financial products. The failure of Lehman Brothers, a major investment bank, spread to other international banks. Lending was dramatically reduced, triggering stock market crashes and a global 'great recession'. According to the IMF, global GDP contracted by 6% in the final quarter of 2008 and the first quarter of 2009. The crisis was contained through coordinated G20 action, including large government-funded bank bailouts and stimulus measures to stabilise the financial system.

Second, the global economy shrank again due to the **Covid-19 pandemic** in 2020. Here, the economic crisis was triggered by the emergence and spread of the SARS virus in China, which was declared a global health pandemic in 2020. The ensuing global lockdowns, disruption to supply chains and reduced demand for global goods and services delivered a serious shock to the global economy and a recession. The IMF estimated that in 2020 global GDP shrank by 2.2 per cent, with the UN estimating that the pandemic led to $8.5 trillion in losses.

However, it is not simply global crises that indicate the level of interconnectedness in the global economy; in a globalised economy, even seemingly localised events can have global ramifications (see **Case Study: The Ever Given Crisis**).

In addition to increased economic interconnectedness in the area of global trade, economic globalisation has also been fuelled by political globalisation, in particular the establishment of a system of global economic governance which helps shape the economic behaviours of states and non-state actors in global politics. Most notably, the liberalisation of trade and resultant reduction in barriers to trade has helped to create a single global economy. The profound interconnectedness of national economies emerged as a defining characteristic of the twentieth and twenty-first centuries.

Driven by the post-Second World War recognition at the Bretton Woods Conference that economic interdependence could serve as a bulwark against future global conflict, the architects of a new economic system deliberately established institutions for global economic governance to help increase the integration of national economies. These organisations were specifically designed to actively promote the growth of free trade and provide a framework for resolving trade disputes (WTO), ensure the stability and health of the global financial system (IMF), and empower developing nations through vital financial and technical assistance (World Bank).

Nowhere has economic integration been stronger than in the area of global finance. Aided by ongoing technological innovations, we now have a truly global financial system. Financial transactions can take place in real-time anywhere across the globe, making it easier to buy and sell goods and services. A

CASE STUDY: THE EVER GIVEN CRISIS

Events

In March 2021, strong winds caused a 400-metre-long container ship, the *Ever Given*, to become wedged diagonally across the Suez Canal in Egypt. The ship was sailing from China to Rotterdam, the Netherlands. It blocked the Suez Canal for a total of 6 days before authorities were able to unblock it.

Significance

The economic impact of the blockage on world trade was significant. The Suez Canal connects the Mediterranean Sea and the Red Sea and provides the shortest sea link between Asia and Europe. Over 12 per cent of global trade passes through it annually. The next shortest sea link is the Cape Route via South Africa, which takes approximately 10 days longer. The economic cost for the closure of the Suez Canal was estimated at $400 million per hour. Losses were caused by many factors, including:

- Some ships had to divert and take the Cape Route, which incurred greater costs (e.g. fuel, salaries, etc.)
- Supply chains were disrupted, leading to production slowdowns (many manufacturing companies use 'just-in-time' systems to manage stock and do not store a surplus of materials used to manufacture their products).
- A number of industries were affected, including the automotive industry (due to component delays), the energy sector (delays to oil and gas delivery) and the retail sector (delay in consumer goods).
- Perishable goods suffered spoilage and became unsellable, leading to significant losses.
- The Suez Canal Authority lost approximately $12–$15 million per day in lost transit fees.

By the time the *Ever Given* was freed, there were approximately 400 ships queuing to pass through the canal. In total, the 6-day disruption held up $60 billion worth of global trade.

The crisis starkly demonstrated the interconnectedness of the global economy, since it showed how a localised event had global ramifications. The fragility of global supply chains was clearly highlighted by the crisis and led to increased awareness of the economic risks of globalisation. Such large supply chains increase the risk that manufacturers are exposed to, and the success of their business is dependent on well-maintained and functioning global transport networks. As a consequence, the incident may have accelerated a shift towards companies using shorter supply chains (e.g. nearshoring) to mitigate the risk of globalised systems of production.

---

globalised banking system also generates capital for investment in business, which in turn generates increased capital in the global economy. Additionally, currencies are traded globally on foreign exchange markets and are determined by global market forces. States also gain access to finance through issuing **bonds**, which global investors can choose to invest in. Whilst this offers states flexible credit at low interest rates, it places states under significant pressure from their creditors, which can in turn affect state policies, for example by insisting on **austerity** measures.

The role of TNCs

TNCs have taken advantage of transnational production. TNCs will draw raw material from one state, produce their products in another, and complete the branding in a third before finally selling their products elsewhere. By doing so, they can take advantage of cheap raw materials, low-wage labour and benefit from basing their activities in countries with lower corporation taxes. Global supply chains have become easier as transport has become both more efficient and dropped in cost. Apple has an infamous global supply chain; it designs its products in California, but outsources manufacturing across a range of countries, including China and India, and its components are sourced from over forty states worldwide.

Cultural globalisation

Cultural globalisation has also escalated in recent years, not least due to improvements in communications technologies and transport. In important respects, cultural globalisation is fuelled by economic globalisation and vice versa, since it is the demand for global goods and services that helps increase economic globalisation and it is the availability and access to global goods and services that

> **Definition**
>
> **Bonds:** A bond is a debt security issued by a state which promises to pay investors a fixed interest over a specific period and repay the principal amount on a specified maturity date. They typically have lower interest rate yields than traditional bank loans for comparable amounts due to their market liquidity and broad investor base.

CASE STUDY: GYMSHARK

Events

Founded in 2012, Gymshark is a British brand founded by university students Ben Francis and Lewis Morgan. The company was based out of Francis's garage and operated on a make-to-order basis, using a sewing machine and a screen-printer. Gymshark went global following one of their products, the Luxe Tracksuit, going viral on Facebook following its exhibition at a fitness trade show in 2012. Within 30 minutes of going viral, £30,000 of sales were generated. From this point onwards, Gymshark has become a significant player in the global fitness apparel market with a revenue of £404 million with £203 million profits (2023–4).

Significance

Gymshark has effectively used the benefits of globalisation to ensure its ongoing success:

- **A global supply chain:** Gymshark uses suppliers from across the globe to make its products. A significant portion of its manufacturing takes place in China, Bangladesh, Turkey and Vietnam (as of 2024). They sell to consumers in over 180 countries across fourteen online stores with their websites in thirteen different languages!
- **Predominantly an online retailer:** Gymshark benefits from the technological innovations driving globalisation, with the majority of its sales coming from online. It does, however, now have a number of physical stores (London, Bicester Village and Dubai) with a fifth due to open in Amsterdam.
- **Use of social media and influencers:** Gymshark has developed a strong brand presence through its successful use of social media and online influencers. As of April 2024, it has millions of followers:
  - Instagram – 7.6 m
  - TikTok – 5.8 m
  - YouTube – 707,000
  - Facebook – 2.1 m

  Gymshark also uses a vast network of influencers from around the world to promote its products, for example, YoungLA and lex_fitness.

- **A global movement:** While closely linked to its social media and influencer strategy, Gymshark's successful brand has been built on its development of a global movement, which focuses on the power of its diverse community and customer engagement. This distinguishes it from its rivals. Gymshark creates opportunities for engagement with its audience through setting up events, hosting virtual exercise classes and expert interviews. It also encourages user-generated content through its use of branded hashtags and competitions; for example, in the summer of 2024, it launched its 'We Do Gym' campaign, celebrating all types of gym-goers.

> **Definition**
>
> **Austerity:** A policy implemented by a government whereby state spending is reduced and/or taxes are increased so that government revenue potentially exceeds or matches spending, aiming to reduce budget deficits and public debt.

helps to drive **cultural globalisation**, demonstrating the interconnectivity that drives the process of globalisation. The main drivers of cultural globalisation are:

1. **Technological advancements and the media.** Both these help to spread products, ideas, values and ways of life across borders which can lead to cultural exchange and the blending of cultures.
2. **International trade and TNCs.** The exchange of global goods and services involves the spread of cultures. TNCs play a crucial role in influencing local cultures through their products and branding.
3. **Global travel and migration.** The movement of people helps to spread ideas, values and ways of life across the world, also helping lead to cultural exchange and the blending of cultures.

Technological advancements and the media

Technological advancements have played an extensive role in the process of cultural globalisation. The broad range of communications technologies means it is easy to communicate across the globe across different mediums. The media has also accelerated the depth of connections between peoples (Table 2.5).

It has had major implications for global politics as it helps to transmit ideas and events in real-time across the globe. Events in one part of the world are seen almost instantly in other parts of the world and can quickly go viral having implications on global politics.

Social media has also been responsible for the growth of social movements such as the #MeToo Movement, #BlackLivesMatter and #FridaysForFuture. Recently, there has been a right-wing social movement attacking so-called 'wokism', which is now used as a pejorative term, as opposed to a term

Photo 2.2 Buddhist monks drink Coca-Cola in a break between classes at Dechen Phodrang Monastery in Thimphu, Bhutan

Source: Roberto Schmidt / AFP via Getty Images

Table 2.5 Monthly Active Users of Social Media in 2025

Facebook	3.1 billion
YouTube	2.5 billion
Instagram	2 billion
WhatsApp	2 billion
TikTok	1.6 billion

> **Chapter Link**
>
> The creation and evolution of the economic global governance system, and the relationship between states and the global banking system is addressed in **Chapter 5: Economic Global Governance.**

> **Spec key term**
>
> **Cultural globalisation:** The increasing interconnectedness between people across the world due to shared ideas, values and ways of life.

identifying an awareness of discrimination against protected characteristics. Figures such as Donald Trump have been figureheads of this movement, and he has begun to attack LGBTQ+ rights, including banning transgender people from serving in the military and issuing an executive order stating that 'anti-American ideologies' such as gender ideology should not be taught in schools, and any teacher supporting a pupil's transition should be prosecuted.

In the past decade, we have seen the rise of a global '**cancel culture**', whereby an individual could encounter a severe online backlash and real-world consequences for their behaviours. This is facilitated by the growth in online users, which has allowed peoples to become mobilised on scales never seen before. There are countless examples of this happening, including:

- **R. Kelly** – In 2019, two women set up the #MuteRKelly Movement as an effort to cancel an Atlanta concert, in response to accusations made against the R&B singer R. Kelly concerning his predatory sexual behaviour towards black women. This movement went international with more than fifteen global chapters of #MuteRKelly established, aiming to encourage a financial boycott of the singer. In 2021, he was convicted of racketeering and sex trafficking.

- **Kim Soo-hyun** – Following the death of K-actress Kim Sae-ron in February 2025, the actor was accused of having had a relationship with the dead actress whilst she was still a minor. Kim Soo-hyun was one of the highest-paid actors in South Korea, but the scandal has seen his public image decline, both within South Korea and internationally. For example, he has lost an endorsement by Prada, lost over 1 million Instagram followers in a short period and the accusations have been covered by many international media outlets.

> **Definition**
>
> **Cancel culture:** A phenomenon where actors (e.g. individuals, groups, TNCs) face widespread online condemnation and real-world consequences for actions deemed unacceptable by a significant number of users.

Component III: Global Politics

CASE STUDY: THE EUROPEAN MIGRANT CRISIS

Events

At the height of the crisis in 2015, an estimated 1.3 million people requested asylum in European states. According to the International Organisation for Migration's Missing Migrants Project, 28,000 people have died whilst crossing the Mediterranean Sea since 2014, and the figure is likely to be far higher.

Cultural globalisation has meant that images and ideas about this crisis have spread in real-time.

In 2015, an image of three-year-old Kurdish-Syrian refugee Alan Kurdi, washed up dead on a Turkish beach, went viral on social media with the Turkish hashtag #KıyıyaVuranİnsanlık, meaning 'flotsam of humanity'. In Europe, there was a huge surge of public anger at political leaders who had allowed the tragedy to escalate.

Other images of **migrants** seeking to cross the Mediterranean Sea and English Channel have also gone viral, such as the photograph of people boarding a smuggler's boat near Dunkirk taken by Sameer al-Doumy in 2022.

Significance

The European Migrant Crisis demonstrates clearly how cultural globalisation enables the real-time transmission of images and ideas about events taking place in global politics.

It also demonstrates how cultural globalisation can affect changes in global politics in different ways.

On the one hand, the image of Alan Kurdi did lead to some policy changes. The language used to describe the crisis became temporarily less hostile, referring to the people as 'refugees' as opposed to 'migrants'. The image led to a surge in donations to Syrian refugee charities. It also led to policy changes from some European states. In Germany, then Chancellor Angela Merkel developed an 'Open Door' Policy allowing refugees to claim asylum in Germany. The UK also offered to resettle 20,000 Syrian refugees.

On the other hand, other images such as those of the 'small boats' have contributed to political changes, in particular the rise of right-wing political parties in Europe Irregular migration has become the most significant policy issue for many European voters. Media coverage has become increasingly hostile, and hate crimes. have increased. In the Netherlands, Geert Wilders' Party for Freedom (PVV) won the largest vote share (23.5%) in the 2023 general election on an anti-immigration platform. In the UK, Reform's anti-immigration stance became similarly popular in 2025.

Definition

Migrant: A person who has changed their country of residence.

Chapter Link

The European migrant crisis prompted lengthy negotiations between the EU Commission and EU member states on a 'Migration and Asylum Pact' finally passed in 2024. It remains controversial. See **Chapter 9: The EU and Regionalism.**

The development of online streaming platforms such as Netflix, Amazon Prime and Disney Plus means that we now have truly global media platforms and, whereas it used to be the case that language restricted access, the sophistication of dubbing and subtitles means that language is no longer a barrier to viewing, and content now has a global audience. Figure 2.2 shows Netflix's most-watched shows (as of April 2025), and 4/10 are non-English language content, with *Squid Game* being exported from South Korea and *Money Heist* from Spain.

Global travel and migration

Another driver of cultural globalisation is the rise in global travel and migration. People are moving more than ever before, and this movement of people is contributing to the spread of ideas, values and ways of life around the globe.

Travel is now easier than ever owing to a number of developments. There are now more direct routes between destinations, via air, rail and boat. It is also easier to travel, with technological developments speeding up the process of checking in, handling baggage and managing traffic. Low-cost travel also makes global travel accessible to more people. Low-cost airlines, buses and trains make travel increasingly easy (e.g. easyJet, Eurolines, Interrail, etc.). According to the UN, there were over 1.4 billion international tourists (overnight visitors) in 2024, which was an increase of 11 per cent from 2022. In 1990, this figure was 0.44 billion. This shows the sheer increase in the frequency of global travel. According to UN Tourism, Europe accounts for 54 per cent of international travel, and China spends the most on international tourism at $256 billion (2024).

The increased ease of global travel has meant that the number of international **migrants** has also increased. In 2024, the number of international migrants globally was 304 million; this figure has

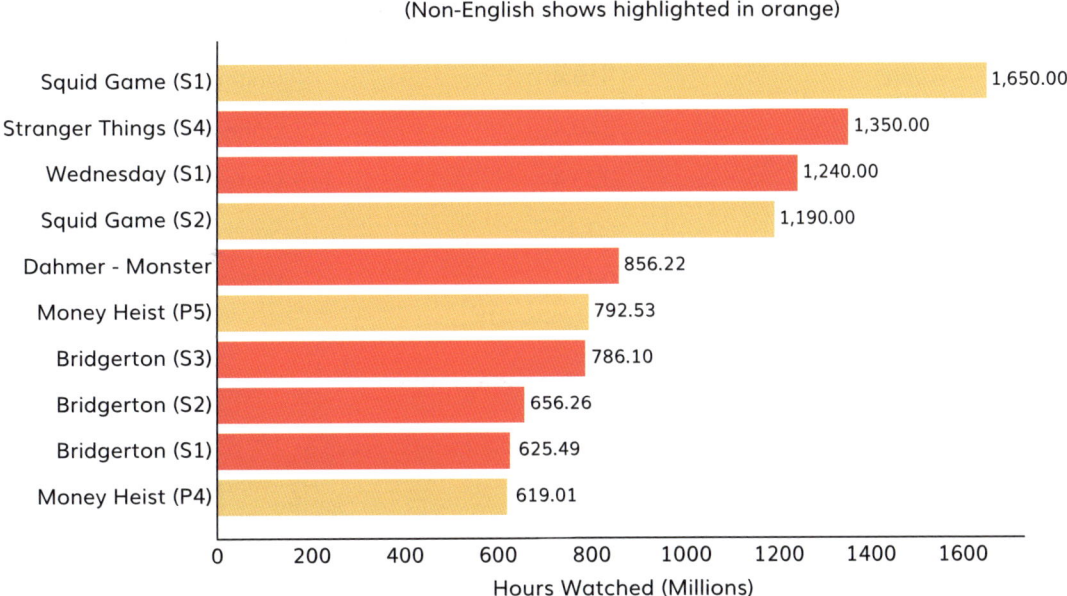

Figure 2.2 Most-watched Netflix shows

Source: Graph created with data from netflix.com

doubled since 1990. However, statistics can be misleading since the number of migrants in relation to the total world population has remained stable since 1990 at roughly 2.7 per cent.

Global brands and TNCs

A final driver of cultural globalisation is the growth of global brands and consumerism. This is closely related to economic globalisation, since it is TNCs that produce these brands (Table 2.6).

The emergence of global brands has helped to promote cultural globalisation, since it means that all peoples, regardless of where they live, have access to the same consumer goods.

Cultural homogenisation

The impact of cultural globalisation is debated. On the one hand, some would argue that cultural globalisation has led to **cultural homogenisation** or a **global monoculture**, in other words, we have seen the emergence of a single global culture.

A middle way has been proposed. The concept of **cultural hybridisation** is used to show how, due to globalisation, elements from different cultures have blended to create new and unique cultural forms, practices and identities (see Table 2.7).

Indeed, some TNCs have adopted a business strategy which has been called '**glocalisation**', tailoring their products to appeal to localised cultural tastes (Table 2.8).

On the other hand, some would argue that cultural globalisation has not led to the emergence of a single global culture. There are many different cultures around the world, each of which have established identities which were formed before their engagement with the different forms of cultural globalisation. Some suggest that due to globalisation we are seeing the rise of identity politics. Following the end of the Cold War, Samuel Huntington (1993) proposed that future conflict would be fought for cultural reasons in the form of a clash of civilisations. He argued that the speed and intensity of globalisation was igniting 'civilisational consciousness' among peoples around the world, leading to a heightened awareness of distinct cultural identities. Huntington suggested that globalisation would lead to a backlash against its perceived homogenising effects, as peoples become more aware of the 'self' (their cultural identity, often within broader civilisational groupings like Western or Islamic) in contrast to the 'other' (different cultural identities). There are many examples which could be drawn upon to support this claim (Table 2.9).

It is not difficult to find examples of growing nationalism around the world and peoples reacting to the notion of belonging to a single global community. The United States has become increasingly anti-globalist, seeing itself as losing out in the game of globalisation. Donald Trump has spearheaded this movement.

Chapter Link

There is a case study on the #FridaysForFuture movement in **Chapter 7: Environmental Global Governance.**

Spec key term

Cultural homogenisation: The coming together of global cultures and development of a single, global culture without diversity or dissension.

Global monoculture: The idea that there is one single global culture.

Definition

Cultural hybridisation: The idea that globalisation has led to the creation of different cultural forms, practices and identities to create new ones.

Table 2.6 The World's Ten Most Valuable Brands 2024

Rank	Brand	Value ($ billions)	State of origin
1	Apple	516.4	United States
2	Microsoft	340.4	United States
3	Google	333.4	United States
4	Samsung	99.4	South Korea
5	Walmart	96.8	United States
6	TikTok	84.2	China
7	Facebook	75.7	United States
8	-T-	73.3	Germany
9	ICBC	71.8	China
10	Verizon	71.8	United States

Source: Graph created with data from Brand Finance

Definition

Glocalisation: Products, services and ideas are adapted to fit the specific cultural preferences of local markets, at the same time as retaining their global identity.

Table 2.7 Examples of Cultural Hybridisation

Genre	Example	Explanation
Music	K-Pop is a form of South Korean pop music. Examples include – BTS, Blackpink and Seventeen.	It blends Korean musical elements with Western influences.
Film	Bollywood is films which are produced in India. Examples include *Dangal* (2016), *3 Idiots* (2009) and *Lagaan* (2001).	It blends Indian traditions with elements of Western storytelling traditions.
	Nollywood is films which are produced in Nigeria. Examples include *The Wedding Party* (2016), *The Figurine* (2009) and *King of Boys* (2018).	Nollywood film blends Nigerian culture and Hollywood techniques to develop its own unique films.
Cuisine	Fusion restaurants combine different culinary traditions to create new ones. Examples include Nobu (Japanese-Peruvian fusion), Roy's (Hawaiian-Asian fusion and using European techniques).	Blends two or more types of cuisine to create a new offering.

Exam Tip: There cannot be an exam question asking specifically about Americanisation, since this concept is not named on the specification. Instead, a question is more likely to ask you about the relationship between globalisation and state power, particularly the power of the United States.

Table 2.8 Examples of Glocalisation

Brand	Glocalisation example
McDonald's	Adapts its menu to local contexts. For example, in **India**, it offers a number of vegetarian options, such as the McAloo Tikki, to take into account the fact that a significant number of its population are vegetarian for religious reasons. In **South Korea**, it offers a Bulgogi Burger borrowing from the traditional Korean recipe, Bulgogi.
Starbucks	Adapts its products and stores to suit local contexts. For example, in **China**, the stores are typically larger to accommodate large groups to reflect the importance of community, and it has offered a broader variety of tea-based drinks based on its cultural affinity with tea. As of 2025, there are currently over 7,600 stores in **China**.

Brand	Glocalisation example
Coca-Cola	Adapts its brand to local contexts in different ways. It offers different flavours, such as Fanta Pineapple in **Brazil**. It also markets its products centred on local customs and traditions. For example, in the **Middle East** during Ramadan, it offered campaigns to emphasise the theme of breaking fast and community, and in India, it has launched campaigns around festivals with limited edition bottles. In India, its Thums Up brand of Cola appeals to local tastes with its extra carbonation and spicy notes.
Nike	Uses 'hyperlocal' advertising strategies to promote its brand. For example, its Nike Rise Concept, which is a city-specific approach whereby large, experience-based stores are built which are unique to the cities they are based in, e.g. Seoul. Also, Nike's 'Nothing Beats a Londoner' campaign in 2018 which used everyday Londoners and local celebrities to promote its products.

Table 2.9 Groups Formed in Opposition to Another Group or Identity

Social movement	Cultural goals
Boko Haram (Nigeria)	Boko Haram literally means 'Western education is forbidden'.
ISIS	Opposed to Western cultural and moral influences brought about due to globalisation.
Right-Wing Extremism (Europe and North America), this can include political parties such as the Party for Freedom in the Netherlands	These groups often have an anti-immigration and pro-national consumer products, believing globalisation and the mass movement of people have led to the loss of national identity in their countries and the loss of jobs. For example, in the Netherlands, Geert Wilders is the founder and leader of the Party for Freedom. This party has an anti-immigration stance and anti-Islam ideology. It also campaigns to exit the EU, and advocates for 'Nexit'.

Political globalisation

Simply speaking, political globalisation refers to the growing importance of international organisations in global politics. It also refers to the growing importance of shared political ideas between different political actors, for example the rule of law, human rights and democracy.

The main drivers of political globalisation are:

1. **The rise of IGOs.** These organisations have proliferated in the last century and are an important platform for multilateral cooperation between states and non-state actors. They help to build consensus about global governance across different issue areas, for example human rights and the environment.
2. **Transnational issues.** Many of the most pressing global challenges today are cross-border issues spanning the sovereign borders of multiple states, or they concern the global commons. Issues such as climate change, terrorism, global pandemics and economic crises require genuinely global solutions because they transcend state borders.
3. **Spread of political ideas.** In particular, the spread of international political ideas concerning the rule of law and humanitarian intervention.

The rise of IGOs

Intergovernmental organisations can exist at the global (e.g. the UN or the IMF) or regional level (e.g. the EU or ASEAN) and help to coordinate state behaviour in different issue areas. The largest and most powerful IGO in global politics is the UN, which seeks to coordinate the behaviour of states across an

> **Chapter Link**
>
> Students sometimes confuse political globalisation with political global governance. Political globalisation is the process of *expansion and increasing importance of IGOs* across all forms of global governance (addressed in **chapters 4 to 7 on political, economic, human rights and environmental global governance** and in **Chapter 8: Analysing and Evaluating Global Governance**).

> **Chapter Link**
>
> Political globalisation arguably also includes increasing regionalism, the focus of a key debate in **Chapter 9: the EU and Regionalism**. The concepts of intergovernmentalism and supranationalism are also explained in more detail there.

Photo 2.3 In 2013, Bolivia brought a case against Chile to the International Court of Justice (ICJ) in the hope of restoring Bolivia's access to the Pacific Ocean. In 2018, the ICJ ruled in Chile's favour. Here, Bolivian people wait for the result of the ruling.

Source: Aizar Raldes /AFP via Getty Images

enormous range of issue areas. IGOs can help to mitigate uncertainty in an anarchic world by creating shared expectations about the behaviour of others. IGOs help to increase the level of interdependence between states in global politics.

IGOs have varying levels of power over states. The majority of IGOs operate on the basis of **intergovernmentalism**. This means that states do not surrender their sovereignty since all decisions are agreed on the basis of consensus or unanimity between its members. For example, the World Trade Organisation cannot force its members to accept trade agreements. Some IGOs contain elements of **supranationalism**. This means that the IGO itself can make decisions which are legally binding on its member states. The UN Security Council can issue legally binding resolutions which UN member states must adhere to. In practice, this is difficult to enforce, especially if a resolution involves a state which possesses significant hard power.

Transnational issues

Closely linked to the formation of IGOs is the growth of increasingly transnational issues. The idea that the world is divided into states is a social construct, i.e. it is not natural. Many of the most pressing problems facing global politics are now transnational, i.e. they span the borders of sovereign states. Some of the biggest issues today include:

- Environmental issues – e.g. exploitation of the global commons (atmosphere, oceans, space, etc.)
- Security issues – e.g. transnational terrorism and crime
- Health issues – e.g. global pandemics

Political globalisation has emerged largely to respond to and resolve these issues, out of recognition that sovereign states alone will be unable to fix the problems. Hence, complex systems of global governance have emerged to develop rules in the absence of a world government.

The globalisation of political ideas

The globalisation of political ideas has challenged the authority of states within their borders. These political ideas have emerged over a period and include the rule of law and humanitarian or forcible intervention.

CASE STUDY: THE UNITED STATES AND THE DEGLOBALISATION MOVEMENT

Events

Trump believes in:

1. **An 'America First' strategy and economic nationalism** – Trump wants to prioritise US business and US jobs by bringing back manufacturing to the United States, a sector which has suffered enormously due to globalisation meaning it is cheaper to manufacture goods elsewhere.

2. **Vocal critic of trade agreements** – In his first presidency, Trump abolished NAFTA to form the United States–Mexico–Canada Agreement. He also pulled out of the Trans-Pacific Partnership (TPP).

3. **Introduction of tariffs on international trade** – Trump has introduced tariffs on many imported goods, arguing that he is levelling the playing field from unfair foreign competition, which includes tactics such as subsidies and dumping products on the global market. In April 2025, he introduced a global tariff regime imposing a 10 per cent baseline on many imported products and higher 'reciprocal' tariffs against states he believes are engaging in unfair trade practices.

4. **Critic of multilateral institutions** – Trump is a vocal critic of multilateral institutions, believing that the United States could achieve its national interests better without them. In his second presidency, he has already withdrawn the United States from the World Health Organisation. He has also reduced US contributions to overseas aid and introduced transactional aid programmes whereby aid is used as leverage to achieve other policy objectives.

5. **Rejection of the principles of international law** – In his second presidency, Trump has expressed views that challenge the principle of state sovereignty. He has repeatedly proposed that Canada should become the fifty-first state of the United States. He has also expressed a desire to acquire Greenland, being quoted saying, 'We'll get Greenland' and refusing to take military action off the table. Finally, in relation to the Russian invasion of Ukraine in 2022, Trump has blamed the Ukrainians for starting the war and has claimed that Zelensky is a 'dictator without elections'.

Significance

The ramifications of US policies under Donald Trump extend beyond simply its implications for globalisation; his policies across a range of issues threaten the very fabric of global governance, a theme which will be returned to throughout the chapters in this textbook.

From the perspective of globalisation, Trump's policies are undoubtedly leading to a reversal of the process of globalisation as it currently exists. Economically, Trump is disrupting patterns of world trade. This is affecting the level of economic interdependence that exists. He is also challenging the extent of economic integration and is moving away from the economic ideas which have shaped globalisation in the twenty-first century, namely the principle of free trade. Politically, Trump's policies are having a profound impact, not just on the institutions of political globalisation, but on political ideas themselves. His rhetoric about 'Make America Great Again' is itself becoming a global movement, its ideas being popular amongst far-right political parties around the world. Culturally, his vision of America is increasingly exclusive – he is anti-migration and anti-foreign. This may have repercussions for US soft power on a global stage.

This does not necessarily mean globalisation is dead; it just means its current form may be changing. Globalisation is not wedded to specific ideologies; it is a process that is in a state of constant flux.

KEY DEBATE: HAS CULTURAL GLOBALISATION LED TO CULTURAL HOMOGENISATION?

- ✅ The spread of so-called 'Western' political ideas and values.
  - Many political ideas practised globally are rooted in 'Western' political traditions.
    - Free-trade capitalism is rooted in Western ideals of individualism, rationalism and free choice.
    - Liberal democracy is rooted in the French Revolution and the Enlightenment and is associated with 'Western' political ideas. In the years following the Second World War and the collapse of the Soviet Union in 1990, we have seen the proliferation of democracies worldwide.

Chapter Link

The impact of the United States on globalisation links closely to the issue of polarity discussed in **Chapter 3: Power and Developments**. In a unipolar system, you would expect to see the US government shape globalisation. Trump's movement away from globalisation has influenced politicians in other states. This contagion effect suggests that the United States continues to have enormous influence on global politics.

Definition

Americanisation: The growing influence of American culture around the world.

❌ Backlash against these ideas and values.
- There has been an enormous backlash against the ideas of free-trade capitalism worldwide. The rise of different economic forms – such as state capitalism – and economic nationalism would suggest that free-trade capitalism is no longer the key economic orthodoxy.
- The number of liberal democracies is now in decline worldwide (see Chapter 3), suggesting the rejection of liberal democracy as an organising principle of states.
- The imposition of so-called 'Western' ideas has led to a clash of civilisations whereby globalisation has led to increased civilisational consciousness. The rise of radical Islam would support this, with groups such as al-Qaeda, ISIS and Boko Haram defining themselves in opposition to the spread of Western ideas within their regions.
- There is also a backlash against the ideas of globalisation in 'Western' states themselves. The rise of populist parties within the EU, such as Alternative Fur Deutschland (AfD) in Germany and Reform in the UK, are in part built around the idea that globalisation (and more specifically immigration) is undermining their own culture and values.

✅ The spread of global brands and TNCs has led to a global consumer culture.
- The spread of global brands, such as fast food outlets, fashion brands and technology, is evidence of cultural homogenisation.
- Naomi Klein (2000) argues that there is a global trend of 'commodity fetishism' whereby the brand has become more important than the product. This is because consumers are buying into the identity or 'lifestyle' offered by the brand, an idea she calls 'corporate transcendence'.
- The spread of global brands has led to the emergence of shared cultural aspirations. Some refer to this as **Americanisation**, reflecting the importance of US culture in shaping cultural.

❌ Global brands have been adapted and reinterpreted by local cultures.
- Glocalisation is a process whereby global products and ideas are adapted to suit local contexts. Global brands and TNCs use culturally friendly media and advertising, a technique which is widely used by global brands in recognition of its importance in building trust with consumers.
- The purchase of global commercial goods does not extend beyond consumerism; it does not mean that local populations are committing to the values of the state of origin. A person may wear Levi jeans and eat McDonald's food, but it does not mean they subscribe to American values.

✅ The spread of English language content worldwide has led to a homogenisation of language.
- English is the most widely spoken global language with over 1.5 billion total speakers.
- The most popular media content is still distributed in English. For example, 6/10 of the top shows on Netflix are in English.
- The use of English terminology worldwide shows the cultural appeal of the English language. This is sometimes called the Anglicism of other languages. Words such as OK, Cool, Internet and Boss are used across many different languages.

❌ English is no longer the dominant language worldwide.
- Technological developments, especially in the field of AI real-time translation, mean that there is no longer a necessity for a single global language. Communication can now take place between speakers of multiple different languages without the need to acquire new spoken languages.
- Social media has enabled non-English film, TV and music to spread and attract global audiences. We are actively seeing a preference for niche and locally specific media, for example the rise of Nollywood, Bollywood, K-Pop, J-Pop, etc.

- Owing to demographic trends, the number of native English speakers is in decline. Mandarin is the most widely spoken language in the world with respect to numbers of native speakers, followed by Spanish.
- Localised adaptations of the English language have meant that the language has adapted rather than dominated. For example, Spanglish is the combination of Spanish and English spoken by some families.

Key Debate Summary: Has cultural globalisation led to cultural homogenisation?

	For	Against
Global Consumer Culture	✓ The spread of TNCs and global brands has led to the development of a single global culture.	✗ Local identities shape global brands to suit their needs and ideas.
The use of English language worldwide	✓ English remains the most influential global language; English language still dominates different media forms.	✗ English is no longer the dominant global language, and this is a trend that has been assisted due to technological advancements in AI; there has been an increase in foreign language media forms.
Global Ideas	✓ Ideas related to free trade and liberal democracy are rooted in Western traditions.	✗ There has been a nationalist backlash against global ideas.

> **Chapter Link**
>
> We return to the role of international law and the courts in **Chapter 6: Human Rights Global Governance**.

The rule of law

International Law refers to the system of laws that guides state-to-state interactions, as well as interactions between states, IGOs and other non-state actors. Since the end of the Second World War, international law has proliferated globally. The **rule of law** is an important tool in global politics for maintaining stability because it creates shared expectations about reasonable (or unreasonable) behaviour by political actors. A number of international (e.g. International Court of Justice and International Criminal Court) and regional courts (e.g. European Court of Human Rights) have been established to uphold and enforce international law in global politics.

Humanitarian and forcible intervention

Political globalisation has also seen the spread of ideas concerning humanitarian and forcible intervention. **Humanitarian intervention** refers to military actions taken in the pursuit of humanitarian objectives. Since the 1990s, we have seen the proliferation of humanitarian intervention, albeit it seems to have halted in the last decade. Globalisation has been a driver in ideas about humanitarian and forcible intervention for a number of different reasons:

- Technology and communications technologies have led to real-time information about human rights abuses across the world, leading to global pressure to stop the suffering of peoples.
- Human rights abuses are often accompanied by large-scale displacement of peoples, which can cause economic disruption due to the level of economic interconnectedness and integration in the global economy.
- Levels of political interconnectedness and integration make it easier to take action against the perpetrators of human rights abuses.

> **Spec key term**
>
> **International law:** The law that governs states and other international actors. It is derived from both treaties and custom (i.e. the behaviour of states).
>
> **Humanitarian intervention:** Military intervention carried out for humanitarian objectives. This is often in response to crimes against humanity or genocide. Humanitarian intervention is distinct from other types of military intervention because of this humanitarian dimension.

> **Chapter Link**
>
> Humanitarian intervention is linked to political globalisation because it results from the idea that states have global responsibilities towards the citizens of other states. In **Chapter 6: Human Rights Global Governance**, we explore the question of whether humanitarian intervention is still a globalised issue.

Comparative Analysis Summary: What are the differences between political globalisation and global governance?

	Globalisation	Global Governance
Conceptual	Refers to the **process** of increasing interconnectedness in global politics between different political actors.	Refers to the political actors and rules that shape behaviour in different issue areas.
Scope	Globalisation has a broad scope, focusing on multiple different aspects of interconnectedness between different political actors.	Has a focused scope looking at the behaviour of different actors in specific issue areas, for example human rights or environmental global governance.
Drivers and Actors	Globalisation is driven by a broad array of drivers and actors, including technology, politics and people.	Global governance is predominantly driven by states and IGOs seeking to find solutions to problems that arise, in part, because of globalisation.
Cause	Globalisation creates the necessity for global governance.	Global governance is a response to globalisation and an attempt to manage its implications.

The impact of globalisation

Comparative Theories: How do realists and liberals view globalisation?

Theme	Realism	Liberalism
Scope of Globalisation	Sceptical about globalisation and view it as intensifying global integration as opposed to the creation of a truly single global economy, global culture or the rule of global institutions.	Positive about globalisation. It allows for deep integration across the economy, cultures and politics.
Importance of the Sovereign State	The sovereign state remains the most important actor in global politics. Globalisation is made by states for states, and its existence is contingent on continued state support.	The role of the sovereign state has changed, and it has found new ways to exert its influence. States choose to 'pool' their sovereignty in IGOs to help resolve global challenges and issues.
Importance of Power Relations	Globalisation is led by the most powerful state(s) in the international system to serve the powerful. Historically, many aspects of globalisation were introduced by the United States to serve its interests, for example, the institutions of global economic governance adopted US-preferred economic systems, and the United States held a disproportionate amount of power within these institutions.	Globalisation helps to bring about a multipolar system whereby all states (weak and strong) can exert influence. In addition to the role of states, IGOs and other non-state actors (such as civil society groups and TNCs) can also influence the different globalisation processes.

The State and Globalisation

Theme	Realism	Liberalism
Impact on the Likelihood of Conflict or Peace	Globalisation increases the vulnerability of states because it makes the success (and failure) of states dependent on the fortunes of others. This was demonstrated in the 2020 Covid-19 pandemic which demonstrated the vulnerability of states to global shocks and increased the competition for resources (e.g. vaccines, personal protective equipment, etc.). Globalisation also increases the rise of nationalism and can create societal conflict between different groups. It therefore increases the likelihood of conflict since states will become more competitive with one another, especially during times of global crisis, therefore escalating the risk of the security dilemma.	Globalisation creates opportunities for peace because deep integration encourages complex interdependence, which has powerful incentives for peace. The spread of global ideas concerning human rights, the rule of law and democracy also promotes peace between states. The ongoing development of a truly global civil society fosters connections between people globally, also reducing the risk of competition and fragmentation.

Globalisation theories

Within the field of globalisation there are a number of competing theories about its impact on global politics. The three theories we need to know about are Hyperglobalisers, Globalisation Sceptics and Transformationalists. These theories debate the extent to which globalisation has transformed global

Photo 2.4 US President Donald Trump and Indian Prime Minister Narendra Modi met in February 2025 to discuss tariffs and trade relations. Transformationalists would argue that Trump's decision to announce heavy tariffs on foreign goods would have a far greater impact globally than the actions of TNCs.

Source: Bloomberg via Getty Images

Component III: Global Politics

Exam Tip: This is likely to appear as a Section A question (for example in 2020). However, it is important to note that if you get asked a question about the 'impact' of globalisation, you should refer to these theories – either briefly in your introduction or throughout the body of your essay. This is to avoid any possible caps on marks.

politics, in particular focusing on the extent and nature of globalisation, its role and significance for state sovereignty, and its impact. The Comparative Analysis table below explores each of the theories in greater depth.

Comparative Analysis Summary: What are the differences between the different theories of globalisation?

	Hyperglobalisers	Globalisation Sceptics	Transformationalists
Extent and Nature of Global Change	Globalisation is a new and profound set of economic, cultural and political shifts. Globalisation is largely irreversible, and it is inevitable, in other words, the process of globalisation will continue unabated.	Question the extent to which globalisation is new, in particular, a globalised economic system. They point to various stages in history, including the Silk Roads (first century BC–fifth century AD), which saw the creation of a network of trade between Asia and Europe. For sceptics, globalisation is a reversible process.	Profound changes have taken place because of globalisation, a process which has sped up from the 1980s onwards. Its future trajectory is uncertain because it is contingent on many factors.
Significance for State	Project an image of a 'borderless world' or 'post-sovereign world'. This means that state borders are increasingly irrelevant (external sovereignty) and the authority of states to govern within their borders is increasingly unnecessary (internal sovereignty). The role of the state is being 'hollowed out' since international actors now carry out the functions of states by shaping the direction of policy.	Sceptical about the extent to which globalisation has challenged either the borders (external sovereignty) or the authority of the state (internal sovereignty). The world continues to be organised around the state, and the majority of economic activity takes place within the state. Globalisation is largely driven by and contingent on the actions of states, in particular, powerful states. Sceptics suggest these states use globalisation as an ideological tool to present their economic policies as inevitable to the rest of the world, i.e. a tool for powerful states to increase their power.	Globalisation has transformed the state, not made it irrelevant. States play a vital role in enabling globalisation to take place, for example, states facilitate and regulate global processes, for example the area of global trade and financial flows. In some areas, the state has become more assertive and in others, it has relinquished control, for example, transformationalists suggest that IGOs and non-state actors are better able to coordinate state action across some of the issues faced today, such as the environment.

	Hyperglobalisers	Globalisation Sceptics	Transformationalists
The Impact of Globalisation	Hyperglobalisers emphasise that globalisation has **positive outcomes**. **Economically**, it has the potential to increase prosperity for all. Where a state is experiencing poverty, it is suggested that it is because they do not have enough globalisation. In other words, they need greater integration into the global economy. **Politically**, hyperglobalisers see a trend towards further cooperation and increasingly supranational forms of governance. **Culturally**, they see the emergence of a global culture (though disagree whether this is homogenised or hybridised).	View globalisation as largely a 'myth', so question its 'global' impact. Sceptics argue that regions are the basis of the majority of economic activity between states, and that in many cases, regions are defensive to protect their members from a global economy. Sceptics highlight how the impact of globalisation is most profoundly felt in the developed world and is therefore not truly a global phenomenon. Globalisation leads to increased inequality and social tensions within and between states and is an exploitative process.	Globalisation is complex and uneven. It creates both opportunities and challenges, and it is not possible to generalise about its impact. Transformationalists caution under or over exaggerating the influence of globalisation. Francis Fukuyama argues that the idea that globalisation has changed everything is 'globaloney', instead emphasising that the role of the state simply changes and evolves over time.
Example Scholars	Kenichi Ohmae (*The Borderless World*). Susan Strange (*The Retreat of the State*)	Paul Hirst and Graham Thompson (*Globalisation in Question*)	Ulrich Beck (*World Risk Society*) Manuel Castells (*The Information Age*)

> **Chapter Link**
>
> We return to the role of international law and the courts in **Chapter 6: Human Rights Global Governance**.

Globalisation and contemporary global issues

The specification defines 'contemporary global issues' as poverty, conflict, human rights and the environment. These issues have grown in significance in recent decades as a consequence of rapid globalisation. Much of global politics addresses collective efforts by states to deal with these dilemmas that they cannot solve alone. Each chapter in this book will consider the impact of global politics on one or more of them.

Component III: Global Politics

CASE STUDY: GLOBALISATION AND AUTOCRATIC STATES – THE CASE OF CHINA

Events

China is undoubtedly a huge beneficiary of globalisation. However, it is also an example of how globalisation can be managed to suit its own specific needs.

Economically, China engages with the global economy and in 2023, was the world's largest exporter of goods. However, instead of practising neoliberal economics it uses a version of capitalism called 'state capitalism'. This has been successful for China as it has enabled it to compete in the world economy whilst at the same time protecting its domestic economy. China is also a key market for TNCs, many of whom base their manufacturing in China, such as Apple, hence why China is sometimes called 'The Factory of the World'. This has helped to create jobs and lift people out of poverty.

Politically, China has also benefited from globalisation. It is a member of many of the world's most significant IGOs (e.g. WTO, IMF, World Bank) and is a Permanent Member of the UN Security Council, meaning that it has the veto power, giving it significant power in global politics.

Culturally, however, China has been able to pick and choose how it has globalised. Crucially, China has been able to 'opt out' of some aspects of cultural globalisation. This has been straightforward for China because it is an autocratic state and exerts enormous control over its citizens. Its internet censorship (called the 'Great Firewall of China', named after the 'Great Wall of China') blocks Western social media platforms (including Facebook, X and Instagram) and internet search providers (e.g. Google). Instead, it offers its own alternatives such as WeChat, Weibo and TikTok, which are subject to government oversight. There is also strict media censorship, and there are quotas placed on the number of 'foreign' media content which is accessible in China. Instead, it promotes its own content which emphasises their key goal of promoting 'cultural confidence' emphasising pride in Chinese history, traditions and culture.

Significance

The example of China shows how globalisation is not a threat to state sovereignty – in the Chinese case, it has carefully selected which parts of globalisation that it wants to be involved with and has created alternatives for those it does not. It shows how states can make globalisation work for themselves.

It is important to remember that the Chinese case may not be generalisable to other states. This is because China is an autocratic state, which means it is easier (and possible) for it to immunise itself from the aspects of globalisation it does not wish to partake in. It is also because China is a powerful state, which means that it can afford to opt out of aspects of globalisation with limited impact on the well-being of its citizens.

KEY DEBATE: DOES GLOBALISATION UNDERMINE STATE SOVEREIGNTY?

Economic globalisation has undermined state sovereignty

 TNCs have undermined state sovereignty and in some cases exert greater power than sovereign states.

TNCs can influence the internal sovereignty of states by affecting their **policies**. This is because states are keen to attract TNCs to operate from their territory because of the benefits they bring to the national economy through employment and tax revenues. They can do this in a number of ways:

1. **Low corporation taxes:** In Europe, Ireland has a corporate tax rate of 12.5 per cent to attract TNCs to establish their European headquarters there. This is in stark contrast to the UK and China, which have a corporate tax rate of 25 per cent and the United States, which has a corporation tax of 25.6 per cent. This has been successful for Ireland, and the following TNCs have their European headquarters there, including Google, Apple, Microsoft, Meta and Amazon.

2. Financial incentives: Many states offer financial incentives to TNCs, including so-called tax holidays. This is a common incentive offered in parts of Southeast Asia (e.g. Vietnam and Thailand) and Africa (e.g. Rwanda and Ghana).

✅ Interdependence increases the vulnerability of states.
- The global economic system is prone to boom and bust cycles (e.g. Global Financial Crisis), and local events can have global implications, as seen by the *Ever Given* crisis. This means that states are not able to guarantee their economic security.
- States are increasingly vulnerable because of global economic forces beyond their control. The extensive use of bonds to finance public projects means that states are beholden to their investors. For example, in 2022, UK Prime Minister Liz Truss's economic policy was to introduce unfunded tax cuts and deregulation to stimulate economic growth; the financial markets responded by increasing government borrowing costs, sparking an economic downturn which led to her resignation only 49 days after being awarded the job!

✅ The existence of a global economy has strengthened terrorist groups and organised crime.
Groups such as ISIS were able to fund their campaign through selling oil in occupied territories on the global market. The ease of global communications and travel has also meant that organised crime can successfully operate worldwide, for example narcotics and people trafficking.

Economic globalisation has not undermined state sovereignty

❌ States can choose to follow their own economic models. This can be seen in the case of China, which practises state capitalism. This effectively allows China to protect its home industries, reducing the vulnerability it faces on the global market.

❌ States can choose their own economic policies, despite neoliberalism emphasising the importance of free trade,

❌ Some regional organisations practise protectionism to protect their members' economies. For example, the EU's Common Agricultural Policy offers subsidies to EU farmers so that they can price their goods competitively, securing trade within the bloc. Otherwise, they could be undersold by foreign exporters.

Political globalisation has undermined state sovereignty

✅ International law has undermined state sovereignty by placing legally binding restrictions upon state behaviour in certain areas. Restrictions on the use of force, for example, prevent a state from attacking another state to gain economic advantage or pre-emptively to protect itself from a perceived adversary.

✅ Ideas about humanitarian or forcible intervention have made sovereignty conditional on upholding human rights, in particular the gravest human rights abuses such as crimes against humanity and genocide. There are many examples of the principle of Responsibility to Protect being invoked, for example NATO's military intervention in Libya in 2011, which saw Gaddafi removed from power.

✅ IGOs have limited state sovereignty in many ways.
- Membership of IGOs can affect a state's authority within its borders. For example, membership of the WTO places restrictions on a state's ability to trade with other states, placing restrictions and rules upon global trade. If a state breaks these rules, it can be subject to an investigation and legal action; failing this, the WTO can authorise economic retaliation.

- IGOs can place conditions on member states which affect their authority to make laws and policies within their borders. For example, the IMF places conditionality on its loans (formerly called Structural Adjustment Programmes) about how the economy should be managed; these states are not in a position to refuse, given that loans are offered in the most urgent economic crises.

- Supranationalism can affect state sovereignty. The United Nations Security Council acts as a supranational body in global politics because it can issue legally binding resolutions on UN member states.

Political globalisation has not undermined state sovereignty

- ✗ International law has not undermined state sovereignty; instead it has strengthened it. This is because international law offers protection to states based on the principle of reciprocity, i.e. a state will not invade another state if in doing so it risks being invaded itself.
- ✗ The backlash against globalisation has meant that states are reasserting their sovereignty. We see this through the US decision to implement tariffs on imports in both Trump's first and second presidencies. We also see this in the move to 'go local', for example to 'buy British' in UK supermarkets.
- ✗ The jurisdiction of IGOs over states is constantly challenged. In the case of the International Court of Justice, in January 2026, it issued a legally binding order against Israel for its conduct in the Gaza Strip; one such order was to take immediate action to restore the provision of humanitarian aid. As of June 2026, this order has not been heeded by Israel, and it is non-compliant with this aspect of the Court's decision.

Cultural globalisation has undermined state sovereignty

- ✓ States can no longer control the flow of information across their borders, threatening their external sovereignty.
- ✓ Globalisation has led to the erosion of national identity within states brought about by cultural homogenisation (see page x). There has been a strong backlash against tourism in recent years due to the impact it is having on local identities (and economies), in particular in Spain and its islands. The growth of Airbnb has priced locals out of the housing market, in turn leaving some unable to afford homes. There have been examples of tourist workers sleeping in their cars in the Balearic Islands because they cannot afford to stay near their jobs in the tourism sector.
- ✓ Cultural globalisation has been accused of cultural imperialism or Westernisation, whereby the cultural norms and products of the 'West' are being imposed on the rest of the world. This has led to a backlash by terrorist organisations such as al-Qaeda, ISIS and Boko Haram, whereby they are seeking to reimplement their own cultural values within their territory. In the case of the latter, terrorist groups use cultural globalisation to their benefit to recruit followers and generate revenue to finance their campaigns.

Cultural globalisation has not undermined state sovereignty

- ✗ States are ultimately in control of their borders, including the flow of information. China is one of many authoritarian states that control the flow of information across its borders. It operates what is called 'The Great Firewall of China', blocking access to Western social media and search engines as well as media which does not promote Chinese values.
- ✗ States still retain their own national identities. The existence of cultural hybridisation and glocalisation business strategies are evidence of how global products can be adapted to fit local contexts.
- ✗ States remain in control of their borders and able to make laws within them to help their local populations. In Barcelona (Spain) a new law has meant Airbnb hosts need a licence, and as of June 2024 the city has announced a plan to ban all short-term rentals by 2028 so that residents can afford housing.

Key Debate Summary: Does globalisation undermine state sovereignty?

	For	Against
Economic Globalisation	✓ TNCs exert enormous power over states and can force them to change their laws and policies. IGOs can also impact state sovereignty by affecting policy decisions. Interdependence limits a state's ability to control its economy.	✗ States can assert economic sovereignty through models like state capitalism (China), choosing policies, and regional protectionism (EU's CAP) to shield domestic industries from global market vulnerabilities.
Political Globalisation	✓ International law and IGOs undermine state sovereignty through legally binding restrictions, conditional sovereignty (R2P), and IGOs' power to set trade rules, impose loan conditions and issue binding resolutions.	✗ International law is seen as strengthening state sovereignty through reciprocity, not undermining it. The backlash against globalisation, shows states reasserting control. Furthermore, IGO jurisdiction is frequently challenged and not always heeded by states.
Cultural Globalisation	✓ Globalisation erodes state control over information and national identity. Cultural homogenisation and over-tourism spark backlash, displacing locals. Western cultural imperialism fuels terrorist groups.	✗ States retain control, exemplified by China's 'Great Firewall' managing information. National identities persist through glocalisation. States also regulate borders.

> **Chapter Link**
> The IGOs responsible for global governance are not explored in this section because they are examined in depth in later chapters. However, the following IGOs could be used to explore the issues below:

Issue	IGOs*
Poverty	Bretton Woods Institutions (World Bank, IMF, WTO), the G7 and G20, ECOSOC and Regional Organisations (e.g. the EU and ASEAN).
Conflict	NATO, the UN, the ICJ and Regional Organisations.
Human Rights	The UN, ICC, International Tribunals, European Court of Human Rights and Regional Organisations.
The Environment	The UNFCCC, IPCC and Regional Organisations.

* Please note this list is not exhaustive.

Globalisation and poverty

The relationship between globalisation and poverty is complex, given the difficulty in measuring both concepts. Poverty can be measured in absolute or relative terms. **Absolute poverty** means being unable to meet basic living standards. The World Bank defines 'extreme poverty' using the 'international poverty line' concept. This was set at $2.15 per day in 2022. Other measures of poverty focus on **relative poverty**. This means a person exists in poverty if their standard of living is less than those in the area they are located. Measuring relative poverty is more challenging because not only can it vary from place to place, but it can also take into account lots of different measures, such as income, access to education, food, water, etc. Relative poverty is closely linked to the issue of **inequality** (Figure 2.3).

> **Definition**
> **Absolute poverty:** Being unable to meet basic living standards.
>
> **Relative poverty:** A measure of poverty that looks at the wealth within an economy and a person's position relative to that wealth.
>
> **Inequality:** Differences in income and/or wealth either within a state or between different states.

Figure 2.3 Share of world population living with less than $2.15 and $3.65 per day, 1990 to 2024

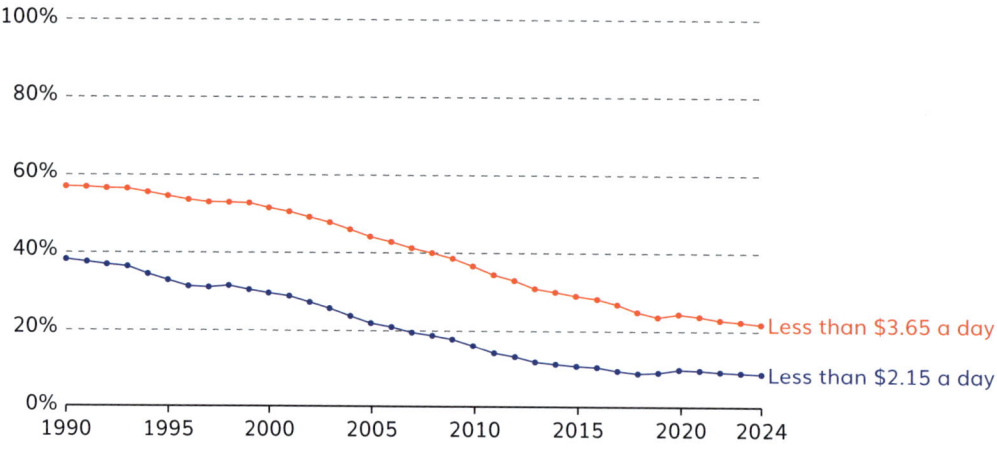

Source: Our World in Data, World Bank Poverty and Inequality Platform (2024) | CC BY

KEY DEBATE: DOES GLOBALISATION INCREASE POVERTY AND INEQUALITY?

Globalisation has reduced absolute poverty globally

✅ By driving economic growth, globalisation has reduced levels of absolute poverty globally, lifting millions out of extreme poverty. The percentage of people living in extreme poverty has declined in the last 35 years. In 1990, the percentage of people living in extreme poverty was 37.9 per cent, and by 2024 this had decreased to 8.5 per cent.

✅ Technological improvements have enabled many people to tap into their entrepreneurial skills. Access to **microfinance** has enabled those without access to traditional banking the opportunity to grow businesses, lifting themselves out of extreme poverty. There are many examples of microfinance organisations, including Microfinancing Partners in Africa, an NGO which offers loans in the African continent and has helped nearly 40,000 individuals access microfinance, of whom 87 per cent have reported increased daily income after receiving loans. Microfinance programmes have also enabled marginalised groups, such as women, to become empowered. NGOs such as the Microloan Foundation have supported women in Malawi, Zambia and Zimbabwe to become financially independent.

> **Definition**
>
> **Microfinance:** An idea coined by Nobel Peace Prize winner Muhammad Yunus, whereby small loans or microcredit is offered to individuals without the need to offer collateral. This money is then used to invest in income-generating activities.

Globalisation still risks poverty for some

❌ The World Bank argues that 700 million people worldwide still live in extreme poverty; this is 8.5 per cent of the global population. The majority of these people are based in sub-Saharan Africa, where 67 per cent of people live in extreme poverty.

❌ Progress in reducing the number of people living in extreme poverty slowed down following the 2020 Covid-19 pandemic. Poverty reduction measures are also slowed down due to the effects of climate change. Of those living in absolute poverty, many are based in regions susceptible to extreme weather events, meaning that they could face severe setbacks in their livelihoods.

❌ Studies show that access to microfinance has not lifted people out of extreme poverty. Instead, it has been criticised for increasing cycles of debt among peoples, aggressive collection methods and in some cases leading to suicides.

Globalisation has reduced economic inequality between states

- ✓ Globalisation has reduced inequality between states by accelerating growth in developing states. Convergence theory argues that developing states will catch up with developed states quickly because they benefit from the technological advancements and knowledge generated by developed states in their development journeys. The Asian Tigers (Hong Kong, Singapore, South Korea and Taiwan), India and China are often cited as successful examples of this in practice.
- ✓ According to the UN, income inequality between states has improved in the last 25 years.

Globalisation has increased inequality between individuals and within states

- ✗ According to Oxfam, in 2024, the top 1 per cent owned more wealth than 95 per cent of the world's total population combined.
- ✗ The amount of wealth concentrated in developed states is still disproportionately high compared to developing states.

Globalisation has improved many people's lives

- ✓ Globalisation has increased the ability of many people to access goods and services. The theory of comparative advantage has meant that goods and services are often produced in the place where they can be produced most effectively (and cheaply), meaning they are accessible to more people.
- ✓ The theory of 'Trickle Down Economics' suggests that benefits offered to wealthy individuals and businesses, such as tax cuts and deregulation, will eventually trickle down to the 'many', leading to advantages for all.

Globalisation has been exploitative of workers and individuals

- ✗ Globalisation has led to a 'race to the bottom' where workers' rights and environmental standards are increasingly abandoned in a bid to attract and retain TNCs.
- ✗ In developed states, globalisation has led to the displacement of many workers due to low-skilled jobs moving overseas. This has been a key policy area for US President Donald Trump, as to attract voters, he has promised to return manufacturing jobs to the United States by the imposition of high tariffs on imported goods.
- ✗ Trickle Down Economics is not universally accepted, with some economists now claiming that subsidies for the rich lead to them getting richer at the expense of workers on low incomes.
- ✗ Globalisation has been accused of corporate violence against poor communities (see Table 2.10).

Globalisation has benefited development globally

- ✓ Immigration brought about by globalisation and the movement of people has benefited economic development in places facing skills shortages or shortages of workers.
- ✓ Foreign aid and foreign direct investment (FDI) can lead to investment in key industries and infrastructural projects globally, which boosts development.

Globalisation has created dependency and neocolonialism

- ✗ According to 'dependency theory', globalisation can lead to a situation where developing states are locked into providing cheap labour and raw materials for developed states, creating a situation of economic dependence.
- ✗ Foreign aid can lead to dependency and increase levels of corruption.
  Foreign direct investment by TNCs benefits themselves more than their host states. They often find ways to circumvent paying taxes, and the majority of revenue generated flows outwards. This is a feature of 'neocolonialism'.

Table 2.10 TNCs and Poverty

	Examples
Environmental degradation and pollution	**United States – 'Cancer Alley'** 85-mile stretch of land along the Mississippi River between New Orleans and Baton Rouge. It is home to over 200 fossil fuel and petrochemical corporations. Human Rights Watch and Amnesty International have documented the health impacts of these corporations on the local residents, in particular black and poor communities, which include cancer, infertility, miscarriage and respiratory problems.
Market and sell harmful products	**Global Obesity Crisis** Large TNCs market harmful ultra-processed foods and sugary drinks across the world. Because these products are cheaper than healthy alternatives, they are disproportionately bought by those from developing states and low-income communities within developed states. According to the NGO World Obesity, by 2035, 79 per cent of adults who are overweight or obese will live in low- to middle-income states. In Brazil, it was said that the consumption of ultra-processed foods led to 57,000 premature deaths in 2019. **Coca-Cola in India** Drinks with a high sugar content, such as Coca-Cola, are shown to increase the risk of obesity and diabetes, and recent discoveries suggest that it can lead to gastrointestinal problems. Coca-Cola is extremely successful in India and in March 2025 experienced double-digit volume growth there, in part due to its sales of over 180 million drinks at the Mahakumbh Mela festival. Correlating to this rise in consumption of sugary drinks such as Coca-Cola, India has experienced a rapid escalation of obesity. In 1990, approximately 53 million people were overweight or obese, and by 2021, this number had risen to 236 million.
Displacement of local communities	**Mining Activities in Zimbabwe** Lithium mining causes mass displacement, which predominantly affects poor rural families. By May 2025, it is estimated that over 3,200 hectares of land has been reclassified as within the lithium mining zone, meaning that many hundreds of people have been displaced, affecting their ability to sustain themselves.

Chapter Link
Dependency theory and the concept of neocolonialism are outlined in **Chapter 5: Economic Global Governance**.

Chapter Link
It is useful to distinguish between the impacts of economic globalisation, which are addressed in this debate, and the impacts of economic global governance, which is addressed in **Chapter 5: Economic Global Governance**. Remember that the increased significance of IGOs – including economic IGOs – is a feature of political globalisation, not economic globalisation. It is in fact, a response to the increasing global challenges posed by economic globalisation.

Key Debate Summary: Does globalisation increase poverty and inequality?

	For	Against
Extreme Poverty	✓ Many millions of people remain in extreme poverty. Their situations are worsened by factors such as bad debt and environmental crises.	✗ Globalisation has dramatically decreased the amount of extreme poverty globally.
Economic Inequality	✓ Globalisation reduces inequality between states, accelerating growth as developing states catch up.	✗ Globalisation increases inequality within states. The top 1 per cent own more wealth than the bottom 95 per cent combined.

	For	Against
Human Well-being	✓ Globalisation fuels a 'race to the bottom', leading to exploitation and corporate violence against peoples.	✗ Globalisation increases access to cheaper goods and services for all. Trickle Down Economics means that everyone is a winner in globalisation.
Development and Dependency	✓ Globalisation benefits development, with the increased movement of people helping to plug labour and skills shortages. Foreign Aid and FDI helps states to develop their economies.	✗ Globalisation creates dependency, trapping developing states in a cycle of underdevelopment and poverty. Foreign Aid and FDI can fuel corruption and fail to bring benefits to the recipient state.

Globalisation and other contemporary global issues

The question of whether globalisation has addressed other contemporary global issues is contested. There is considerable debate about the extent to which globalisation is a cause of or resolves conflict, human rights and environmental issues. As you read through this textbook, you will start to develop your own ideas about this complex issue, and the answer is by no means straightforward. The Key Debate below outlines some of the key strengths and weaknesses of globalisation in addressing and resolving contemporary global issues.

KEY DEBATE: DOES GLOBALISATION RESOLVE CONTEMPORARY GLOBAL ISSUES?

Globalisation increases the risk of global conflict

- ✗ Realists believe that globalisation can increase the risk of conflict because it increases mutual vulnerabilities. This was illustrated clearly during the Covid-19 pandemic, which highlighted clear divides between developed and developing states, whereby the former retained vaccines at the expense of the latter. It also showed how fragile global supply chains were. High levels of interdependence have certainly not always acted to prevent conflict. Russia invaded Ukraine in 2022, despite high levels of economic interdependence between itself and Ukraine, and itself and Ukraine's allies.

- ✗ A further effect of globalisation has been its impact on the proliferation of criminal and terrorist groups. Whilst states have been able to capitalise on the benefits of improved communications technologies and infrastructure, so too have non-state actors. Such ideas are also shared by Mary Kaldor in her 'New Wars' thesis, where she suggests that globalisation has helped lead to globalised war economies, whereby non-state actors can recruit and raise finance from all over the world to fuel conflict. In Iraq and Syria, ISIS used social media, such as Facebook, extensively to recruit members, especially from Western states. At its height, it was estimated that over 40,000 foreign nationals from over 100 states joined ISIS. It was also able to exploit improved infrastructure and the global economy to sell oil from within its illegally captured territory, and between 2014 and 2015 was estimated to be generating up to $3 million from illegal oil trade. These proceeds were then used to fund the ongoing conflict in the region.

- ✗ The spread of globalisation has helped fuel many identity-based conflicts. Samuel Huntington suggests that a 'Clash of civilisations' will occur as groups become threatened by others. We are also seeing such identity-based conflicts playing out within civilisations as contestation over ideas and values becomes particularly fierce. In his book *Grave New World*, Stephen King argues how complex algorithms used by social media platforms mean that peoples are only exposed to ideas they agree with, which polarises society between 'them' and 'us'. This was poignantly seen in the UK during and post the Brexit referendum, whereby neither vote leave or vote remain were able to engage with the debate on the other side. It is also seen today in the

'Far Right', whereby the proliferation of the 'Make America Great Again' movement adopted by right-wing groups has led to a backlash against so-called 'expert knowledge', and they use ever new social media technologies to spread their messages outside of the mainstream; for example Trump launched 'Truth Social' in 2022 after being banned from X and Facebook following the 2021 Capitol Hill attacks.

Globalisation helps reduce the risk of global conflict

- ✅ The liberal argument is that by promoting interdependence (in particular, economic interdependence) between states, globalisation has helped to reduce the likelihood of conflict because states are connected by a complex web of relations. This idea has been expanded on by Thomas L. Friedman, who proposed in the 'Golden Arches Theory of Conflict Prevention' that no two states with a McDonald's had fought a war against each other. This was to demonstrate the high costs of conflict when states share economic ties.
- ✅ Political globalisation helps to increase interdependence between states because it creates forums where cooperation can take place. It has also helped to establish international law, which regulates conflict between states; in particular, wars of aggression are outlawed and the use of force is only permitted in self-defence or with a UN Security Council Resolution providing a mandate for the use of force. Finally, it has also created shared democratic norms, and from the 1990s, led to a spread of liberal democracies. Liberals argue in the 'Democratic Peace Theory' that democracies do not wage war against other democracies, hence showing that the globalisation of democracy has helped foster peace.

Globalisation increases the risk to human rights in global politics

> **Chapter Link**
>
> The spread of liberal democracy is discussed in **Chapter 3: Power and Developments**, whilst 'Democratic Peace Theory' is discussed in **Chapter 1: Comparative Theories**.

- ❌ Globalisation's increased interdependence between states makes it difficult to challenge human rights offenders; this is because if a human rights offender is a major trading partner, it is economically difficult to challenge them. In the 1990s and 2000s, so-called 'Western states' frequently made relations with others conditional on upholding human rights norms; however, now we are undoubtedly in a period of power transition, whereby the 'West' is in decline relative to others; it is more difficult for it to challenge others. It faces the dual threat of demands from populations for improved living standards (i.e. trade promotes jobs and cheaper economic goods) as well as the necessity to do business with human rights violators. This was seen in May 2025, when the UK signed an explicitly 'values-free' £1.6 billion trade deal with the Gulf states.
- ❌ The global spread of ideas and interconnectedness has, paradoxically, fuelled a backlash against universal human rights. In particular, it is increasingly highlighted that there are different cultural versions of human rights, known as cultural relativism. It is also increasingly seen as an attack on the sovereignty of other states to criticise their human rights violations.
- ❌ Globalisation has led to the exploitation of workers' rights and increased poverty. Globalisation has also seen Indigenous peoples forced from their homes. For example, Indigenous communities in the Amazonian rainforest have been driven from their land for timber.

Globalisation helps promote human rights in global conflict

- ✅ Globalisation has led to the spread of ideas about universal human rights – this is the idea that human rights are applicable to all human beings by virtue of being human. The UN Declaration on Human Rights forms the basis of ideas about human rights in global politics.
- ✅ Globalisation has challenged traditional views of state sovereignty and has led to the idea that sovereignty is conditional based upon fulfilment of human rights. This has formed the basis of ideas of humanitarian or forcible intervention, which is permitted under the doctrine of 'Responsibility to Protect'.
- ✅ Cultural Globalisation has helped to promote peace and stability through its real-time reporting on global events as they take place. This helps act as a restraint on state behaviour when it comes to human rights violations. It also helps to foster a sense of global civil society, which fosters a sense of common humanity amongst peoples.

Globalisation increases environmental degradation in global politics

- Globalisation increases environmental degradation through waste. The increased production and consumption of fast fashion and disposable products has led to unprecedented levels of waste. According to the UN, there are over 92 million tonnes of clothing waste every year, which ends up either incarcerated or in landfills. Much of this waste is made using plastic materials, which are produced using fossil fuels. In addition to waste from the products themselves, enormous waste is created through single-use packaging. Developed states have typically shipped lots of their waste to developing states to dispose of, leading to pollution, amongst other health hazards. In 2018, China's 'National Sword' policy reduced its import of foreign waste, but in turn, many other states, especially in Southeast Asia, saw a massive surge of imports. The shipment of e-waste (i.e. used electronic goods) has been especially devastating for developing states. For example, a 2024 study showed that in Ghana and Nigeria, there are increased child mortality rates near e-waste sites due to the release of highly toxic chemicals into the air, soil and water.
- Globalisation has led to the loss of ecosystems. The demand for natural resources such as minerals, water and timber has had huge implications. Since 1990, it is estimated that there have been 420 million hectares of deforestation. This has been carried out due to demand for palm oil and soy cultivation, for example. For our oceans, globalisation has had a dramatic impact. It is estimated that between 1 and 2 million tonnes of plastic are dumped in the sea each year. The Great Pacific Garbage Patch, located between Hawaii and California, is the largest accumulation of ocean plastic in the world.
- Globalisation has led to increased CO_2 emissions worldwide and contributes to global warming and increasingly severe weather incidents and pollution (Figure 2.4).

Globalisation enhances environmental protection in global politics

- In important ways, globalisation has led to increased research and innovation, which helps to protect the environment. It has led to rapid information exchange and technology transfer, for example in non-renewable energy sources.

> **Chapter Link**
>
> Ideas about human rights are discussed in **Chapter 6: Human Rights Global Governance**.

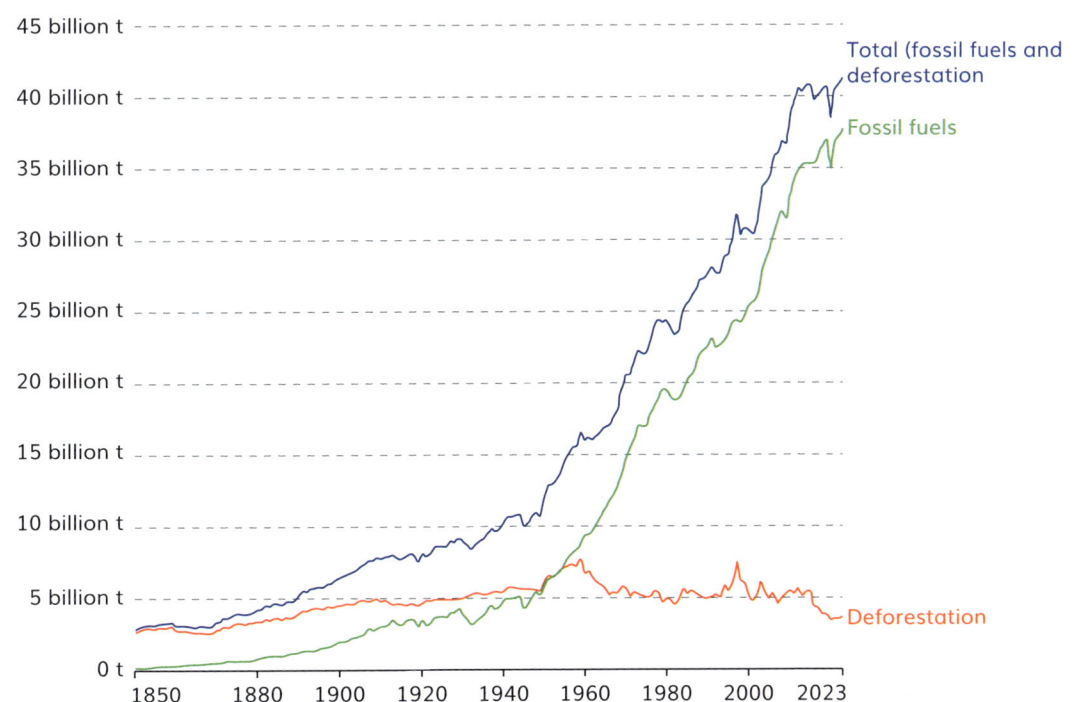

Figure 2.4 Global CO_2 Emissions, 1850–2024

Source: Our World in Data (2025), 'Global CO₂ emissions from fossil fuels and industry (1850–2024)', CC BY licence

> **Chapter Link**
>
> The issue of global environmental damage is discussed in **Chapter 7: Environmental Global Governance**.

✓ Whilst globalisation may have placed pressure on the environment, the tools of globalisation have facilitated the spread of knowledge and debate about the issues. There has been a significant growth in global media and activism, which helps to raise public awareness. NGOs such as Greenpeace and social movements such as Extinction Rebellion and Fridays for Future have helped raise awareness and put pressure on states and IGOs to take action. There has also been increased demands for 'green' or eco-friendly products through a rise in so-called 'conscious consumerism'. For example, the brand 'Faith in Nature' initially began in Scotland in 1974 and is now available in over forty states worldwide.

✓ There is increasing pressure on TNCs and businesses to implement sustainable business models. This is sometimes done through increased use of renewable energy to power business operations. For example, IKEA aims for 100 per cent renewable energy across its operations. Brands are also using sustainable sourcing for their broader supply chains. For example, Tony Chocolonely is produced using entirely 100 per cent slave-free chocolate. It is now increasingly common for businesses to publicise their sustainability reports. For example, large TNCs such as Nestle and Apple produce annual reports.

Key Debate Summary: Does globalisation resolve contemporary global issues?

	For	Against
Conflict	✓ Globalisation reduces conflict via economic interdependence, political cooperation and the spread of international law and democratic norms.	✗ Globalisation can increase conflict by fostering vulnerabilities, enabling non-state actor proliferation and fuelling identity-based clashes.
Human Rights	✓ Globalisation spreads universal human rights ideas, challenges sovereignty for R2P, and real-time reporting fosters global civil society, restraining human rights violations.	✗ Globalisation hinders human rights protection by making it hard to challenge key trading partners, fuelling cultural relativism and enabling worker exploitation and indigenous displacement for resources.
Environment	✓ Globalisation boosts environmental protection through rapid knowledge exchange, increased public awareness and putting pressure on TNCs to adopt sustainable practices.	✗ Globalisation increases environmental degradation through exploitation of the global commons.

Chapter Summary

- ✓ The nation-state is a key actor in global politics.
- ✓ Whilst the state is legally sovereign, its sovereignty is increasingly challenged by the process of globalisation.
- ✓ Globalisation – the process of increasing interconnectedness between political actors in global politics – is a complex process of broadening and deepening, which is driven by people (social), countries, institutions, culture, economics, technology and politics.
- ✓ Globalisation reached its peak in the decade following the end of the Cold War, but has increasingly come under challenge in the 2020s; a process called deglobalisation.
- ✓ Globalisation includes different types – economic, cultural and political – all of which impact state sovereignty in different ways.
- ✓ There is debate among globalisation theorists – including realists and liberals – about the impact of globalisation.
- ✓ There is debate about the extent to which globalisation addresses and resolves contemporary global issues – poverty, conflict, human rights and the environment.

Exam Style Questions

- Examine the distinctions between political and cultural globalisation. (12)
- Examine the differences between hyperglobalisers' and globalisation sceptics' explanations of the impact of globalisation. (12)
- Examine the different perspectives on globalisation of realists and liberals. (12)
- Evaluate the extent to which economic globalisation has had a greater impact on the world than any other form of globalisation. (30)
- Evaluate the extent to which cultural globalisation has created a global monoculture. (30)
- Evaluate the view that globalisation has failed to resolve contemporary global issues. (30)

Further Resources

https://www.youtube.com/watch?v=0seMlf57nWo 'Corporate Nations'. A documentary by TRT World exploring the power of TNCs versus states.

https://www.youtube.com/watch?v=a5qt5fFOJI0 'Economic Decoupling: Is globalisation dying or transforming'. A documentary by DW exploring current trends in globalisation.

https://www.youtube.com/watch?v=yoZiTCz_wYA 'Winners and Losers in World Trade'. A DW documentary exploring the impacts of economic and cultural globalisation.

https://www.youtube.com/watch?v=gIYaSEwoblY 'Profits over People'. A DW documentary exploring the impact of economic globalisation.

https://www.theguardian.com/us-news/2025/may/08/can-we-reform-global-capitalism-trump-tariffs This Guardian 'long read' explores the implications of globalisation and global capitalism.

Stephen D. King, *Grave New World: The End of Globalisation and the Return of History* (Yale University Press, 2017). This book explores the pressures on globalisation and possible alternatives.

Visit https://bloomsbury.pub/essentials-of-global-politics to access additional materials to support teaching and learning.

3 POWER AND DEVELOPMENTS

Chapter Preview

With the end of the Cold War, the United States entered the 1990s in a position of unchallenged hegemony, possessing a level of dominance that is largely incomparable in history. Why states are powerful, how we classify their position within international relations and the impact this has on the geopolitical system are key aspects of global politics.

Historically, the main way that states were seen to influence other states was by hard power, forcing or coercing states and other actors into doing what they wanted. In more recent times, soft power has also started to play an equally key role. Soft power is the ability for states to persuade other states to follow a certain route or policy through diplomacy or cultural appeal.

States that wield significant influence in global politics tend to be categorised as 'Great Powers'. Great powers are states that possess considerable economic, military and structural power. Since the 1990s, some states in the developing world have gained 'emerging power' status, signifying their recent increase in power and influence. Great powers that have influence at a truly global level can be classified as 'superpowers'.

How individual states are governed also impacts the international system. The spread of democracy was a defining feature of the second half of the twentieth century, associated as it is with the spread of peace and liberal capitalism. Comparing the relative instability that autocratic, non-democratic, rogue and failed states all have on the geopolitical scene is also key to understanding why different parts of the globe exist under different conditions.

One of the themes of this chapter in modern global politics has been the extent to which US dominance is in decline. The rise of China, as well as internal shifts within the US political system, has meant that US hegemony is shifting. We are arguably entering a period of multiple superpowers within international relations.

Key Questions and Debates

» How do states wield power?
» What are the different ways in which we can classify states within the international system?
» How does the number of superpowers present within international relations relate to different types of polarity within global politics? How has this changed over time?
» What impact does the nature of a state's government have on its conduct within the international system?

Specification Checklist

4.1 Different types of power
» The use and effectiveness of:
  - Hard power: military and economic
  - Soft power: diplomatic and cultural

4.2 Differing significance of states in global affairs
» State power classifications:
  - Great powers
  - Superpowers, including the United States
  - Emerging powers, including BRICS (Brazil, Russia, India, China and South Africa)

4.3 Polarity
» The implications of the following polar structures
  - Unipolarity/hegemony
  - Bipolarity
  - Multipolarity
» Consideration of the changing nature of world order since 2000

4.4 Different systems of government
» The characteristics, examples and consequences of for global order of:
  - Democratic, semi-democratic, non-democratic, autocratic states, failed states and rogue states

4.5 Development and spread of:
» Liberal economies
» Rule of law
» Democracy

4.6 The ways and extent to which changing state power and other developments address contemporary global issues such as conflict, poverty, human rights, and the environment

Source: NurPhoto via Getty Images

Power

Spec key term

Hard power: The ability of one actor (usually, but not necessarily, a state) to influence another through the use of threats or rewards, typically involving military or economic actions.

In international relations, power is the ability of states to achieve their goals and interests. The aims of each state differ depending on the country's geopolitical position, and each government will have its own priorities and agenda that it wants to achieve. A state's success within international relations is dependent on how it goes about achieving these goals.

The aims of states have developed considerably in modern times. Rather than simply being focused on the expansion of their territory and consolidation of power within their borders, governments now have a wide range of priorities that the exercise of power can help them to achieve. At the most basic level, this can still be the acquisition of new territory, at the expense of other states. Far more likely, however, as conflict has become less of an option, is that states will try to exert influence through institutions, diplomacy and economic power. Acquiring better trading relations, providing a secure environment for their citizens or promoting their world-view are more likely to be priorities for nations in the twenty-first century.

Hard power

Hard power, or the ability to force or coerce another state or actor to do as you wish, is traditionally seen as the main way in which states try to achieve their aims within international relations. While the term 'hard power' has only been applied to these types of actions in recent times, as an approach, it has always existed. Hard power has often been categorised as 'command power' – the ability to change what others are doing by either using 'carrots' or 'sticks' – rewards or threats.

The use of military power by states is a very clear example of hard power. States largely remain the only actors in international relations who are capable of using armies to achieve their aims, certainly in a large-scale manner. The acquisition of territory, either through conquest or annexation, played a major role in the wars of the twentieth century and earlier. Military conquests have become less common in the twenty-first century, but Russia has continued to take this approach with mixed success (see **Case Study: Russian Annexation of Crimea, 2014** for more detail). Military power can not only be used in regard to territorial disputes. The United States spends more on its military than any other nation (by some calculations, more than the next nine highest-spending countries combined). America regularly deploys its military overseas, but the United States has not increased in size since 1947. Rather than looking to acquire more land, the United States uses its substantial military might for a number of other aims:

- Encouraging a regime change in another state, as in the case of Iraq (2003) and Afghanistan (2001).
- Humanitarian intervention, as in Syria (2014), Libya (2011) and Kosovo (1998).
- As a member of NATO (North Atlantic Treaty Organisation), supporting other states within the alliance and coordinating military drills. NATO has carried out military practices within the Baltic states in 2022, 2023 and 2024, in opposition to Russia. America also offers a 'nuclear umbrella' for NATO states, with US nuclear weapons being placed in a number of European states, such as Germany and Turkey.
- To counter China's and Russia's military threats. US military force offers protection against China for Taiwan and other states in the South China Sea, as well as protection against Russia for the Baltic states.

Definition

Economic sanctions: Restrictions placed on trade and economic relations between states. Sanctions could involve placing a blanket ban on trade between two states, or a more focused one on certain types of trade or on certain individuals who hold important positions within society, such as in government.

The increasingly globalised nature of international relations has had an impact on the use of hard power. As the world economy has become more interlinked and interdependent, the use of **economic sanctions** and trade tariffs have become common as a tool to exert influence and achieve a state's aims. Direct conflict has become a far less practical option, as globalisation has meant that war would have considerable economic, political and cultural fallout. Nuclear weapons have made waging war even riskier. Other methods of coercing states have, as a result, become an important aspect of international relations.

Economic sanctions aim to damage a foreign power's economy to the point that it feels pressured to agree to certain terms or aims. For example, the EU and the United States both try to avoid the use of force as a first reaction (particularly so in the case of the EU), but both also possess significant economic power. For them, sanctions present a practical way of making use of that economic power in international relations. When Russia invaded Ukraine in 2022, the EU and America both placed significant economic sanctions on the Russian economy – on a scale that is arguably unprecedented in global political history. Trade between the EU and the United States with Russia was massively restricted in several different areas, such as a ban on the provision of technology for oil and gas exploration and a ban on credit to Russian oil companies. Prominent Russians who were close to Russian President Vladimir Putin had their Western bank accounts closed and funds frozen. The Russian economy suffered, as a result, with the rouble losing 50 per cent of its value within days. It is worth noting that despite the significant economic sanctions put on Russia, the sanctions did not initially succeed in making Putin withdraw his troops from Ukraine.

Other forms of hard power also could include the use of bribes, payments or even funds from international organisations such as the IMF and the World Bank, which often come with strings attached. During the East Asian Financial Crisis of 1997, the United States was accused of using IMF loans as a 'hard power' tool. By forcing several states, such as Thailand and South Korea, to remove restrictions on foreign ownership in exchange for loans, the IMF allowed US businesses to buy corporations in these states at a significant discount. This was seen by some as an example of hard power in action – though it is worth noting that since then, the IMF has admitted to handling this crisis poorly. Under President Trump, the United States has dramatically increased its use of hard power. In 2025, 'Trump tariffs' have been used as a coercive tool in trade negotiations. The United States conducted air strikes on Iran's nuclear facilities. Trump has also talked of making a deal with the Taliban to re-establish a US base at Bagram, 60 km north of Kabul in Afghanistan, close to Chinese nuclear bases.

Soft power

'Whose story wins?' is often how **soft power** is presented as a force in international relations. If hard power is the ability to force another actor to do as you wish, soft power is the ability to persuade them. The term was popularised by Joseph Nye, a liberal theorist, in the 1990s, but it has existed in global politics for as long as hard power has. Unlike hard power, states have never historically focused on their ability to project soft power. More so than hard power, the sources of soft power can be quite diverse. Soft power can be represented by:

- a strong economic system and citizens of the country experience a high quality of life, through, for example, access to housing, technology and healthcare, as in Germany.
- a substantial international media presence and reputation for reliable reporting, as with the UK.
- a spread of culture internationally, as in the case of India.

With growing interdependence facilitated by globalisation, the ability for states to achieve their goals via soft power has become more important. War, as a means to achieve their aims, has for many states ceased to be a legitimate option. Even other versions of hard power, such as economic sanctions, cannot be deployed as readily or swiftly as in the past. With the world becoming more interconnected and interlinked, states' ability to use soft power has increased.

A state's economic output is one of the clearest methods of soft power. States with a thriving, successful economy are seen positively by the rest of the world. They may be viewed as a potential trading partner, but states may also think that mirroring the actions of the state in question will result in similar economic success. When other countries admire a state's way of life, they are more likely to willingly align their own interests and actions with that state's goals.

As well as economic soft power, soft power is often wielded through diplomatic and cultural means. The pope arguably wields significant diplomatic soft power, as he holds support from 1.36 billion Catholics internationally. His intervention in international affairs carries no military or economic weight, but he is still likely to be listened to by a number of governments and individuals. Similarly, cultural power is a useful example. India is notable for wielding significant cultural influence globally. The widespread nature of practices such as yoga and Indian cuisine, is an example of how Indian culture acts as a form of soft power. India has actively leveraged yoga as a diplomatic tool. The successful campaign to establish 21 June as the International Day of Yoga by the United Nations (with unprecedented co-sponsorship from 177 countries) is a prime example. This initiative,

Exam Tip: Despite economic sanctions not being a direct conflict between two actors, it remains an example of hard power, not soft. The state issuing the sanctions is trying to coerce the other actor through this action.

Spec key term

Soft power: The ability to influence other actors by persuading them to follow or agree to norms and aspirations that produce the desired behaviour. It is the power of attraction and co-opting other actors into working towards your aims.

CASE STUDY: RUSSIAN ANNEXATION OF CRIMEA, 2014

Map 3.1 Donbass and Crimea, disputed areas between Ukraine and Russia

Source: PeterHermesFurian/iStock via Getty Images

Context

Ukraine was a Soviet Socialist Republic within the USSR during the Cold War. In 1954, Crimea, an area of land between Ukraine and Russia (see Map 3.1), was given to Ukraine by the leader of the Soviet Union, Nikita Khrushchev. Crimea had previously been part of Russia, and like some of the regions in eastern Ukraine, continued to have a large Russian-speaking population living within it.

In 2014, Vladimir Putin claimed he was acting in the interest of these ethnically Russian groups when he invaded Crimea to put it under Russian control.

Earlier in the year, a series of protests and uprisings had resulted in the replacement of the former, pro-Russian president of Ukraine (President Yanukovych) with a pro-EU and pro-West president (President Petro Poroshenko). In the aftermath of this, there was a series of pro-Russia protests within Ukraine, in part due to support from Putin.

Intervention

As the protests continued, Russian Special Forces began to occupy key positions within Crimea, making this initially a covert, unannounced occupation. There was no official declaration of war by Russia; instead, Russian troops focused on taking key infrastructure and government points. The Supreme Council of Crimea was taken over on 27 February 2013. Despite protests from the international community, most notably the UN and the United States, the whole of the peninsula was then brought under Russian control. A referendum on 16 March confirmed that Crimea had left Ukraine and voted to become part of Russia.

The referendum vote, and the Russian actions it supported, were both seen as illegitimate by much of the wider international community. Despite this, the **annexation** can only really be seen as a success for Russia. In practice, Crimea has been part of Russia since 2014, and Western media sources have struggled with reporting on the reality of Crimea as an occupied territory in contrast to how the situation is represented internationally. The annexation of Crimea was, largely, a smooth and unchallenged process. Russia's secondary aim was the destabilisation of eastern Ukraine to prevent Ukraine from later joining the EU and NATO. If it was not internally sovereign, then it would be unable to join either institution. Russia's continued presence in Crimea meant that the Ukrainian government was unable to bring the region back under its control. The situation progressed with the subsequent invasion of Ukraine by Russia in 2022.

Significance

The annexation of Crimea is a very clear example of a state using hard power to achieve its aims. Russia had two priorities – to destabilise Ukraine so that it could not join NATO or the EU and to bring Crimea into Russia for strategic reasons. In both of these, it was, at least in the short term, completely successful. It is also an example of a state needing to use coercion or force to achieve its aims, as it is unlikely that Ukraine would have given up Crimea voluntarily.

Aftermath

The full-scale Russian invasion of Ukraine began in February 2022, with initial attempts to seize Kyiv failing due to Ukrainian resistance and Western military aid. Throughout 2023, a Ukrainian counteroffensive yielded limited territorial gains. By 2024 and into 2025, the conflict remained largely a war of attrition. In contrast to the initial annexation of Crimea, the extent to which this has been a successful use of hard power is less clear currently.

---

championed by Prime Minister Narendra Modi, cemented yoga's global status and India's role as its custodian, projecting an image of India as a peaceful nation promoting global harmony and wellness. In turn, this makes it more likely that other states would want to work with India and cooperate on the international stage.

The EU is a great example of the potential of soft power. It depends on its members for defence, so its hard power options are limited in comparison to those of a sovereign state. It can, and does, use economic sanctions, but relies far more on its use of soft power to influence world affairs. One of the clearest examples is the former Soviet Bloc states joining the EU after the end of the Cold War. To join the EU, a state must meet certain criteria, including having a functioning democracy and a capitalist economic system with limited state involvement. Theoretically, the EU could have used hard power to enforce these ideals, threatening economic sanctions on the new governments unless they embraced the Western ideals of the EU. Instead, the draw of possible EU membership, and the requirements that came with that, meant that the majority of former Soviet Bloc countries have adopted liberal democracy and laissez-faire economic systems.

Soft power can be even more implicit than this. In one sense, it is simply the global appeal that a state has, which in turn makes it more likely for other actors to view interactions with them positively. The soft power index (https://softpower30.com/) ranks how well a state is perceived internationally, both by other governments and their citizens. In these rankings, the UK has scored highly, although Brexit and other events have resulted in a slide downwards towards the end of the 2010s. Factors influencing Britain's soft power:

- It has a functioning democracy, with a relatively free press and competition between different parties in its electoral system.
- Its education system, in particular at university level, is world renowned and prestigious. Oxford and Cambridge rank amongst the top universities globally, with four of the top ten international universities being British.
- Culturally, the UK has a number of television programmes that are watched or copied internationally, such as Doctor Who, the Great British Bake Off and Strictly Come Dancing. The BBC also has worldwide recognition.

> **Definition**
>
> **Annexation:** Taking territory from another state by seizing it, normally through military means.

> **Chapter Link**
>
> See **Chapter 1: Comparative Theories**, for details on the competing views on power between realism and liberalism.

- The Premier League increases the UK's soft power. For example, in 2017, the Egyptian player Mo Salah joined Liverpool Football Club, meaning that within Egypt, there is more active support for Liverpool, and therefore the UK.
- The British monarchy is predominantly viewed in a positive light globally, and its role in diplomacy offers the UK more potential soft power. Donald Trump, in his first term as US president, set up a meeting with Queen Elizabeth II as swiftly as he could.
- English is, at the moment, the most commonly used language in diplomacy and business in the world. The UK has significant soft power through this, too.

As demonstrated above, the UK possesses soft power to a considerable extent. Although the reality of this is harder to measure in quantifiable terms, it is nonetheless important in international relations. From the 2010s onwards, China made attempts to increase its soft power, establishing Confucius Institutes around the globe. These institutions seek to spread Chinese values, making them be perceived in a more favourable light by other states, increasing China's soft power appeal.

Other types of power: smart, sharp and structural

Smart power

While Joseph Nye popularised the term 'soft power' to describe a type of power which has existed and been actively used for centuries, Nye actively developed the concept of 'smart power' himself. In his book *Soft Power: The Means to Success in World Politics* (2005), Nye established the concept of **smart power** as being a combination of hard and soft power.

> **Definition**
>
> **Smart power:** A combination of both 'hard' and 'soft' power to achieve foreign policy objectives. It acknowledges that in certain situations neither hard power nor soft power may be sufficient on its own to address the complex challenges of the twenty-first century.
>
> **Sharp power:** The use of manipulative diplomatic policies by one country to influence and undermine the political system of a target country.

Nye was initially writing in 2004, but during the rest of the 2000s, smart power really gained traction as a concept. When the United States became embroiled in conflicts in Iraq and Afghanistan, there was a recognition that hard power by itself was often not sufficient. There was also an acceptance that soft power alone was often not sufficient. Rogue states, which are states that operate outside international rules and norms, such as Iran or North Korea, would not respond to soft power by itself (rogue states are covered in more detail later on in the chapter, see p. 102). Therefore, Nye's belief was that for states to effectively achieve their aims in international relations, they needed to use hard and soft power in combination.

This attitude gained a lot of traction during President Barack Obama's administration from 2008 to 2016, as he was seeking to learn from the issues his predecessor, President George Bush, had faced in foreign policy. Obama and Hilary Clinton, as his Secretary of State, tried to adapt their foreign policy to include a combination of soft and hard power. The agreement that the United States, and other states, made with Iran in 2015 over a lifting of sanctions in return for Iran restricting its nuclear programme was arguably an example of this attitude. In the process of achieving this deal, Obama treated Iran with a level of respect that it had not received from the US administration for years. Obama spoke to the Iranian president, Rouhani, by phone; it was the first time since the Iranian Revolution of 1979 that a US president had done this. This was a clear effort at using soft power to try to make the American demands more enticing. However, this was always combined with the potential threat of continued economic sanctions by the US government, which is an example of hard power. In this way, Obama was making use of subtle influence and threatened punishment to try to persuade the Iranian government to agree to his terms, which it ultimately did. The subsequent breakdown of the treaty in 2018 under Donald Trump is, in part, a reflection of Trump's belief that hard power is the only legitimate and effective tool of foreign policy.

Sharp power

Sharp power is a very new term used to describe the actions that authoritarian states increasingly take to interfere in the actions of democratic states. Sharp power refers to these states, such as China or Russia, using their own propaganda to try to misinform the citizens of other nations although it involves persuasion, it is not soft power. The intent is not to make other states, or their citizens, necessarily view Russia or China in a more positive light, but rather to sow dissent or distrust within these countries. These states' intent here is to covertly influence other states for their own interests, rather than through open persuasion. Sharp power, therefore, can be seen as a form of hard power.

Russian interference in Western elections is a clear demonstration of sharp power in action. Both the 2016 US election and the Brexit referendum of the same year were found to have been heavily influenced by Russian money and intervention. The election of President Donald Trump in the United States and the withdrawal of Britain from the EU suited Russian aims, as they were aiming to make the West less united. To achieve this, Russian bots on social media, particularly X (formerly Twitter), spread misinformation aiming to influence the views of the voting public. There was also a significant number of meetings between Russian businessmen and leading figures within both the 'Vote Leave' Brexit campaign and Trump's election team. Trump's more positive attitude towards Putin is reflected in Photo 3.2.

Structural power

Structural power, unlike smart power and sharp power, is less about direct actions that states take. Structural power in global politics refers to the ability of a state to shape the global political and economic system. Structural power can be defined in four key ways:

- Knowledge – shaping the perception of global events and the spread of knowledge, through news channels and social media. Consider Russian and Chinese promotion of far right views on 'X', as well as the role of news network RT/Russia Today.

- Financial – setting the rules for global finance and international lending institutions, such as the International Monetary Fund and World Bank.

- Security – helping to establish global security rules and norms, influence international security organisations (like NATO or the UN Security Council), and dictate the acceptable uses of force.

Chapter Link

The dominance of the United States within the International Monetary Fund and World Bank and the impact of this on global politics are both considered in Chapter 5: Economic Global Governance.

Photo 3.1 US President Donald Trump, left, receives a soccer ball from Russian President Vladimir Putin, right

Source: Bloomberg via Getty Images

KEY DEBATE: IS HARD POWER REDUNDANT IN GLOBAL POLITICS?

A globalised economy has made hard power undesirable to deploy

✓ As the global economy has become increasingly interconnected, it has become harder to take coercive action against other states. Two of the chief weapons that states can use to deploy hard power, military action and economic sanctions, risk economic blowback for the state taking the action. International trade has grown to the extent that there are few states that are not fully interlinked to the global economic system – possibly North Korea as a singular exception. For Western states, this has been seen most clearly in their interactions with China. Much as they might want to deploy economic sanctions in retaliation for some of China's recent actions, such as the treatment of the Uighur population in the Western Xinjiang province, they have been reluctant to do so for fear of the economic damage that their own economies will receive if they do.

The impact of economic sanctions has become greater due to this interconnectedness

✗ Although economic sanctions (an example of hard power) have always been a tool that states have been able to make use of, in less interconnected times, their impact was not as great. As the international economy has become truly global in nature, the ability for states to make their own market immune from sanctions has become much harder. In comparison to an economy that was relatively isolated from the West during the Cold War, Russia now has strong trade links with the West. This is why the recent sanctions in the aftermath of the illegal invasion of Ukraine by Russia have been so impactful, sending the rouble's value plummeting and causing severe economic problems in Russia. Although this has caused economic problems in the West, notably in a cost-of-living crisis, it nonetheless demonstrates the greater impact that economic sanctions can now have.

Growth of norms and international law against conflict

✓ Citizens are less likely to accept the need for states to deploy hard power. This is due to a rise in cultural awareness of other nations, to the spread of democracy and the increased media coverage of the impact of military and economic sanctions. The Iraq War caused remarkably few casualties among the coalition forces deployed. Combined official figures stated that 4,809 people died during the invasion – around 1 per cent of lives lost during the Second World War for the United States alone. However, every individual death was seen as a needless loss of life. This attitude, particularly present in Western states, has limited certain types of hard power as options. These views have also been cemented in a range of international treaties that lay out a number of restrictions on the use of military power in international affairs. Notably, the International Criminal Court (ICC) attempts to try individuals who have committed war crimes.

Military power remains a unique tool to achieve a state's aims

✗ The deployment of military might remains in some circumstances the only option that a state has to achieve their aims. Despite the setbacks that the United States experienced in its deployments in Iraq and Afghanistan, the only way that they would have been able to remove Saddam Hussein and the Taliban was via hard power, in particular, military force. No amount of soft power diplomacy and persuasion would have achieved these aims. Similarly, the annexation of Crimea by Russia (see **Case Study: Annexation of Crimea by Russia, 2014**) was an example of a state using hard power to achieve a primary aim in a manner that would not have been possible by other means.

Soft power's increasing impact

✓ Alongside the declining ability to use hard power, there is also the greater way in which states can utilise soft power to achieve their aims. Globalisation has resulted in the spread of culture, which has led to states such as the UK having their soft power developed. There has also been an increased level of investment by certain powerful nations in other states, in part designed to alter the way in which they are perceived and their soft power as a result. China has been most active in this area in recent years, investing heavily in Africa, spending money on infrastructure, hospitals and sporting venues through the Belt and Road Initiative (BRI). This investment has economic benefits, but also leads to these states viewing China in a more positive light, increasing their ability to achieve their aims when working with these states.

Hard power is evolving

✖ Although traditional methods of hard power, such as economic sanctions and military power, are becoming more limited, states are using other methods to carry out aggressive actions. States have been using new technology to increase the ways in which they can utilise hard power. The increased use of drone technology by the United States in the Middle East is one example of this, but so is cyberwarfare: the ability to attack, or threaten, other states' internet systems. This is a way in which countries can covertly deploy hard power. Rogue states, such as North Korea, see it as a way in which they can act to destabilise and threaten other countries, without receiving direct blame. In the past, North Korea has carried out cyberattacks on Sony Pictures, the NHS and Bangladesh's central bank.

Key Debate Summary: Is hard power redundant in global politics?

Key Criteria	For	Against
Has economic interdependence stopped hard power from being a valid choice for states?	✓ Hard power is increasingly hard to deploy, as the international system has become ever more interdependent and interconnected.	✖ Economic sanctions arguably have a greater impact now, due to the economic interdependence that exists between states.
Is the deployment of military power still a viable option for states?	✓ Citizens of states are more reluctant to accept conflict as an option when pursued by their governments and will object to the consequences of hard power being used.	✖ Military power remains a unique tool that states possess to achieve certain geopolitical goals.
Is hard power being replaced by soft power?	✓ Soft power is increasingly being used by states to achieve their aims, as they take advantage of greater opportunities to project a positive world-view of their country.	✖ Hard power is evolving, and the way in which it is deployed by states is changing, making it easier to use without risking direct retaliation.
Exam Tip:		
When considering your AO3 for this question, looking at the relative successes of the annexation of Crimea (2014) and the subsequent invasion (2022) of Ukraine by Russia can offer an interesting point of comparison for judgement.		

Spec key term

Great power: A great power is a state deemed to rank amongst the most powerful in a hierarchical state system, based upon its military and economic power.

Superpower: A power that is greater than a traditional 'great power'. A superpower has the strengths of a great power, but with much greater mobility of power, as well as even more significant military and economic strength.

Emerging power: A broad category for state that are thought to be in the process of increasing their economic and military power faster than other actors, and are therefore in the process of becoming great powers.

Unipolarity: When there is a single superpower or significant actor in the international system, without any major rivals.

Definition

Hegemon: An unchallenged superpower, which exists without competitors in the international system.

- Production – influencing the global production network and how goods are produced. Establishing the respective roles within the international economy, such as 'developing' nations producing raw materials and providing cheap labour, whilst 'developed' economies produce manufactured goods, technology and advanced services like finance and information technology.

Economic global governance institutions show America's structural power most clearly. Within the IMF and the World Bank, which both lend out money to states that are either struggling economically or are seeking development funds, the United States wields a great deal of power. Within the IMF, the United States possesses an effective veto as it has 16–17 per cent of the vote, where 85 per cent of the vote is required to authorise any loan. This is an example of how the structural setup of international relations can bring power to certain states. Structural power is hard to possess by itself, as it is normally acquired through a state's hard power capabilities.

Classification of state power within global politics

International relations is at times referred to as 'great power politics'. This reflects the importance of certain states, which possess greater economic, military and structural power at a level above other states. These states exert a disproportionate level of influence within global politics. Traditionally, these 'great powers' have been seen as the focus of international relations.

Other classifications of states have emerged over time, including 'superpower', 'emerging power' and 'hegemon'. Table 3.1 illustrates the difference between these various classifications.

Polarity

Polarity is one way of describing how power is distributed within the international system. The different types of system, dependent on the amount of superpowers present, are known as **unipolarity**, **bipolarity** and **multipolarity**.

Unipolarity

Unipolarity is when there is a single superpower or significant actor in the international system, without any major rivals. A unipolar power is sometimes termed a 'hegemon'. Whilst their power may not be completely absent from any restraints, they will exert significant influence across the geopolitical stage.

When did it exist?

In the 1990s, after the end of the Cold War, the United States was the sole superpower. With Russia struggling domestically and China just beginning its economic growth, the United States could act unchallenged in international relations. No other state could come close to matching US military power, and it occupied a central position in the global economy. It is up for debate whether this period of unipolarity has ended. For some international relations analysts, the recession of 2008 signalled the end of the unipolar period. For others, it has been a steadier transition as China has begun to challenge the United States in the 2010s and 2020s.

Potential strengths of the system

The benefits of unipolarity, in theory, are that one dominant actor can act as the 'world's police officer', settling disputes and preventing conflict from taking place and potentially acting as a hegemon within the international system. This can be positive for smaller states that may have been susceptible to interference from nearby, more powerful countries. The United States played this 'police officer' role during the 1990s. The clearest encapsulation of this was their intervention against Iraq in the First Gulf War, after Saddam Hussein invaded neighbouring Kuwait, causing instability in the region, as shown in Photo 3.3. The United States, with NATO support and UN backing, intervened on behalf of Kuwait,

Table 3.1 Classification of States

Classification of state power	Criteria	Examples of states	An example of how a state meets these criteria
Hegemon	• Hegemonic status is based on the possession of structural power, particularly the control of economic and military resources. This theoretically enables the hegemon to shape the preferences and actions of other states. • The hegemon will also tend to have an ideological aspect to its dominance, which other states adopt and follow.	• United States – though we can question if this is still the case.	The United States in the 1990s was a prime example of a hegemon. With the USSR's collapse, resulting in the newly formed Russia experiencing a number of difficulties, alongside China still in the early stages of its resurgence, the United States was truly unchallenged. The manner in which it deployed military forces across the world showed this – most notably in its intervention against Serbian forces in Bosnia and Kosovo in the mid-1990s, with Serbia being allied to Russia. Similarly, the adoption of capitalism and democracy by a number of formerly communist states was reflective of the dominant structural position that the United States possessed.
Superpower	• A superpower has many of the same features as a great power, but to an enhanced level. • Military power that they are able to project internationally. As part of this, they must possess nuclear weapons. • An economy that is dominant within its economic sphere. • International influence and the ability to influence events globally. • Ability to exert significant structural power, both through institutions and wider international presence. • Must not possess an isolationist foreign policy.	• United States • USSR (during the Cold War). • China (China sits between superpower and great power status. It meets elements of the criteria for a superpower, but not as clearly as the United States does).	Since the end of the Cold War, the United States has been the only state to definitively meet the criteria of superpower status. Its military is a level above other nations, spending more on its armed forces than the next nine states combined, with military bases spread across the world, along with the second largest nuclear arsenal in the world. Within the international economic system, the United States is the key economy. So, for example, in 2008, a crisis of bad debt in the US housing market triggered a global financial crisis, causing the collapse of banks in Europe and elsewhere. The phrase 'when America sneezes, the world catches a cold', was applied in the aftermath of the 1929 depression, but is still true today. The United States has a dominant role in institutions, with a P5 seat on the United Nations Security Council (UNSC), controlling influence in the World Bank and the IMF, as well as prominent positions in the G7 and G20.

Component III: Global Politics

Classification of state power	Criteria	Examples of states	An example of how a state meets these criteria
Great power	• Significant military power. • A strong and developed economy. • Substantial regional influence, within their local area – their 'near abroad'. • Wider diplomatic and institutional influence, including major roles in international organisations.	• Germany • Japan • The United Kingdom • France • Russia • China (China sits between superpower and great power status. It meets elements of the criteria for a superpower, but not as clearly as the United States does).	France has a strong, developed economy, ranked seventh in the world, with a Gross Domestic Product (GDP) of just under $3 trillion in 2022. Within the European area, aided by its role within the EU, it wields significant influence and power. It has a substantial military, which it has deployed in humanitarian interventions in recent history, most notably in Mali in 2019. Also being one of the Permanent 5 (P5) of the UN, it has considerable institutional influence here too.
Emerging power	• An emerging power will tend to meet some of the criteria of a great power, but not all of them. • For example, it may have a rapidly developing economy, but not yet have a military that matches this. • Alternatively, it may have a developed economy and military, but its international presence may be severely lacking, with little representation in global institutions. • There is an expectation that an emerging power would have influence within its local region, however.	• India • Brazil • South Africa • Indonesia	India's economic growth and expansion has been second only to China since the 1990s. It has significant regional influence within South Asia, being the dominant presence in that region. Frequent clashes with China, where their two spheres of influence meet, demonstrate this. However, India's large GDP hides, to an extent, the reality that it is still a largely poor nation. India's **GDP per capita** is still only $1,900, around 10 per cent of China's. India also lags behind in terms of wider international influence, lacking presence in global institutions.

destroying the Iraqi army and restoring peace to the area. The dominant superpower is also meant to guarantee economic and financial stability, as it has an interest in maintaining the system that benefits its state. The dominant state would also look to enforce a shared economic approach by all states, such as supporting largely free trade, attempting to challenge states if they do not stick to this.

Potential weaknesses of the system

Critics of unipolarity emphasise that so much power lying with one state can lead to difficulties. The idea that 'Power corrupts, absolute power corrupts absolutely', as the famous quote from Lord Action states, is relevant here. An unchallenged superpower may start to carry out actions that have negative effects on other states. This is particularly a worry for those states that do not align with the same world-view as the dominant superpower and may find themselves forced to 'toe the line' with their actions. Indeed, whilst the 'Pax Americana' of the 1990s was good for Kuwait, Kosovo and Bosnia, it would be seen as less of a positive for Serbia and Iraq. The challenging of the US system by China and Russia in the modern age is in part a retaliation to the dominance that the United States wielded over these states during the 1990s.

Bipolarity

Bipolarity is when there are two superpowers in the international system, with the global political structure revolving around these two states. For the system to be genuinely bipolar, the powers of the two should be broadly equivalent, particularly in terms of military capacity.

When did it exist?

The concept of bipolarity is heavily linked with the Cold War period. The United States and the USSR were balanced against each other, with two spheres of influence building around them. Although

> **Definition**
>
> **GDP per capita:** Represents the average value of goods and services produced by each individual in a country.
>
> **Pax Americana:** A term used to describe the relative peace and stability the US dominance has brought to the Western world.

> **Spec key term**
>
> **Bipolarity:** When there are two superpowers existing in the international system, with the global political structure revolving around these two states.

Photo 3.2 People flee Iraq after the Iraqi invasion of Kuwait. The United States, with NATO support and UN backing, intervened on behalf of Kuwait, destroying the Iraqi army and restoring peace to the area

Source: Alain Nogues/Sygma via Getty Images

Component III: Global Politics

KEY DEBATE: DOES THE UNITED STATES REMAIN A GLOBAL HEGEMON?

Exam Tip: It can be helpful to approach essay questions by dividing your essay into different themes.

For this question, it is best to approach it through the extent to which the United States remains a hegemon in terms of military, economic, structural and soft power.

US military power

✅ The United States' military dominance is arguably a greater advantage than any state has had in the history of international relations. The United States outstrips other states in terms of its spending, putting more money into its military than the next nine highest spenders combined – the majority of whom are states allied with the United States. The United States has been in this position of strength for the past three decades, meaning that it has a significant amount of military resources stockpiled as an advantage over any state that does start to challenge it in military spending. Alongside this, the United States has an unrivalled ability to deploy military force globally. The United States has approximately 750 military bases across the world, in over 80 different states, on all 6 continents. There are few areas that the United States could not realistically deploy troops, and few adversaries that could stand up to it in conventional warfare. The United States also has a large nuclear arsenal, deployed across the world.

The declining importance of military power

❌ The issues that the United States faced in its military interventions in the Middle East in the 2000s and 2010s highlighted the limitations of military power. Although the United States was swift to win conventional wars in both Iraq (2003) and Afghanistan (2001), it then got bogged down in conflict in both places. Modern warfare has made it harder for a state as powerful as the United States to achieve dominance, due in part to the spread of powerful weaponry to all sides. The humiliating retreat by the United States from Afghanistan in 2021 symbolised defeat for the United States in its aims in the country, particularly in the light of the Taliban's rapid reconquest of the country since then. If the United States had remained truly hegemonic, it would arguably not have lost its influence in the area in such a dramatic manner.

Chapter Link

The dominance of the United States within these Bretton Woods Institutions is addressed in Chapter 5: Economic Global Governance.

The United States remains the central figure within the global economy

✅ The United States' role within the global economy remains central, and the United States is still the largest in the world in terms of nominal GDP. The recession that hit the United States in 2008 onwards highlighted this clearly, as the United States' downward spiral triggered a global economic crisis. From the establishment of the **Bretton Woods Institutions**, such as the IMF and the World Bank, to the acceptance of capitalism as the global economic system, the structure that the United States established as a hegemon remains in place. In economic terms, the United States' rivals, such as China and Russia, are not seeking to challenge the US economic establishment, but rather to place themselves in a more dominant position within it.

China's economic growth presents the first serious challenge to the United States' economic status

❌ Unlike the USSR, which never posed a genuine economic threat to the United States, China's rapid economic development may overtake the United States. We can argue that this has already happened if we measure GDP in PPP (Purchasing Power Parity) terms, and China will most likely overtake the United States in terms of nominal GDP towards the end of the 2020s or beginning of the 2030s. China's economic growth has resulted in the benefits that are associated with economic dominance, which allows it to challenge the United States in certain areas. In particular, China is now the largest trading partner for sixty economies in 2023, almost twice as many as for the United States, which was the largest bilateral trading partner for thirty-three economies. This reflects the way China is starting to play as significant a role as the United States in the global economy.

US structural power remains in place

✅ The global structure remains crafted in the United States' image, reflecting its position as a hegemon. The framework by which global politics operates is still the one that was established and developed by the United States in the aftermath of the Second World War. Nowhere is this clearer than in global governance institutions. The United States continues to wield considerable influence and play a key role in the chief institutions within international relations. The IMF provides an example of the clever way in which the United States has this power, where the United States contributes enough funds to be granted 16–17 per cent of the vote. With 85 per cent of votes needed to pass any funding resolution, this effectively gives the United States a veto within the IMF. The United States possesses similar power within the World Bank, suggesting that US hegemony remains present.

Within this structure, the United States is being challenged

❌ China, the United States' most significant challenger, is not seeking to replace the existing structural system. Instead, China is trying to replace the United States as the chief operator within the system. It has begun to achieve this through economic strength, but it is also challenging the United States through institutions. At a very basic level, this has involved China increasingly using its veto within the UN. Prior to 2007, China had used its veto three times, and since 2007, it has deployed it sixteen times, as of 2025. Alongside this, China has also created the Asian Infrastructure Investment Bank (AIIB). This is a direct rival institution to the IMF and the World Bank, which allows China to control offers of investment to other states. Despite the United States' pleas for other states to not join the Bank, over 100 members have joined, including long-time US allies such as the UK and Germany. If the United States was an unchallenged hegemony, then other states would have complied with US requests.

US soft power still has significant appeal for large portions of the world

✅ Although US **liberal democracy** has not quite become dominant enough to bring in the 'End of History', where, in 1992, Francis Fukuyama claimed that with the end of the Cold War, liberal democracy had emerged victorious it remains the system with the most amount of appeal for the rest of the world. It is US TV programmes and films that remain the most watched, with the worldwide viewership of Marvel films reaching around 350 million views worldwide. Not only this, but there is still continued demand for the democratic values that the United States represents. Protests such as the Arab Spring (2011) (see **Chapter 2: State and Globalisation** for more details) and the Hong Kong protests of 2019–20 had demands for democracy and 'Western' style human rights as some of their key priorities. No such protests take place in democratic states demanding Chinese- or Russian-style authoritarianism. In this way, the appeal of the United States' cultural and democratic values is still strong, representing the United States' continued hegemonic status.

The decline in US soft power and the reaction against globalisation

❌ Globalisation has been a key aspect of US hegemony. It has allowed the United States to project its soft power, through cultural globalisation, as well as underpinning its economic dominance. The reaction against this has challenged US hegemony in a few different ways. The United States has undermined its own soft power with its military actions of the 2000s and 2010s, particularly Iraq (2003) and Afghanistan (2001), leading to the Muslim world developing considerable anti-US feeling. A secondary aspect of this was the election of Donald Trump in 2016 and again in 2024, who actively pursues a more isolationist policy that alienates a number of US allies. This has all been combined with a more widespread rise of **populism** that is arguably a reaction to the previously established US system.

> **Definition**
>
> **Liberal democracy:** A term used for modern democracies that embrace, alongside free and fair elections, entrenched human rights, freedom of the press and the rule of law.
>
> **Populism:** A political stance that divides society into 'the people' and 'the elite', with the populist leader claiming to represent the unified will of the people. Often includes policies from both left and the right of the political spectrum.

Key Debate Summary: Does the United States remain a global hegemon?

Key Criteria	For	Against
Does the United States' military dominance have relevance in modern-day international relations?	✓ The United States' military spending remains miles ahead of any of its rivals, and it possesses a military force that is unchallengeable.	✗ It has become harder to deploy military forces effectively. This is reflected in issues that the United States has faced in wars in both Iraq and, most notably, Afghanistan.
Has China successfully replaced the United States as the world's chief player in the economic system?	✓ The global economy is still built around the United States as an economic power. The United States still has an incredibly powerful economy that is central to the international financial system.	✗ China has replaced the United States as the largest economic power by some definitions and is now doing more trade with the majority of states than the United States.
Is the structure of international relations still established in a manner that supports the United States?	✓ The manner in which international relations is conducted still reflects the system that the United States established. This is most notable within the global governance institutions, which continue to be dominated by the United States and act in the United States' interest primarily.	✗ Although China does not seek to challenge the international relations structure itself, China has begun to put pressure on the United States within the system. Within the institutional setup, China has begun to carry out actions that challenge the United States as a global hegemon.
Does the United States still possess significant soft power?	✓ The United States' story continues to have international appeal, both in terms of its governmental system and the culture that the US produces.	✗ Recent actions by the United States, as well as a general trend globally, have undermined the strength of the United States' story as actors retaliate against globalisation.

Exam Tip:

It is important in a question such as this to define what you mean by a hegemon in the introduction.

CASE STUDY: THE DECLINE OF US GLOBAL POLITICAL INFLUENCE

Events

One way in which US hegemony was clear in the 1990s and early 2000s was the extent of its global influence. In part, this was clear in the way they could intervene internationally, most notably in the Balkans. Interventions in Bosnia and Kosovo (1994–95 and 1999) involved the deployment of US military force in an area close to Russia's borders, and against a state (Serbia) that had historically been closely tied with Russia. The United States' influence was also demonstrated by the number of states that contributed troops to the operation, numbering over twenty and including countries such as Germany and France.

Decline in influence

During the 2000s, 2010s and 2020s, the United States' influence can be seen to be in decline in several ways:

- Protest and lack of involvement in the Iraq War (2003). Many key allies, notably Germany and France, criticised US intervention in Iraq and refused to send troops to support the invasion.
- The United States did not intervene directly or significantly to counter Russian intervention.
- Alternative international institutions. China created the AIIB, a multilateral development bank providing financing for infrastructure projects. The AIIB is seen as a challenge to the existing global institutional order centred on US-dominated bodies such as the IMF and World Bank – see Chapter 6 for more details.
- Allies, including Israel, acting against US criticism. Israel's action in Gaza and across the Middle East have resulted in repeated calls from both Biden and Trump for a different approach in the region. Biden condemned Israel over high civilian casualties and insufficient humanitarian aid in Gaza, whilst Trump was more critical of Israel's actions regarding Iran, expressing a desire for de-escalation and cautioning against being drawn into wider Middle East conflicts. These calls have been largely ignored by Netanyahu, the Israeli prime minister.

Significance

American hegemony did not rest on a territorial empire, in comparison to previous hegemonic powers such as the British or Roman empires. Instead, power has been wielded through institutional dominance, a broad alliance, and robust foreign interventions. As these have declined, so too has US hegemonic power declined. It is giving way to an increasingly multipolar world order.

---

economically the two powers were not on equal footing for the duration of the Cold War, militarily they were seen as well balanced. Events, such as the Cuban Missile Crisis, can be seen in this context, with both sides reacting to actions taken by the other superpower.

Potential strengths of the system

The concept of a 'balance of power', which is also associated with the idea of **Mutually Assured Destruction (MAD)**, suggests that if neither superpower is willing to aggravate the other and deal with large-scale conflict, a form of peace will exist. This was seen during the Cold War, where, despite around 50 years of frosty relations, direct conflict never broke out between the USSR and the United States. China and the United States have been in a similar situation since the 2010s. Supporters of bipolarity suggest that this Cold War was due to both states' fear of nuclear destruction if conflict did take place between them. Bipolarity supporters highlight the rarity of two states being directly in competition with each other for such a prolonged period without war taking place.

Definition

Mutually Assured Destruction (MAD): A condition in which a nuclear attack by either state would only ensure its own destruction, as both possess an invulnerable second-strike capacity.

Potential weaknesses of the system

Critics of bipolarity focus on the associated tension and insecurity that the system breeds. The nature of bipolarity results in two 'sides' forming in global politics, with the two dominant superpowers forcing other states to be either with or against them. They in turn emphasise that although direct conflict

> **Definition**
>
> **Proxy war:** A conflict in which rival powers support opposing factions, often through funding and arms, to fight on their behalf without engaging in direct combat.

between the two superpowers is unlikely, there are knock-on effects that do lead to wider conflict within international relations, most notably through increased **proxy wars**. Although the United States and the USSR were never directly at war during the Cold War, they were both involved in a number of proxy wars. The Korean War in 1950, the Vietnam War in the 1960s and 1970s and the Soviet–Afghan War in the 1980s are all examples of conflicts taking place despite the supposed peaceful influence of bipolarity. A wider criticism is also levelled at MAD, arguing that despite there being no conflict between the United States and the USSR, this was as much due to luck, with a number of very close calls, as some inbuilt security within bipolarity.

Multipolarity

> **Spec key term**
>
> **Multipolarity:** When three or more significant actors or power centres are present in the international system.

When three or more significant actors are present in the international system, the term multipolar is applied. To a greater extent than with unipolarity or bipolarity, the categorisation of significant actors may be more blurred, and there is less need for the actors to be at very similar levels to each other. If there are multiple power centres in global politics, then a multipolar system can be said to exist.

When did it exist?

The interwar periods, as well as the immediate build-up to the First World War, have traditionally been interpreted as multipolar. In the build-up to the First World War, the European empires of Britain, France, Germany, Russia and Austro-Hungary were seen to be on similar levels, particularly within Europe. It is arguable that we are also now in a multipolar period, with the US hegemony being in decline, the rise of China and the EU wielding major influence internationally.

Potential strengths of the system

The chief argument in favour of multipolarity is that by stopping one state from dominating, it promotes cooperation and coordination. Powerful actors are unable to take unilateral action, as that would risk the other chief players banding against them. As a result, states will work together and pursue multilateralism, seeking to achieve mutually beneficial results. In a multipolar system, actions such as the invasion of Iraq in 2003 by the United States would not be possible. Although the United States acted with some support from other nations, its actions went against the will of several powerful states, such as Germany, France and China. The invasion of Iraq undoubtedly had negative long-term consequences, with instability in the region leading to the rise of ISIS. Supporters of multipolarity argue that actions like this would be less possible in a multipolar system, as states could not risk alienating other powerful actors.

Potential weaknesses of the system

Critics argue that multipolarity creates too much fluidity within the international system, resulting in an increased amount of instability. Powerful states are uncertain of the actions of other key players in international relations, which in turn makes conflict far more likely. Arguments against multipolarity state that, with international relations being anarchic in nature, multipolarity enhances this aspect of global politics. In the current international system, a multipolar system would arguably lead to more confusion in the 'hotspots' of potential global conflict. Areas such as the South China Sea, where China is looking to challenge US influence and possibly annexe Taiwan, have greater potential to be triggers of war under multipolarity.

Different systems of government

In Francis Fukuyama's 1992 work *The End of History*, he suggests that the end of the Cold War signalled the United States' ideological triumph. In time, all other states would adopt liberal, capitalist democracy as their governmental system, signalling the 'end of history'. In the last 30 years, Fukuyama's theory has proven to be quite inaccurate. Whilst democracy did spread in the immediate aftermath of the Cold War, there has been no unification around one type of governmental system. Instead, global politics can be seen to be highly influenced by the different types of government that exist within the international system. The Democracy Index in Map 3.3 shows the current spread of democracy across the globe.

Power and Developments

CASE STUDY: BRICS – BRAZIL, RUSSIA, INDIA, CHINA AND SOUTH AFRICA

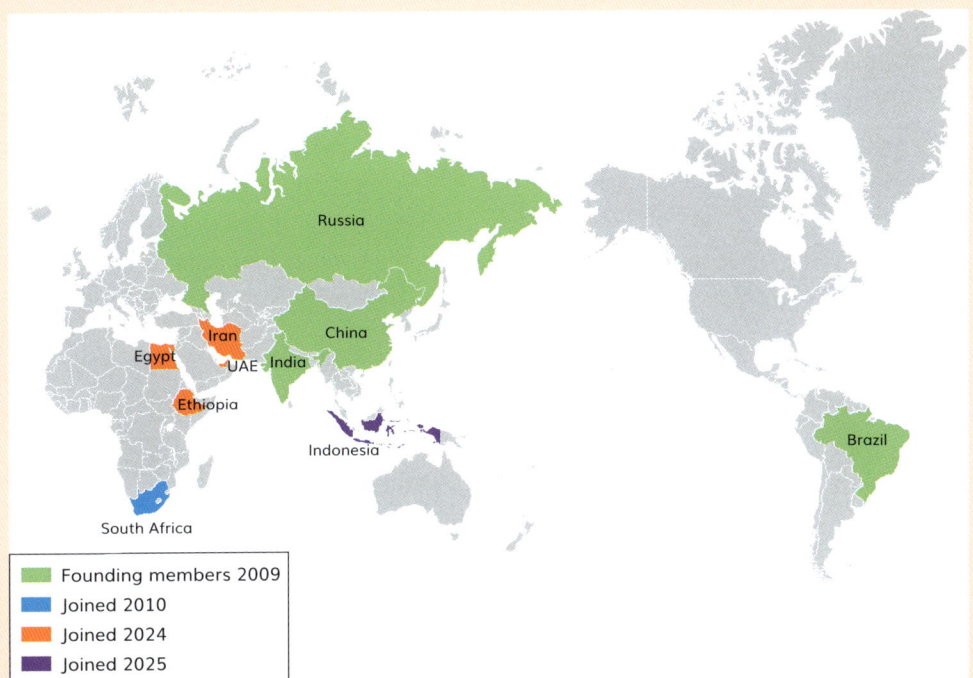

Map 3.2 **BRICS members**

- Founding members 2009
- Joined 2010
- Joined 2024
- Joined 2025

Context

BRIC (later BRICS) is a term originally coined in 2001 in a report by Goldman Sachs, meant to highlight the significance of four large, fast-growing economies and the challenge they represented to the dominance of Western influence (see Map 3.2). This was predominately an economic shift, but was followed by a growing political dimension. The original four states, Brazil, Russia, India and China, were firstly joined by South Africa (2010), before BRICS more recently expanded to include Egypt, Ethiopia, Iran and the United Arab Emirates (2024) and Indonesia (2025). The agendas and aims of the BRICS are very different from those of Western states. Attempting to present themselves as 'guardians of the interests of developing countries', they have offered criticism of the IMF's funding methods. They have sometimes gone as far as to present themselves as an alternative for funding, known as the BRICS Contingent Reserve Arrangement.

Criticisms of the term

There are several issues with the term BRICS. Firstly, bundling the ten different states together ignores a range of differences between the states. On a simple power level, there are significant differences between the position that China occupies within international relations and that of Ethiopia. The use of the term BRICS suggests a regular cooperation between the different nations that does not exist. The states also have different economic and political systems. Brazil, South Africa and India are all democracies (to a greater or lesser extent), whilst Russia, China and Iran are all authoritarian regimes. China's economic system, combining socialist and capitalist elements, differs significantly from the predominately capitalist systems of Brazil and India. This difference is further reflected in their economies. At a simple level, this can be seen in their respective **GDP per capita**. There is massive difference between the UAE ($49,000), Russia ($14,000) and Ethiopia ($1,300).

Significance

Historically, these combined differences meant that the BRICS were not seen as a genuinely effective counter to Western influence. Indeed, they have often been accused of not acting as an alternative to Western power, but rather to strengthen their own position within the existing system. This argument was supported by the decline in BRICS activity as the G20 has increased in importance, and the G20 has become a vehicle for political influence for non-Western states. The recent expansion of the BRICS from five to ten states reflects the renewed desire by the member states of the BRICS to use the body as a method to coordinate against Western global authority. A clear demonstration of this was in 2024 when the BRICS summit focused on reducing reliance on the US dollar, through exploring alternative payment systems, and strengthening trade relations within the bloc. This challenge feeds into the growing debate around whether the United States remains a global hegemon.

Component III: Global Politics

🚩 MILESTONES: DIFFERENT SYSTEMS OF POLARITY 1939 TO PRESENT

1939	Multipolar	Start of Second World War
		World war between a number of different countries of very close strength. Japan, Germany, USSR, the United States and the UK all play key roles in the fighting
1945	Bipolar	End of Second World War, start of Cold War
		Second World War ends with victory for the Allies. Soon after the world enters into a Cold War, between the two superpowers of the United States and USSR. They never fight directly, but a number of 'proxy wars' take place, with the two powers supporting one side or the other.
1989–1992	Unipolar	End of Cold War
		USSR collapses and is disbanded. It loses its grip over Eastern Europe and shrinks in size, to become Russia once again. The United States triumphant across the globe.
2000–present	Unipolar or multipolar?	Rise of China
		China's economy develops to the point where it is starting to be seen as a rival to the United States. Its military is very large, and it is starting to develop its reach in places like Africa.

Comparative Theories: Realist and liberal views on different types of polarity

Realist views on polarity	Liberal views on polarity
• Realists, neo-realists in particular, see that in the absence of a global government, a hegemon emerges as the most effective solution to impose and maintain this necessary order. • This is associated with the concept of 'Hegemonic Stability Theory' (HST), which argues that a dominant hegemon brings stability to international relations. According to this theory, a hegemon can squash actions by rogue states and enforce international rules and norms. • Bipolarity is largely supported by realists and neo-realists. They see bipolarity and the balance it brings as allowing for some level of stability and peace within global politics. • The idea of a 'balance of power', as described above, is one that is integral to realist thought. Both states being wary of the damage they would take if war took place fits within the anarchic and violent view that realists have on global politics.	• Multipolarity is largely seen in a positive light by liberals. • Liberals see this largely through the potential for increased cooperation and multilateralism. With more major powers, no single state can dominate, making collective action through international institutions more appealing for all. • States may recognise that their interests are best served by collaborating on shared challenges like climate change, pandemics or economic stability. This encourages the strengthening of multilateral institutions like the UN, WTO and regional organisations. • John Ikenberry, a liberal theorist, offered a different perspective on HST. He argued for the concept of a 'constitutional' or 'liberal hegemony'. • This is a type of hegemonic order where the dominant state deliberately binds itself to rules and institutions, thereby limiting its own power. By operating within multilateral institutions and upholding liberal values (like democracy, human rights and free trade), the hegemon creates an order that is more attractive and legitimate, encouraging other states to 'buy in' rather than balance against it.

Map 3.3 Democracy Index 2024

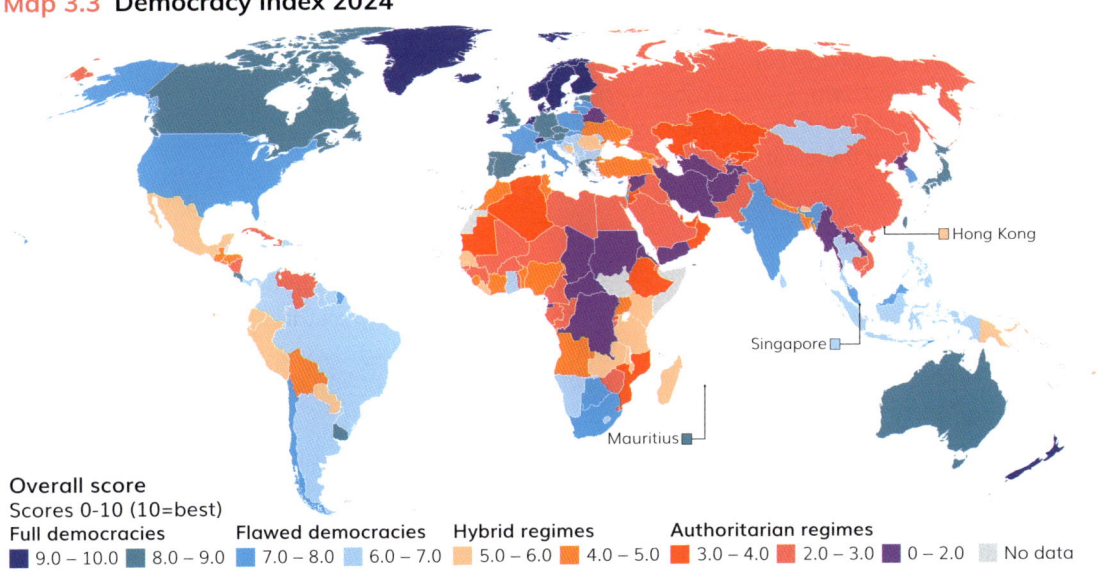

Source: *The Economist Intelligence Unit*

Democracy

A **democracy** is a state where the government is elected in some manner by its citizens, or when the citizens have a direct say in the lawmaking process. Alongside a fair and free electoral process, there should also be a respected rule of law within the legal system of the state, as well as strong protection of human rights. A free press is also considered a prerequisite.

Example: New Zealand has elections every three years, where voters use proportional representation (PR) to vote in their government. The rule of law and human rights are protected through New Zealand's entrenched constitution. It also has a press that is free to criticise the government.

Tables 3.2 to 3.7 explain how different states impact the global system.

Semi-democratic states

Semi-democratic states, on the surface, have the same features as democratic states. However, democracy is undermined in some way by the ruling party or dominant interests within the state. There might, for example, be heavy interference in the press, or state control of the judiciary. Normally, the electoral system will also be under some pressure from the controlling groups, with opposition parties' campaigns and actions being restricted.

Example: Turkey, under their President Recep Erdoğan, has steadily become less democratic over the last two decades. Erdoğan has outlawed opposition parties that directly opposed him, using a failed coup in 2016 as justification for doing so, as well as temporarily halting access to internet sites such as Wikipedia, Twitter/X and YouTube – alongside heavy interference in the press and the judiciary. The reaction to this can be seen in Photo 3.4.

Non-democratic states

Non-democratic states can be states that are either legally or in reality lacking in democracy. Although their number has declined in the modern age, absolute monarchies do still exist, where all power in theory resides in the monarchy. Alongside this, there are the states whose citizens have no choice between different parties or a real functioning democracy, even if the state pretends to have one. These types of government tend to be called single-party states.

> **Spec key term**
>
> **Democracy:** A state where the government is elected by its citizens, or when the citizens have a direct say in the law-making process. A democracy has a fair and free electoral process, respected rule of law, protected human rights and a free press.
>
> **Semi-democratic states:** On the surface, these have the same features as democratic states. However, democracy is undermined in some way by the ruling party or dominant interests within the state.

Spec key term

Non-democratic states: States that are either legally or in reality lacking in democracy.

Autocratic state: An autocratic state wields absolute authority over the governmental setup and the citizens of the nation, through complete control of political, military and economic power.

Failed state: A failed state is when the government no longer wields authority across the entire country, with large sections of the nation being in such a state of civil unrest that the regime in charge is no longer the sole ruler of the country.

Example: Saudi Arabia is a clear example of a prominent non-democratic state. It is ruled as an absolute monarchy, with power lying with the House of Saud. The royal family makes all the decisions for the state, with little outside consultation. There is no form of democratic voting, and wider human rights are very restricted, with Saudi Arabia basing its constitution on the Qur'an, the Muslim religious book. As an example of this, women's rights within Saudi Arabia have historically been very restricted, and women only gained the ability to learn to drive in 2018.

Autocratic states

Autocratic states have a great deal of overlap with non-democratic states. Indeed, all autocratic states are non-democratic by nature (it is in theory possible to be non-democratic, but not autocratic, such as the Vatican City, but there are few examples of this). An autocratic state wields absolute authority over the governmental setup and the citizens of the nation, through complete control of political, military and economic power.

Example: China is the archetype of an autocratic state in global politics in the twenty-first century, with a one-party state in place, under the Chinese Communist Party (the CCP). Elections do take place, but only for the selection of candidates from the CCP. Chinese Premier Xi Jinping has further consolidated power in his own hands. This is reinforced with a strong police state that monitors and controls citizens' lives heavily.

Failed states

A **failed state** is when the government no longer wields authority across the entire country, with large sections of the nation being in such a state of civil unrest that the regime in charge is no longer the sole

Photo 3.3 Protesters in Istanbul, August 2017, march in opposition to a referendum that boosted President Recep Tayyip Erdoğan's powers, claiming blatant vote-rigging had swung the result.

Source: Yasin Akgul /AFP via Getty Images

ruler of the country. Within these failed, or failing, states, there will be a number of competing actors and warlords, each with their own sources of support, authority and power, often in military conflict with each other.

Example: Yemen's civil war began in 2014. By 2025, the UN described Yemen's situation as 'deeply fragile'. The UN-recognised government controlled only a fraction of the country, with a rival Iranian-backed Houthi 'Supreme Political Council' controlling the North and a UAE-backed separatist 'Southern Transitional Council' dominating the South. Continuing conflict has created one of the world's worst humanitarian emergencies in Yemen.

> **Rogue states:** States that operate outside the international norms and conventions of global politics.

Rogue states

Rogue states are states that operate outside the international norms and conventions of global politics. Normally due to actions or stances they have taken in the past, they have alienated themselves from the majority of states in international relations. These states act in a way that reflects this, pursuing policies that threaten other states and the international order.

Example: North Korea accelerated its nuclear weapons programme in the early 2000s, and has continued to do so in defiance of UN sanctions. It regularly provokes its neighbours Japan and South Korea, creating regional instability. It has provided military support to Russia in Ukraine. It has therefore been labelled a rogue state by democratic states, who also deplore its severe human rights abuses.

> **Chapter Link**
>
> The Democratic Peace Theory is covered in more detail in **Chapter 1: Comparative Theories**.

Table 3.2 Characteristics of a Democratic State

Impact on conflict	Democracies tend to be associated with greater chance of peace, particularly with other democracies. Democratic Peace Theory, suggests that democracies are less likely to go to war. Citizens resent the additional cost and burden of conflict, and so are likely to retaliate by voting out the government at the next election. As governments are aware of the potential of this, they are less likely to go to war.
Impact on the environment	The connection between democracies and the fight against climate change is mixed. In theory, democracies are some of the most progressive when it comes to action on the environment. Member states of the EU have been central figures in climate change conferences, notably with all twenty-eight (now twenty-seven) member states sticking to the Kyoto Protocol of 1997 (see Chapter 7: Environmental Global Governance for more details). However, there is a secondary element here, which is that democratically elected governments are aware that they can be voted out of office, and voters often prioritise their economic well-being over the environment.
Impact on poverty	Democracies tend to stand for the promotion of human rights internationally, which means that they ostensibly make efforts to help deal with poverty on an international scale. The majority of international aid comes from democratic states – of the top twenty donors, sixteen are democracies.
	In a similar manner to the environment, there is the potential for voters to protest against this. In the United States and the UK in recent years, voters have given support to candidates who have campaigned on reducing international aid and focusing on their own citizens' difficulties instead.
Impact on human rights	Democracies are overwhelmingly a boon for the existence of human rights in the international system. By their definition, they should have a strong rule of law with good protection of human rights for minorities. Whilst some democracies are guilty of varying levels of hypocrisy over human rights, such as the United States' continued use of the death penalty, it is overwhelmingly the case that human rights are protected in democracies to a far greater extent.

Table 3.3 Characteristics of a Semi-democratic State

Impact on conflict	States that carry out these changes to their democratic setup often need a reason to enable them to make these adjustments, which often increases their tendency towards a more incendiary attitude in their approach to global politics. Turkey under Erdoğan has portrayed the Kurds that live in eastern Turkey as one of the chief threats, leading to Turkey's involvement in the conflicts of the Middle East.
Impact on the environment	The leaders of semi-democratic states tend to focus on securing their own position, so the environment is not always a point of concern. In some ways, these countries represent the worst aspects of democracies when it comes to environmental policy, focusing far more on economic growth than climate change mitigation.
Impact on poverty	Whilst there is some overlap between semi-democratic states' attitudes to poverty and the environment, they are more likely to have significant international aid programmes. As part of the need to strengthen their position within their nation, international aid as a form of soft power can lead to support from other countries for their regime. Turkey donates the ninth-highest amount of international aid globally.
Impact on human rights	In terms of human rights, semi-democratic states can be seen to play a significant role in their diminishment internationally. By giving the impression that human rights are being respected, but in fact undermining them domestically, it encourages other states to take the same approach. The degradation of human rights within the EU, by populist leaders and parties, can be in part a reflection of the attitudes of semi-democratic states. The policies restricting press freedom, the judiciary and opposition parties, which have been enacted by the Law and Order party in Poland and Viktor Orbán in Hungary are very similar to those undertaken by Erdoğan.

Table 3.4 Characteristics of a Non-democratic State

Impact on conflict	Non-democratic states can be linked with increased likelihood of conflict, as they are less likely to need to worry about pushback if they support or carry out war-like actions. A key example of this is Saudi Arabia's active support for the government in Yemen in the ongoing civil war there. The Saudi government has not had to worry about being held to account for the deaths in the region or the instability that the war has brought.
Impact on the environment	Historically non-democratic states have often been associated with increased CO_2 emissions. Without democratic pressure, many non-democratic states have not taken steps to move away from fossil fuels. Saudi Arabia is one of the most prominent examples of this, having the second-largest oil reserves in the world and playing a key role in oil's continued central role in the geopolitical system.
Impact on poverty	Non-democratic states tend to be linked with increases in poverty. Without democratic representation, there is less need for the ruling government to think of poorer groups in society and take care of them. This is also the case with giving support to other states internationally, where aid will often be offered only to states that have similar attitudes or policies to the non-democratic state in question.
Impact on human rights	Non-democratic states often restrict human rights. In Saudi Arabia, women have only recently gained basic rights such as divorce, property ownership, and access to education and healthcare without male permission. Meanwhile, Sunni Islam is the only permitted religion. Other forms of religious worship are not permitted.

Table 3.5 Characteristics of Autocratic States

Please note, these share a lot of similarities with non-democratic states.

Impact on conflict	In the same manner as with non-democratic states, autocratic states are less likely to need to worry about pushback if they support or carry out war-like actions. Xi Jinping, the president of China, has made the annexation of Taiwan a long-term goal of his rule. He has been able to do this in part due to the autocratic nature of his governance.
Impact on the environment	Although autocratic states are similarly free of democratic pressure, there is a counterargument that states where a single party or figure has complete control have the potential to carry out swifter action on climate change, if they do have the desire to do so. China, having realised the threat that climate change poses to it in the last decade, spent $760 billion on renewable energy between 2010 and 2019. This quick reversal in policy would be harder for a democracy to carry out.
Impact on poverty	As with the environment, although there is very little democratic pressure to resolve issues around poverty, the lack of checks and balances on decision-making can lead to positive impacts on a state's poverty levels. There are practical and pragmatic reasons for wishing to reduce poverty in a state, which autocratic nations may pursue.
Impact on human rights	Autocratic states, by their nature, need to suppress human rights within their states. The type of rule that the single party or figure has instituted rests on this. China restricts human rights in a number of ways, including concentration camps in the western region of Xinjiang, various limitations on the rights of workers and severely limited freedom of speech.

Table 3.6 Characteristics of Failed States

Impact on conflict	Conflict within international relations in the twenty-first century tends to focus on these failed states. The majority of serious recent international conflicts, such as in Yemen, Afghanistan and Syria, have all been in states that can be seen as failing or failed states.
Impact on the environment	Although failed states do not have the governmental capacity to pursue environmental policies, they also do not tend to have the economic growth that is associated with policies that are damaging to the environment. There is a link between an increase in a state's GDP and its production of CO_2 emissions. Therefore, although these states are not playing an active role in dealing with climate change and environmental issues, they arguably are not contributing to them.
Impact on poverty	The existence of failed states leads to increases in poverty, if indirectly. The reason states fail to begin with is often associated with problems that cause poverty, such as poor governance, lack of stable government or corruption. Failing states lack the governmental infrastructure to take on or implement foreign aid and support, meaning that failed states are often centres of the most serious global poverty.
Impact on human rights	Breakdown in governance, as well as the bloodiness of the violence taking place within these states, tends to result directly in serious human rights violations. According to the United Nations, during the civil war in Yemen from 2014 onwards, up to 80 per cent of the population were in need of humanitarian aid, due to the situation in this failed state.

Table 3.7 Characteristics of a Rogue State

Impact on conflict	Rogue states tend to not be as interconnected or interdependent as other states are. As a result, they tend to be more willing to carry out hostile and intimidatory actions. North Korea's repeated missile tests are a pertinent example of this. Since Kim Jong-Un became leader of the state in 2011, 119 tests have been carried out. A large number of these have been directed into the Sea of Japan, which lies between North Korea and Japan. These tests are seen as threatening to Japan and certainly heighten tensions around conflict in the region.
Impact on the environment	In a similar manner to failed states, rogue states often have undeveloped economies due to their relative isolation from global politics. As a result of this, their CO_2 emissions are often lower than other similar states; however, this is not due to the active pursuit of green policies. In fact, the energy consumption of these states is likely to be based around entirely non-renewable sources, and they are unlikely to engage in international climate change conferences.
Impact on poverty	Due to rogue states' isolation from the international economy and wider political system, they also tend to be associated with higher levels of poverty. In the case of North Korea, this is quite severe – North Korea's GDP is fifty-four times smaller than South Korea's. In other rogue states, such as Cuba and Iran, this is less severe. Nonetheless, there is a tendency for rogue states' relative political isolation to lead to an increase in poverty.
Impact on human rights	International human rights are built around, in the large part, an acceptance of the norms and rules associated with universal human rights. As rogue states choose to cut themselves off from the international system, it is unsurprising that they also tend to ignore these human rights conventions. North Korea is one of the worst actors here, with a UN report commenting on how it continued to sharply curtail all basic liberties, including freedom of expression, religion and conscience, assembly and association. North Korea also bans political opposition, independent media, civil society and trade unions.

Comparative Theories: Views on different types of states

Realist views on different types of states	Liberal views on different types of states
• Realists argue that there is less difference between democracies and autocracies in their impact on the international system. Realists primarily view states as self-interested actors operating in an anarchic international system. Both democracies and autocracies seek power, security and survival. • Realists are especially sceptical of the Democratic Peace Theory (see Chapter 2 for more detail). They see the foreign policies of liberal democracies as not significantly different from autocratic states when it comes to national interest. • Many realists would view the term 'rogue state' itself as an inaccurate label often used by powerful states (like the United States) to demonise adversaries and justify certain foreign policy actions.	• Liberals have a positive view on democracy. They see a world with more democracies as a more peaceful and prosperous one. The emphasis that democracies have on human rights, civil liberties and the rule of law supports this, from a liberal perspective. • Linked to the above, liberals also believe in the idea of the Democratic Peace Theory, which suggests that democracies rarely, if ever, go to war with each other. • In contrast, liberals see rogue states as being very damaging to the international system. As liberals emphasise the importance of institutions and shared norms, the way in which rogue states ignore this is perceived as particularly harmful by liberals.

KEY DEBATE: ARE LIBERAL DEMOCRACIES IN DECLINE?

In 1992, Francis Fukuyama published his work *The End of History*, in which he claimed that with the end of the Cold War, liberal democracy had emerged victorious. This has not ended up being the case. The geopolitical stage of the 2020s finds itself dramatically changed by the rise of China, an illiberal autocracy.

China represents an alternative model to liberal democracy

- ✅ In China, the West has its first genuine competitor to its governmental and economic system. China has no pretence of being a liberal democracy, basing its government around a non-democratic autocratic system. This system of government rejects individual rights and the need for free and fair elections. It instead focuses on the collective good of the community and ensuring stability within the nation to support this. The Chinese model has understandable appeal to other nations that do not wish to give a voice to their citizens. For certain parts of the globe in particular, such as sub-Saharan Africa or the Middle East, the focus is on the Chinese model of government rather than liberal democracy. Autocratic governments like China are also arguably better placed to deal with long-term issues, such as the environment, that need decision makers to accept the short-term costs of fixing them.

Since the 1990s, democracy has spread to a significant extent and remains the most dominant governmental system in global politics

- ❌ There is a risk of focusing too much on the recent appeal that China has offered and neglecting to consider the wider trend towards democracy that has taken place since the end of the Cold War. Large sections of the world that did not previously have democratic governments have now embraced them, with democracies thriving in Eastern Europe and South America in particular. Prior to the end of the Cold War, the majority of states were non-democracies, and there are now more democracies than non-democracies (though not all of these are full-functioning liberal democracies).

Populist democratic governments have abandoned some of the key principles of liberal democracy

- ✅ A major argument supporting the decline in liberal democracies is that many states carry out practices that arguably break from democratic norms. The actions of states such as Hungary and Poland, both within the EU, undermine their credentials as liberal democracies, with both states interfering with their judiciaries and the voting systems to a certain extent. This trend can also be seen with Donald Trump's dismissal of the 2020 election result as fake. These actions suggest that the values of liberal democracies have become less entrenched even within Western nations, where the concept of liberal democracy originated.

International institutions continue to support and promote liberal democracies

- ❌ Despite this, the international system continues to support and promote the idea of democracy, in particular through global bodies. Most notable of these are the UN and the EU, who within their own framework insist that their member states should be democracies. Whilst the UN has little enforceability in this respect, the EU does still insist on democracy from its members. Although in Hungary and Poland, governments have undermined the judicial system and the rule of law, the EU has taken action against them, withdrawing their right to vote within the EU for a time.
- ✅ Alongside this, the EU attempts to support and promote democracy on a more global scale.

Liberal democracy has been classified as a 'Western' model for government

✅ One of the reasons for a potential decline in liberal democracies is a growing view in certain parts of the globe that they are representative of 'Westernisation' or 'Americanisation' and are not reflective of other cultures. The failures of the attempts to create democracies in Iraq and Afghanistan after the invasions of the 2000s, as well as the Arab Spring uprisings, largely resulting in a return to autocracy in Arab states, have led to many claims that other parts of the world are either not ready or not a fit for liberal democracies.

Citizens still demand liberal democracy around the globe

❌ The claim that liberal democracies are a solely Western phenomenon ignores the continued demands for their implementation across the globe. Protests in the Arab world in 2011, known as the Arab Spring, were a particularly large-scale example of this, despite their ultimate lack of resolution. In more recent years, pro-democracy protests have taken place in Thailand, Hong Kong and Sudan. The demand for the rights, freedoms and choice that liberal democracy brings still exists on a global scale.

Key Debate Summary: Are liberal democracies in decline?

Key Criteria	For	Against
Does the Chinese model of government signal an end to the shift towards democracy since the end of the Cold War?	✓ The Chinese model of autocratic rule has significant appeal to large sections of the globe, far more than liberal democracy does.	✗ Since the end of the Cold War, the most successful and dominant form of government has been liberal democracy, which is reflected in the manner in which it has spread internationally.
Does the rise of populism within the West signal a dissatisfaction there with liberal democracy?	✓ The actions of states such as Hungary and Poland, as well as individuals such as Donald Trump, suggest that even within the West, there is a move against the values and principles that liberal democracies are meant to uphold.	✗ International institutions, most notably the EU, still promote the use of democracy and insist upon it by member states, taking actions against Hungary and Poland for their undermining of liberal democracy.
Is liberal democracy fundamentally Western in its nature?	✓ Liberal democracy has proven to be a product that often does not seem to export well. In the Middle East, as well as the Arab world in North Africa, democracies that have tried to have been implanted do not appear to have worked.	✗ There is still significant demand internationally from citizens who live in non-democratic states for liberal democracy, and the bonuses that they bring.

Chapter Summary

- Power in international relations relates to the ability to force other actors in global politics to act as you wish. It has historically focused around hard power, which involves using coercion to achieve its aims. In more recent times, soft power has become a more commonly used tool, using persuasion instead.

- States within the international system can be classified at different levels depending on the amount of power they wield. Countries that possess a significant level of both economic and military power are defined as great powers. If states possess truly international reach, as well as having a dominant military and economy, then they can be seen as superpowers, whilst a superpower that operates unchallenged across the geopolitical system can be defined as a hegemon. States that are beginning to meet great power criteria in some ways, but not all, are seen as emerging powers.

- The number of superpowers operating within global politics relates to the nature of the global order in place within the international system, which is known as polarity. If there is just a single superpower, then it is known as unipolarity. If there are two superpowers of similar strength, particularly in military terms, then the system is seen as being bipolar. Finally, if there are three or more superpowers of roughly similar levels, then the international system is considered to be multipolar.

- International relations is also heavily impacted by the different types of states that exist within it. Democratic states have seen a notable increase in their prevalence since the end of the Cold War, with their basis of free and fair elections, the rule of law and a free press. Semi-democratic states have a lot of these same features in theory, but in reality, many of them do not fully exist. Non-democratic states and autocratic states both tend to exist through ignoring these features, or outright not having them, often through a strong police force or state interference. Rogue and failed states, which are respectively states operating outside the international system and states where the government does not possess full internal sovereignty, both have a destabilising effect on global order.

Exam Style Questions

- Examine the different impacts of democratic and autocratic states on the international system. (12)
- Examine the differences between hard and soft power. (12)
- Analyse the divisions regarding world order that exist between realists and liberals. (12)
- Evaluate the extent to which the United States remains a hegemon in international relations. (30)
- Evaluate the extent to which hard power is no longer relevant in international relations. (30)

Further Resources

https://fragilestatesindex.org/. A think tank that produces a ranking system of how close states are to collapse or conflict.

https://freedomhouse.org/. A non-profit organisation that produces a report on the relative democracy, human rights and political freedom internationally.

http://brics2022.mfa.gov.cn/eng/. The website for the BRICS organisation, noting the outcomes of their summits and their aims.

https://www.youtube.com/watch?v=JsE_1sY0lfU. Joseph Nye gives a TED Talk on global power shifts: hard power, soft power and smart power.

Visit https://bloomsbury.pub/essentials-of-global-politics to access additional materials to support teaching and learning.

4 POLITICAL GLOBAL GOVERNANCE

Chapter Preview

This chapter looks first at the United Nations: its creation in the traumatic aftermath of the Second World War, how it works and whether it is fit for purpose in a twenty-first-century world of unprecedented global challenges. We assess the UN's progress on the four ambitious aims of maintaining peace and security, upholding international law, protecting human rights and promoting social progress and sustainable development.

We then consider how NATO was created for Europe's collective defence against the Soviet Union, how it shape-shifted into a global humanitarian enforcer for the United Nations and then pivoted back to deal with a resurgence of war in Europe. We compare different views on its significance to global peace and security, and how effective it is at supporting the UN's work.

Key Questions and Debates
» How has the United Nations developed, and what does it do?
» What are the roles, significance, strengths and weaknesses of the main Organs of the United Nations?
» Is the United Nations effective?
» How has NATO's role and significance in global politics developed, and what are its strengths and weaknesses?
» How effectively have the United Nations and NATO worked together to maintain peace and security?

Specification Checklist

2.1.1 The United Nations (UN)
» Origins and development of the UN, including its 1945 charter
» Role and significance of the UN to include the Security Council, General Assembly, Economic and Social Council, International Court of Justice, including their strengths and weaknesses

2.1.2 North Atlantic Treaty Organisation (NATO)
» Role and significance of NATO, including its changing role, particularly since the end of the Cold War, and strengths and weaknesses

2.3 The ways and extent to which these institutions address and resolve contemporary global issues, such as those involving conflict, poverty, human rights and the environment

2.3.1 In particular, to focus on how the following prevents the UN Security Council from effectively addressing and resolving the issues above:
» the membership and structure
» the use of veto

2.3.2 The role and significance of global civil society and non-state actors, including non-governmental organisations (NGOs) in addressing and resolving the issues above

Source: Eyad Baba/AFP via Getty Images

The United Nations (UN)

The origins, development, structure and roles of the United Nations

Why the United Nations?

> *We, the peoples of the United Nations, determined to save succeeding generations from the scourge of war, which twice in our lifetime has brought untold sorrow to mankind, and to reaffirm faith in fundamental human rights, in the dignity and worth of the human person, in the equal right of men and women and of nations large and small .... And for these ends to practice tolerance and live together in peace with one another as good neighbors ...*
>
> 'Preamble', Charter of the United Nations, 1945

After the First World War in 1919, US President Wilson proposed a 'League of Nations': a permanent international body to help maintain peace. However, with no powers to punish its members, it was destined to fail. The United States never joined, and Germany, Japan, Italy and the Soviet Union had all left by 1939.

As the Second World War came to an end, the Allies, led by US President Roosevelt, decided to create a replacement for the failed League to ensure that such a war could never happen again. **The United Nations** was created on 26 June 1945 with fifty-one founding members.

Many more states joined in the following decades, including Germany, Italy and Japan. It has become the world's most complex intergovernmental organisation, with 193 member states. Adlai Stevenson, former US ambassador to the UN, described it as 'a world society of nations under law, not merely law backed by force, but law backed by justice and popular consent'.

The creation of the UN was intended to bring about Immanuel Kant's ideal of 'perpetual peace', (see pages 16-17) through cooperation between independent, equal states under international law.

The Charter of the United Nations

The Charter is the founding document of the United Nations.

Article 1 sets out the UN's purposes, including:

- Maintain international peace and security
- Uphold international law
- Encourage respect for human rights
- Promote social progress and solve international economic, social, cultural and humanitarian problems
- Develop friendly relations amongst nations

Article 2 sets out the rights and responsibilities of states in relation to the UN.

- The UN is governed by the principles of sovereign equality and non-intervention.
- The UN is not authorised to intervene in 'domestic' matters within states without their consent, except to enforce international peace and security.
- States are required to assist the UN in its work.

Article 103 states that the Charter takes precedence over any other international agreement. This makes it a primary source of international law.

With 193 member states, the UN is the closest thing we have to a **'world government'**. However, a world government would take all sovereignty away from states, imposing order on them through force. That does not exist. The UN has the power to require states to act to preserve international peace and security, but, significantly, that request is made collectively by the members of the UN Security Council. Military force is applied by states, on a voluntary basis. This makes it primarily an **intergovernmental organisation** (IGO), with a few **supranational** characteristics.

Spec key term

The United Nations: An organisation created in 1945 following the Second World War to promote international cooperation and to prevent another such conflict.

Chapter Link

Intergovernmentalism and supranationalism are important concepts for understanding the impacts of both global governance and regionalism on state sovereignty. Intergovernmentalism preserves state sovereignty, whereas supranationalism undermines it. See **Chapter 9: The EU and Regionalism** for discussion of these concepts within regional organisations.

Spec key term

World Government: The idea of a common political authority with legislative and executive power over states.

The structure of the United Nations

The UN Organs

The UN Charter established six 'principal organs' of the United Nations (of which five remain in operation), based at its headquarters in New York:

- A Security Council (UNSC), tasked with maintaining international peace and security. It is intergovernmental, but the Council's decisions have authority over states in international law, giving it some supranational characteristics.
- A General Assembly (UNGA), the main representative, deliberative and policy-making body at the centre of the UN system. It is the collective voice of the international community of states, allowing all states an equal voice, no matter their size or power. It oversees various subsidiary councils, including the Economic and Social Council (ECOSOC).
- An ECOSOC, which oversees the wider UN system that provides humanitarian and development support to member states.
- A Trusteeship Council, which oversaw decolonisation and is no longer in use.
- The International Court of Justice (ICJ), based in The Hague, Netherlands, hears disputes between member states. Its judges do not represent member states, but instead oversee their compliance with international law, meaning that it has supranational authority. It also advises the UN Organs on matters of international law.
- Finally, there is the Secretariat, a huge 'civil service' with a permanent staff, led by the Secretary-General, who is based in New York. It has subsidiary bodies around the world. The Secretariat is not intergovernmental. It plays a supporting role, carrying out policies that member states decide on together.

The UN system

This is a vast organisation with a huge range of social, humanitarian and sustainable development bodies, based in many countries and overseen by ECOSOC and the Secretariat.

Specialised agencies

ECOSOC coordinates its work with external independent organisations, including the International Monetary Fund (IMF) and World Bank in Washington DC and the World Trade Organisation and World Health Organisation in Geneva.

The aims and roles of the United Nations

The purposes laid out in the Charter have translated into five main roles for the UN.

1. Peace and security

With its roots in the Second World War, the UN's primary aim is to maintain international peace and security through conflict prevention, responding to threats, peacekeeping and peacebuilding.

Conflict prevention: the UNGA builds consensus on disarmament, regulation of weapons and approaches to counterterrorism. The ICJ helps states to resolve disputes peacefully, and the Secretariat provides diplomacy to resolve disputes 'in the field'.

Responding to threats: the UNSC can impose economic sanctions and authorise military intervention to stop state aggression, fight terrorist regimes and restore security.

Peacekeeping: the UN authorises peacekeeping missions when fighting has stopped. These maintain the ceasefire, support the rule of law and allow humanitarian aid to be delivered.

Peacebuilding: the UN supports fragile post-conflict states to build the social, political and economic foundations for sustainable peace.

2. Upholding international law

Making law: the UNGA recommends the drafting of treaties and conventions by legal experts. These are negotiated and signed by state governments at UN conferences.

Upholding law: the International Court of Justice settles legal disputes between states, upholding and creating precedents in international law. The UN Charter, the fundamental treaty in international law, allows the UN to enforce international peace and security.

> **Spec key term**
>
> **Intergovernmentalism:** A form of cooperation between states in which decisions are made collectively, based on the principle of sovereign independence.
>
> **Supranationalism:** A form of cooperation between states in which they transfer their sovereign decision-making powers to a central, transnational authority.

> **Definition**
>
> **Decolonisation:** The transition of a territory from foreign control to achieving independence.

Chapter Link

The UN has coordinated the creation by states of a large body of international humanitarian law, and created the international courts and tribunals that are addressed in **Chapter 6: Human Rights Global Governance**.

Most economic global governance organisations are separate from the UN. These include the International Monetary Fund, World Bank, World Trade Organisation, G7 and G20 (see **Chapter 5: Economic Global Governance**). However, whilst independently run, the IMF and World Bank are 'specialised agencies' of the UN. This means that they coordinate with UN bodies such as ECOSOC and the UN's Peacebuilding Commission (see **Chapter 8: Analysing and Evaluating Global Governance**).

3. Protecting human rights

Human rights work is woven throughout the UN system, from UNSC and UNGA resolutions to peacekeepers in conflict zones. The UN's human rights work focuses on:

Promoting human rights: a large body of international human rights laws has developed from the UNGA's 1948 Universal Declaration of Human Rights. The Office of the High Commissioner for Human Rights (OHCHR) in Geneva, Switzerland, has overall responsibility for the UN's human rights work and promotes respect for human rights around the world.

Accountability on human rights: the Human Rights Council holds states to account publicly for their human rights record and any violations. It reports to the UNGA and UNSC. The UN has created international tribunals and the International Criminal Court to bring war criminals to account.

4. Social progress and development

As the UN expanded after 1945 to include many newly independent developing states, its economic and social development roles expanded too. The most important of these are supporting sustainable development and the delivery of humanitarian aid (see Photo 4.2). This work is overseen by the ECOSOC, which coordinates across the UN and works with the Washington DC-based International Monetary Fund and World Bank.

5. Developing friendly relations among states

The UN provides an inclusive intergovernmental forum 'to develop friendly relations amongst nations based on respect for the principle of equal rights and self-determination'.

The Organs of the United Nations

General Assembly (UNGA)

The General Assembly is the hub of the UN system. It is the main representative, deliberative and policy-making organ of the UN. However, it does not have legislative power.

Photo 4.1 Children receive humanitarian aid organised by the UN.

Membership and representative role

Only sovereign states may be full members of the UNGA

- In 2025 there were 193 full member states and two non-member observer states, Palestine and Vatican City, who may speak but not vote.
- The European Union is a non-member non-state observer, with the right to speak but not vote on behalf of its members.

The UNGA can admit new members, in co-decision with the UNSC

- Permanent members of the UNSC (China, France, Russia, United States, UK) can veto membership applications. Palestine's full membership application has been vetoed by the United States, overruling the UNGA (see **Case Study: Support for Palestinian Statehood**).
- The threat of a veto is enough to stop an application. Taiwan has been denied representation by China, which views Taiwan as its own sovereign territory. Kosovo is not recognised by Russia or China, and almost half of the other states.

Revolutions and military coups can confuse representation

- After governments were overthrown in Myanmar and Afghanistan in 2021 and Niger in 2022, their representation in the UN was disputed, meaning neither side could speak in debates. This situation was not yet resolved by the UNGA in 2025.

The UNGA has a central role in electing the other organs

- Member states are organised into five broadly regional groups. Each group elects representatives to the other UN councils. See Figure 4.1.

Deliberative role and decision-making process

State leaders meet at the UN headquarters in New York each year in September (see Photo 4.3). Every member state has a team of United Nations ambassadors based year-round in New York.

> **Chapter Link**
>
> Since the UN Charter set out these initial aims in **1945, sustainable development** has become the focus of most of the UN's work. This is addressed in both **Chapter 5: Economic Global Governance and Chapter 7: Environmental Global Governance**.

Figure 4.1 The UN General Assembly's central role in the UN System

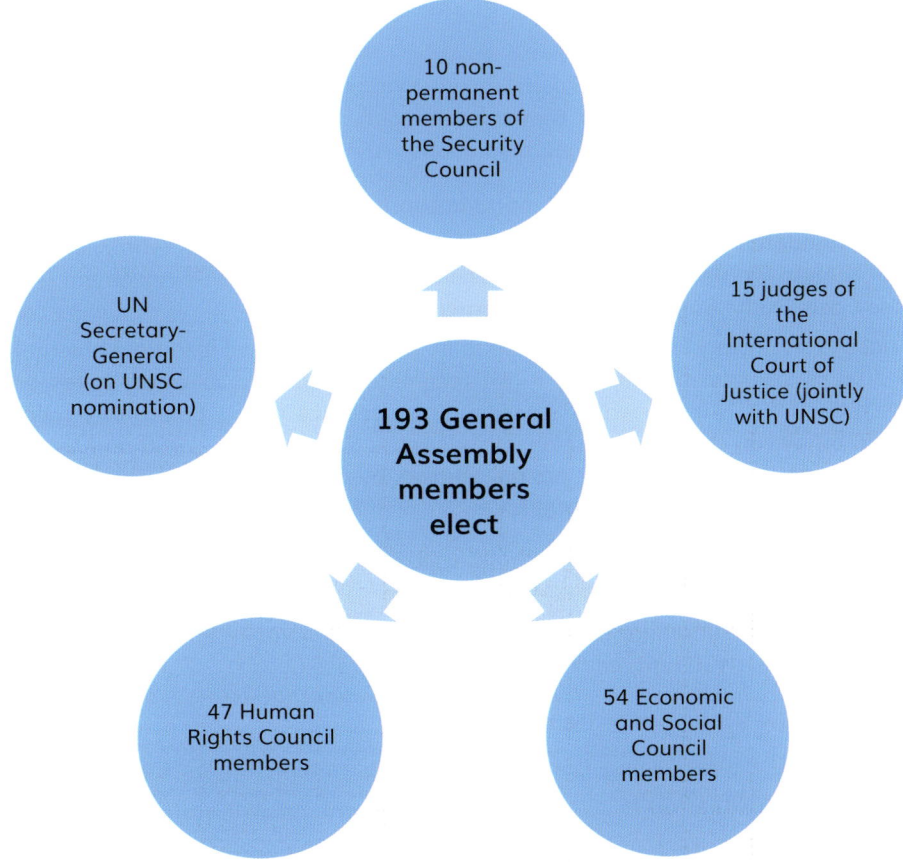

Photo 4.2 President of Ukraine, Volodymyr Zelenskyy gives a speech at the UN General Assembly on 23 September 2024.

The UNGA debates and votes on the budget, membership applications and reports from UN bodies, and can debate conflicts if the UNSC cannot agree a way forward. Committees draft resolutions to be voted on in the UNGA. Records of meetings and documents are publicly available. Voting is 'one country, one vote', upholding sovereign equality. Most decisions are carried with a simple majority or by consensus, but votes on the budget, new members and conflicts require a two-thirds majority.

Policymaking role

The UNGA makes **resolutions** (policy decisions) on any matter covered by the Charter. Resolutions may apply to specific states or all states, but they are not legally binding on states. As well as admitting new members and agreeing the UN budget, resolutions may:

Act as a source of collective intention and moral authority

The UNGA sets standards and targets for the UN and its members to work towards, e.g. the Universal Declaration of Human Rights 1948, and the Millennium and Sustainable Development Goals of 2000 and 2015 (see **Case Study: Sustainable Development Goals**).

The UNGA passed a 'Uniting for Peace' resolution in 1950. This allows it to hold emergency special sessions to discuss security matters and make recommendations to member states on action to uphold peace, if the UNSC is unable to pass a resolution (see pp119-124). Emergency special sessions have been held on eleven conflict situations, including the Suez crisis of 1956 and the Ukraine and Gaza wars. Uniting for Peace resolutions are not binding, but they show the strength of opinion in the international community.

- The UNGA passed a resolution condemning Russia's invasion of Ukraine in 2022 after Russia vetoed a UNSC resolution.
- It also called for a humanitarian ceasefire in Gaza in October 2023, after three weeks of negotiations in the UNSC had resulted in three vetoed resolutions.

Propose setting up new UN bodies or treaties

- For example, the Peacebuilding Commission (2005), Human Rights Council (2006) and UN Environment Assembly (2012).

- It can ask legal experts to draft treaties and conventions, to be negotiated and signed by states at world summits, e.g.
  - Humanitarian laws such as the Genocide Convention of 1948 and the Geneva Conventions of 1949
  - The Rome Statute of 1998, which set up the International Criminal Court.
  - Weapons treaties, such as the Nuclear Non-Proliferation Treaty of 1968.
  - Environmental treaties such as the Paris Climate Change Agreement of 2014.

Request advisory opinions from the International Court of Justice

- In 2019, the Court gave an advisory opinion as requested by the UNGA, that the UK had acted unlawfully by retaining sovereignty over the Chagos Islands when granting independence to Mauritius (see **Case Study: Britain's Last Colony in Africa**).
- In 2025, the Court gave an advisory opinion to the UNGA that all states have legally binding duties under international law to take effective action on climate change. This ruling provides a legal basis for civil society to challenge governments on inadequate climate actions.

Significance

The UNGA is not the most powerful body in the UN, but it is significant

Its inclusive membership and decision-making make it the most important representative body in global politics, upholding the UN Charter's fundamental principle of sovereign equality.

States often vote in 'blocs' from the global North and South

- Global North blocs include NATO, the EU and G7 members. They often vote with the United States, but not uniformly.
- Global South blocs include the overlapping groups of the African Union (54 members) and G77 (set up in the 1960s, now 134 members). They outnumber the Global North and increasingly vote with China and India on shared interests such as postcolonial reparations or climate change.
- The ideologically diverse BRICS emerging economies group includes Brazil, Russia, India, China and South Africa, from both North and South. They sometimes cooperate against the United States and Europe in the UNGA.

The question of Palestinian statehood has been deeply controversial in the UNGA. The Global South tends to identify with Palestinians. These states have argued that Palestinians have the right to self-determination and that a legitimate state exists. Palestine should therefore have equal voting and representation rights in the UN. The United States, Israel and a dwindling number of allies oppose the idea, arguing that peace must precede full membership.

This evolving situation demonstrates both the significance of the UNGA as the voice of the international community, dominated by the large number of states from the Global South, and its subordination to the five permanent members of the UNSC. Without the weight of the US veto, Palestine might have been granted full membership in 2012. It would certainly have been agreed by September 2025 with the support of 81% of UNGA members (see Milestones: Support for Palestinian Statehood).

Security Council (UNSC)

The **Security Council** fulfils the most significant role of the UN: the maintenance of international peace and security. It is a political body rather than a court, but its decisions do have legally binding status. The legitimacy of its membership, structure and decision-making have been strongly challenged.

Membership and representation

The Council has fifteen member states. The five Allies who designed the UN at the end of the Second World War have permanent seats. These are the United States, the UK, France, Russia (then the Soviet Union) and China. They are known as the 'P5'.

Another ten members (the elected 10, or 'E10') are elected by the UNGA. Seats are allocated within regional blocs, e.g. Africa has three seats, Latin America and the Caribbean have two. They serve two-year terms, with five seats being elected each year to provide continuity. Some states are quite

> **Chapter Link**
>
> The world is becoming increasingly multipolar, meaning that no single state can dominate because power is distributed between a number of powerful states, who build alliances and compete to outrank each other. See **Chapter 3: Power and Developments** for more on increasing multipolarity

> **Spec key term**
>
> **Security Council (UNSC):** The United Nations' most powerful body, with primary responsibility for the maintenance of international peace and security.

MILESTONES: SUPPORT FOR PALESTINIAN STATEHOOD

1974 — The UNGA voted to recognise the Palestine Liberation Organisation as an 'observer entity' and invited it to participate in discussions on Palestine.

1988 — The UNGA acknowledged Palestine's declaration of statehood and gave it the right to speak in the UNGA and co-sponsor resolutions. Since then UNGA has passed many resolutions supporting Palestinian statehood.

2011 — The United States said it would veto Palestinian membership at the UNSC.

2012 — The UNGA voted by 138–9 with 41 abstentions to upgrade Palestine to a non-member observer state. This allowed Palestine to sign treaties as a state. It signed the Genocide Convention in 2014 and joined the International Criminal Court in 2015, which opened an investigation in 2019.

Dec 2022 — The UNGA requested an advisory opinion from the International Court of Justice on the legality of Israel's settlements in the occupied Palestinian territories.

Oct 2023 — On 7 October, Hamas, the Palestinian group which has governed Gaza since 2007 and is widely designated as a terrorist organisation, attacked Israel. They killed thousands of Israelis and took hundreds of hostages. This triggered a retaliatory attack by Israel on Gaza, aiming to destroy Hamas and retrieve the hostages. Most of Gaza has been destroyed and almost the entire population displaced. The civilian death toll has been massive.

Dec 2023 — South Africa raised a dispute with Israel at the ICJ, stating that under the Genocide Convention, it had an obligation to prevent genocide in Gaza.

April 2024 — Palestine again asked the UNSC to consider granting full membership. Algeria presented a resolution to the Council, which was vetoed by the United States.

May 2024 — The UNGA voted by 143–9 with 25 abstentions to grant Palestine most of the member state rights, including proposing resolutions. It stated that Palestine was eligible for full membership and called on the UNSC to reconsider. The United States vetoed a UNSC resolution, saying that recognition must follow peace.

May 2024 — The chief prosecutor of the ICC applied for arrest warrants for the military and political leaders of Hamas for crimes against humanity and war crimes, and the president and defence ministers of Israel for war crimes.

June 2024 — Palestine accepted the jurisdiction of the ICJ, allowing it to participate in the South Africa v Israel case.

July 2024 — The ICJ advised that Israel's settlements do violate international law.

Nov 2024 — The ICC issued arrest warrants for Israeli Prime Minister Binyamin Netanyahu, Defence Minister Yoav Gallant and Hamas commander Mohammed Deif. The other Hamas leaders, Ismail Haniyeh and Yahya Sinwar, had already been killed.

Feb 2025 — US President Trump proposed that the United States take over Gaza, displacing 2.3 million Palestinians to other countries. This idea was widely condemned.

July 2025 — France and Saudi Arabia planned a conference at the UN in New York, to discuss a pathway to Palestinian statehood. Several US allies said they would recognise Palestine. The conference was postponed to UNGA Leaders' week in September.

September 2025 — Ten states including US allies Australia, Canada, UK and France recognised Palestine, bringing the total to 157 of 193 members (81%). The USA responded by removing Palestinian leader Mahmoud Abbas' US visa, effectively banning him from the UNGA (all states must be allowed diplomatic access to the UN). The UNGA then granted an exception to the rules, allowing Abbas to speak by video link.

Political Global Governance

Comparative Analysis: Strengths and weaknesses of the General Assembly

	Strengths	Weaknesses
Equity	✓ It is the only truly global forum. Full membership confers recognition of legitimate statehood by the international community. ✓ The UNGA gives all member states an equal voice in international relations, upholding the principle of sovereign equality. ✓ The one-country-one-vote system means it is unique in global governance in allowing developing states to counterbalance powerful states.	✗ Fragile states may have their rights suspended if their government's legitimacy is challenged, which may do further harm, e.g preventing aid. ✗ Disputed claims to statehood deny a voice to some nations, e.g. Taiwan. ✗ The 11,000 people of Tuvalu have equal voting power to the 1.4 billion people of India. Arguably, sovereign equality is highly undemocratic. ✗ Regional voting groups have not been updated since the Cold War. EU and NATO members are still split into East and West groups.
Authority	✓ Resolutions show international opinion and have moral authority. ✓ The UNGA has the power to create new UN bodies, e.g. a resolution in 2005 created the Human Rights Council and Peacebuilding Commission.	✗ Resolutions are not legally binding on states and can easily be ignored. ✗ The UNGA has no legislative power of its own and can only make recommendations to the more powerful UNSC.
Impact	✓ Resolutions set universal goals, such as the Universal Declaration of Human Rights in 1948, and the Millennium and Sustainable Development Goals. ✓ Resolutions have led to successful actions, e.g. a 1998 resolution led to work on the Rome Statute, which set up the International Criminal Court. ✓ If the UNSC is paralysed by the veto, the UNGA can make emergency 'uniting for peace' resolutions: it did this on Gaza in October 2023. A similar resolution was later agreed by the UNSC, showing UNGA's influence.	✗ The UNGA's inclusiveness and deliberative approach slows negotiations and results in weakened resolutions, reducing its impact. ✗ The 2/3 majority requirement can make it difficult to resolve peace and security, budget and membership matters. ✗ A resolution condemned the Russian invasion of Ukraine in 2022, but many states in the Global South did not support it, showing their anger at UK and US hypocrisy, given the ongoing occupation of the Chagos Islands (see **Case Study: Britain's Last Colony in Africa**).

> **Exam Tip:**
> In Section A 12-mark questions, you may be asked to examine the strengths, weaknesses or controversies of two of the main organs of the UN. One way to do this is to select two or three paragraph themes, such as the criteria of equity, authority and impact used in this table. Remember that there are no introductions and no conclusions in Section A questions.

frequently elected, notably Japan, Germany, India and Brazil – all significant regional powers. Around sixty small states have never sat on the Council.

States that are not members of the Council may attend meetings and speak with the agreement of the Council, but they cannot vote. As a non-member observer state, Palestine cannot be elected to the Council but can attend relevant meetings. Israel has not sat on the Council, despite hundreds of resolutions dealing with its situation. However, the United States reliably represents Israel's interests.

Deliberation and decision-making

- The Council meets throughout the year. Meetings are usually public (see Photo 4.4) but can be closed if the situation requires confidentiality.
- There are briefings by UN staff and meetings to debate resolutions.
- In between meetings, ambassadors negotiate over the precise wording of resolutions.

Photo 4.3 A UN Security Council meeting on the first anniversary of the conflict between Russia and Ukraine on 24 February 2023.

- Decisions require nine votes in favour to pass.
- The 'P5' have the power to veto any decision. The ten non-permanent members do not.
- This means that a decision supported by fourteen members can be blocked if a P5 state votes against it.

Role and significance of the Security Council

Under the Charter, member states must accept and implement the UNSC's decisions.

Chapter V of the UN Charter lays out the authority of the UNSC to:

- Act on behalf of states in maintaining peace.
- Make resolutions that states must accept and follow.

Chapter VI says that

- States must seek to resolve disputes peacefully.
- States may bring their disputes to the UNSC, and the Security Council will decide whether to act.

Chapter VII empowers the Council to decide when peace is threatened or breached by an act of aggression, and on measures to restore peace.

The Council will first try to find a political resolution with consent from both parties. It may:

- Dispatch a mission to investigate or a special envoy to mediate.
- Require a ceasefire to allow for humanitarian aid and provide personnel to monitor it.
- Set out principles for a peace agreement.
- Provide peacekeepers to maintain calm so that peace talks can be established.

If a state continues to disrupt international security, the UNSC has the authority to require UN members to contribute resources and assistance to enforce peace:

- Cut off diplomatic relations.
- Impose economic sanctions and financial penalties (e.g. freezing assets of individuals).

- Impose travel bans and cut off means of communication.
- Take military action to enforce peace and provide resources to the UN for such action.

Security Council Actions under Chapter VII

Beyond mediation, which the Secretary-General can initiate without UNSC authorisation, the level of action taken by the UNSC under Chapter VII depends on four main factors.

1. Whether a ceasefire can be agreed or not.
2. The humanitarian impacts of the war on civilians.
3. Whether the state or states involved consent to UN action or not.
4. Whether the UN can agree action.

Wherever possible, the Council tries to work with the consent of the main parties in the conflict. It will try to ensure that measures impact those responsible rather than the mass population wherever possible. Military peace enforcement is the very last resort (see Table 4.1).

The UNSC can also refer a situation to the International Criminal Court for investigation and prosecution, as it did with President al-Bashir of Sudan in 2004. It can also refer situations to the UN Peacebuilding Commission. See **Chapter 8 Case Study: The UN's Peacebuilding Commission** for the UN's wider work on maintaining peace and security and upholding international law.

The significance of the veto

As of June 2024, the UNSC has passed 2,736 resolutions, whilst the veto has been used 321 times to block 265 resolutions. Vetoes show how the balance of power in the Council has changed over time see Figures 4.2 and 4.3).

1946–1991: Cold War superpowers

The Cold War saw high geopolitical tension between the United States and the USSR, and rapid decolonisation. Up to the 1960s, the USSR used its veto 118 times, blocking new UN memberships to constrain the United States, while from the 1970s, the United States focused on protecting Israel. The UK used its veto 28 times, often protecting ex-colonial apartheid South Africa and Rhodesia from sanctions. France used its veto 16 times. China's UN seat transferred from Taiwan to mainland China in 1971. The mainland People's Republic of China only used the veto twice in 1972. During the Cold

Table 4.1 Peacekeeping vs Peace Enforcement under Chapter VII of the UN Charter

Peacekeeping	Peace enforcement
Principles: • Consent of the main parties in the conflict. • Impartiality. • Minimal force used only in self-defence or defence of the UNSC mandate. **Traditional peacekeeping (1940s onwards)** deploys lightly armed forces to monitor a ceasefire and any disputed borders. **Multidimensional peacekeeping (1990s onwards).** Alongside military forces, civilian support helps maintain peace and establish democracy. **Robust peacekeeping (1990s onwards)** allows 'all necessary measures' including, as a last resort, the use of force against armed groups to protect civilians, in self-defence and to maintain peace.	**Principles:** • Does not require consent. • Significant force may be applied by states on behalf of UNSC. • A last resort. **Peace enforcement** involves coercive action by other states on behalf of the UNSC to restore peace. This might include economic sanctions or military action such as air strikes. **Humanitarian intervention** is peace enforcement that aims to stop atrocities – genocide, crimes against humanity and war crimes. See **Chapter 6: Human Rights Global Governance** for discussion of the evolution and use of this concept.

Figure 4.2 UNSC vetoes by P5 members to June 2024

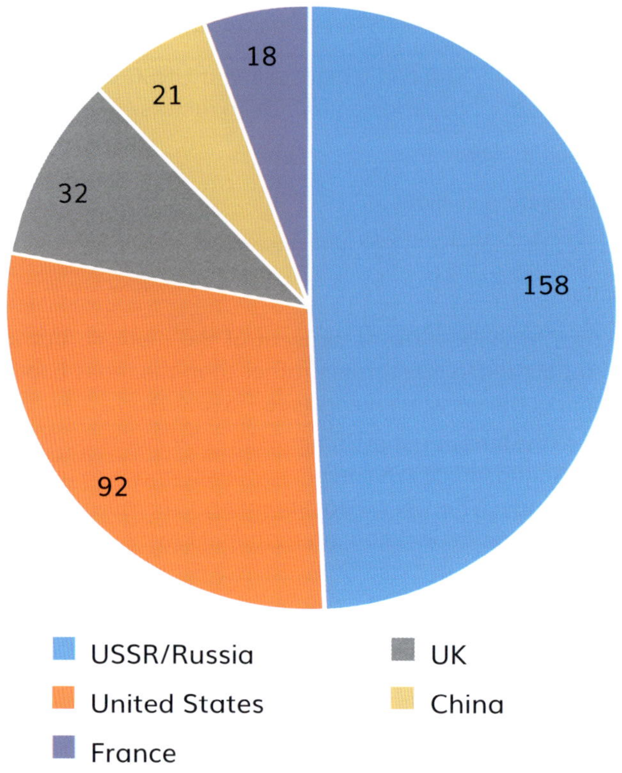

- USSR/Russia: 158
- United States: 92
- UK: 32
- China: 21
- France: 18

Graph created with data from the UN Peace Security Data Hub

War, resolutions on conflicts were rare, because at least one P5 member often had a clear vested interest. The anticipation of P5 vetoes meant that the Council rarely moved beyond condemnation or calls for ceasefires.

1991–2011: post-Cold War US hegemony

In 1991, after the Soviet Union collapsed, the United States became the sole superpower, with President George H.W. Bush envisioning a 'New World Order' of liberal peace and cooperation. However, civil wars became more common, especially in Africa. The Security Council saw increased cooperation from some of the P5: The United States used 69 vetoes, Russia 6, China 4 and the UK and France none. The overwhelming majority of US vetoes were on Israeli-Palestinian matters, whilst China used its vetoes against states that had recognised Taiwan.

This cooperation meant that many more peacekeeping and peace enforcement missions were authorised. High-profile failures in countries including Somalia, Bosnia and Rwanda prompted the development of **multidimensional** and **robust peacekeeping** (see below).

In the 2000s, US political influence started to decline, due to the controversial 'War on Terror' against the Taliban in Afghanistan and then Iraq. Then the 2008–9 global financial crisis hit the US economy. These developments reduced public support for costly foreign interventions in the United States. Meanwhile, China and Russia's economies had been rapidly developing, and they became more assertive internationally.

2011–2024: From hegemony to multipolarity

Major divisions reappeared following a failed intervention in Libya in 2011, in which Russia and China believed that NATO had overstepped its humanitarian mandate from the UNSC by allowing rebels to kill the Libyan dictator, Muammar Gaddafi.

Russia began to challenge the United States in the Council more often, with 32 vetoes, mostly shielding the Syrian dictator Bashar al-Assad from accountability for attacking civilians. China sometimes

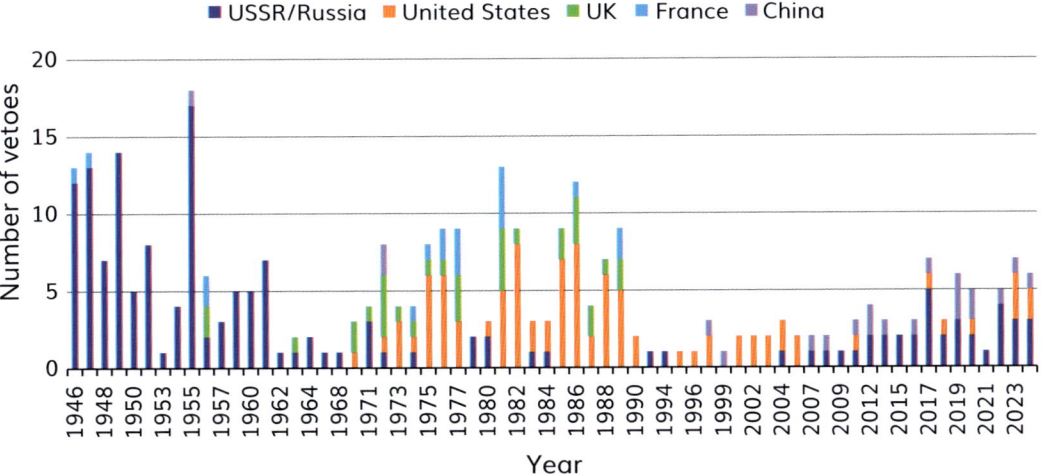

Figure 4.3 UNSC P5 vetoes per year to June 2024

Graph created with data from the UN Peace Security Data Hub

> **Chapter Link**
>
> There is a discussion of the failures of UN peacekeeping and the evolution of a new peacebuilding approach later in this chapter and a case study on the UN Peacebuilding Commission in Chapter 8 Analysing and Evaluating Global Governance.

supported Russia (14 vetoes) but more often abstained. The United States cast only eight vetoes, mostly on Israeli-Palestine issues.

Since 2011, the UNSC has authorised no new peace enforcement missions and only three peacekeeping missions – in Mali in 2013, in the Central African Republic in 2014 and in Haiti in 2017. Partly this was due to the renewed dysfunction in the Council, but failures of peacekeeping were a significant factor too.

Since 2020, the UK and France, having not used their vetoes since 1989, have both supported a campaign in the General Assembly to restrict the use of vetoes in humanitarian situations. See the companion website for a case study on the use of the veto over the war in Gaza.

Resolving inter-state wars

The UN was set up primarily to prevent and resolve wars between states. It has succeeded to some extent, as inter-state wars are not common. During the Cold War, just one inter-state peace enforcement in the Korean War, in 1950. This action was not vetoed because at the time, the USSR was boycotting the Security Council in protest at the UN's failure to recognise the People's Republic of China.

It also authorised several peacekeeping missions. Just once, following the 1956 Suez Crisis (Second Arab–Israeli War), the General Assembly used its powers under its 'Uniting for Peace' resolution to authorise a peacekeeping mission when the UNSC could not agree.

After the Cold War, the UNSC authorised peace enforcement to end Iraq's invasion of Kuwait in the Gulf War of 1991. See Figure 4.4.

Resolving civil wars (intra-state wars)

However, since the Second World War, and especially since the Cold War, more wars have occurred within states than between them. Civil wars tend to be between states and insurgents (armed rebels). They are often more complex and difficult to resolve than wars between states, and the number of civilian casualties is often very high. UN peacekeeping missions need to be robust and tailored to the specific circumstances of the conflict.

If the UNSC decides to enforce peace to protect civilians from attacks by an insurgent group, and the state consents to action, its sovereignty is not undermined. However, if the UNSC decides to enforce peace to protect civilians from attacks by their own state, the state's sovereignty would be undermined.

The P5 failed to agree to enforce peace in the Syrian Civil War. Instead, it became a complex proxy war, lasting 13 years. Russia supported Assad, whilst the United States, the UK and France supported various rebel groups. Turkey and Iran became involved. All sides fought ISIS, which emerged in Iraq and exploited the Syrian conflict to seize territory. The war ended in late 2024 when Assad's regime collapsed, weakened by Israeli attacks on Syria's allies Hezbollah and Iran. Assad was granted asylum in Russia.

By late 2025, the UNSC had failed for over two years to authorise peace enforcement in the Sudan Civil War and the Gaza War. See Figure 4.4.

Component III: Global Politics

Figure 4.4 Examples of UNSC authorised actions and failures to act to restore peace

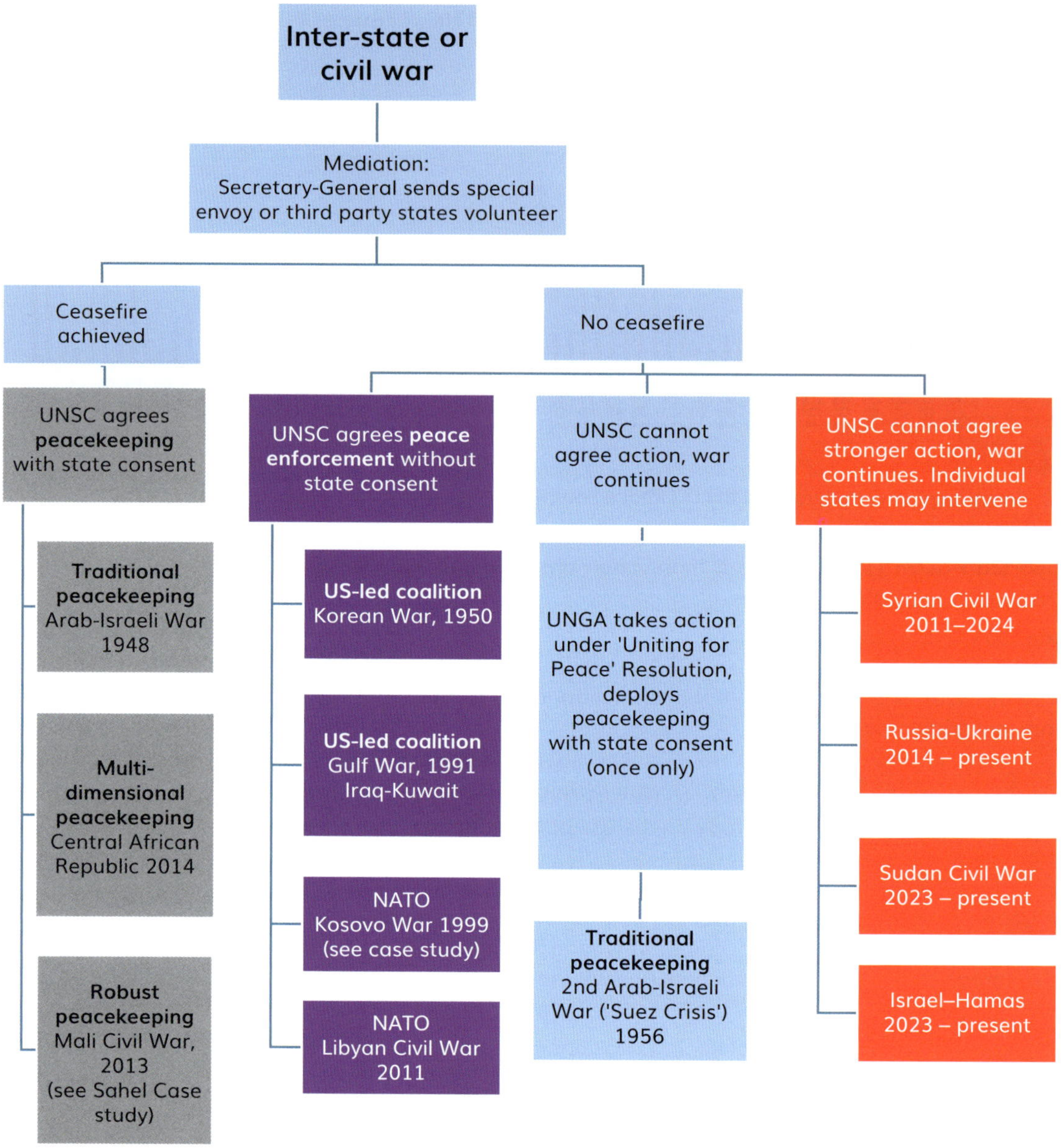

```
Inter-state or civil war
         │
Mediation: Secretary-General sends special envoy or third party states volunteer
         │
    ┌────┴────┐
Ceasefire   No ceasefire
achieved        │
    │      ┌────┼────────┬──────────┐
```

Ceasefire achieved:
- UNSC agrees **peacekeeping** with state consent
  - Traditional peacekeeping: Arab-Israeli War 1948
  - Multi-dimensional peacekeeping: Central African Republic 2014
  - Robust peacekeeping: Mali Civil War, 2013 (see Sahel Case study)

No ceasefire:
- UNSC agrees **peace enforcement** without state consent
  - US-led coalition Korean War, 1950
  - US-led coalition Gulf War, 1991 Iraq-Kuwait
  - NATO Kosovo War 1999 (see case study)
  - NATO Libyan Civil War 2011
- UNSC cannot agree action, war continues
  - UNGA takes action under 'Uniting for Peace' Resolution, deploys peacekeeping with state consent (once only)
  - Traditional peacekeeping 2nd Arab-Israeli War ('Suez Crisis') 1956
- UNSC cannot agree stronger action, war continues. Individual states may intervene
  - Syrian Civil War 2011–2024
  - Russia-Ukraine 2014 – present
  - Sudan Civil War 2023 – present
  - Israel–Hamas 2023 – present

KEY DEBATE: IS THE USE OF THE VETO JUSTIFIABLE?

Maintaining the system vs evading accountability

A functioning **multilateral** system needs to keep the P5 engaged; the veto is necessary for this.

✓ The P5 are least in need of protection and are asked to carry the greatest burden of collective security. They pay for 55 per cent of the peacekeeping fund. They should therefore have the right to say no.

✓ Abolishing the veto would make the UN no more effective than the League of Nations, which failed because states did not see it as protecting their interests.

However, it appears that Russia and the United States do not use their power responsibly, using the veto to shield themselves and their allies from accountability.

✗ In 2017, Russia used the veto several times to protect the Syrian government from an investigation into the use of chemical weapons in the Syrian war, and in 2022, it vetoed a resolution on its own invasion of Ukraine.

✗ The UK and France have repeatedly argued that the veto should not be used in humanitarian situations, but in 2023–24, the United States continued to veto humanitarian and ceasefire

> **Definition**
>
> **Multilateralism:** Multiple countries pursuing a common goal, usually within an IGO and usually bound by a code of conduct that upholds principles of inclusivity, equality and cooperation.

resolutions on the Israel–Gaza conflict that did not condemn Hamas, whilst Russia vetoed those that did not condemn Israel.

Multilateral vs unilateral action

The veto helps to maintain multilateral consent for action, which is important for legitimacy.

- ✓ Military intervention should be a last resort when political solutions have failed. The veto allows action to be taken only when there is unanimous agreement between great powers, providing a legal basis for intervention.
- ✓ A legitimate intervention with multilateral support is more likely to result in lasting peace.

However, the veto can actually encourage *unilateralism* or bandwagoning rather than multilateralism.

- ✗ A threatened veto actually hastened a pre-emptive unilateral invasion of Iraq by the United States and the UK in 2003.
- ✗ The power of the veto does not stop states from forming competing alliances, which can escalate hostilities. Russia's war on Ukraine has been supported to varying extents by China, Iran and North Korea – the last with armed troops – whilst Ukraine has been supported by NATO, the EU, UK, Japan, Australia and South Korea with military aid.

> **Definition**
>
> **Unilateralism:** One-sided action. Unilateralism in international relations is generally seen as acting in narrow self-interest and with disregard to the impacts on other states.

The risk of escalating conflict

The veto helps to avoid a misjudged escalation of conflict.

- ✓ Military intervention should be a last resort when political solutions have failed. The veto allows action to be taken only when there is unanimous agreement between great powers, providing a legal basis for intervention.
- ✓ It allows each P5 member to warn other states away from provocative interventions that would threaten their interests: it gives an indication of their strength of feeling without resorting to force.

The veto fails to decrease unilateral P5 aggression or escalation.

- ✗ After using its veto to block condemnation of its own actions in 2022, Russia accused the Ukrainian government and its allies of being the aggressors by expanding NATO and threatening ethnic Russians in Ukraine. It then escalated its own campaign.
- ✗ After using its veto to block condemnation of Israel's attacks on Gaza, the US government has continued to supply arms to Israel, supporting it in further hostilities in Gaza and Lebanon.

The humanitarian impacts

The problem of the veto is overstated, and humanitarian action does happen.

- ✓ The world's media focuses on relatively infrequent vetoes on the most contentious matters such as Syria or Gaza, but in general, around 90 per cent of resolutions pass, often with a high level of consensus, without significant media attention. By 2024, the UNSC had authorised seventy-one peacekeeping missions around the world, and eleven of these were currently active.
- ✓ This negative media focus obscures the hard work of 'penholder' states in drafting resolutions and building consensus. In 2024, the UK representative in the Council spent a year working on a ceasefire resolution for Sudan. By June, two resolutions had passed with no vetoes: the first for a temporary truce during Ramadan and a second for a local ceasefire in a city in Darfur.

However, time and effort are spent on weakening drafts to the point that they will not be vetoed, costing many lives.

- ✗ The UNSC debated eleven resolutions on Gaza over eight months. It eventually passed five humanitarian resolutions and approved a ceasefire plan in June 2024, after an estimated 35,000 deaths. At no point then or in the next year did it authorise peace enforcement.
- ✗ In Sudan, when the UNSC passed its first resolution for a temporary truce, the year-long civil war had caused 15,000 civilian deaths and 8 million displaced people at risk of famine. There was already evidence of a second genocide in the Darfur region (following an earlier one in 2003). By October 2025 there was strong evidence of genocide in El Fashur, Darfur, but still no UNSC resolution.

Key Debate Summary: Is the use of the veto justifiable?

	For	Against
Maintaining the system vs evading accountability	✓ A functioning multilateral system needs to keep the P5 engaged; the veto is necessary for this.	✗ Russia and the United States do not use their power responsibly, using the veto to shield themselves and their allies from accountability.
Multilateral vs unilateral action	✓ The veto helps to maintain multilateral consent for action, which is important for legitimacy.	✗ However, the veto can actually encourage unilateralism or bandwagoning rather than multilateralism.
Risk of escalation	✓ The veto helps to avoid a misjudged escalation of conflict.	✗ The veto fails to decrease unilateral P5 aggression or escalation.
Humanitarian impact	✓ The problem of the veto is over-stated, and humanitarian action does happen.	✗ However, time and effort are spent on weakening drafts to the point that they will not be vetoed, costing many lives.

Exam Tip:
When considering the word 'justifiable' in the question, you could consider what is justifiable within a realist view of the world, and what is justifiable from a liberal view.

Comparative Theories: The use of the veto

Realist view	Liberal view
States prioritise narrow self-interest, and the stability of the international system depends on a balance of hard power between great powers.	Liberals believe that states can create the conditions for multilateral cooperation, and if they do, they will be inclined to seek peaceful solutions to conflict.
The veto preserves this balance.	The veto disrupts the principle of equality that underpins multilateralism.
States do not operate on the basis of morality or the universal concept of human rights.	It also has moral consequences for humanitarian action.

KEY DEBATE: SHOULD THE SECURITY COUNCIL BE REFORMED?

Chapter Link

Chapter 6: Human Rights Global Governance
For more on the Responsibility to Protect Doctrine.

Should the veto be removed for humanitarian actions?

The veto could be replaced by a supermajority on humanitarian intervention, a compromise that could gain P5 support by allowing them to maintain national interests on all other matters.

- ✓ When the UNGA agreed the 'Responsibility To Protect' in 2005, a code of conduct was drafted urging the P5 not to use their vetoes against humanitarian intervention. By 2020, 120 states had signed it, including the UK and France.
- ✓ US President Joe Biden agreed in Sept 2022 that the use of the veto should be restricted to 'rare, extraordinary situations'.

The veto could not be abolished or reformed unless all the P5 agree, which is unlikely.

- ❌ Russia has vetoed more humanitarian interventions than any other state and has not signed up to the code.
- ❌ US vetoes by the Biden administration on humanitarian resolutions in Gaza in 2023–24 undermined President Biden's statement of support and the Trump administration continued to veto ceasefire resolutions in 2025. The United States instead worked outside the UNSC with its regional allies on a peace deal, highlighting the irrelevance of the UNSC.

Should the size of the Council be increased?

The number of elected members increased from six to ten seats in 1965, because the UN had grown. Since the 1990s, there have been regular calls to add more permanent members, providing stronger continuity and expertise, broader representation and responsibility-sharing.

- ✅ In 2004, Germany, Japan, India and Brazil formed a 'P4' group to campaign for permanent seats.
- ✅ Indian Prime Minister Narendra Modi said in 2015: 'The UN reflects a century which we left behind and not the century we live in.'

However, whilst this would expand representation, it could increase rather than decrease the Council's dysfunction.

- ❌ It is not clear which states should be chosen and how many, nor which states should have the authority to choose. The P5 would veto their own rivals.
- ❌ More vetoes would only make it harder to agree, as outlined below.

Should more states from the Global North gain permanent seats?

Regional economic powers Germany and Japan are both willing and able to play a greater security role.

- ✅ They have larger economies than the UK and France and already contribute more to peacekeeping costs. Japan also contributes significantly to UN peacebuilding.
- ✅ Germany is a major source of civilian humanitarian support, and since 2022, it has radically expanded its military spending.

These states lack military deterrent power and would not be likely to gain unanimous P5 support.

- ❌ Neither states possesses their own nuclear deterrent. Arguably, it is the nuclear deterrent that legitimises the permanent status of the P4.
- ❌ Russia would veto its regional rival, Germany, and China would veto its regional rival, Japan.

Should more states from the Global South gain permanent seats?

- ✅ India has the military strength to be a permanent member: in 2023, its military spending and power was ranked fourth in the world, and it has nuclear weapons. It is a democracy and provides financial support to the African Union. It is emerging as a diplomatic and economic leader in the Global South.
- ✅ Brazil could represent the whole continental area of Latin America and the Caribbean. It is wealthier than India and has contributed to humanitarian missions in Haiti.
- ✅ Africa suffers from more conflicts than anywhere else, and most African peacekeeping is already done by African states, so they should have a voice on these matters. President Biden endorsed the idea of two permanent seats for Africa, without vetoes, in 2022.

Global South representation could present political difficulties.

- ✅ India's tensions with Pakistan are a threat to regional stability rather than a stabilising force. It is also a regional rival to China, so would probably be vetoed.
- ✅ Brazil is not a nuclear power and does not have regional support from Mexico and Argentina.
- ✅ Even the two most powerful African states, South Africa and Nigeria, would not necessarily 'represent' a continent of such diverse interests.

Key Debate Summary: Should the Security Council be reformed?

	For	Against
Veto	✓ Restricting use in humanitarian situations would reduce obstructive behaviour.	✗ The P5 are very unlikely to agree to any reform and A voluntary code of conduct would fail.
Membership structure	✓ Expansion of P5 has growing support. The G4 are obvious candidates.	✗ Increasing the number of veto powers would make decision-making more not less difficult.
Global North	✓ Germany and Japan already contribute more to peacekeeping than the UK and France.	✗ They are not nuclear powers and would be vetoed by Russia and China.
Global South	✓ India is a major military power with growing economic and diplomatic influence. Latin America and Africa deserve representation and would help to resolve problems.	✗ There would be political difficulties with adding any of the regional powers that have been suggested.

Exam Tip:

In this case, no matter how strong the arguments in favour of reform, they are all outweighed by one point – that P5 members remain very unlikely to agree to reforms as long as they are opposed to each other on ideological and strategic grounds.

Comparative Analysis: Strengths and weaknesses of the UN Security Council

	Strengths	Weaknesses
Equity	✓ The E10 can persuade the P5 when they work together, e.g. proposing a successful resolution on Gaza in March 2024. This improves the legitimacy of the Council. ✓ Any member state can stand for election. Smaller states have made very effective contributions, e.g. Malta proposed a successful humanitarian resolution on Gaza in November 2023.	✗ The P5 powers reflect world power as it was in 1944. But the world has changed. Their legitimacy has been challenged in the Global South. ✗ The 'G4' of Japan, India, Germany and Brazil claim they have as much right to a permanent seat as the UK and France, and they often seek and gain re-election, meaning that other states have even less chance of a seat.
Authority	✓ The Council is the most powerful global body, with the right to enforce state compliance with its resolutions.	✗ The veto makes the Council powerless to prevent or punish aggression by the P5 and their close allies, e.g. in Iraq, Syria or Ukraine.
Impact	✓ The streamlined membership and veto make the UNSC more effective than the League of Nations. Without the ability to veto, the P5 could act unilaterally, ignoring diplomacy. ✓ Only a tenth of resolutions are vetoed, and the UNSC has authorised 71 peacekeeping missions, mostly to maintain ceasefires, since 1948. ✓ Successful economic sanctions have been imposed on 31 states and terrorist regimes, including ISIS, al-Qaeda and the Taliban. Since 2005, sanctions have increasingly been used to facilitate peacebuilding and constrain individuals rather than punishing whole states.	✗ The UN relies on member states for intervention. With tension rising between the P5, this makes UN interventions less likely and unilateral interventions more likely. ✗ The threat of veto means that some resolutions are abandoned before a vote, others are weakened or agreed too late to prevent suffering. The UNSC failed to act quickly or robustly enough on genocide in Rwanda and Bosnia. From 2023 to date (2025), no enforcement action was taken on alleged genocides in Gaza and Sudan. The UNSC has never imposed economic sanctions on P5 members.

International Court of Justice (ICJ)

Membership and representation

The International Court of Justice is in The Hague Peace Palace, in the Netherlands (see Photo 4.5). It is composed of fifteen judges from different legal systems around the world. Judges sit for nine-year terms, and five are elected every three years. They are elected jointly by the UNSC and UNGA. The five permanent members of the UNSC usually have a sitting judge. Any state involved in a dispute may appoint a temporary judge to the panel if they do not already have a sitting judge. These 'ad hoc' judges are required to be impartial, as all judges are. This makes sure that there is relevant expertise from both states' legal systems and avoids the perception of bias if only one of the state parties had a judge on the panel.

Deliberation and decision-making

Cases can take from six months to two or more years to conclude. Rulings are carried by a majority decision. Judges give their reasoning for their majority decision and any dissenting views.

Role and significance

The court has two main functions: settling disputes between member states in **contentious cases** (around 80 per cent of its work) and issuing **advisory opinions** at the request of UN bodies.

The jurisdiction of the court is strictly limited to states and UN bodies, and so most of its cases have concerned territorial and sovereignty disputes. In a contentious case, both state parties must accept the court's jurisdiction. This can happen in three ways:

- The state signs an optional clause giving the court binding jurisdiction in advance. Seventy-four of 193 member states have done this.
- The state signs a treaty which gives jurisdiction to the court to resolve disputes on that treaty.
- The two states involved in a dispute agree to give jurisdiction to the court in that case.

These three options fundamentally uphold the principle of state sovereignty. However, there is debate about whether states can be held to account by the court on 'customary international law', which is principles that are so widely accepted that they are deemed to apply to all states. See the companion website for a case study on the ICJ's failure to hold the USA to account for a disputed intervention in Nicaragua in the 1980s.

Photo 4.4 The Peace Palace in The Hague, the Netherlands, is the seat of the International Court of Justice

Source: iStock.com/thehague

CASE STUDY: BRITAIN'S LAST COLONY IN AFRICA

Map 4.1 Indian Ocean with Chagos Islands

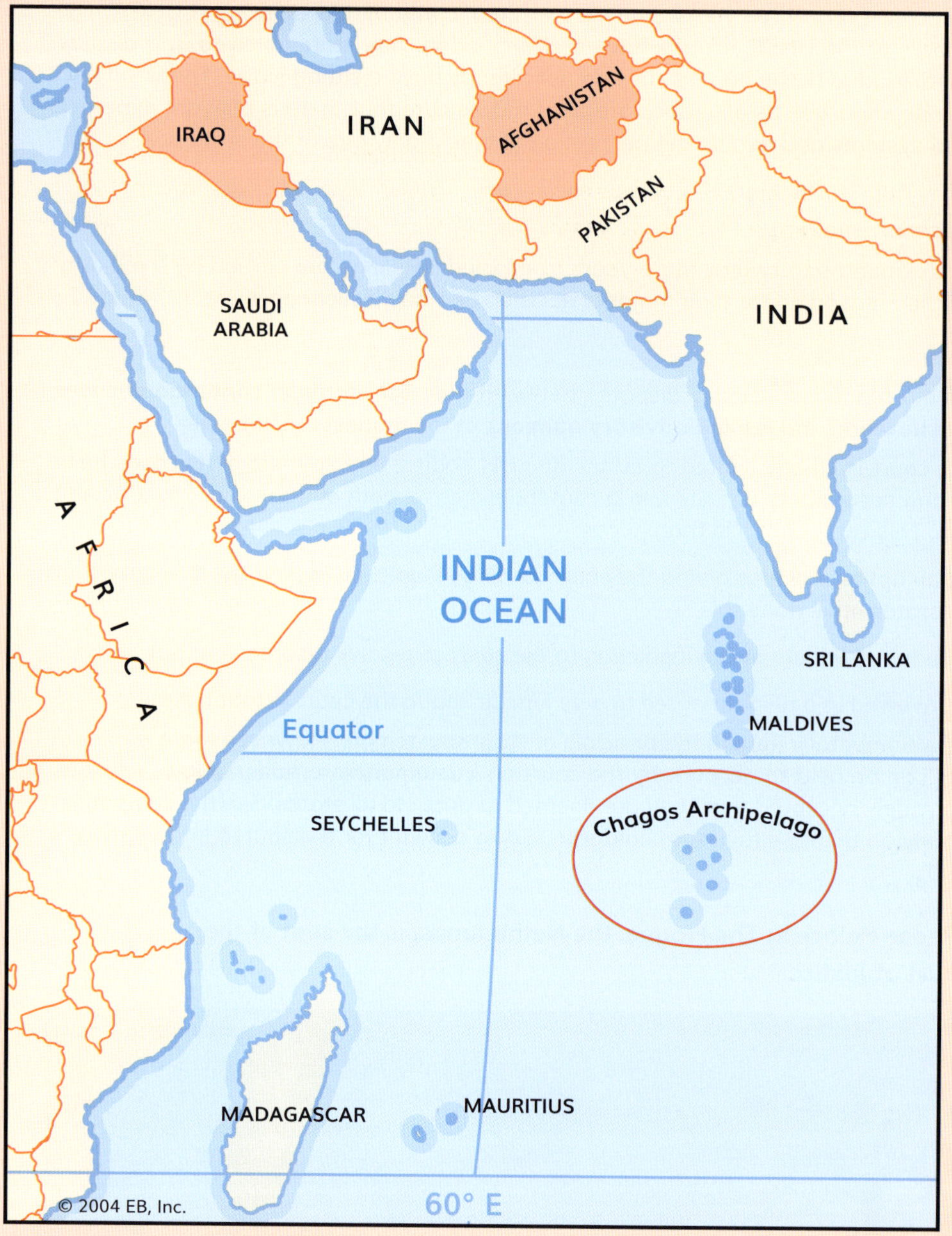

Context

The Chagos Islands are a tiny, remote archipelago in the Indian Ocean (see Map 4.1). In 1814, they were added to the colony of Mauritius and handed over by the French to the British Empire. In 1965, the UK purchased the Chagos Islands for £3 million and a promise of independence for Mauritius. The UNGA passed a resolution asking the UK not to divide Mauritian territory, which the UK ignored. It deported the Chagos islanders and leased Diego Garcia, the largest island, to the United States for a military base. In 2016, the UK renewed the lease for 20 years.

In 2017, the UK rejected a General Assembly resolution asking for the islands to be returned, saying that they would be returned when no longer needed by the military, and that the UK would not consent to a dispute at the ICJ. The UNGA voted to ask the ICJ to give an advisory opinion on the matter, led by states from the African Union. In 2019, the court ruled that keeping the islands was unlawful and that the UK should complete decolonisation of Mauritius by returning its islands. The UK rejected the ruling, arguing that Mauritius had never had sovereignty over the islands.

The UNGA voted in agreement with the court, calling for complete decolonisation. The vote was carried with 116 to 6, with 56 abstentions. The UK retained control of the islands, but in 2022, they agreed to negotiate. In 2024, an agreement was reached with Mauritius. The UK agreed to return the islands, whilst Mauritius agreed to extend the lease to the United States for 99 years.

Significance

This case demonstrates the ability of the Global South to outvote the Global North in the UNGA. It also shows that the UNGA only has moral authority over states, not legal authority. The UNGA can bolster that moral authority by seeking advisory opinions from the IC. However, advisory opinions are not binding, so the UK could ignore both bodies.

Eventually, the UK acknowledged the legitimacy of the Mauritian claim. The process was begun by Conservative Prime Minister Liz Truss in 2022 and concluded in 2025 under Labour Prime Minister Keir Starmer, who had promised to repair the UK's international reputation for complying with international law. The UK has signed a 99-year lease agreement with Mauritius for continued use of Diego Garcia, costing £101 million per year. The deal does not permit Chagos Islanders to return to Diego Garcia, which has been challenged in the courts.

Contemporary developments

The work of the court is constantly evolving. In recent years, the court has heard more cases relating to international humanitarian law and to environmental law. For example, In 2025, the Court gave an advisory opinion to the UNGA that all states have binding duties under international law to take effective action on climate change. The ruling had been requested by Vanuatu, supported by 132 states and many youth groups. The ruling provides a legal basis for civil society to challenge governments on inadequate climate actions. See the companion website for a case study of this ruling.

Comparative Analysis: Strengths and Weaknesses of the International Court of Justice

	Strengths	Weaknesses
Equity	✓ All 193 UN members have equal rights to access justice. Non-UN member states can also access the court if they sign a declaration accepting its jurisdiction. Palestine accepted the ICJ's jurisdiction on the Genocide Convention in May 2024. ✓ Judges represent different legal systems rather than member states, maintaining their independence, neutrality and inclusivity.	✗ Victims of atrocities can only access justice if a member state will raise a dispute on their behalf. A case was brought in 2019 by Gambia on the Rohingya genocide in Myanmar, because signatories to the Genocide Convention have a responsibility to prevent genocide. South Africa brought a similar case in 2023 on Gaza (see the ICJ contentious case: South Africa vs Israel in Chapter 6: Human rights Global Governance. No country has attempted to do this for the Uighurs in China, despite some, including the United States, calling their treatment genocide.
Jurisdiction/ Authority	✓ The court can arbitrate in contentious disputes between states if both parties consent to its jurisdiction in that dispute. ✓ States that consent to jurisdiction are required by the Charter to comply with the court's rulings, upholding the rule of law. ✓ The court's impartiality and neutrality uphold the liberal principle of sovereign equality and give its rulings legitimacy and moral authority. ✓ The organs of the UN can ask the Court for advisory opinions.	✗ The ICJ cannot initiate cases or force states to participate. Iran refused its jurisdiction over its hostage-taking in the US Embassy in 1979 and the United States withdrew consent in 1984. ✗ It has no jurisdiction to deal with insurgents and terrorists, limiting its ability to uphold the rule of law. ✗ Only 74 of 193 states have signed the optional clause accepting the court's jurisdiction in advance, limiting both its equality and authority. ✗ Only UN bodies can request advisory opinions, not NGOs or individuals.

Component III: Global Politics

Chapter Link

States have begun to use the ICJ to try to hold states that are not members of the International Criminal Court accountable for violating international humanitarian law. This development is addressed in **Chapter 6: Human Rights Global Governance**. The use of international law and courts for environmental protection is also increasing, see **Chapter 8: Analysing and Evaluating Global Governance**.

	Strengths	Weaknesses
Impact	✓ It upholds important liberal principles of the rule of law, human rights and peaceful resolution of conflicts in a world that desperately needs this. It can request that the UNSC enforce its rulings if needed. ✓ It has resolved violent disputes over territory, e.g. in 2011, it helped to end a three-year war between Thailand and Cambodia over the sovereignty of an ancient Hindu temple; later ruling in favour of Cambodia.	✗ The UNSC has never enforced a dispute ruling. The Charter only allows intervention when international peace and security are threatened, plus the P5 states can veto a resolution. ✗ Advisory opinions are not binding. Israel ignored an advisory opinion in 2004, regarding its security wall in the West Bank, and the UK ignored another in 2019.

Economic and Social Council (ECOSOC)

Membership, representation and decision-making

ECOSOC was established by the UN Charter in 1944. It began as a much smaller body of eighteen states. As UN membership grew through decolonisation, it was expanded to twenty-seven and then to fifty-four members in 1973, giving developing states more of a voice in its work. Its members are elected for three-year terms. They nominate themselves in regional groups, and then nominations are voted on by the whole General Assembly. Powerful states often renominate themselves and are re-elected for multiple terms. Decisions are made by resolutions on a simple majority vote.

Role and significance

ECOSOC's main role is to oversee the UN's work on three dimensions of sustainable development: economic, social and environmental. In practice, some work overlaps with the UNGA's committees, such as on gender equality, but the UNGA sets overall policy, and ECOSOC is responsible for its implementation and reporting to the UNGA.

ECOSOC is the central coordinating body for the UN's huge system of subsidiary bodies:

- Funds and Programmes that deliver aid and development projects, e.g. the World Food Programme, the UN Development Programme and the UN Environment Programme.
- Commissions that encourage cooperation and research on issues such as the status of women, protection of refugees and trade and development.

It coordinates with:

- Specialised agencies, including the IMF and World Bank.
- Civil society organisations (NGOs) which have 'consultative status'.
- Representatives from the private sector.

It supports collective action by member states:

- Since 2016, it organises an annual High-Level Political Forum (HLPF) to review collective and individual progress on the Sustainable Development Goals (see case study).

Significance

Within the UN: ECOSOC is subordinate to the UNGA and UNSC, but it has an enormous role in overseeing the UN system, in partnership with the Secretariat (see Figure 4.5).

Figure 4.5 The roles and significance of ECOSOC in the wider UN System

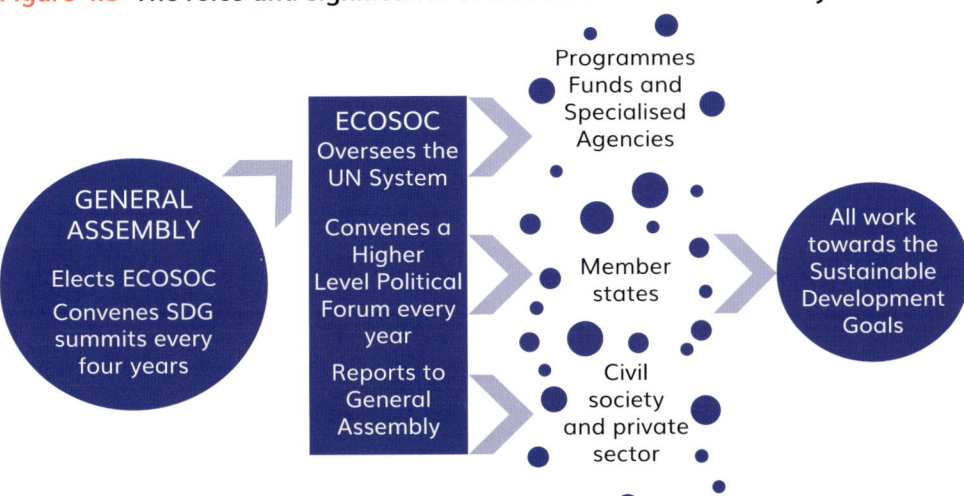

Beyond the UN: It plays an important role as the 'public facing' council of the UN, consulting with private sector associations and civil society organisations.

Working with civil society organisations: these are local, national or international non-profit, voluntary citizens' groups or NGOs. Around 6,500 organisations have formal 'consultative status' which allows them to provide briefings and speak in debates at ECOSOC and the Human Rights Council. These include Oxfam International, The International Committee of the Red Cross, Human Rights Watch and Greenpeace International. Civil society organisations have had significant impacts on the UN's work – in exposing human rights abuses and highlighting what needs to be done to prevent them; in advancing international humanitarian and environmental law and in campaigning to establish new IGOs such as the International Criminal Court.

Secretariat and Secretary-General

It is useful to understand the difference between the UN as an intergovernmental body of states and the UN Secretariat, which implements its development and humanitarian work. The Secretary-General oversees the Secretariat and can serve two five-year terms. The UN describes the Secretary-General as 'equal parts diplomat and advocate, civil servant and chief executive'. They are the public face of the UN and must uphold its values and moral authority, a role that sometimes creates tension with member states. An important role is the use of their 'good offices' of independence, impartiality and integrity to try to prevent and resolve conflict between states, for example by sending a special envoy to mediate, or by urging the UNSC to take humanitarian action.

Each Secretary-General shapes their own 'agenda':

- Kofi Annan, Secretary-General from 1997 to 2006, initiated significant reforms and developments, including the Millennium Development Goals, the 'Responsibility to Protect' declaration, the Human Rights Council and the Peacebuilding Commission. He was awarded a Nobel Peace Prize in 2001 for revitalising the UN's work on human rights.
- Antonio Guterres, Secretary-General from 2017 to 2027, has driven work on the Sustainable Development Goals and climate justice, and reformed the UN's peacekeeping approach, developing its capacity for peacebuilding. In the face of climate change and increased divisions, he has encouraged states to re-commit to multilateralism.

CASE STUDY: THE SUSTAINABLE DEVELOPMENT GOALS

Figure 4.6 The Sustainable Development Goals

Source: United Nations

Context

In June 1992, at the Earth Summit in Rio de Janeiro, Brazil, more than 178 countries adopted Agenda 21, a plan drafted by civil society organisations and UN bodies to agree to work together on sustainable development.

In the late 1990s, Secretary-General Kofi Annan began work on a Millennium Declaration. The UN again invited civil society to help draft the document, and more than 100 organisations contributed. Member States unanimously adopted the declaration in September 2000. It included eight Millennium Development Goals (MDGs) to reduce extreme poverty by 2014. The goal of halving extreme poverty was met five years early, due to the rapid development of China. Good progress was made on the other goals, although they were not all achieved.

In January 2015, the UNGA began negotiations on the next set of goals. The 2030 Agenda for Sustainable Development, with its seventeen Sustainable Development Goals, was adopted in September 2014. The annual High-level Political Forum on Sustainable Development was set up to review progress. The goals combine ending poverty with strategies to improve health and education, reduce inequality and spur economic growth, while tackling climate change and preserving oceans and forests (see Figure 4.6).

Significance

The SDGs build on decades of work by civil society, states and the UN. The MDGs significantly spurred efforts to promote development and reduce the debt of developing countries. They influenced the work not just of the UN but also of the World Bank, International Monetary Fund, member states and other global and regional organisations. They brought the world together to work on a shared agenda. It was hoped that the SDGs would step progress up further and faster. However, after a strong start, things have not progressed well.

In 2023, Secretary-General Antonio Guterres warned that progress on half of the SDGs was weak. Progress on poverty, hunger and climate had stalled, due to the Covid-19 pandemic and the triple crises of climate change, biodiversity loss and pollution.

The Ukraine war has caused a global cost-of-living crisis affecting billions of people, but this is worse in developing countries, with more than half facing unsustainable debt, for two reasons. Financial markets charge developing countries interest rates up to eight times higher than developed countries, and developed countries had delayed meeting their commitments on aid.

Political Global Governance

Comparative Analysis: Strengths and weaknesses of ECOSOC

	Strengths	Weaknesses
Equity	✓ ECOSOC includes many different civil society groups and minority groups who struggle to be heard in many states. They have helped ECOSOC to change its thinking on development.	✗ ECOSOC's state representation is based on the outdated UNGA regional groupings. Arguably, African states should have more representation, as they receive most development aid.
Authority	✓ ECOSOC is the front-facing body of the UN which coordinates many organisations. ✓ It contributes to the UN's cross-system work on peacebuilding and human rights.	✗ ECOSOC has no power to compel states to follow its resolutions. ✗ The roles of ECOSOC and the UNGA overlap, causing some confusion about responsibility.
Impact	✓ ECOSOC stimulated global development with the Millennium Development Goals and Sustainable Development Goals. MDG 1 to halve global poverty was achieved five years early in 2010. ✓ Led by ECOSOC, since 2015, the UN has been working in a more coordinated way with external bodies such as the World Bank. ECOSOC promoted a multidimensional concept of human development. This led the World Bank to broaden its understanding of poverty in 2015 when it adopted the SDGs. ✓ ECOSOC responds to criticisms. A 'Co-ordination Segment' was created in 2021 to improve coordination on the Sustainable Development Goals across its subsidiary bodies.	✗ The Millennium Development Goals were only partly achieved by 2014. Since the pandemic, progress on the ambitious 2030 SDGs has been weakened. The climate crisis is escalating, and poverty is increasing. ✗ ECOSOC's coordination has been criticised, and it has no control over independent 'specialised agencies' such as the World Bank, which has its own priorities and still does not use as broad a concept of poverty as the UN. ✗ ECOSOC's many programmes must compete for voluntary contributions from states. The United States and, to a lesser extent, the UK have drastically cut their development aid in 2025, when the need for support is higher than ever. This is making the SDGs more difficult to achieve.

Summary comparison of the main strengths and weaknesses of UN Organs.

	Strengths	Weaknesses
UN General Assembly	Fully inclusive, upholds the principle of sovereign equality, holds moral authority and sets aspirational standards for states.	A bureaucratic 'talking shop' with non-binding resolutions which have no legal authority over states.
UN UNSC	Significant powers of intervention with a streamlined membership that includes major military powers for negotiations in crisis situations.	The veto is used to evade accountability and prevent humanitarian action. The P5 fails to represent the Global South.
International Court of Justice	All member states of the UN can access justice, upholding sovereign equality and the rule of law between states. Judges represent the main legal systems in the world to achieve impartiality.	Minority groups that are not recognised as states cannot access justice for themselves. States do not have to accept jurisdiction, and the court cannot enforce its own rulings.
ECOSOC	Coordinates a huge number of organisations, includes civil society, good progress on some Millennium Development Goals.	Coordination has been criticised, and voluntary funding is insufficient. Progress has faltered on Sustainable Development Goals.

The UN's impact on conflict

> *It has been said that the United Nations was not created in order to bring us to heaven, but in order to save us from hell.*
>
> Secretary-General Dag Hammarskjöld in 1954

In this section we move away from the workings of the UN's organs to address how effective the UN is on its primary aims of maintaining international peace and security and upholding international law.

The work of the UN is governed by the Charter, which aims to uphold state sovereignty and non-intervention, except to maintain international peace and security under Chapter VII.

All UN Organs contribute to peace and security, from law making and conflict prevention to peacebuilding after a conflict.

- **ECOSOC** works to promote human rights, social progress and cooperation, aiming to prevent disputes and conflict.
- Ideally, if a dispute arises. states would use the **International Court of Justice** to resolve it peacefully.
- If tensions escalate, the **UNGA** can pass resolutions condemning conflict and promoting peaceful dialogue.
- If conflict breaks out, the **Secretary-General** can call for a ceasefire and send an envoy to mediate, notifying the UNSC rather than requesting authorisation. This speeds up the process. In recent years, envoys have been sent to numerous difficult conflicts, for example in Yemen, Gaza and Sudan.
- Under Chapters VI and VII, the **UNSC** should restore peace by supporting ceasefire negotiations and a peace agreement, sending peacekeepers or as a last resort, authorising peace enforcement (see Security Council, p. x).
- If the UNSC cannot agree, the **UNGA** 'Uniting for Peace' resolution allows it to authorise peacekeeping – if the main parties in the conflict agree. It has only done this once, in 1956, but has used the resolution to condemn aggression and call for ceasefires numerous times.
- Societies that have been devastated by civil war and atrocities need long-term peacebuilding support to prevent the resurgence of conflict. This is overseen by the UN **Peacebuilding Commission**.

Figure 4.7 United Nations peacekeepers on active missions by type

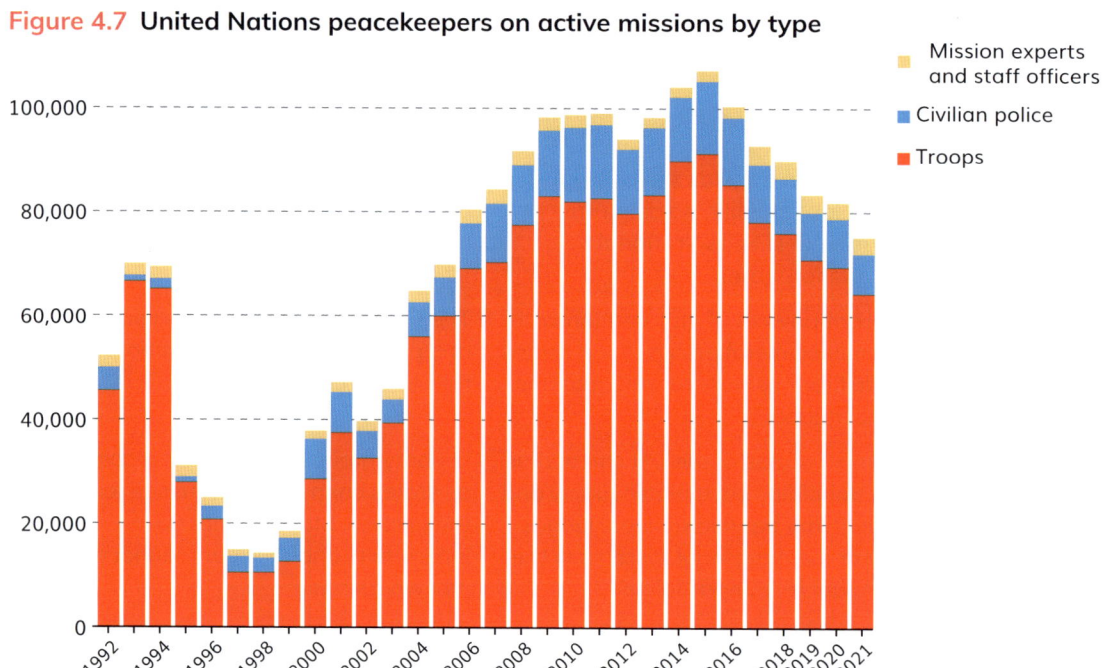

Source: Our World in Data

> **Exam Tip:**
> 'Evaluate the view that the UN provides effective global governance.' You could evaluate:
> 1. Each organ separately, using the individual strengths and weaknesses tables.
> 2. The UN as a whole, using three criteria: equity, authority and impact.
> 3. The UN's impacts on conflict, poverty, human rights and the environment, relating these to the UN's aims.

> **Exam Tip:**
> This section helps you to address the impact of global governance on the specification's overarching theme of conflict. The next three chapters look at the impacts on poverty, human rights and the environment, whilst **Chapter 9, Analysing and Evaluating Governance**, takes an overview of the four themes.

The rise and decline of peacekeeping

In response to the increasing complexity of civil wars, genocide and the failures of the traditional peacekeeping model, in the 1990s, 'multidimensional' and 'robust' peacekeeping were adopted (see Table 4.1). More missions were authorised (see Figure 4.7), and they were more ambitious and more expensive. The UN peacekeeping budget grew from $0.4 billion in 1991 to $8.5 billion in 2014.

No new UN peacekeeping missions have been established since 2014, and by 2022, the budget had declined to $6.45 billion. There are several reasons for this. Some reasons are related to states' willingness to accept peacekeepers:

- Robust peacekeeping has become more difficult due to terrorism and jihadist insurgencies, with increasing attacks on peacekeeping troops, who are then unable to fulfil the mandate of protecting citizens. Mali asked failed UN peacekeeping missions to leave in 2023.
- The UN published a review of peacekeeping in 2020, which acknowledged many reports of violent crimes, sexual exploitation and abuse committed by peacekeepers in the Central African Republic, the Democratic Republic of Congo, Sudan, Haiti, Bosnia and Cambodia. Many were not punished. UN peacekeeping suffered a legitimacy crisis.
- Some conflict-afflicted authoritarian governments have sought military support from Russia instead (see **Case Study: Intervention, Peacekeeping and Peacebuilding in the Sahel**).
- Another example of ineffective peacekeeping can be seen in the Democratic Republic of Congo, where more than 6 million people have died in a series of civil wars since 1996. In 2024, 7 million people were internally displaced in an area the size of Western Europe. DRC's wars have involved many rebel groups, and multiple foreign powers, including Rwanda and Russia. UN peacekeepers have become preoccupied with self-defence, failing to protect civilians and have sometimes abused them. In around 2021, DRC, like Libya, Mali and the Central African Republic, turned to Russia for weapons and military training. The government ordered the ineffective MONUSCO mission to leave in late 2023. In 2025, a minerals-for-security deal was under discussion with the United States.

Other reasons are related to the UN's reluctance to provide peacekeepers:

- Increasing attacks on peacekeepers have made some states reluctant to put their own soldiers in harm's way.
- The UNSC's dysfunctionality has prevented robust action.

In 2021, UN Secretary-General Antonion Guterres initiated peacekeeping reforms. The UN now relies mostly on regional organisations, including the African Union and Economic Community of West African States for peacekeeping missions. The EU also provides financial support, military training and civilian support for the rule of law.

A new focus on peacebuilding

The UN is also doing more peacebuilding. Teams based within fragile states organise long-term projects to build democratic institutions, supervise elections, reintegrate fighters into society and support civil society efforts on reconciliation.

Peacebuilding is a small but increasingly important part of the UN's overall work, overseen by the Peacebuilding Commission since 2006. This includes representation from the UNSC, the UNGA and the ECOSOC. The UN added $50 million to its Peacebuilding Fund in 2023. This is small, but projects are mostly funded by the World Bank, the African Union and the European Union. There have been projects in 26 fragile states.

> **Chapter Link**
>
> See **Chapter 9: The EU and Regionalism** for more detail on how the African Union and the European Union have taken over peacekeeping in Africa on behalf of the UN, and see **Chapter 8: Analysing and Evaluating Global Governance** for a case study on how the UN Peacebuilding Commission coordinates a range of global and regional governance organisations to support fragile post-conflict states.

CASE STUDY: INTERVENTION, PEACEKEEPING AND PEACEBUILDING IN THE SAHEL

Map 4.2 Sahel region: a semi-arid ecological zone (marked in orange)

Context

The Sahel region is a semi-arid area below the Sahara Desert (see Map 4.2), traditionally populated by nomadic livestock herders. After decolonisation by France, Chad, Burkina Faso, Mali, Mauritania and Niger, the formed a group called the 'G5 Sahel'. These states have remote, hard-to-govern borders. The region has long been unstable, with twenty-five military coups from 1960 to 2022.

Civil war erupted in Mali in 2012. The UN Security Council authorised an African Union (AU) intervention, which failed, leading to French intervention in 2013. The UNSC then authorised MINUSMA, a UN peacekeeping mission including African peacekeepers, French counterterrorism forces, and the 'United Nations Integrated Strategy for the Sahel' (UNISS), a peacebuilding operation in collaboration with the Economic Community of West African States (ECOWAS), the AU, the EU and the World Bank. Despite these efforts, conflict continued, with two military coups in 2020 and 2021. The new government hired the Russian paramilitary Wagner Group to combat the terrorist groups, al-Qaeda and ISIS. Coups followed in Burkina Faso and Niger in 2022. ECOWAS suspended the three states.

Why has this happened? The region is highly vulnerable to climate change, with drought devastating agriculture. Livestock moving into cultivated land for food, destroy crops and trigger conflict between herders and farmers. Birth rates remain high due to early marriage for girls, and a population boom has caused high unemployment. Unemployed youth are susceptible to trafficking and insurgent recruitment, spreading instability.

There have been localised successes. For example, in 2021, UNISS set up an early warning system for herd movements and trained village committees to resolve tensions and tackle extremism. This reduced conflict on the Mali-Mauritania border by 80 per cent.

However, broader regional conflict continues. With its counterterrorism forces under increasing attack, France withdrew from Mali in 2022, and from Burkina Faso and Niger in 2023. Mali asked MINUSMA to leave in 2023, frustrated that it prioritised self-defence over civilian protection. In 2024, the three states accused ECOWAS of serving French colonialism, and formed a Russian-backed 'Alliance of Sahelian States'. Russia's new 'Africa Corps' (replacing the defunct Wagner Group) deployed troops in exchange for resources, including uranium, which were historically controlled by France.

Significance

This case study shows how civil wars have become complex and internationalised due to climate change, terrorism and foreign interventions and that P5 involvement, with or without UN authorisation, may be driven by strategic motives. It is a factor driving emigration from the Sahel to wealthier states. It shows that large-scale militarised peacekeeping is not necessarily the best way to build long-term social trust and political legitimacy for sustainable peace.

KEY DEBATE: CAN THE UN EFFECTIVELY RESOLVE CONFLICT, REDUCE POVERTY, PROTECT HUMAN RIGHTS AND THE ENVIRONMENT?

Preventing and resolving conflict

Preventing conflict

- ✅ States can resolve disputes peacefully at the International Court of Justice.
- ❌ Some states refuse to accept the ICJ's jurisdiction: only seventy-four states had signed declarations making jurisdiction compulsory in 2024.

Promoting non-violent resolution

- ✅ The UNSC and the Secretariat use diplomacy and mediation as their first response. The UNSC has authorised seventy-two peacekeeping missions in the Middle East, Africa, Europe and Asia, many from 1991 to 2011.
- ❌ Since 2011, the UNSC has been paralysed by the veto again. It has failed to stop wars in Syria, Sudan, Gaza, Ukraine and more.

Recovering from conflict

- ✅ Peacebuilding in fragile states is a relatively new approach, small-scale but growing. It is locally coordinated, civilian-led and long-term, focusing on building sustainable peace.
- ❌ Many interventions and peacekeeping missions have failed to stabilise conflict zones, such as in Libya, Yemen, the DRC and Mali.

Protecting human rights (see Chapter 6)

The development and promotion of human rights.

- ✅ The Universal Declaration of Human Rights led to a huge body of international human rights law.
- ❌ The UN Human Rights Council scrutinises states on all human rights violations, not just atrocities.

- ✅ The UN International Children's Emergency Fund (UNICEF) and the World Food Programme provide urgent humanitarian aid during crises and natural disasters.

UN peacekeeping has often failed to prevent the worst atrocities.

- ❌ The UNSC peacekeeping mandates in Rwanda and Bosnia were inadequate to prevent or stop genocide.
- ❌ The UNSC has failed to protect millions of civilians in Sudan and Gaza.
- ❌ Military peacekeepers in civil wars have often failed to protect civilians, being preoccupied with self-defence. Some have abused civilians instead of protecting them.

Reducing poverty (see Chapter 5)

Millennium Development Goals

- ✅ MDG 1 'halve extreme poverty' was achieved in 2010, and there was good progress on most goals by 2014.
- ❌ MDG 1 was achieved mainly by China's development, not the UN's work. Although global poverty rates have declined dramatically since the 1990s, the total number of people in poverty in sub-Saharan Africa has increased due to rapid population growth, conflict and climate change.

Sustainable Development Goals

- ✅ The seventeen ambitious SDGs that followed the MDGs set global standards, including ending poverty and hunger, good health and education, gender equality, clean water, clean energy, sustainable cities and climate action. They encouraged the World Bank to take a broader view of human development.
- ❌ In 2024, half of the developing countries had unsustainable debt. Development aid and climate finance are insufficient. There was little progress on poverty and hunger. In 2025, the United States and the UK dramatically cut development aid.

Protecting the environment (see Chapter 7)

Climate action

- ✅ The 2015 Paris Agreement on climate change, negotiated within the United Nations Framework Convention on Climate Change, was a significant step towards the SDG climate action goal.
- ❌ UN climate summits fail to reconcile the interests of developed and developing states – especially the most climate-vulnerable states. Divisions remain on reducing fossil fuel use and climate finance. The UN cannot meet all the needs of developing countries and needs more support from developed states, but this is not forthcoming, as developed states prioritise defence and national interests.

Protecting the natural world

- ✅ The UN created the UN Environment Assembly in 2012 to develop the profile of environmental issues within the UN. The Sustainable Development Goals of 2015–2030 included reducing pollution and protecting biodiversity, forests and oceans alongside climate action.
- ❌ Progress on governance has been outpaced by climate heating, pollution and declining biodiversity.

Key Debate Summary: Can the UN effectively resolve conflict, reduce poverty, protect human rights and the environment?

Key criteria	For	Against
Resolving conflict	✓ The UN has options to prevent conflict, promote non-violent dispute resolution and the power to enforce peace. It works collaboratively on peacebuilding.	✗ States often reject non-violent means of dispute resolution. The UNSC fails to authorise robust actions. Some peacekeeping missions fail to stabilise conflict zones.
Protecting human rights	✓ Creates standards for states to work towards (the Universal Declaration of Human Rights), international law, and public accountability (the UN Human Rights Council).	✗ Humanitarian interventions sometimes fail. Some peacekeepers have abused civilians.
Reducing poverty	✓ MDG 1 'halve extreme poverty' achieved in 2010. Good progress on some MDGs.	✗ MDG 1 achieved mostly in China, not globally. Progress has slowed on Sustainable Development Goals.
Protecting the environment	✓ SDGs created global standards. Paris Agreement 2015 introduced universal targets, monitoring and reporting on carbon emissions.	✗ Damage on climate, biodiversity and pollution is outpacing progress. The need for development aid and climate finance is outpacing supply.

Exam Tip:

The UN's conflict and human rights work overlap, but for conflict, you can include any of conflict prevention by UNGA and the ICJ, mediation, UNSC authorisations, peacekeeping, enforcement and peacebuilding. For human rights, focus on human rights laws and accountability, humanitarian interventions and protecting civilians from abuse.

You could also highlight that these four themes are integrated into the SDGs.

NATO

The North Atlantic Treaty Organisation is a collective security alliance. It is a product of the Cold War between the United States and Western Europe on one side, and the Soviet Union and Eastern Europe on the other. Its headquarters are in Brussels, Belgium.

Membership

Twelve states, including the United States, Canada, the UK and nine Western European states, signed the North Atlantic Treaty in 1949 to establish NATO. It grew significantly after the Cold War, expanding to the east. Finland joined in 2023 and Sweden in 2024, bringing the total to thirty-two members (see Map 4.3).

Decision-making

The main principle in the North Atlantic Treaty is Article 5, which states that an attack on one state will be considered an attack on all members and will be met with a collective response. Article 5 does not require every member to participate in conflict, because, unlike the EU, NATO does not direct the

Map 4.3 NATO enlargement in Europe, 1949-2024.

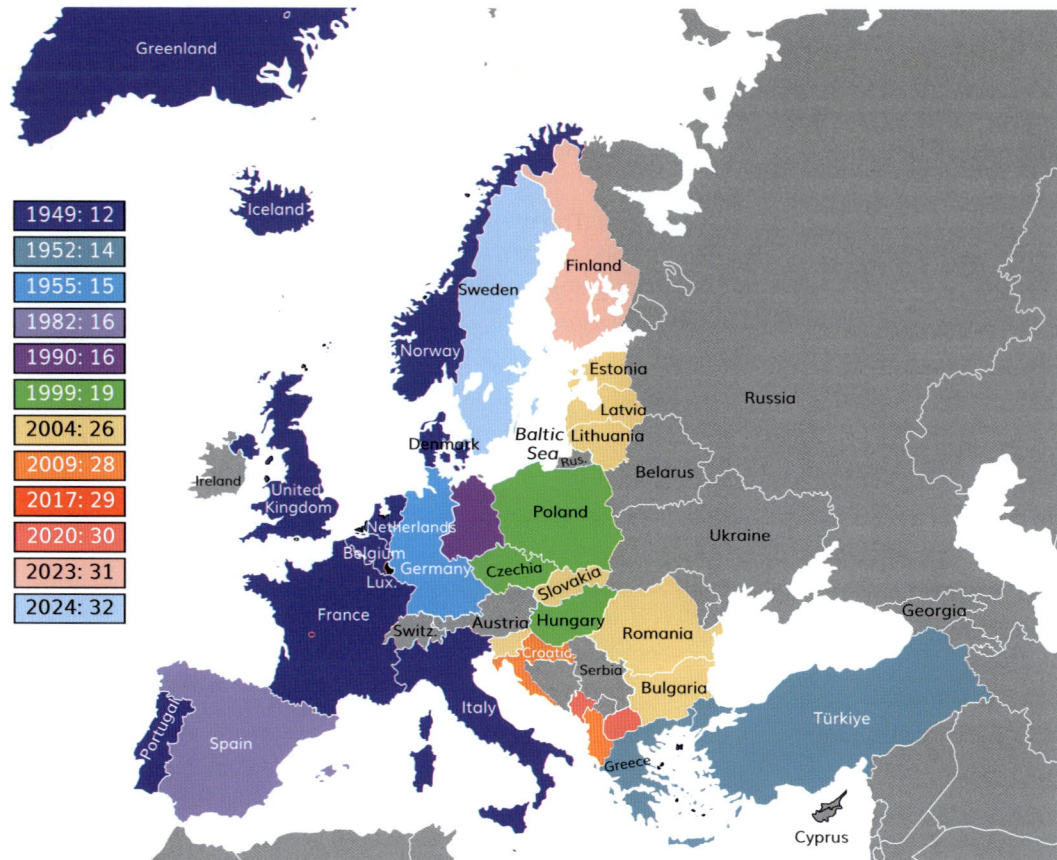

Source: Korwin, 'History of NATO enlargement animation', Wikimedia Commons (2023). Licensed under CC BY-SA 4.0. Membership numbers include USA and Canada, which are not shown on the map

policy of its member states. It is a firmly intergovernmental arrangement which makes decisions by consensus as far as possible. States can opt out of operations, for example Germany opted to provide humanitarian aid instead of participating in a NATO intervention in Libya in 2011. The collective defence purpose of NATO and a desire for consensus explains why the P5 members – the United States, the UK and France usually take on UN Chapter VII enforcement action without wider NATO support, for example in Somalia, Sierra Leone and the Sahel region.

The changing role and significance of NATO

Cold War, 1949–1991

NATO's first Secretary-General, Lord Ismay of the UK, described its role in post-war Europe as being to 'keep the Russians out, the Americans in and the Germans down'. Following the partition of Germany, it formalised the collective defence alliance between the United States and the Western European states, underwritten by US military power.

1955 saw the signing of the 'Warsaw Pact', a Soviet-led counter-balancing security pact with seven Eastern European states. The rivalry between NATO and the Warsaw Pact maintained a balance of power in Europe for four decades.

Post-Cold War, 1991–2001

As the Soviet Union collapsed and relations thawed in 1991, NATO suddenly found itself without a role. From 1992, it took on a new humanitarian intervention and peacekeeping role in the former Yugoslavia (see **Case Studies: NATO in Bosnia** and **Intervention to independence in Kosovo**). Several former communist states in Eastern Europe joined.

CASE STUDY: THE UN AND NATO IN BOSNIA

Context

The Socialist Federal Republic of Yugoslavia collapsed in 1992 after the death of dictator Josip Broz 'Tito'. After a short war, Slovenia declared independence. The more multicultural republics suffered long civil wars: two years in Croatia and three in Bosnia and Herzegovina.

Almost half of Bosnians were Muslims, a third were Serbs, and the rest were mostly Croatian. Muslims and Croats voted for independence, but the Serb minority wanted to stay within Serb-controlled Yugoslavia, which backed the Bosnian Serbs. The UNSC authorised an arms embargo and a NATO no-fly zone, and sent UNPROFOR, a peacekeeping mission to secure 'safe havens' for civilians. However, in July 1995, Bosnian Serb forces overran the safe haven of Srebrenica, abducting 8,000 men and boys from the small town, executing them and concealing the bodies in unmarked mass graves. UN peacekeepers were not permitted to use force to stop the genocide, and despite their frantic requests, the UNSC and NATO took too long to authorise peace enforcement.

Following another massacre in Sarajevo, the Muslim-held capital, which had endured a three-year siege by Bosnian Serbs, NATO launched Operation Deliberate Force in August, bombing Serb military targets to enforce peace. In November, the United States brokered a peace settlement, the 'Dayton Accords', to partition the country, creating an autonomous Serb region and a power-sharing government in the larger multicultural area. The UN authorised NATO to oversee the implementation of the peace agreement and to stay on to maintain peace.

In the 2000s, the United States wanted to redeploy its forces into Iraq and Afghanistan. So, by 2004, the EU's humanitarian EUFOR mission took on the long-term peacebuilding and law enforcement work, whilst, under EU and media pressure, NATO continued to arrest Bosnian war criminals.

Significance

This case shows how traditional peacekeeping failed in Bosnia, prompting NATO's first humanitarian intervention and more robust peacekeeping missions in the future.

It shows how NATO evolved into an international peace enforcer, but also how NATO's European regional stabilisation priorities became dominated by US strategic global goals.

It also shows how NATO missions differ from the EU's humanitarian and peacebuilding approach.

CASE STUDY: FROM INTERVENTION TO INDEPENDENCE IN KOSOVO

Context

In 1989, Slobodan Milosevic became president of Serbia, aiming to retain Serb dominance in the Socialist Federal Republic of Yugoslavia. Kosovo, a majority-Albanian province, was taken under Serb control in 1990. In 1995, the Kosovo Liberation Army began attacking Serb police. By February 1998, Milosevic began a campaign against Kosovo's ethnic Albanians.

UNSC resolutions in 1998 imposed a weapons embargo, demanded a ceasefire, access for monitoring missions and cooperation with the International Criminal Tribunal for the Former Yugoslavia (ICTY). NATO threatened air strikes on Serbia if Milosevic did not comply. He agreed to a temporary ceasefire and allowed observers in, but they withdrew in early 1999, fearful for their own safety. Genocide followed, and hundreds of thousands of refugees fled to neighbouring countries.

NATO proposed the 'Rambouillet Agreement', which would require Serbia to accept armed NATO peacekeeping forces with immunity from Yugoslav law. Milosevic rejected it.

With Russia threatening a veto, NATO leaders considered intervening without UNSC approval. The situation worsened, so NATO launched 'Operation Allied Force' in March 1999, with air strikes on Belgrade. Russia condemned this for undermining Serbia's sovereignty and attempted a resolution to stop it, but was outvoted by twelve members. In April 1999, UK Prime Minister Tony Blair justified the action on both humanitarian grounds and in the interests of regional stability and security, asserting that 'genocide can never be a purely internal matter'.

The P5 dispute was resolved in private by foreign ministers at a G8 summit, paving the way for a UNSC resolution. In June 1999, they authorised a UN-run interim government (United Nations Interim Administration Mission in Kosovo (UNMIK)). It was agreed that NATO would continue to maintain peace (KFOR) and that reconstruction would be funded by the EU.

Kosovo declared independence in February 2008, and UNMIK was replaced by an independent government, whilst the EU helped to maintain the rule of law (EULEX). Serbia said that Kosovo's Declaration of Independence contravened the Serbian constitution. The UNSC was divided again, with Russia supporting Serbia, whilst the United States, the UK and France supported Kosovo. Serbia, through the UNGA, requested an advisory opinion from the International Court of Justice. The court advised that international law did not cover declarations of independence. By April 2025, Kosovo was recognised by 108 states, including most, but not all NATO and EU members. It was not a UN member state.

Significance

There is debate over whether it is legitimate for NATO to conduct a military intervention without UNSC authorisation, as it did at first with Operation Allied Force. The position of the United States was that NATO did not require a UN mandate to act, whereas France argued that it did.

Like Bosnia, this case study shows how the UN relies on other organisations for peace enforcement (NATO: KFOR), support for the rule of law (EULEX) and long-term peacebuilding activities, including reconstruction (EU) and truth and accountability (ICTY).

Expansion and global role, 2001–2011

In 2001, Article 5 was invoked for the first time, to defend US airspace after the 9/11 attacks. In 2004, NATO welcomed Russia's neighbours, Estonia, Latvia and Lithuania, with Georgia also expressing interest. Relations with Russia deteriorated. In 2008, NATO supported Kosovo's independence, ignoring Serbia and Russia's objections. Russia intervened in Georgia, perhaps in retaliation.

NATO supported African Union missions in Sudan (2005) and Somalia (2007). In 2008, it launched a counter-piracy operation to protect ships carrying UN humanitarian food supplies from Somali pirate raids.

Rising tensions, 2011–2021

In 2011, NATO was authorised by the UNSC to impose a 'no-fly zone' in Libya. The intervention resulted in the death of Libya's dictator and the collapse of the state, worsening Russia–NATO relations. Russia annexed Crimea in 2014, prompting NATO to triple its response force, sending enhanced battlegroups to the Baltic states to deter direct aggression.

NATO members are required to spend 2 per cent of GDP on defence; however, by 2016, only four European members met this goal, leading President Trump to criticise Germany and threaten NATO withdrawal. In 2018, Russian agents' Novichok poisonings in the UK resulted in NATO expelling Russian diplomats.

In 2021, President Biden honoured a Trump-Taliban deal to withdraw from Afghanistan, leading to a botched exit, the Taliban's return, a humanitarian crisis and anger within NATO.

War in Europe, 2022 onwards

The Ukraine war has returned NATO's focus to collective defence and deterrence, with an increased military presence in Eastern Europe and massive military and humanitarian aid to Ukraine. Ukraine applied to join NATO, which was agreed in principle, but not before the end of the war. Russia's demands included Ukraine committing not to join.

In 2023, the Stockholm International Peace Research Institute found that NATO accounted for 55 per cent of global military spending. It is, by far, the most significant military alliance in the world, as long as the United States and Europe remain united.

Controversies over NATO's changing role

Legitimacy of humanitarian interventions

The United States has argued that consensus within NATO on humanitarian grounds provides legitimacy for intervention, as it did in Kosovo, whilst France has argued that intervention requires multilateral agreement from the UNSC.

Furthermore, despite giving UNSC authorisation for intervention in Libya, Russia and China argued that because NATO's no-fly zone weakened Gaddafi's forces to the extent that rebels were able to assassinate him, NATO, in effect, allowed regime change, overreaching the UN's humanitarian mandate.

Changing relationship with Russia

The NATO–Russia relationship was relatively stable in the 1990s. This was tested by NATO's intervention in Kosovo in 1999 (see case study). Realist theorist John Mearsheimer argued that NATO expansion was the cause of rising tension. President Putin justified invading Ukraine as a response to NATO expansion:

> *There were promises to our country not to expand NATO even one inch to the east. I repeat – they deceived us.*
>
> President Putin, 24 February 2022

However, NATO disputed that claim:

> *He wanted us to sign that promise, never to enlarge NATO. He wanted us to remove our military infrastructure in all Allies that have joined NATO since 1997, meaning half of NATO ... We rejected that.*
>
> Jens Stoltenberg, NATO Secretary-General, September 2023

European 'free riders' and declining US commitment

Successive US presidents have criticised Europe's lack of commitment to defence spending, but did not waver on their commitment to collective defence. President Trump changed that, casting doubt on US commitment:

> *You didn't pay, you're delinquent. I would not protect you. In fact, I would encourage them to do whatever the hell they want. You got to pay.*
>
> Donald Trump, February 2024

President Biden reaffirmed the US commitment:

> *NATO stands more united, determined, and dynamic than ever—now 32 nations strong. Our shared democratic values—and our willingness to stand up for them—is what makes NATO the greatest military alliance in the history of the world.*
>
> US President Joe Biden, March 2024

By 2024, twenty states had committed to spending at least 2 per cent of GDP, but in 2025, the US ambassador to NATO demanded 5 per cent, with 3.5 per cent on defence and 1.5 per cent on intelligence and infrastructure. NATO's leader, Mark Rutte, proposed to achieve this by 2032. Whilst European leaders are taking a realist view that they can no longer depend on the United States, they would like to maintain the transatlantic alliance if at all possible.

Table 4.2 NATO Strengths and Weaknesses

	Strengths	Weaknesses
Collective defence of Europe	NATO is a hugely powerful collective defence alliance, which maintains a state of constant readiness. It accounts for 55 per cent of global military spending. Almost 70 per cent of that is spent by the United States. The war in Ukraine has prompted a strengthening of the alliance with stronger commitments and higher defence spending. It provides a huge boost to the security of more vulnerable Eastern European and Baltic states.	European states have become reliant on US power and skimped on their own defence commitments. US presidents have criticised freeloading by states who have not met the required 2 per cent defence spending, in particular Germany, although this has recently changed. Trump has undermined European trust in US commitment. John Mearsheimer has argued that NATO expansion provoked Russia into war in Ukraine. Putin has also made this claim.
Shared values and interests	Almost all members share commitment to the values of liberal democracy, which encourage cooperation and strengthen states' commitment to the alliance.	Some members have diverging values and interests. Turkey has been criticised for its poor human rights and democracy, and has acted against US interests in Syria. Turkey also delayed Sweden's membership over protection of Kurdish refugees.

	Strengths	Weaknesses
Humanitarian and counter-piracy role	Successful intervention and peacekeeping helped to bring peace to Bosnia and Kosovo. Counter-piracy operations around the Horn of Africa succeeded in protecting World Food Programme shipments bound for the region.	NATO intervention resulted in Libya collapsing into a failed state, allowing ISIS and al-Qaeda to spread across North Africa and into the Sahel region, causing long-term instability. The chaotic withdrawal of the United States from Afghanistan in 2021 forced NATO allies to withdraw, allowing the Taliban to return to power.

Comparative Analysis: NATO and the UNSC

	NATO	UNSC
Structure and authority	NATO is not a representative body; it works on consensus and does not hold supranational authority in international law.	The UNSC is partly representative, has a two-tier voting system (with P5 veto) and does have supranational authority in international law.
Significance for global peace and security	NATO emphasises regional collective defence but broadened its role to humanitarianism after the Cold War. NATO is a hegemonic military alliance: in 2024, it accounted for around 55 per cent of global military spending.	The UNSC is partly elected by the UNGA's almost universal membership and seeks international cooperation. The UNSC has definitive authority over member states and can call on them to take military action but has no military power of its own.
Controversies and criticisms	NATO's focus on regional defence displays state egoism but its humanitarian interventions have also been motivated by liberal values. There have been debates in NATO over whether it must operate within the legitimacy of a UNSC mandate (France said yes, the United States said no). Russia has objected to NATO expansion and interventions.	After the Cold War, the UNSC became more cooperative for around a decade, until Russia objected to NATO expansion and pursued unilateral interventions instead of multilateral cooperation. The UNSC became dysfunctional again from around 2011.

KEY DEBATE: DOES POLITICAL GLOBAL GOVERNANCE FAIL TO MAINTAIN PEACE AND SECURITY?

Scale and types of conflicts

✓ The UN was established to prevent a third world war, and it has succeeded so far, even during the tense Cold War.

✓ Since 1945, inter-state wars have been relatively infrequent and despite superpower interventions, none have escalated into global conflicts.

✗ Realists would argue that this relative Cold War stability was not due primarily to the UN, but to the balance of power between the superpowers. The inter-state Russia–Ukraine war has caused instability, with NATO supporting a proxy war in Ukraine.

Map 4.4 Countries where armed conflicts took place in 2022

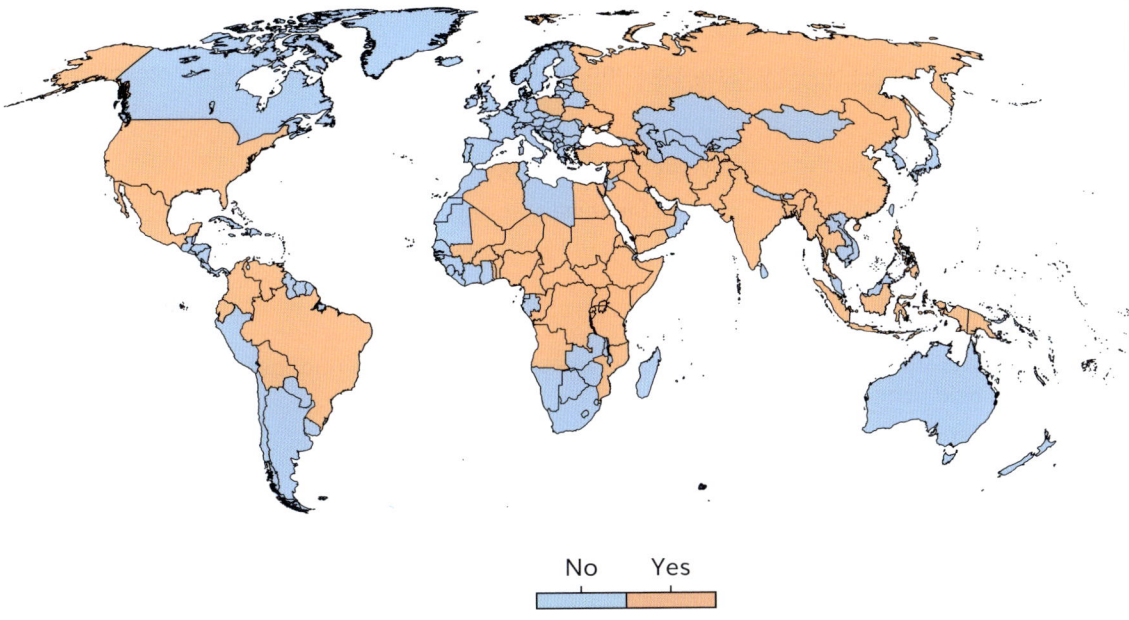

No   Yes

Source: Our World in Data, 'Locations of ongoing armed conflicts', CC BY. Retrieved from https://ourworldindata.org/grapher/locations-of-ongoing-armed-conflicts

- ❌ The world has become much more dangerous with the decline of US hegemonic power since the 2010s (see Map 4.4). According to the Global Peace Index, in 2024, there were fifty-three conflicts between states and non-state actors. These are prone to foreign interventions, which can prolong conflict (e.g. Libya, Syria).

Ability to agree collective action (UNSC veto)

Cold War

- ✅ During the Cold War, the UN authorised peacekeeping missions to Palestine, India and Cyprus and a military intervention in the Korean War.
- ❌ The UNSC did not prevent or resolve proxy wars, e.g. in Vietnam or Afghanistan.

Post-Cold War

- ✅ The UNSC cooperated on the 1991 Gulf War and on weapons inspections in Iraq.
- ❌ Since 2011, it has become dysfunctional again on Syria, Gaza and Ukraine. There have been no new peacekeeping missions since 2014. The UNSC has failed to protect the Rohingya of Myanmar, the Uighurs of China and civilians in Ethiopia and Sudan.

UN peacekeeping and peacebuilding efforts

- ✅ After failing to protect civilians from genocide in Rwanda and Bosnia, the UN reformed peacekeeping to include 'multidimensional peacekeeping' and 'robust peacekeeping'.
- ❌ UN peacekeeping still failed to protect civilians. Governments in Mali and in the DRC both ordered ineffective long-term peacekeeping missions to leave in 2023. Peacekeepers left Sudan in 2020, 13 years after genocide in Darfur, but widespread attacks on civilians started again in 2023.
- ✅ The UN has shifted its priorities towards civilian peacebuilding projects to help fragile post-conflict states avoid relapsing into conflict. These oversee disarmament, fund reconstruction, reintegrate soldiers into society and support reconciliation efforts.
- ❌ Despite fifty-three active civil wars in the world, in 2024 the UN had only eleven active UN peacekeeping operations, with a peacekeeping budget of just over $6 billion – less than

0.25 per cent of global military spending. The peacebuilding budget is much smaller again, with only $50 million in ringfenced funding.

NATO's contribution to resolving conflict

Stability in Europe

- ✅ NATO has maintained the collective defence of Europe since 1949.
- ❌ However, it has been claimed by John Mearsheimer and Vladimir Putin that NATO's eastward expansion after the Cold War provoked the Ukraine war.

Wider humanitarian and counter-terror roles

- ✅ NATO successfully intervened in Bosnia, where UN peacekeepers had failed. It also intervened and achieved peace in Kosovo.
- ✅ It helped to stabilise Afghanistan and root out al-Qaeda, which had been sheltered by the Taliban.
- ✅ It successfully eliminated piracy against World Food Programme shipments around the Horn of Africa and has supported African Union missions in Sudan and Somalia.
- ❌ NATO failed to rein in the US 'War on Terror', creating the conditions for ISIS to form in Iraq, and it failed to stabilise Libya, allowing ISIS and al-Qaeda to expand across North Africa.
- ❌ NATO's legitimacy as a military enforcer of global peace and security has been questioned, and it has not engaged in any new military interventions.
- ❌ The botched withdrawal from Afghanistan by the United States forced NATO partners to withdraw suddenly too, creating a humanitarian crisis and allowing the Taliban to regain control.

Key Debate Summary: Does political global governance fail to maintain peace and security?

	For	Against
Scale of conflicts	✓ There has been no third world war and inter-state wars are relatively infrequent since 1944.	✗ Intra-state wars are more common, more complex, more difficult to end. Terrorism and insurgency have increased.
Ability to agree collective action (UNSC veto)	✓ Seventy-two peacekeeping missions and some interventions have been authorised. Cooperation was possible in the 1990s but declined after 2011.	✗ The UNSC has often been paralysed by veto, particularly on the Middle East (Syria, Israel, Palestine) and Ukraine.
UN peacekeeping and peacebuilding	✓ The UN has reformed peacekeeping over the years, with an increased focus on long-term peacebuilding.	✗ No new missions since 2014. Peacekeeping still frequently fails to protect civilians, and foreign states have intervened.
NATO's contribution to resolving conflict	✓ The world's most powerful military alliance has succeeded in stabilising Bosnia, Kosovo and in countering piracy.	✗ Eastwards expansion and botched interventions have not helped to calm tensions with Russia. US commitment has been questioned.

Exam Tip:

Students tend to emphasise high-profile failures. The UN aims to maintain international peace and security, and clearly, it has not fully achieved this. But perhaps a fairer standard to apply would be whether the UN can provide a forum for states to resolve conflict if they are prepared to do so, and that it learns from experience, reforming and strengthening what it does.

Chapter Summary

- The UN was created to bring peace and security, uphold international law, protect human rights and promote development, and it has since added environmental protection to those aims.
- It is a primarily intergovernmental organisation that seeks to uphold state sovereignty, with the exception of the use of force to maintain peace.
- The UNSC is dysfunctional because it is dominated by great powers that use the veto with impunity.
- The UNGA is inclusive and has moral authority, but has no legally binding authority over states.
- The International Court of Justice provides a valuable dispute resolution process but is similarly limited by a lack of enforcement power.
- ECOSOC does valuable work in including many non-state voices, but manages a large, complicated and underfunded system.
- The world is becoming more dangerous, and UN peacekeeping is often ineffective. Regional organisations are taking on peacekeeping roles, and the UN is shifting towards peacebuilding.
- NATO is a powerful regional collective defence alliance which provides military force for UN interventions, but it sometimes acts without a UN mandate, causing controversy.

Exam Style Questions

- Examine the main controversies relating to the International Court of Justice and the General Assembly. (12)
- Examine the strengths of ECOSOC and the UN General Assembly. (12)
- Examine the different roles and significance of the United Nations Security Council and NATO. (12)
- Examine the changing role of NATO during and after the Cold War. (12)
- Evaluate the view that the United Nations Security Council veto can help to maintain peace. (30)
- Evaluate the view that it is not possible to reform the United Nations Security Council. (30)
- Evaluate the view that the United Nations is able to effectively resolve conflict, reduce poverty, protect human rights and the environment. (30)
- Evaluate the view that political global governance fails to maintain peace and security. (30)

Further Resources

The Council on Foreign Relations provides articles on the UN and NATO.

The United Nations website can be overwhelming, but these are useful overviews:

https://www.un.org/en/about-us/main-bodies. UN Organs.

https://www.un.org/en/about-us/history-of-the-un. Historical overview.

https://www.un.org/en/about-us/un-system. The wider UN system.

https://peacekeeping.un.org/en/our-history. The history of peacekeeping.

https://www.un.org/sustainabledevelopment/sdg-fast-facts/. Sustainable development.

Foreign Affairs Magazine and *Foreign Policy* – the *Global Magazine of News and Ideas* are very useful for students who are interested in regular further reading on international relations from a US perspective. *Foreign Affairs* gives limited access to one article per month. *Foreign Policy* requires registration for a weekly newsletter, or a subscription.

The **Foreign Affairs Interview.** https://www.foreignaffairs.com/podcasts/foreign-affairs-interview is a free podcast, interviewing experts and academics on topics from the magazine.

The **Conflicted** podcast (available on usual platforms) is hosted by an ex-al-Qaeda jihadi-turned-MI6 agent, who analyses the global implications of fundamentalism and wars.

Visit https://bloomsbury.pub/essentials-of-global-politics to access additional materials to support teaching and learning.

5 ECONOMIC GLOBAL GOVERNANCE

Chapter Preview

The 1944 'Bretton Woods System' was created by the United States and its European trading partners to set up a stable rules-based trading system. It brought huge economic prosperity to the United States and Europe.

In the 1960s, newly independent states were encouraged to join this system. Some benefited, but many did not, creating a 'North–South divide'. The economic turbulence of the 1970s pushed many states in the Global South into debt crisis. Dependency theorists argued that the system was rigged against developing states. The Bretton Woods Institutions disagreed, saying their underdevelopment was due to overspending in state-run economies. They offered loans to states in crisis. These came with Structural Adjustment Programmes (SAPs): strict free-market reforms that increased poverty and inequality.

In 2000, the UN agreed eight Millennium Development Goals, and then in 2005, the G8 agreed to cancel the debts of the poorest states. Globalisation and economic reforms created rapid growth and reduced extreme poverty in China and India. However, globalisation also allowed economic crises to spread rapidly. In response, a new 'G20' group emerged to lead the governance system. Since 2020, a 'poly-crisis' of pandemic, conflict and climate shocks has created spiralling inflation and a renewed debt crisis: worsening global instability and testing the system's resilience as never before. Global South demands for system reform have grown louder and more insistent.

This chapter will analyse and evaluate the responses of states and IGOs to these problems, asking whether they have been effective enough in resolving crises and sharing prosperity, and asking also whether and how the system should be reformed.

Key Questions and Debates

- » What is economic global governance?
- » How can governance promote economic stability and growth?
- » How can governance reduce poverty and inequality?
- » Is there a North–South divide?
- » What are the aims, roles, significance, strengths and weaknesses of the economic IGOs?
- » Have economic IGOs reformed in response to crisis and criticism from civil society?
- » What are the views of liberals, realists and neo-Marxists on economic global governance?
- » Is economic global governance effective?

Specification Checklist

2.2 Economic Global Governance

2.2.1 International Monetary Fund (IMF) and the World Bank

- » Role and significance of these institutions, including their strengths and weaknesses

2.2.2 The World Trade Organisation (WTO) and G7/G8 and G20

- » Role and significance of these institutions, including their strengths and weaknesses

2.2.3 Significance of how economic global governance deals with the issue of poverty, including:

- » The North–South divide and other measurements to include world systems theory, dependency, orthodox and alternative measurements of poverty
- » Classical economic development theory, structural theory, neoclassical development theory

2.3 The ways and extent to which these institutions address and resolve contemporary global issues, such as those involving conflict, poverty, human rights and the environment

2.3.1 In particular, to focus on how the following prevents the IMF and World Bank from effectively addressing and resolving the issues above

- » pressure for reform and criticism, including Structural Adjustment Programmes (SAPs), global economic crisis

2.3.2 The role and significance of the global civil society and non-state actors, including non-governmental organisations (NGOs) in addressing and resolving the issues above

Source: Matt Cardy/Getty Images News via Getty Images

Introducing economic global governance

What is economic global governance?

The term economic global governance encompasses **actors** such as IGOs, states and non-state actors (see Figure 5.1); **processes** such as international meetings and voting systems, and **decisions** such as international agreements. It is a liberal concept, based on three main ideas:

- Interdependence: states can become interdependent, peaceful and prosperous by trading freely with one another.
- Institutions: they need institutions to create a stable, rules-bound trading system.
- Equality of opportunity: some states need support to develop and to access the benefits of the trading system.

> **Definition**
>
> **Trade barriers:** These include tariffs that tax imported goods and services, quotas that limit imports or exports and state subsidies that protect industries from external competitors.

The Bretton Woods System

In 1944, the United States and its capitalist European allies met in Bretton Woods, New Hampshire, to establish a new international economic order (see Photo 5.2). They recognised that putting up **trade barriers** during the Great Depression of the 1930s had created more problems than solutions. Worse, they had severely impacted Germany's economy, contributing to the rise of the Nazis. The United States wanted to create a stable global economy based on free trade. Devastated by war debt and in need of support, Europe and Japan had little bargaining power. It was clear that

Photo 5.1 English economist John Maynard Keynes attends the United Nations International Monetary and Financial Conference in July 1944.

the United States would dominate the system, giving itself the **structural power** to veto major decisions.

How did the Bretton Woods System work?

The system included two institutions and a treaty:

- **International Bank for Reconstruction and Development (IBRD)**: Initially aimed at reconstructing Europe, IBRD evolved into a global development bank (the World Bank) that sourced foreign investment and provided loans and advice to developing countries. In 1960, it created the International Development Association (IDA) to support the poorest nations.
- **International Monetary Fund (IMF)**: Based in Washington DC, the IMF maintained stable currency exchange rates and provided emergency bailout loans. It was underpinned by the US dollar 'gold standard', which meant that most international trade was conducted in dollars. That gave the United States considerable powers over the trading system. British economist John Maynard Keynes had proposed a neutral currency but was overruled.
- **General Agreement on Trade and Tariffs (GATT)**: GATT was a 1947 treaty providing rules to liberalise international trade by reducing tariffs.

The evolution of the contemporary economic global governance system

In the United States, decades of high spending caused inflation to rise. In 1971, the government was forced to abandon its 'gold standard' guarantee of the dollar's exchange value. This meant that exchange rates between different currencies fluctuated as they were bought and sold, as they do today. It left the IMF, which had overseen the fixed exchange rate system, without a job. It was the end of the post-war Bretton Woods System.

Fluctuating global currencies meant greater economic risks at times of global crisis. In 1973, Arab oil-producing states stopped exporting oil to the United States because it had provided Israel with weapons for the Arab Israeli wars. This caused oil prices to spike, triggering a global recession. Many developing states had borrowed heavily from global banks and could not repay their debts.

The leaders of the United States, the UK, France, Germany and Japan met in the White House library in 1973 to discuss how to maintain global economic stability without fixed exchange rates. These five called themselves the 'Library Group'. With the addition of Canada and Italy, by 1975, they became a 'Group of 7' or G7. They met annually to coordinate their economic policies.

By 1978, the IMF had a new role: monitoring the new system of fluctuating exchange rates, providing crisis loans and advising on currency policies. By the 1980s, the Bretton Woods Institutions (World Bank and IMF) adopted a neoliberal approach to development called the Washington Consensus. This rapidly accelerated economic globalisation, but also increased global poverty and debt.

By the 1990s, the increasingly complex global economy needed to be governed more effectively. In 1995, a World Trade Organisation was set up to oversee GATT, managing trade negotiations and disputes. In 1999, the G20 emerged: a group of major economies that met regularly to coordinate their economies to maintain global stability and respond to crises.

Following sustained criticism from civil society, in 2000 the Bretton Woods Institutions developed a more flexible Post-Washington Consensus, which was more focused on poverty reduction and good governance. The IMF continued to give crisis loans, whilst the World Bank focused more on longer-term development in poor states. This system remains.

What are the contemporary aims of economic global governance?

- **From 1944: Promoting economic stability and growth:** maintaining a predictable global economy to encourage trade and increase prosperity.
- **From 1960: Reducing extreme poverty:** helping more people to access basic living standards.
- **From 2015: Sustainable development:** reducing social and economic inequalities and promoting growth whilst protecting the environment.

Definition

Gold Standard: The United States guaranteed to exchange dollars for gold at a fixed rate, so that businesses could use it with confidence for international trade.

Tariff: A tax or duty imposed by a government on imported or exported goods, intended to protect domestic industries, control trade flows or generate revenue.

Definition

Bretton Woods Institutions and System: The IMF and World Bank are Bretton Woods Institutions. Along with GATT they formed the Bretton Woods System.

The Washington Consensus: Was a set of policy ideas emphasising market liberalisation, fiscal discipline and structural reforms imposed by the IMF and World Bank.

Component III: Global Politics

Definition

Civil society: The collective term for organisations, networks, movements and individual activists that scrutinise, advise and lobby states and IGOs. It does not include businesses.

The Post-Washington Consensus: Replaced SAPs with more flexible 'Poverty Reduction Strategy Papers' (PRSPs).

Good governance: Is effective, transparent, accountable and responsive government, that upholds the rule of law, combats corruption and protects democracy and social justice.

Chapter Link

ECOSOC is covered in **Chapter 4: Political Global Governance** but can be included in essays on poverty reduction. Emerging economies are covered in **Chapter 3: Power and Developments**, but the BRICS forum can be included in essays in this topic to highlight the need – and the failure – to reform representation in the institutions.

Figure 5.1 Main economic global governance organisations: Spec key terms and definitions

Institutions
Formal multilateral organisations with constitutional rules on membership and decision-making, and a permanent location and staff

International Monetary Fund (IMF)*
Established in 1944, lends money to states in an economic crisis, provides surveillance and forecasting to help to prevent and contain crises.

World Bank*
Established in 1944, sources finance for development from private investors and donor states and provides low-cost loans and aid to developing countries.

World Trade Organization (WTO)
Established as an institution in 1995 to support the General Agreement on Trade and Tariffs (1947). Provides a forum for states to negotiate trade rules and resolve trade disputes.

ECOSOC
Established in 1945, 54-member council that oversees the UN system's work on the Sustainable Development Goals. It coordinates with the IMF, World Bank, WTO, states and civil society.

Forums
Informal organisations, with flexible ways of working, regular summit meetings and channels of communication between governments but no permanent location or staff.

G7
A forum set up in 1975 by leaders of the seven largest liberal democratic capitalist states. The EU joined later. They cooperate on trade, aid, climate crisis, terrorism, conflict, etc.

G20
Originally a forum for finance ministers of the 19 largest economies and the EU, set up in 1999 to co-ordinate economic, financial and trade policies. Since the 2009 global financial crisis, state leaders meet annually. It is the most powerful global economic body.

BRICS
A forum for emerging economies. Brazil, Russia, India, China and South Africa set in 2009. Iran, UAE, Ethiopia and Egypt joined in 2023. BRICS is a loose economic cooperation forum that aims to counter the influence of the G7 in global governance.

ECOSOC and the BRICS are addressed elsewhere in the specification but have links to this topic.

How do economic global governance organisations aim to achieve these goals?

- **A rules-based trading environment:** Stability and predictability should encourage businesses to trade and invest internationally, stimulating economic growth. The World Trade Organisation's job is to reduce tariffs and resolve disputes.

- **Managing globalised risk:** In a highly interconnected global economy, a crisis in one state can have unpredictable ripple effects. Global coordination helps to manage those risks. The IMF tries to predict and avert crises and help states recover. The G20 step in when needed to help the IMF to steer the global economy away from potential disasters.

- **Investment for development:** Investors can use their capital internationally to generate profit and – it is hoped – help poorer countries to develop. The World Bank promotes investment for development.

- **Reducing poverty:** The IMF and World Bank support poor states in crisis. The World Bank advises on poverty reduction strategies in developing countries and provides low-cost finance and aid for development. The G7 has helped the World Bank with debt cancellation.

- **Sustainable, inclusive growth:** Shared growth in developing countries can support political stability, reducing internal conflict and irregular migration, which is a policy challenge for wealthy states. Inspired by the UN's Sustainable Development Goals, the World Bank now aims for environmentally and socially sustainable development, but it has some way to go.

How states achieve economic growth and stability

The global economy is made up of deeply interconnected national economies. To understand how economic global governance promotes global growth and stability, it is therefore useful to understand how individual states promote growth and stability, and why they might need help at times. Some of the basics of this are addressed in Component 1: Core Political ideas.

How can a state promote economic growth?

A developed economy requires infrastructure such as roads, railways, ports, energy and communications systems. Social democrats argue that these should be provided by a mix of state and private investment. In contrast, classical (liberal) economists want to minimise the role of the state, allowing private investors to compete to meet these needs for greater efficiency. They advise reducing taxes and regulations on businesses to encourage them to invest.

How can a state promote economic stability?

Almost all states allow some free-market activity. Free-market economies experience cycles of expansion (growth) and contraction (recessions). Economic cycles are influenced by factors including:

- levels of inflation (price increases),
- demand (spending),
- employment,
- fiscal policy (government tax, spending and debt),
- external 'shocks' (global economic crises and natural disasters).

Managing inflation for stability

Monetarist economists argue that the government's main job is to vary interest rates – the cost of borrowing – to manage inflation. Uncontrolled inflation increases living costs and devalues savings.

Managing demand and employment for stability and growth

Keynesian economists argue that the state should aim to manage the ups and downs of the economic cycle. A global economy means that recessions can quickly spread between states. During a recession, a state government should stimulate growth by investing in infrastructure projects to create jobs. This generates a 'multiplier effect': employed people spend more. Higher spending and new infrastructure both support businesses in growing and creating more jobs. The government's investment is rewarded with more tax income, and it can then spend more in future.

Government fiscal policy and sovereign debt

When a business struggles, its share price drops as shareholders sell. If a country faces sudden economic instability, investors may remove their money to safer investments in other countries. Therefore, all governments must carefully balance their fiscal policy: their tax and spending. If a state increases public spending without raising taxes to a similar level, it has a 'budget deficit' and, over time, can get into debt. There are two types of debt: long-term loans to stimulate growth, which are generally seen as positive if it is not too high, and short-term loans to help balance the budget or get through a crisis, which are seen as risky.

All governments borrow long-term fixed-interest loans called 'bonds' to stimulate growth. These are traded by investors in global 'bond markets'. The fixed-interest rate that a government will pay on any new bonds depends on whether investors see it as high or low risk now. Governments that 'balance the budget' and borrow mostly for long-term growth are seen as low risk – likely to repay their debts. This keeps their bond interest rates low. States with large budget deficits or debts are high-risk. They pay more interest and can struggle to find investors.

The impact of global 'shocks' and financial markets

In an emergency, such as when global energy prices spiked in 2022, a government may need to take emergency fiscal measures to protect its own people. UK Prime Minister Liz Truss imposed a cap on energy prices, massively increasing government spending, and at the same time announced tax cuts. She did not publish plans to repay the emergency spending. Investors in bond markets became concerned that the UK would become unable to repay its debts. UK bond interest rates shot up, with knock-on effects across the economy. Events like this show that governments must try to balance their budgets if they want to borrow from global financial markets, even in a global emergency.

How the World Bank and IMF help states with growth and stability

The World Bank helps with long-term development finance: The World Bank helps poor states that struggle in bond markets. It offers fiscal advice, guarantees loan repayments and supports the poorest states with loans and aid.

The IMF provides short-term crisis finance: If a state borrows too much, or if interest rates go up suddenly, it may experience a 'debt crisis'. In this situation, the IMF can step in as 'lender of last resort' with a crisis loan and support to stabilise the economy. This is called a 'bailout'.

The IMF manages globalised crises: If banks do not lend carefully enough, they can collapse, and because the global banking system is highly interconnected, if one bank collapses, others may follow. The IMF monitors and stabilises this global financial system, with support from the G20. They aim to prevent a recurrence of the Global Financial Crisis of 2007–9 and the Eurozone crisis of 2010–15.

Poverty and development

Reducing poverty has been a goal for the UN since 1945 and the World Bank since 1960. In 1990, 38 per cent of the world's population lived in extreme poverty. In 2000, the UN Millennium Development Goals committed to halving extreme poverty. By 2010, rapid globalisation and Chinese development achieved this goal five years ahead of schedule. Optimism soared. The World Bank's 2013 goals and the UN's 2015 Sustainable Development Goals both aim to end extreme poverty by 2030. By 2018, extreme poverty fell to 8.7 per cent, but progress has slowed since the pandemic. The estimated rate was 8.5 per cent in 2024. While globalisation lifted many in Asia out of poverty, most of those in extreme poverty now are in sub-Saharan Africa. Economic governance appears to be failing these regions. We need to uncover the reasons behind this.

Definitions of poverty, inequality and development

Poverty can be narrowly defined as low income or more broadly as access to services such as clean water, education and healthcare.

- **Absolute poverty** means being unable to meet basic living standards.

- However, how those standards are judged, and the income needed to reach them, varies widely between households and places, so sometimes the concept of **relative poverty** can be useful. In developed countries, the relative poverty rate is often set at 60 per cent of the median national income.

Relative poverty is one element of **inequality**: systematic patterns of advantage and disadvantage between individuals, social groups and states in incomes, wealth and opportunities.

Development involves progress towards higher living standards and well-being. Again, it can be conceptualised narrowly or more broadly:

- Economic Development: growth in a country's economy (Gross Domestic Product, or GDP) and average income (Gross National Income per capita, or GNI per capita). A broader economic view also considers wealth and income distribution.

- Structural Development: broader distribution of resources due to government tax and spending, plus good governance (democratic rights, constitutional protections, effective institutions, rule of law).

- Social Development: increased equal opportunities in education, healthcare and employment for individual well-being.

- **Human Development:** Indian economist Amartya Sen's approach combined these economic, structural and social elements.
- **Sustainable development** underpins the UN's Sustainable Development Goals. It is a broad view of development as economic and social progress that fulfils current human needs, fairly, while safeguarding the environment and resources for future generations.

What are the seventeen Sustainable Development Goals?

These goals, agreed by the member states of the United Nations, guide all development work from 2015 to 2030.

SDG 1: 'No poverty': defined as people living below the extreme 'international poverty line' of $2.15 per day and reducing by half the number of people living in poverty above that level.

SDGs 2–6: Human rights: ending hunger (food insecurity), health and well-being, quality education, gender equality, clean water and sanitation.

SDGs 7–10: Economic rights: affordable clean energy, decent work and economic growth, industry, innovation and infrastructure, reduced inequalities.

SDGs 11–15: Environmental protection: sustainable cities, responsible consumption and production, climate action, life below water and on land.

SDGs 16 and 17: Governance: peace, justice and strong institutions, working in partnership to meet these goals.

Measuring poverty and inequality

There are two broad approaches to measuring global poverty and inequality. The 'orthodox' approach focusses on narrow economic measures, whilst the alternative 'human development' approach takes a broader view.

1 The World Bank's 'orthodox' economic approach

Gross National Income (GNI) per capita

GNI per capita is a measure of the average living standard in a state. The World Bank uses it to classify states in four income bands and to direct different levels of support to the states in each band (see Map 5.1). It is useful for comparing the inequality between states, but it tells us nothing about inequality within each state.

International poverty line and extreme poverty rate

The World Bank's 'international poverty line' was introduced in 1990 at $1 per day per person and updated over the years to $2.15 per day in 2022 (see Figure 5.2). It is used for simplicity rather than accuracy. It is an estimate of the minimum income necessary to meet basic living needs (clean water, shelter, food security and clothing) in the world's fifteen poorest countries. It uses a calculation called **purchasing power parity (PPP)** to account for differences in the cost of living. The Bank also calculates the national poverty line in each state. Since 2013, the Bank has used this data to check progress on its twin goals. These are:

- to end extreme poverty at less than $2.15 per day by 2030,
- to build 'shared prosperity' for the bottom 40 per cent of the income scale in each country.

Gini index (inequality within a state)

A Gini coefficient measures inequality within a country. A higher score out of 100 means greater inequality. The World Bank uses Gini coefficients to compare levels of inequality between different states, but there is often missing data. Map 5.2 shows a North-South divide in inequality, especially sub-Saharan Africa and in Latin America.

2 The 'alternative' human development approach

In the 1980s and 1990s, Indian economist Amartya Sen challenged the World Bank's narrow economic approach. Sen, a modern liberal, proposed that rather than simply measuring income and economic growth, policymakers should try to understand poverty more broadly, looking at people's access to opportunities such as education, healthcare, employment and political participation. This understanding would help them to promote meaningful human development.

> **Chapter Link**
>
> See **Chapter 4: Political Global Governance** For a case study on the creation of and progress on the Sustainable Development Goals. See **Chapter 7: Environmental Global Governance** For a detailed examination of sustainable development, and **Chapter 8: Analysing and Evaluating Global Governance** for a discussion of 'good governance'.

> **Definition**
>
> **Purchasing power parity (PPP):** Is a tool used by economists to compare prices across different states. It helps them account for differences in the cost of living when making international comparisons. It is updated every six years or so.

Map 5.1 The World Bank's four income groups according to GNI per capita, 2023

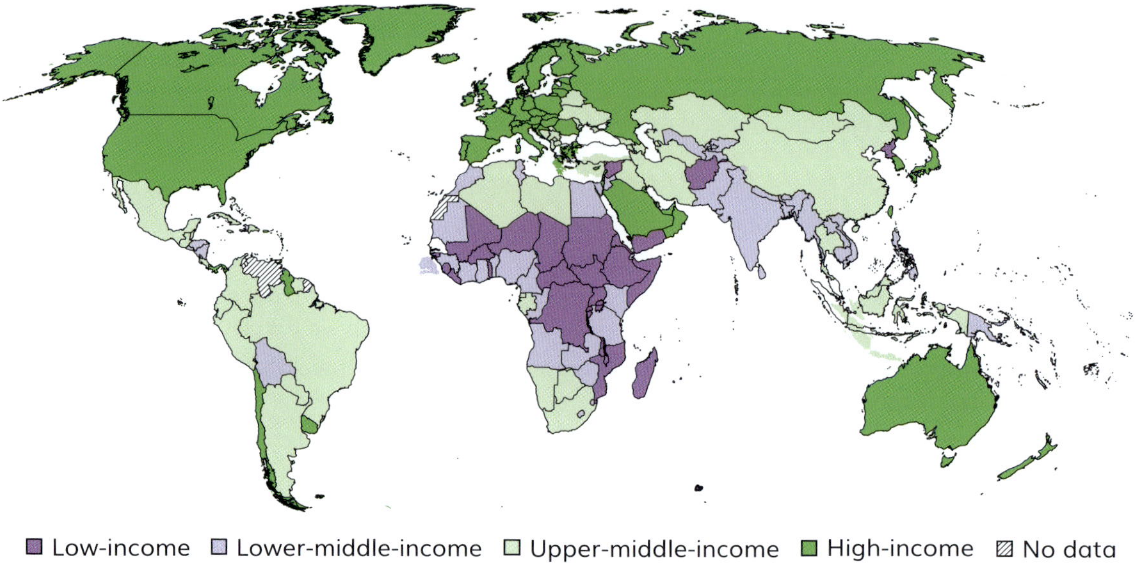

■ Low-income ■ Lower-middle-income □ Upper-middle-income ■ High-income ▨ No data

Source: Our World in Data, 'World Bank income groups', CC BY. Retrieved from https://ourworldindata.org/grapher/world-bank-income-groups

Figure 5.2 Extreme poverty rates: the percentage of population living on $2.15 per day (2107 PPP) from 1990 to 2022 in the world, in China, India and sub-Saharan Africa

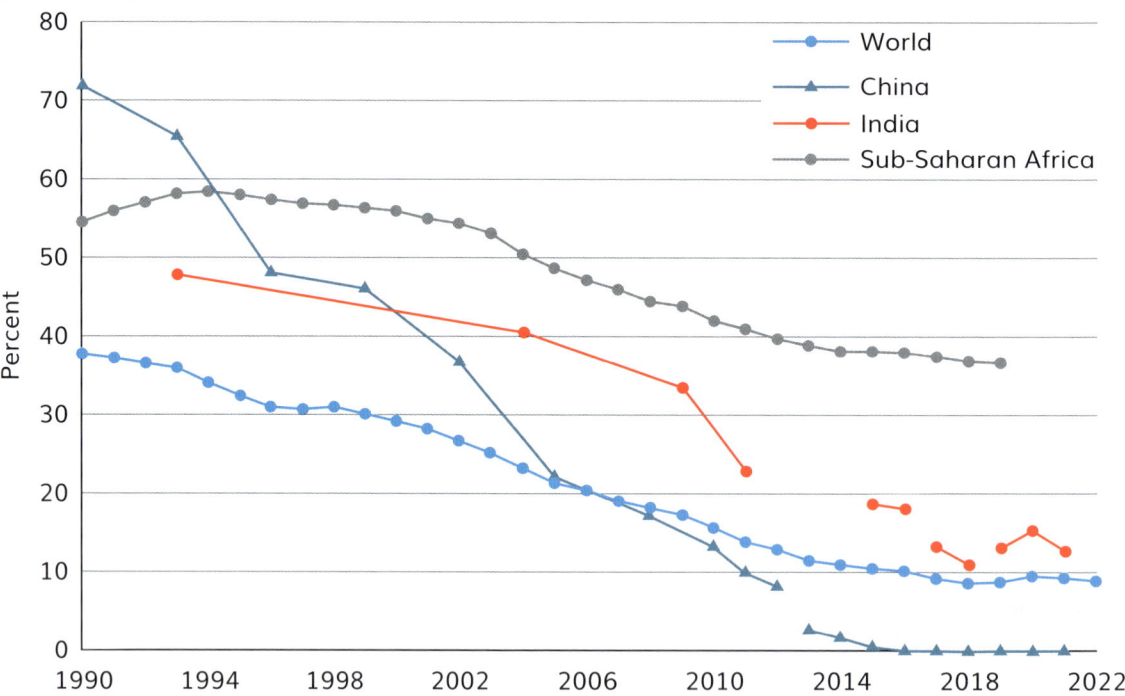

Source: World Bank, Poverty and Inequality Platform (PIP) – Poverty Calculator, CC BY 4.0. Retrieved from https://pip.worldbank.org/poverty-calculator. Note: World Bank data for China and India is incomplete

Multidimensional Poverty

Sen's approach inspired the UN Development Programme to introduce a **'Human Development Index' (HDI)** in 1990. It produces a development score for each country based on average income (GNI per capita), health (average life expectancy) and education (average length).

In 2010, the UNDP introduced a broader **'Multidimensional Poverty Index' (MPI)** alongside the HDI to support their work in developing countries. The MPI measures health, education and living standards of households, including access to basic services such as electricity, sanitation and clean water.

Map 5.2 **Global map of high inequality countries**

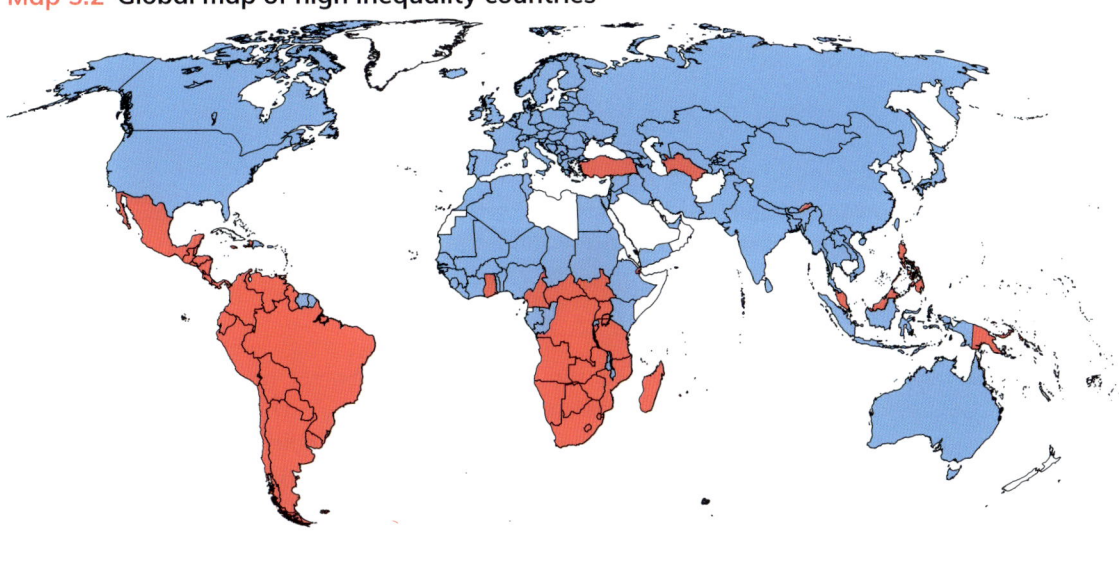

■ Low/moderate inequality   ■ High inequality

Source: Pleninger et al. (2024), 'Figure 1: Global map of high inequality countries', *World Bank Data Blog*, based on Poverty and Inequality Platform (PIP); licensed under CC BY 3.0 IGO

The World Bank developed its own '**Multidimensional Poverty Measure' (MPM)** in 2020. This includes the extreme poverty rate at the international poverty line, years of education and access to basic services but does not include health indicators.

Theories of development and global inequality

Classical economic development theory (classical liberalism)

Adam Smith's idea of the **'invisible hand of the market'**, has come to define classical economics. He argued that if producers could compete freely to sell their products, levels of supply and demand for each product would determine its price. If businesses invested in equipment to improve productivity, they could lower their prices to beat competitors: one person working by hand could make a few pins a day, but ten people operating ten machines could create thousands of pins per day. Each business would try to innovate in order to reduce costs and maximise profits. If the state left the market alone, it would become efficient and productive.

David Ricardo's 1817 theory of **comparative advantage** argued that states should not try to discourage imports by imposing tariffs (taxes on foreign goods). States will have a surplus of their most efficiently produced goods, which should be traded internationally for products produced more efficiently by other countries. This would reduce prices and increase profits, which would encourage investment and stimulate economic growth. This is the foundation of the global economy.

For instance, Brazil's climate and low labour costs provide a comparative advantage in coffee production compared to Germany. Germany's high-tech industries efficiently produce machinery. So, Brazil should trade coffee for machinery and vice versa, and both should allow tariff-free access to their markets. However, relying solely on coffee exports would overexpose Brazil to volatile agricultural markets. A bad harvest could create serious economic difficulties. Hence, Brazil needed to industrialise and diversify for more reliable economic growth.

Modernisation theory

The Western post-1945 'modernisation' theory of development supported the idea that developing countries need to modernise themselves, becoming less reliant on agriculture and raw materials, and industrialise by copying wealthy capitalist states. They should increase foreign trade, which would bring investments, technology and business expertise. At the height of the Cold War, US foreign policy adviser Walt Rostow proposed a version of this approach. In 'The Stages of Growth: a Non-Communist Manifesto' (1960), he explained five stages of development:

1. Traditional subsistence agriculture
2. A basic domestic market
3. Industrialisation
4. Diversification
5. Mass consumption

He argued that US development aid should encourage international trade and investment, but also argued that it should encourage states to invest in infrastructure to speed up industrialisation. The benefits would encourage developing states to reject communism.

Neoclassical development theory (neoliberalism)

Neoclassical development theory was part of the late-1970s neoliberal revolution promoted by US President Ronald Reagan and UK Prime Minister Margaret Thatcher. This view disagreed with Rostow, proposing that state-owned and subsidised industries were the cause of poor development. State spending made businesses less competitive, slowing economic growth. Neoclassical theorists also rejected Rostow's ideas about development aid, which they said created dependency. Instead, they proposed that all states should open their markets to foreign trade and investment to promote economic growth. The Bretton Woods Institutions embraced a neoclassical policy package called the '**Washington Consensus**', which included:

- **Market reforms:** deregulation (fewer constraints on businesses such as planning laws and workers' rights) and privatising state-owned industries and utilities.
- **Free-trade reforms:** welcoming foreign investment, removing trade tariffs and subsidies.
- **Fiscal reforms**: reducing government spending and taxes to encourage investment.
- **Monetary reforms:** Control inflation by varying interest rates. Allow free movement of capital in and out of the country and allow markets to determine the currency value.

These policies were imposed as a condition of lending, in packages called **Structural Adjustment Programmes**. They had mixed results – they did increase trade but also increased debt and poverty.

Structural theories of inequality and development

Structural theories challenged the neoclassical view that the state was the obstacle to its own development. They argued instead that the structure of the global economy created and entrenched inequality. A 'core' of industrialised states with high-wage, mass consumption economies, has exploited a 'periphery' of underdeveloped states with low-wage, agricultural and resource-extraction economies. This structural approach is sometimes described as 'neo-Marxist', because it criticises capitalist exploitation in the post-colonial global economy. There were two main theories:

Dependency theory

This explained how European imperialism (the core) halted the development of African, Asian and Latin American economies (the periphery) by extracting their resources and wealth, creating **underdevelopment**. This contrasted with modernisation theory, which saw underdevelopment as an early stage of development that all states go through before they modernise. Despite gaining their political independence through **decolonisation**, underdeveloped states remained dependent due to an exploitative system of **neocolonialism**, which kept them dependent on wealthy states for markets, finance, investment and manufactured goods (see Photo 5.3).

- **Global markets:** Underdeveloped states sell agricultural products and natural resources in global markets, where prices can fall below the cost of production, causing poverty and debt. They want to industrialise to use these resources themselves, but may lack the capital to do so.
- **International debt:** Developing countries borrow from global banks. Debt crisis forces severe public spending cuts, perpetuating poverty and inequality.
- **Global governance:** The Bretton Woods Institutions are dominated by wealthy states. They offer aid for market liberalisation, including opening up to foreign investors and privatising state industries.

Spec key term

Structural Adjustment Programme (SAP): The conditional loans provided by the International Monetary Fund (IMF) and World Bank to countries that experienced economic crises.

Definition

Underdevelopment: In dependency theory, underdevelopment means that the natural development of a state's economy has been prevented through exploitation, enforcing dependence on wealthier states for investment, finance, markets and manufactured goods.

Decolonisation: The transition of a territory from foreign control to achieving independence.

Neocolonialism: Indirectly controlling a country, typically a former colony after independence, by exploiting its resources and labour for profit and maintaining economic dependency.

Photo 5.2 Anti-US demonstrators opposing global trade liberalisation burn the Stars and Stripes during a rally near the US Embassy in Manila, 16 September 2003, to denounce the recently concluded WTO talks in Mexico.

Source: Romeo Gacad/AFP via Getty Images

> **Definition**
>
> **Protectionism:** Is the economic policy of restricting imports to protect domestic industries through tariffs, quotas and other trade barriers.
>
> **Import substitution industrialisation (ISI):** A form of protectionism involving investing in key industries such as steel, cement, heavy machinery and vehicles, and protecting domestic manufacturing from foreign competition with high tariffs.

- **Foreign investment:** Wealthy shareholders extract profits from multinational corporations (MNCs). MNCs exploit workers by driving down pay to maximise profit and exploit the environment by turning raw materials into profitable manufactured goods.
- **Exploitative elites:** Privatisation of state industries can provide opportunities for corrupt elites to profit from buying undervalued state assets. They may evade local taxes by hiding their wealth in offshore tax havens.

The route out of dependency was therefore not free trade and foreign investment. In fact, the answer was less of these. The state should practise **protectionism** to reduce dependence on imports and promote industrialisation. So, for example, from the 1950s to the 1990s, both India and Brazil used **import substitution industrialisation**. However, whilst this protectionism did protect businesses by reducing imports, it also raised prices and stifled innovation and growth. By the 1990s, many countries abandoned these policies for economic liberalisation. However, in the crisis-prone 2020s, protectionist industrial investment has come back into fashion.

World systems theory

This was proposed by Immanuel Wallerstein in 1974. He agreed that the global capitalist system perpetuated structural inequalities, but with two important differences.

He described the semi-periphery as a buffer between the core and periphery: partly industrialised with a lower-paid, lower-skilled workforce than the core, but better off than the periphery. Semi-periphery elites exploit the periphery, while core elites exploit both (see Figure 5.3).

He argued that the system was more dynamic than dependency theorists believed, and that states could break free of dependency to reach the semi-periphery. Wallerstein's semi-periphery theory fits emerging economies like India and Brazil. A good example is China's rapid move from periphery in the 1970s, to semi-periphery in the 1990s, to core status in recent years. It is building a global power base and adopting neocolonial economic policies.

Both **dependency theory** and World Systems theory encourage awareness of global inequalities. They seek fairer trade to support economic diversification, and most importantly, they seek to reform the Bretton Woods Institutions and create a more equitable economic global governance system.

> **Spec key term**
>
> **Dependency theory:** Explains that European imperialism created 'under-development' in colonised states, and that inequality is maintained through neocolonial trade, finance and global governance.

> **Chapter Link**
>
> The exploitative system of neocolonialism is linked to the negative impacts of multinational corporations on communities and the environment, discussed in **Chapter 2: The State and Globalisation**.

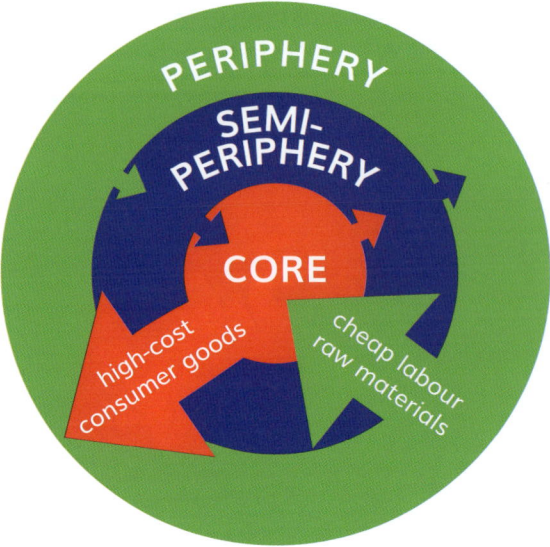

Figure 5.3 Wallerstein's World Systems theory

Source: 'Wallerstein's Core–Periphery Model'. Adapted from Wikimedia Commons, by Ali Zifan, licensed under CC BY-SA 3.0. https://commons.wikimedia.org/wiki/File:Wallerstein%27s_Core-periphery_model.png

The North–South divide

This concept has its origins in the core–periphery model. In the 1960s, industrialised states experienced sustained economic growth, doubling their share of global income, whilst newly independent states remained poor. Inspired by dependency theory and frustrated by their lack of voice in the Bretton Woods Institutions, a group of developing states formed the G77 group in the UN General Assembly, where they held a majority. In the oil crisis of 1974, they passed a resolution calling for a 'New International Economic Order' (NIEO) to end neocolonialism by:

- radically reforming economic global governance.
- introducing 'fair trade' rules, including price controls on natural resources.
- redistributing wealth, including aid from the North to support industrialisation in the South.

The states of the Global North were unmoved. However, in 1977, World Bank president Robert McNamara asked Willy Brandt, a former social-democratic German chancellor, to lead an international commission on international development.

The Brandt Reports

In 1980 and 1983, Brandt published reports on the 'North-South divide' (see Map 5.3), arguing that the prosperity of the North depended on sharing that prosperity by supporting sustainable development in the South. He recommended that:

- Developed states should share technology to support industrialisation in developing states.
- Free trade should be fair, with rules to limit the impacts of MNCs in developing states.
- Developed states should give 0.7 per cent of Gross National Product in aid by 1985 and 1 per cent by 2000.
- A global taxation system should increase funding for the World Bank.

Brandt said that failure to cooperate across the divide would end in disastrous inequalities, mass unemployment, conflict, environmental decline and famine. But instead, the World Bank adopted the Washington Consensus, and its recommendations were largely ignored. Four decades on, these predictions have become a grim reality for many people in the Global South.

Map 5.3 The Brandt Line showing the North–South divide in 1980

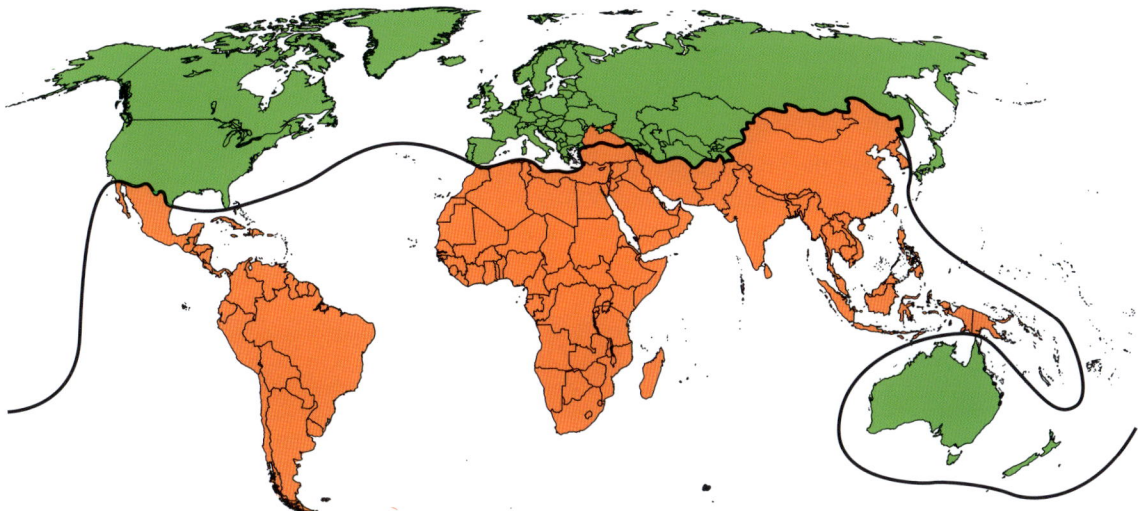

Does the North–South divide still exist?

The North–South divide has narrowed. In 1980, the North's share of global GDP was 4.5 times that of the South. In 2020, it was 2.5 times greater. However, 'the South' is not a single entity.

Emerging powers like China, India, Brazil, Mexico and Indonesia are catching up, with China's global economic share growing tenfold from 1980 to 2015. Despite its recent slower growth, China's GNI per capita is approaching high-income status. But growth has not been inclusive. The World Bank reported that the twenty-two poorest states in 1987 have made some progress on extreme poverty rates, which fell from 70 per cent in 1994 to 40 per cent in 2019 – but overall, they have failed to prosper, with low GDP per capita. Most are landlocked countries in sub-Saharan Africa, such as the Democratic Republic of the Congo or Niger. They are trapped in poverty due to political instability, conflict, corruption, challenging geography and poor trade infrastructure.

The divide is therefore better explained by World Systems theory as a three-level system of core, semi-periphery and periphery. The semi-periphery is catching up to the core, whilst the periphery is falling behind both. The semi-periphery includes some of the world's most unequal states, such as South Africa and Brazil, with both exploitative elites and exploited workers.

Furthermore, rising inequality within many states is becoming more significant than inequality between Global North and South. Globalisation creates winners and losers across income levels, e.g. US manufacturers moved car factories to Mexico, leaving behind deindustrialisation and unemployment, whilst Mexico has exploited migrant workers from poorer neighbouring states.

Globally, 44 per cent live below the poverty line (set at $5.85 per day for middle-income states), whilst extreme wealth is concentrated among a tiny global elite.

> **Chapter Link**
>
> The political divisions between the developed Global North, the emerging economies, and the least developed and most climate-vulnerable states of the Global South are a significant obstacle to progress on climate change. These divisions are addressed in **Chapter 7: Environmental Global Governance**.

Economic global governance institutions

The International Monetary Fund

Overview

The IMF, based in Washington DC, aims to maintain stability in the international financial system. This role is explained in table 5.1: the IMF's Contemporary Roles, and in the Milestones box: Changing Role and Significance of the IMF. Also see 'How states achieve economic growth and stability' pp155–156.

Membership, representation and decision-making

- The International Monetary Fund (IMF) has 190 member states, which fund its work.
- It is overseen by the Board of Governors, a group of finance ministers from the member states.

Table 5.1 The IMF's Contemporary Roles

	Responding to crisis	Preventing future crises
Assistance to states	Provides loans to stabilise low and middle-income states.	Provides economic forecasts. Advises states on economic management.
Global economy	Stabilises the financial system, e.g. in the Global Financial Crisis of 2008–9.	Provides surveillance, warning of risks in its Global Financial Stability Reports.

MILESTONES: CHANGING ROLE AND SIGNIFICANCE OF THE IMF

1944 States attending the Bretton Woods Conference agreed to establish the IMF.

1970s After states abandoned fixed exchange rates, the IMF adapted to a new role. It advised and gave crisis loans to states and, if necessary, stabilised currency exchange markets.

1980s The IMF and World Bank worked together on a developing world debt crisis, creating Structural Adjustment Programmes requiring market reforms to access loans.

1990s Globalisation gathered pace. The IMF used SAPs to rapidly transition ex-communist states to market economies and following the Asian Financial Crisis (AFC).

2000s The IMF started monitoring its members' economies. It failed to avert the Global Financial Crisis (2007–9) because it did not expect problems to begin in the United States.

2010s The IMF helped the EU and European Central Bank to bail out troubled European economies such as Greece in 2010 and 2015. After 2015, it stopped advising states to cut spending on public services, acknowledging that it was counterproductive.

2020s During the Covid-19 pandemic, the IMF temporarily increased lending with help from the G20. In 2022, it created a Resilience and Sustainability Trust for longer-term crisis loans for vulnerable states. In 2023, it doubled quotas to permanently increase borrowing limits.

Comparative Analysis: Strengths and weaknesses of the IMF

	Strengths	Weaknesses
Representation and equity in decision-making	The quota voting system reflects the principle that states with the most responsibility should have more say in how funds are spent. There is a (weak) argument that, as the United States is the anchor of the international financial system, its consent is important. Although the United States has veto power, its vote share is less than its share of global GDP, so it is not over-represented. The United States provides more funding than China, which prefers to invest in developing states directly, on its own terms. States that can elect their own Executive Directors are those that are most significant to the global economy.	Quota voting does not uphold the principle of sovereign equality and is outdated. On IMF measures, the EU has 18 per cent of the global economy but 25 per cent of votes, Africa has 2.7 per cent but 5.5 per cent of votes, and China has 14 per cent but 5.5 per cent of votes. The United States blocked quota reforms from 2010 to 2016, fearing a loss of power to China and its allies. More reforms have been delayed until 2025. Most states dislike the supermajority rule that gives the United States a veto. They want reform but disagree on how to reform. The executive board is unequal. Saudi Arabia has 2 per cent of quota votes and its own director, whilst 22 African states with 3 per cent of quota votes share a director.

	Strengths	Weaknesses
Impact on borrowing states	The IMF used SAPs successfully to stabilise Mexico in the early 1990s. Poland's 'shock therapy' SAP transition to liberalism also succeeded. In 2005, it provided debt cancellation for very poor states. Since 2015, it has advised against welfare-reduction policies. Poor states with weak governance are the highest risk borrowers. The IMF provides low-cost loans to high-risk borrowers that cannot raise finance elsewhere.	The 'one-size-fits-all' Washington Consensus template caused more harm than good in the 1980s and 1990s. In the Asian Financial Crisis of 1997–8, China and Malaysia's state-controlled capitalist economies were more resilient than the IMF's neoliberal reforms imposed in Indonesia and South Korea. The IMF's fairness has been questioned by poor states and civil society. It requires more reform from poor states than others, and unlike the World Bank is not accountable to communities who are negatively impacted by its policies.
Impact on regional and global stability	The IMF has reformed in response to international economic crises. It prioritises global financial surveillance. Lending capacity was increased to $1 trillion in 2023–24. In 2022, the IMF created the Resilience and Sustainability Trust to provide longer-term loans for fragile low and middle-income states to help prevent crises from escalating into social conflict that may draw in neighbours.	The IMF failed to predict the Asian Financial Crisis in 1997, and despite stepping up surveillance, it was 'asleep at the wheel' when the unexpected global financial crisis began in the United States in 2008. The IMF's lending conditions still require fragile states to prioritise private debts despite the debt crisis. A new full debt cancellation programme is needed.

- Governors' vote shares and state borrowing limits are determined by quotas. These vary depending on the size of the state's economy and its contribution to IMF funds. However, voting power has not kept pace with changes in contributions and borrowing limits.
- Quotas are reviewed every five years if the governors agree. Reform requires an 85 per cent vote in favour. The United States has an effective veto, with 15.5 per cent of the votes.
- Day-to-day work is led by 24 Executive Directors and a Managing Director. Seven members appoint their own directors: the United States, Japan, Germany, France, the UK, China and Saudi Arabia. The rest are elected by groups of states.
- The managing director has always been European.

External relationships

- The IMF has a formal partnership with the World Bank.
- It is an independent specialised agency of the United Nations.
- The Managing Director of the IMF attends G7, G20 and UN summits.
- The G20 advise and provide financial support to the IMF and begin negotiations on reforms.

The World Bank

Overview

- The **World Bank** has two main bodies: the **International Bank for Reconstruction and Development** (IBRD) and **International Development Association** (IDA) headquartered in Washington DC, with offices around the world.

CASE STUDY: ARGENTINA AND THE IMF

Photo 5.3 Street vendor Alberto Diaz, 63, sells flowers in Avellaneda, Argentina, September 2024: 52.9 per cent of Argentina's population were in poverty in 2024.

Source: Luis Robayo /AFP via Getty Images

Context

Argentina is the IMF's biggest debtor. In 2000, the government defaulted on its debts, so the IMF lent it $88.3 billion. That loan was repaid, but high spending left-wing populist 'Peronist' governments rejected the IMF's advice, and by 2014, Argentina had defaulted again, with spiralling inflation.

From 2015, a centre-right government cut public spending and negotiated a $57 billion IMF loan. This failed to reassure international investors who continued to withdraw capital from the country.

President Fernandez, a Peronist, was elected in 2019 and took a $44 billion IMF loan in 2022. Pro-investment policies improved growth, but Argentina struggled more than most countries with the global inflation crisis. Annual inflation soared to 210 per cent by 2023. Fernandez borrowed from China to repay $18 billion to the IMF and accepted an invitation to join the BRICS. This worried the United States, which negotiated with the IMF to adjust the terms of Argentina's loans.

In late 2023, hard-right populist Javier Milei was elected. He abandoned the BRICS, made deep public spending cuts and devalued the currency. The IMF praised efforts to restore stability but noted Argentina's long-term difficulties and a 'fragile social situation', with very high rates of poverty (see Photo 5.4). $41 billion was still owed to the IMF.

Significance

Argentina shows how changes of government in a politically polarised state can be both cause and effect of economic instability. High public debt can frighten international investors away, but the IMF's required reforms are often controversial with voters. It also shows how a struggling middle-income state can become caught up in great power rivalry.

- IBRD is a global development bank, giving loans and economic advice to low and middle-income states. It raises funds mostly from bond markets (see 'How states achieve economic growth and stability', p155–156).
- IDA provides grants and low-interest loans to around sixty low-income countries. It also issues bonds but is mostly funded by forty donor states.

Membership, representation and decision-making

- The World Bank has 189 member states.
- It is overseen by the Board of Governors, normally finance ministers from member states, who meet annually.
- Governors' voting power is weighted according to shareholdings. Vote shares are reviewed every decade. Reform to voting requires an 85 per cent vote in favour. The United States has at least 16 per cent in IBRD, giving it an effective veto. At IDA it can cooperate with wealthy allies to block reforms.
- Day-to-day work is led by 25 Executive Directors. The United States, Japan, China, Germany, the UK, France and Saudi Arabia each appoint a director. The rest are elected by groups of members.
- The president of the World Bank Group is elected by a majority of the directors, who have always accepted the US government's nominee.

External relationships

- The World Bank has a formal partnership with the IMF.
- It is an independent specialised agency of the United Nations, working alongside ECOSOC. Since 2015, it has aligned its work with the UN's Sustainable Development Goals.

Table 5.2 The World Bank's Contemporary Roles

Extreme poverty reduction
The Bank aims to end extreme poverty by 2030, focusing on shared prosperity for the bottom 40 per cent.
Raising finance
Bank spending doubled during the pandemic to $160 billion per year, then declined to $120 billion annually. Donor states gave $93 billion for 2022 to 2025. Around ¾ of funding comes from private investors.
Debt relief, development loans and aid
The Bank helps states raise investment bonds and gives advice on economic reforms. It gives aid and low-interest loans to the poorest states.
Climate resilience projects
Most infrastructure projects funded by the Bank are now for climate protection. From 2019 to 2022, the Bank's annual climate project costs doubled to $32 billion. From 2023, all projects must comply with the 2015 Paris Agreement.
Crisis response
In 2023, the Bank approved $73 billion for 322 crisis response operations in ninety countries. It has provided $37.5 billion in emergency financing to Ukraine alone.

MILESTONES: CHANGING ROLE AND SIGNIFICANCE OF THE WORLD BANK

1944	The IBRD was created to support the reconstruction of post-war Europe. It broadened its focus to global development in 1947.
1960	The IDA was established to help the poorest states.
1970s	By 1970, 40 per cent of people in low-income countries were in absolute poverty. Bank President Robert McNamara broadened the focus from economic growth to poverty reduction, increasing spending twelvefold by raising finance from private investors.
1980s	Amidst a developing world debt crisis, the Bank adopted the 'Washington Consensus'. It imposed neoliberal Structural Adjustment Programmes (SAPs) on loans. It began to advise China and India on trade reforms.
1990s	In 1991, the Bank added 'good governance' to its SAPs. In 1996, the Bank and IMF set up the Heavily Indebted Poor Countries (HIPC) Initiative to provide debt relief in exchange for SAPs. In 1999, it replaced SAPs with Poverty Reduction Strategy Papers, negotiated with borrowers in what became known as the 'Post-Washington Consensus'.
2000s	After 2000, the Bank aligned with the UN's Millennium Development Goals. Good governance became its main lending requirement. From 2005, HIPC cancelled debts for countries that tackled corruption, introduced market reforms and reduced poverty.
2010s	From 2013, the Bank set its two poverty reduction goals, linked to the UN's 2015–30 Sustainable Development Goals. These began to guide all of its work.
2020s	It broadened its understanding of poverty, using a 'multidimensional poverty measure'.

- The Bank's president attends G7, G20 and UN summits, and these influence its work. For example, at COP28 in 2023, UN members agreed to establish a new 'Loss and Damage Fund' to support reconstruction and resilience projects in climate-vulnerable states. The World Bank agreed to host this independently governed fund for four years.

Comparative Analysis: **Strengths and weaknesses of the World Bank**

	Strengths	Weaknesses
Equity in decision-making and representation	In 2010, reforms increased developing states' governors' vote shares to 47 per cent. An Executive Director was allocated to sub-Saharan African states, improving representation of developing states in lending decisions. The Bank is required to engage with civil society. It has a Civil Society Team that works with the Civil Society Policy Forum and in the states it works in.	The World Bank does not uphold the principle of sovereign equality. Its Board of Governors is dominated by the United States, which holds veto power at IBRD. BRICS are underrepresented. The United States effectively appoints the President, and the largest five economies each appoint their own Executive Directors.
Impact on states and communities	The Bank's Heavily Indebted Poor Countries Initiative (HIPC) cancelled more than $100 billion of debt from thirty-seven of the poorest states. The Bank has responded to criticism with reforms. It works in partnership with states to develop projects with local control and accountability. It requires good governance as a condition of lending. Since 2015, communities have been able to complain to the Bank if a project negatively affects them or the environment. Since Covid-19, the Bank has doubled its support for climate resilience projects.	A 1994 review found that a third of SAPs had failed. Expanding agricultural exports whilst cutting health and education caused unemployment, poverty and debt to rise. The Bank's record on environmental sustainability and human rights is poor. Until the 1990s, it supported dictators and did not tackle corruption. It supported state-led infrastructure projects that displaced communities and damaged the environment, such as the Narmada Dam in India and Polonoroeste Road in the Amazon. The debt crisis is growing. In 2024, 60 per cent of low-income states were at risk of or in debt crisis.
Impact on global development	The extreme poverty rate has fallen from 38 per cent in 1990 to 8.5 per cent in 2024 after a slight rise during the pandemic. That is over a billion people, mostly in China and India, who were both advised by the Bank, helping them to successfully liberalise their economies, generating rapid growth for themselves and many developing country trading partners. The Bank provides a comprehensive open data platform for development economists and produces regular expert reports. It carefully evaluates the impact of its projects.	The North–South divide and extreme poverty rate increased during the 1980s and 1990s. Progress on extreme poverty has stalled at 8.5 per cent, and there are more people in extreme poverty in sub-Saharan Africa than in 1990. The World Bank maintains the neocolonial dependence of the Global South. Low growth means that poor states cannot increase their voting power in the Bretton Woods Institutions to effect reforms. The Bank's budget is tiny. In 2023, an expert group at COP28 estimated that developing states need £2.4 trillion per year. Its budget is $120 billion. The rest must come from private finance.

Economic Global Governance

Comparative Analysis: What are the differences between the IMF and World Bank and their significance in global politics?

Key criteria	IMF	World Bank
Membership, representation and decision-making	The IMF has 190 member states and is overseen by the Board of Governors: member states' finance ministers. Voting shares and borrowing limits are based on economic size, but voting power has not kept pace with changes. Quotas need 85 per cent approval for reform, giving the United States (15.5 per cent of votes) an effective veto. Daily operations are managed by 24 Executive Directors and a Managing Director. Seven members appoint their own directors, while the rest are elected by groups of states. The Managing Director has always been a European. The IMF is not required to engage with civil society, although it does consult.	The World Bank has 189 member states and is overseen by a similar Board of Governors. Voting power is organised similarly – weighted by shareholdings, and like the IMF, reforms require an 85 per cent vote. The United States holds at least 16 per cent in IBRD, enabling a veto, and, although it cannot veto at IDA, it can, with its allies, dominate decisions at both bodies. Day-to-day work is led by 25 Executive Directors, similarly to the IMF. The President has always been the US nominee. The World Bank has a Civil Society Team, Civil Society Policy Forum and a complaints procedure for people affected by its policies.
Aim and Roles	The IMF responds to economic crisis by stabilising the financial system e.g. in the Global Financial Crisis of 2008–9. It provides surveillance, with annual Global Financial Stability Reports. It provides economic forecasts and gives loans and advice to stabilise low and middle-income states in crisis. It includes poverty reduction in its broader economic stability programmes. It works with governments, but not on in-country projects.	The Bank aims to end extreme poverty by 2030 and create shared prosperity for the bottom 40 per cent. It helps states to source investment and gives advice on economic reforms. It gives aid and low-interest loans to the poorest states. Most of the Bank's work is on in-country projects, now mostly for climate protection: From 2019 to 2022, the Bank's annual climate project costs doubled to $32 billion. In 2023, the Bank approved $73 billion for 322 crisis response operations in ninety countries.
Significance	The IMF works with states and at the global level. It stabilised the global economy during the Covid-19 pandemic and in 2022, it established the Resilience and Sustainability Trust to help vulnerable states with longer-term lending. Member states cover its budget. In 2023, it doubled borrowing quotas to $1 trillion, highlighting its continued role in maintaining global economic stability.	The Bank spends much less than the IMF: spending doubled during the pandemic to $160 billion per year, then declined to $120 billion annually. Donor states cover only a quarter of its budget; the rest comes from private investors. It is a fraction of the $2.4 trillion a year that it estimates is needed to resolve global challenges that disproportionately impact developing countries.

> **Exam Tip:**
> Students often confuse the roles of the IMF and World Bank. They do sometimes work together but their roles are different. Compare the case studies on the IMF in Argentina and World Bank in North Africa. The IMF only lends and advises on economic stability. The World Bank supports development projects.

Exam Tip:

If the question asks for similarities, these are clear. They have similar membership, structure and ideology; they both support developing states with loans and advice. If it asks for differences, highlight the subtle differences in organisation structure, and focus mainly on the differences in purpose, roles and global significance.

CASE STUDY: THE IMF AND WORLD BANK IN ZAMBIA

Context

When Zambia became independent in 1964, its vast copper reserves were the dominant export of its state-run economy. However, oil price rises triggered a global recession in the mid-1970s, causing copper prices to fall. Instead of reducing its high spending, the government took on debt, hoping prices would rebound. They did not, and by the early 1990s, Zambia was one of Africa's poorest countries. Protests ended the one-party system, and in 1992, an elected government implemented a structural adjustment programme (SAP) with the World Bank.

The SAP required currency, trade, fiscal and market reforms, including hundreds of privatisations. Zambia's market became the most open in Southern Africa, but it did not help. Inflation hit 183 per cent in 1993. High interest rates meant that despite repaying $5.6 billion, Zambia's debt grew from $4.5 billion in 1985 to $5.8 billion in 1995. Copper prices tumbled to a 13-year low in 1998. Frequent droughts added to the troubles. In 1999, an international buyer was eventually found for the copper mines after the IMF threatened to withdraw aid; but the investor pulled out in 2001.

Debt repayments outpaced public spending, and AIDS devastated the nation. Extreme poverty reached 73 per cent in 1998. By 2001, 20 per cent of the adult population were HIV positive, and 570,000 children were orphaned. Life expectancy dropped ten years in two decades; primary school enrolments fell 20 per cent in one decade. Zambia's government was weak and riddled with corruption.

In 2000, Zambia joined the IMF/World Bank Heavily Indebted Poor Countries Initiative and agreed new reforms for debt relief. A Poverty Reduction Strategy Paper was negotiated with conditions on trade, infrastructure investment, governance and anti-corruption, public services, HIV/AIDS and environmental projects. The World Bank gave aid and advice and monitored progress on the Millennium Development Goals.

By 2004, copper prices rebounded with rising demand from China. An Indian buyer purchased the mines, and economic growth improved. Debt relief in 2005 and Chinese investments accelerated growth until 2015. However, Covid-19, persistent droughts, fluctuating copper prices and inflation have brought continued challenges. Extreme poverty increased from 61 per cent in 2015 to 64 per cent in 2022.

Zambia has since had more help. With IMF support, it restructured its debt, reduced inflation and attracted more foreign investment. World Bank projects support small businesses, public health, gender inclusion, electricity access and climate resilience. The outlook in 2024 was improving.

Significance

Zambia's story encapsulates the devastating impact of depending on one resource in volatile commodity markets, excessive debt and austerity policies on public health and welfare. Yet it bounced back in the 2000s. There are three main reasons for this: the painful economic reforms coming to fruition, a reformed 'Post-Washington Consensus' approach centred on debt cancellation, poverty reduction and good governance, and an improved global economic outlook due to rising demand for copper. It is essential to appreciate that SAPs were only part of a broader picture.

Zambia also shows that escaping the poverty trap is not necessarily a one-time challenge. It demonstrates how governance organisations collaborate to support governments in the poorest countries on their own development goals. It highlights the continuing dependence on foreign investment, and the impact of the 'poly-crisis' of Covid-19, inflation and climate change on poor countries.

The World Trade Organisation

Overview

The World Trade Organisation was created in 1995 to provide an institution for the General Agreement on Tariffs and Trade. It aims to maintain a rules-based global free-trade system, creating predictability for businesses and promoting fair competition. It is based in Geneva, Switzerland.

Two key rules are **non-discrimination:** imports from all states must be treated the same, except developing states can be given free-trade access and regional free trade deals are permitted; and **reciprocity**: if a state acts unfairly by manipulating global markets, trade partners are allowed to take steps to rebalance the deal (this is the justification given for the US Trump administration's imposition of widespread tariffs of 2025).

CASE STUDY: WORLD BANK PROJECTS ON NORTH AFRICAN FOOD INSECURITY

Events

Since 2014, a food crisis has developed due to climate change, unsustainable agriculture and conflicts, accelerating in the 2020s due to Covid-19 and the war in Ukraine. In 2023, the UN World Food Programme estimated 221 million people across fifty-four state members of the World Bank's International Development Agency (IDA) faced acute food insecurity, a 71 per cent increase since 2019.

Before Russia's invasion, Ukraine produced more than half of the world's sunflower oil and was also a major exporter of barley and wheat. Port blockades by Russia in 2022 disrupted global food supplies. Prices spiked. Worse, shipments of grain for World Food Programme aid to people suffering drought were blocked.

The impact was severe in the sub-Saharan Sahel and Horn of Africa regions, which have been heavily dependent on food imports from Ukraine. By 2023, there were 10 million food-insecure people in the G5 Sahel states of Burkina Faso, Chad, Mali, Mauritania and Niger and 36 million in the eastern states of Ethiopia, Kenya and Somalia.

The World Bank responded by scaling up efforts, making $45 billion available for food security projects and providing technical policy support.

Supporting governments with short- and long-term policies, e.g.

- $420 million funding for emergency measures in the G5 Sahel states.
- Working with UN agencies to help governments develop Food Security Crisis Preparedness Plans (FSCPPs).

Supporting short-term projects to help the most vulnerable households, e.g.

- Food vouchers in Mali and cash benefits in Somalia during severe droughts.

Supporting long-term projects to help farmers' climate resilience, e.g.

- A long-term sustainable agriculture project supporting 1.5 million farmers in Ethiopia.

Supporting international projects to deal with regional emergencies, e.g.

- An Emergency Locust Response Program across the Horn of Africa after a plague of locusts devastated crops in 2020.

Significance

This case study demonstrates the World Bank's 'multifactorial' approach to food insecurity.

- Rather than just giving aid, the Bank helps governments to develop, monitor and evaluate projects that will have the greatest impacts on the poorest households.
- It supports short-term crisis response, medium-term recovery and long-term resilience-building projects.
- As a global organisation, the Bank can coordinate 'official development aid' from donor states, and it can subsidise interest rates on loans from private investors. It also works with regional organisations on multi-state projects such as the Emergency Locust Response.
- However, with 221 million people facing food insecurity, the World Bank can only deal with the tip of the iceberg of the global hunger crisis. In 2024, war in Sudan had created widespread famine. The challenge has increased.

Membership and decision-making

- In 2025, the WTO had 166 member states, accounting for 97 per cent of world trade.
- EU states are members but are represented in negotiations by the EU Commission.
- There is a biennial Ministerial Conference, where trade rules and reforms are finalised.
- A group called the 'Quad' – the United States, the EU, India and Brazil – negotiates trade reforms in packages called 'single undertakings'. These must be accepted or rejected in full by the ministerial conference, giving other states little input.
- India and Brazil replaced Canada and Japan in 2009 in an effort to give emerging economies a greater voice. They have positioned themselves as leaders of the Global South.
- The WTO operates on consensus. Every member can veto proposed trade rules.
- Two states can take a trade dispute to the WTO Dispute Settlement Body. This resembles a court, although disputes are heard by a panel of trade experts rather than judges. States can appeal to an Appellate Body if they disagree with the decision.

External relationships

- The WTO Director General attends meetings of the G20 and UN.

MILESTONES: THE CHANGING ROLE AND SIGNIFICANCE OF THE WTO

1947	The GATT was signed in 1948. It would reduce average tariffs to 5 per cent by the 1990s.
1995	The Marrakesh Agreement set up the WTO with initial agreements on trade in goods (GATT), services (GATS), intellectual property (TRIPS), agricultural trade and subsidies. It created a dispute resolution process.
1996–2010	SAPs highlighted unfair agricultural trade rules, and the AIDS pandemic highlighted unfair intellectual property rules. The 1999 WTO conference on fair trade in Seattle, USA, was abandoned after disruption by 70,000 anti-globalisation protesters demanding fair trade.
2001	China joined the WTO, and the Doha 'Development' Round of talks on agriculture began.
2015	The agriculture talks failed. Fishing subsidy talks continued.
2017	The WTO's **Trade Facilitation Agreement** was completed to make cross-border processes easier: the first multilateral agreement since 1995. The United States started systematically blocking nominations to the Appellate Body, so it could not hear dispute appeals (see case study).
2018	A trade war began between the United States and China (see case study).
2020–2021	The trade war ended, but the United States continued to block nominations. Ngozi Okonjo-Iweala became the first African and first female Director General. She urged cooperation.
2022	The first ministerial conference in five years was held. An **Agreement on Fisheries Subsidies** (known as 'Fish 1') bans fisheries subsidies, which contribute to global overfishing. It was the first WTO agreement to focus on environmental sustainability, partly fulfilling SDG14.
2025	The second Trump administration imposed high unilateral trade tariffs on trading partners. Rising tensions posed a risk to global trade and to the future of WTO reform.

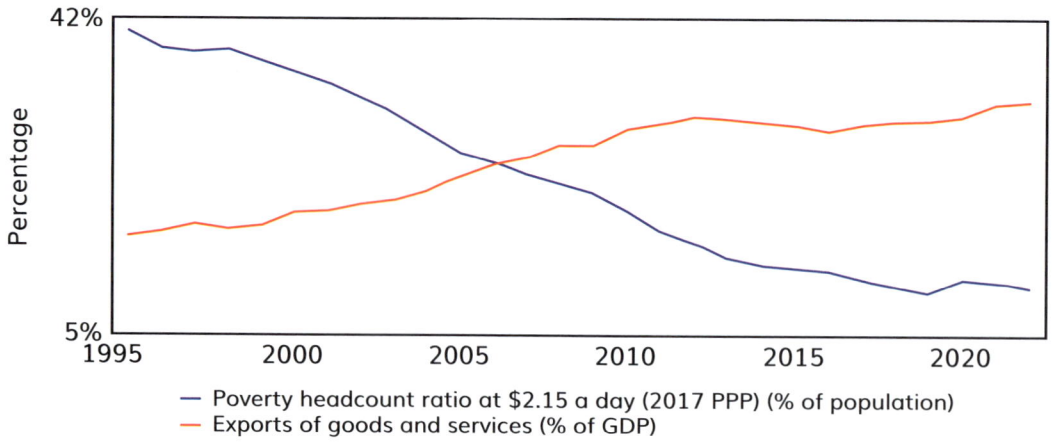

Figure 5.4 Substantial poverty reduction alongside increased trade participation of low and middle-income economies, 1995–2022

— Poverty headcount ratio at $2.15 a day (2017 PPP) (% of population)
— Exports of goods and services (% of GDP)

Source: World Economic Forum, World Trade Organisation (2024)

Comparative Analysis: Strengths and weaknesses of the WTO

	Strengths	Weaknesses
Equity and representation	Unlike at the IMF and World Bank, every state in the WTO has an equal voice at the ministerial conference. India and Brazil were brought into the Quad in 2009 to give a voice to the Global South. Developing countries can access preferential tariff-free terms, promoting shared prosperity. The EU offers these only to the Least Developed Countries.	Poor states lack permanent representation, expert negotiators and bargaining power. The Quad system undermines equality. India and Brazil claim to represent the Global South but have little in common with the poorest states. Countries can designate themselves as developing, which can cause controversy and block negotiations.
Impact of dispute resolution	The multilateral dispute resolution process is essential to avoid tension spilling over into conflict.	The United States blocked nominations to the Appellate Body due to frustrations over Chinese state subsidies, preventing appeals from being heard until reforms are agreed (see case study).
Impact of trade agreements	The WTO's consensus-based multilateral system is crucial for maintaining the liberal rules-based free-trade system, supporting peace. Simply joining the WTO has benefits for developing countries, regardless of further progress. According to the 2024 World Trade Report, implementing the trade reforms required before joining has boosted members' trade by an average of 140 per cent. Increased trade participation is strongly linked to reduced poverty rates in low- and middle-income countries (see Figure 5.4). The Fish 1 agreement in 2022 bans fisheries subsidies for illegal, unreported and unregulated fishing. It was the first WTO agreement to focus on environmental sustainability, partly fulfilling SDG14.	Consensus decision-making among so many states is slow and difficult. The WTO has failed on fair trade. Intellectual property rules caused immense human suffering in the AIDS pandemic by denying affordable drugs. By 2010, 40 million children in Africa had lost at least one parent to AIDS. The Doha Development Round failed over disagreements on EU and US agricultural subsidies. Chinese industrial subsidies remain high, distorting global markets. Some countries become more unequal when they open to the global market. Fish 1 was a partial response to the problem of global overfishing, compared to 'Fish 2', which would have a much greater impact on sustainability. It was still under negotiation in 2025. If not agreed by 2026, both agreements would expire.

> **Chapter Link**
>
> The problem of overfishing is a good example of the 'tragedy of the commons', and the WTO fishing agreements represent an attempt by states to overcome the tragedy in accordance with the SDGs, by creating legally binding trade regulations. See **Chapter 7: Environmental Global Governance**.

CASE STUDY: US–CHINA TRADE DISPUTE AND THE WTO APPELLATE BODY

Context

China subsidises some of its industries, including steel, solar panels and aluminium. This encourages high production and reduces prices. Using export subsidies to deliberately flood global markets with cheap products to damage global competitors and drive them out of business is unfair market manipulation, which is against WTO rules. It is known as 'dumping'. In 2010, the United States put anti-dumping tariffs on Chinese steel pipes, solar panels and aluminium, using the principle of 'reciprocity'.

China, however, argued that it was not dumping products and that US tariffs violated WTO non-discrimination rules. It took the case to the WTO Dispute Settlement Body for resolution.

In 2012, the panel ruled in favour of China, finding that the United States had not adequately demonstrated that the Chinese products were being dumped or subsidised against WTO rules.

In 2013, the United States appealed to the WTO Appellate Body. In 2014, it upheld the panel's decision, ruling that the US tariffs were inconsistent with WTO rules.

The US government criticised the Appellate Body's ruling as 'judicial activism', arguing that it was creating new obligations for WTO members that should only be agreed by states, not judges. The government said that the WTO Appellate Body needed to be reformed and demanded reforms. This strained US–China trade relations even more.

In 2018, the Trump administration, frustrated at the WTO's failure to stop Chinese subsidies, decided to take unilateral action. They initiated a trade war with China. In tit-for-tat retaliation, both states imposed tariffs of up to 25 per cent on a wide range of products, disrupting global supply chains and affecting industries around the world, including in Europe.

The US blocked appointments to the Appellate Body, saying that it would do so until reforms to the dispute settlement process were agreed, in an effort to persuade other states to agree to reform. By 2019, the Appellate Body could not operate. The G20 agreed to negotiate reforms but could not agree what they should be.

In 2020, the WTO dispute resolution body again ruled that the US tariffs were against WTO rules. Ironically, the United States was unable to appeal against the decision. In 2025, reforms were still under negotiation.

By 2025, US–China trade relations had not improved. US President Trump imposed significantly increased tariffs of up to 145 per cent on China, with China retaliating with tariffs of up to 125 per cent. Alongside these, Trump imposed a universal 10 per cent tariff and much higher 'reciprocal' tariffs on many US trade partners to try to coerce them into making new trade agreements that would encourage US exports.

Significance

This case highlights rising tensions between the United States and China in their competition for global economic dominance. It demonstrates the challenges facing the multilateral trading system in an increasingly tense world. The difficulty is that almost all states agree that the system needs reform, but the breadth and depth of reforms needed and the painfully slow system for achieving them means that the chances of consensus are low.

Chapter Link

The rising tensions between the United States and China as a result of China's increasing global significance are dealt with throughout **Chapter 3: Power and Developments**.

The G7/8

Overview

The G7 coordinates economic and foreign policies between the seven wealthiest liberal democracies to address challenges and promote global stability and prosperity. It is flexible, responding to need.

Membership and decision-making

- The G7 is a forum for cooperation between the governments of the United States, the UK, France, Germany, Japan, Canada and Italy and the EU Council and Commission presidents.
- Each member state holds the presidency for a year, on rotation. Each president sets their own agenda and chairs the annual summit meeting.
- Government ministers and officials meet throughout the year.

Economic Global Governance

- Like the G20, the G7 does not have a headquarters or permanent staff.
- States join if invited. With Russia, they were the G8 from 1998 to 2014.
- In the 1970s, the G7 members were the seven largest capitalist economies, but GDP is not the defining feature: Russia was ranked twentieth by GDP in 1998, China and India are ranked second and fifth by GDP in 2024 and are not members.
- Meetings are closed, allowing frank discussions to achieve consensus.
- There are regular press releases and a joint 'communiqué' (summary report) of the annual summit meeting.
- Businesses, thinktanks and civil society meet in 'engagement forums' to produce recommendations for the G7.

External partnerships

- IGO leaders and guest states are often invited, to build alliances and resolve problems.

MILESTONES: CHANGING ROLE AND SIGNIFICANCE OF THE G7/8

1973-1975	The group began with informal meetings to coordinate responses to global economic problems. The G7 formed with annual summit meetings in 1975.
1990s	The G7 focused on economic stability, market liberalisation and development aid. Leaders of the UN, IMF, World Bank and WTO were invited. Meetings in the 1990s and early 2000s attracted significant public protest.
1998	Russia joined, and the group was renamed G8.
1999	After the Asian Financial Crisis of 1997-1998, the G8 set up the G20 group of finance ministers, to try to contain future crises.
2000s	After 9/11, the G8 broadened its focus to security and counterterrorism. It invited leaders from developing states and the African Union to discuss development. Following earlier protests, summits were held in resorts with high security.
2005	The G8+5 formed with China, Brazil, India, Mexico and South Africa. Responding to the Make Poverty History campaign, the G8 agreed to cancel all outstanding debts of forty Heavily Indebted Poor Countries (HIPC).
2009	In the global financial crisis, the G8 decided to bring together the G20 states' leaders. The G8 became less significant as a result, and protests declined further.
2014	After annexing Crimea from Ukraine, Russia was suspended and then left the group. They reverted to the G7.
2020s	The G7 discussed global health matters, including pandemic responses. From 2022, discussions increasingly focused on security threats from Russia and China.

Comparative Analysis: Strengths and weaknesses of the G7/8

	Strengths	Weaknesses
Equity and representation	Over the years the G7 has invited additional states to discussions, for example the African Union, African leaders, and IGOs were invited to discussions on development aid, and emerging economies have also been invited at times.	The G7 is a self-appointed elite 'club' which undermines the liberal principle of equality. A failure to include emerging economies as members in 2005 caused resentment.

	Strengths	Weaknesses
Significance and authority	The G7 still takes a legitimate leadership role in the Western world. Its' leaders have the power to allocate resources to respond to rising security threats such as counterterrorism.	The economic significance of the G7 has declined relative to the significance of the G20, and its share of global GDP is predicted to decline further as the significance of the BRICS rises.
Impact	The closed meetings allow frank and open discussion at the highest level, which helps leaders build relationships that they can rely upon when needed. In 2005, the G8 solved a decade-long developing world debt crisis, offering full debt cancellation to countries in the IMF and World Bank's HIPC Initiative. By 2008, 80 per cent of HIPC debt was cancelled. Liberal democracies cooperate to promote their shared values. The G7/G8 does this better than the rival BRICS, which is less likely to form a strong, deep alliance. The group is flexible and responsive in comparison to the formal institutions, which are outdated and dysfunctional. In 1998, the G8 achieved consensus on humanitarian intervention in Kosovo, paving the way for a Security Council resolution that had previously seemed unlikely. In 2009, the G8 recognised its own limitations in convening the G20 to deal with the financial crisis.	The group's closed meetings in remote, high security locations means that it does not act in a transparent manner. The G7 have been criticised by civil society for entrenching global inequalities. There is no accountability for following through on its decisions. Repeated promises on climate finance have not been fulfilled. The perception that the G7 control the Bretton Woods Institutions in their own interests has led to resentment in the Global South and pushback from emerging economies, prompting the creation of the rival BRICS in 2009 to rebalance global economic power. The group became divided during the first Trump presidency. They disagreed on climate change after Trump withdrew from the Paris Climate Change Agreement in 2017, on Trump's aim to re-admit President Putin, and on trade during the US-China trade war of 2018–20. This continued in the second Trump Presidency from 2025.

The G20

Overview

The G20 promotes discussion between the governments of major economies, regional organisations and economic global governance institutions to support global economic stability.

- The G20 is a forum for continual economic cooperation between its members.
- Each member state holds the presidency for a year, on rotation. Each president sets their own agenda and chairs the annual summit meeting.
- Government ministers and officials meet throughout the year.
- Like the G7, the G20 does not have a headquarters or permanent staff.

Table 5.3 Membership, Representation and Decision Making of the G20

G7	BRICS	Other states	Regional organisation members	IGOs attend but are not members
France Germany United States UK Japan Italy Canada	Brazil Russia India China South Africa	Argentina Australia Indonesia Mexico Saudi Arabia South Korea Turkey	European Union: Commission and Council Presidents African Union: Council and Commission Chairpersons (since 2023)	International Monetary Fund World Bank World Trade Organisation

- Members are invited to join. Since 2023, there are nineteen state members and two regional organisation members.
- Meetings are closed, allowing frank discussions to achieve consensus.
- There are regular press releases and a joint 'communiqué' (summary report) of the annual summit meeting.
- Businesses, thinktanks and civil society meet in 'engagement forums' to produce recommendations for the G20.
- Unofficial protests and events sometimes occur, depending on the host country.

External relationships

- IGO leaders attend. The G20 provides a forum for their most powerful members to discuss potential reforms.
- Guest states and other regional organisations, such as ASEAN, may be invited to attend.

Photo 5.4 G20 leaders at the Summit on Financial Markets and the World Economy at the National Building Museum in Washington, DC on 15 November 2008

Source: Handout/Getty Images News via Getty Images

MILESTONES: CHANGING ROLE AND SIGNIFICANCE OF THE G20

1999	The G7 proposed a G20 of finance ministers, in response to the Asian Financial Crisis.
2008	The G7 proposed leader's summits of the G20 to respond to the global financial crisis.
2009	The G20 became the most influential group in economic global governance, preventing global banking system collapse and agreeing extra funding for the IMF (see Photo 5.5).
Early 2010s	The G20 worked on trade and financial market regulation. It began negotiating reform of the Bretton Woods System.
Late 2010s	The group broadened its focus, but it failed to find consensus on climate change and institutional reform. It spent two years dealing with a US-China trade war.
2020	The G20 met remotely and pulled together to an extent on Covid-19.
2021	The group agreed to a global minimum corporate tax rate: a significant achievement.
2022	President Zelenskyy of Ukraine was invited by Indonesia to discuss the Russian invasion of his state. President Putin of Russia did not attend in person and has not done since due to an arrest warrant from the International Criminal Court.
2023	India's agenda focused on sustainable development, climate finance and global governance reform. The African Union became a full member.
2024	Brazil's presidency again focused on sustainable development and governance reform.
2025	South Africa's presidency set an agenda on African development concerns: sustainable development, food security, the debt crisis and strengthening climate resilience.

Comparative Analysis: Strengths and weaknesses of the G20

	Strengths	Weaknesses
Equity and representation	The G20 is more inclusive than the G7 and even more so since the African Union joined in 2023. Half of the world's states are represented either individually or by the EU and AU. It is economically diverse, with established and emerging powers. Politically diverse, with democracies and non-democracies. Geographically, with representation from every continent. This diversity is a strength in solving global challenges.	There are two tiers of representation – states and regional organisations. Only two regional organisations are members, which impacts representation and diversity. Member states represent their own interests. France, Germany, Italy and South Africa have their own membership as well as being represented collectively by the EU/AU. South Africa and Argentina are not in the twenty largest economies. Their participation is questionable.
Significance and authority	The G20 is large enough to be significant and small enough not to become stuck in endless negotiations, unlike the WTO. Even without the AU, its members' combined economies made up 85 per cent of the global economy, giving its significant power and authority.	The G20 acts as a means to consolidate economic power. These self-appointed 'guardians' of the global economy make far-reaching decisions without scrutiny or accountability.

	Strengths	Weaknesses
Impact	The G20 brings states, regional organisations and global institutions together in a flexible way to solve problems. It reduced the impacts of the global financial crisis. It achieved agreement to reform the WTO's dispute resolution process. Four consecutive summits in 2022–25, chaired by members from the Global South (Indonesia, India, Brazil, South Africa), have maintained the group's focus on sustainable development and the need to reform the economic governance institutions and energised civil society participation.	The G20's communiqués are often unimpressive, with the need to achieve consensus producing weak agreements. It has attracted criticism from civil society for prioritising global free trade over the needs of disadvantaged groups, especially in the Global South. The G20 has become less productive since the mid-2010s due to rising tensions. Decisions on climate change have been weak. Its Covid-19 response was inadequate for public health challenges in developing countries. It has been arguing over economic governance reform for years without significantly resolving the issues.

> **Chapter Link**
>
> The EU and AU's membership of the G20 has enhanced their global significance. In the EU's case, there is a complex mix of supranational and intergovernmental representation at both the G7 and G20, with France, Germany and Italy retaining their own representation as well as having a collective EU representative. See **Chapter 9: The EU and Regionalism** for more on the global role of the EU.

Analysing and evaluating economic global governance

Table 5.4 Summary of Main Strengths and Weaknesses of Economic Global Governance Organisations

	Strengths	Weaknesses
IMF	• States with most responsibility and most significance in global economy have the most say. • Some SAP success in Mexico and Poland. • Some reform in response to criticism – debt cancellation, poverty reduction, global surveillance, longer-term loans for fragile states.	• Quota voting on the boards is outdated and unrepresentative. • The US veto is unfair. • SAPs generally unsuccessful, e.g. Indonesia, South Korea. • Less reform than World Bank. • No accountability to communities. • Fewer governance reform conditions in larger states.
World Bank	• States with most responsibility have most say. • Supported extreme poverty reduction, debt cancellation for the poorest states. • Reform to lending conditions and improved accountability to civil society and communities. • Increased focus on sustainability since 2023.	• Poor representation of developing countries on its boards. Major Western economies dominate. • 1/3 of SAPs had failed by 1994 and Sub-Saharan poverty has increased. • Poor historical record on environment and human rights. • Much more financing needed.

> **Exam Tip:**
> When comparing different organisations, use terms such as 'similarly', 'both' or 'in contrast'. Explain reasons and impacts. For example, *similarly* unequal voting power in *both* the IMF and World Bank has created a bias towards the interests of the Global North at the expense of the Global South, leading to a failure to adequately address the debt crisis.

	Strengths	Weaknesses
WTO	• India and Brazil represent Global South in the Quad. • Preferential free trade for developing states in EU. • Free trade and multilateralism should reduce conflict risk. • Joining WTO boosts trade and is linked to reduced poverty in low–middle-income states.	• Poorer states not well represented. • Self-designation for developing countries is controversial. • US has blocked dispute resolution since 2009. • Trade openness does not consistently reduce inequalities.
G7/8	• Includes a wide range of guests in discussions including Global South leaders. • Resolved developing world debt in 2005. • Sufficient power to allocate resources for rising security threats. • Flexible and responsive.	• Self-appointed elite club undermines equality, creates resentment in Global South. • Failure to include BRICS. • Economic significance has declined relative to G20. • Lack of transparency, accountability and follow-through on climate finance.
G20	• AU membership since 2023. • G20 is more inclusive economically, politically and geographically than G7. • It is more flexible and responsive than the global institutions.	• The G20 consolidates its own power. • Unequal representation of states. • There is a lack of accountability. Consensus decision-making has produced weak outcomes.

Comparative Theories: Liberal, realist and structural views on economic global governance

Liberal view	Realist view	Structural view (see pages 158-60)
States will seek global cooperation for peace and economic stability. The desire for progress shapes governance.	States prioritise self-interest. Power dynamics shape governance: 'The strong do what they can, the weak suffer what they must' (Thucydides).	Structural inequality in the global capitalist system perpetuates underdevelopment, and these unequal power dynamics shape governance.
Classical and interdependence liberals support free trade, rule of law and IGOs to support these. Modern liberals advocate for inclusive and equitable growth and better Global South representation.	IGOs serve as tools for powerful states rather than as forums for mutual benefit. They will resist reforms that are not in their own interests (e.g. Doha development trade talks, voting reform).	The Global South remains dependent on the Global North due to neocolonial IGOs, trade, debt and aid. Any reforms tend to be superficial and do not challenge this dominance.
Civil society plays a role in holding power accountable and driving progress.	Civil society is not significant.	Civil society plays a role in holding power accountable and driving progress.

> **Exam Tip:** Economic global governance involves IGOs, the states that set their rules, and non-state actors like businesses and civil society that influence the decisions of states and their IGOs. Consider the contributions of each type of actor when analysing the system from these different perspectives.

KEY DEBATE: IS ECONOMIC GLOBAL GOVERNANCE EFFECTIVE?

The idealism and institutionalism of liberalism is reflected in the argument in favour, whilst realist and structural views on development are reflected in the counterarguments.

Economic stability

The IMF and G20 have played a crucial role in stabilising the global economy during financial crises.

- ✅ The IMF learned from earlier crises, stepping up monitoring of states' economies, changing its advice on austerity and introducing its Global Financial Stability Reports.
- ✅ In the 2008–9 financial crisis, the IMF worked with the G20 to stabilise the banking system and increase lending capacity to $1 trillion to support states.
- ✅ They repeated the increase during the Covid-19 pandemic, rapidly supporting states in difficulty, including Egypt and Zambia.

Crisis-prevention efforts usually fall short:

- ❌ The IMF failed to act swiftly enough to prevent the Asian Financial Crisis from spreading.
- ❌ Dependency theorists argue that the IMF's austerity measures exacerbated economic instability rather than alleviating it in Asia.
- ❌ It was 'asleep at the wheel' in the 2008–9 financial crisis and in the Eurozone sovereign debt crisis, exposing leadership failures.

Trade and economic growth

Economic global governance has supported economic growth by liberalising trade and investment.

- ✅ Trade reforms required when states join the WTO boost trade on average by 140 per cent, creating growth.
- ✅ GATT and the Trade Facilitation Agreement of 2017 helped to streamline international trade and encourage competition, promoting economic growth. India, for example, benefited hugely from free trade in telecommunications and IT, achieving significant growth.
- ✅ The IMF and World Bank have worked closely with many states to successfully integrate them into global markets. These include Poland, India and China in the 1990s.

However, critics argue that the benefits of trade are unevenly distributed and that the WTO is dysfunctional.

- ❌ Trade liberalisation has led to neocolonialism, with powerful states benefiting from the exploitation of poorer countries' resources and labour.
- ❌ The Doha 'Development' Round failed to achieve its objectives of fairer agricultural trade for the Global South.
- ❌ The WTO fails to rein in unfair and obstructive behaviour by powerful states. Its dispute resolution appeals process was blocked by the United States from 2017, with the issue still unresolved in 2025. It was unable to tackle a trade war between the United States and China in 2018–20 and unilateral 'Trump tariffs' in 2025.

Poverty reduction

Economic global governance has had a positive impact on extreme poverty reduction.

- ✅ Global extreme poverty rates halved between 1990 and 2010 from 38 per cent to 16 per cent. Over a billion people were lifted out of extreme poverty, around three-quarters of them in China. Rates fell more slowly to 8.5 per cent by 2024. Since 2010, the greatest gains have been in India.
- ✅ Poverty Reduction Strategy Papers from 1999 better supported countries like Zambia that had struggled under a heavy debt burden with SAPs.
- ✅ The cancellation of debts for up to forty HIPC states by 2008, driven by the G8's agreement under Tony Blair and Gordon Brown, resulted in significant progress in poverty reduction in countries such as Zambia.

Despite these initiatives, economic global governance has often been criticised for its inadequate focus on poverty reduction.

- ❌ Progress on poverty paused during the Covid-19 pandemic. From 2020 to 2025 it has increased in sub-Saharan Africa.
- ❌ Structural Adjustment Programmes imposed by the IMF and the World Bank in the 1980s and 1990s exacerbated poverty in heavily indebted countries by forcing cuts to health, education and pensions.
- ❌ Many developing states missed out on debt relief in the 2000s. In 2024, the developing country debt crisis had grown, with 60 per cent of low-income states at risk of or in debt crisis.

Sustainable development

The UN Sustainable Development Goals guide development work by IGOs, states and NGOs. Alongside poverty reduction, the SDGs include human rights, environmental protection, good governance institutions and collective action on sustainable development.

- ✅ Good governance and anti-corruption measures in lending practices supported countries such as Ghana and Zambia towards democracy, protecting human rights.
- ✅ The World Bank doubled its climate project funding from 2019 to 2023, and from 2023, it requires all new infrastructure projects to comply with the 2015 Paris Agreement.
- ✅ Since 2022, the IMF Resilience and Sustainability Trust has provided longer-term crisis loans for vulnerable countries.
- ✅ Since 2015, the World Bank has had a complaints system for communities that are negatively affected by its projects, e.g. due to environmental damage.
- ✅ Indonesia, India, Brazil and South Africa chaired the G20 in 2022–25, and the AU joined in 2023, increasing pressure for sustainable development and IGO reforms.

However, sustainable development efforts under economic global governance have often fallen short, as organisations have prioritised economic stability over environmental and social concerns.

- ❌ China's lending to developing countries does not prioritise governance and human rights.
- ❌ World Bank compliance with Paris Agreement targets should have started from 2015.
- ❌ Climate-vulnerable states have called for climate funding for years, and provision by 2024 was still far from adequate.
- ❌ IGO reform has been delayed and was overdue by 2025.
- ❌ The UN Secretary-General was so concerned in September 2024 that he held a 'Summit of the Future' to try to invigorate multilateralism.

Key Debate Summary: Is economic global governance effective?

Key criteria	For	Against
Economic stability	✓ IMF and G20 have stabilised economies during crises by increasing lending during the 2008–9 financial crisis and Covid-19.	✗ The IMF was criticised for failing to prevent the 1997–8 Asian Financial Crisis and mismanaging the 2008–9 global financial crisis and Eurozone debt crisis.
Trade and economic growth	✓ Trade and investment liberalisation boosts trade for WTO members, with significant benefits in India.	✗ Trade liberalisation has increased neocolonialism; WTO has struggled with fair trade and dispute resolutions.
Poverty Reduction	✓ Extreme poverty rates halved between 1990 and 2010. IMF and World Bank cancelled debts for HIPC states and introduced Poverty Reduction Strategy Papers.	✗ SAPs worsened poverty in the 1980s and 1990s. Progress stalled during Covid-19, and the debt crisis has increased.
Sustainable Development	✓ The World Bank uses the SDGs and has increased climate funding. The IMF has introduced a Resilience and Sustainability Trust. Global South G20 presidents have kept a focus on development from 2022 to 2025.	✗ World Bank delayed compliance with the Paris Agreement. Climate funding remains inadequate. China provides alternative lending without good governance.

Exam Tip:

When debating effectiveness, consider governance's impact on poverty, conflict, human rights and the environment, but you do not need to debate them all or in equal depth unless specified. The economic governance aims of economic stability, growth, poverty reduction and sustainable development encompass these four themes.

Table 5.5 The Roles and Significance of Civil Society and Non-state Actors in Economic Global Governance

Scrutiny and accountability	**The Bretton Woods Project**: A UK-based civil society watchdog of the IMF and World Bank. The project was established in 1995 to 'advocate for a multilateral system that is democratic, inclusive, transparent, accountable and responsive to people, especially the poorest and most vulnerable'. It brings together scrutiny and accountability work from many NGOs, publishing accounts of meetings and advocating for reforms to the institutions' appointments and voting, lending conditions and advocates for human rights, sustainability and debt cancellation.
Media engagement and public mobilisation	**Jubilee Debt Campaign** and **Make Poverty History** were two related successful coalition movements. The Jubilee Debt Campaign human chain around the G8 in 1998 helped achieve debt relief in 1998 and the Make Poverty History music events and protests in 2005 helped to persuade the G8 and WB to give full debt cancellation to the 40 HIPC states in 2005.

Research, lobbying and consultation	**Oxfam International** is known for its annual reports released at the World Economic Forum, where the global elite and world leaders gather each January in Davos, Switzerland. These reports highlight the growing wealth gap and push for progressive taxation. They have influenced discussions at the G20 on financial transaction taxes and profit-shifting to tax havens by MNCs.
	Oxfam has formal consultative status at ECOSOC and was included in drafting the MDGs and SDGs. It also actively engages with the World Bank and to a lesser extent, the IMF. It scrutinises the World Bank's performance and directly lobbies managers to reform policies. They sometimes collaborate on development projects. Oxfam also presents reports and organises sessions at the IMF/World Bank's joint Civil Society Policy Forum, which is held alongside their biannual governors' meetings in Washington DC.

KEY DEBATE: HAS ECONOMIC GLOBAL GOVERNANCE REFORMED IN RESPONSE TO CRISIS AND CRITICISM?

This debate demonstrates the breadth of neocolonial dependency and highlights the role of civil society in supporting the Global South's demands for change. It also demonstrates the tensions between liberal hopes for genuine global progress and self-interested resistance by the Global North.

Crisis and criticism: Structural Adjustment Programmes and debt

In the 1980s and 1990s, Structural Adjustment Programmes failed to prevent corruption and tax evasion, and poor states suffered from volatile global prices. Many could not protect health, education and pensions, worsening poverty. The developing world debt crisis escalated throughout the 1980s and 1990s. The Jubilee Debt Campaign demanded full debt cancellation by the millennium. In the early 2000s, the 'Make Poverty History' campaign kept up the pressure.

Reforms

- ✓ In 1996: The World Bank and IMF introduced the Heavily Indebted Poor Countries (HIPC) Initiative, reducing debt to sustainable levels.
- ✓ In 1999, the Washington Consensus was reformed, replacing SAPs with flexible Poverty Reduction Strategy Papers, focusing on poverty reduction and good governance.
- ✓ In 2005, the G8 agreed to cancel all outstanding debts to themselves, the IMF and World Bank for up to forty HIPC states, if they met reform conditions. By 2008, 80 per cent of those debts were wiped out.
- ✓ The IMF and World Bank have reformed their approaches over time. In 2013, the World Bank prioritised poverty reduction, in 2015, the IMF advised states against deep spending cuts, and in 2023, the IMF set up a Resilience and Sustainability Trust for longer-term crisis loans for vulnerable states.

Failure to reform

- ✗ In the 1990s, the IMF and World Bank were slow to reform lending conditions despite rising poverty, inequality and debt. A 1994 World Bank review found that 1/3 of SAPs had failed. They only changed SAPs to PRSPs in 1999 under public pressure.
- ✗ Full debt cancellation did not come until 2005, and then only for the very poorest, most indebted states. Many heavily indebted states, such as Zambia, still struggled with required economic reforms. The main reason that Makes Poverty History succeeded was arguably that it did not seek to fundamentally change the neocolonial global economic system.

Economic Global Governance

Crisis and criticism: trade

SAPs had required developing countries to open their borders to trade and investment. On joining the WTO in 1995, developing countries sought fairer trade rules on agriculture and intellectual property. They could not compete against subsidised agricultural products from the EU and the United States, and an uncontrolled AIDS pandemic spread through Africa. AIDS drugs were unaffordable due to the intellectual property rights of US pharmaceutical companies. Anti-globalisation movements emerged, leading to the disruption of the 1999 WTO conference in Seattle, USA.

Reforms

- ✅ The Doha 'Development' Round began in 2001 with hopes for fairer agricultural trade.
- ✅ The World Trade Report 2024 argued that, on average, trade reforms required on joining the WTO have boosted members' international trade by 140 per cent and reduced poverty as a result.

Failure to reform

- ❌ The two sides could not agree on most trade reforms – with tragic consequences in the case of AIDS drug patents: by 2010, 40 million children in Africa had lost at least one parent to AIDs. In 2015, the Doha agriculture talks were abandoned.
- ❌ Trade openness does not always reduce inequality – in fact, it sometimes increases inequality within a state as lower-skilled jobs are outsourced and offshored to states with lower labour costs, increasing unemployment.

Crisis and criticism: globalised financial crises

Rapid globalisation in the 1990s also increased the risks of financial crises spreading from state to state and from bank to bank. The IMF was widely criticised for not responding to contain the Asian Financial Crisis quickly enough. It was accused of being 'asleep at the wheel' during the global financial crisis of 2008-9 and the Eurozone sovereign debt crisis in 2010.

Reforms

- ✅ In 1999, the IMF stepped up monitoring of developing states' economies.
- ✅ In 2009, it worked with the G20 to maintain the global trading system and increase lending to states in crisis. It also stepped up surveillance and reforms in the global financial system.

Failure to reform

- ❌ Since 2009, as the IMF's role has become more focused on stability in the financial system, it has narrowed its governance lending requirements. It only requires effective financial governance and is much more flexible on democratic governance.

Crisis and criticism: continued neocolonialism

The Global South see neocolonial domination of IGOs by the Global North as the cause of stalled progress on extreme poverty and delays on climate finance. These resentments are amplified at the G20 by the BRICS, who seek institutional reform as part of their efforts to rebalance global power.

Reforms

- ✅ In 2010, some reforms were made to voting power and directors in the World Bank to give emerging and developing countries a little more influence.
- ✅ In 2016, similar reforms, delayed by the United States, were made at the IMF.
- ✅ In 2023, the African Union was accepted as a full member of the G20.
- ✅ In 2022–25 four members of the Global South have chaired the G20, pushing for voting reforms. These were due to be negotiated in the IMF and World Bank in 2025.

Failure to reform

- China has stepped up its lending to developing countries. China does not ask awkward questions about governance, unlike the World Bank.
- The 2010 and 2016 reforms were a token effort, inadequate for any kind of democratic legitimacy. IMF quota reforms were delayed until 2025 and were well overdue.
- The G20 and G7 are still unrepresentative.
- Negotiations to reform the dysfunctional WTO have been under way since 2019. In 2025 they were still unresolved.

Key Debate Summary: Has economic global governance reformed in response to crisis and criticism?

Crisis and Criticism	Reforms	Failures
Structural Adjustment Programmes and debt (1980s–1990s): Failed to prevent corruption and tax evasion, increased poverty	HIPC Initiative (1996), PRSPs (1999), G8 debt cancellation (2005)	Slow reforms, full debt cancellation only in 2005, many states still struggled
Trade (1990s–2015): Unfair trade rules, AIDS drug patents, increased inequality	Doha Round (2001), trade reforms boosted trade by 140 per cent	Doha talks abandoned (2015), increased inequality, AIDS crisis
Globalised financial crises (1990s–2010): IMF slow to respond to crises	IMF monitoring (1999), G20 cooperation (2009)	Narrowed governance requirements, flexible on democratic governance
Neocolonialism (2010–2025): Global South sees domination by Global North	World Bank voting reforms (2010), IMF reforms (2016), African Union in G20 (2023)	Token efforts, delayed reforms, unrepresentative G20 and G7

Chapter Summary

- Economic global governance began with the 1944 Bretton Woods System, which collapsed in the 1970s.
- IMF and World Bank SAPs had mixed impacts on poverty and inequality, leading to civil society criticism and calls for debt cancellation.
- Trade liberalisation boosted growth but often benefits powerful nations, creating inequality.
- Economic growth in BRICS, Poverty Reduction Strategy Papers, HIPC debt relief and improved focus on governance improved poverty reduction after the millennium.
- The IMF and G20 aim to stabilise economies during crises but have struggled to prevent them. The G7 has become less significant since 2009.
- Since 2015, UN SDGs guide development, and the World Bank has focused more on poverty, inclusive growth and climate funding.
- Since 2019, progress on poverty has stalled, with rising debt and food crises in low-income countries intensified by climate change, Covid-19 and the Ukraine war.
- Calls for greater representation and fairness in global governance persist.

Exam Style Questions

- Examine the differences between the IMF and World Bank and their significance in global politics. (12)
- Examine responses to criticisms by the International Monetary Fund (IMF) and the World Bank. (12)
- Examine the differences between the G7 and G20 organisations and their impact on global politics. (12)
- Examine the strengths of the World Trade Organisation and the G20. (12)
- Evaluate the view that economic global governance has effectively reformed in response to crisis and criticism. (30)
- Evaluate the view that economic global governance has prevented the development of the Global South. (30)
- Evaluate the view that economic global governance is effective. (30)

Further Resources

https://pip.worldbank.org/home. The World Bank's Poverty and Inequality Platform is a useful interactive resource.

https://ourworldindata.org/poverty. Our World in Data also has useful interactive charts.

https://www.worldbank.org/ext/en/who-we-are. The World Bank's organisation page.

https://www.imf.org/en/About. The IMF has plenty of information about its work here.

https://www.brettonwoodsproject.org/. The Bretton Woods Project website provides in-depth critical analysis of the IMF and World Bank.

https://www.wto.org/english/thewto_e/whatis_e/whatis_e.htm. The WTO has useful explainers and a video here.

https://www.un.org/sustainabledevelopment/youth/ and https://www.un.org/sustainabledevelopment/sdg-fast-facts/. The UN has many useful web pages on the Sustainable Development Goals.

Andrew Heywood and Ben Witham, *Global Politics*, 3rd edition (Bloomsbury, 2023) is an excellent and very comprehensive undergraduate level book for those who want more depth. Chapters 16 and 20 expand on many of the issues here.

Visit https://bloomsbury.pub/essentials-of-global-politics to access additional materials to support teaching and learning.

6 HUMAN RIGHTS GLOBAL GOVERNANCE

Chapter Preview

This chapter explores the post-Second World War system of human rights global governance: a rules-based order shaped by international law. It considers the nature of human rights and international law and liberal and realist views on these.

A complex system of international courts and tribunals has been established to deal with human rights violations by states and individuals, including the International Court of Justice (ICJ), the International Criminal Court (ICC), UN Special Tribunals and the European Court of Human Rights (ECHR). They play a significant role in the development of human rights law, but there are controversies over their roles and significance in global politics.

Since the 1990s, humanitarian intervention has gained prominence, later reinforced by the Responsibility to Protect doctrine. We explore the features of humanitarian intervention and examples of successful (and unsuccessful) interventions, and evaluate whether humanitarian intervention remains relevant or not.

Finally, the chapter explores accusations of Western hypocrisy and double standards over human rights abuses. For realists, this is simply realpolitik in action, with states prioritising their own national interests above those of individuals. For liberals, it is unjustifiable. Recent events in Gaza, Lebanon, Ukraine and China raise important questions about whether hypocrisy makes global governance irrelevant in a newly emerging multipolar world order.

Key Questions and Debates

- What is the post-Second World War system of human rights global governance, and how is it shaped by international law?
- What are the liberal and realist perspectives on human rights and international law?
- How do international courts and tribunals (ICJ, ICC, UN Special Tribunals, ECHR) address human rights violations, and why are they controversial?
- What are the key features of humanitarian intervention, and how successful or unsuccessful have such interventions been since the 1990s?
- How did the Responsibility to Protect doctrine reinforce humanitarian intervention, and does it remain relevant in global politics today?
- Do accusations of Western hypocrisy over human rights abuses undermine the effectiveness of global governance in an emerging multipolar world order?

Specification Checklist

3.1.1 Origins and development of international law and institutions (International Court of Justice, International Criminal Court, Special UN Tribunals and European Court of Human Rights) in creating the concept of global politics

- Sources of authority, including the 1948 Universal Declaration of Human Rights

3.1.2 The key issues of these institutions in dealing with human rights:

- Impact on state sovereignty
- Rise of humanitarian interventions and growth in 1990s, with examples of successful and unsuccessful intervention
- Reasons for selective interventionism, development of responsibility to protect and conflict with state sovereignty
- Examples of alleged Western double standards/hypocrisy

3.3 The ways and extent to which these institutions address and resolve contemporary global issues, such as those involving conflict, poverty, human rights and the environment

3.3.1 How the following issues affect international law from effectively addressing and resolving the issues above:

- Debate about the effectiveness and implications for state sovereignty and the extent to which international law is accepted and enforced
- Performance of the international courts, including controversies

3.3.3 The role and significance of the global civil society and non-state actors, including non-governmental organisations (NGOs), in addressing and resolving the issues above

Source: Clay Banks/Unsplash

Human rights

Human rights are a contested concept, historically shaped by various cultures and religious beliefs. The Western concept of 'natural' or 'God-given' rights originated with seventeenth-century philosophers such as Hugo Grotius and John Locke. Human rights have evolved to encompass a moral dimension, emphasising what individuals 'should' be entitled to by virtue of being human. The modern concept of human rights is that they are *universal*, applying to all individuals regardless of race, gender, sexuality or religion; *fundamental*, meaning they cannot be taken away by states or institutions; and *absolute*, meaning they must not be diminished or compromised.

The universality of human rights is contested, particularly by *cultural relativists*, who argue that rights should reflect cultural differences. Scholars identify three types of rights:

1. Civil and political rights protect freedom from state interference, such as the right to freedom of speech, assembly and religion. These are contentious in authoritarian states.

2. Economic, social and cultural rights require state provision, like healthcare and education. They are contentious due to their economic burden.

3. Collective rights protect the rights of minoritised groups such as indigenous populations and women. These are contentious when they are perceived to prioritise group identities over individual merit or the goal of national unity.

However, liberal proponents of human rights view them as universally applicable, and have created a complex web of human rights global governance to promote and protect them. This has brought the concept of human rights into conflict with the core organising principle of global politics: the sovereignty of states. Realists therefore challenge this idea of universality.

> **Definition**
>
> **Human rights:** Rights to which people are entitled by virtue of being human. They are universal, fundamental and absolute.

Liberal and realist views on human rights

Liberal views

The idea of human beings as 'rights bearers' derives from liberal individualism.

For liberals, human beings are inherently good, moral creatures, capable of altruistic behaviour. The suffering of fellow human beings is considered abhorrent, and all people have an obligation to prevent the suffering of others.

Liberals see the primary role of the state as protecting the rights of its citizens. If a state fails to do this, the social contract between the state and its citizens is broken, and people would be entitled to rebel against the state.

Human rights are also a source of legitimacy within IGOs. Supporting human rights is seen as a precondition for joining the international community, offering benefits like preferential trade and collective security. Hedley Bull and the English School view human rights protection as essential for membership in an international society of states.

Liberals support the universal promotion and enforcement of human rights. They therefore view **sovereignty as conditional** or *earned*, and if a state violates the human rights of its citizens, the principle of non-intervention no longer applies because the state has forfeited its sovereignty. It is on this basis that liberals support the principle of humanitarian intervention.

Realist views

Realists dismiss the liberal belief in human rationality and the respect for human life that underpins liberals' conception of human rights. For realists, it is unthinkable that human beings would willingly sacrifice their own security to protect the well-being of others.

Realists fundamentally disagree with the liberal view that the sovereign state should serve the individual. They do not concern themselves with the inner workings of states and believe that the national interest is the state's first and only priority.

Because the international system is anarchic, realists believe that a state would not sacrifice its own resources to protect human rights, as the utilisation of vital economic resources could leave a state vulnerable to attack from its enemies.

Because state sovereignty is absolute, there can be no obligation upon states to protect the human rights of either their own citizens or citizens living in another state. Where humanitarian intervention does take place, this is simply a smokescreen for the promotion of national interests. Those might be the acquisition of power or the prevention of instability from refugee flows and economic disruption.

As evidence of these views, realists point to selective application of humanitarian intervention and hypocrisy by states that supposedly uphold the idea of universal human rights.

Comparative Theories: Realist and liberal views on human rights

Liberal view	Realist view
Supports the existence and promotion of human rights.	Sceptical about the existence and importance of human rights.
Human rights are a source of legitimacy for states and international organisations.	States should prioritise national interests above all else. The rights of citizens are not significant.
State sovereignty is conditional on the upholding of human rights; if a state violates the human rights of its citizens, it could be subject to humanitarian intervention.	States are concerned about their power relative to other states and will not sacrifice their power to uphold human rights elsewhere, unless their security or prosperity are impacted.

International law

International law is very different from domestic law because, in the absence of a world government, it is very difficult to enforce due to the principle of state sovereignty.

There are two key sources of international law. Increasingly, international law is codified in international treaties, formal legal agreements reached between political actors which are written and signed. States sign and ratify international treaties voluntarily. This is why international law is not necessarily universally applicable. Confusingly, treaties can have several names; for example the UN Charter, the Genocide Convention and the Rome Statute, discussed in this chapter, are all types of treaty.

The second key source of international law is customary international law. Customary law is based on what is actually practised by states; a common 'custom' rather than a signed document. A legal principle gains customary status when it is seen as a universal norm based on consistent, widespread and well-established legal practice by states. Customary international laws are viewed as legally binding, whether or not an individual state has explicitly consented to them. So, for example, whilst there are a few UN member states that have not ratified the Genocide Convention, the prohibition of genocide is considered to apply universally.

The problem with customary international law is that it can be difficult to define and apply and requires expert interpretation by lawyers and judges. This is why the last century saw many efforts to codify international law into a huge number of international treaties, making this task easier. However, customary international law constantly evolves and therefore requires constant monitoring, especially in the field of human rights.

> **Spec key term**
>
> **International Law:** The law that governs states and other international actors. It is derived from both treaties and custom (i.e. the behaviour of states).

> **Exam Tip:** Students are often confused about the differences between signing and ratifying international treaties, and it is important to be able to distinguish between the two when measuring the effectiveness of international treaties.

International law and state sovereignty

In the absence of a world government, one might expect that international law would be weakened by continual violations by sovereign states. Yet this has not been the case: realist scholar Hans Morgenthau noted that 'international law has in most instances been scrupulously observed'. Why is this the case?

- Firstly, it is in their interests to do so. States prefer order to disorder, and international law helps to reduce uncertainty in the anarchic international system. Conforming to international law allows states to become members of the international society described by Hedley Bull.
- Secondly, states also fear punishment. Although the UN cannot enforce international law, states themselves, acting collectively through the UNSC or other organisations such as NATO, can, under the UN Charter, punish a state that breaks international law.

> **Definition**
>
> **Convention:** The word 'convention' has multiple meanings. It can mean a customary practice such as the UK's **constitutional conventions**, a formal political assembly such as the Democratic and Republican National Conventions in the United States, or an international treaty, e.g. the Genocide Convention (1948).
>
> **Ratification:** Unless an international treaty is ratified by a signatory state, it is not legally binding on that state. Ratification takes place at the domestic level and in some states requires approval from the legislature.

- Thirdly, states do so because they accept the moral values that underpin international law, and because international law reflects their own practices.

The significance of international law is evident in the way that states justify and respond to violations. Most states – even authoritarian ones – justify their actions in legal terms, even when breaking the law. For instance, Russia cited the legal norm of self-determination to justify its 2014 annexation of Crimea, referring to a referendum where 95.5 per cent voted for union with Russia with a turnout of 85 per cent. Similarly, Western states accused Russia of violating Ukraine's sovereignty and territorial integrity under Article 2(4) of the UN Charter. Clearly states consider it important to be seen as acting within international law.

The impact of international humanitarian law on state sovereignty

International humanitarian law (IHL) is a controversial area of international law, because it represents a shift towards supranational law. The rapid growth in humanitarian treaties such as the Genocide Convention and the Refugee Convention after the Second World War aimed to regulate states' treatment of citizens within their own borders – previously considered to be a matter for states themselves to decide. Furthermore, the Rome Statute of 1998 established the principle that a state leader could be held personally accountable for human rights abuses by the international community. IHL has therefore posed greater challenges to the principle of sovereignty than many other forms of international law.

However, many powerful states have chosen not to sign or have delayed ratification of these treaties. For example, the United States finally ratified the Genocide Convention in 1988, forty years after its creation, and along with China, Russia and India, has not signed the Rome Statute. Whilst the Genocide Convention has achieved customary status, the Rome Statute has not.

More recently, IHL has arguably also been used to undermine the principle of sovereign equality in the international state system. For example, in 1998, some African countries signed the Rome Statute and joined the International Criminal Court to meet the conditions of the EU's preferential trade scheme for developing countries. This implies that the EU used its economic power to gain the consent of those states to a law that, in a more equal world, they may not have freely chosen to adopt. Whilst they are bound by the statute, more powerful states are not.

Sources of authority in international human rights law

The UN system and human rights treaties

The UN Charter

The preamble of the **Charter of the United Nations** commits member states to 'universal respect for, and observance of, human rights and fundamental freedoms for all without distinction as to race, sex, language, or religion'. Whilst the preamble itself is not legally binding on states, it is significant because it shows the UN's intention to protect human rights, to avoid the human rights catastrophe caused by the First and Second World Wars, and countless other conflicts.

The Universal Declaration of Human Rights

The **Universal Declaration of Human Rights** (UDHR) was adopted by the UN General Assembly in 1948 (Table 6.1). This was the first time that human rights were codified in a single international document, so it is a foundational text for human rights. As a decision of the UNGA, it is not legally binding, but it has had a profound influence on the development of international law. Many of its thirty 'articles' have since become human rights treaties, and because of their widespread acceptance by states, they have assumed the status of international customary law. These include the right to equality and non-discrimination (Article 2), right to life (Article 3), prohibition of slavery (Article 4), and torture (Article 5).

Comparative Theories: Liberal and realist views on international law

Liberal view	Realist view
Liberals argue that states identify with and have helped create international law, based on the liberal belief in human dignity and on the social contract. They believe adherence to international law enhances mutual trust and global cooperation to the benefit of all. Liberals argue that compliance with international law enhances a state's soft power, because being seen as law-abiding builds trust and improves diplomatic relationships. For example, the United Kingdom has tended to uphold international law, strengthening its global influence. Violating international law damages the soft power of states. When the UK rejected the ICJ decision in 2019 that its occupation of the Chagos Islands was illegal, this was seen as reviving British imperialism, significantly damaging its soft power in the Global South. This explains why, in February 2022, most African states did not vote with the UK and the United States in a UN General Assembly (UNGA) resolution condemning Russia's occupation of Ukraine.	Realists emphasise self-interest as a primary motivator for states. Violations of international law create disorder, so states only follow international law because it creates predictability in an anarchic system. Realists highlight the use of hard power coercive tools such as sanctions, which are imposed by economically powerful states on those that violate legal norms. For example, Russia faced sanctions from the EU and G7 after annexing Crimea in 2014, which were increased when it invaded Ukraine in 2022. Realists note that powerful states often justify their actions within legal norms even when violating them. For example, the United States' justification for its Iraq invasion without a UNSC resolution referred to the Treaty on the Prohibition of Nuclear Weapons, the human rights of the Iraqi people and their right to democratic government. Russia similarly argued that its invasion of Ukraine was to protect human and civil rights in Russian majority areas of the country.

> **Chapter Link**
>
> International law is relevant to any discussion of state sovereignty. A hegemonic state will shape or reject international law to meet its own interests: the United States refused to sign the Rome Statute. It may also violate international law, as when the United States invaded Iraq in 2003 without a UNSC mandate. See **Chapter 3: Power and Developments** for more on hegemony, **Chapter 4: Political Global Governance** for more on UNSC resolutions, and **Chapter 7: Environmental Global Governance** for more on environmental laws.

Table 6.1 Strengths and Weaknesses of the UDHR

Strengths	Weaknesses
• UN member states reached a collective understanding of human rights, providing a foundational text that can hold states to account. • The declaration recognises that human rights are 'the foundation of freedom, justice and peace in the world'. • Despite lacking enforcement powers, the Declaration has formed the basis of subsequent international human rights treaties and covenants. • Despite the enormous complexity of the task, it only took two years to draft the Declaration and at the time and out of 58 member states, 48 states voted in favour (the Soviet Union abstained). • The declaration remains influential after eight decades, suggesting that states consider it to be an important source of human rights law.	• The declaration is not legally binding upon UN member states, and many continue to abuse the human rights of their own citizens. • The rights contained in the declaration are considered secondary to national interests such as security (see **Case Study: Human Rights vs National Security**). • The Declaration represents a 'Western' liberal interpretation of human rights and is seen by some as a form of cultural imperialism. • The declaration was not universally supported. Saudi Arabia and some other Islamic states rejected the protection of religious freedom, undermining sharia law. This led to a rival, more restrictive 'Cairo Declaration' of Human Rights in 1990. • The Declaration has not been updated to reflect current human rights concerns, such as the protection of LGBTQ+ rights.

CASE STUDY: HUMAN RIGHTS VERSUS NATIONAL SECURITY – THE CASE OF SHAMIMA BEGUM

Photo 6.1 **Shamima Begum in Roj camp, Syria, 2021.**

Source: Sam Tarling /Getty Images News via Getty Images

Events

In 2015, then 15 years old, Shamima Begum travelled to Syria to join ISIS (Photo 6.1). She immediately married an ISIS fighter who was 24 years old, and they had three children, all of whom died.

In 2019, then Home Secretary Sajid Javid stripped Begum of her nationality as a British citizen, effectively rendering her stateless. The British government justified this on the basis that she was a threat to national security. In 2019, Begum had shown no remorse about her decision to join ISIS and supported their extensive use of extreme violence and Islamic ideology. In 2020, a tribunal ruled that the government's decision was lawful because Begum was Bangladeshi by descent and could claim citizenship there, albeit that state refused to grant her citizenship. In 2021, the Supreme Court ruled that Begum could not return to the UK to appeal against the decision. A 2023 hearing at the Special Immigration Appeals Commission also ruled that, despite their acceptance of the probable truth in Begum's lawyers' claims that she was a victim of trafficking and sexual exploitation, she could not regain her citizenship on the basis that she continued to be a threat to national security. Begum appealed this, and in 2024, the Court of Appeals upheld this decision.

At the time of writing, Begum was living in a refugee camp in Northern Syria.

Significance

The decision to strip Begum of her British citizenship is controversial from the perspective of the UDHR. Article 15 states that 'everyone has the right to a nationality. No one shall be arbitrarily deprived of his nationality nor denied the right to change his nationality.' In this case, the UK unilaterally decided to remove her citizenship without expressly informing her of the decision, a matter which was later legalised by the passing of the Nationality and Borders Act (2022). Moreover, the decision violates Article 13, which states that 'everyone has the right to leave any country, including his own, and to return to his country'. In this case, not only has she been stripped of her citizenship, but she is not allowed to return to the UK to participate in the legal process.

The decision by the UK government highlights that when it comes to human rights, the national interest of security takes precedence. In this case, the individual rights afforded to Begum are held as less important than the collective rights of UK citizens to be safe.

Martha Gill, a UK journalist, argued that this case was essentially political. It highlights how political concerns override concerns about the application of international law. This was because the government was afraid to reinstate Begum's citizenship because the decision would have been deeply unpopular amongst the British public. For Begum, by initially showing no remorse for her decision to join ISIS, she lost the support of the British public, regardless of the hardships she has endured.

Human rights treaties

The UDHR is incorporated into a collection known as the 'International Bill of Human Rights', alongside two other treaties:

- The Covenant on Civil and Political Rights (1966), which originates in classical liberalism, emphasising 'negative' rights such as freedom of speech, religion and conscience.
- The Covenant on Economic, Social and Cultural Rights (1966), which originates in the socialist tradition, emphasising 'positive rights' such as the right to health care, education and protection from economic exploitation.

These were separated into two treaties, because states could not all agree on both elements. For example, the United States rejects the Covenant on Economic, Social and Cultural Rights, whilst China rejects the Covenant on Civil and Political Rights.

The UDHR has inspired the creation of many other treaties. Often, a civil society campaign will pressure states to propose a resolution at the UN General Assembly, calling for a treaty to be drafted to protect a UDHR right in law. If the UNGA agrees, the Secretariat works with legal experts and NGOs to draft the treaty text. The UN Secretariat then organises summits, or 'conventions', where diplomats negotiate the final text of the treaties, and they are signed by state leaders. Then the treaty is ratified. This process can take many years (Table 6.2).

Judicial precedents from international courts and tribunals

The final source of authority is the international courts and tribunals. Like domestic courts, these create **judicial precedents** that influence the development and interpretation of the law.

Examples of these precedents are considered in the next section. Sources of judicial precedent in international law include:

Within the UN system:
- The International Court of Justice (ICJ)
- UN Special Tribunals

Non-UN Courts:
- The International Criminal Court (ICC)
- European Court of Human Rights (ECHR)

Judges in international courts are appointed from member states but are not appointed to represent their state's interests. Instead, they are expected to be impartial. They are appointed for their expertise within different legal systems. In the International Court of Justice (ICJ), which adjudicates disputes between states, if a state involved in a case does not have one of its citizens serving as a judge on the Court, it may appoint an ad hoc judge – for that case alone. States do not have this privilege in the other international courts. Instead, their judges are elected by an assembly of member states of the court.

> **Exam Tip:**
> The specification refers to 'sources of authority', including the UDHR. It is therefore important to familiarise yourself with the UDHR and some human rights treaties. These can help strengthen your analysis of the effectiveness of human rights global governance and states' adherence to global governance architecture.

> **Definition**
> **Judicial precedent:** A legal principle where courts are bound to follow the legal principles established in previous decisions made by courts in similar cases.

> **Exam Tip:**
> It is important to be clear that the ICC is not part of the UN system. If an essay question asks you about the success of the UN in upholding human rights, you should not consider the ICC. This has been a common error in exams.

Table 6.2 Significant Treaties in International Human Rights Law

Treaty	Aim	Strengths	Weaknesses
Convention on the Prevention and Punishment of the Crime of Genocide (1948)	Genocide is a crime under international law. This includes committing genocide or conspiring to commit genocide.	+ Defines genocide broadly to include acts committed with intent to destroy, in whole or in part, a national, ethnic, racial or religious group. + Prohibits genocide in international law. + Places a duty on state parties to punish the perpetrators of genocide. + civil society groups investigate and alert the international community to the risk of genocide.	- Does not include political, economic or cultural groups as possible victims of genocide. - Scope was limited by great power politics at the time, e.g. the Soviet Union prevented the inclusion of political groups in the definition. - Lacks enforcement powers. - The UN has only recognised three genocides – Rwanda (1994), Bosnia (1995) and Cambodia (1975–9). Others remain unrecognised, e.g. China (Uighur Muslims), Myanmar (Rohingya Muslims) and Ethiopia (Tigrayans).

Treaty	Aim	Strengths	Weaknesses
The Geneva Convention (1949)	Regulates the conduct of armed conflict, including humane treatment of prisoners of war, and protection of civilians and civilian infrastructure.	+ increased accountability for states in conflict; violation of conventions can result in prosecution. + The first convention is ratified by all UN member states: showing universal support for regulating the use of armed force. + A major step in regulating how combatants and non-combatants should be treated in armed conflict.	- Conventions lack an enforcement mechanism and depend on the willingness of states to enforce them. - Subsequent protocols to the convention have received less support than the first: Protocols I and II (1977) on protecting civilians have not been signed or ratified, including by the United States (not ratified), Israel (not signed or ratified) and Iran (not ratified). - Many conflicts now are characterised by sexual violence and attacks on civilian safe havens (e.g. schools, hospitals).
The Rome Statute (1998)	Establishes the International Criminal Court (ICC) to prosecute individuals (including state leaders) responsible for genocide, crimes against humanity, war crimes and the crime of aggression.	Provides a permanent international tribunal for serious crimes. Promotes accountability and deters future atrocities. Complements national judicial systems when they are unwilling or unable to act.	Limited jurisdiction, as non-member states are not bound by it. Reliance on state cooperation for enforcement, which can hinder effectiveness. Accusations of bias, particularly against African states.

International courts and tribunals

The International Court of Justice (ICJ)

> **Chapter Link**
>
> The ICJ is one of the main UN Organs. Its structure, membership, wider role, including settling disputes between states over sovereignty and territory, and its overall significance in global politics, are all examined in **Chapter 4: Political Global Governance**.

Whilst the ICJ predominantly deals with political disputes between states, for example border disputes, it is being increasingly used by states to attempt to protect human rights in other states. It has created judicial precedents on international humanitarian law, both in its rulings on contentious disputes between states and in its advisory opinions, requested by the UNGA.

Contentious case: Bosnia and Herzegovina vs Serbia and Montenegro (initiated 1993)

In 1993, the newly independent Bosnia and Herzegovina filed an application to the ICJ accusing the then Federal Republic of Yugoslavia (FRY) of having committed genocide during the Bosnian War, violating its obligations under the Genocide Convention. Initially, the FRY refused to engage with the case and challenged the jurisdiction of the ICJ. Following protracted submissions of evidence, responses and public hearings, the ICJ finally reached a verdict in February 2006. The court ruled that whilst there was evidence of massive killings and atrocities throughout the war, these were not accompanied by the intent to commit genocide. Only in the case of the Srebrenica killings in 1995 did the court find that genocide had taken place, and, in this case, the perpetrators were not acting on behalf of the FRY.

Comparative Theories: Realist and liberal views on judicial precedents

Realist view	Liberal view
Judicial precedents can be controversial as they may override decisions made by states when **signing** treaties, thereby undermining the principle of state sovereignty – a key preoccupation of realists.	On the other hand, liberals argue that the supranational authority of international courts has the consent of their state members, gained through the signing of treaties and election of judges.
Politicians who are concerned primarily with state sovereignty often criticise *judicial activism*: where judges apply laws broadly or in new ways in international law. Instead, they tend to demand *judicial restraint* – where judges interpret laws narrowly and leave policy-making to state legislatures.	They emphasise the legitimate authority of judicial precedents, which update the law in response to changing circumstances. They uphold the independence of international courts from state interference.
This critique has been evident in the attitudes of British Conservative politicians to the European Court of Human Rights and US decisions to impose sanctions on the International Criminal Court for opening an investigation into US war crimes in Afghanistan and issuing arrest warrants for Israeli leaders for alleged war crimes in Gaza.	This critique has been evident in the British Labour government's statement in 2024 that it respects the independence of the International Criminal Court and would not challenge its investigation in Gaza, regardless of its belief that Israel was entitled to act in self-defence.

> **Definition**
>
> **Signing:** By signing an international treaty, a state expresses its approval of it. It also creates an obligation for the state to act in accordance with the treaty.

The court therefore concluded that Serbia and Montenegro had not met their obligations to prevent genocide in this case, nor had they met their obligation to punish the perpetrators of genocide (see section on ICTY).

Advisory opinion – Israel's construction of the wall in the Occupied Palestinian Territory (initiated 2003)

In December 2003, the UNGA submitted a request for an advisory opinion from the ICJ concerning Israel's construction of a wall around the Occupied Palestinian Territory (Map 6.1). Considering the case, the ICJ judges issued an advisory opinion in July 2004, which was agreed by 14–1, that the construction of the wall was contrary to international law. In reaching this decision, the opinion outlines that:

- The wall violates the right of the Palestinian people to self-determination.
- The purpose of the wall is to change the borders of a Palestinian state.
- Israel should cease construction of the wall and pay reparations to those affected by its construction, e.g. for loss of land and property.
- The construction of the wall violates international human rights laws, including the right to freedom of movement and the right to access vital services such as water, healthcare and education.

The judges' advisory opinion shows how the ICJ can play a significant role in shaping international human rights laws. It is not legally binding on Israel, but advisory opinions are seen as 'soft law' with moral authority.

There was a dissenting opinion from a US judge on the panel, showing that, despite the impartiality principle, national interests do impact judicial decisions. In this case, the national interest of supporting their ally, Israel, overrode humanitarian laws and principles. Israel chose to ignore the advisory opinion.

Map 6.1 The West Bank Wall

Source: iStock.com/filo

Contentious case: the Gambia vs Myanmar (initiated 2019)

In 2019, on behalf of the fifty-seven members of the Organisation of Islamic Cooperation (OIC), the Gambia submitted an application to the ICJ in relation to the alleged genocide of the Rohingya Muslims in the Myanmese state of Rakhine, arguing that Myanmar had violated its obligations under the Genocide Convention. The Gambia has accused Myanmar of the following violations:

- Denial of legal rights, including the right to marry and bear children.
- Subjecting the Rohingya to systemic hate campaigns designed to incite genocide.
- Clearance operations including mass executions of men, women and children, burning Rohingya villages.
- Commissioning a mass campaign of rape and sexual violence

In 2023, the Gambia and the OIC were supported by a joint declaration under Article 63 of the Court's statute by Canada, Denmark, France, Germany, the Netherlands and the United Kingdom, citing their obligations to prevent and punish the crime of genocide.

Myanmar initially replied by challenging the jurisdiction of the ICJ, but the ICJ has ruled that Myanmar must prevent further acts prohibited by the Genocide Convention and protect evidence related to previous alleged crimes by late 2025 11 countries had supported the Gambia's case, making this one of the most legally significant genocide cases in history. The case continued.

Contentious case: South Africa vs Israel (initiated 2023)

"In December 2023, South Africa brought a case to the ICJ relating to its duty as a signatory of the Genocide Convention to prevent acts of genocide in Gaza. In early 2024, the ICJ agreed that this case could be pursued. On 8 October 2024, South Africa filed an application to the ICJ accusing Israel of violating the Convention on the Prevention and Punishment of the Crime of Genocide in its military operations in Gaza since 2023. South Africa submitted 750 pages of evidence outlining alleged acts of genocide and genocidal intent, with over 4,000 pages of annexes. The South African presidency stated that 'the evidence will show that undergirding Israel's genocidal acts is the special intent to commit genocide, a failure by Israel to prevent incitement to genocide, to prevent genocide itself and its failure to punish those inciting and committing acts of genocide'. South Africa accused Israel of:

- killing civilians
- causing serious bodily and mental harm
- mass expulsion and displacement
- depriving civilians of access to food, water, shelter, clothing, hygiene products and medical assistance.

Several UN member states have joined in support of South Africa's application under Article 63 of the Court's statute. Hearings began in 2025, and Israel was given until early 2026 to submit its response.

UN Special Tribunals

Origins and development

International tribunals are ad hoc (temporary) courts created to deal with human rights atrocities that occur in specific places, or conflict. After the Second World War, the Nuremberg and Tokyo trials marked the first use of international tribunals to prosecute individuals for wartime atrocities. The Nuremberg Trials (1945–1946) convicted 19 of 21 Nazi defendants tried, sentencing 12 to death and 3 to life imprisonment (Photo 6.3). The Tokyo Trials (1946–1948) tried Japanese military and political leaders. All 25 defendants were convicted, with 7 sentenced to death. These trials were pivotal in shaping international law, establishing the principle that individuals – as opposed to states – can be held accountable for war crimes and crimes against humanity.

Photo 6.2 Nazi Hermann Goering during his trial as part of the Nuremberg Trials, 1946.

Source: Bettmann via Getty Images

UN Special Tribunals are established by and report to the UNSC (Table 6.3). They apply relevant domestic and international law when prosecuting individuals accused. Whilst there were no further tribunals during the Cold War due to the dysfunction in the UN system, after the Cold War, a number of international courts and tribunals were established. They have a number of aims:

- To investigate and prosecute individuals responsible for war crimes, crimes against humanity and genocide.

- Provide justice and accountability for victims of human rights atrocities which can help to contribute to post-conflict reconciliation and peacebuilding efforts by the international community.

- Establish an impartial court to hear matters of international law in areas where the state is unable or unwilling to do so.

- Help to develop customary international human rights laws.

International courts and tribunals were used extensively throughout the 2000s; however, in recent years their use has significantly declined. There are a number of strengths and weaknesses to addressing human rights.

Strengths of international courts and tribunals

The development of international human rights law

The courts and tribunals were critical in influencing the development of international human rights law. Table 6.4 outlines the unique contributions of the different international courts and tribunals. Critically, the courts and tribunals established personal culpability for war crimes, crimes against

Table 6.3 **International Tribunals**

Tribunal	When	Objectives	Precedents in international law
International Tribunal for the Former Yugoslavia (ICTY) (see case study)	Established 1993 and dissolved in 2017	To investigate and prosecute those responsible for war crimes and crimes against humanity in the territory of the Former Yugoslavia.	First verdicts on genocide and recognised that rape is a means of perpetrating genocide. First to indict a head of state.
International Criminal Tribunal for Rwanda (ICTR)	Established 1994 and dissolved in 2015	To investigate and prosecute those responsible for genocide and crimes against humanity in Rwanda and neighbouring states between January and December 1994. To help bring about national reconciliation.	Delivered verdicts on genocide and recognised that rape is a means of perpetrating genocide. First to convict a head of government.
Special Panels for Serious Crimes (East Timor) (SPSC)	Established in 2000 and dissolved in 2006	To investigate and prosecute crimes, including but not limited to genocide, war crimes and crimes against humanity.	First to prosecute forced marriage and child soldier recruitment.

Tribunal	When	Objectives	Precedents in international law
Special Court for Sierra Leone (SCSL)	Established in 2002 and dissolved in 2013. Replaced by the Residual Special Court for Sierra Leone in 2013 (to protect witnesses, supervise sentences)	To prosecute individuals responsible for human rights atrocities in the Sierra Leone civil war.	Created a 'hybrid' model of international and domestic law for investigating and prosecuting human rights crimes, strengthening the legitimacy of the court. First to **convict** a head of state. The first tribunal to prosecute for forced marriage and the recruitment of child soldiers.
The Special Tribunal for Lebanon (STL)	Established 2007 (opened in 2009) and shut in 2021 due to financial difficulties	To investigate and prosecute those responsible for the terrorist attack on 14 February 2005, which killed former prime minister, Rafik Hariri.	The first tribunal to prosecute terrorism offences.
The Extraordinary Chambers in the Courts of Cambodia (ECCC)	Established 2006	To investigate and prosecute those responsible for crimes committed during the Khmer Rouge regime (1975–9).	Sentenced a head of state to life imprisonment.

> **Exam Tip:**
> You must be clear on the differences between indictments, prosecutions and convictions. An indictment is when a court wants to investigate a claim against an individual accused of a crime, a prosecution is the process through which an individual is either found guilty or not guilty (i.e. the court case itself) and finally, a conviction is when an individual is found guilty of a crime.

humanity and genocide. They also show that no organisation is beyond reproach, for example, in Rwanda the ICTR established that the media was responsible for broadcasts which incited people to commit genocide.

Justice and reconciliation

The courts and tribunals play a significant role in facilitating justice and reconciliation in post-conflict societies. They do this in numerous ways.

They promote justice through the prosecution process. Irrespective of whether an individual is found guilty, following due process against indicted individuals shows victims and their families that the rule of law is being applied to the crimes. The courts and tribunals also promote justice by convicting the perpetrators of war crimes, crimes against humanity and genocide.

The fact that the majority of courts and tribunals make their evidence publicly available helps to ensure transparency and legitimacy. It also helps post-conflict societies to acknowledge and address shared trauma through truth-telling about what happened. This also provides an official historical record, which helps to challenge denial in the future.

These courts and tribunals support the development of legal expertise in post-conflict societies by employing and training local people. For example, the International Criminal Tribunal for Rwanda (ICTR) recruited more than 1,200 local employees.

CASE STUDY: INTERNATIONAL CRIMINAL TRIBUNAL FOR THE FORMER YUGOSLAVIA (ICTY)

Context

In 1992, the Socialist Federal Republic of Yugoslavia collapsed. Some of its republics declared independence. Conflict broke out between the remaining Serb-dominated Federal Republic of Yugoslavia (FRY) and Slovenia in 1992, and a civil war was fought between Bosnian Serbs, Croats and Muslims in 1992–95, with the FRY providing support to Bosnian Serbs. There was another war between the FRY and Kosovo in 1997–99. There were widespread atrocities, including mass killings, ethnic cleansing, rape, torture, starvation and the use of concentration camps. Most – but not all – of the atrocities were committed by Bosnian Serb forces against other ethnic groups.

In response, the UNSC established the ICTY in May 1993 at The Hague in the Netherlands. The tribunal had a broad mandate: to deter future crimes in the territory and to contribute to lasting peace by bringing justice to thousands of victims.

Significance

In total, 161 indictments were issued, 111 trials were conducted, and 90 individuals were convicted, including Bosnian Serb General Ratko Mladic, the so-called 'Butcher of Bosnia', who was sentenced to life imprisonment for genocide and crimes against humanity.

From the outset, the ICTY faced problems in securing arrests because it lacked its own police force. NATO claimed the whereabouts of indictees were unknown, yet high-profile perpetrators such as Mladic moved freely across the former Yugoslavia. Human Rights Watch investigated and submitted evidence of atrocities to the tribunal and mapped all known suspects in their 'Arrest Now' campaign in 1997, applying political pressure on NATO to arrest them.

Indictees were arrested all over the world, including Croatian General Ante Gotovina in the Canary Islands. The EU encouraged Croatia's compliance with the tribunal with an offer of EU membership.

However, despite giving voice to thousands of victims, the location of the court in The Hague, in the Netherlands, was remote and victims and their families were, in practice, often denied access. It seemed to many that the tribunal was more concerned about the international community 'saving face' than bringing justice to victims and their families.

Furthermore, a lengthy process meant that justice was not always served. Serbian President Slobodan Milosevic died in custody before being sentenced. In November 2017, Bosnian Croat General Slobodan Praljak swallowed poison in the dock following his conviction and died, rather than face his sentence.

The ICTY may not have achieved a sustainable peace. Many Serbs felt unfairly targeted by the tribunal. Indeed, over 60 per cent of convictions were Serbs and Bosnian Serbs, receiving sentences totalling over 1,000 years. Although Muslims and Croats committed fewer atrocities, they were also less likely to be convicted for their crimes. Russia criticised the court as 'victor's justice'. In Serbia, Milosevic remains a national hero.

Despite these criticisms, the ICTY significantly developed customary international humanitarian law. There were multiple convictions for rape as a crime of genocide, for example, three Bosnian Serbs sentenced for organising and running 'rape camps' in the town of Foca. It was also the first tribunal to prosecute sexual violence against men and boys within a conflict.

Table 6.4 Actions of International Courts and Tribunals

Prosecutions	Convictions
• Slobodan Milosevic, former leader of Serbia, was indicted and prosecuted by the **ICTY** for crimes against humanity and genocide committed during the conflicts in Croatia, Bosnia and Kosovo. He died whilst being prosecuted. • The **SCSL** indicted and prosecuted Issa Sesay, commander of the Revolutionary United Front; however, he was later acquitted.	• The **ICTR** was the first tribunal to convict a head of government, former prime minister, Jean Kambanda, for the crime of genocide. • The **SCSL** was the first tribunal to convict a head of state, President Charles Taylor, for war crimes and crimes against humanity. • The **ECCC** handed out the sentence of life imprisonment to former head of state, Khieu Samphan for crimes against humanity and genocide.

Procedural strengths

Owing to the complexity and sensitivity of the cases, courts and tribunals and better able than national courts to address war crimes, crimes against humanity and genocide. They are impartial and independent, often free from political pressure. The courts and tribunals benefit from a wealth of legal personnel and generous financial resources. This enables them to manage large caseloads. For example, the ICTR indicted 93 individuals and convicted 62 of these.

Weaknesses of international courts and tribunals

Struggle to achieve justice and reconciliation

The courts and tribunals have been accused of implementing a 'victors justice', meaning that the crimes of victors are often ignored, eroding the principle of legal equality. The ICTR did not prosecute a single Tutsi rebel, some of whom now occupy important positions within Rwandan society. The International Criminal Tribunal for the Former Yugoslavia (ICTY) was also accused by Russia and Serbia of being politically biased. This was because the majority of individuals prosecuted and convicted were Bosnian Serbs. Their criticisms were further fuelled by the fact that some non-Serbs were acquitted, for example Kosovar commander Ramush Haradinaj. The Special Tribunal for Lebanon (STL) was also accused of victor's justice being established to investigate the murder of twenty-two individuals in a terrorist attack, but not being mandated to investigate the crimes committed in the broader context of the Lebanon Civil War.

In some cases, the courts and tribunals were not complemented by local efforts to promote reconciliation. Whereas in Rwanda, the efforts of the ICTR were complemented by the efforts of the local 'Gacaca' open-air community justice courts; in the former Yugoslavia, this never happened, meaning that only the high-level perpetrators of human rights crimes were prosecuted. This is because the tribunals did not have the capacity or the capability to investigate all those accused of human rights violations. The the absence of community-based justice and reconciliation processes alongside the ICTY is one of the reasons why peace in Bosnia even today remains in such a fragile state because there are still long-held animosities between the former warring parties some of who have already served their sentences, others who were never prosecuted in the first place.

High operating costs

The courts and tribunals have been accused of having too high operational costs. The high cost per conviction is also criticised as being an inefficient use of funds in post-conflict societies. The following examples illustrate these points:

- Both the ICTY and the ICTR took over two years to begin prosecuting cases. The length of time to prosecute individuals ranged from months to years in some cases. In 2000, these trials accounted for over 10 per cent of the UN's regular budget! The ICTR alone cost in excess of $1 billion.
- The cost per trial for the ICTY and ICTR was considered too high. For the ICTY, it is estimated that each prosecution cost in excess of $700,000. For the ICTR, this figure is even higher at $25 million.
- The STL cost $970,000 in its 15-year history and only secured one conviction tried in absentia.

Procedural limitations

The courts and tribunals struggled to fulfil their mandates owing to the difficulties of operating in conflict or post-conflict societies. Criminal indictments at the ICTY during the Bosnian War put peace negotiations at risk. Consequently, the ICTY had to issue sealed indictments so that individuals would not be incentivised to continue the war. The threat of indictment also failed to prevent the ongoing violence. The Srebrenica genocide was committed after the ICTY had been established.

Whilst there are benefits to holding tribunals in stable and neutral third-party states such as the ICTR in Tanzania and the ICTY in the Netherlands, these arrangements have been criticised for their remoteness from the post-conflict societies they served.

> **Chapter Link**
>
> The use of international tribunals is linked to polarity, discussed in **Chapter 3: Power and Developments**. In the US-dominated unipolar system of the 1990s, the UNSC agreed to set up several international tribunals (see **Chapter 4: Political Global Governance**). However, as multipolarity has emerged, the UNSC has become more dysfunctional, and so its use has declined. There are disagreements about where a tribunal could be used, but there are also more fundamental disagreements over universal human rights.

The International Criminal Court (ICC)

Origins and development

Calls for a permanent international criminal court began in the late 1980s. In 1998, delegates from 160 countries and 33 organisations and a coalition of NGOs met in Rome to make it happen. The Rome Statute (1998) established a court of last resort to investigate and prosecute individuals guilty of committing four types of atrocities:

- **Acts of genocide**: the intention to destroy a national, ethnic, racial or religious group, in whole or in part, by killing, deliberately causing serious harm, preventing births and removing children. Genocidal intent is very difficult to prove as it requires evidence of orders given from the top of the chain of command.

- **Crimes against humanity**: a much broader concept of 'widespread' and 'systematic' attacks on groups of civilians, including killing, enslavement, imprisonment, deportation, torture, rape and more. These crimes are easier to convict than genocide.

- **War crimes**: these are committed in situations when war has been declared. They include the use of poison gas, taking hostages, attacking civilians, enlisting child soldiers and torturing prisoners of war.

- The **crime of aggression** – planning and executing an attack on another state in violation of the UN Charter – was added to the statute in 2010, and the ICC was given jurisdiction over this crime from 2018.

The Rome Statute was initially ratified by only 120 states, with 21 abstentions and 7 votes against. The United States, China, Israel, Iraq, Libya, Qatar and Yemen all voted against it and refused to join the court.

The ICC came into being in 2002. It is based in The Hague, the Netherlands. Unlike the ICJ, which deals with states, the ICC can investigate and prosecute individuals. It cannot apprehend indicted criminals for itself and so it relies on its member states to arrest fugitive indictees. It can detain indictees before trial, but after sentencing, they are usually taken into custody by a member state. The court is overseen and funded by its member states. Their contributions are based on their economic size (Table 6.5).

The ICC has eighteen judges, each from a different member state and elected by member states for nine-year non-renewable terms. The most high-profile and controversial figure is the prosecutor. British lawyer Karim Khan QC took on this office in 2021 for a non-renewable nine-year term.

As of October 2024, the International Criminal Court (ICC) has 124 member states. Notably, three of the P5 are not members of the court. The newest member to join the ICC, in 2024, was Armenia.

Critically, the ICC can only investigate issues that have arisen since its establishment in 2002. It will only take action where the national courts of a state are unwilling or unable to investigate or prosecute crimes. It has three ways of opening an investigation into crimes:

(1) Member states can refer any situation that is within the jurisdiction of the court for investigation by its prosecutors.

(2) The UNSC can refer any case to the court, irrespective of whether the state is party to the Rome Statute. They did this in the case of Omar al-Bashir, the now-deposed president of Sudan, who was accused of genocide.

Table 6.5 ICC Annual Budgets

Year	Annual budget in millions (in euros)
2018	128
2022	154
2023	169.6
2024	187
2025 (proposed budget)	202.6

(3) The ICC prosecutor can initiate cases on their own initiative. This is important because it means that, unlike the ICJ, the ICC can initiate cases of its choosing.

Significantly, the Rome Statute allows the ICC to investigate an individual who is a national of a non-member state if the individual has committed the crimes in the territory of a member state. This is the part of the statute that has been most unpopular with the United States, leading to the sanctioning of ICC prosecutors by two Trump administrations for initiating investigations into atrocities alleged against US forces in Afghanistan, and against Israeli forces in Gaza.

The ICC has a complicated relationship with the UN Security Council. The United States proposed that UNSC permission should be required for the ICC to investigate and prosecute crimes. However, this was overruled by other states on the basis that its veto powers could probably paralyse the court. Instead, the 'Singapore Compromise' agreed that the UNSC can pass a resolution to postpone an ICC investigation for 12 months. That said, the UNSC does refer cases to the ICC.

Strengths of the ICC

Global reach and accountability

A key strength of the ICC is its ability to hold those guilty of human rights crimes to account in both conflict and post-conflict scenarios. It also has a truly global reach. The ICC demonstrates continued relevance by being involved in ongoing conflicts and issues, including:

- **Venezuela (2021 investigation):** Following a referral from six states, the ICC opened an investigation into crimes against humanity. This investigation was initially delayed due to Venezuela's wish to investigate in its national courts, but the ICC overruled this in March 2024, asserting its jurisdiction over the matter.

- **Russia and Ukraine:** The ICC launched an investigation after a referral from over forty member states, despite neither Russia nor Ukraine being full member states (Ukraine accepted the court's jurisdiction for crimes committed since the annexation of Crimea). In March 2023, the court issued an arrest warrant for Russian President Vladimir Putin for forcibly deporting hundreds of children from Ukraine into Russian foster families. In March 2024, further arrest warrants were issued for two Russian commanders.

- **Israel and Palestine:** The ICC first became involved in 2018 when the Palestinian Authorities asked the ICC to investigate crimes committed in the Gaza Strip and the West Bank. In late 2023, South Africa submitted a referral to the ICC, supported by other member states, to investigate further crimes committed during Israeli military operations against Hamas. This was followed by an application by the ICC prosecutor, Karim Khan, for arrest warrants for Israeli Prime Minister Benjamin Netanyahu and three Hamas leaders, based on 'reasonable grounds to believe' they bear criminal responsibility for war crimes and crimes against humanity.

Legitimacy

The ICC is designed to be an inclusive organisation. Every state has the option to join the ICC, ensuring it is accessible to all states should they wish to join it. Procedurally, it also gains legitimacy from the process of selecting judges. The court requires a gender-balanced bench and representation from each of the UN's five regions, aiming for broad geographical and gender diversity. Whilst not a part of the UN, the ICC gains further legitimacy through its endorsement by the UNSC. Referrals to the ICC by the UNSC suggest that both the UN and the P5 states view the court with some legitimacy. Examples include the UNSC referral of Sudan to the ICC in 2005, and the referral of the situation in Libya in 2011 in response to the killing of unarmed civilians during the Arab Spring. The latter led to arrest warrants for Prime Minister Muammar Gaddafi and his son, Saif al-Islam.

Strengthening international human rights law and protection

Similar to international courts and tribunals, the ICC also contributes to and strengthens international human rights law. The ICC has codified and provided the most authoritative and detailed definitions of genocide, crimes against humanity and war crimes available to date, strengthening the normative framework of international law. It also helps tackle the global justice gap by being able to protect human rights in states that are unable or unwilling to do so, providing a crucial avenue for accountability. It can help to deter future atrocities by shaping the behaviour of political and military leaders; the threat of legal proceedings may have persuaded leaders of the Lord's Resistance Army in Uganda to attend peace talks in 2007, and prompted Australia to launch its own inquiry into its soldiers' conduct in Afghanistan.

Powers

The ICC has broad-ranging powers to investigate and prosecute offenders, and unlike courts and tribunals, is a permanent institution based in The Hague. The court is permanently in session and can respond quickly to events as they occur, ensuring a continual mechanism for justice. It also demonstrates that not even heads of state or government, or senior officials, are immune from prosecution. Omar al-Bashir was the first sitting president of a state to be indicted for allegations of genocide, crimes against humanity and war crimes in Sudan's Darfur region, setting a powerful precedent for the future.

Weaknesses of the ICC

Weak representation and legitimacy

The ICC's legitimacy is undermined by significant gaps in its membership. Over 60 per cent of the world's population is not represented by the ICC; for example, India and China alone account for approximately 33 per cent of the world's population. The court has also experienced two significant withdrawals: Burundi in 2017 following an investigation into a government crackdown, and the Philippines in 2019 after an inquiry into Duterte's 'War on Drugs', demonstrating states' willingness to exit if national interests conflict with ICC investigations. These withdrawals undermine the legitimacy of the court.

The ICC also faces strong accusations of being Western-dominated, impacting its legitimacy and relationship with parts of the world. In its early years the Court focused primarily on African conflict situations. This was criticised by some African leaders, who labelled it a 'colonial court' for perpetuating damaging stereotypes about the region. In 2016, the African Union (AU) urged its members to collectively withdraw from the court due to this perceived bias. Only Burundi did so, in 2017. South Africa and Gambia also initiated but then cancelled withdrawal. Since 2016 the ICC's case load has expanded significantly, for example to situations in Afghanistan, Palestine, Ukraine and the Philippines.

Expensive and inefficient

The ICC is frequently criticised for its high operating costs. Its budget significantly exceeds the ICJ's (approximately $25 million to $30 million per year), and its costs increase year-on-year.

- It took until 2006 for the ICC to begin its first trial and until 2012 to secure its first conviction, indicating lengthy procedural timelines.
- In its first 20 years, the ICC had a budget of over $1.5 billion but secured only ten convictions and four acquittals, suggesting high costs relative to judicial outcomes.
- As of May 2024, the ICC had indicted fifty individuals and convicted only six individuals who were either imprisoned or forced to pay reparations.

The ICC has faced criticism for inefficiency, politicisation and a toxic internal culture. Human Rights Watch has accused the Court of allowing vote trading in judicial elections—raising serious concerns about its transparency and legitimacy. An Independent Expert Review highlighted a 'culture of fear' among staff.

Weak Powers

The ICC has limited power due to its complete dependence on state cooperation. The court is dependent on states to apprehend suspects because it cannot try them in absentia (unlike some of the international tribunals). For example, after his indictment, the Sudanese President Omar al-Bashir travelled overseas freely, receiving assurances from states he visited that he would not be extradited to the ICC. Even since his overthrow in 2019, Sudanese authorities have still not extradited him, preventing his prosecution. Even investigating human rights crimes requires the cooperation of states. Again, in the case of Sudan, the ICC had to drop investigations into war crimes in Darfur because the Sudanese government would not cooperate.

Challenges to State Sovereignty

The court's jurisdiction is perceived by realists as a direct threat to state sovereignty. This is because its powers of prosecution extend to citizens of all states. Even the citizens of non-signatory states can be investigated and prosecuted if their alleged crime was committed in a signatory state. The fact that the UNSC can refer to the ICC individuals from any state means that no one is truly immune from the court's reach, regardless of their state's ratification status. Finally, the ICC prosecutor enjoys enormous powers to prosecute, further contributing to concerns about an overreach of authority relative to state sovereignty. This is because the prosecutor has the power to initiate investigations on their own initiative based on information they receive, for example, from victims or NGOs. Some liberals might argue that this is a positive feature of the court, extending some protection of fundamental human rights to people living under non-signatory regimes.

CASE STUDY: THE UNITED STATES' UNEASY RELATIONSHIP WITH THE ICC

Context

The United States' relationship with the International Criminal Court (ICC) has been fraught with tension. In 2000, President Clinton signed the Rome Statute but did not seek congressional ratification, arguing it was flawed.

In 2002, the Bush administration withdrew from the Rome Statute, and Congress passed the American Service Members' Protection Act (ASPA). This law authorised the US president to use 'all means necessary' to secure the release of American or allied personnel detained by the ICC – a provision that led to it being called the 'Hague Invasion Act'. It aimed to show the US government's commitment to protecting its citizens and allies from politically motivated prosecutions. However, it was a unilateral statement of the United States' presumed right to invade an allied state, to the distaste of the Netherlands. The ASPA also withholds military aid from ICC member states unless they sign bilateral immunity agreements ensuring neither extradites the other's citizens to the ICC.

In 2005, Senator Hillary Clinton argued that although she thought that the United States should engage with the court, 'Europe must acknowledge that ... we are more vulnerable to the misuse of an international criminal court because of the international role we play and the resentments that flow from that.' The Obama administration said that it would cooperate with the ICC and participated as an observer at the ICC's Assembly.

In 2020, National Security Advisor John Bolton strongly criticised the ICC, and President Trump imposed sanctions on ICC officials, including then-Chief Prosecutor Fatou Bensouda, in response to her investigations into alleged war crimes in Afghanistan and Palestine.

President Biden lifted these sanctions in 2021, yet the United States remains deeply critical of the court's actions relating to Afghanistan and Palestine, in particular its investigations in Gaza.

In 2025, President Trump reimposed sanctions on Prosecutor Karim Khan over the ICC's prosecution of Israeli leaders for alleged war crimes in Gaza, reaffirming US objections to the court's jurisdiction over non-member states like Israel.

Significance

ASPA has faced widespread criticism for its coercive nature and its rejection of international law. US sanctions aimed at ICC officials have further compromised the court's autonomy. Condemnation has been strong in Europe, where the ICC is based and where a robust tradition of human rights protection is upheld by the European Convention on Human Rights.

On the other hand, the United States believes the ICC is deeply politicised and that there are insufficient checks and balances to limit its supranational powers.

The strained relationship demonstrates the limits of the ICC's authority in constraining state power and enforcing international accountability. By refusing to recognise ICC jurisdiction, the United States set a precedent for other powerful states to disregard the court, limiting its legitimacy and effectiveness as an international court of last resort.

The ICC's ability to uphold human rights globally depends not only on legal mechanisms but also on collective political will, which is difficult in a world of competing national interests. Cases involving powerful non-member states expose the court's vulnerability: it is unable to enforce its own indictments of Israeli Prime Minister Netanyahu and Russian President Putin. This complicates efforts to achieve consistent, impartial justice across the globe.

The European Court of Human Rights (ECtHR)

Origins and development

The ECtHR was established to promote human rights and the rule of law in Europe. It upholds the rights outlined in the European Convention on Human Rights (ECHR), which came into force in 1950 (Photo 6.4). The ECtHR became operational in 1959. Based in Strasbourg, the court initially had twelve member states, each of which nominated a judge to be based at the court (Table 6.6). In 2025 it had forty-six member states.

Article 46 of the ECHR states that member states must follow the final decisions of the court. So, on the surface, it appears that the decisions of the court take precedence over the sovereignty of states. Indeed, approximately 90 per cent of ECtHR judgments are acted on. States must justify any delay or modification when implementing a ruling. Consistent non-compliance could lead to suspension or expulsion from the Council of Europe.

However, under Article 15, in exceptional circumstances of war, public emergency or other strict necessity, a member state can decide to temporarily derogate (disapply) some provisions of the ECHR. In those circumstances, derogated measures must not conflict with the state's other obligations under international law and must be notified to the Council of Europe. The right to life, prohibition of torture, slavery and punishment without law cannot be derogated.

The Court is extremely busy. At its height in 2013, the Court allocated 65,800 applications. Between 2011 and 2021, applications averaged at just under 42,000 per year. In the same period, the Court issued an average of 965 judgements per year.

Article 6 of the ECHR, right to a fair hearing, makes up 25 per cent of the Court's work. A further 25 per cent concerns serious breaches of the ECHR, such as the right to life and prohibition of torture and inhuman treatment. Much of the Court's work has been to consider applications against the Russian Federation. In 2021, these cases made up a quarter of the Court's caseload. In February 2022, the Russian Federation was expelled from the Council of Europe, following its invasion of Ukraine. It later withdrew from the ECHR.

Photo 6.3 Pro-Kurdish and pro-Islamic students protest against the ban on Islamic-style headscarves at Turkish universities, December 2010. The ECHR ruled that wearing the headscarf on campus 'is not protected as part of freedom of religion and is not compatible with the principle of secularism'.

Source: Adem Altan /AFP via Getty Images

Table 6.6 Strengths and Weaknesses of the ECtHR

Strengths	Weaknesses
The independence of judges is protected. In the recruitment process, each member state nominates three national judges. These are assessed, and one of them is elected by the Council of Europe.	The selection of judges can still be influenced by political factors. Nominated candidates might all reflect political biases or interests rather than ensuring absolute judicial independence.
Member states can derogate from (not apply) the ECHR in times of 'war or other public emergency threatening the life of a nation'. This encourages states to stay in the ECHR whilst prioritising national security. For example, in 2022, Ukraine notified the court of its derogation from several articles of the ECHR in response to Russian aggression.	Derogation can significantly impact human rights. In response to the 9/11 terrorist attacks, the UK derogated from Article 5, to detain non-nationals suspected of terrorism who could not be deported due to risk of torture. The court later ruled in A v. UK that this was disproportionate and discriminatory towards non-nationals.
The Court can grant urgent interim measures when an applicant is at risk of 'irreversible harm'. When the court issues an interim measure, the offending member state must comply.	Member states have ignored interim measures. Prior to its expulsion, the Russian Federation said it would ignore any interim measures which were contrary to its will.
The Court has established a robust human rights culture within Europe. It can effectively protect the human rights of individuals because it receives applications from individuals as opposed to only from state parties. It is the only international court that can do this. Approximately 90 per cent of its judgements are adhered to, showing good compliance by member states and respect for its authority.	Some states are slow to comply with the court. Hungary has implemented only 28 per cent of judgments. The UK takes, on average, three years to comply. It took a decade to address the court's 2005 ruling on prisoners' voting rights in Hirst v UK (No 2). In 2015, it finally adopted minimal measures by granting the vote only to a few categories of prisoners. This complied with the ruling but did not fulfil the principles of the ECHR.

> **Chapter Link**
>
> The European Court of Human Rights is part of the Council of Europe. These should not be confused with the European Court of Justice, the European Council and the Council of the EU – which are all European Union Institutions. Although not listed as a regional organisation in the specification, the Council of Europe is an important regional actor. You could include its impact on human rights in questions about the impact of regionalism alongside the other regional actors discussed in **Chapter 9: The EU and Regionalism**.

The roles and significance of non-state actors in scrutinising human rights

UN human rights bodies

Since 1945, the UN has developed bodies to support the implementation of the UDHR and monitor state compliance with human rights treaties. They are not a source of international law, but they do scrutinise adherence to the law.

Comparative Analysis: The differences between the International Court of Justice and the International Criminal Court

	ICJ	ICC
The subject and process of prosecutions	The ICJ investigates human rights charges against states, not individuals. The ICJ is unable to initiate contentious cases or advisory opinions unless it is requested to do so by states.	The ICC investigates individuals suspected of carrying out war crimes, crimes against humanity and genocide. The ICC Prosecutor can initiate cases on their own accord.
Membership	All UN member states are members of the ICJ, since it is a part of the UN.	The ICC is a voluntary court which is not part of the UN. It has 125 member states.

	ICJ	ICC
Contribution to international human rights law	The ICJ does not contribute to international human rights law significantly.	The ICC pioneers international human rights law.
Impact on state sovereignty	Whilst in theory the judgements of the ICJ are legally binding in states, states can opt out of this. Unless they consent to jurisdiction, it is not binding.	The judgements of the ICC are legally binding on its members.

The UN Human Rights Commission (UNHRC), established in 1946, worked on setting international human rights standards. It was involved in drafting the Universal Declaration of Human Rights and many of the human rights treaties. Following the adoption of the International Bill of Human Rights in 1966, the Commission shifted its focus to monitoring and investigating treaty violations.

The UNGA held a World Conference on Human Rights in 1993, which agreed to set up the Office of the High Commissioner for Human Rights. The High Commissioner's job is to ensure that human rights protection is at the centre of the UN's work and to support states to improve their human rights records. Meanwhile, the Human Rights Commission lost credibility. It was regularly accused of being biased against Israel, whilst ignoring other states with poor human rights records, who would seek election to the commission as a way to avoid scrutiny.

The UN Human Rights Council (HRC) was set up by the UNGA in 2006 to replace the discredited Commission. It is responsible for setting international human rights standards and conducting a four-yearly periodic review of the human rights situation within every member state. It is advised by 'special rapporteurs', independent, unpaid human rights lawyers.

The Council does not have the legal authority to compel states to stop their human rights abuses, but it can refer states to the UNSC and the UNGA. The periodic review and special rapporteurs are an improvement on the work of the old Commission, but the HRC still suffers from politicisation and evasion by states.

Global civil society and other non-state actors

NGOs can lobby states to prompt the creation of treaties and institutions. They can expose and monitor human rights abuses, and they can provide evidence and expert testimony to IGOs and international courts and tribunals.

The International Committee of the Red Cross played a leading role in writing the Geneva Conventions and Genocide Conventions, and successfully persuaded states to sign up to these, ensuring their global significance. Alongside its partner organisation, the International Committee of the Red Crescent, it works with the UN to provide humanitarian aid in conflict zones and to monitor the treatment of civilians and the conduct of war under these conventions.

The International Campaign for the ICC was a Global South movement which was involved in drafting the Rome Statute and successfully lobbied states to agree the statute in 1998, creating an International Criminal Court of last resort at The Hague in 2002. It also lobbied for the addition of the crime of aggression to the statute in 2010.

Human Rights Watch (HRW) is an international NGO based in New York that has consultative status at ECOSOC and can speak in UNHRC debates. Its reporters monitor human rights abuses around the world, researching and publishing reports for the media, state governments and IGOs. HRW played a critical role in helping to locate war criminals across the world after the wars in the former Yugoslavia. It was a significant leader in the International Campaign for the ICC, alongside Amnesty International and many NGOs from Global South countries. It has provided expert testimony and evidence that has helped to secure convictions at the international tribunals and at the International Criminal Court. In recent years, it has investigated the treatment of unaccompanied asylum-seeking children in France, and human rights abuses in conflict zones such as Mariupol in Ukraine, Gaza and Tigray in Ethiopia.

Humanitarian intervention

What is humanitarian intervention?

In global politics, intervention means military action taken by one state or a group of states to force compliance by another state. The UN Charter says that the UN is not authorised to 'intervene in matters which are essentially within the domestic jurisdiction of any state'. Yet, as we have seen, after the Second World War, the question of how civilians were treated changed from being essentially a domestic matter to an international one. The problem then became, how could states that abuse their citizens be held to account?

Like the rule of law, the concept of *humanitarian intervention* originates in the liberal principle that the state must serve the individual. In this view, sovereignty is not *absolute*, as Thomas Hobbes would have argued, but *conditional* on the state fulfilling its responsibilities to protect human life and liberty, as proposed by John Locke's social contract. States must therefore protect their populations from genocide, crimes against humanity, war crimes and disasters. In human rights governance, the principle of the *responsibility to protect* (R2P) makes that responsibility universal. If a state deliberately perpetrates atrocities or is unable to protect its people from war crimes or natural disasters, the responsibility to protect them passes to the international community, which should intervene to restore order and save lives.

Ideally, this would be done peacefully, with the consent of the state concerned. Military support in this situation may be commonly described as an *intervention*, but strictly speaking, it is not, because it does not undermine that state's sovereignty. If the state refuses its responsibilities, the international community should apply pressure to the state. In the first instance, this would be diplomatic pressure in the form of the UNGA and the UNSC resolutions condemning the state's actions and calling for change. A second strategy would be to impose a collective non-military coercive measure, such as economic sanctions. As a last resort, the UNSC could authorise the use of collective military force under Chapter VII of the UN Charter – in other words, *humanitarian intervention*.

When and how should the international community intervene?

When there is clear evidence that a government is engaging in mass killings, rapes and ethnic cleansing of its own or another state's citizens, the case for forcible intervention should be clear-cut. In the 'fog of war', that is not always the case.

Even if there is clear evidence of the need for intervention, should the international community simply secure 'safe havens' for some citizens, whilst leaving the hostile government in power? Should the state leader be removed and brought to justice? If this requires the destruction of the existing regime, things are not so simple. Rebuilding a government from the ground up is a long, difficult task, and democracy cannot be imposed by force. The international community may ask wealthy democracies to take on that responsibility.

Secondly, what should be done about the larger number of countries where civil liberties are not respected, where political prisoners are mistreated, or where there is an apartheid regime? In these situations, there might be a strong case for lower-level interventions such as economic sanctions, but the case for forcible military intervention is less clear. The desire to create political stability, democratic governance and respect for civil and political rights are justifiable moral goals for liberals, but they are not necessarily humanitarian goals, unlike ending genocide. There is a possibility of causing greater harm through forcible intervention.

The rise of humanitarian intervention in the 1990s

The 1990s marked a shift towards humanitarian intervention, with the United States emerging as the sole superpower (Table 6.7). President George H.W. Bush declared a 'New World Order', leading to US intervention in the 1991 Gulf War to protect Kuwait and Iraqi Kurds.

A humanitarian crisis in Somalia in late 1992 prompted 'Operation Restore Hope'. This evolved into military action, but a 1993 helicopter shoot-down and US casualties led to withdrawal in 1994, leaving Somalia a failed state.

Simultaneously, the civil war in Yugoslavia from 1992 saw widespread atrocities. UN peacekeepers established 'safe havens' in Bosnia, yet Clinton's reluctance and the EU's hesitation meant atrocities continued.

In mid-1994, the Rwandan genocide saw at least 800,000 Tutsis and moderate Hutus killed. The world watched, but UN reinforcements arrived too late, drawing global condemnation.

Later, in 1994, the United States intervened in Haiti ('Operation Uphold Democracy') to restore its elected president, easily justified by curbing refugee flows to the United States.

The 1995 Srebrenica massacre, where 7,000 men and boys were killed in a UN 'safe haven', sparked outrage. UN Secretary-General Kofi Annan questioned state sovereignty in the face of such atrocities.

Srebrenica was a turning point for Bill Clinton. In 1995, NATO launched 'Operation Deliberate Force', ending the Bosnian genocide. The United States brokered the 'Dayton Accords', establishing peacekeepers and an interim government.

By 1997, Clinton and UK Prime Minister Tony Blair advocated robust interventionism. In 1999, NATO bombed Belgrade over Kosovo genocide reports without a UNSC mandate, with Clinton arguing genocide was a national interest. Blair's 'Blair Doctrine' asserted a moral responsibility to prevent genocide, leading to the 2000 'Responsibility to Protect' (R2P) concept, adopted by the UNGA in 2005. However, R2P's high point passed with Kosovo, becoming muddled with the 'War on Terror', which caused irreparable damage to the principle.

Was the war on terror a humanitarian war?

Following 9/11, the US-led intervention in Afghanistan was swiftly approved by the UNSC, primarily justified as self-defence to remove the Taliban for harbouring al-Qaeda. A secondary humanitarian argument to restore women's rights was also made. After 20 years, over a trillion dollars spent, and many casualties, the coalition withdrew in 2021, and the Taliban regained control and quickly reestablished the human rights restrictions it previously had in place, especially for women.

In Iraq, the justification for intervention was weaker. The United States and the UK claimed Saddam Hussein possessed weapons of mass destruction, but the evidence was questionable. The UNSC did not authorise the invasion, but the United States and the UK proceeded anyway, controversially aiming to impose democracy on the state. Saddam was quickly overthrown, but without a long-term plan for nation-building, Iraq descended into chaos, leading to a brutal insurgency and eventually paving the way for ISIS.

Neither intervention brought peace or stability. Both were largely regime change efforts, initially framed as self-defence but augmented with humanitarian justifications. They significantly damaged the international reputations of the United States and the UK, and by tainting the concept, contributed to the decline of the 'responsibility to protect' doctrine.

Reasons for success and failure of humanitarian intervention

There are certain conditions that support effective intervention. If these conditions are absent, interventions are more likely to fail.

1 A UNSC mandate and sufficient political will from the P5

The intervention should be authorised by the UNSC, with the political will amongst the P5 to quickly authorise and implement sufficient force. This accounted for successes in Iraq in the 1991 'Operation Provide Comfort', and in Bosnia from 1995 and Kosovo, where NATO members were on standby to force compliance.

This contrasts with the situation in Bosnia in 1993, when the United States and EU states were reluctant to get involved and when the UN peacekeepers were given insufficient powers by the UNSC. An intervention without UN consent looks very like imperialism, causing huge resentment. The lack of a UNSC mandate in Iraq in 2003 made the war highly controversial from the start and has resulted in a lack of political will for military intervention in subsequent situations needing humanitarian intervention, such as Sudan's most recent civil war from 2023.

2 Supporting a legitimate government

If intervention is requested by an elected government that has been overthrown, it is more likely to be seen as legitimate by the majority of the population and by the international community, meaning that it will probably face less resistance. For example, successful interventions in Sierra Leone and Côte d'Ivoire were requested by the legitimately elected governments.

In comparison, interventions that seek to overthrow an established government, even if unelected, will probably face stronger resistance, for example those in Afghanistan, Iraq and Libya.

Table 6.7 Significant Humanitarian Interventions, 1991–2013

Date and location	Intervention force	Humanitarian goal	UNSC mandate	Significance
1991, Northern Iraq	United States, UK, France 'Operation Provide Comfort'	Defend a no-fly zone to establish 'safe havens' for the Kurds from chemical attack by Saddam Hussein.	Yes	A successful intervention which highlighted the new US hegemony.
1993, Somalia	United States 'Operation Restore Hope'	To secure UN humanitarian aid from rebel raids.	Yes	A failure. US troops were lost in the Battle of Mogadishu, leading to a more cautious US foreign policy for the next two years.
1994, Haiti	United States 'Operation Uphold Democracy'	At the request of the deposed president, to restore the elected government after a military coup.	Yes	Short-term success restored the elected government, but Haiti has struggled with long-term lawlessness, leading to state failure.
1994, Rwanda	France 'Operation Turquoise'	Following the genocide of Tutsis by Hutus, once Tutsis had gained control, France created safe havens for Hutu refugees.	Yes, but delayed	This intervention was too little, too late to prevent the genocide. It succeeded in reducing reprisals, but the Hutu refugee crisis led to long-term problems in neighbouring DRC.
1995, Bosnia	NATO 'Operation Deliberate Force'	Following the failure of UN peacekeepers to stop genocide in Srebrenica, NATO aimed to end atrocities, including the three-year siege of the capital, Sarajevo by Serbs.	Yes	The intervention succeeded, forcing an end to the siege and other atrocities. The United States brokered a peace deal later the same year.
1999, Kosovo	NATO 'Operation Allied Force'	Intervention to end ethnic cleansing of the Albanian population, which appeared to be an act of genocide.	No	Successful but controversial. NATO forced the Serbian withdrawal. Russia proposed a UNSC vote to stop intervention but was outvoted. NATO claimed implied UNSC consent. Serbia and Russia reject Kosovo's statehood.

Date and location	Intervention force	Humanitarian goal	UNSC mandate	Significance
1999, East Timor	Australia and the UN	Stop atrocities by pro-Indonesian militias backed by the Indonesian government, following an independence referendum in East Timor.	Yes	As the regional power, Australia led a UN force to avert the potential refugee crisis. They restored peace and facilitated the transition to independence.
2000, Sierra Leone	UK 'Operation Palliser'	UK intervention, initially to protect foreign citizens, and later the elected government, after a prolonged civil war.	Yes	Successful. Like Haiti, the intervention supported an elected government against insurgents accused of atrocities.
2011, Côte d'Ivoire	France	Incumbent president Laurent Gbagbo refused to cede power after the 2010 election, leading to civil war. France was authorised to destroy his military power.	Yes	Successful. France's intervention allowed the democratic government to resume, bringing peace and stability. Gbagbo was convicted by the ICC.
2011, Libya	US-led coalition, followed by NATO, 'Operation Unified Protector'	US coalition air strikes against Libyan forces to stop attacks on civilians alongside rebel insurgents. NATO then maintained a 'no-fly zone'.	Yes, but limited	Controversial. Russia and China agreed on the condition that the intervention would only give humanitarian protection, but it enabled rebels to capture and kill Gaddafi. Libya became a failed state. A long-term failure.
2012 and 2013, Mali	African Union, then France	Intervention at the request of the state to restore control from the rebels. The AU intervention failed, so France stepped in to support UN peacekeepers.	Yes	There were military coups in 2020 and 2021. France left in 2022, and the UN left in 2023 due to increasing attacks on their soldiers. Mali's military government brought in Russian mercenaries. A long-term failure.

3 Supportive engagement by neighbouring countries, regional powers and regional organisations

The United States, the EU and Australia, as regional powers, were all motivated to make a success of their interventions in Haiti, Kosovo and East Timor to stem the potential flow of refugees into their own countries. In Côte d'Ivoire, there was also good engagement between the UNSC and the African Union.

In contrast, again, the situation in Bosnia in 1993 did not have sufficient support from the EU.

4 Professionalism and cultural awareness of military personnel

Peacekeepers and occupying forces should be trained to use proportionate force and remain impartial. Furthermore, former colonial powers with a common language and cultural awareness among their forces might have a better chance of success – for example French and British interventions in the ex-colonies of Côte d'Ivoire and Sierra Leone.

If soldiers, trained for war, are not carefully trained in the very different job of policing communities with consent, this can create unintended problems, as in Somalia, where US troops were seen as an occupying force rather than a humanitarian presence. Afghanistan had questionable humanitarian objectives and legitimacy, and was hampered by a poor understanding of the religious, ethnic and tribal dynamics in those countries.

5 A commitment to long-term peacebuilding

Regime change requires a long-term plan for peacebuilding and a democratic transfer of power. Interventions in Bosnia and Kosovo succeeded because NATO and the EU both made long-term commitments. NATO provided policing functions, and the EU helped to build a new constitution and democratic institutions.

In contrast, in Somalia, US troops were not trained in police work; in Afghanistan, there were insufficient forces to police a huge and largely inaccessible terrain and insufficient understanding of tribal loyalties that undermined the democratic institutions that were set up. In Iraq, the United States failed to plan at all for long-term reconstruction of the political system after toppling Saddam Hussein. The same mistake was made in Libya by the coalition of the United States, the UK and France.

The development of selective intervention – has R2P failed?

Since its signing in 2005, R2P has only been invoked and fully implemented three times – in Libya and in Côte d'Ivoire in 2011, and in Mali in 2013 (Photo 6.5). Of these, only Côte d'Ivoire could be considered a success. Intervention in Libya caused great resentment in Russia and China, who believed that NATO had overstepped its mandate from humanitarian protection into regime change.

Sometimes, instead of full military intervention by a P5 member, the UNSC has agreed to establish 'stabilisation missions'. These are more robust than traditional peacekeeping, as they are authorised under Chapter VII of the UN Charter, which allows the use of force to protect civilians. However, they stop short of a full-scale military occupation or airstrikes. These were established in Sudan from 2007, in the Democratic Republic of the Congo from 2010, and in the Central African Republic from 2013. However, they have generally failed to improve humanitarian situations because of obstruction by the government concerned or its neighbours (particularly in the DRC), and a lack of political will from the international community to rapidly overcome those obstructions with sufficient force. As a result, the African Union has increasingly taken over peacekeeping roles in Africa from the UN, deploying peacekeeping troops from other African states. The AU does not tend to engage in full military intervention without the consent of states. Since 2023, Mali and DRC have both told UN forces to leave their countries, and their roles have since been filled by Russian mercenaries. Humanitarian situations have worsened in both states.

The continuing dysfunction of the UNSC means that humanitarian intervention has now become very rare. Russia and China vetoed proposed Western interventions in Syria throughout the duration of its civil war from 2011. Since 2022, Russia and China have vetoed Western-proposed sanctions on North Korea and a resolution of concern over the escalating humanitarian crisis in Myanmar. Since 2023, the Sudanese and Gaza conflicts have further highlighted this dysfunction. The UNSC failed to agree to a sufficient renewal of the stabilisation mission in Sudan during its devastating recent civil war, and Russia and the United States vetoed each other's proposed resolutions for humanitarian ceasefires in Gaza.

Photo 6.4 Soldiers from the West African Republic of Togo arrive in Mali in January 2013, to provide military support to the fledgling Malian government in its battle with Islamic militants. The African-led International Support Mission to Mali (AFISMA) was an Economic Community of West African States (ECOWAS) organised military mission, authorised by the UN Security Council.

Source: The Washington Post/via Getty Images

KEY DEBATE: ARE HUMAN RIGHTS ARE MORE EFFECTIVELY PROTECTED BY HUMANITARIAN INTERVENTION THAN BY INTERNATIONAL COURTS AND TRIBUNALS?

✅ **Humanitarian Intervention responds to human rights violations quickly and immediately, putting an end to war crimes, crimes against humanity and genocide. It offers an effective short-term solution.**

Interventions with clear mandates and sufficient force have demonstrated the ability to immediately end ongoing war crimes, crimes against humanity or genocide, such as NATO's 'Operation Deliberate Force' in Bosnia (1995) which ended the siege of Sarajevo and other atrocities, or 'Operation Provide Comfort' in Northern Iraq (1991) which established safe havens from chemical attack.

In situations where the objective was to re-establish stability or restore a legitimate government, interventions could be swiftly successful in their immediate aims, as seen in the US 'Operation Uphold Democracy' in Haiti (1994), which restored the elected government, or France's intervention in Côte d'Ivoire (2011), which allowed democratic government to resume.

By deploying forces quickly, humanitarian interventions can provide immediate protection to civilian populations facing imminent threats of mass violence, as was the goal and initial impact of operations like NATO's in Kosovo (1999) to end ethnic cleansing, or the UN/Australian force in East Timor (1999) to stop atrocities by militias.

Human Rights Global Governance

❌ **However, humanitarian interventions can often make the situation on the ground worse, increasing human rights suffering.**

Humanitarian interventions often worsen human rights suffering. In Iraq (2003), overthrowing Saddam Hussein without a plan led to chaos, insurgency and ISIS's rise. Similarly, the Libya (2011) intervention resulted in a failed state and prolonged instability. After 20 years, the Afghanistan intervention ended with the Taliban regaining control, effectively returning the population to brutal rule. These instances show that poorly executed interventions, lacking understanding or long-term commitment, can exacerbate crises rather than resolve them.

In contrast, whilst the courts and tribunals can be slow to respond, the effects are lasting and can be done in conjunction with wider peacebuilding efforts.

While international courts and tribunals operate slowly, their effects are durable and complement broader peacebuilding. The ICTY, established in 1993 during ongoing conflict, meticulously built a legal framework for international crimes, prosecuting high-level perpetrators like those in Bosnia, fostering an enduring historical record. This sustained judicial process, as seen with the ICTR's efforts complemented by Rwanda's Gacaca courts, contributes to long-term accountability, truth-telling and eventually, reconciliation, which are vital components of lasting peacebuilding.

✅ **Humanitarian Intervention demonstrates the collective will of states to take action against war crimes, crimes against humanity and genocide. It acts as a long-term deterrent.**

When the international community intervenes to stop mass atrocities (as in Bosnia 1995 or East Timor 1999), it clearly signals a collective rejection of war crimes, crimes against humanity and genocide, thereby strengthening these international legal norms. It also strengthens the norm that sovereignty is conditional on upholding human rights norms. Successful interventions create precedents for future interventions, signalling to would-be perpetrators that their crimes will not go unpunished.

❌ **However, humanitarian interventions can often lack a clear mandate and can be viewed as neocolonial.**

Humanitarian interventions frequently face legitimacy issues, especially when lacking a clear UN Security Council mandate. As shown by the 2003 Iraq War, where the United States and the UK proceeded controversially without explicit UN authorisation, such actions are often perceived as a unilateral imposition of will. This fosters resentment and strengthens accusations of neocolonialism, particularly when powerful Western states intervene in the internal affairs of developing nations. These perceptions undermine the humanitarian intent and international cooperation, as seen in the resentment from Russia and China over the perceived overreach in Libya (2011).

In contrast, courts and tribunals are considered more legitimate due to their reliance on established international law and formal, often UN-backed, mandates, which provide a stronger basis for their actions.

Courts and tribunals are considered more legitimate due to their reliance on established international law and formal, often UN-backed, mandates, which provide a stronger basis for their actions. For instance, the ICTY and ICTR were explicitly created by UN Security Council resolutions under Chapter VII, making their jurisdiction binding on all states. This foundation in formal international legal instruments and adherence to fair trial standards gives them widely recognised authority. Their actions are thus perceived as upholding a rules-based order, unlike interventions potentially driven by unilateral interests.

✅ **Humanitarian intervention when combined with long-term peacebuilding can help restore good governance and end human rights suffering.**

When interventions are followed by a commitment to peacebuilding, they can provide the security and resources necessary to build new political and democratic institutions, as exemplified in

Bosnia and Kosovo, where the UNSC authorised an international administration to rebuild democratic institutions and restore good governance.

By providing security, supporting legitimate authorities, and investing in post-conflict reconstruction, interventions combined with long-term peacebuilding can help to break cycles of violence and human rights abuses, promoting an environment where good governance can take root and address the root causes of suffering.

✗ However, the selectivity of humanitarian intervention and the reaction to NATO's intervention in Libya suggest that R2P is in decline.

Russia and China, having consented to the Libya intervention solely for humanitarian protection, believed NATO overstepped its mandate to achieve regime change, causing deep resentment. The fact that there continue to be places in the world where war crimes and crimes against humanity take place, with no humanitarian intervention, undermines the principle in its entirety. It suggests that it only takes place in areas of strategic importance to the intervening powers. It also suggests that intervening powers protect their allies and target their 'enemies'.

In contrast, courts and tribunals directly target the perpetrators of these crimes and hold them accountable, something which humanitarian intervention does not do.

Courts and tribunals are specifically mandated to investigate, prosecute and try individuals responsible for genocide, war crimes and crimes against humanity. They hold high-ranking officials and commanders personally responsible, as seen with numerous indictments by the ICTY, including the prosecution of a former head of state, Slobodan Milosevic. This process establishes judicial truth, combats impunity and contributes to a lasting historical record, aiming for a more profound and enduring form of justice than military action alone.

Key Debate Summary: Are human rights more effectively protected by humanitarian intervention than by international courts and tribunals?

	For	Against
Ending suffering	✓ Humanitarian Intervention responds to human rights violations quickly and immediately, putting an end to war crimes, crimes against humanity and genocide. It is a short-term solution.	✗ However, humanitarian interventions can often make the situation on the ground worse, increasing human rights suffering. In contrast, whilst the courts and tribunals can be slow to respond, the effects are lasting and can be done in conjunction with wider peacebuilding efforts.
Collective strengthening of legal norms	✓ Humanitarian Intervention demonstrates the collective will of states to take action against war crimes, crimes against humanity and genocide. It acts as a long-term deterrent.	✗ However, humanitarian interventions can often lack a clear mandate and can be viewed as neo-colonial. In contrast, courts and tribunals are considered more legitimate due to their reliance on established international law and formal, often UN-backed, mandates, which provide a stronger basis for their actions.

	For	Against
International commitment to long term reconciliation and accountability	✓ Humanitarian intervention when combined with long-term peace building can help restore good governance and end human rights suffering.	✗ However, the selectivity of humanitarian intervention and the reaction to NATO's intervention in Libya suggest that R2P is in decline. In contrast, courts and tribunals directly target the perpetrators of these crimes and hold them accountable, something which humanitarian intervention does not do.

Western hypocrisy and double standards on human rights

This chapter has shown that Western democracies, especially the UNSC members the United States, the UK and France, have often presented themselves as champions of human rights and the rule of law in the international community. This was undermined spectacularly in the case of the United States and the UK by the questionable legality and brutality of their war in Iraq. There have been many other examples of human rights abuses by these states.

Western hypocrisy

Guantanamo Bay

The United States has often criticised China, Myanmar, North Korea and Iran for their human rights records, particularly regarding arbitrary detention and torture. Yet, the United States' Guantanamo Bay detention facility, located offshore in Cuba since 2002 to avoid being subject to US laws or ICC accountability, demonstrates its breathtaking hypocrisy. It has been widely condemned by NGOs and the international community for the use of indefinite detention without trial, torture and inhumane treatment, including waterboarding, sleep deprivation and force-feeding of hunger strikers. While the US government initially portrayed mistreatment at US-run detention facilities as isolated incidents, a subsequent investigation showed a systematic endorsement of abuse at many facilities, including [name] in Afghanistan and Abu Ghraibh in Iraq.

The death penalty in the United States

The United States has criticised Saudi Arabia and China for their use of capital punishment. However, it remains one of the few Western nations to retain the death penalty, with executions often marred by racial bias, wrongful convictions and inhumane methods. Cases of botched executions and the prolonged psychological torment of death row inmates have drawn international condemnation. This inconsistency undermines the United States' position as a global advocate for human rights.

UK immigration policy

The UK has criticised Belarus for its treatment of migrants and refugees. However, its own immigration policies have faced significant backlash for being inhumane. The controversial Rwanda deportation scheme, which sought to send asylum seekers to Rwanda for processing, was ruled unlawful due to concerns over Rwanda's human rights record. The UK has also been criticised for putting asylum seekers into extremely poor living conditions in detention centres and failing to safeguard vulnerable unaccompanied children.

Western double standards

In addition to these cases, the United States, UK and France have frequently condemned human rights abuses in one country whilst turning a blind eye to abuses by their own allies for strategic reasons. For example:

Russia and Israel

The United States and Europe have strongly condemned Russia's actions in Ukraine and repeatedly demanded that it respect Ukraine's territorial integrity and the human rights of its people. However, they have failed to condemn Israel's human rights violations in Palestine, where Israel has faced accusations of breaching international law and has not respected the territorial integrity of Palestine. Whilst they justify this by claiming Israel's right to self-defence from Hamas, they have failed to address the disproportionality of Israel's response. Furthermore, Israel's settler attacks on Palestinians in the West Bank predate Hamas's October 2023 attack and cannot be attributed to its campaign against Hamas.

Syria vs Egypt

The UK, the United States and France have all raised concerns over human rights abuses of political dissenters in Syria, yet maintain strategic cooperative relationships with Egypt, where political opposition and religious minorities are harshly suppressed by the dictatorship. This is because Egypt's control of the Suez Canal and lower Nile and its strategic location alongside the Red Sea are critical to its economic and security interests.

CASE STUDY: THE UK'S ARMS SALES TO SAUDI ARABIA

Context

From 2015 to 2021, Saudi Arabia, which led a coalition in support of the government in Yemen against the Houthi rebels, has been accused of violating international humanitarian law (IHL). Saudi forces have used UK-manufactured and licensed arms, including Typhoon aircraft, missiles and bombs in many operations targeting civilians and critical infrastructure. Human Rights Watch, Amnesty International, the UN and Yemeni rights groups have repeatedly documented war crimes – including attacks on markets, schools, hospitals and homes. Thousands of civilians have been killed.

Campaign groups, such as the Campaign Against Arms Trade (CAAT), have actively lobbied MPs to halt these sales. Despite mounting pressure from opposition parties and backbenchers, the Conservative UK government continued to allow exports to Saudi Arabia. In 2017, CAAT sought a judicial review of the government's decision, but the High Court rejected their claim. However, in June 2019, the Court of Appeal ruled that the government's process for granting export licences was 'irrational' and 'unlawful', as it failed to properly assess the risk of IHL violations.

Following the ruling, the government announced a review of all licences and temporarily halted new arms exports to Saudi Arabia and its coalition partners. Yet, in September 2019, then-International Trade Secretary Liz Truss admitted that new licences had been granted in breach of the Court of Appeal's ruling. By July 2020, the government resumed granting licences, claiming that a revised methodology showed no 'clear risk' of IHL violations. Opposition MPs called it 'morally indefensible', especially as it coincided with sanctions against Saudi officials implicated in the murder of dissident journalist Jamal Khashoggi by the Saudi state. In October 2020, CAAT filed another judicial review challenging the renewed arms sales. Meanwhile, in January 2021, the United States suspended some arms sales to Saudi Arabia, increasing pressure on the UK to reconsider its stance. At the time of writing, the UK was still exporting arms to Saudi Arabia.

Significance

While the UK often condemns human rights abuses, such as Russia's actions in Ukraine or China's treatment of Uyghurs, it continues to supply arms to a nation accused of war crimes in Yemen, contributing to what the UN described as the world's worst humanitarian crisis. Despite overwhelming evidence of violations of international humanitarian law, the UK government continued these sales because they support its economic and strategic interests. This has undermined its credibility as a defender of human rights and attracted much condemnation from NGOs.

This case shows that even in the case of a state that claims to respect human rights, strategic alliances outweigh justice and accountability. It raises questions about the effectiveness of global governance in holding powerful states to account.

China's human rights vs trade relations

Western countries frequently criticise China's human rights record, including its treatment of Uighur Muslims and suppression of dissent in Hong Kong. Despite this, the EU, the United States and the UK maintain extensive trade relations with China, prioritising their economic interests over their human rights concerns.

Conclusion

Whilst it is fair to say that there is strong evidence of hypocrisy by Western powers, including the UK, the United States and France, it should be noted that in most – although not all – cases these are of a very different magnitude to the human rights abuses that they condemn in other countries. It is also fair to say that any state that takes on the responsibility of helping to uphold international peace and security and which seeks to maintain an ethical foreign policy in doing so will be held to higher standards than countries that do not attempt to take on these responsibilities or adopt any kind of moral leadership. There will inevitably be mistakes and failures. This was the reasoning of US Senator Hillary Clinton when she justified the United States' rejection of the Rome Statute in 2005.

However, the question remains – how many repeated or continual 'mistakes' are acceptable? In 2025, Guantanamo Bay was still open after 23 years. The UK was still selling arms to Saudi Arabia, 10 years after the Yemen civil war began. These no longer look like isolated mistakes.

Yet, in an increasingly multipolar world in which these states are becoming more focused on their own defensive power rather than on foreign humanitarian interventions, accusations of outright hypocrisy on human rights might actually decrease. Instead, criticism will more likely focus on a growing tendency to condemn enemies whilst turning a blind eye to the actions of allies. It is also likely that states will increasingly ignore human rights abuses in other countries entirely.

Chapter Summary

- Human rights are universal, fundamental and absolute.
- International human rights governance evolved after the Second World War, shaped by international law and by the international courts and tribunals.
- International courts and tribunals like the ICJ and the ICTY have made important contributions to the development of international humanitarian law, but have been criticised for their costs and perceived lack of impartiality.
- The Doctrine of Responsibility to Protect (R2P) emerged from failures in Rwanda and Bosnia.
- Humanitarian interventions have been effective in some cases (Bosnia, Kosovo) but also controversial and ineffective in others (Somalia, Libya).
- The concept of humanitarian intervention has been tainted by associations with the War on Terror, especially in Afghanistan and Iraq.
- Humanitarian intervention became more selective after the adoption of R2P.
- UNSC dysfunction and increased multipolarity have led to a failure of R2P in recent years.
- Western countries exhibit hypocrisy and double standards in human rights advocacy, often prioritising strategic interests over humanitarian principles. This undermines the credibility of their international human rights advocacy.

Exam Style Questions

- Examine the criticisms that have been made of both the International Criminal Court and the special UN tribunals. (12)
- Evaluate the view that global governance has been more united than divided in dealing with human rights. (12)
- Evaluate the view that global governance has failed in its responsibility to protect human rights. (30)
- Evaluate the view that international human rights law is widely accepted and respected by states. (30)

Further Resources

https://www.youtube.com/watch?v=SQ6uF19KOJg. 'What is Humanitarian Intervention?' A short documentary explaining humanitarian intervention.

https://www.youtube.com/watch?v=Uc_1VlcEpv8. 'What is the ICC, and is it fair?' A useful summary of the ICC and some of its strengths and weaknesses.

https://www.youtube.com/watch?v=VuqPwdb-56I. 'Yugoslavia trial explained' – this documentary examines the ICTY in greater depth.

https://research.reading.ac.uk/ungop/wp-content/uploads/sites/13/paths-to-intervention_Binder_JPR.pdf. 'Selective Humanitarian Intervention' – this article explains why humanitarian intervention has been selective. It is a more academic article.

https://www.icc-cpi.int/. The ICC website is very useful in explaining the work of the court and the cases it is investigating.

https://unwatch.org/. This NGO examines the performance of the UN and offers a useful critique of its humanitarian work.

https://www.hrw.org/. Human Rights Watch is an NGO that examines human rights violations across the world. It is very informative.

 **Visit https://bloomsbury.pub/essentials-of-global-politics to access additional materials to support teaching and learning.**

7 ENVIRONMENTAL GLOBAL GOVERNANCE

Chapter Preview

Climate change is the greatest challenge faced by humanity. It is now widely recognised that greenhouse gases from human activity cause climate heating, with catastrophic consequences. Global civil society has repeatedly demanded collective action from states.

The UN holds international conferences to support states in taking collective action. The first was in Stockholm in 1972, followed by a second in Rio de Janeiro in 1992, when states agreed to hold annual meetings.

There were hopes for strong international agreements at conferences in Kyoto (1997), Copenhagen (2009) and Paris (2015). However, disagreements between developed and developing states over responsibilities for emissions and financial support for climate action made it difficult to achieve significant progress. Greenhouse gas emissions continued to rise.

With the emergence of Russia, China, India and Brazil as powerhouses of the global economy, the old division of developed versus developing states has become too simplistic. We must consider the political division between governments who seek collective action and those who reject such constraints on their sovereignty. A significant division has arisen between the most climate-vulnerable developing states and those want fossil fuels to power their own development.

Key Questions and Debates

» What is the 'tragedy of the commons' and how can it explain the climate emergency?
» What is sustainable development, and how is it viewed by 'shallow-green' and 'deep-green' ecologism?
» How has environmental governance been developed by the UN and who are the main actors?
» What are the origins, roles and significance of the UNFCCC and IPCC in climate change governance?
» What are the strengths and weaknesses of international agreements made at the UN's Conference of Parties (COP) meetings?
» What are the obstacles to international cooperation on climate change?
» How has global civil society contributed to international cooperation on climate change?

Specification Checklist

3.2.1 The role and significance of the United Nations Framework Convention on Climate Change (UNFCCC)

» The creation of the Intergovernmental Panel on Climate Change (IPCC) and its role and significance

3.3 The ways and extent to which these institutions address and resolve contemporary global issues, such as those involving conflict, poverty, human rights and the environment

3.3.2 How the following issues affect global environmental governance from effectively addressing and resolving the issues above:

» Competing views about how to tackle environmental issues to include shallow-green ecology versus deep-green ecology, sustainable development and the tragedy of the commons
» Strengths and weaknesses of international agreements, including key highlights from Rio, Kyoto, Copenhagen, Paris
» Obstacles to international cooperation and agreement, including sovereignty, developed versus developing world division and disagreement over responsibility and measurement

3.3.3 The role and significance of the global civil society and non-state actors, including non-governmental organisations (NGOs) in addressing and resolving the issues above

Source: Abstract Aerial Art/DigitalVision via Getty Images

The climate crisis

At the UN's annual climate summit in Dubai in 2023, the global effort to address climate change came down to a battle over a few words. Should the world agree to 'phase out' fossil fuels, as the most climate-vulnerable states demanded, or 'transition away from' them, a much slower approach favoured by major oil and gas producers? It was a step forward: the first time that fossil fuels had even been mentioned in a COP agreement. But the choice over those few words was critical for our hopes of staying within relatively safe levels of global warming. The climate-vulnerable states lost the argument.

Their struggle continued the following year in Baku, Azerbaijan, but this time the battleground was finance. They sought trillions of dollars in urgent funding to help them adapt to climate change, but the wealthy developed states offered less than half of what they needed. In deep frustration, the Alliance of Small Island States (AOSIS) and Least Developed Countries (LDC) delegations walked out of the negotiations, before resentfully accepting the offer.

The stakes could not be higher. If we do not dramatically reduce our use of fossil fuels by 2040, some of these vulnerable states will be wiped out by rising sea levels. The challenge remains: how can almost 200 states with wildly differing interests and resources agree on a solution quickly enough to prevent catastrophic levels of global warming?

> **Spec key term**
>
> **The Intergovernmental Panel on Climate Change (IPCC):** Is the global authority for evaluating climate science, the impacts of climate change and strategies to deal with these. It communicates an evidence-based consensus to build a shared understanding between states, supporting collective action.

How is the climate changing and what are the risks?

In 1990, the Stockholm Environmental Institute said that to avoid the worst impacts of climate change, an absolute limit should be set at 2°C average increase from pre-industrial temperatures, warning that an increase beyond 1°C could extensively damage ecosystems. The 2°C limit was agreed at COP15 in 2009 in Copenhagen, but states did not agree measures to ensure it. Six years later, the Paris Agreement of 2015 kept the 2°C limit, along with 'efforts' to limit warming to a safer 1.5°C.

This 'safety limit' of 1.5°C may already have been reached. In January 2025, the World Meteorological Organisation (WMO) reported that 2015 to 2024 were the ten warmest years on record, with 2024 the warmest year ever at 1.55°C higher than pre-industrial levels (see Figure 7.1).

In 2023, the **Intergovernmental Panel on Climate Change** said that if our **greenhouse gas emissions** continue unchecked, the global temperature will rise 2°C by the 2040s. At 2°C, the effects will be severe. Polar ice and glaciers will shrink dramatically. Sea levels could rise by 7 metres, destroying low-lying islands and coastal regions. Deserts will expand. Heavy rainfall and flooding will cause widespread destruction. Many more areas will become uninhabitable, massively increasing human migration. Many more species will become extinct. **Ecosystems** will be irreversibly lost.

Fossil fuel production must be cut by 75 per cent by 2050 to remain within the safety limit of 1.5°C.

> **Definition**
>
> **Greenhouse gas emissions:** The release of carbon dioxide (CO_2), methane (CH_4), nitrous oxide (N_2O), and other gases that trap the sun's heat, causing a 'greenhouse effect' which drives global warming.
>
> **Ecosystem:** A balanced, self-sustaining system made up of living organisms interacting with each other and their physical environment, including air, water, soil and climate.

Is climate change caused by human activity?

In its first report in 1990, the IPCC reported that climate change was driven by greenhouse gases, produced by human activities. By 2022, it said that it was 'unequivocally' human-driven – with a virtually universal consensus. The main sources of greenhouse gas emissions are:

- Burning fossil fuels: coal, oil and gas for energy.
- Industrial processes: e.g. emissions from mining or landfill waste.
- Destruction of 'carbon sinks': ecosystems that absorb carbon, such as forests and peat bogs.
- Agriculture: e.g. methane emissions from livestock and nitrous oxide from fertilisers.

Figure 7.1 Average global temperatures, 1850 (pre-industrial) to 2025

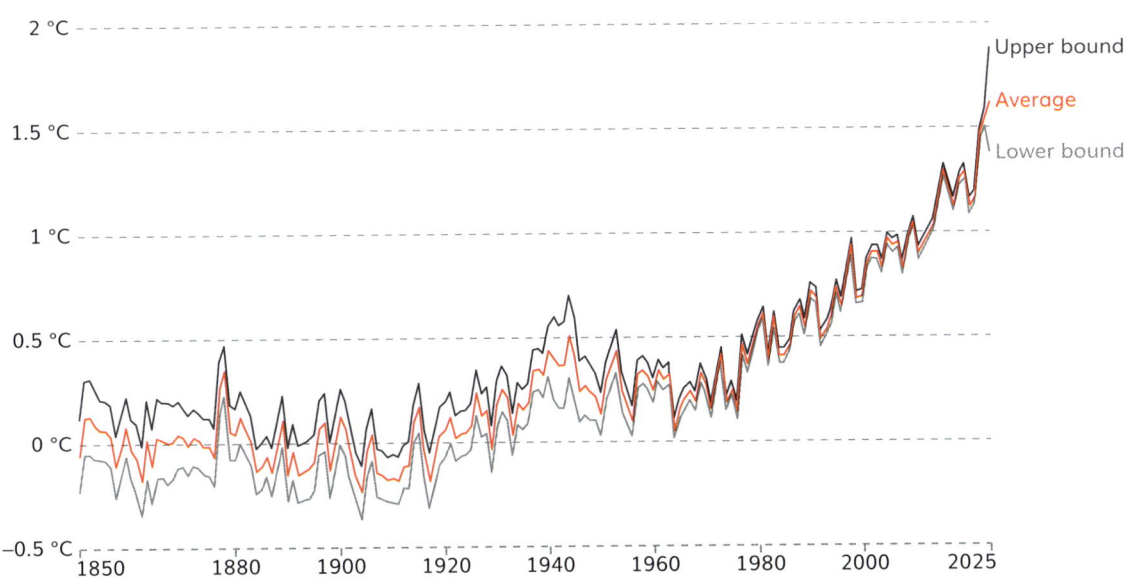

Source: 'Annual temperature anomalies relative to the pre-industrial period', Our World in Data. Based on data from the Climate Research Unit (University of East Anglia) and Berkeley Earth. Licensed under CC BY 4.0. Available at: ourworldindata.org/co2-and-greenhouse-gas-emissions.

Competing views on environmental issues

The tragedy of the commons

The 'tragedy of the commons' dates back to the ancient Greek philosophers. It is the idea that human nature makes the destruction of shared resources inevitable. It happens like this. If a piece of common land provides enough grass for sixteen cows, and access to the land is shared between four villagers, each villager can keep four cows on the common indefinitely. However, a rational villager would soon realise that they could add another cow to their herd. If they do, they gain one extra cow's worth of meat or milk, whilst the cow eats grass that everyone shares. This maximises their own benefit and minimises their own costs. Seeing this, other villagers become tempted to add more cows, but the common land cannot support them. Over time, the grass will not re-grow. Without another food source, the cows would starve. Overfishing, which has threatened some species with extinction, is another example of the tragedy of the commons (see Photo 7.1).

The tragedy of the commons is that although everyone benefits in the long term from conserving limited shared resources ('the commons'), there is no incentive for any individual to limit their own consumption because they would lose out to 'free riders' who selfishly take more than their share. The result is that the resource that they depend upon for survival is destroyed. Whilst at first sight such selfishness seems rational for the individual, collectively it becomes self-defeating.

In 1968, Garrett Hardin revived the concept, arguing that pollution, a consequence of population growth, was another type of tragedy of the commons. In this case, the environment is degraded because of excess waste: individuals profit from operating factories, but everyone suffers from the waste they discharge into rivers and the air. Furthermore, whilst common land could be divided and individually allocated so that owners bear responsibility for conserving their own resources, the 'global commons' – our shared atmosphere and oceans – cannot be privatised in this way. The environmental impacts must therefore be shared, and will therefore, inevitably, be degraded (see Figure 7.2). Hardin said the only way to prevent this would be through 'mutual coercion': everyone must enforce restrictions on each other.

Spec key term

Tragedy of the commons: Without regulation, individuals acting in self-interest will deplete shared, finite resources rather than conserving them for the common good.

Global commons: Shared global resources that are not 'owned' by states and therefore are beyond national control. These include the earth's oceans, polar regions and atmosphere.

Photo 7.1 Overfishing is a clear example of the tragedy of the commons. This image shows Mexican fishermen discarding unwanted fish.

Definition
Mutual coercion: Hardin's term for how society must create accountability with agreed restrictions on our use of the global commons.
The free rider problem: Occurs when individuals or groups benefit from a shared resource or collective effort without contributing. This can lead to depletion of the resource and a breakdown in trust and cooperation.

Soon afterwards, in 1972, the Club of Rome, a civil society group of senior diplomats, business leaders and policy experts, published a highly influential report 'The Limits to Growth', which used computer simulations to show that economic growth could not continue indefinitely. However, pollution and environmental destruction have continued. Although the EU's member states have created a '**mutual coercion**' system of binding environmental regulations, at the global level, no environmental authority can override state sovereignty or contain the actions of transnational corporations. **The free rider problem** is built into the anarchic international state system, and the tragedy of the global commons is very difficult to overcome.

Sustainable development

Sustainable development is the idea that economic growth must be limited, safeguarding environmental resources to meet human needs fairly in the present without compromising the needs of future generations. This idea, highlighted by the UN's Brundtland Report of 1987, influenced the 1992 Rio Declaration and **UN Framework Convention on Climate Change**. It is fundamental to environmental global governance.

The Sustainable Development Goals (SDGs) are non-binding targets agreed by the UN General Assembly in 2015. They sit alongside the legal UNFCCC process that creates international agreements on climate change, and are used by states, the UN and non-state actors. SDG 13 'Climate Action' sets out the urgent need to take collective action. The UN raises awareness and educates people on climate change, helps states take climate action and manages a Climate Fund. This is paid for by developed states, who have responsibility under the UNFCCC to support developing states with sustainable development. Support can be financial or technical – for example, affordable wind and solar power designs that help to increase access to electricity and create jobs; or advice on introducing building regulations for energy efficiency and water management.

Ideas associated with sustainable development include the **circular economy**, in which waste is minimised by designing products for reuse and recycling – for example electronics that can be easily disassembled and refurbished. However, whilst this reduces waste, it does nothing to promote social justice, which is fundamental to sustainable development.

Spec key term
Sustainable development: Economic progress that fulfils current human needs, fairly, while safeguarding the environment and resources for future generations to meet their needs.
UN Framework Convention on Climate Change (UNFCCC): An international environmental treaty negotiated 1992. It set out the process for states to cooperate on climate change.

Figure 7.2 The tragedy of the global commons in the climate emergency

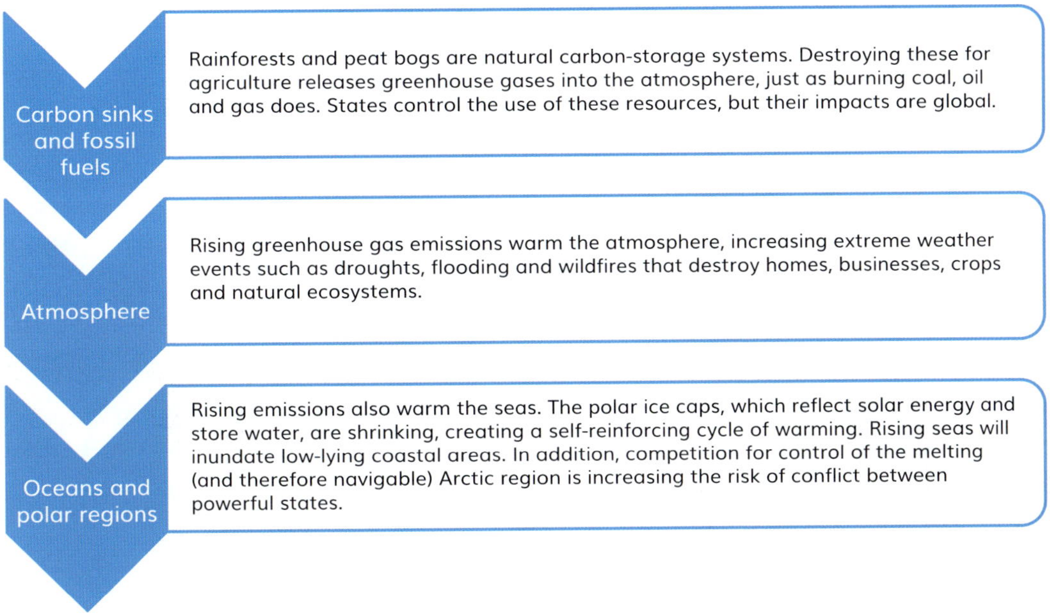

Carbon sinks and fossil fuels: Rainforests and peat bogs are natural carbon-storage systems. Destroying these for agriculture releases greenhouse gases into the atmosphere, just as burning coal, oil and gas does. States control the use of these resources, but their impacts are global.

Atmosphere: Rising greenhouse gas emissions warm the atmosphere, increasing extreme weather events such as droughts, flooding and wildfires that destroy homes, businesses, crops and natural ecosystems.

Oceans and polar regions: Rising emissions also warm the seas. The polar ice caps, which reflect solar energy and store water, are shrinking, creating a self-reinforcing cycle of warming. Rising seas will inundate low-lying coastal areas. In addition, competition for control of the melting (and therefore navigable) Arctic region is increasing the risk of conflict between powerful states.

A stronger theory of **sustainability**, known as the **steady-state economy**, proposes that the entire global economy must be kept stable rather than allowing it to grow. Natural resources must be sustained at stable levels, and population growth must end. This would require 'degrowth' in some states, reducing production and consumption to fair and sustainable levels. Further development must focus on well-being rather than wealth.

Doughnut economics, proposed by Kate Raworth in 2017, provides a framework for sustainable development. She argues that the global economy must operate within a 'doughnut' shaped 'safe and just space for humanity': with production and consumption levels that are high enough to secure basic human needs for all (the 'social foundation'), but low enough to be sustainable (the 'ecological ceiling') (see Figure 7.3). Every state should stay within these limits.

> **Spec key term**
> **Sustainability:** The capacity to endure over time.

Comparative Theories: sustainable development

Realist view	Liberal view
Realists argue that states are concerned with power, not morality.	Liberals believe in human rationality, so they emphasise the possibility of cooperation.
States act in self-interest, prioritising their own short-term national interests and sovereignty.	States will see that sustainable development is rational and will be inclined to collectively manage shared resources for the benefit of all.
States see global environmental issues as secondary to national economic and security concerns, will exploit shared resources and are not concerned with supporting sustainable development in other states.	Their belief in foundational equality means that developed states will be willing to support sustainable development in poorer states.
They will resist international agreements and environmental regulations if they see them as economically harmful. The tragedy of the commons is inevitable.	Liberal institutionalism: the theory that international institutions, laws, and norms help states cooperate, reduce conflict, and manage anarchy by promoting transparency, trust, and mutually beneficial outcomes; sees mutual agreements and regulations as critical for preventing the tragedy of the commons.

Debates on climate change and sustainable development

Climate debates have evolved over decades between fossil fuel lobbyists and right-wing libertarian politicians who have taken a more realist view, on one side, and the environmental movement, climate scientists and liberal politicians on the other.

Figure 7.3 The Doughnut of social and planetary boundaries

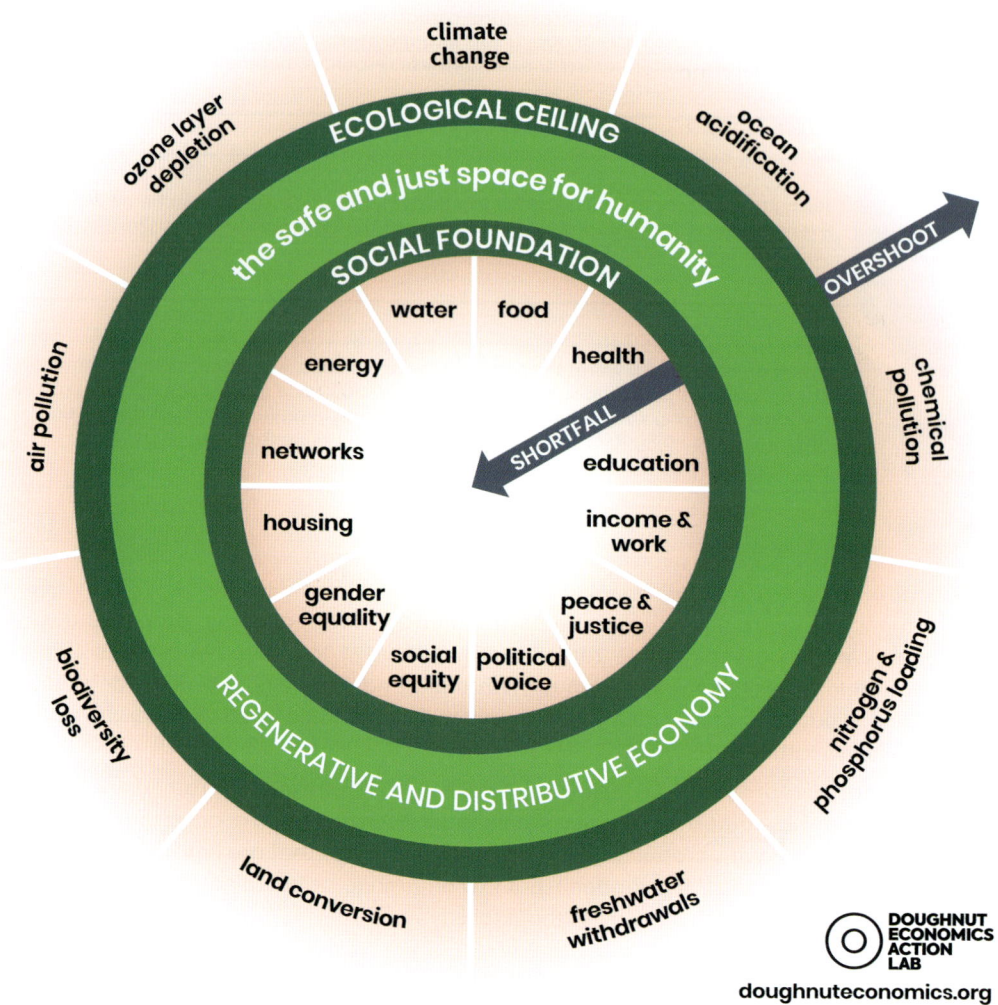

Source: Raworth, K. (2017), Doughnut Economics: Seven Ways to Think Like a 21st Century Economist. London: Penguin Random House. CC-BY-SA 4.0

From the 1950s, fossil fuel companies have funded research disputing climate change, its human causes and exaggerating the economic impacts of reducing fossil fuel use. They have funded US Republicans, influencing them to reject domestic climate legislation and international agreements.

Meanwhile, from 1990, the IPCC regularly reported on a growing scientific consensus that those claims were incorrect. As a result, the idea of sustainable development became more influential, particularly in Europe. In 2008, the UK became the first developed state to set legally binding climate emissions targets. In 2015, the Sustainable Development Goals and then the Paris Agreement were universally accepted by states. When the IPCC highlighted the risks of inaction in 2018 and 2019, environmentalists lobbied authorities to declare a 'climate emergency' and governments in the UK, Europe, the United States and more than 100 other countries set targets to reach 'net-zero' by 2050. Sustainable development projects multiplied.

However, from around 2022, the Covid-19 pandemic and the Ukraine war caused energy and food prices to soar. Some right-wing voices, including the UK Global Warming Policy Foundation and the US Heritage Foundation, continue to challenge the idea of a climate crisis, but most, including the US Trump administration, now highlight the economic risks of transition. They argue that renewable energy is unreliable and that net-zero efforts will threaten energy security and increase energy bills, severely impacting poorer families and destroying jobs. They follow the fossil fuel industry in arguing for gas production rather than renewable energy.

On the other hand, many governments that have made net-zero commitments stand by their arguments that the transition presents opportunities for investment, economic growth and strengthened energy security.

Ecologism

Shallow ecologism

Shallow ecologism includes the ideas of enlightened anthropocentrism, sustainable development, green capitalism and state management of the commons.

Enlightened anthropocentrism

Anthropocentrism means prioritising human needs and rights over those of other species. Shallow ecologism combines anthropocentrism with an 'enlightened' awareness that human well-being depends on conserving the rest of the natural world too, although this is done for our own future benefit, not for other species.

Sustainable development

Shallow ecologists accept that we need to limit – but not end – growth, reduce pollution and replace our use of non-renewable resources with renewable ones. They focus on intergenerational equity: the idea that our descendants should be able to live in a prosperous capitalist world, avoiding the tragedy of the commons. They argue that businesses and states have an important role in creating sustainable development.

Green capitalism – technological and market solutions

Companies invest in technological and market-driven solutions, adopting sustainable practices in pursuit of profit. They might, for example, develop cheaper solar panels or electric vehicles. Technological development creates jobs in renewable energy, leading to sustainable economic growth that, if managed carefully, can replace growth powered by fossil fuels. The idea of a circular economy is compatible with green capitalism.

Carbon markets as an example of green capitalism: Both states and the private sector can trade in carbon markets. Half of the world's largest 2,000 companies have set 'net-zero' emissions targets in support of national targets set by states. Some companies make pledges to consumers, like planting a tree for every product sold. Because trees absorb carbon dioxide from the atmosphere, businesses can offset their carbon emissions by paying for trees to be planted – often in developing states. This can redistribute wealth, although projects are not always sustainably managed, for example trees may not be watered once planted.

State management of the commons

Shallow ecologists argue that the state can manage the global commons through regulation, legislation and state investment in technologies to support the transition to net-zero. For example:

- Locally, London has introduced ULEZ (ultra-low emissions zone), which imposes charges on highly polluting vehicles. Democrat-controlled cities across the United States have implemented net-zero policies.
- At a national and regional level, governments in the UK, the United States and the EU have made huge state investments and encouraged private investments in an approach known as the 'Green New Deal'. The UK and the EU have passed legislation enshrining their 2050 net-zero targets in law.
- States also work globally. In 2024, states agreed international regulations for carbon markets to ensure that carbon emissions are offset properly.

Deep ecologism

In 1972, Norwegian philosopher Arne Naess distinguished between what he called the 'shallow ecology' and 'deep ecology' (or ecologism) movements. He criticised the mainstream shallow ecology or environmental movement for focusing only on technological fixes that benefit developed capitalist states. Naess instead proposed a radical, egalitarian 'deep ecology' philosophy.

Ecocentrism and egalitarianism

Deep ecologism is ecocentric: focusing on the needs of the earth's ecosystems, and ecologically egalitarian – respecting the equal worth of all species. That also implies human egalitarianism: celebrating diversity and rejecting hierarchy and domination.

> **Definition**
>
> **Net-zero emissions:** Reducing the amount of greenhouse gases emitted into the atmosphere and offsetting the rest by, for example, planting trees to absorb carbon dioxide, ensuring that the overall impact on global warming is neutral.
>
> **Ecology:** Is a branch of biology that studies the relationships between organisms and their environment and the processes that sustain life within ecosystems.
>
> **Ecologism:** Is a political and philosophical ideology or 'green' political movement that emerged in the late 1960s. It emphasises the importance of preserving and protecting the natural environment.

Strong sustainability

Deep ecologism says that conserving resources and reducing pollution are necessary but not enough to protect the natural world. They call sustainable development 'weak sustainability', because as long as the economy grows, it consumes more resources. 'Strong sustainability', on the other hand, argues that environmental preservation cannot be balanced with economic priorities, and so there must be 'zero growth'. The idea of a steady-state economy is compatible with 'strong sustainability'.

Anti-industrialism

Deep ecologists oppose 'industrialism': an economic system that encompasses both capitalism and socialism, which pursues endless growth through large-scale production. Deep ecologists argue that industrialism is dedicated to materialism, science and technology at the expense of the earth's ecosystems. Instead, deep ecologist Schumacher argued for economics 'as if people mattered': promoting well-being and collaboration rather than materialism and consumerism.

Localism

Deep ecologists say that we should live, work and buy locally to reduce our ecological impact. So, for example, rather than buying a new electric car which uses materials and needs power, we should adapt our lifestyles, travel less and use public transport.

Decentralised governance

Deep ecologists say that governance should be decentralised, empowering local communities to manage their own environments sustainably. Deep ecologist Peter Berg challenged the whole idea of the nation-state, arguing for human societies based on naturally defined 'bioregions' – for example the Amazon and Alpine regions. Communities in these bioregions could practise local democracy focused on the needs of their local ecosystems.

Comparative Analysis: Shallow and deep ecology

	Shallow Ecology	**Deep Ecology**
Overall approach	**Enlightened anthropocentrism:** human-centred view that long-term human prosperity depends on conserving the environment and its resources for the benefit of future generations.	**Ecocentrism and egalitarianism:** focused on the needs of the earth's ecosystems, respecting the equal worth of all species. Rejects hierarchy and domination, advocating for deep human egalitarianism and collective stewardship of the land.
Sustainability	**Sustainable development:** ensuring future generations will not suffer reduced living standards by limiting growth, reducing pollution and using renewable resources. Criticised as **'weak sustainability'** by deep ecology.	**Strong sustainability:** environmental preservation is non-negotiable, rejecting shallow ecologist notions of sustainable development. Advocates for zero-growth economics and proposes substantial reduction in the global population.
Economy and society	**Green capitalism:** works within the existing system, pursuing sustainability through technological and market solutions. Companies invest in new technologies, creating jobs and growth.	**Anti-industrialism:** a rejection of exploitative industries, with an economic system that promotes well-being rather than materialism and consumerism. **Localism:** advocates for living and working locally to reduce ecological impact.
State	**State management of the commons:** state regulation, such as ULEZ and the UK Climate Change Act. State investment to support businesses in the transition to net-zero.	**Decentralised governance:** empowers local communities to manage their environments sustainably. Berg proposes 'bioregions' for sustainable governance of an ecosystem.

Environmental global governance

Environmental governance brings states together to make international agreements on climate change, biodiversity loss, and pollution and supports them to meet their commitments. It has a short history, with fewer and less powerful institutions than other forms of governance. There are no complex voting systems, biased towards powerful states. Instead, binding international agreements are made through consensus.

> **Chapter Link**
>
> For more on the environmental impacts of these regional organisations, see **Chapter 9: The EU and Regionalism.**

The main actors in environmental global governance

States

Are the primary actors in global politics: they set up IGOs, they attend international conferences, they agree international laws, and they choose whether or not to enforce them. Environmental global governance is no different from other forms of global governance in this respect. The UN Framework Convention on Climate Change was signed at the Rio Earth Summit in 1992. In doing so, the state 'parties' to the convention agreed to hold annual international Conference of the Parties (COP) meetings to negotiate future collective action. Each COP is hosted by a member state. The consensus-based COP process respects the sovereign equality of states but also means that a single state can block progress by diluting or refusing to sign agreements.

Regional organisations

The European Union has become a global leader on environmental regulation. Its supranational authority has helped it to impose binding 'net-zero' targets, although it cannot do so without the consent of its member states. One – although not the only – reason for the EU's investment in climate action was its members' realisation that they had become dependent on Russian oil and gas. Since imposing sanctions on Russia in 2022, the EU has invested heavily in renewable energy, supporting the net-zero target and making energy supplies more secure. However, in 2023 and 2024, farmers and lorry drivers protested about the costs of environmental regulation.

The African Union has had some success in coordinating a collective voice in global negotiations on climate finance. ASEAN coordinates climate resilience projects such as flood defences in member states that are vulnerable to typhoons in the Pacific and tropical cyclones in the Indian Ocean.

Sub-national governance: e.g. city authorities

Many city authorities have acted on climate change and are learning from each other. A notable example is the C40 Cities Climate Leadership Group. Many have developed local 'net-zero' strategies. Sub-national governance is particularly important in the United States, where state and city authorities share power over environmental policy with the federal government. Cities control transport, energy efficiency and building regulations, which are significant levers for climate action. For example, the Democrat-dominated cities of San Francisco, New York and Los Angeles consistently pursue net-zero commitments, despite changes in federal environmental policies.

Non-state actors

Non-state actors include businesses, academics, think tanks and global civil society

Businesses lobby governments over regulations. Fossil fuel companies have pushed for ongoing investment in oil, gas and coal. According to NGO Global Witness, at COP29 in Azerbaijan, fossil fuel lobbyists outnumbered scientists, with some lobbyists attending within state delegations (see **Case Study: Global Witness: Human Rights, Corruption, Conflict and Climate Change** in **Chapter 8 Analysing and Evaluating Global Governance**). In contrast, renewable technology companies lobby for faster decarbonisation policies. Even without enforcement from governments, many companies have voluntarily adopted Environmental, Social and Governance (ESG) policies, and the B-Corp initiative

CASE STUDY: GRETA THUNBERG AND THE FRIDAYS FOR FUTURE MOVEMENT

Photo 7.2 Greta Thunberg at a 'Fridays For Future' protest outside the Swedish parliament Riksdagen in Stockholm, 2019.

Source: Pontus Lundahl/AFP via Getty Images

Context

The Fridays for Future movement (FFF) is a global grassroots environmental movement founded by Greta Thunberg, a Swedish teenager who began skipping school in 2018 to sit outside the Swedish parliament every Friday to demand climate action (see Photo 7.2). Thunberg's solitary protest inspired a movement of students around the world. Within months, school climate strikes involving millions became global news events. They demanded collective state action to improve the monitoring and enforcement of states' commitments under the 2015 Paris Agreement, whilst also advocating more broadly for climate justice and scientific evidence-based policy-making.

In May 2019, European students protested during the EU Parliament election, setting off a 'green wave' of political debate across Europe. In Germany, politicians and the media discussed climate policies more frequently during FFF strikes. In 2021, the Greens made it into government as a junior coalition partner. Thunberg was awarded the first Gulbenkian Prize for Humanity in 2020 and was nominated for a Nobel Peace Prize three years running. She was subjected to a torrent of online abuse from climate change deniers, to which she responded, 'this shows that we're winning'.

However, since then, FFF has lost momentum. The pandemic forced young people inside. The Black Lives Matter campaign then became a priority for many progressive activists. By 2023, participation in climate protests had dropped sharply, with events drawing thousands rather than millions. Greta Thunberg stepped back from media engagements. Many of the movement's activists became more involved in the Palestinian solidarity campaign, and a hard-right anti-climate action movement is gaining influence in Europe.

Significance

The social media-driven #FridaysForFuture movement is a good example of how cultural globalisation has sped up the process of achieving and losing global cultural influence. It also shows how global civil society actors collaborate to amplify campaigns: its activists collaborated with scientists and environmental organisations, and Greta Thunberg was invited to speak at the UNGA and at the World Economic Forum. Young people's anger attracted widespread attention, encouraging older policy makers to give much more serious consideration to their intergenerational responsibilities.

As a result, in 2024, states that signed the UN's Plan for the Future committed to actively involving youth in national and global decision-making. Perhaps the greatest legacy of the school strikes will be a greater willingness to listen to young activists in future.

has certified around 10,000 companies worldwide for their sustainability. Initiatives like this help to promote a culture of sustainability. However, some corporations exaggerate their ESG commitments for marketing purposes – a practice criticised as 'greenwashing', and since a change of government in the United States in 2025, there is less corporate interest in promoting ESG.

Global civil society includes scientists, think tanks, activists and non-governmental organisations (NGOs). In recent years, there has been extensive global civil society pressure on environmental global governance, including the lobbying of states domestically and at the annual UN summits.

Scientists work with state representatives in the IPCC to produce reports that communicate the international consensus on climate science and ways to tackle the issues. These reports inform negotiations on international agreements.

Think tanks aim to influence media debate and provide policy ideas for policymakers, leaning either towards research or advocacy. Climate sceptic think tanks include the Heritage Foundation and American Enterprise Institute in the United States, and the Global Warming Policy Foundation and Institute for Economic Affairs in the UK. Pro-sustainability think tanks include the influential Club of Rome, a global network of senior diplomats, ex-heads of state, business leaders and scientific and economic experts. The Institute for European Environmental Policy and the US-based World Resources Institute also have significant profiles. However, their influence depends on whether they have links to the government in power. The Heritage Institute has deep connections with the US Trump administration, whilst the Institute for Economic Affairs is linked to ex-British Prime Minister Liz Truss.

Activists and NGOs influence media debates, lobby governments and mobilise public support for campaigns. They investigate corporate and state behaviour and try to hold them publicly accountable. For example:

- Greenpeace and Friends of the Earth have been influential in the environmental movement since the 1960s. Both are known for mass participation campaigns: petitions and letter writing. Greenpeace is also known for direct actions against the fossil fuel and whaling industries.

- Extinction Rebellion (XR) is a global disruptive non-violent protest network. Its UK spin-off Just Stop Oil used similar methods to challenge North Sea oil and gas expansion plans between 2022 and 2024. The radical newsworthy nature of their publicity stunts (blocking roads, damaging famous artworks) faced media criticism, punitive legislation and heavy-handed policing. In 2024, it abandoned its disruptive tactics. Extinction Rebellion returned to mass protests, and Just Stop Oil ended operations when the new Labour government pledged not to issue fossil fuel exploration licences.

- The Stop Ecocide movement lobbies governments to strengthen criminal laws on ecological destruction. Vanuatu and the Maldives have proposed adding ecocide to the Rome Statute, which would make it punishable at the ICC. This would be a long process as two-thirds of Rome Statute signatories have to agree.

- Many NGOs have campaigned for 'fossil fuel divestment': urging investment funds to withdraw from fossil fuel companies in favour of sustainable development projects. Whilst this might be more impactful than a street protest, consumer boycotts alongside pressure from remaining investors may have more influence on corporate behaviour.

The United Nations (UN)

The UN provides forums for states to negotiate action and supports them in meeting their commitments. The two most important elements in supporting collective action are the Intergovernmental Panel on Climate Change, which has provided the scientific basis for climate action, and the United Nations Framework Convention on Climate Change, which provides the legal framework for climate action.

> **Chapter Link**
>
> See **Chapter 8: Analysing and Evaluating Global Governance** for more explanation of the different ways that civil society influences global governance, including a case study of the work of the NGO Global Witness and the Stop Ecocide movement.

Exam Tip:
Although examiners expect you to focus mostly on climate change negotiations, it is useful to know how these fit into the UN's broader work on the environment. The effectiveness of global action on the environment is a theme throughout global politics.

MILESTONES: THE DEVELOPMENT OF ENVIRONMENTAL GOVERNANCE BY THE UN

1972: The Stockholm Conference on the Human Environment. States agreed that they needed to protect the global commons but would do so individually.

1972: The UNEP was set up in Nairobi, Kenya, to coordinate environmental action, providing scientific research and guidance to governments, civil society and businesses.

1979: The First World Climate Conference gathered scientists, recognised climate change as a serious problem and called on governments to tackle it.

1987: The Montreal Protocol was signed, creating a landmark agreement committing states to phasing out the use of ozone-depleting chlorofluorocarbons (see case study).

1988: UNEP noted that despite growing concern, many politicians had limited understanding of climate science. With the World Meteorological Organisation (WMO), it set up the Intergovernmental Panel on Climate Change (IPCC) to build consensus among climate scientists and provide summaries that all states could agree on.

1990: The IPCC published its first consensus report on climate change. This guided discussions at the Second World Climate Conference, which called for a framework treaty on climate change. It established the ideal of sustainable development and the principle that developed and developing states should have different responsibilities. The UNGA agreed that treaty negotiations should begin.

1992: At the Rio Earth Summit, the United Nations Framework Convention on Climate Change (UNFCCC) was signed by UN member states, laying the foundation for future collective action and establishing annual international climate negotiations.

1997: The Kyoto Protocol was the first legally binding agreement made under the UNFCCC, setting emission reduction targets for developed nations. However, its acceptance and impact were limited.

2009: Climate finance was agreed at COP15 in Copenhagen to help developing nations cut emissions and adapt to climate change. Developed states pledged $100 billion of investment by 2020.

2012: Recognising the need for stronger environmental governance, the UNGA established the 193-member Environment Assembly (UNEA) to oversee the UN's environmental work, granting it equal status to the UNGA.

2015: World leaders adopted the Sustainable Development Goals (SDGs). These include climate action (Goal 13), life below water (Goal 14) and life on land (Goal 15).

2015: The Paris Agreement was signed at COP21. This established voluntary national targets and agreed to limit global temperature increases to below 2°C, with efforts to cap warming at 1.5°C. Unlike the Kyoto Protocol, the Paris Agreement was signed by all states.

Chapter Link

See **Chapter 4: Political Global Governance,** which explains how the UN's work on the SDGs fits into the wider role of ECOSOC.

The Intergovernmental Panel on Climate Change

Origin

By the late 1980s, strong evidence was emerging on global warming and its human causes. However, there was limited coordination between scientists in different states, and the world's leaders did not have a shared understanding of the risks. In the face of fossil fuel industry research designed to downplay the risks, policymakers needed reliable evidence to inform their collective decisions. As a result, the Intergovernmental Panel on Climate Change (IPCC) was established in 1988 by the World Meteorological Organisation (WMO) and the United Nations Environment Programme (UNEP), which both oversee its work.

CASE STUDY: THE ROLES OF SCIENTISTS, STATES AND THE UN IN THE MONTREAL PROTOCOL (1987)

Context

The ozone layer in the earth's atmosphere provides protection from the sun's harmful UV radiation. In the 1970s, scientists discovered that this layer was being depleted by rapidly rising levels of chlorofluorocarbons (CFCs) in the atmosphere. CFCs were man-made gases, widely used in industry and emitted by fridges and aerosol sprays. A corresponding increase in skin cancers and crop damage was soon noted. A political battle followed between environmentalists and the chemical industry. Then, in 1985, the British Antarctic Survey revealed a large hole in the ozone layer over Antarctica. Scientists predicted that the protective ozone layer could be gone within a lifetime.

In response, the UN Environment Programme brought together governments, scientists and industry representatives to write the Vienna Convention of 1985: a framework agreement for solving the problem internationally. It soon became clear that a 'protocol' – an additional binding agreement was needed to enforce action. The Montreal Protocol was signed in 1987 and entered into force in 1989. It committed signatories to phasing out CFCs over fifty years.

Parties to the Vienna Convention and Montreal Protocol meet annually. The protocol has been amended several times, phasing out more than 100 damaging gases.

Significance

Environmental governance can succeed. Five factors can explain the Protocol's success:

- By the 1980s, there was strong scientific consensus that ozone depletion was a significant problem with severe human consequences.
- The UNEP provided effective coordination, bringing together governments, scientists and industry.
- There was united, pragmatic leadership from three powerful conservative leaders: Brian Mulroney in Canada, Margaret Thatcher in the UK and Ronald Reagan in the United States. It was said that Thatcher – a trained research chemist – had been quick to grasp the scientific evidence, and that Reagan – who had himself twice suffered from skin cancer – was easily persuaded of the need to act.
- Alternatives to CFCs were easily found, and action required fewer economic sacrifices than are needed for climate action now.
- The protocol was universally adopted, avoiding the 'free rider problem' that causes the 'tragedy of the commons', and providing a foundation for ongoing collective action.

Role and significance

The IPCC provides a bridge between the worlds of science and politics. The international panel has 195 state representatives who direct the work of several hundred scientists and social scientists. Experts are nominated by states, relevant IGOs and NGOs. Almost half of the panel for the sixth report came from developing states. Whilst the evidence is supplied by scientists, the summary reports are written collaboratively by scientists and state representatives. UN bodies and experts appointed by NGOs can observe IPCC meetings and comment on its draft reports.

The IPCC does not carry out research studies. Its role is to assess, on a comprehensive, transparent and regular basis, the latest scientific literature from across the world on four areas:

- The physical science of climate change
- Impacts of climate change, adaptation and vulnerability of states
- Mitigation of climate change – options to reduce greenhouse gas emissions
- Methods for monitoring emissions

The IPCC has published six assessment reports from 1990 to 2025, with a seventh in 2027. States request 'special reports' too, for example a special report in 2018 on the probable impacts of 1.5°C versus 2°C warming.

> **Exam Tip:** Whilst examiners often prefer to see contemporary examples, the Montreal Protocol is the best example to date of successful environmental governance, illustrating how weak progress has been since. A comparison can be made to highlight the reasons why climate action is much more difficult.

Component III: Global Politics

Table 7.1 Effectiveness of the IPCC in Resolving Environmental Issues

	Strengths	Weaknesses
Validity of conclusions	It is normal for scientists to disagree on evidence: in fact, it is an important part of the scientific method and does not invalidate the IPCC's role. The 2007 errors should be judged in the context of the rest of the report, which was accurate. The IPCC has achieved universal consensus on human-caused climate change. Its broad membership and reputation for objectivity makes it credible amongst policy makers.	The IPCC's fourth Assessment Report (2007) was criticised for minimising some claims and overstating others. For example, underestimating the speed of ice-melting in the Arctic; whilst saying that Himalayan glaciers would disappear by 2035. That claim was from unverified sources and retracted in 2010. ICIMOD, an intergovernmental institution for the Himalayas said in 2025 that the glaciers are substantially retreating but not at that speed.
Timeliness of reports	Assessment Reports are published before each major COP, helping to inform negotiations. Since 2021, Assessment Reports have been published in stages, speeding up the release of findings and ensuring maximum attention on each one.	The IPCC has been criticised for the length of its assessment reporting cycle, resulting in conclusions that have been well out of date by publication, and which have arguably contributed to slow political progress.
Impact of science on politics	The IPCC's role is to support political agreements based on scientific consensus, so it is reasonable for states to contribute. Furthermore, IPCC Special Reports respond to questions raised at COPs, helping to resolve polarisation. For example, negotiations became stuck when the EU and developing states saw US and Canadian support for planting forests as an excuse to avoid cutting their emissions under the Kyoto Protocol. An IPCC special report was requested in 1998. It explained the scientific reasoning, helping to move negotiations on.	The summary report that most politicians and journalists read is subject to political oversight and negotiated by state representatives, reducing scientific impartiality. At an IPCC meeting to discuss the draft 1995 summary report, NGO observers and developing states misinterpreted economists' conclusions about how much people would pay to reduce the risk of death as an ethical judgement that the lives of rich and poor people were not of equal value. They were outraged, slowing progress on the negotiated draft.

> **Exam Tip:** Note the difference between the IPCC table on page 238 and the UNFCCC table on page 240. Here, strengths respond to weaknesses because the IPCC makes corrections when criticisms of its work are justified, and when they are not justified, you should point that out. Careful sequencing of your paired arguments shows how ideas develop logically towards the conclusion.

In summary: Without the IPCC, policymakers would lack a common understanding of the problems they face. During the very polarised times of the early 2000s, criticisms of its role, methods and conclusions were frequent, and some of them were valid. However, the panel has evolved in response to criticism. As the consensus on climate change has strengthened, it has become widely respected as a source of knowledge.

The UN Framework Convention on Climate Change (UNFCCC)

Origin

In the late 1980s, the international campaign for a treaty on climate action gathered momentum. At the 1990 Second World Conference on Climate Change, states agreed fundamental principles. Over 150 states helped to draft the UN Framework Convention on Climate Change, which was signed in 1992 at the Rio 'Earth Summit'.

Role and significance

The UNFCCC was signed by all UN member and observer states, who agreed that there was a scientific basis for climate action and to:

- act collectively to stop greenhouse gas emissions from reaching dangerous levels.
- create a legal framework for further agreements.
- attend annual Conferences of the Parties (COP) to negotiate further commitments.
- establish the UNFCCC Secretariat to coordinate this work.

The UNFCCC's principle of **common but differentiated responsibilities (CBDR)** acknowledged that all states must 'mitigate' (reduce) greenhouse gas emissions, adapt and develop resilience to climate change, but recognised that states all have different capabilities and historical emissions levels, so their responsibilities to other states would vary. Developed states were asked to take stronger action and support less developed states.

Accordingly, the UNFCCC categorised states into groups. The most industrialised group (Annex I and II) committed to reducing their greenhouse gas emissions below 1990 levels and accepted financial responsibilities to support climate action. Those 'in transition' to capitalist economies were not expected to provide or receive financial support. The rest were developing states, entitled to financial support (see Map 7.1).

> **Exam Tip:**
> Note the difference between this table on the UNFCCC and the table on the IPCC on page 238. Here, weaknesses follow strengths, to create paired arguments that contrast strong early ambitions with weak later developments. This might lead to the conclusion that overall, the weaknesses outweigh the strengths. See Chapter 10: Exam Skills for more on this technique.

International conferences and agreements

The 'Earth Summit': The Rio Declaration and UNFCCC, 1992

Held in Rio de Janeiro, Brazil, over two weeks in June 1992, the Earth Summit was at that time the largest ever gathering of state leaders, plus NGOs, scientists and thousands of activists (see 12 June). Discussions included sustainable development, biodiversity and climate change.

Map 7.1 UNFCCC state categories

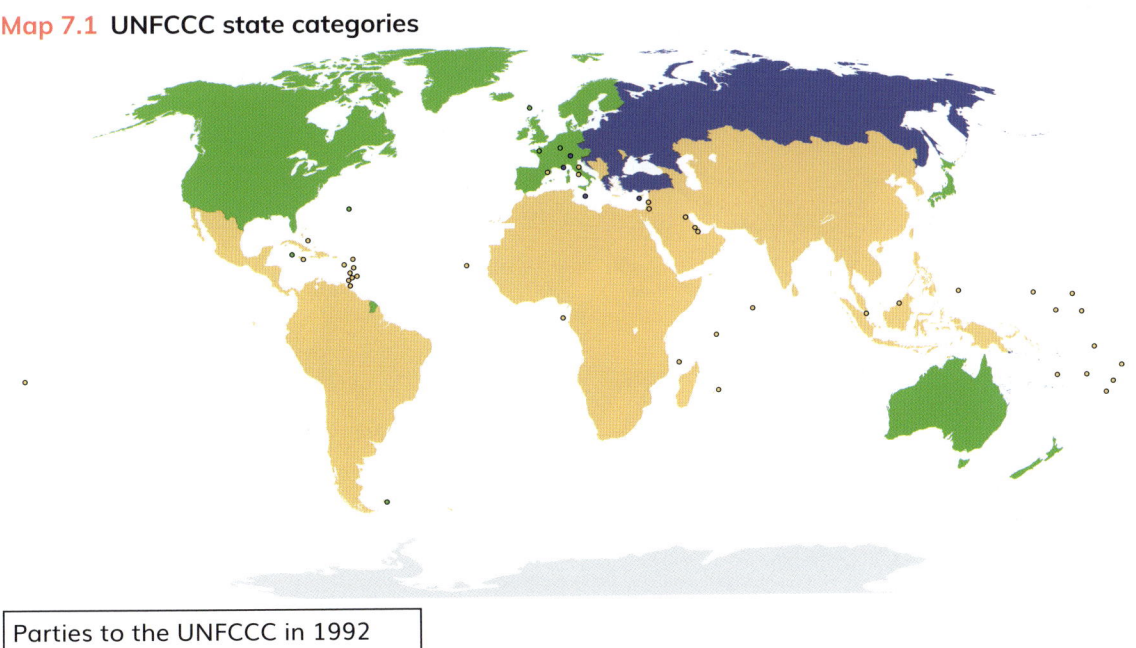

Parties to the UNFCCC in 1992
- Developed states (Annex I and II)
- Transitioning states (Annex I)
- Developing states (non-annex)

Table 7.2 **Effectiveness of the UNFCCC in Resolving Environmental Issues**

	Strengths	Weaknesses
Universal membership and consensus decision-making	The universal membership of the UNFCCC ensures that all states are involved in climate change negotiations, providing a platform for inclusive global cooperation.	It is almost impossible to achieve consensus between 193 states. Negotiating blocs such as the Association of Small Island States and the Like-Minded Developing Countries group have entrenched divisions.
Different treatment of developed and developing states	The UNFCCC recognises the different responsibilities of developed and developing states, with the most industrialised states accepting a greater share of the burden, including financing climate action and sustainable development in developing states.	The UNFCCC's categorisation of states stored up problems for the future, as states remained in these groups regardless of economic progress. China insists that it is still a developing state, refusing responsibility for finance, despite being the second-largest economy in the world.
Outcomes	The UNFCCC provided a basis for future collective action with annual Conference of the Parties (COP) meetings to assess progress and negotiate new commitments. This led to the adoption of important agreements: notably the Kyoto Protocol and the Paris Agreement.	The UNFCCC did not require emerging economies to start reducing their emissions quickly enough. Despite most developed states complying with the Kyoto Protocol, global fossil fuel use and greenhouse gas emissions have increased significantly. By 2024 emissions were still growing, although more slowly.

Photo 7.3 US President George Bush signs the Earth Pledge at the Earth Summit in Rio de Janeiro, 12 June, 1992.

Source: AFP via Getty Images

Environmental Global Governance

Table 7.3 Strengths and Weaknesses of the Earth Summit's UNFCCC and Rio Declaration

	Strengths	Weaknesses
Participation and significance of the UNFCCC	The Earth Summit brought together representatives from 179 states, including 112 state leaders to agree ways forward for collective action. It established the UNFCCC's annual COP meetings to continue negotiations.	Despite its historic significance and inclusive nature, states have not all continued to cooperate, and many of its goals have still not been realised. Greenhouse gas emissions have increased significantly.
Common but differentiated responsibilities in the UNFCCC	The common but differentiated responsibilities principle was a step forward in redressing the inequity between developed and developing states. The most industrialised states accepted greater responsibilities on both emissions and on financial support.	The UNFCCC's categorisation of states into groups stored up problems for the future, as states remain in their allocated groups, with the same responsibilities regardless of the economic progress they have made.
Impact of the Rio Declaration	The Rio Declaration set out twenty-seven principles to guide states in promoting sustainable development, broadening the impact of the summit to include biodiversity and sustainable development.	The principles outlined in the Rio Declaration were non-binding, which limited their effectiveness in driving meaningful action for states.

The two main outcomes were the Rio Declaration and the UNFCCC (see above). The Rio Declaration was a non-binding agreement on twenty-seven principles to guide states on sustainable development, while the UNFCCC was a legally binding treaty to stabilise greenhouse gas emissions.

In summary, Rio created a legal framework for making binding agreements in the future, but it was just the first step.

COP3: The Kyoto Protocol, 1997

Following the IPCC's second assessment report of 1995, setting out the risks of climate change, expectations in Kyoto were high that developed states would take the next step, accepting binding targets to reduce their emissions by just 5 per cent below 1990 levels.

The Kyoto Protocol respected the UNFCCC's 'common but differentiated responsibilities' by requiring developed states to take compensatory action for their historical emissions. But with the loss of the United States and the absence of China, it was not exactly a success.

Table 7.4 Strengths and Weaknesses of the Kyoto Protocol

	Strengths	Weaknesses
Participation and significance	The Kyoto Protocol was eventually signed by 192 states. To encourage states to work together, the Protocol required signatures and ratification from states representing at least 55 per cent of global emissions before it could come into force. The Protocol's focus on reducing developed states' emissions had to be the first UNFCCC priority, to show that they were serious about their greater responsibilities.	China, India, Brazil and South Africa were exempt, despite their large and increasing emissions, causing resentment. 37 of 192 signatories did not ratify the protocol (make it national law). The US Senate refused due to economic concerns, and in 2001, the United States, then responsible for 25 per cent of global emissions, withdrew, although did make smaller voluntary cuts. Australia joined late in 2007, when its 1990 baseline level was altered to make its target easier.

	Strengths	Weaknesses
Overall ambition – Legally binding emissions reductions	The Kyoto Protocol set legally binding emissions reduction targets for the thirty-seven most industrialised states. It set up UN monitoring and imposed penalties: missed phase 1 targets would mean stricter phase 2 targets. The EU and Japan achieved their targets of 8 per cent reductions by 2012. The EU went on to reduce its emissions by 23 per cent compared to 1990 levels by 2020.	The measures lacked ambition, and implementation was delayed until 2008, meanwhile, by 2005, emissions were rising four times faster than in the 1990s. The penalty for missing phase 1 targets could be avoided by withdrawing from the Protocol. Canada, Japan, Russia and New Zealand all withdrew before the next phase.
Carbon trading schemes	The Kyoto Protocol allowed states to meet their emission targets through carbon trading. This meant that by reducing emissions, some states could accumulate carbon credits and sell them to those that exceeded their allowances.	Carbon trading was controversial. Some argued that developed states wanted to maintain existing emissions levels by purchasing credits rather than doing the hard work of reducing persuading their own people to reduce their fossil fuel consumption.

COP15: The Copenhagen Accord, 2009

There were hopes of more progress at the Copenhagen Climate Summit. In 2007, the IPCC had starkly highlighted the risks of global warming. A new Climate Vulnerable Forum of around seventy states formed, calling for urgent climate action by all, phasing out fossil fuels to secure a 1.5°C warming limit, compensation for loss and damage due to climate disasters and long-term development support. The presence of newly elected US President Barack Obama raised hopes that the United States and the BASIC states (Brazil, South Africa, India and China), would work together.

It was difficult. Towards the end of the two-week conference, talks looked close to collapse. Obama, determined to get a deal at almost any cost, decided to negotiate privately with the BASIC group, reaching a deal called the 'Copenhagen Accord'.

Despite a vague promise on finance, the Accord was widely criticised as a failure.

Table 7.5 Strengths and Weaknesses of the Copenhagen Accord

	Strengths	Weaknesses
Participation and significance	45,000 people attended COP15. Substantial civil society presence added pressure on negotiators to reach a meaningful agreement. Despite its weaknesses, 192 states signed the Accord.	The Copenhagen Accord's weak, non-binding targets were presented at the final hour. The Climate Vulnerable Forum resented it but had to accept if they wanted finance. The Accord was 'taken note of' but not 'adopted'. Its status in international law was unclear.

	Strengths	Weaknesses
Overall ambition – limiting global warming	For the first time, a COP 'recognised' the scientific case for limiting warming to 2°C above pre-industrial levels. China and India agreed for the first time to make voluntary reductions and agreed to monitoring emissions.	Even with 'recognition' of the 2°C limit the voluntary targets would lead to highly dangerous 3°C warming. Sixteen years on from Rio, there were still no enforceable targets. An agreement to reduce CO_2 emissions by 80 per cent on 1990 levels by 2050, so as to keep warming within 1.5°C, was vetoed by China.
Finance	Developed states agreed support for developing states to reduce emissions and adapt to climate change. They would mobilise $100 billion per year by 2020 with a Green Climate Fund and private finance.	There was no detail on how the promised $100 billion in financial support would be delivered, and this had to be settled at later COPs. Eventually, it was mostly private finance rather than aid.

COP21: The Paris Agreement, 2015

By 2015, there was near universal agreement that climate change needed a genuinely global response. In 2014, the United States and China made a bilateral deal with significant emissions reduction targets, reflecting a change in attitude under the new Chinese president, Xi Jinping. There was a good chance that the world's two largest polluters might help to pass a universal agreement.

The Paris Agreement was widely seen as a high point in climate governance. Its universal acceptance, clear roadmap and efforts to improve monitoring of emissions were widely celebrated. However, these came at a cost: allowing states to set their own targets, which have not been sufficiently ambitious, and a lack of enforcement for failing to meet targets.

In 2018, in its requested special report, the IPCC highlighted stark differences between the probable consequences of 1.5°C and 2°C warming. Then in 2019, it said that limiting warming to 1.5°C would require greenhouse gas emissions to decline before 2025 and reach net-zero by 2050.

These reports had a significant impact. In June 2019, the UK government set a global precedent with its legally binding 2050 'net-zero' target, following the IPCC's recommendations. The EU and the United States followed in 2021. However, China, now the world's largest polluter, pledged in 2020 to start reducing emissions from 2030 and reach net zero by 2060, whilst India pledged in 2021 to reduce emissions in the 2040s and reach net-zero in 2070.

Table 7.6 **Strengths and Weaknesses of the Paris Agreement**

	Strengths	Weaknesses
Participation and significance	Like Kyoto, the Paris Agreement is legally binding, but unlike Kyoto, the targets would be applicable to every state. All 198 state parties signed the agreement; it was quickly ratified by 55 per cent of states and was in force within a year. By 2023, it was ratified by 195 states.	Donald Trump gave notice in 2017 that the United States would leave as soon as permitted in 2020. Joe Biden rejoined on his first day in office in 2021. On assuming office in 2025, Trump gave notice to withdraw again from 2026. By 2025, Iran, Libya and Yemen had still not ratified the deal.
Overall ambition – limiting global warming	The agreement set a goal to limit the temperature increase to 2°C and pursue efforts towards 1.5°C. States agreed a long-term planning process for future climate action, with a 'Global Stocktake' in 2023 to assess collective progress and plan next steps.	It is widely agreed that a +2°C increase would have severe consequences, making this a weak target. But the IPCC had not yet reported on the impacts at different temperatures, so the goals were not yet based on comprehensive understanding (this report was requested at Paris).

Component III: Global Politics

Definition

Nationally Determined Contributions (NDCs): Are commitments made by states under the Paris Agreement to reduce their own greenhouse gas emissions. Unlike the Kyoto Protocol's targets, NDCs allow states to retain sovereignty by setting their own targets.

State accountability	The 'Paris Rulebook' for setting and monitoring targets allows states to set their own five-year plans called '**Nationally Determined Contributions**' (NDCs). Plans have to be transparent, accurate data must be collected, and progress is monitored by the UN. States then review and set more ambitious targets for the next cycle.	The targets are voluntary, and although there is monitoring, there are no penalties for missing targets. This meant that the Kyoto approach to binding targets on developed countries was dropped. Disputes over measurements meant that some rules were not agreed until the Glasgow summit in 2021, six years later.

COP26: The Glasgow Climate Pact, 2021

COP26 was delayed for a year by the Covid-19 pandemic. The stakes were high. Collectively, states' NDCs were not ambitious enough to achieve the Paris Agreement's goal of limiting warming to 2°C. In its sixth report ahead of the conference, the IPCC stressed that halving emissions by 2030 and reaching net-zero by 2050 could limit warming to 1.5°C, but only with immediate and transformative collective action. The UK's aim for the summit was therefore to 'keep 1.5 degrees alive'. With the United States and China once more agreeing to overcome their tensions and cooperate on climate action, perhaps that goal could be achieved.

The main hopes in Glasgow were that all states would:

- agree to phase out coal and end deforestation.
- submit new, ambitious NDCs showing that overall emissions could be halved by 2030.
- finalise the Paris Rulebook.

Table 7.7 Strengths and Weaknesses of the Glasgow Climate Pact

	Strengths	Weaknesses
Participation and significance	The Pact was signed by 197 parties. Civil society involvement was strong. 130 states, covering 90 per cent of the world's forests, agreed to reverse deforestation by 2030.	Fossil fuel lobbyists were included in some state delegations. Accountability was weak. No enforcement methods were agreed for preventing deforestation.
Overall ambition	For the first time, the Glasgow Climate Pact explicitly called for the 'phasing down' of coal power and ending fossil fuel subsidies. 151 states produced more ambitious NDCs, including the United States, Canada and India.	Following resistance from India and China, the agreement on coal was watered down from 'phasing out' to 'phasing down'. Pledges were inadequate to keep within the 1.5°C limit. States were asked to come back with more ambitious NDCs next time.
Finance	The Adaptation Fund was boosted by $356 million, with an agreement to double finance by 2025. Developed states agreed to discuss increased support for climate-related damage in the future.	The adaptation funding was billions of dollars less than needed, and the need for a loss and damage fund was already evident, but developed states rejected the idea that they were 'liable' for climate-related damage due to their historical emissions.

Environmental Global Governance

On finance, it was hoped that developed states would:

- meet the overdue 2020 target for $100 billion a year.
- promise to raise the target for the adaptation fund to meet growing needs.
- agree to a much-needed Loss and Damage fund.

The IPCC repeated its warning in 2022, saying that 'without immediate and deep emissions reductions across all sectors, limiting global warming to 1.5°C is beyond reach'. They said it would be possible to almost halve emissions by 2030, and that net-zero emissions must be achieved by 2050.

Strengths and weaknesses of recent COPs

Can we still meet the Paris Agreement's 1.5°C limit?

The net-zero transition requires a complete transformation in the ways that we produce and consume goods and energy. Three-quarters of greenhouse gas emissions are from the energy sector, so the most urgent step is to replace coal, oil and gas with renewable sources. Renewable energy capacity doubled in 2024 to 92 per cent of all new energy, but demand for fossil fuels was still growing. More than 100 states have now made net-zero 2050 pledges, but also, many states have resisted phasing out fossil fuels for fear of inconsistent supply.

The 2023 'Global Stocktake' found that collective action to reduce emissions had been insufficient, with many states failing to meet their first NDC targets. According to Climate Action Tracker in late 2024, the 'real world actions' taken by states so far suggest a possible increase of around 2.7°C by 2100. Their most optimistic scenario – if states fulfil all the promises and targets made so far – would be an increase of around 1.9°C by 2100. The IPCC's call for immediate and deep emissions reductions will be difficult to reach voluntary national targets.

> **Exam Tip:** Whilst the specification names the four agreements made in Rio, Kyoto, Copenhagen and Paris, you also need to evaluate whether environmental governance has been successful or not since these summits. Summarise key themes from more recent COPs, such as NDCs/net zero targets, ending fossil fuel use, state accountability for NDCs and financing.

Table 7.8 Strengths And Weaknesses of Recent COPs

	Strengths	Weaknesses
COP27: Sharm El-Sheikh, 2022	Established a **Loss and Damage Fund** to support vulnerable nations affected by climate disasters. Commitments to double adaptation funding by 2025. Largest ever attendance at a COP.	Insufficient ambition on emissions reductions to meet the 1.5°C target. No clear commitments to reduce oil, gas or coal use. Heavy policing of protesters. Fossil fuel lobbyist attendance increased.
COP28: Dubai, 2023	Significant commitments to cut methane – a potent greenhouse gas. Implemented the Loss and Damage Fund, with the first $100 million donated by conference host UAE.	Continued failure to agree phasing out fossil fuels, with fossil fuel lobbyists heavily influencing negotiations. Financing for climate adaptation remained inadequate.
COP29: Baku, 2024	Developed states agreed on a new climate finance goal of $300 billion annually by 2035. Agreed regulations for global carbon markets, which will support net-zero targets.	$300 billion was far short of the trillions needed by developing countries. Still no agreement to end fossil fuel use by a specified date. A draft agreement on reducing gas was blocked by Saudi Arabia.
COP30: Belem, 2025	A target to triple adaptation finance by 2035, initiatives to speed up progress on NDCs and a 'just transition mechanism' to protect human rights.	States failed to agree a global roadmap to end fossil fuel use and deforestation, so voluntary steps will be taken outside the COP process.

> **Definition**
>
> **Loss and Damage Fund:** A global fund, paid for by developed states, to help climate-vulnerable states recover from destructive extreme weather events and cope with the economic problems caused by gradual changes such as less predictable rainy seasons.

KEY DEBATE: IS ENVIRONMENTAL GLOBAL GOVERNANCE EFFECTIVE?

Global governance can prevent dangerous levels of global warming

The 1992 UN Framework Convention on Climate Change set expectations for states to prevent dangerous levels of global warming, and the IPCC set out to provide the knowledge base for states to help them achieve this goal.

- ✓ In 1992, the signing of the UNFCCC laid important groundwork for later collaborative efforts, just as the Vienna Convention of 1995 had done for the Montreal Protocol. States agreed a goal to limit climate heating to 2°C at COP15 in Copenhagen in 2009 and added the intention to 'pursue efforts' towards 1.5°C warming in the Paris Agreement in 2015.

- ✗ Meanwhile, global emissions continued to rise by 44 per cent between 1990 and 2015, largely due to rapid development in China and India.

- ✓ The IPCC has succeeded in establishing a credible scientific consensus, putting the existence of climate change beyond doubt. From 2018 to 2022, it reported the clear dangers of 2°C warming, set clear targets for halving emissions by 2030 and achieving net-zero by 2050 to stay within 1.5°C. A majority of states have made plans to meet these targets.

- ✗ However, the IPCC can only advise states. It has become clear that their voluntary approach is unlikely to 'keep 1.5 degrees alive' as hoped for in Glasgow in 2021. The Global Stocktake in 2023 showed that actual progress on state NDCs falls short of this goal.

Global governance holds developed states to account for their historical emissions

The UNFCCC set out 'common but differentiated responsibilities' for state parties, meaning that whilst all states have a responsibility to contribute, industrialised states were largely responsible for existing CO_2 levels so they should carry the greatest burden of reducing them.

- ✓ The Kyoto Protocol was to be the first step. Developed states would submit to binding emissions, and if they missed their first target, they would face a penalty of stricter targets later.

- ✗ However, its impact was constrained by the absence of the United States. President Clinton signed the Protocol in 1997, but the Senate would not ratify it. President G.W. Bush withdrew the US signature in 2001, citing his concerns for the economy and that developing states were not required to reduce emissions. This is a good example of the free rider problem associated with the 'tragedy of the commons'.

- ✓ Despite the absence of the United States, the Kyoto Protocol encouraged the EU and Japan to take responsibility – both achieved their targets, and the EU went on to make further reductions.

- ✗ The Protocol failed to hold other developed states sufficiently to account: Russia did not sign until 2005. Australia would not ratify it until its baseline measure was changed to allow it to increase its emissions. Canada failed to meet its target and withdrew in 2011. Japan also withdrew in 2011, complaining about the non-participation of large emitters (the free rider problem again).

Global governance requires all states to work collectively to reduce greenhouse gases

- ✓ At Copenhagen, large greenhouse gas emitters, including the United States, China and India, proposed voluntary emission reductions for the first time since the United States had rejected the Kyoto Protocol. This was a significant step towards more inclusive agreements in the future.

- ✗ However, this agreement was non-binding, limiting the chances of sustained emissions reductions from these large emitters. It created divisions between large developing states and more climate-vulnerable states.

✅ The Paris Agreement's flexible approach to target setting allows states to protect their sovereignty, whilst its near universal support addressed free rider concerns. It also introduced a long-term planning process, better transparency and some monitoring of progress.

❌ However, the Paris Agreement allows states to set and pursue targets that are too modest. There are no penalties for missing the targets, and so it still allows free riding to undermine the collective goal.

Global governance has provided finance for developing states to adapt and become resilient

One reason that collective action has been so hard to achieve is the difficulties with agreeing an acceptable level of financial support and the slow rate at which it has been delivered.

✅ In the UNFCCC, developed states agreed that they should support developing states to adapt to climate change, to mitigate their emissions and adapt to climate change.

❌ However, finance was not agreed until 17 years later at Copenhagen. The promise of $100 billion a year by 2020 did not include details on how it would be delivered. Climate-vulnerable states were excluded from negotiations but compelled to accept the Accord if they wanted access to the promised funds, creating resentment.

✅ Considering the costs of Covid-19, the 2020 $100 billion finance target was achieved just two years late, which could be seen as a success. A Loss and Damage Fund was also agreed at COP27 in 2022 and introduced at COP27. COP29 introduced a new climate finance goal of $300 billion annually by 2035.

❌ However, the growing need for climate finance has vastly outstripped contributions. Finance commitments made by 2025 were far below the trillions needed to tackle the climate crisis.

Key Debate Summary: Is environmental global governance effective?

	For	Against
Prevent dangerous levels of global warming	✓ Set 2°C and 1.5°C limits, aiming to stabilise global temperatures. The IPCC has built a credible consensus on climate science.	✗ Emissions are still rising, although more slowly, undermining these limits. The IPCC can only advise states and cannot enforce targets.
Collective action to reduce greenhouse gases	✓ Despite earlier failures, the Paris Agreement had almost universal support and strengthened measurement and accountability for emissions.	✗ The Paris Agreement achieved universal support at the cost of meaningful commitments. Its voluntary approach is inadequate, with no binding enforcement mechanisms.
Acknowledge historical responsibilities	✓ Some developed states reduced their emissions under the Kyoto Protocol, recognising their greater responsibility.	✗ Before Paris, the United States, several other wealthy states and the BASIC states did not submit to meaningful targets, causing tension and slowing progress.
Finance for developing states to adapt and become resilient	✓ The $100 billion climate finance goal was achieved, and a Loss and Damage Fund, established in 2022 to support vulnerable states.	✗ Funding promised is far below needed levels, leaving many developing states highly vulnerable to accelerating climate change.

> **Exam Tip:**
> In answering this debate, you should acknowledge the important contribution of the IPCC and the limitations of its role. You should also focus on the aims of the UNFCCC and judge the outcomes of the summits against those aims. Comparing outcomes against aims is a useful approach to take in evaluating any area of global governance.

Obstacles to meaningful progress on international cooperation

Achieving consensus is extremely difficult. There is wide variation in states' approaches to international cooperation, their historical and projected contributions to climate change, their vulnerability to climate impacts and their economic interests and capacity for climate action.

CASE STUDY: SHOULD OIL-PRODUCING STATES HOST COPS?

Photo 7.4 Activists stage a protest against fossil fuel usage and profits during COP29 in Azerbaijan.

Source: SOPA Images/LightRocket via Getty Images

Context

COP29 in 2024 was hosted by Azerbaijan in its capital, Baku. Azerbaijan is a 'petrostate': oil and gas make up 90 per cent of its export revenues and 60 per cent of its national budget. The IPCC said in 2023 that no new oil and gas licences should be allowed if we are to limit global warming to 1.5°C.

Yet, just before the summit, an undercover Global Witness investigation discovered Azerbaijani Deputy Energy Minister and COP29 Chief Executive Elnur Soltanov negotiating oil and gas contracts with sponsors. Shortly afterwards, during the COP opening speech, Azerbaijani President Ilham Aliyev hailed his state's oil and gas reserves as a 'gift from God'. The environmental movement was appalled (see Photo 7.4).

COP28 in Dubai, United Arab Emirates, was similarly controversial. Its president, Dr Sultan Al Jaber, was head of the state-owned National Oil Company in neighbouring Abu Dhabi, the most fossil-fuel dependent Emirate.

At both COPs, Global Witness reported that fossil fuel lobbyists far outnumbered delegates from the ten most climate-vulnerable states.

Significance

It can be argued that petrostates do not make good COP hosts. It is easy to see how they might want slow progress on decarbonisation. Appointing a fossil fuel industry leader to set the agenda for COP negotiations does appear to show a conflict of interest.

That said, at least half of UNFCCC state parties produce fossil fuels, and it is difficult to know where the line would be drawn. Furthermore, producing fossil fuels need not prevent other commitments to climate action. The UAE demonstrated leadership during its COP presidency by providing the first $100 million for the new Loss and Damage fund. In February 2025, the UK, COP26 host and a minor oil-producing state, was the only government in the world that had submitted a new NDC, on time, which was compatible with the Paris Agreement's 1.5°C limit.

Following COP29, the Club of Rome – an organisation of prominent climate scientists and policy experts advocating for climate action – addressed an open letter to the UN calling for reforms to the COP process. They argued that only states that demonstrate their commitment to the Paris Agreement should host a COP, and they urged the UN to restrict fossil fuel delegations while supporting representation for climate-vulnerable states. Such measures would not be hard to implement and would significantly redress the balance of representation.

Comparative Theories

The realist view: sovereignty and the national interest	The liberal view: multilateral cooperation for the common good
Realists believe that states prioritise their own sovereignty and economic interests and assume that they rarely align with other states.	Liberals believe that rational states will seek positive-sum goals – mutually beneficial long-term solutions.
States pursue 'zero-sum' goals, where one state's gain means another's loss; rather than 'positive sum' or mutually beneficial solutions.	States can be encouraged to pursue collective action on climate change and will make sacrifices for the common good, if they can trust that others will do the same.
Powerful states will not make sacrifices that would allow other states to outrank them economically. If COPs do not serve their purposes, state leaders will either disregard them or withdraw from agreements.	Liberal institutionalists argue that, despite the anarchic international system, states can pool sovereignty, using institutions to establish shared norms and build trust.
Environmental governance is unlikely to provide a lasting solution to the tragedy of the commons.	This makes them hopeful that in time, the COP process can produce multilateral agreements that overcome the tragedy of the commons.

Different realist and liberal approaches can be seen in the United States since Republican George H.W. Bush signed the UNFCCC in 1992. Democrats have taken a positive-sum multilateral approach to COPs, whereas Republicans have taken a zero-sum egoistic approach to sovereignty, rejecting the Kyoto Protocol and the Paris Agreement as unfair constraints that benefit China at their expense. This inconsistency in the world's most powerful state and second-largest emitter is a major obstacle to progress. The fossil fuel industry and right-wing think tanks have contributed to these obstructions (see p. 236). Meanwhile, the EU has taken a more consistently liberal institutional approach to pooling sovereignty by creating supranational targets for itself and working multilaterally at COPs. However, the rising influence of hard-right politics casts doubts on whether that can continue. Refer back to p. 232 for detail of how this debate has evolved.

Developed versus developing world divisions

Developed states

In climate governance, **developed states** officially refers only to the most industrialised capitalist states in 1992 that were listed in the UNFCCC's 'Annex II' category. Most developed in the nineteenth and twentieth centuries followed by rapid deindustrialisation from the 1980s due to globalisation. Their high fossil fuel consumption is the primary cause of historical global warming. They have relatively robust economies, large financial sectors and advanced technologies that allow them to invest in climate adaptation. They agreed in 1992 to provide financial and technical support for developing states. There are different approaches within this group, for example the UK, the European Union and Japan have made faster progress on reducing emissions than the United States, Canada and Australia have done.

Developing states

Most of the UNFCCC's **developing states** are united in anger at the injustice of climate change, in which wealthy states have contributed most to climate change but suffered least from its impacts. They argue for their right to fully industrialise, insisting they should not have to reduce their own emissions before the developed states fulfil their UNFCCC financial obligations.

However, there are significant divisions here, too. China has become the world's second-ranked power and largest greenhouse gas emitter, yet it is still classified under the UNFCCC as developing, with no responsibilities to support the world's poorest states. Saudi Arabia and South Korea also have high emissions, yet are classified as developing. Some of the 'transition' states in 1992 are now part of the EU, and Russia is extremely powerful – these states have no financial responsibilities.

In 2009, around seventy states set up the Climate Vulnerable Forum to strengthen their collective voice at the Copenhagen summit, demanding greater ambitions from all states on reducing emissions and from developed states on finance and compensation. They resented their exclusion from US-BASIC negotiations and were angry about the weak Copenhagen Accord.

In contrast to the CVF's demand for universal climate action, the Like-Minded Developing States coalition of more powerful developing states aims to push finance up the agenda before agreeing to reduce their own emissions. Some of the least developed states, such as Mozambique, which discovered gas fields in 2011, have also sought to delay the net-zero transition, citing their right to develop.

Since Paris in 2015, the 120-member High Ambition Coalition of developed and developing states has sought to overcome divides between developed and developing states, and to strengthen collective ambitions. See Table 7.9 for more detail on these and other negotiating blocs.

Disagreements over responsibility for greenhouse gas emissions and the right to develop

Historical versus future emissions

The UNFCCC required developed states to take more ambitious climate action because of their greater historical emissions and powers. The question of whether historical or current emissions should be used to compare contributions to climate change and determine targets and financial contributions was debated at Copenhagen, Paris, Glasgow and Abu Dhabi.

Developing states argued that developed states had the benefit of growth without environmental regulations and that they too have the right to develop without that constraint. Developed states argue that they did not know the impacts, and – particularly the EU – have argued that now the science is established, and they have developed and shared new technologies, all states have a responsibility to develop sustainably.

Table 7.9 Some Overlapping and Competing COP Negotiating Blocs

The Organisation of Petroleum Exporting States (OPEC) was first formed in the 1960s by oil-rich states including Saudi Arabia, Iran, Iraq, Kuwait and Venezuela. Most argue for retaining fossil fuel use with carbon capture, utilisation and storage (CCUS) to reduce emissions.	The Alliance of Small Island States (AOSIS) was established by the Maldives in 1990. The thirty-nine members' extreme vulnerability to climate change gives them influence in COP negotiations. They wanted global emissions to peak before 2025 and demanded loss and damage compensation.	Least Developed States Group (LDC) Around fifty states were identified in this group in the UNFCCC, they are low income, highly vulnerable to climate change and in need of the most support. They campaign for more ambition on aid, including loss and damage compensation.
The Climate Vulnerable Forum, founded in the Maldives in 2009, represents around seventy states, with 1.7 billion people who are responsible for only 5 per cent of global emissions. It includes AOSIS and LDC members and campaigns for universal action to keep within the 1.5°C limit, finance for sustainable development and loss and damage compensation.	Like-Minded Developing States (LMDC) is a coalition of large developing states including India, China, Malaysia and Iran, representing around half of the global population. It formed after the 2009 Copenhagen summit. LMDC wants the most developed states to fulfil their responsibilities on climate finance before they reduce their own emissions.	The High Ambition Coalition (HAC) set up by the Marshall Islands in 2015 includes around 120 states from other groups. It calls for ambitious emissions targets from all states under the Paris Agreement. Members range from tiny Vanuatu to the EU. The US joined in 2022, but the Trump administration has withdrawn from the Paris Agreement.

After 1997, the United States rejected the Kyoto Protocol until other large emitters agreed to binding reductions, whilst China refused even to allow the UN to monitor its greenhouse gas emissions, repeatedly pointing to US historical emissions. There was little meaningful progress until they started cooperating in 2014. Neither has ever agreed to be bound by imposed targets.

This obstacle was finally overcome at Paris by allowing states to set their own targets. The voluntary approach has spurred some progress: despite being outside the Kyoto Protocol, the United States has made steady progress in reducing emissions, and significant progress under the 2021–25 Biden administration, with over a trillion dollars of state investment in renewable energy and climate action. China is now the world leader in wind and solar power, and India's renewable energy boom has brought affordable power to many whilst reducing reliance on coal. However, it is not enough: their fossil fuel usage was still growing in 2024 (see Figure 7.4).

Further disagreements on how to measure emissions

Under the Paris Agreement, the internationally accepted approach for measuring emissions is based on production rather than consumption, which underestimates the contributions of developed states to climate change. Globalisation allowed developed states to significantly reduce their emissions by outsourcing manufacturing to China and developing states, who are then held responsible for the emissions caused by production. This should be kept in mind when assessing the growth of Chinese emissions seen in Figure 7.5.

A further disagreement is over whether to compare states on their total emissions, as in the Paris Agreement, or per capita emissions, which would highlight global inequities. For example, achieving net-zero in the UK will require citizens to make significant lifestyle changes for little overall impact on global warming compared to what India could achieve (Figure 7.5). However, per capita (per person) emissions are much lower in India than in the UK (Figure 7.6). This strengthens India's argument that it has the right to develop before reducing its emissions.

Different ways of comparing greenhouse gas emissions

Total greenhouse gas emissions: According to the UN, in 2023, the six largest total emitters in order are: China, the United States, India, the EU, Russia and Brazil (Map 7.2). They accounted for 63 per cent of global emissions, whilst together the G20 states are responsible for about 77 per cent of global emissions, which is comparable to their share of the global economy. In contrast, the forty-five least developed states accounted for only 3 per cent.

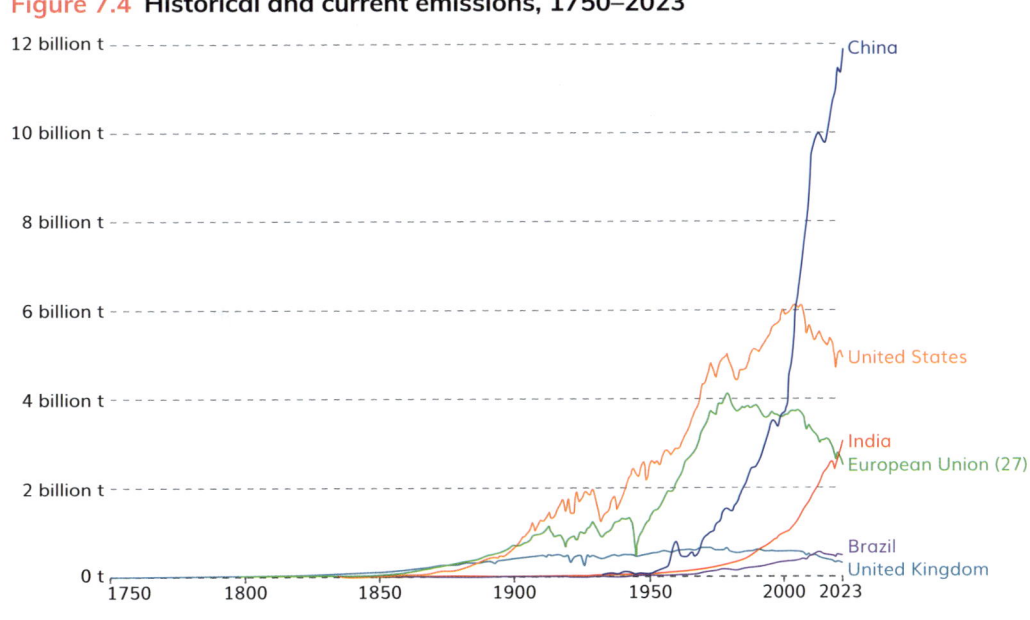

Figure 7.4 Historical and current emissions, 1750–2023

Source: 'Annual CO₂ emissions per country', Our World in Data. Based on data from the Global Carbon Project. Licensed under CC BY 4.0. Available at: ourworldindata.org/grapher/annual-co2-emissions-per-country

Definition

Total greenhouse gas emissions: All the greenhouse gas emissions produced each year in a state.

Per capita greenhouse gas emissions: Average emissions per person in a state.

Per capita greenhouse gas emissions: Greenhouse gas emissions per capita is a measure of how much, on average, each person in a state contributes to global warming. Emissions per capita are highest in major oil, gas and coal-producing states with low-density populations, such as Saudi Arabia, Canada and Australia. People in Sub-Saharan Africa and South Asia produce the lowest emissions per capita (Map 7.3).

Resentments over inequitable climate vulnerability

The negative impacts of climate change are very unevenly distributed. The IPCC reported that 13 million vulnerable people lost their homes in 2019, and by 2022, people were fifteen times more likely to die from extreme weather in more vulnerable states than in developed states. For example, Pakistan was hit by floods in 2022 that affected 33 million people, killing 1,700. Pakistan relied on international aid. Two years later, many homes had not been rebuilt, and malaria and waterborne diseases had created a health emergency. In 2024, almost half a million Europeans were affected by severe floods, and 335 people lost their lives. However, unlike Pakistan, European states can afford to help their people rebuild and adapt for the future.

The Global North has, on the whole, suffered less, because of its greater wealth (Figure 7.5). This does not necessarily mean that everyone in the Global North is safe – for example, after Hurricane Katrina flooded New Orleans in 2005, poorer black communities suffered disproportionate deaths due to poorer housing and inability to evacuate quickly. However, since the mid-2010s, wildfires and floods have regularly destroyed communities in North America, Europe and Australia, bringing these impacts much closer to home.

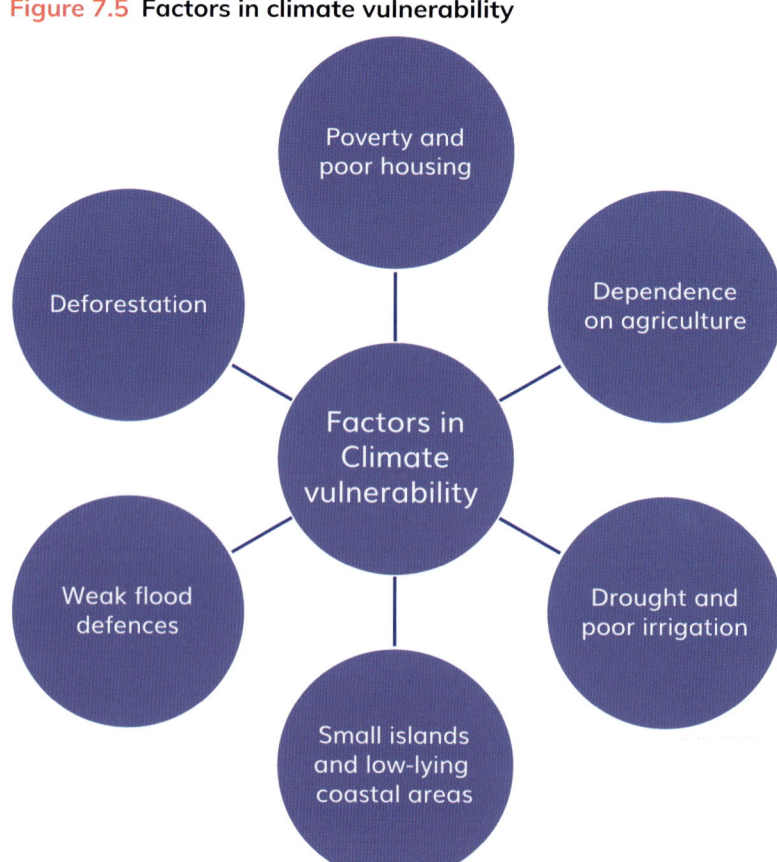

Figure 7.5 Factors in climate vulnerability

Map 7.2 Total greenhouse gas emissions by state, 2023

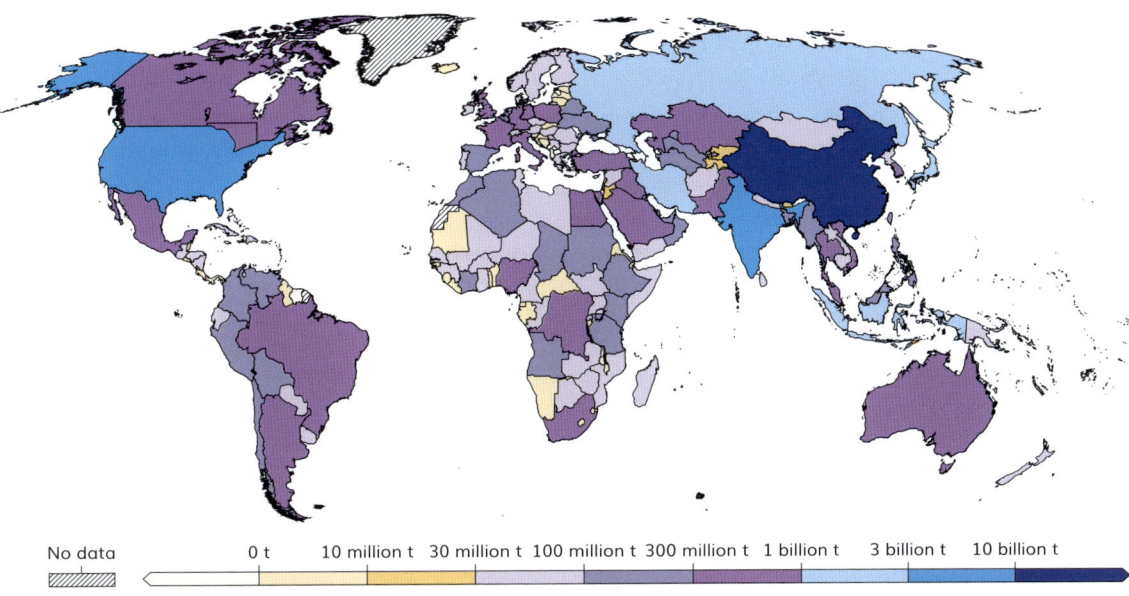

Source: Jones et al. (2024), Our World in Data. Map and legend adapted from 'Greenhouse gas emissions, 2023'. Licensed under CC BY 4.0. Available at: ourworldindata.org/co2-and-greenhouse-gas-emissions

Map 7.3 Map of carbon emissions per capita by state, 2023

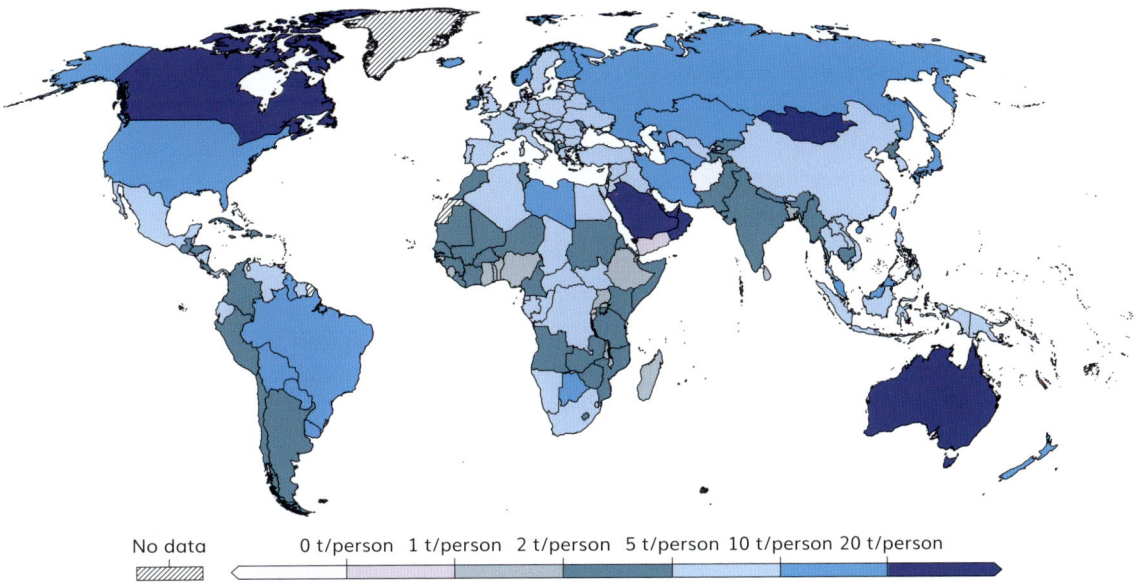

Source: Jones et al. (2024), Our World in Data. Map and legend adapted from 'Greenhouse gas emissions, 2023'. Licensed under CC BY 4.0. Available at: ourworldindata.org/co2-and-greenhouse-gas-emissions

Disagreements over responsibility for financing

Differences over the most developed states' responsibility to support developing states in reducing emissions and adapting to climate change has long been an obstacle to progress. Developed states argue that their main responsibility is to support access to finance and technology to help with sustainable development and that they have reached the $100 billion finance target agreed in 2009. Developing states want more international aid for adaptation and a 'loss and damage' fund to compensate them for climate-related disasters. Developed states have repeatedly rejected the loss and damage demand, fearing that giving compensation implies that they accept liability. As a result, many developing states have been resentful and unwilling to do more to reduce emissions until developed states take more responsibility.

However, attitudes in the Global North have shifted as more people have witnessed climate disasters and understood the need to support developing states to become more resilient. After the Pakistan floods in 2022, a small loss and damage fund was agreed at COP27 and funded a year later at COP27. China refused to contribute, arguing that as a developing state it was not obliged to pay. This has been a source of tension with the EU.

By 2024 at COP29, developing states said they faced a funding gap of around $1.4 trillion and asked the most developed states to provide half of this in international aid. With China eventually agreeing to make voluntary contributions, these states agreed to take the lead on raising $300 billion per year but would not specify the types of funding. Delegations from AOSIS and the LDC group walked out of negotiations before angrily accepting the offer.

Comparative Analysis: Divisions between developing and developed states

	Views of developing states	Views of developed states
Contribution to climate change	Developing states argue that developed states have contributed more historical greenhouse gases and should therefore reduce their emissions faster and further – a matter of global justice. A division has emerged between the most vulnerable states and powerful fossil fuel-dependent states – China, India, Brazil.	Under the UNFCCC, developed states acknowledged their responsibility for historical emissions, and most submitted to Kyoto requirements. Developed states emphasise the need for all states to reduce emissions. The United States consistently demands that China reduce its huge current emissions.
Right to develop	Some developing states, notably India, insist on their right to use fossil fuels to catch up with developed economies, while others want sustainable development. Views differ even within the climate-vulnerable group between those that seek a fast phase-out (e.g. the Maldives, Vanuatu) and those that want to delay (e.g. Mozambique).	Developed states argue that growth in all states should be sustainable now that renewable energy technologies exist. They have shared new technologies with developing states and supported access to investment. However, Trump's United States insists on the right to develop further without restriction.
Measuring current emissions	Developing states prefer consumption and per capita measures. In the 2000s, whilst the United States rejected Kyoto, China refused to even measure its emissions.	Developed states won the argument to use production-based total measures at Paris, instead.
Climate vulnerability	Developing states are disproportionately vulnerable to the impacts of climate change, yet have contributed the least to the problem: the Climate Vulnerable Forum (CVF) covers 1.7 billion people who are responsible for only 5 per cent of greenhouse gas emissions. They seek much more compensation and financial aid from developed states.	Developed states have been reluctant to admit liability for compensation, but floods and wildfires in Europe, North America and Australia have helped some to recognise that loss and damage funding is needed for states with less capacity to rebuild. Most now agree that support is needed for resilience in climate-vulnerable states, but the Trump administration does not.

> **Chapter Link**
>
> These divisions reflect global power dynamics discussed in **Chapter 3: Power and Developments**. In particular, the views of developing states are strongly influenced by dependency theory's concepts of underdevelopment and neocolonialism, addressed in **Chapter 5: Economic Global Governance**.

Environmental Global Governance

	Views of developing states	Views of developed states
Climate finance	Developing states have long demanded more financial aid. Climate finance was promised in 1992, not agreed until 2009 and not fully delivered until 2022, by which time need had outstripped supply. Most has been private investment rather than aid as requested. For decades, climate-vulnerable states demanded loss and damage compensation for historical emissions. They resent the developed states' refusal to fulfil UNFCCC responsibilities. China does not accept responsibility here.	Developed states argue that they meet their responsibilities. They achieved the goal of $100 billion a year in 2022. They believe that, realistically, private investments should play a significant role in financing sustainable development and have supported access to lending. They agreed to a loss and damage fund in 2022. In 2024, they agreed to increase climate adaptation financing by $300 billion per year. They resent China's claim that it is still a developing state without financing responsibilities.

KEY DEBATE: IS THE SLOW RATE OF PROGRESS ON CLIMATE ACTION DUE PRIMARILY TO GLOBAL ECONOMIC INEQUALITIES?

Contribution to climate change and the right to develop

A significant reason for slow progress has been disagreements over inequitable historical emissions:

- ✓ Developed states have historically contributed the most to climate change. The Kyoto Protocol should have accounted for historical emissions, but some powerful states did not fully accept their responsibilities.
- ✓ Developing states such as India argue that they have the right to use fossil fuels to catch up with developed economies, given these historical contributions and their unfulfilled responsibilities under the UNFCCC.

However, states' current dependence on fossil fuels arguably has a greater impact on their willingness to cooperate:

- ✗ Many states have been reluctant to make cuts to their own fossil fuel production regardless of their level of development and historical emissions. The United States, Saudi Arabia, China, India and Mozambique, to name a few, have all obstructed negotiations on phasing out different fossil fuels because they reserve the right to exploit their own natural resources for future growth.
- ✗ In contrast, the EU and small island developing states (SIDS), who do not depend on fossil fuel production, have allied in pushing for more ambition on universal cuts.

Disagreements over measurement of emissions for comparisons

Differences over which measurements of emissions would provide for equitable comparison were an obstacle to progress for many years.

- ✓ Developed states benefit from using production-based rather than consumption-based measures and from comparing national total emissions rather than per capita emissions. They tend to argue that they have reduced their historic emissions and that now all states have a responsibility to develop sustainably.
- ✓ Developing states push for consumption and per capita measures and incorporation of historical emissions in comparisons to highlight global inequalities.

> **Exam Tip:**
> The title of this key debate is adapted from a more complex question on climate action that appeared in the 2022 exam paper. When using past papers, note that the exam board made a change after 2022 to simpler question styles. When using past papers as a guide for revision, we advise you to ignore the 2022 paper.

These disagreements have become less important since 2015. The biggest problem now is a lack of accountability.

- ✖ The Paris Agreement overcame these disputes by allowing states to set their own nationally determined contributions towards an agreed goal of limiting warming to 2°C and working towards 1.5°C.
- ✖ However, by February 2025, only the UK had submitted an updated NDC that would be sufficient to achieve that goal. Regardless of their stage of development, no other state had submitted on time.

Inequalities in climate vulnerability

The poorer developing states are disproportionately vulnerable to climate change impacts, yet have contributed the least to the problem. This causes great resentment:

- ✔ The Climate Vulnerable Forum (CVF) covers 1.7 billion people responsible for only 5 per cent of greenhouse gas emissions. Small island states, and those impacted by monsoon flooding and extreme heat are concentrated in the Global South. These states seek compensation and financial aid from developed states to help them recover from climate-related disasters.
- ✔ Less vulnerable states in the Global North, and large states at a higher level of development, such as China, Brazil and India, have been more likely to block ambitious action with their reluctance to cut their own emissions.

However, climate vulnerability makes states less likely to obstruct negotiations to reduce emissions, unlike fossil fuel dependence:

- ✖ As climate change has accelerated since 2015, climate vulnerability has started to affect more people in the wealthy Global North. Floods and wildfires in Europe, North America and Australia have helped these states to recognise a shared vulnerability. Yet despite this awareness, progress has remained slow.
- ✖ Both wealthy and poorer states with climate vulnerabilities have blocked progress during this time; for example, the US South is vulnerable, but Trump has withdrawn from the Paris Agreement and is promoting more oil drilling. Extreme heat has caused many deaths in India, yet its government still resists phasing out coal.

Climate finance and compensation for loss and damage

Delays by developed states in negotiating and delivering on financing promises have caused resentment, blocking progress.

- ✔ Financial support was promised in 1992, agreed in 2009, but not fully delivered until 2022. By then, need had outstripped supply, and most of the finance came from private investments rather than aid as requested.
- ✔ Climate-vulnerable states demanded loss and damage funding for decades before it was finally agreed in 2022.

There has been inadequate progress made on finance, but it is not the states that need the most financial support that have blocked progress on reducing emissions; it is those that depend on fossil fuels.

- ✖ The CVF have promoted universal reductions and developed states agreed to a loss and damage fund in 2022 and to triple climate finance in 2024, suggesting that inequalities are not the main obstacle.
- ✖ In contrast, China and India have continued to block the phase-out of coal and delayed their net-zero targets to 2060 and 2070. They have sought to retain fossil fuels for long enough to support their own economic growth, suggesting narrow self-interest was the main driver rather than global inequalities.

Environmental Global Governance

Key Debate Summary: Is the slow rate of progress on climate action due primarily to global economic inequalities?

	For	Against
Contribution to climate change and the right to develop	✓ The Kyoto Protocol failed to hold some developed states to account, while developing states argue for the right to use fossil fuels for development.	✗ Fossil fuel-producing states have been most likely to refuse to phase out fossil fuels, regardless of their level of development.
Disagreements over measurements	✓ Disagreements between developed and developing states over measures have slowed progress.	✗ The Paris agreement resolved some disputes over measurements. States' reluctance to accept enforcement mechanisms is now a greater problem.
Inequalities in climate vulnerability	✓ Small island states in the Global South are most vulnerable. Less vulnerable states are more likely to block emissions cuts.	✗ All states are now at risk. Fossil fuel interests appear to be more significant than vulnerability, regardless of levels of development.
Climate finance and compensation	✓ UNFCCC financial support promises have been slow and inadequate, especially for climate-vulnerable states – causing resentment.	✗ Progress on finance has been inadequate, but it is not the states most in need of support that block progress, but those who want to retain fossil fuels for their own narrow economic self-interest.

Exam Tip:

Students sometimes struggle to structure an essay like this when a question asks if one factor (e.g. inequality) is more important than others. Find different ways that the factor has been influential. Directly counter each point by explaining why a different factor may be more important – in this case fossil fuel interests and state sovereignty are also significant.

Conclusion

Global surveys in the 2020s have consistently shown that an overwhelming majority of people are worried about the climate emergency, and want their governments to take decisive action, even at cost to themselves. Yet voluntary actions by states are unlikely to even keep us within the 2°C upper warming limit.

The Montreal Protocol showed us that even if a relatively small number of well-informed leaders in powerful states are prepared to show global leadership and prioritise action, they can move global environmental governance forward. However, climate sceptic Donald Trump's second withdrawal from the Paris Agreement in 2025 makes it harder for the rest of the world to find the collective will to set more ambitious targets and accept enforcement. It will be extremely difficult, but vital, to persuade major fossil fuel producers and large emitters that they must sacrifice their short-term interests for the common good.

Chapter Summary

- Tragedy of the commons: individuals acting in self-interest deplete shared resources and cause environmental degradation, as shown in the climate crisis.

- Sustainable Development: 'Shallow-green' ecologism supported by many governments promotes sustainable development to manage resources for future human use, while 'deep-green' ecologism calls for a more radical ecocentric approach.

- The UN supported the creation of the UNFCCC and its subsequent Kyoto Protocol and Paris Agreement to promote global climate action. Main actors include member states, the IPCC, which provides guidelines, support and scientific assessments, and non-state actors, including industry and civil society.

- Global civil society has raised awareness, influenced policies and mobilised public support for climate action, playing a vital role in fostering international cooperation.

- The UNFCCC was established to provide a framework for states to work together to avoid dangerous levels of global warming, while the IPCC provides scientific assessments on climate change. Both play crucial roles in informing and shaping international climate agreements.

- COP meetings achieved the Kyoto Protocol, the Copenhagen Accord and the Paris Agreement, but progress has been slow. The principle of state sovereignty slows progress on reducing greenhouse gas emissions and makes it difficult to enforce agreements.

- Obstacles to collective action have included disagreements over responsibilities for historical and future emissions, ways of comparing national emissions, inequitable climate vulnerabilities and disagreements over finance. The most significant obstacle now is fossil fuel interests, leading to blocked negotiations and weak accountability.

Exam Style Questions

- Examine the differences between shallow ecology and deep ecology in their approaches to the environment. (12)
- Examine the differences between developing and developed states on climate governance. (12)
- Examine the significance of the Kyoto Protocol and Paris Agreement. (12)
- Examine the impacts of the Rio and Copenhagen COP summits. (12)
- Examine the criticisms/strengths of the UNFCCC and IPCC. (12)
- Analyse the divisions between realists and liberals on environmental governance. (12)
- Evaluate the view that environmental global governance has been effective. (30)
- Evaluate the view that the slow rate of progress over climate change results primarily from economic inequalities. (30)

Further Resources

https://ourworldindata.org/climate-change. An excellent source of graphs and charts on climate change, regularly updated.

https://www.youtube.com/watch?v=zbEnOYtsXHA. *Before the Flood*, a National Geographic documentary from 2016 featuring Leonardo DiCaprio, examining the impacts of climate change.

https://www.bbc.co.uk/iplayer/episode/m00049b1/climate-change-the-facts. *Climate Change: The Facts*, a BBC documentary from 2019 featuring Sir David Attenborough, examining climate science and impacts.

https://footprint.wwf.org.uk/. Calculate your own carbon footprint.

https://doughnuteconomics.org/about-doughnut-economics. A clear and accessible explanation of the 'doughnut economics' approach to sustainable development.

https://www.cfr.org/backgrounder/paris-global-climate-change-agreements. A very useful overview of global climate agreements.

https://cvfv20.org/. The Climate Vulnerable Forum.

https://www.aosis.org/. The Alliance of Small Island States.

https://www.highambitioncoalition.org/. The High Ambition Coalition.

https://www.theguardian.com/us-news/2024/apr/14/climate-disinformation-explainer. 'Explainer: How to spot five of the fossil fuel industry's biggest disinformation tactics', by climate journalists Amy Westervelt and Kyle Pope for *The Guardian*.

https://www.theguardian.com/environment/2025/apr/22/spiral-of-silence-climate-action-very-popular-why-dont-people-realise. *The Guardian* is a member of the 89 per cent project, aiming to correct public misperceptions on how much support there is for more climate action.

 Visit https://bloomsbury.pub/essentials-of-global-politics to access additional materials to support teaching and learning.

8 ANALYSING AND EVALUATING GLOBAL GOVERNANCE

Chapter Preview

This chapter pulls together the threads from the four preceding chapters. We begin by answering the tricky question 'what is global governance', briefly revisiting learning from Comparative Theories by defining it as a liberal ideal and contrasting it to realist ideas about the way that the international state system is ordered.

We then consider the impact of global governance on state sovereignty and compare it to the hypothetical concept of world government.

We'll look back at how states have developed and expanded global governance to address emerging global problems, and how and when this has been challenged over the years, highlighting the tensions between national interests and collective global action.

We will then review the actors involved, considering how the significance of each type of actor varies between the four areas of global governance, and how they work with and against each other.

Finally, we explore ways to compare the effectiveness of governance across the four areas of conflict, poverty, human rights and the environment.

Key Questions and Debates
- » What is global governance and what is it not?
- » How do liberals and realists view global governance?
- » What is the difference between global governance and world government?
- » How has global governance developed and changed over time, and what are its prospects?
- » How effective are IGOs, and how do states and non-state actors contribute to and obstruct their work?
- » How can we evaluate the effectiveness of IGOs across the four themes of conflict, poverty, human rights and environment?

Specification Checklist

This chapter helps you to address the following skills in Section C questions that ask you to compare two different forms of governance:

- » Students must identify parallels, connections, similarities and differences between the content studied, providing a basis for comparing contemporary global issues, such as conflict, poverty, human rights and the environment and how these are affected by the content in each of the sections.
- » Students must construct and communicate arguments and explanations with relevance, clarity and coherence, and draw reasoned conclusions about global politics.

Source: kolderal/Moment via Getty Images

Component III: Global Politics

Chapter Link
Section C exam questions are explained further in **Chapter 10: Exam Skills**.

Analysing global governance

In this chapter, we will be drawing together and comparing governance across the four themes of conflict, poverty, human rights and the environment to help with the broad questions that are sometimes asked in Section C of the Global Politics examination.

Recap: What is global governance?

Global governance is a complex process where states work together to make decisions.

States normally have sole sovereignty over their own territories. In global governance, they work together to create and maintain institutions, laws and norms to address issues they cannot solve alone, like resolving conflicts, promoting economic development and stability, protecting human rights and tackling the climate crisis.

Governance is different from government. At the global level, governance means the process of negotiating collective agreements that states then agree to implementing collectively or individually. Sometimes, global governance involves creating international law in the form of treaties signed by states. Other times, decisions are made informally.

Sometimes, non-state actors like civil society or businesses are invited by states and international organizations to participate in global governance processes (see Table 8.1).

Table 8.1 Actors and Processes in Global Governance

Actors	Processes
States are often seen as the 'primary actors' in global politics. The principle of state sovereignty means that it is states that create intergovernmental organizations, and states that collectively make decisions within them.	States make **international law** by signing **treaties**, conventions and **protocols**. These laws are often drafted with the help of legal and policy experts at the UN. The UN also facilitates state negotiations by organising international **summit meetings**: conferences of state leaders where treaties are signed. Treaties are often named after the location of the summit.
Intergovernmental Organizations (IGOs) include: **Institutions** such as the United Nations (UN), which has councils for deliberation and decision-making, a judicial system and a secretariat that fulfils its executive functions. **Informal forums** such as the G7 and G20, which are exclusive 'steering groups'.	**Charters and statutes** are international laws that establish the rules and powers of international institutions. Institutions have regular formal deliberative meetings where **resolutions** are agreed. **International summits** can be informal, for example, annual G7 and G20 meetings where powerful states discuss solutions to crises and try to agree what the future goals of global governance should be.
International courts such as the International Court of Justice (part of the UN) and the International Criminal Court are not intergovernmental. They are led by panels of judges who do not represent individual states.	International law is constantly developing as **judicial precedents** provide new interpretations of treaties, **customary international law** (common legal practise) and **general legal principles**. States often challenge the legitimacy of 'judge-made law'.

Definition

Treaties: Formal agreements between states. A treaty may be bilateral – between two states, or multilateral conventions and covenants open to all states.

Protocols: Additions to previous treaties.

A charter or statute: A treaty that establishes an institution and the laws that govern it.

Security Council Resolutions: Under Chapter VII of the UN Charter, these are binding on all UN members, so have the status of international law.

Judicial precedents: Decisions made by international courts or tribunals that serve as guidance for future cases.

Table 8.1 Continued

Actors	Processes
Multinational corporations such as banks, oil or tech companies and their lobbyists.	These non-state actors aim to influence decision-making by states. Liberal ideology argues that broad participation in decision-making is important. Non-state actors often attend meetings on the 'fringes' at COPs and G20 summits. They may be invited to work alongside states and IGOs in informal **policy networks**. They might support the UN in providing aid and advice to states. NGOs with 'consultative status' can address ECOSOC meetings.
Civil society includes **non-governmental organizations** (NGOs) such as the International Red Cross or Amnesty International, professional associations and trade unions, expert advisers, philanthropists such as Bill Gates and activists such as Malala Yousafzai or Greta Thunberg and the social movements that they inspire.	

> **Definition**
>
> **Customary international law** Generally accepted practises and general principles of law such as the principle of equality are applied by judges if there is no other form of international law to apply.

How do realists and liberals view state sovereignty?

Realist view: Hobbes	Liberal view: Locke
Hobbes's version of the social contract imagines sovereignty as *absolute*.	On the other hand, John Locke argued that the social contract was *conditional*.
The state – or Leviathan – has supreme power over its subjects and must guard its sovereignty as its highest priority – never allowing it to be surrendered to a higher authority.	The state must serve its citizens and has no right to give its sovereignty away to a higher power without their ongoing consent.

> **Spec key term**
>
> **Intergovern-mentalism:** Is interaction between states based on sovereign independence.
>
> **Supranation-alism:** Refers to a large amount of power given to an authority, which, in theory, is placed higher than the state.
>
> **Complex interdependence:** The broad, overlapping web of relations between states and with non-state actors in global politics. States become dependent on one another which helps to reduce the risk of conflict.

How does global governance impact on state sovereignty?

State sovereignty is the organising principle of global politics, as laid down in the Charter of the United Nations. This has two important implications:

- *Participation in global governance is voluntary.* A state can choose whether to sign up to international law and whether to join international organizations.
- *It is difficult to enforce international law.* A state can choose not to comply with its international obligations. This might happen if a government that signs a treaty is replaced by another with a very different ideology or leadership style. States can resist scrutiny, and international organizations do not have the power to enforce collective decisions. The UN can ask the UNSC member states to enforce international law on behalf of the international community, but they may not agree to do so.

Decision-making in global governance is therefore usually **intergovernmental** rather than **supranational**. So, another term for international organization is 'intergovernmental organization' (IGO). The question of how far state sovereignty is impacted by any organization, decision or law is fundamental to the analysis of global governance.

How is global governance different from other forms of world order?

Global governance is a liberal concept, associated with the idea of **complex interdependence**. One way we can help to define it is by contrasting it against other theories, or models, of international relations: international anarchy and global hegemony, which come from the realist tradition, the imaginary liberal idea of world government, and the Anarchical Society, which is drawn from both realism and liberalism.

International anarchy is the idea that we met in **Chapter 1: Comparative Theories**, that there is no supranational authority that is capable of regulating the behaviour of states, meaning that states must therefore look after themselves and prioritise their own security. As a result, the international state system is prone to periods of conflict interspersed with periods of relative stability whenever a balance of power can be achieved. It is a core assumption of realism, based on the 'Westphalian' state system that emerged in Europe from 1648.

Global hegemony is the idea that we met in **Chapter 3: Power and Developments**. It is the realist idea that one power – 'a hegemon' – will stand above other states and impose its will on them. It will gather allies, who accept its leadership in return for protection (bandwagoning). It will seek to maintain stability by providing a reliable currency to support international trade, by establishing IGOs with rules that give it dominant structural power and by using its military power to maintain stability around the world. After the Second World War, the United States was hegemonic in the Western Hemisphere. It led to the establishment of the Bretton Woods Institutions, giving it structural power to dominate in both the International Monetary Fund and the World Bank.

With the collapse of the Soviet Union in 1991, the United States became the global hegemon. It intervened in conflicts around the world and drove the establishment of the World Trade Organization and G20, both of which promote its free-trade ideology. The intention may have been to entrench its own economic hegemony, but these actually encouraged the rise of China as a challenger and the United States' relative decline.

If it existed, **World Government** would be a supranational authority with power over all nation-states. The closest thing we have to a world government is the United Nations. However, it is not a government because it depends entirely on the states that created it and that provide its resources. Only the Security Council can take enforcement action against states, and that council is in turn largely controlled by its five permanent members.

> **Spec key term**
> **World Government:** The idea of a common political authority with legislative and executive power over states.

Comparative Analysis: Differences between global governance and world government

	Global Governance	World Government
Structure and actors	Global governance is complex and flexible. It includes: • Multiple IGOs with overlapping powers and responsibilities, set up by states to formalise collective decision-making. • Summit meetings, informal forums and policy networks in which non-state actors help states and IGOs to solve problems. • International laws that states choose to sign up to – or not.	World government could be either: • A single, centralised government with global jurisdiction (authority over every state). • A federal world government holding some powers (perhaps environmental law and military intervention) while states or regional bodies retain other powers (perhaps human rights and development). Some powers might be shared, e.g. taxation.
Impact on state sovereignty	**Intergovernmental** decision-making protects the principle of state sovereignty, allowing states to decide on a case-by-case basis whether they wish to cooperate or make their own decisions.	• A unitary **supranational** government could make and enforce international law on any matter it chooses. • A **federal** world government would have sole sovereignty within its reserved constitutional powers.

Analysing and Evaluating Global Governance

	Global Governance	World Government
Strengths	• The flexible global governance system can adapt and respond to emerging global problems. • Global governance has encouraged liberal values such as support for human rights and democracy to spread around the world. • Its flexibility allows states to prioritise their own needs, interests and values, respecting diversity.	• A world government could provide more streamlined, efficient decision-making. • Cosmopolitan liberals (those in favour of world government) have argued that it could be designed to ensure democratic accountability to states and their citizens. • It could legally constrain powerful states from abusing their power and would have its own security forces to enforce this.
Weaknesses	• Global governance often fails to constrain powerful states from exploiting or attacking weaker states or their own citizens. • Many IGOs do not uphold the sovereign equality of states in their decision-making processes, e.g. IMF, World Bank, in their membership, e.g. G7 and G20, or in both, e.g. UNSC.	• A world government carries the risk of uncheckable power. • Full democratic accountability to both states and their citizens is unrealistic at the global level. Democratic accountability to citizens is therefore best achieved by protecting state sovereignty through intergovernmentalism.

How do realists and liberals view global governance?

Realist view	Liberal view
Realists believe that all states, no matter their regime type, are fundamentally only interested in their own power and security.	Liberals aim to make the world more peaceful and prosperous by encouraging states to work together co-operatively for the common good.
They believe that states use institutions to serve their own purposes. If that approach fails, they will bypass or undermine IGOs, weakening them.	They argue that global governance can help maintain stability in the international system. Global governance is a liberal concept. Institutions help states to act according to liberal assumptions rather than realist ones.
Realists argue that IGOs provide a platform for empty promises and threats but produce little of substance: in the famous words of the ancient Greek historian Thucydides, 'the strong do what they will, and the weak suffer what they must'. IGOs therefore cannot constrain powerful states from violating the rights of their own people or the sovereignty of other states.	Liberal institutionalists argue that IGOs create rules, procedures and norms such as transparency. They monitor state activity, making international relations more predictable. They provide opportunities for repeated interaction, helping states to build diplomatic relationships with each other.
'Good governance' is simply not relevant to a realist view of the international system 'as it is'. Realists would argue that when states provide aid, they are not motivated primarily by altruism; instead, they impose conditions on aid primarily to serve their own interests, for example, enforcing free trade and foreign investment in exchange for debt relief.	Liberals argue that IGOs encourage states to practise good governance within their own territories, enhancing equity and freedom. They see weak governance as highly destabilising to global order due to the risk of conflict, which might spread. They see support for good governance in fragile states as a moral responsibility. Good governance is an important focus of aid from the UN, the World Bank, and the EU (see **case study: the UN Peacebuilding Commission**).

CASE STUDY: THE LIBERAL IDEAL OF 'GOOD GOVERNANCE'

Context

The concept of good governance refers to the effective, transparent, accountable and inclusive management of resources and decision-making processes. The aim is to reduce the risk of corruption by political elites, promoting equity and responsiveness to the needs of the people.

The World Bank started to make good governance a condition of lending in the late 1980s and early 1990s. Initially, the concept was narrowly targeted at economic institutions in developing countries, to crack down on bribery and waste, to ensure that privatization of state assets was done without corruption, and to safeguard the assets of investors from being seized by the state.

In the 1990s, the concept was broadened to include respect for the rule of law more broadly, democratic accountability and constitutional checks and balances on executive power. Good governance also requires the participation of various stakeholders, including governments, civil society, and the private sector, in making and implementing government policy, giving rise to the concept of policy networks. The World Bank and the EU started to use this broader approach as a condition for development aid, and the EU also made it a condition of its preferential trade scheme for developing countries.

In the early 2000s, the UN recognised that good governance was key to achieving the Millennium Development Goals, and it was also built into the debt cancellation criteria on the IMF/World Bank Highly Indebted Poor Countries Initiative. However, the IMF was not as fully committed to the idea as the World Bank was. After the Global Financial Crisis, it loosened its requirements for good democratic and constitutional governance in favour of tighter financial governance.

The idea of good governance was written into the UN's Sustainable Development Goal 16 in 2015: 'Promote peaceful and inclusive societies for sustainable development, provide access to justice for all and build effective, accountable and inclusive institutions at all levels.'

Significance

Good governance requirements for loans and aid have helped to spread democracy, particularly in Africa. However, this practise has provoked resistance by some authoritarian governments, who have turned to Russia and China for 'values-free' loans and aid instead of the Western-dominated IGOs.

China is often accused of neocolonialism in Africa, by investing for its own purposes and imposing unaffordable debt repayments. However, 'good governance' requirements can also be seen as neocolonialism, because they protect the interests of foreign investors by ensuring their assets are protected by the rule of law in the states they invest in.

The concept of good governance as a requirement of loans and aid is relevant to both the political and economic aspects of global governance, as well as to the impact of the European Union's Common Foreign and Security Policy (see Chapter 9, p. 325).

> **Spec key term**
>
> **Global governance:** A complex, mostly 'intergovernmental' process where states work together to make decisions. States create and maintain the institutions, laws and norms of global governance to address issues they cannot solve alone, Non-state actors are sometimes involved.

World government is not a realistic prospect. Understandably, states – and particularly powerful states – are very wary of the idea of giving up their sovereignty to any superior authority. What if they created a world government which became tyrannical over them, and they could not take that sovereignty back? This concern is why, when EU member states signed the Lisbon Treaty in 2007 (this gave the European Union a single legal identity in international law and enhanced its supranational powers), they also included the 'Article 50' clause that allows states to leave the union.

Anarchical society: In **Chapter 1: Comparative Theories**, we considered the anarchical society, which was Hedley Bull's challenge to the theory of international anarchy. Bull explained how groups of states will cooperate on the basis of shared norms and rules, despite a lack of supranational authority. He blended realist ideas about power with liberal ideas about cooperation to explain how intergovernmental decision-making – in other words, **global governance** – can emerge from the anarchical system, without the imposition of a supranational authority or world government. Bull's theory provided an update for the post-Second World War era, in which states in the West built a system characterised by cooperation and interdependence.

How has global governance developed over time?

The post-war era of global governance
History shows that global governance evolves in response to crisis. The establishment of the United Nations and Bretton Woods Institutions marked a new post-war era: promoting state sovereignty, peace and security, human rights and economic development through collective, rule-bound decision-making. However, this soon degenerated into the Cold War, which saw powerful states persistently blocking and bypassing the UN much as they do today.

Early 1990s: The evolution of multi-actor and multilevel governance
The early 1990s saw dramatic expansion and evolution of global governance, driven by the United States as the unchallenged global hegemon. The UN started work on sustainable development and humanitarian assistance. States were still primary actors, but with non-state actors increasingly participating. The 1992 Rio 'Earth Summit' saw thousands of NGOs contribute to drafting the UN Framework Convention on Climate Change.

The liberal European Union, created in 1993, became a sophisticated supranational authority with a single market to rival that of the United States. With the development of EU aid programmes, the concept of 'good governance' in international development (see **Case Study: The Liberal Ideal of Good Governance**) was expanded from anti-corruption measures to encompass constitutional safeguards, democratic accountability, rights and the rule of law.

Late 1990s: The rise of global social movements
Humanitarianism: Images of genocide in Yugoslavia and Rwanda led to a global civil society campaign throughout the 1990s, calling for greater humanitarian efforts by the United States and Europe and for the establishment of an International Criminal Court. Humanitarian intervention increased, and the Rome Statute was agreed in 1998, leading to the establishment of the International Criminal Court in 2000.

Anti-poverty and anti-globalisation: the World Trade Organization opened in 1995, and the rapidly developing internet allowed grassroots activists to organise global social movements calling for change to unfair trade practises and neocolonialism. A wave of mass protests took place at international summits (see Photo 8.2). These movements spurred the UN's Millennium Development Goals (MDGs) in 2000 and, in 2005, debt cancellation for the world's most heavily indebted poor countries, conditional on 'good governance'.

2000s: Globalisation and global governance reach their peak
As globalization continued to accelerate in the early 2000s, non-state actors such as multinational corporations and policy consultants played an ever-increasing role in global governance. The term 'global public policy networks' (GPPNs) was popularised by liberal theorists. These networks bring together governments, international organizations, civil society and businesses to solve global issues.

However, globalisation also led to the rise of Chinese power and the decline of the United States as global hegemon. In 2009, the G20 set up a global leaders' forum, including China, to avert the collapse of the global banking system and sustain trade.

2010s: Humanitarianism declines; conflict, climate change and migration surge
Despite the universal adoption of the UN's 'responsibility to protect' in 2005, there have been few interventions since. Following failed interventions in Iraq, Afghanistan and Libya, the P5 states' appetite for humanitarian intervention has certainly declined, whilst conflicts have multiplied. In the 2010s,

Photo 8.1 The Make Poverty History rally, along with protests around Edinburgh, were organised to coincide with the G8 Summit in 2005. 100,000 people turned up to protest, and many clashed with the police.

Source: Scott Barbour/Getty Images News via Getty Images

intensifying climate change added to conflicts to increase migration from the Global South to the North to unprecedented levels.

The period from 2011 to 2014 might be seen in retrospect as the beginning of a decline in global governance as hostility between the United States, the UK and France on one side, and Russia and China on the other slowly ramped up. In the UNSC, Russia continually vetoed intervention in Syria, and then, following chemical weapons attacks by the Syrian government on its citizens, the UK and France failed to support the United States in proposed airstrikes against Assad. In parallel, the US government became increasingly unhappy with the WTO's failure to curb China's trade practises, whilst China launched its successful Belt and Road Initiative. Russia annexed Crimea in 2014. It was suspended from and later left the G8.

2015–2019: Environmentalism and isolationism

2015 saw the universal adoption of the Sustainable Development Goals and the Paris Climate Change Agreement, but, viewed in the context of the previous few years, these achievements looked more like a 'blip' than a trend in multilateralism. The decline became more evident when both the UK and the United States took an isolationist turn in 2016 with the Brexit vote and the election of US President Donald Trump. In the same year, an increasingly assertive China, resentful of the US veto on quota reform at the Western-dominated Bretton Woods Institutions, established its own Asian Infrastructure Investment Bank. By 2018, the United States, China and the EU were engaged in a trade war.

2020s: Crisis after crisis and the Global South push back

The Covid-19 pandemic exposed the increasing fragility of global supply chains. In 2021, Democratic President Biden replaced Donald Trump, leading to a temporary return of US multilateralism, but, hard on the heels of Covid-19, Russia's invasion of Ukraine in 2022 set off a global inflationary spiral, stoking a wave of far-right nationalism in response and triggering a renewed developing world debt crisis.

Global governance achieved some successes, for example in expanding the lending capacity of the IMF and World Bank between 2020 and 2024, but these were few and hard-won. The Bretton Woods

Institutions remained dominated by the G7, who repeatedly ignored calls for significant voting reform. In response, the BRICs group of emerging economies has deepened its cooperation and expanded its membership. The UNSC has been largely paralysed for more than a decade. Many developing states have chosen to abstain from votes, such as a UNGA resolution condemning Russia for invading Ukraine. Western outrage at Russian imperialism is increasingly perceived by postcolonial states as hypocritical, given the history of European imperialism and European support for Israel's destruction of Gaza.

Will global governance fail?

Some argue that in an increasingly multipolar world, global governance has already failed. In 2025, nationalist leaders lead some of the world's most powerful states, promoting a view of international relations as a zero-sum game involving trade wars and hybrid warfare. After years of complaints about European freeloading on its military deterrent investments, the United States has signalled that it will no longer be an unconditional defence partner for Europe. Trump's realignment towards Russia in early 2025 simply reconfigures the divisions between the UNSC permanent members so that the UK and France can no longer count on US support. The council's paralysis is likely to continue.

If the UN and NATO cannot function, states will bypass them, either working within regional organizations or setting up ad hoc 'coalitions of the willing' to cooperate on single issues. This is already happening. In Europe, states are seriously considering the prospect of a European defence alliance, and stepping up cooperation with the UK, Turkey and Norway to support Ukraine.

In the past decade, Chinese foreign investment has significantly increased. Unlike Western powers, China does not require democratic and human rights reforms as a condition of investment. In 2024, the United States provided 40 per cent of all international humanitarian aid tracked by the UN. Much to Ukraine, but also to other conflicts, global public health and economic development. However, in 2025, the United States and the UK both reduced their international aid spending. As a result, multilateral international development aid has an uncertain and much-reduced role to play. Humanitarian aid will continue at a reduced level. High-cost spending on development projects may be replaced by more low-cost provision of expert advice. Consequently, developing states have fewer incentives to adopt human rights and democratic principles in exchange for protection or financial support.

That being said, UN peacebuilding, climate negotiations and international courts continue to operate. Litigation against irresponsible states could be a growth area. Frustrated civil society leaders and climate-vulnerable states have begun to use the International Court of Justice to try to shift the dial on climate change commitments.

We may therefore witness a significant re-ordering of global governance. The post-war, US-led liberal model of global governance could join Western imperialism in the history books, but Chinese-led neocolonialism looks set to continue. States may increasingly turn to regional cooperation and to international courts.

Evaluating global governance

The relationships between states and international organisations

When we consider the relationships between states and international organisations, we must always remember that states remain in the driving seat. They create IGOs to serve them, rather than to rule over them. The job of the IGO is to help, by providing advice and a rules-based, predictable forum in which relationships can be built. How well, then, do they do this job?

Your evaluative toolkit

Throughout this book, we have used evaluative criteria such as *equity, authority, accountability* and *impact* to help us make judgements about IGOs. Let's recap these to ensure that you have understood them fully. This will help you to access the all-important AO2 and AO3 marks.

> **Chapter Link**
>
> **Chapter 4: Political Global Governance discusses** the failures of the UN Security Council and UN peacekeeping, and Secretary-General Antonio Guterres's decision to move towards peace-building work.

> **Exam Tip:**
> You can use liberal and realist perspectives to evaluate these concepts. Liberals argue that equity and accountability are possible and desirable within institutions, realists disagree. Liberals believe that state sovereignty can legitimately be overruled if a state breaks international law or its social contract with its own citizens, but realists see sovereignty as a fundamental principle that should not be overruled.

CASE STUDY: THE UN PEACEBUILDING COMMISSION

Context

The UN's Peacebuilding Commission (UNPC) was created in 2005. Its role is to guide and help states recover from conflict to prevent them from becoming failed states. Once a ceasefire has been established, peacebuilding is the long, civilian-led process of supporting reconciliation to prevent conflict from re-emerging. This will involve justice for victims, reintegrating fighters into work and communities, and building or strengthening democratic institutions.

The UNPC is a 31-member advisory body made up of member-state representatives from the UNSC, the UNGA, ECOSOC, donor countries, troop contributing countries, the country being supported, along with officials from the Secretariat, the IMF, the World Bank and relevant regional organisations, such as the African Union.

It coordinates the UN's efforts with those of interested parties in the affected region – governments, the African Union and civil society groups – to agree strategy, provide guidance and mobilise resources for peacebuilding projects, with the help of the World Bank. It is also supported by the UN's Peacebuilding Fund.

The UNPC has considered twenty-six conflict situations since 2006, including fourteen in 2022. However, according to the US Institute of Peace, a non-partisan think tank, there were fifty-five state-based and eighty-two non-state conflicts around the world in 2022, so this is a fraction of what is needed. Conflicts are becoming more common, more complex and more deadly to civilians.

Significance

Today's global security challenges from terrorism and internal conflicts involving non-state actors are deeply intertwined with human rights, political inequalities, cultural divisions and underdevelopment. However, the UNSC and UN military peacekeeping have often failed. In response, the UN has reformed and integrated its political, economic and human rights work, collaborating more with other IGOs, regional organisations and non-state actors to produce joined-up solutions to these problems.

The UNPC helps the Organs of the UN to work together better. It advises the Security Council – doing so seventeen times in 2022. Unlike the Security Council, it works by consensus and its meetings often have a cooperative atmosphere, supported by the inclusion of non-state actors. Initially, some states were dismissive of the Commission, which they saw as inefficiently duplicating the Security Council's work. Since 2015, the UNPC's role has become more distinctively focused on preventing future conflicts.

Strengthening the UN's peacebuilding work is part of Sustainable Development Goal 16, and UN Secretary-General Antonio Guterres's top priority. In 2023, he secured the agreement of UN members to expand the voluntary Peacebuilding Fund with an additional $50 million a year in assessed contributions from all states. Strengthening peacebuilding was a key theme of the 'Pact for the Future', agreed by members in 2024.

In summary, the UNPC provides a great example of the evolution of global governance from formal, intergovernmental bodies towards flexible, collaborative, multi-actor ways of working.

Equity is about inclusive membership and equal access to decision-making. States that establish and finance an organisation can design it to centralise structural power to their advantage. That is arguably justifiable: the UNSC permanent members bear the majority of peacekeeping costs, and the IMF and World Bank voting quotas are related to an extent to what states pay in. However, it means that the more numerous developing states are affected by decisions that they have very little influence over. This has led to demands for reform.

It is important to understand the difference between inclusivity and representation in global governance. A fully inclusive organisation would include and give equal powers to all states that identify as states, including places such as Kosovo, Palestine and Taiwan. No organisation does that. A representative organisation is one where some states sit as representatives of other states, rather than representing their own interests. Arguably, there are processes for this in the election of the UN's councils by the regional groups of the UNGA, but these, as with many electoral systems, do not provide equitable representation. There is an incomplete system of representation in the G20, with the EU and AU providing some representation for their members, whilst the nineteen member states represent their own interests.

Accountability refers to whether international organisations or states can be scrutinised and challenged. IGOs should be accountable to the states and citizens they serve, ensuring transparency by providing records of meetings. On the other hand, states are accountable to one another, not IGOs. When a state breaches international law, the UN Secretary-General may issue a public condemnation but cannot enforce compliance. Only the UNSC can enforce international law on a UN member state, requiring unanimous agreement from its five permanent members and four of its ten non-permanent members. If states choose not to impose accountability measures, then accountability does not exist. This is one of the main areas for development in the UNFCCC's COP process.

Authority is legitimate power: in this case, the powers granted to an IGO by its member states through a treaty, statute or charter. States are reluctant to give up their own authority, so supranational authority is rare. The UNSC's enforcement powers and the EU's legislative powers are the only clear forms of supranational authority in the global system. Intergovernmental decisions in the UNGA only have moral, not legal authority.

Jurisdiction is the authority to administer justice, so it applies only to judicial bodies. It includes rules about what cases can be heard, who can participate in a case (for example states or non-state actors) and the territorial scope of the court's authority. In international law, states choose whether or not to accept the jurisdiction of an international court.

Legitimacy: Equity, accountability and authority or jurisdiction all have an impact on the perceived legitimacy of an organisation. States that perceive IGOs as lacking legitimate authority due to unfair rules or the adoption of excessive powers will leave and undermine those IGOs – for example the UK leaving the EU due to a perception that it had become too powerful.

Effectiveness is judged by whether an organisation meets its aims. Some organisations regularly miss their targets, failing to make progress towards the aims of peace, global equity, human rights and sustainable development. For example, during the 1980s and 1990s, the IMF and World Bank's Structural Adjustment Programmes failed in many states that adopted them. However, sometimes global governance aims are hugely ambitious and difficult to fulfil; for example 'maintaining international peace and security', so it is important to judge whether the aims are realistic as well as judging progress towards them.

Always remember when making judgements on effectiveness that the IGOs only have the powers that states give them. They often fail because states have given them insufficient authority, or because powerful states have refused to reform decision-making, or because they have bypassed the IGO completely in favour of their own national sovereignty.

> **Exam Tip:**
> Try evaluating equity and effectiveness from the perspectives of developed and developing states. For example, the Global North see quota voting as equitably reflecting their greater responsibilities, whereas the South argue for sovereign equality. Neoliberal economists have typically viewed the World Bank as reducing unhelpful dependency, whereas dependency theorists from the Global South have criticised its neocolonial exploitation.

The role and significance of global civil society and other non-state actors

Non-governmental organisations play multiple roles in global governance. They investigate, scrutinise and raise awareness of state and business practises. They mobilise the public to participate in global campaigns for change. They are consulted by deliberative intergovernmental forums such as ECOSOC. They draft international laws and lobby governments collectively and individually to adopt them. They participate in policy networks, developing policy recommendations to solve collective problems. They are an integral part of the global governance process (see Table 8.2).

You may be familiar with the methods and **access points** used by pressure groups from the democracy topic in component 1. The concept of insider and outsider status is more complex at the international level: an international NGO such as Oxfam International might be an insider with some governments but an outsider with others. It may have formal consultative status within one IGO (ECOSOC) but less formal arrangements with another (IMF).

> **Definition**
>
> **Access point:** A place or person that pressure groups target to influence legislation or policy decisions.

How significant are the contributions of global civil society?

It is easy to think that the 'little people' cannot do much against the multinational corporations that can pay for professional lobbyists, often have the ear of business-friendly governments and can easily shift their activities and profits between states.

Table 8.2 The Roles of Civil Society Actors in Global Governance

Role	Description	Main access points for influencing decisions
Scrutiny	Researching issues and producing reports, including monitoring and exposing unethical behaviour by businesses or states.	ECOSOC International policy networks Global media, public opinion
Media engagement and public mobilisation	Creating issue coalitions or networks, initiating campaigns, participating in social movements, mobilising mass participation events, especially at international summits.	Summits Global media, public opinion
Advocacy (lobbying)	Developing policy recommendations, designing interventions, drafting legislation, campaigning for legal reforms and lobbying supportive states to influence other states.	Summits International policy networks Individual states
Consultation	Obtaining 'consultative status' at ECOSOC, gaining access to international policy networks to lobby states collectively.	ECOSOC International policy networks

The World Bank is highly influenced by the global finance industry because it depends on banks and investment funds to raise funding for developing states. Foreign investors demand strict budget discipline. This limits the public spending options available to loan-dependent governments, making it more difficult for them to reduce poverty and improve public health and well-being. The fossil fuel industry has considerably slowed progress on phasing out fossil fuels, often through discreet interactions with national governments or individual politicians rather than through transparent processes. MNCs have been complicit in widespread abuses of human rights and environmental degradation – for example allowing child labour in factories and palm oil produced through deforestation. They have engaged in 'profit-shifting' to avoid paying taxes. These are all enormous global problems.

However, civil society has had significant impact at times. NGOs have exposed evidence of human rights abuses to the media and used their consultative status at the UN to advance international humanitarian law. They are regularly consulted in the World Bank's Civil Society Policy Forum, and some, like Oxfam International, collaborate on projects with the World Bank, helping to guide outcomes. Civil society campaigns, including the Bretton Woods Project, were instrumental in changing World Bank policies in the 1990s to focus more on protecting health and education and reducing poverty, and the Jubilee Debt Campaign and Make Poverty History were critical in achieving debt cancellation for thirty-seven heavily indebted countries in 2005. Activist and NGO networks have organised protests to apply pressure at COP summits, helping to achieve the Rio Declaration, the Kyoto Protocol and the Paris Agreement. The Fridays for Future school strikes and efforts of youth climate activists around the world persuaded UN members to sign a pact to improve youth engagement in decision-making in 2024.

Like the UN, increasingly, NGOs are also working to find and apply solutions across the four main areas of global governance. Stop Ecocide International is building on the work of the International Campaign for the International Criminal Court in the 1990s to build a body of international environmental law. The NGO Global Witness works across the domains of economic, political, human rights and environmental governance to hold states and businesses to account and to develop innovative forms of global governance that enhance transparency and accountability.

CASE STUDY: CAMPAIGN TO MAKE ECOCIDE AN INTERNATIONAL CRIME, ALONGSIDE INTERNATIONAL HUMANITARIAN LAW

Photo 8.2 Palestinian children hold hands at the Gaza city beach, strewn with rubbish; just one example of environmental damage in Gaza.

Source: Paula Bronstein/ The Image Bank Unreleased via Getty Images

Context

In June 2021, an independent expert panel defined 'ecocide' as knowingly causing widespread, long-term damage to the environment through acts such as deforestation, pollution and the destruction of habitats and endangered species. Within two months, France encoded ecocide into its national law. At COP26 in Glasgow later that year, the first global citizens' assembly proposed to make ecocide an international crime by amending the Rome Statute to include it alongside the four humanitarian crimes of genocide, crimes against humanity, war crimes and the crime of aggression. This inclusion would make ecocide punishable at the International Criminal Court (ICC), which has so far dealt only with international humanitarian law.

Since then, Stop Ecocide International has been lobbying national governments to amend the Rome Statute. The campaign is gathering momentum, with over 70 per cent of people in the world's twenty-two largest economies supporting the prosecution of business leaders and governments who commit ecocide, and the crime has been proposed in several national legislatures. In March 2024, the EU adopted an environmental crime directive, which must be incorporated into its member states' laws.

Also in early 2024, International Criminal Court Prosecutor Karim Khan signalled the Court's commitment to addressing environmental harm during armed conflict as an international crime – this was already covered within the Rome Statute's war crimes but had not at that point been used. This means that the court may prosecute individuals for severe environmental damage in Gaza (see Photo 8.3). Then in September 2024, the crime of ecocide was formally introduced to the Assembly of State Parties to the Rome Statute by Vanuatu, Fiji and Samoa for consideration.

Significance

Criminalising ecocide would significantly expand the scope of the Rome Statute and the role of the International Criminal Court into a new area of global governance. It would address significant gaps in international law and demonstrate the international community's commitment to environmental protection. This would shift the focus of international environmental law from reporting and transparency over climate change emissions to strengthening accountability for actual impacts on the environment. It would hold individuals and corporations accountable, rather than just states. It would create a deterrent to prevent business leaders from making decisions that they know will lead to environmental destruction rather than relying on post-damage reparations.

However, for ecocide to be included in the Rome Statute, two-thirds (or 83 out of 124) of the statute's signatories must agree, meaning the process might take a decade or more. There are legal difficulties to resolve, notably that ecocide, unlike genocide, has not been recognised as existing under customary international law, meaning it is not binding on states without international treaty obligations.

Conclusion

Jubilee 2000 and Make Poverty History were professionally organised with clear, specific and quite modest demands, they were supported by celebrities who attracted media attention, they built on momentum that had been created over a decade of activism, and, most crucially, they took advantage of a pivotal moment in time, with G8 meetings chaired by an ideologically aligned world leader (Tony Blair).

CASE STUDY: GLOBAL WITNESS: HUMAN RIGHTS, CORRUPTION, CONFLICT AND CLIMATE CHANGE

Photo 8.3 Workers mining blood diamonds in Sierra Leone.

Source: José Nicolas/Sygma via Getty Images

Context

Global Witness was founded in 1993 with a focus on exposing human rights and environmental abuses due to the extraction of natural resources, corruption and conflict. It exposed the trade in blood diamonds that fuelled civil wars in Angola and across Africa (see Photo 8.4) and was nominated for the Nobel Peace Prize in 2003. Its 'publish what you pay' campaign led to the 'Extractive Industries Transparency Initiative' (EITI) being set up in 2002, now with over fifty-seven state members. This initiative supports good governance by monitoring mining and drilling companies so that profits can be kept and taxed in the country of production rather than hidden away in tax havens.

However, widespread corruption and conflict remain an issue in plenty of states with weak governance that have not joined EITI. For example, the Democratic Republic of the Congo has vast mineral resources, including cobalt, copper and diamonds, but the exploitation of these resources has fuelled corruption, and mismanagement of revenues has hindered the country's development. Armed groups continue to fight for control of lucrative mining areas. Nigeria has also suffered long-running conflict between armed groups for control of the oil-rich Niger delta. Global Witness has recently turned its attention to investigating and exposing the scale of fossil fuel lobbying at COPs. In 2022, at COP27, twenty-nine of the state delegations included oil and gas corporations. Its research has successfully prompted media condemnation and political advocacy by other organisations. After more than 1,800 fossil fuel lobbyists outnumbered scientists and climate-vulnerable state delegations at COP29 in 2024, the Club of Rome, a think tank of high-profile former state leaders, senior diplomats, policy experts, scientists and business leaders, published an open letter to the UN calling for fundamental reforms to COP processes, including limiting the number of fossil fuel lobbyists and requiring delegates to demonstrate their commitment to decarbonisation.

Significance

As Thomas Jefferson, one of the United States' Founding Fathers, said, 'the price of freedom is eternal vigilance'. People with power must be scrutinised carefully. Global Witness and the EITI have made a significant difference to the lives of people in many developing countries.

In global governance, transparency is the first, and therefore the most important step in improving the way that organisations operate. By exposing the fossil fuel lobbyists to public scrutiny, Global Witness mobilised the influential Club of Rome to generate policy ideas and lobby decision makers to ensure that the interests of the most vulnerable are represented. However, the next steps are more difficult.

The main obstacle to COP reform is that states would need to reach consensus to change the process laid down in the UNFCCC. Because many fossil fuel lobbyists attend as part of state delegations, this will not be easy. There is also a counterargument that it is legitimate and important for fossil fuel lobbyists to participate at COPs, because the oil and gas industries are where the greatest changes must happen. They also provide important industry expertise. However, the principle of pluralism should be upheld by keeping their numbers proportionate to those of climate scientists and the most vulnerable stakeholders whose interests they oppose.

The Occupy and World Social Forum, in contrast, wanted fundamental change in the global political and economic power structures. Whilst they both did take advantage of pivotal moments – WSF followed the adoption of the Millennium Development Goals whilst Occupy followed the Global Financial Crisis and G20 bank bailout packages – they failed to capitalise on them because they demanded a revolution rather than tinkering around the edges of the system. They also lacked any kind of leadership or communications strategy – a key failure in the fast-paced twenty-first-century media environment.

These examples show that civil society campaigns tend to succeed when they can seize a pivotal moment. A large coalition of NGOs with clear leadership and communications strategies, making very specific and coherent demands on a single issue, can apply direct and focused pressure to state leaders. They can mobilise public protest and celebrity endorsement as part of their strategy: in effect, 'embarrassing' leaders into action.

Most importantly, civil society campaigns have succeeded when they have campaigned for reforms within existing power structures rather than seeking revolutionary change.

KEY DEBATE: HAS GLOBAL CIVIL SOCIETY HAD A SIGNIFICANT IMPACT ON GLOBAL GOVERNANCE AND INTERNATIONAL LAW?

1. Public mobilisation on poverty, inequality and debt

Public mobilisation campaigns in the 1990s and 2000s successfully lobbied state leaders to take decisive action on global poverty and inequality.

- ✓ The **Jubilee 2000 Debt Campaign** demanded debt cancellation for poor countries suffering from the debt crisis in the 1990s. In May 1998, 50,000 peaceful protesters created a human chain around the G8 summit in Birmingham, UK. British Prime Minister Tony Blair, who chaired the meeting, agreed to meet the leaders of the protests. The campaign did not immediately succeed, but it was a turning point.
- ✓ The next time the G8 met in the UK in 2005, NGOs were ready with a more ambitious Make Poverty History campaign. This time, huge protest marches were supported by Live 8 benefit concerts, featuring celebrity activists Bob Geldof and Bono and televised globally. This time, Tony Blair and Gordon Brown persuaded the G8 and World Bank to give full debt cancellation to states in the Heavily Indebted Poor Countries Initiative.

However, other campaigns have struggled to make an impact:

- ✗ The World Social Forum began in 2001 as an annual grassroots forum for the anti-globalisation movement, to counter the elite World Economic Forum. It struggled to make an impact because activists rejected hierarchies, with leadership or spokesperson roles. This prevented it from setting a clear agenda or communicating specific demands.
- ✗ Similarly, the Occupy movement in 2011 aimed to address economic inequality and corporate influence over politics. Despite its initial success in capturing global attention, again, the lack of a clear agenda, leadership and concrete demands meant that it resulted in failure. Its 'tent cities' by New York's Wall Street and by London's St Paul's Cathedral were cleared by the police.

2. Disarmament movements

There have been two very effective disarmament movements:

- ✓ The International Campaign to Ban Landmines (ICBL) persuaded 164 states to join the 1997 Ottawa Convention (Mine Ban Treaty). The campaign was supported by Diana, Princess of Wales, who in 1997 was filmed meeting landmine survivors and walking through a partly cleared minefield in Angola.
- ✓ The International Campaign to Abolish Nuclear Weapons (ICAN) is a coalition of over 600 NGOs in 110 countries, launched in 2007. It used massive public mobilisation and direct lobbying to persuade states to sign the Treaty on the Prohibition of Nuclear Weapons (TPNW) in 2017.

However, although both were awarded the Nobel Peace Prize, the hardest tasks remain incomplete:

- ✗ The Mine Ban Treaty cannot unearth all of the millions of buried landmines remaining in sixty post-conflict countries, which still indiscriminately kill and injure civilians. Several countries have not signed the treaty and continue to produce landmines, including the United States, China, Russia, India and Pakistan. The United States has exported landmines to Ukraine.
- ✗ In addition, the world's nuclear powers show no sign of willingness to give up their existing weapons, and the TPNW has failed to prevent efforts by Iran and North Korea to develop nuclear capabilities.

3. Human rights monitoring and consultative status

Some international NGOs successfully use research, monitoring and consultative status at the UN to draw the attention of states to human rights abuses:

- ✓ Global Witness has a successful track record of exposing unethical trade, corruption and human rights abuses to the media, helping to raise public awareness (see case study).
- ✓ Human Rights Watch uses its consultative status at ECOSOC and the UN Human Rights Council to bring human rights abuses to the UN's attention. It contributes to HRC country reviews, for example, calling repeatedly for an independent body to hold the Taliban accountable for its human rights abuses in Afghanistan.

However, whilst monitoring abuse and unethical behaviour is necessary, it is only a first step in the process of influencing states to act.

- ✗ As of early 2025, there is still no independent body commissioned by the UN to investigate the human rights situation in Afghanistan. The Taliban can only be forced to allow investigators in by the UNSC.
- ✗ Despite the 'responsibility to protect' doctrine being established in 2005, the political will of the P5 states to intervene has declined in recent years.

4. Political advocacy for IGOs

International NGOs have also lobbied states to create and join international organisations to strengthen their governance:

- ✓ Global Witness's 'Publish what you pay' campaign led to the creation of the Extractive Industries Transparency Initiative, which has helped to crack down on corruption in many mineral-rich states.
- ✓ The International Campaign for the International Criminal Court was a global coalition that successfully lobbied 124 states to agree the Rome Statute in 1998. The court of last resort opened in 2000 at The Hague: a significant win for global civil society.

However, states with poor records are unlikely to accept supranational accountability:

- ✗ The EITI has fifty-seven members, but there are many other states where the theft of mineral wealth funds authoritarian regimes or fuels conflict. The Rome Statute has 124 signatories, but around 70 per cent of the world's population live in non-member states, many of which have poor human rights records e.g. China, Russia, the United States, Israel.
- ✗ It is also easier to make law than it is to enforce it. Genocide has been a crime since the Nuremberg Trials of 1945, but it requires evidence of intent, which is very hard to prove. Genocide continues with impunity, e.g. in Myanmar and in China.

5. Legal advocacy on environmental damage

In a recent development, environmental campaigners, frustrated by continuing failures to create a robust accountability system for climate change emissions, have turned to legal advocacy, following the example of the ICFICC.

- ✓ The **Stop Ecocide International** campaign to include 'ecocide' as an international crime within the Rome Statute has been gathering momentum around the world between 2021 and 2024. Prominent international human rights barrister Professor Philippe Sands KC, and former prosecutor and UN jurist Dior Fall Sow, chaired the panel that drafted the legal amendment.
- ✓ There is growing interest in adopting ecocide into national laws. France was the first state to do this in 2021, and the EU passed an environmental crime directive in 2024.

However, a change to the Rome Statute is unlikely to happen very soon.
- ✗ For ecocide to be included in the Rome Statute, two-thirds (or 83 out of 124) of the statute's signatories must agree. The process of lobbying them might take a decade or more.
- ✗ There are also legal difficulties to resolve, notably that, like genocide, it could be difficult to prove. It would require evidence that an individual knew in advance that their actions would result in widespread environmental damage.

Key Debate Summary: Has global civil society had a significant impact on global governance and international law?

Theme	Successes	Failures / not yet succeeded
Public mobilisation on poverty in the 1990s and 2000s	✓ Jubilee 2000: G8, 1998 Make Poverty History G8: 2005 Achieved HIPC debt cancellation. Strong leadership, focused goal, state support.	✗ World Social Forum (2001) and Occupy Movement (2011): No leadership. Poorly defined, unachievable goals.
Disarmament movements	✓ International Campaign to Ban Landmines: Ottawa Treaty 1997. International Campaign to Abolish Nuclear Weapons: Treaty on the Prohibition of Nuclear Weapons 2017. Both campaigns won the Nobel Peace Prize.	✗ These treaties are not universal. TPNW does not apply to nuclear states and failed to prevent North Korea nuclear programme.
Human rights monitoring and consultative status	✓ Global Witness exposes unethical states and businesses to public scrutiny. Human Rights Watch contributes to UN Human Rights Council debates.	✗ Monitoring alone does not create political will to act. P5 states' political will to intervene has declined since R2P in 2005.
Political advocacy for IGOs	✓ Publish What You Pay Campaign: Extractive Industries Transparency Initiative (EITI). International Campaign for the International Criminal Court: Rome Statute.	✗ States with poor records less likely to accept accountability. Law vs Enforcement: Genocide difficult to prove.
Legal advocacy on environmental damage	✓ Stop Ecocide International proposal to amend Rome Statute is gathering momentum. Ecocide adopted into some domestic laws, e.g. France (2021), EU (2024).	✗ Rome Statute change requires two-thirds of signatories (83 out of 124). Ecocide may be hard to prove, like genocide.

Exam Tip:

Consider the themes of conflict, poverty, human rights and the environment in turn, discussing the successes and failures of NGOs in each. Or focus on the different methods used by NGOs, such as research and monitoring, public mobilisation, consultation and lobbying. This debate does both, so it features five themes, but you could choose three or four.

Comparing the effectiveness of different areas of global governance

How to approach comparative evaluation questions on global governance

In the global politics component, some section C 30-mark questions require you to compare and evaluate global governance on two of the four main themes: conflict, poverty, human rights and the environment. For these questions, it is necessary to contrast both the strengths and the weaknesses of both areas of governance.

You could start each paragraph by showing how the side you reject is the weaker argument and then showing how the side you accept is the stronger argument, which then leads directly into your interim judgement.

Alternatively, start each paragraph with a summary statement of the judgement, then explain why the side you reject is weaker and why the side you accept is stronger.

Either way, all the comparisons must be systematically evaluated to form the overall judgement. That means it is sensible to cover fewer themes in more depth, and to include a more substantial final concluding paragraph, so that you can do more analysis and evaluation (see Table 8.3).

In this chapter, we therefore include three themes in the last two key debates instead of our usual four. However, if time is a concern, you might choose to address just two themes in greater depth, with a more substantial concluding paragraph. For more advice on different essay structures, see **Chapter 10: Exam Skills**.

Types of comparative questions about global governance

These comparative governance questions fall into two broad types:

1. Questions about the comparative effectiveness of global governance in dealing with the four main issue themes.
2. Questions about the concern for (or attention to) those issue themes within global governance.

With questions that ask you to compare effectiveness, the main focus should be on what has actually been achieved or not achieved. From there, you can analyse the reasons why the initiatives have succeeded, or why it has been difficult to achieve collective agreement to act. For example, problems with membership or the structural power imbalances within IGOs that create resentment, or consensus decision-making processes that make it easy for individual states to block collective action.

> **Chapter Link**
>
> For debates on these matters, see **Chapter 4: Political Global Governance** on the failures of the UNSC to agree humanitarian interventions and the debate on reforming the veto; and **Chapter 5: Economic Global Governance** on the US refusal to accept IMF and World Bank voting reform and delays to debt cancellation. See also **Chapter 7: Environmental Global Governance** on powerful states avoiding accountability for greenhouse gas emissions and delaying commitments on climate finance.

Table 8.3 A Possible Structure for Comparative Evaluation Questions on Global Governance

	Argument	Counter argument	
Theme 1	Why A is more effective than B	Why B is more effective than A	Interim judgement
Theme 2	Why A is more effective than B	Why B is more effective than A	Interim judgement
Optional theme 3	Why A is more effective than B	Why B is more effective than A	Interim judgement
Drawing the three themes together, explain why they justify your clear overall judgement			Final conclusion

Analysing and Evaluating Global Governance 279

With questions on attention or concern for the issues, consider efforts first, before outcomes. You could begin with the collective efforts made by states to build equitable and functional IGOs, to negotiate treaties and accept accountability under international law. You could include the extent to which powerful states are prepared to take decisive collective action for the benefit of others, such as debt cancellation or humanitarian intervention. You could include the extent to which civil society has influenced states and IGOs to take those actions.

KEY DEBATE: HAS GLOBAL GOVERNANCE THROUGH THE UNITED NATIONS (UN) ADDRESSED HUMAN RIGHTS ISSUES MORE SUCCESSFULLY THAN ENVIRONMENTAL CONCERNS?

Theme 1. Progress on developing international law and governance

In favour of the view: Human rights law and governance have a longer tradition and have developed further than environmental law and governance in the UN:

- ✓ Human rights have been fundamental to the United Nations since the Universal Declaration of Human Rights was agreed in 1948. This was later enshrined in international law alongside the covenants of the International Bill of Human Rights in 1976.
- ✓ In 2006, the UNGA voted by 170–4 to replace the politicised and much-criticised United Nations Commission on Human Rights with an elected 47-member Human Rights Council (UNHRC). Since 2009 this subsidiary council of the General Assembly has reviewed states' human rights records every four years.

In comparison

- ✓ The UN Framework Convention on Climate Change, agreed in 1992, *only* committed states to work together towards sustainable development through annual meetings and to acknowledge that developed states needed to take more responsibility for climate change than developing states.
- ✓ There have been no substantial developments of the Conference of Parties (COP) process laid down in the UNFCCC, and they do not work effectively. Fossil fuel lobbyists influence the intergovernmental process. Oil and gas-producing states have repeatedly watered down agreements until they are almost meaningless, whilst the climate crisis has escalated.

Countering the view: despite the legal framework being undoubtedly weaker around environmental concerns, it can be argued that the UN has made faster progress on raising the status of environmental governance:

- ✗ The UN Environment Programme created the International Panel on Climate Change, when the Montreal Protocol negotiations in 1987 showed the need for impartial scientific expertise to guide states' negotiations. Since then, the IPCC has published regular reports on climate change, providing states with a common framework of expertise.
- ✗ In 2012, the 193-member UN Environment Assembly was established. It has equivalent status to the UNGA, showing the UN's increasing focus on environmental protection.

In comparison

- ✗ Despite replacing a politicised Human Rights Commission, the UNHRC still suffers from politicisation, as human rights abusers such as China seek election to try to avoid being held accountable on human rights.
- ✗ The UNHRC is subordinate to the UNGA, reflecting its lower priority in comparison to the UNEA.

Theme 2. Collective will of powerful states to act

In favour of the view: In the 1990s and 2000s, powerful states made more efforts to support human rights than they did to strengthen the response to climate change.

> **Exam Tip:** Include ONLY the work of UN bodies and member states in answer to this question. The International Criminal Court, the European Court of Human Rights and the international tribunals are not relevant. Using these bodies in the answer is a common error.

- ✅ Many peacekeeping and peacebuilding operations were authorised by the UNSC in the late 1990s and 2000s – in Bosnia, Kosovo, Sierra Leone, Timor-Leste, Afghanistan, Côte d'Ivoire and Libya. US hegemony and global civil society activism on humanitarianism played a role in persuading the P5 to act during these years.

In comparison
- ✅ Under the UNFCCC process, it took 17 years to agree a climate finance fund. Despite the demands of climate-vulnerable states, a loss and damage fund took even longer to agree, being established in 2023. Both funds are inadequate. Developed states agreed to half of the finance that was asked for in 2024, with no commitment on what types or sources of funding. With the United States withdrawing again from the Paris Agreement and slashing its aid budget in 2025, that funding is very unlikely to materialise.

Countering the view: on the other hand, it can be argued that efforts by powerful states within the UN to support developing states on climate change have increased, whilst efforts on human rights were temporary and have declined:
- ❌ The Rwanda and Srebrenica genocides in the 1990s were followed by stronger UNSC action for a while, but since 2011, they have failed to stop civil wars in Syria, Yemen and more. There have been no UN interventions to protect civilians in recent genocides in Myanmar, Gaza or Sudan.

In comparison
- ❌ Although nowhere near the level needed, the finance commitments made at Copenhagen, and at COP28 in the UAE and COP29 in Azerbaijan, have made some progress on supporting sustainable development, and since COP28, there is better understanding of the scale of support needed.

Theme 3: Accountability of states

In favour of the view: Arguably, the UN has better processes to hold states to account on human rights than on greenhouse gas emissions.
- ✅ The HRC scrutinises the human rights records of each state every four years.
- ✅ The ICJ has been used to hold states accountable for genocide. Cases can be brought on behalf of citizens of one state by another state that is not directly involved (e.g. Senegal against Myanmar and South Africa against Israel) because the Genocide Convention requires its signatories to take action to stop genocide. In this way, the UN's ICJ can address some limitations of the ICC.

In comparison
- ✅ The UNFCCC process does not effectively hold states to account for their emissions. The Kyoto Protocol, which imposed binding emissions reduction targets on developed states, did not demand reductions from the emerging giants, China and India. The United States, Canada and Russia signed but later withdrew.
- ✅ There is no enforcement of Nationally Determined Contributions (NDC) emissions targets under the 2015 Paris Agreement, and there was no automatic requirement for states to improve their targets over time.

Countering the view: Ultimately, intergovernmental accountability processes are voluntary. Powerful states can evade accountability on both human rights and greenhouse gases if they so choose.
- ❌ Alongside their rejection of the Kyoto Protocol, the United States, Russia and China have faced no accountability for abusing human rights; for example, the United States' detention without trial and torture in Guantanamo Bay and Iraq; China's genocide of the Uighurs; and despite an ICC arrest warrant, Vladimir Putin is unlikely to stand trial for the abduction of children from Ukraine. These P5 states can veto any resolution against them.

In comparison
- ❌ The more liberal states of the EU and Japan have stronger commitments both to the protection of universal human rights and to their duties under the UNFCCC than the United States, Russia and China. They have fulfilled their legally binding targets under the Kyoto Protocol, providing a model for other states to follow.

Analysing and Evaluating Global Governance

Key Debate Summary: Has global governance through the United Nations (UN) addressed human rights issues more successfully than environmental concerns

Theme	For	Against
Development of international law and governance	✓ Human rights law and governance have a longer tradition and have developed further than environmental law and governance.	✗ The UN has made faster progress on raising the status of environmental governance.
Collective will of powerful states to act	✓ In the 1990s and 2000s, powerful states made more efforts to support human rights than they did to strengthen the response to climate change.	✗ Efforts by powerful states within the UN to support developing states on climate change have increased, whilst the collective will of P5 states to intervene in human rights abuses was short-lived.
Accountability of states	✓ There is more effective scrutiny of states' actions on human rights by UN bodies than there is of their climate change emissions.	✗ Ultimately, intergovernmental accountability processes are voluntary. Powerful states can evade accountability on both human rights and on greenhouse gases if they so choose.

Exam Tip:

In your conclusion, you could note that this artificial choice between human rights and environmental work is outdated. Since 2015, Agenda 2030 and the SDGs have guided the UN's work. They integrate human rights, environmental, political and economic goals into the concept of sustainable development. All are equally important. However, you must clearly state that one has been more effective *overall* than the other.

KEY DEBATE: IS GLOBAL GOVERNANCE REDUCING POVERTY BUT FAILING TO PROTECT THE ENVIRONMENT?

Theme 1: Effectiveness of governance structures

In favour of the view

Global governance has a stronger and longer tradition of poverty reduction than environmental protection:

- ✓ Economic governance organisations are well established. The World Bank and ECOSOC both have specific goals on poverty reduction and international development. These goals are supported by the IMF, which promotes economic stability, and the WTO, which promotes free trade and shared prosperity. Developing countries have usually seen increased prosperity after joining the WTO.

In comparison

- ✓ There is a much more limited institutional structure for environmental governance. The consensus-based COP process is slow, unwieldy and prone to obstruction and weakening of targets by fossil-fuel dependent states.

Countering the view:

Economic global governance has a legitimacy problem. Multilateral aid for poverty reduction is under the control of developed states, whereas decision-making in the environment-focused COP process is more equitable and inclusive.

> **Exam Tip:**
> This is a similar style of question, focusing on outcomes, but there are important differences in scope. It is not restricted to the UN, but it is restricted to poverty reduction rather than free trade or stability. If you discuss the IMF, WTO, G7/8 and G20, include only their poverty reduction and environmental protection efforts

- ✗ ECOSOC's many funds and programmes struggle for funding, and the inequitable Bretton Woods Institutions established by the United States and Europe marginalise the voices of developing countries, affecting their legitimacy.

In comparison
- ✗ The UN's consensus-based COP process is more equitable than the Bretton Woods Institutions. COPs aim to strengthen commitments from every state, every year, with unanimous agreement.

Theme 2: Progress from 1990 to 2015

In favour of the view: Better progress was made on poverty reduction than on environmental protection between 1990 and 2010.

- ✓ Globalisation promoted by the World Trade Organization and World Bank has lifted millions out of poverty between 1990 and 2010, especially in China.
- ✓ Following anti-poverty and anti-debt campaigns in the 1990s, Tony Blair and Gordon Brown persuaded the G8 to agree to support the World Bank in giving debt cancellation for up to forty HIPC states in 2005.
- ✓ All states signed the UN's ambitious Millennium Declaration in 2000, which established the MDGs. There were some significant achievements – notably on halving extreme poverty and on broadening access to primary education for girls. The target to halve extreme poverty was met five years early in 2010. Building on this success, SDG1 aimed to end extreme poverty at the World Bank's international poverty line – $2.15 income per day in 2025: a highly ambitious goal.

In comparison
- ✓ Despite civil society pressure, the UNFCCC did not stimulate rapid progress towards ambitious universal binding targets for climate change emissions. Agreements at Rio (1992), Kyoto (2001) and Copenhagen (2009) COP summits were weak.
- ✓ Despite its huge and rapidly rising emissions, China did not engage at all in the Kyoto agreement. The United States withdrew before it came into effect. Russia joined late, and Canada withdrew after breaking its commitments.

Countering the view: arguably, global governance made greater steps on climate change than on poverty in the lead up to 2015.

- ✗ After 15 years, the WTO failed to reach agreement on the Doha 'development round' in 2015. It therefore failed to address US and EU agricultural subsidies that harm poor countries' competitiveness, increasing poverty.
- ✗ The significant reduction in global extreme poverty can be attributed primarily to economic development in China, which adapted market economics to suit its own circumstances rather than accepting a top-down 'neocolonial' process of structural adjustment.

In comparison
- ✗ A target to achieve $100 billion in climate finance by 2020 was agreed at the Copenhagen COP in 2008. This eventually helped to persuade developing states to begin negotiations on reducing their own emissions.
- ✗ The 2015 Paris Agreement was a significant step forward. For the first time, both the United States and China, the world's two largest carbon emitters, signed up. States collectively aimed to limit global heating to 2°C above pre-industrial levels, with a 1.5°C target. All states agreed to measure emissions and set reduction targets over five years (nationally determined contributions). They agreed in principle to a 'loss and damage' fund to support recovery in states hit by climate-related disasters.

Theme 3: Progress since 2015

In favour of the view: Developed states have made more commitments to economic stability and recovery since the pandemic than they have to reducing their greenhouse gas emissions.

- ✓ More recently, G20 states have significantly boosted post-Covid-19 recovery and climate resilience funds for developing countries at the IMF and WB.

Analysing and Evaluating Global Governance   283

In comparison

✓ There has been little progress at COPs on NDCs. Oil and gas-producing states have watered down agreements to move away from fossil fuels. Developed countries have weakened their commitments. The Trump government has withdrawn twice from the Paris Agreement. Since 2024, the primary focus of the EU Commission and Council has shifted from emissions reductions to defence, due to a combination of the Russian threat, US disengagement and electoral pressure from hard-right parties over EU net-zero policies.

Countering the view: The challenges of poverty reduction and climate change are both increasing, whilst the commitment of developed states to both issues has started to decline.

✗ Despite the boost to IMF and World Bank funds, poverty remains stubbornly high in sub-Saharan Africa. Debt crisis has returned to the continent, fuelled by climate change, the Covid-19 pandemic, the Ukraine war and a strong US dollar. In 2025, both the United States and the UK have made severe cuts to their international aid budgets.

In comparison

✗ Developed states fulfilled their $100 billion climate fund target by 2023, and a separate loss and damage fund has been established at the World Bank. These amounts are too little too late for developing countries, but with these states increasingly focused on their own defence, further progress on both areas has become less likely.

> **Exam Tip:** You could mention in your conclusion that poverty reduction and environmental protection have become inseparable, and that it is increasingly difficult to make progress on both of them because of the growing divide between emerging economies and climate-vulnerable states over future fossil fuel use. However, you must make a clear statement that progress on one has been stronger *overall* than on the other.

Key Debate Summary: Is global governance reducing poverty but failing to protect the environment?

Theme	For	Against
Effective governance structures	✓ More established IGOs for reducing poverty – ECOSOC and World Bank, supported by IMF for stability and the WTO for free trade; compared to the slow and frequently obstructed annual COP process.	✗ ECOSOC struggles for funding and Bretton Woods Institutions are dominated by wealthy states. In comparison, there is a more equitable process at COPs.
Progress from 1990 to 2015	✓ More progress made on poverty from the late 1990s to the late 2000s: MDGs, Chinese development, G8 and WB debt cancellation. SDG1 to eradicate extreme poverty was very ambitious. COP agreements at this time were weak and incomplete.	✗ More progress was made on environmental protection after climate finance was agreed in 2008. The Paris Agreement of 2015 was a significant step forward.
Progress since 2015	✓ Developed countries have given a huge boost in post-Covid-19 recovery funding for developing countries at the IMF and World Bank. Whereas progress on reducing carbon emissions has stalled.	✗ The challenges of poverty reduction and climate change are both increasing, whilst the commitment of developed states to both issues has started to decline.

Component III: Global Politics

KEY DEBATE: IS GLOBAL GOVERNANCE MORE CONCERNED WITH ECONOMIC ISSUES RATHER THAN HUMAN RIGHTS ISSUES?

> **Exam Tip:**
> This question is about the level of concern for the issues in global governance, rather than its effectiveness. The answer uses similar content to the previous two and begins in the same way with an overview of governance structures, then focuses on efforts rather than progress.

Theme 1: Development of governance institutions

In favour of the view: Global governance has a well-established system of IGOs with complementary roles to support the reduction of poverty, whereas the human rights system of organisations evolved much later.

✅ Economic institutions have a long history. Since the 1940s, the IMF has worked to maintain stability in the global financial system, the World Bank has invested in economic development, and the General Agreement on Trade and Tariffs (GATT) has supported the process of reducing trade tariffs between states.

In comparison

✅ Although in 1945 the UN Charter set out human rights protection as one of its main aims, human rights IGOs evolved much later. After the Nuremberg Trials, there were no special tribunals until the 1990s. The International Criminal Court was established in 2000 and the UN's Human Rights Council in 2008.

Countering the view: The well-developed body of universal international humanitarian law has arguably had a greater, more universal impact.

❌ Although economic institutions were established in the 1940s, these were not at first intended to be global institutions; rather they were intended to support a US-dominated Western trading system.

In comparison

❌ The UN's Commission on Human Rights, established in 1946, and its Universal Declaration of Human Rights, 1948, initiated a significant post-war development in international humanitarian law. The UDHR is part of international customary law, and therefore universally applicable.

Theme 2: State membership of IGOs

In favour of the view: Economic global governance has almost universal membership, unlike human rights governance.

✅ After the Cold War, the IMF and World Bank grew to almost universal state membership, and almost all states have joined or have applied to join the WTO. In 2023, the G20 consisted of states accounting for 85 per cent of the global economy – with the addition of the African Union, that percentage has increased.

In comparison

✅ The ICC has failed to attract universal state membership. In 2025, it had 124 members: around two-thirds of all states. However, because most states with the world's largest populations – e.g. China, India, the United States and Russia – have not joined, only around 30 per cent of the world's population are fully protected by the Rome Statute.

Countering the view: productive engagement is a better indicator of concern than universal membership.

❌ Although the economic institutions have broader membership, this does not mean that all those members engage productively in them. The United States' refusal to accept voting reforms at the World Bank and the IMF has been resented by China, India and other developing states. The WTO's dispute settlement appeals process has been blocked by the United States for years.

In comparison

❌ Some states have found alternative ways to bring state leaders to account within the more multilateral UN system, overcoming the problem of limited membership at the ICC. For example, under the Genocide Convention, signatory states have a responsibility to act to stop genocide. In 2019, Gambia brought a genocide case against Myanmar, and at the end of 2023, South Africa brought a genocide case against Israel to the International Court of Justice.

Theme 3: Bypassing or ignoring the multilateral system
In favour of the view: powerful states remain more engaged with the economic system than they do with the 'responsibility to protect'.
- ✓ A huge boost in post-Covid-19 recovery funding at the IMF shows that the multilateral economic global governance system is still important to powerful states.

In comparison
- ✓ The responsibility to protect doctrine was unanimously agreed at the UNGA in 2005 but it has been ignored more often than it has been observed because of the P5 veto. The United States and Europe have provided extensive military aid to Ukraine, and the United States to Israel, instead of engaging in a responsibility to protect civilians elsewhere. There have been no meaningful humanitarian interventions in recent wars in Myanmar, Gaza or Sudan.

Countering the view: on the other hand, multilateral economic IGOs have been bypassed by states, whereas the system of international law works flexibly alongside domestic laws.
- ✗ The BRICS have set up rivals to the World Bank: the Chinese-dominated New Development Bank and Asian Infrastructure Investment Bank, suggesting that when economic IGOs lack legitimacy states will bypass them. A similar process can be seen in trade with regionalisation and 'friendshoring' (favouring trade with 'friendly' states).

In comparison
- ✗ International humanitarian law is intended to support national laws where possible, and to allow alternative routes when IGOs fall short. Under the international legal principle of 'universal jurisdiction', national courts can prosecute human rights crimes committed against citizens of other states. The ex-president of Chad, Hissène Habré, was convicted in 2016 by an African Union-backed court in Senegal for crimes against humanity against his own citizens. Similarly, between 2021 and 2023, Germany has prosecuted ISIS members in its national courts for genocide of the Yazidi in Syria.

Key Debate Summary: Is global governance more concerned with economic issues rather than human rights issues?

Theme	For	Against
Development of governance institutions	✓ Poverty reduction: a well-established system of IGOs with complementary roles. Human rights IGOs evolved much later.	✗ The well-developed body of universal international humanitarian law has arguably had a greater, more universal impact than poverty reduction IGOs.
State membership of IGOs	✓ Economic global governance has almost universal membership, unlike the ICC.	✗ Broader membership does not mean more productive engagement. The United States has often blocked reforms of economic IGOs. States have recently used the ICJ instead of the ICC.
Bypassing or ignoring the multilateral system	✓ Powerful states remain more engaged with the economic system than they do with the 'responsibility to protect'.	✗ Multilateral economic IGOs have been bypassed by powerful states, whereas the system of international law works flexibly with domestic laws.

Exam Tip:

An alternative third theme could be the efforts made by civil society to influence states to take action on poverty and inequality in comparison with human rights abuses.

Table 8.4 Summary of Global Governance Organisations, Laws and Agreements

	Political global governance	Human rights global governance	Economic global governance	Environmental global governance
Decision-making councils and forums	UN Security Council UN General Assembly	UN Security Council UN General Assembly (UN Human Rights Council)	International Monetary Fund and World Bank Boards of Governors World Trade Organization (ECOSOC)	Conference of Parties (COPs) ECOSOC (UN Environment Assembly)
Advice, support, intervention	NATO intervention UN peacekeepers	NATO intervention UN peacekeepers	IMF, WB finance and advice WTO advice UNDP and other funds	IPCC – advice UN Environment Programme – support for states
Courts, tribunals and dispute resolution	International Court of Justice	International Criminal Court International Court of Justice European Court of Human Rights Special Tribunals	WTO Dispute Resolution Process	ICJ (starting to hear state disputes)
International laws	UN Charter UNSC resolutions	Rome Statute Genocide Convention International Bill of Human Rights European Convention on Human Rights	WTO Agreements Bilateral Trade Agreements	Montreal Protocol UN Framework Convention on Climate Change Kyoto Protocol Paris Agreement
Non-binding agreements	UNGA resolutions	Universal Declaration of Human Rights Responsibility to Protect	Millennium Development Goals Sustainable Development Goals	Climate finance 'Loss and damage' funding Emissions targets (NDCs)

Conclusion

In 2021, the global think tank Chatham House surveyed the state of global governance and proposed ten 'insights' about the current state of the system and possibilities for improving it in the future. These were:

1. **The power for change lies with states**

    Sovereign states remain 'the anchor of the international system'. They have the authority to create IGOs and enforce international agreements. Non-state actors can influence change, but significant progress depends on state leadership and cooperation, most importantly, a willingness by the United States and its powerful rivals to act multilaterally (see Photo 8.5).

2. **Multilateral IGOs give weaker states a platform – but not a fair one**

    The UN gives marginalised states a voice, for example the Alliance of Small Island States led the Paris Agreement. However, powerful states always have the resources to take part; developing states often do not. Power imbalances in voting systems must be reformed.

Photo 8.4 A Greenpeace activist protests President Trump's withdrawal from the Paris Climate Agreement. The banner highlights the fact that civil society and other non-state actors can influence change, but significant progress depends on state leadership and cooperation.

3. **Balancing inclusion and effectiveness is difficult but necessary**

   Inclusion is important, but if too many voices are involved, organisations can become ineffective. The inclusion of the African Union in the G20 is a good compromise.

4. **Transparency and outcomes are important for building trust**

   Transparent processes and clear communication are essential for fair decision-making in IGOs. The Global South will only engage if they believe that they can influence meaningful outcomes.

5. **Civil society can drive change if it is given access**

   Public data can empower civil society to hold governments and organisations accountable, and this can drive change, but institutions must also listen.

6. **Regional blocs and coalitions can bypass multilateral gridlock**

   Like-minded groups of states, such as the EU and climate-vulnerable states, can set examples for others to follow and build momentum for global change.

7. **Local governments can drive efforts on climate change**

   The C40 network of forty major global cities is an important coalition for sharing expertise on sustainable transport and public health. Whilst US President Trump has twice withdrawn from the Paris Agreement, US cities are still making progress towards net-zero goals.

8. **Global challenges demand a commitment to intergenerational participation**

   Half of the global population is under 30. The next generation wants and needs effective governance. Governance organisations must invest in developing young leaders.

9. **Global governance needs to be better at including civil society from poorer countries**

   Civil society consultation efforts can often favour well-funded organisations such as Oxfam International, whilst grassroots activists from the Global South cannot afford to participate. More support should be provided to include more diverse voices.

10. **Rapid change requires flexible governance – but rules remain important**

    Flexible coalitions, digital participation and litigation in the international courts should add to rather than undermine the existing rule-based system.

Adapted from **'Ten insights: reflections on building more inclusive global governance'**, Chatham House (2021).

In summary, global governance must continue to evolve and become more inclusive if it is to succeed in dealing with conflict, poverty and inequality, human rights abuses and environmental degradation and climate change. Only states can make this happen. Powerful states must agree to share their power fairly.

# Chapter Summary

- Global governance is a collaborative process of decision-making, in which states address shared issues through institutions, laws and norms.
- Global governance is different from world government. It is largely intergovernmental rather than supranational. State participation is voluntary. Their sovereignty is generally upheld by the intergovernmental organisations that they create. The main exception to this is the UNSC.
- Liberals view global governance as a means to promote transparency, rule-bound behaviour and cooperation for the common good, while realists argue that institutions are dominated and undermined by powerful states.
- Global governance has evolved and expanded to include greater participation by non-state actors, a wider range of institutions, more protection of human rights, and the promotion of sustainable development, but rising geopolitical tensions make its future uncertain.
- Global civil society has been a driving force for progress on the four global issues of reducing conflict and poverty, protecting human rights and the environment. However, states and non-state actors can also create obstacles to effective governance.
- When evaluating the effectiveness of different forms of governance, it is useful to consider the overall development of international organisations and international law, the willingness of states to cooperate within IGOs and be bound by international law, and progress over time or the effectiveness of accountability mechanisms.
- When evaluating the attention or concern for different forms of governance, it can be useful to address these same themes but with a greater focus on how much states engage in the processes and organisations rather than the progress made. It would also be relevant to consider the efforts of civil society to drive change.

Exam Style Questions

- Examine the role and significance of global civil society in economic and environmental global governance. (12)
- Examine the role and significance of global civil society in human rights and political governance. (12)
- Evaluate the view that environmental issues have received greater attention than economic issues in global politics. (30)
- Evaluate the view that global governance has been more successful at resolving poverty than reducing conflict. (30)
- Evaluate the view that global governance is reducing poverty but failing to protect the environment. (30)

# Further Resources

https://www.cfr.org/. Council on Foreign Relations (CFR): CFR is an independent, non-partisan US-based think tank and publisher on foreign relations, with accessible resources on global governance, international politics and foreign policy.

https://www.brookings.edu/. Brookings is a highly respected think tank that publishes research and analysis on global governance, international relations and policy issues.

https://www.chathamhouse.org/2021/04/reflections-building-more-inclusive-global-governance/03-ten-insights-reflections-building. Chatham House is a respected, UK-based non-partisan think tank on global politics. This chapter referenced their article 'Ten insights: reflections on building more inclusive global governance', Chatham House (2021).

https://carnegieendowment.org/research/2023/09/rules-of-order-assessing-the-state-of-global-governance. The Carnegie Endowment Fund is another well-respected non-partisan think tank on global governance. There is a challenging extended read here.

Visit https://bloomsbury.pub/essentials-of-global-politics to access additional materials to support teaching and learning.

9 REGIONALISM AND THE EUROPEAN UNION

Chapter Preview

Since the mid-twentieth century, regionalism has shaped political, security and economic relationships between states, sometimes protecting states from globalisation and sometimes promoting it. The Arab League, founded in 1945, aimed to unify Arab states. The European Union has evolved to become the most integrated political-economic regional bloc in the world, providing a model for other organisations to emulate or reject. The Association of Southeast Asian Nations (ASEAN), set up in 1967, set out a similarly broad set of goals, but works in its own distinctive 'ASEAN way' to protect its members' independence. The African Union, created in 2001 to enhance African unity and development, has adopted some EU features but with less supranational authority. It has become a major peacekeeping force. NAFTA – renegotiated as USMCA – is much less integrated, aiming simply to promote trade and protect its members' industries.

Regionalism can shift the global balance of power. A united EU can rival the United States, China and Russia. It has taken on a significant role in its 'sphere of influence', working to reduce poverty, resolve conflict, promote human rights and protect the environment, and has become the world's largest source of humanitarian and development aid. ASEAN's efforts to integrate economies and support social cohesion have enhanced stability in Southeast Asia. Africa's regional free-trade area is strengthening the continent as a more powerful global actor.

Key Questions and Debates
- » What is regionalism and what forms does it take?
- » How and why have different regional organisations developed?
- » Does regionalism protect against globalisation?
- » How and why has the EU become the most integrated regional organisation in the world?
- » Is the EU federal?
- » Is the EU a significant global actor?
- » Does regionalism undermine state sovereignty?
- » Have regional organisations impacted positively on poverty, conflict, human rights and the environment?

Specification Checklist

5.1 Regionalism

5.1.1 The different forms
- » Growth of regionalism and regionalism in different forms, including economic, security and political

5.1.2 Debates about and the reasons for and significance of regionalism
- » The relationship between regionalism and globalisation
- » Prospects for political regionalism and regional governance
- » The impact on state sovereignty

5.2 Development of regional organisations, excluding the EU
- » North American Free Trade Association (NAFTA)
- » African Union (AU)
- » Arab League
- » Association of Southeast Asian Nations (ASEAN)

5.3 Factors that have fostered European integration and the major developments through which this has occurred
- » Formation, role, objectives and development of the European Union (EU)
- » Establishment and powers of its key institutions and the process of enlargement
- » Key treaties and agreements
- » Economic and monetary union
- » Debates about supranational versus intergovernmental approaches

5.4 Significance of the EU as an international body/global actor, including the constraints and obstacles affecting:
- » Its political, economic, structural and military influence in global politics

5.5 The ways and extent to which regionalism addresses and resolves contemporary global issues involving conflict, poverty, human rights and the environment

Source: Ben Stansall/AFP via Getty Images

Regionalism

The chapters on global governance have shown that it is hard to achieve consensus in a world of almost 200 states, all with different interests, capabilities and world views. One only needs to consider three decades of tense and unproductive climate conferences. Or even to consider the five permanent members of the Security Council, where fundamental divides continue to block collective action on conflict and genocide. However, not every problem needs a global solution, and regionalism provides an easier route for states that want to work together.

Regionalism describes the formation of 'blocs', or organisations of states within a geographical area (see Map 9.1). Sometimes, regional organisations encompass a geographical continent, like the African Union and the North American Free Trade Organisation, renamed USMCA in 2018. They may be subcontinental, like the European Union and the Association of Southeast Asian Nations (ASEAN). Or they may be transcontinental, like the Arab League which spans North Africa, the Middle East and the Arabian Peninsula.

The growth of regionalism

People sometimes feel a sense of regional identity or belonging based on a shared language, religion, ideology or experience like colonialism, that crosses nation-state boundaries. These shared identities are what theorist Samuel Huntington referred to as civilisations (see **Chapter 3**).

The idea of state-based regionalism emerged in the mid-twentieth century, when the collapse of empires after the Second World War re-ordered global power into a bipolar capitalist West and communist East (see **Chapter 4**).

In that context, regional groups of states decided to collaborate as equal partners: defending shared identities, protecting themselves from geopolitical rivalries in the anarchic international state system

> **Definition**
>
> **Regionalism:** The creation of institutions that express a particular identity and coordinate collective action between states in a geographical region
>
> **Regional bloc:** A group of states in a geographical region that cooperate on economic, political or security matters. Also called a regional organisation (RO).

> **Spec key term**
>
> **Proxy war:** A conflict in which rival powers support opposing factions, often through funding and arms, to fight on their behalf without engaging in direct combat.
>
> **Intergovernmentalism:** A form of cooperation between states in which decisions are made collectively, based on the principle of sovereign independence.
>
> **Supranationalism:** A form of cooperation between states in which they transfer their sovereign decision-making powers to a central authority.

Map 9.1 Trade blocs

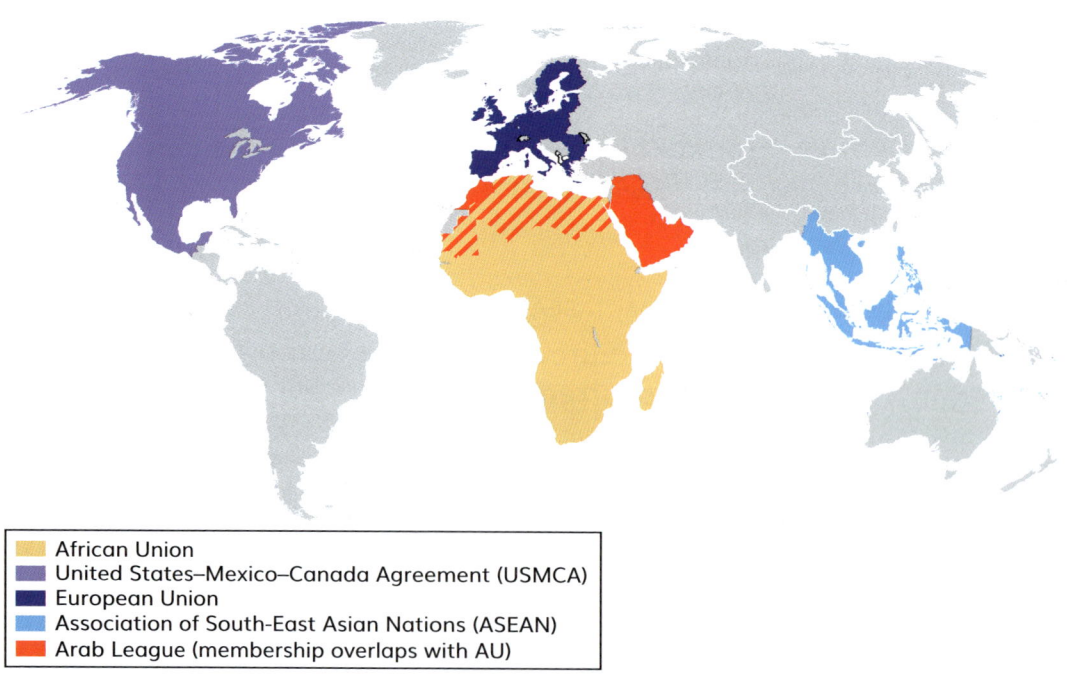

- African Union
- United States–Mexico–Canada Agreement (USMCA)
- European Union
- Association of South-East Asian Nations (ASEAN)
- Arab League (membership overlaps with AU)

and strengthening their collective voices in international relations. These included the Arab League (AL), formed in 1945, and the Organisation of African Unity (OAU), created in 1963.

In Southeast Asia, several of Vietnam's neighbours watched as the United States and China, then the Soviet Union, engaged in a *proxy war* in Vietnam. They created the Association of Southeast Asian Nations (ASEAN) in 1967 to contain the spread of communism and prevent superpower intervention through economic, social and cultural cooperation.

The members of these regional groups were almost all ex-colonies of European powers, who greatly valued their hard-won sovereignty. As a result, they created *intergovernmental* organisations that would not undermine their individual voices.

In Europe in the early 1950s, however, the biggest concern was to prevent another war between France and Germany. The European Coal and Steel Community (ECSC) anchored its economies together with other states, creating the first *supranational* organisations to avoid competition over the resources needed to make war (see pp. 308–309).

By the 1980s, it became clear that accelerating globalisation was reshaping national economies, creating new winners and losers and making it more difficult for governments to maintain economic stability. Then, suddenly, the Soviet Union collapsed in 1991, and the ideological rivalry of the Cold War seemed to be over. The Cold War security-focused 'old' regionalism gave way to a 'new' regionalism, which focused on trade integration to enhance states' competitiveness in the global economy and support economic growth.

In 1992, three significant developments took place. The Maastricht Treaty was signed, establishing the European Union's single market, which aimed to promote competitiveness and was overseen by strong supranational institutions. Free-trade agreements were also signed by ASEAN (AFTA) and by Canada, Mexico and the United States (NAFTA). These agreements reduced *tariffs* and increased trade integration among member states while maintaining full intergovernmentalism.

Inspired by the EU, the African Union (AU) replaced the Organisation of African Unity (OAU) in 2002. It created intergovernmental institutions for economic development and peacekeeping, recognising that peace was the foundation for economic integration.

> **Spec key term**
>
> **Old regionalism:** mid-twentieth century intergovernmental regional integration focused on economic recovery and security cooperation in the context of the Cold War.
>
> **New regionalism:** A more flexible approach to economic, political, social and environmental cooperation that emerged in response to globalisation.
>
> **Tariffs:** Are taxes on imported goods and services, which aim to protect domestic producers from international competition.

Different forms of regionalism: features and impacts

The three forms of regionalism that we study are political, security and economic integration, although states do also pursue social and cultural integration.

Political regionalism

Political regionalism aims to defend shared identities, values and interests, forming a collective voice to strengthen member states' diplomatic influence. These range from simple intergovernmental forums to intergovernmental institutions, to, in the EU, strong supranational institutions. This form challenges state sovereignty, so it is difficult to achieve.

Defending identities and independence: For example, after the First World War, the Ottoman Empire collapsed, giving way to European colonial rule in Arab states. At the end of the Second World War, the Arab League was created, calling for independence and Arab unity, whilst the OAU and ASEAN did the same for African and Southeast Asian states in the 1960s.

Promoting values: Alongside unity, ASEAN's intergovernmental councils promote mutual respect and non-interference in each other's affairs. The EU promotes shared liberal values including freedom, democracy and the rule of law.

Institutions for collective decisions: The EU is the world's most advanced regional organisation with a complex institutional structure, blending supranational and intergovernmental decision-making. However, its integration and expansion have come at the cost of losing the UK, its second-largest economy. The African Union has created mostly intergovernmental forms of the EU's institutions. Political divisions between democracies and autocracies and a strong desire to protect sovereignty make supranationalism difficult in Africa, but its Peace and Security Council has some supranational authority.

Collective external action: The EU tries to coordinate its members' foreign policies, provides collective representation at the WTO, G7 and G20, and contributes to debates as an observer at the UN. However,

> **Exam Tip:**
> NATO has both global and regional roles. Its military interventions on behalf of the UN Security Council (e.g. in Libya and Afghanistan) are part of *political global governance*. You could use NATO's *regional collective defence role in Europe and North America* in a 30-mark essay on regionalism. If you do, use it alongside, not instead of, the listed regional organisations.

the election of hard-right governments in recent years, for example in Hungary, Poland and Italy, has made it more difficult for the EU to maintain a collective position in these institutions. The African Union joined the G20 in 2023 and also coordinates a collective voice at the UN. It too has significant internal divisions, especially on climate change.

Security regionalism

Security regionalism can involve military alliances, but none have the depth of cooperation seen in NATO. Security is the most fundamental role of the sovereign state, and so regional security organisations are always intergovernmental. Usually, regional security cooperation includes intelligence-sharing, counterterrorism, humanitarian and peacekeeping missions.

Collective security against external threats: States might seek a military alliance against a rival bloc, as NATO did in 1949. In a broader security sense, they might band together to protect themselves from superpower interference, as ASEAN did in 1967, during the Vietnam War.

Collective internal security: Regional security organisations support members with regime stability and counterterrorism, as the Shanghai Co-operation Organisation does, and in conflict resolution and peacekeeping, helping to stabilise fragile states, as the African Union has done since 2002. They can also assist in disaster relief, as ASEAN does.

Wider partnerships: Since the 1990s, regional security organisations have pursued wider partnerships in response to global challenges. The EU conducts military peacekeeping and civilian peacebuilding missions to support regional and international security (see pp. 398–320). NATO maintains partnerships with thirty-five non-member states. It collaborates with the EU and increasingly with the AU, which participated in NATO exercises in 2025. The 'Quad' (Quadrilateral Security Dialogue) of Australia, India, Japan and the United States aims to maintain maritime security in the vast Indo-Pacific ocean region.

Economic regionalism

Economic regionalism typically involves a sequence of steps to promote trade and support prosperity. First, states establish a **free-trade area** to strengthen trading relationships within the bloc, as NAFTA, now the USMCA, has done. They might go further, creating a **customs union** with a common set of external tariffs. They may continue by building a **common market** or even a **single market**, as the EU has done. Trade negotiations typically take years, and trade agreements are rarely 'complete'. A complete single market needs supranational authority over trading regulations, with judicial authority to ensure compliance (see Figure 9.1).

Figure 9.1 Stages of economic integration

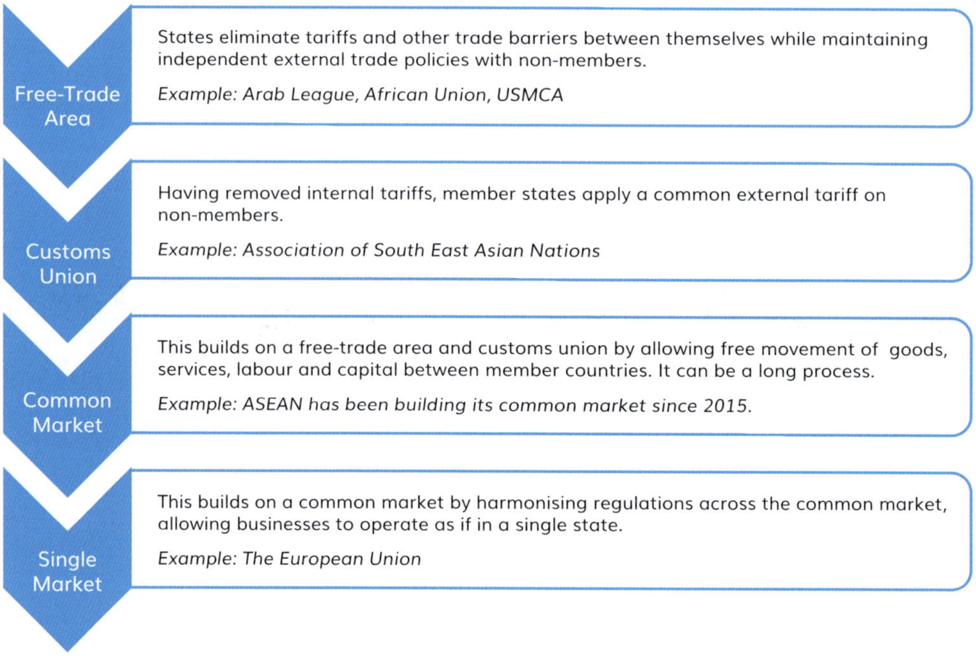

Free-Trade Area: States eliminate tariffs and other trade barriers between themselves while maintaining independent external trade policies with non-members.
Example: Arab League, African Union, USMCA

Customs Union: Having removed internal tariffs, member states apply a common external tariff on non-members.
Example: Association of South East Asian Nations

Common Market: This builds on a free-trade area and customs union by allowing free movement of goods, services, labour and capital between member countries. It can be a long process.
Example: ASEAN has been building its common market since 2015.

Single Market: This builds on a common market by harmonising regulations across the common market, allowing businesses to operate as if in a single state.
Example: The European Union

Reducing prices for consumers: The main reason for removing trade barriers is that it will increase competition and reduce costs for businesses; in theory leading to lower prices for consumers. However, reducing tariffs on trade also removes a source of government funding.

Protecting workers: Economic regionalism can create rules that improve living standards, but does not necessarily support all workers. Under NAFTA, many US and Canadian companies shifted their production to Mexico, taking advantage of lower labour costs and weak labour rights. There were corresponding job losses in US 'rust belt' states. Furthermore, like the EU, the United States subsidises farmers' incomes. Cheap, subsidised US corn has been exported to Mexico, damaging Mexico's agricultural economy.

In 2018, NAFTA was renegotiated. The new USMCA required 40 per cent of passenger car parts to be produced in factories paying at least US$16 per hour. This directly benefited Mexican automotive workers with higher wages. It reduced the incentive for US companies to relocate for cheap labour, protecting US jobs. It did not solve Mexico's problem with subsidised US food.

Protecting farmers, promoting sustainable agriculture: The EU's Common Agricultural Policy (CAP) was created in the 1960s to boost food production and support farming incomes. However, in the 1990s, EU subsidies made some agricultural products cheaper than products from developing countries in the global markets, contributing to a developing world debt crisis. The CAP was reformed in 2000, and EU export subsidies were phased out by 2009. Now, the Least Developed Countries (LDCs) are given free access to EU markets in its 'Everything but Arms' (EBA) scheme. The CAP still subsidises farmers' incomes, with the intention of promoting sustainable farming and helping manage climate-related damage.

Despite these subsidies, farmers across the EU have engaged in escalating protests since 2020. Farmers' grievances include EU environmental regulations that restrict pesticides and nitrate fertilisers and require them to conserve water and set aside land for nature (see Photo 9.2). Powerful supermarkets have cut food prices whilst farmers' fuel costs and the risks of crop failure due to extreme weather have increased, pushing many into debt.

Increasing internal trade with barriers to external trade: Economic regionalism sometimes increases trade among member states at the expense of global trade. For example, the EU's external tariffs encourage consumers to buy beef produced within the customs union. The EU also imposes non-tariff

Photo 9.1 Polish farmers drive their tractors in a column to block public roads in Krakow, as part of the European farmers' protest against the EU's Green Deal regulations in 2024.

Source: NurPhoto via Getty Images

> **Chapter Link**
>
> The EU's EBA scheme supports global governance efforts on poverty reduction in the Least Developed Countries (see **Chapter 5: Economic Global Governance**). The farmers' protests against EU environmental regulations threaten the EU's role as a global climate leader (see **Chapter 7: Environmental Global Governance**).

barriers, for example EU food safety standards ban chlorine-washed raw chicken. Most US chicken is chlorine-washed, so it cannot be sold in Europe. Meanwhile, cars sold in the United States, Canada and Mexico must be 75 per cent domestically manufactured. Mercedes, for example, must create jobs in North America if it wants to sell into these markets.

Increasing external trade: Economic regionalism may also promote external trade. The EU makes trade agreements on behalf of its members, for example, with Canada, Australia and Japan. ASEAN has created a wider free-trade area with its larger neighbours, China, South Korea and Japan. External trade deals increase competition, benefiting consumers but increasing pressure on primary producers, especially farmers. In 2024, EU farmers protested against a planned EU-MERCOSUR free-trade deal. MERCOSUR is the South American common market. It has lower environmental and animal welfare standards than the EU, so a free-trade deal could expose European farmers to unfair competition at a time when many are already struggling. (Note: MERCOSUR is not on the specification, but it is useful to know about this trade deal with the EU).

Comparative Analysis: Different forms of regionalism

	Political	Security	Economic
Purposes	Aims to defend shared identities, values and interests by amplifying a collective voice and strengthening diplomatic influence in global governance.	Cooperation to protect against internal and external security threats.	Promote trade and prosperity. Can reduce prices, protect workers and businesses from or promote global competition, promote wider social and environmental goals.
Drivers	Power imbalances – Initially a response to Cold War superpower rivalry. Now seeks to strengthen the political influence of weaker states in a globalised world.	Power imbalances – Initially a response to Cold War superpower rivalry. Now it is driven by the need to counter non-traditional security challenges created by globalisation.	Economic globalisation, which has created global markets for products, services and state borrowing (bond markets).
Common features	Promoting unity and independence (AL, AU). Promoting shared values (EU, ASEAN). Collective decision-making bodies: Councils (AL, AU, ASEAN, EU). Institutions (AU, EU). External representation (AU, EU).	Intelligence-sharing and counterterrorism (EU, ASEAN). Disaster relief (EU, AU, ASEAN). Humanitarian and peacekeeping missions (EU and AU). Wider partnerships (EU, AU, NATO). Deep military integration (NATO).	1. Free Trade Area (USMCA, AL, AU): No/low internal tariffs. 2. Customs Union (ASEAN): common external tariffs. 3. Common Market: free movement. 4. Single Market (EU): full alignment.
Intergovernmental or supranational	Varies from basic intergovernmental forums to highly supranational structures like the EU.	Some deep military alliances, but more often cooperation and coordination of separate resources. Control remains intergovernmental.	Free trade areas are purely intergovernmental, but other forms of economic integration involve varying levels of supranational authority over states.

The relationship between regionalism and globalisation

Is regionalism a direct consequence of globalisation?

Regionalism and globalisation are deeply intertwined, but this does not mean that regionalism is *only* a direct consequence of globalisation. As we have seen, in the Cold War, regionalism was often a response to superpower rivalry. On the other hand, the wider and deeper integration since then has been a response to accelerating economic globalisation.

Since then, regional bodies have protected their members from globalisation, for example by creating external trade barriers and coordinating their responses to global challenges like climate change and terrorism. They have also used globalisation to their advantage and promoted further global integration, for example having access to the EU's large consumer market helps its member states to attract foreign investment.

On the other hand, the rapid rise of China as a global manufacturer and India as a global IT services provider demonstrates that integration into global trade networks can create significant global power without deep regional integration. That said, the populations and economies of these two states are far larger than most regional organisations. Regionalism is a useful tool for smaller and middle-ranking economies, helping them to compete with dominant states. Ultimately, regionalism can be seen as both a reaction against and a driver of globalisation.

KEY DEBATE: DOES REGIONALISM PROTECT STATES FROM GLOBALISATION, OR DOES IT PROMOTE IT?

Political regionalism
Political regionalism helps members to find their own collective solutions, tailored to their regional needs and values, as an alternative to global governance.
- The Arab League has long held a common position on Palestinian statehood, which the UN is unable to do.
- The EU and AU have strengthened their members' voices, pushing for more climate action from the world's largest greenhouse gas emitters at the G20. EU states created a European Climate Law in 2021, binding them to achieve their 'net zero' emissions target by 2050, which the UN's COP process has failed to do.

Political regionalism promotes political globalisation (global governance).
- The EU explicitly states its liberal global political objectives in its Lisbon Treaty, seeking to promote sustainable development, international peace, human rights and the rule of law beyond its own borders. It promotes these principles in multilateral forums.
- The EU and AU's participation in the G20 and observer status at the UN supports global governance (political globalisation) by streamlining decision-making and making it more inclusive.

Security regionalism
Regional organisations make their members more resilient to globalised security threats.
- Both ASEAN and the EU promote cooperation between members on disaster response and transnational crime. The African Union leads peacekeeping operations that once would have been led by the UN.
- They can also protect strategic interests from global risks posed by dominant global powers such as China. For example, in 2023, the EU agreed a collective 'de-risking' strategy, which ended reliance on China for products that were important for members' national security.

Regional organisations promote global cooperation in the interests of international peace and security.
- Regional organisations increasingly form wider international partnerships to manage transnational threats more effectively. NATO and the AU have participated in joint exercises in 2025.
- The EU provides military training, humanitarian missions, ceasefire monitoring and civilian peacebuilding missions outside its own area, supporting both the AU and UN.

Economic regionalism
Economic regionalism protects its members against global competition and exploitation.
- Regionalism establishes 'fortress' customs unions with common external tariffs and subsidies, shielding internal producers from external competition, e.g. the EU's agricultural subsidies and common external tariffs protect its farmers and strengthen members' bargaining power in global trade deals.
- Regional organisations can also protect against neocolonialism or a 'race to the bottom' by multinational corporations, for example the EU has imposed a carbon tax on imports from places with weaker environmental protections, and a 'digital services tax' on transnational technology corporations, whilst the USMCA imposed minimum wages for car manufacturers.

Economic regionalism promotes globalisation by promoting wider trade integration.
- Regionalism attracts greater global investments into larger, more integrated markets, offering economies of scale and reduced transaction costs. The EU's single market attracts massive amounts of foreign investment. It also pursues trade deals with other regional blocs, for example MERCOSUR.
- Regionalism also sometimes promotes external trade deals and engagement with global markets. ASEAN, through agreements like RCEP, is creating vast interconnected trade networks that drive global commerce and integrate its member states into globalised supply chains.

Cultural regionalism
Cultural regionalism helps states to resist Americanisation or hybridisation.
- Regional organisations can protect their distinctive culture. This has been more apparent in the Arab League than anywhere else. The Arab League promotes the teaching of Arabic and supports pan-Arab cultural heritage projects, resisting Americanisation, whilst the EU respects members' linguistic diversity with twenty-four official languages.

Cultural regionalism contributes to hybridisation and the global spread of values and ideas.
- European regionalism has promoted the global spread of liberal social values like feminism and LGBTQ+ rights. Protecting these values has helped the EU to gain soft power, encouraging immigration. When migrants return to their countries of origin, they spread those values globally.

Exam Tip: Whilst you are not required to know about cultural regionalism, you do need to know about political, economic and cultural globalisation, Understanding cultural regionalism can help you to explain how regionalism and globalisation are linked.

Key Debate Summary: Does regionalism protect states from globalisation, or does it promote it?

Type of Regionalism	Protects from Globalisation	Promotes Globalisation
Political	Helps members find collective solutions tailored to regional needs and values (e.g. Arab League on Palestinian statehood, EU Climate Law 2021)	Promotes global governance (e.g. EU and AU climate action at G20, EU's Lisbon Treaty objectives)
Security	Makes members more resilient to global security threats (e.g. ASEAN and EU on disaster response, AU peacekeeping, EU 'de-risking' strategy 2023)	Forms wider international partnerships (e.g. NATO and AU joint exercises 2025, EU's support for AU and UN missions)

Type of Regionalism	Protects from Globalisation	Promotes Globalisation
Economic	Protects members against global competition and exploitation (e.g. EU customs unions, carbon tax, digital services tax, USMCA minimum wages)	Promotes wider trade integration, e.g. ASEAN and the RCEP, and the planned EU and MERCOSUR trade deals
Cultural	Helps states resist Americanisation (e.g. Arab League on Arabic teaching, EU linguistic diversity)	Contributes to hybridisation and global spread of values (e.g. EU liberal social values, encouraging immigration)

> **Chapter Link**
>
> This debate can be linked to the impact of globalisation on state sovereignty in **Chapter 2: The State and Globalisation**. When regionalism protects against globalisation, it can help to uphold de facto state sovereignty. When regionalism promotes globalisation, it may undermine de facto state sovereignty.

Prospects for political regionalism and regional governance

On one hand, the trend begun in the EU for deeper political integration may continue. States increasingly recognise that global challenges like climate change, financial crises and cyberattacks do not respect national borders and require collective action, but global governance institutions have become dysfunctional. Regional bodies, through enhanced political institutions, offer an alternative platform for more effective decision-making and policy coordination, allowing their members to better represent their individual interests, and actively resisting or shaping globalisation to suit their own purposes. States in the EU customs union, for example, are better protected from the United States' unpredictable tariff wars by their internal single market than many other states.

However, NAFTA, the Arab League and ASEAN do not aim to pursue supranational integration, and the African Union is not making fast progress towards its aim of emulating the EU. Political institutions are perhaps the most difficult form of regionalism for states to sustain, as they present a more direct and obvious challenge to state sovereignty than trade rules or security cooperation. State sovereignty has emotional significance for many people. The rise of populist nationalism since the mid-2010s has eroded the political will for integration in numerous states. If hard-right nationalism begins to dominate in the EU as it has done in the United States, the supranational powers of EU institutions are likely to be eroded.

Development of regional organisations excluding the EU

The Arab League (AL)

Formation
Date: 1945
Context: a rise in Arab nationalism, seeking unity and independence from colonial rule.

Membership
Founding members (7): Egypt, Iraq, Lebanon, Saudi Arabia, Syria, Transjordan (Jordan), Yemen. 2025 membership: **22 states** across North Africa and the Middle East.

Key measurements (2024 estimates)
Population: 472 million; GDP: $3.5 trillion; GDP per capita: $7,500.

Table 9.1 Has the Arab League Achieved Its Aims?

	Political	Security	Economic
Aims	Safeguard sovereignty, promote Arab unity, coordinate on regional and global issues. Protect Arab culture and Arabic language.	The 1950 Joint Defence Treaty commits states to defence policy coordination, although not military integration.	Promote free-trade, aiming for a **common market**.
Success	It supported struggles to free Arab states from colonial rule (e.g. Sudan, 1956, Algeria, 1962). It has protected Arabic heritage and language. It suspended Libya and Syria in 2011 due to attacks on civilians. It held a united position on Palestinian independence until 2020. The first China-Arab States Summit in Riyadh in 2022 increased strategic and economic engagement with China.	The AL backed UN-authorised interventions in civil wars in Libya and Yemen. There have been 'coalitions of the willing' between some member states e.g. the Saudi-led coalition of several Arab states that intervened in Yemen against Houthi rebels from 2015.	Established the Greater Arab Free Trade Area (GAFTA) (1997), eliminating most tariffs on goods by 2005.
Failure	Limited collective action due to divisions between rival autocracies with conflicting foreign policies. While Libya was readmitted after the overthrow of Gaddafi, several members boycotted a League summit in Libya in 2023 – its disputed government was seen as illegitimate. The AL readmitted Syria in 2023, despite continued attacks on civilians.	Collective military action is rare. The AL failed to resolve or contain internal conflicts in Libya, Syria and Yemen. A voluntary Joint Arab Force announced in 2015 has never been created. Humanitarian support for Gaza has not been coordinated between members.	Despite early aims for a common market, there is a lack of political will to broaden or deepen GAFTA.

Structure and purpose

Main body: Council of the League. Foreign ministers set policy and meet twice a year.

Other bodies: General Secretariat, Economic and Social Council, Joint Defence Council.

Decision-making: Intergovernmental, with national veto powers.

Primary purpose: A political forum for discussion and diplomatic coordination.

Developing issue: Palestine

Until the United States brokered the 'Abraham Accords' in 2020, the Arab League held a unified stance: no diplomatic relations with Israel before a comprehensive Israeli-Palestinian peace.

After the Abraham Accords, the UAE, Bahrain, Sudan and Morocco normalised relations with Israel, and there were signs that Saudi Arabia might do so too. The AL still expresses solidarity with Palestinians, but these actions weakened its collective position.

From 2023, the League coordinated responses to the Israel–Gaza conflict. It collectively condemned Israel's actions and called for an end to the humanitarian crisis. Several members have given humanitarian aid, Qatar and Egypt have mediated between Israel and Hamas during negotiations and contributed to international planning for post-conflict reconstruction in Gaza.

Photo 9.2 Palestinians in the West Bank city of Ramallah march in solidarity with those in the Gaza Strip after the Arab League chief demanded an end to military operations in Gaza on 16 October 2023.

Source: Jaafar Ashtiyeh/AFP via Getty Images

The Association of Southeast Asian Nations (ASEAN)

Formation

Date: 1967

Context: A response to Cold War regional instability and the expansion of communism.

Membership

Founding Members (5): Indonesia, Malaysia, Philippines, Singapore, Thailand.

2025 Membership: 10 member states (Brunei Darussalam, Cambodia, Indonesia, Laos, Malaysia, Myanmar, Philippines, Singapore, Thailand, Vietnam). Timor-Leste is an observer.

Key measurements (2024 estimates)

Population: 685 million; GDP: $4 trillion; GDP per capita: $5,800.

Structure and purpose

Main Body: ASEAN Summit (Heads of State and Government).

Other Bodies: ASEAN Coordinating Council (Foreign Ministers); ASEAN Community Councils (Political-Security, Economic, Socio-Cultural); Secretariat.

Decision Making: Primarily intergovernmental. Decisions are traditionally made by consultation and consensus (the 'ASEAN Way'), emphasising non-interference in internal affairs. There is no supranational enforcement.

Primary purpose: Promote peace, stability, prosperity and resilience. ASEAN organises its work across three 'pillars': political-security (separated here), economic, and socio-cultural (combined here).

Table 9.2 Has ASEAN Achieved Its Aims?

	Political	Security	Economic & socio-cultural
Aims	Promote principles of non-interference, mutual respect and peaceful conflict resolution 'the ASEAN Way'.	Promote regional peace and stability, coordinating cybersecurity, counterterrorism, crisis management.	Create a common market, and wider trade deals with regional neighbours. Reduce inequalities in health, education and welfare.
Success	The 1976 Treaty of Amity and Cooperation set out the principles of non-interference, mutual respect and peaceful conflict resolution, strengthening relations and supporting regional stability. An ASEAN Charter in 2008 turned the informal group into a rules-based organisation.	Regional disaster management and public health cooperation have strengthened resilience, reducing triggers for conflict. The ASEAN Regional Forum set up in 1994 allows dialogue with the United States, China, Russia and the EU. In 2022 ASEAN warned China and the United States over the risks of conflict over Taiwan.	Since 1992, ASEAN free-trade area (AFTA) has boosted trade and investment, producing steady economic growth. In 2015, ASEAN agreed to work towards a common market. A trade deal was agreed in 2020 with China, Japan, South Korea, Australia and New Zealand (RCEP: see Case Study: Regional Free Trade in Africa and Asia).
Failure	Non-interference weakens collective political action. After its 2021 military coup, Myanmar's military government was barred from summit meetings, and its turn to chair and host in 2026 has been postponed, signalling disapproval, but the principle of non-intervention prevents stronger action.	Consensus decision-making has weakened collective security action on Chinese expansionism in the South China Sea. Limited integration means that disaster responses have sometimes been delayed, only arriving after local services have been overwhelmed, for example when a typhoon hit the Philippines in 2013.	Large income and infrastructure differences among member states affect solidarity and complicate deeper economic integration. Difficulty harmonising national regulations between members has slowed progress on the single market.

USMCA (previously NAFTA)

Formation

Date: Originally formed as the North American Free Trade Agreement (NAFTA) in 1994; renegotiated as the United States–Mexico–Canada Agreement (USMCA) in 2018 to 2020.

Context: Designed to correct perceived imbalances under NAFTA while deepening trade integration, updating the agreement to include digital commerce, intellectual property rights, workers' rights and environmental standards.

Membership

United States, Canada, Mexico.

Key measurements (2024)

Population: 503 million; GDP: $32.8 trillion; GDP per capita: $65,000.

Structure and Decision Making

It is an intergovernmental agreement with just periodic reviews every six years. There is no organisation except for dispute resolution panels.

Table 9.3 Has USMCA Achieved Its Aims?

	Economic	Political
Aims	Eliminating trade barriers, increasing investment, improving global competitiveness and promoting competition between members.	As a free-trade area, NAFTA did not have a political aim as such. President Trump demanded renegotiation as USMCA to favour US manufacturing jobs, many of which had been lost in so-called 'swing states' that he relied upon for political support.
Success	Streamlined customs processes have made supply chains more efficient and boosted cross-border trade.	NAFTA created intergovernmental procedures for implementing the free-trade agreement. The USMCA resolved a trade dispute between the first Trump administration and its neighbours.
Failure	Long-running trade disputes on automotive, dairy and steel industries that periodically require renegotiation. The economic gains are not uniformly distributed. The agricultural sector in Mexico for example has struggled, compared with those in the United States and Canada which are more heavily subsidised.	Tensions resurfaced in 2025 with unilateral and unpredictably fluctuating tariffs imposed by the Trump administration on its free-trade partners as well as on other states around the world. A lack of consistent enforcement of labour and environmental protections due to divergent national priorities.

The African Union (AU)

Formation

Date: 2002

Context: Successor to the Organisation of African Unity (OAU, 1963–2002).

Formed to address Africa's challenges more effectively than the OAU, focusing on integration, peace and development. Due to their colonial history, African states tend to be highly protective of their national sovereignty.

Membership

Founding Members: All 53 OAU member states at the time of its formation.

2025 membership: 55 member states (all African countries).

Key measurements (2024)

Population: 1.36 billion; GDP: $2.8 trillion; GDP per capita: $2,100.

Structure

Main Body: Assembly of the Union (Heads of State and Government).

Other Bodies: Executive Council (Foreign Ministers); Peace and Security Council (PSC); Pan-African Parliament (PAP); AU Commission; African Court on Human and Peoples' Rights.

Decision-making

Primarily intergovernmental. The Assembly drives decisions and it requires consensus.

The AU Commission is more like the UN Secretariat than the EU Commission – it has fewer powers and does not have sole authority to propose legislation. The 15-member PSC aims for consensus but, if necessary, it can act on a two-thirds majority to intervene in a member state – there is no veto power. Its decisions are legally binding on states. This gives it some supranational characteristics.

Table 9.4 Has the African Union Achieved Its Aims?

	Political	Security	Economic
Aims	Promote unity, safeguard sovereignty/territorial integrity, promote democracy and human rights.	Promote peace and stability, prevent conflicts, defend common positions on international security issues.	Promote sustainable economic development, create a common market, introduce a single currency, strengthen Africa in the global economy.
Success	The AU has suspended members after military coups (e.g. in Burkina Faso, Mali, Niger, Gabon), to uphold democratic norms. States are readmitted if they return to democratic rule. The AU joined the G20 in 2023, enhancing Africa's collective diplomatic influence.	The AU rejected the OAU's non-interference principle, with 'the right to intervene' in war crimes, genocide and crimes against humanity. It has a Peace and Security Council (PSC) and African Standby Force (ASF). It has largely replaced UN peacekeeping. It has deployed missions in Somalia, the Sahel region and central Africa.	NEPAD (New Partnership for Economic Development) helps states to negotiate aid and investment and meet donor/lender rules on governance. The African Continental Free Trade Area (AfCFTA) was set up in three years, by 2021. Existing economic communities have joined together, speeding progress.
Failure	It is less effective at dealing with other undemocratic acts: refusing to concede elections, constitutional manipulations and a power grab by the son of the deceased president of Chad in 2021. Divisions between democratic and authoritarian states have slowed progress on human rights.	Peacekeeping challenges in Africa are significant, and the A's resources are limited. It relies on funding from the EU, UN and states including China. Despite its powers to intervene in war crimes and genocide, member states often lack capacity and political will to do so.	Africa struggles with poorly integrated energy and transport infrastructure which are significant barriers to economic development and continental free-trade, despite tariff reductions (see **Case Study: Regional Free Trade in Africa and Asia**) The AU's hope to create a single currency with a single central bank by the 2020s was over-ambitious.

> **Spec key term**
>
> **European integration:** Process of 'deepening' the industrial, political, legal, economic, social and cultural integration of states in Europe.
>
> **European Union (EU):** Political-economic union of twenty-seven European member states (2025). It should not be confused with the 46-member Council of Europe, which is entirely separate.

The European Union (EU)

Factors that have fostered European integration

Realists recognise that in an anarchic state system, powerful sovereign nation-states will naturally tend towards nationalism and conflict, whilst liberals hope to create ways to avoid conflict through cooperation, interdependence and rules-based institutions. After the Second World War, there were fears in Europe that conflict would re-emerge, and a liberal solution was attempted.

The European Coal and Steel Community (ECSC) was founded by France, Germany, Italy, Belgium, the Netherlands and Luxembourg in 1952, on the initiative of Jean Monnet, adviser to the French foreign minister, Robert Schuman. The 'Schuman Declaration' of 9 May 1950, said the plan was to make war between the six states 'not merely unthinkable but materially impossible'. This was a clear example of the Kantian Triangle theory that peace can come from interdependence (see p16-17). The ECSC promoted interdependence by removing **trade barriers** on coal and steel, ensuring free collective access to strategic industrial resources. This helped to alleviate tensions over resource-rich areas that spread across borders (see Map 9.2).

CASE STUDY: REGIONAL FREE TRADE IN AFRICA AND ASIA

Context

Regional organisations are increasingly reshaping global trade into regional trade, particularly in Africa and Asia.

The African Continental Free Trade Area (AfCFTA) began operating in 2021. The African Union provided the impetus and framework for negotiations. The AfCFTA is the largest free-trade area in the world by number of members, with 54 out of 55 AU member states, covering a market of 1.3 billion people and a combined GDP of approximately $3.4 trillion.

The colonial economic system established in Africa promoted specialisation in a few raw materials for export to the imperial powers of Europe. Transport networks connected inland areas to coastal ports, and roads and railways rarely crossed administrative boundaries, hindering internal African integration. This colonial legacy has remained a problem. The AfCFTA has knitted together existing trade agreements in parts of the continent. It will gradually reduce tariffs on 90 per cent of goods and remove non-tariff barriers to increase the proportion of intra-African trade from a low level of 15–18 per cent. This will encourage new infrastructure and keep more raw materials in the continent to support manufacturing, creating more wealth.

In Asia, the Regional Comprehensive Economic Partnership (RCEP) was signed in November 2020 and in operation by January 2022. Like Africa, the ten economies of ASEAN (the Association of Southeast Asian Nations) were impacted by colonialism. However, ASEAN has a longer history of economic integration and development, in part due to its smaller size and better maritime trade links. Having made progress on internal integration, in 2012 ASEAN decided to initiate talks with five major Asia-Pacific trade partners: Australia, China, Japan, New Zealand and South Korea, hoping to form a consolidated free-trade area. The resulting RCEP is the world's largest trade agreement by economic significance and population, accounting for nearly 30 per cent of global GDP, population and trade. Over 20 years, members will eliminate 90 per cent of tariffs, reducing costs and administration for businesses across the region.

Significance

These two huge trade deals are highly significant developments in the global economy. They also show two different approaches towards globalisation.

In the short term, AfCFTA is inwardly focused, aiming to protect its members from globalisation. By developing the continental market, the AU hopes to reduce African dependence on volatile global commodity prices, which will protect them from global recessions and support their development. In the long term, a unified African market could eventually become a major global trading partner on more equal terms with ASEAN, China, the EU or USA.

ASEAN is at a more advanced stage of integration, and so its RCEP is more outwardly focused: promoting globalisation. It links ASEAN countries to major global economies, improving their access to large consumer markets and attracting foreign investment. Globally, RCEP has accelerated the rebalancing of global trade towards the East, away from its historical centre between Europe and the United States.

The ECSC was also a bold experiment in liberal institutionalism (see pp. 16–17), creating supranational organisations to manage integration. It was followed in 1957 by the Treaty of Rome, which set out the goal of 'ever closer union between the peoples of Europe', created a European Economic Community: a free-trade area with plans to create a customs union and common market (these economic models are outlined on p. 298). In 1967, a merger treaty combined the ECSC and EEC with a third body, EURATOM, into the European Communities under a single set of supranational institutions: a European Commission, European Parliament, European Court of Justice, alongside an intergovernmental Council of Ministers.

These experiments were a success. Growing prosperity in the 1970s and 1980s encouraged more states to apply for membership. The members decided on further integration into a single market that would completely remove barriers to trade and would require political and legal institutions to oversee common regulations. Freedom of movement would require greater security cooperation. This process of '**spillover**' seemed to create its own momentum, resulting in unprecedented – and ever-increasing – levels of supranationalism.

Amidst accelerating globalisation, the Soviet Union collapsed in 1991, and in 1992, the Maastricht Treaty establishing the European Union was signed, along with the ASEAN and North American Free Trade Agreements. These marked the rise of a 'new regionalism' that promoted deeper trade

Definition

Spillover: A process in which the deepening of integration in one economic area creates a desire for integration in other areas of the economy and prompts political integration to help manage economic integration.

Map 9.2 The main coal and steel producing areas of the ECSC

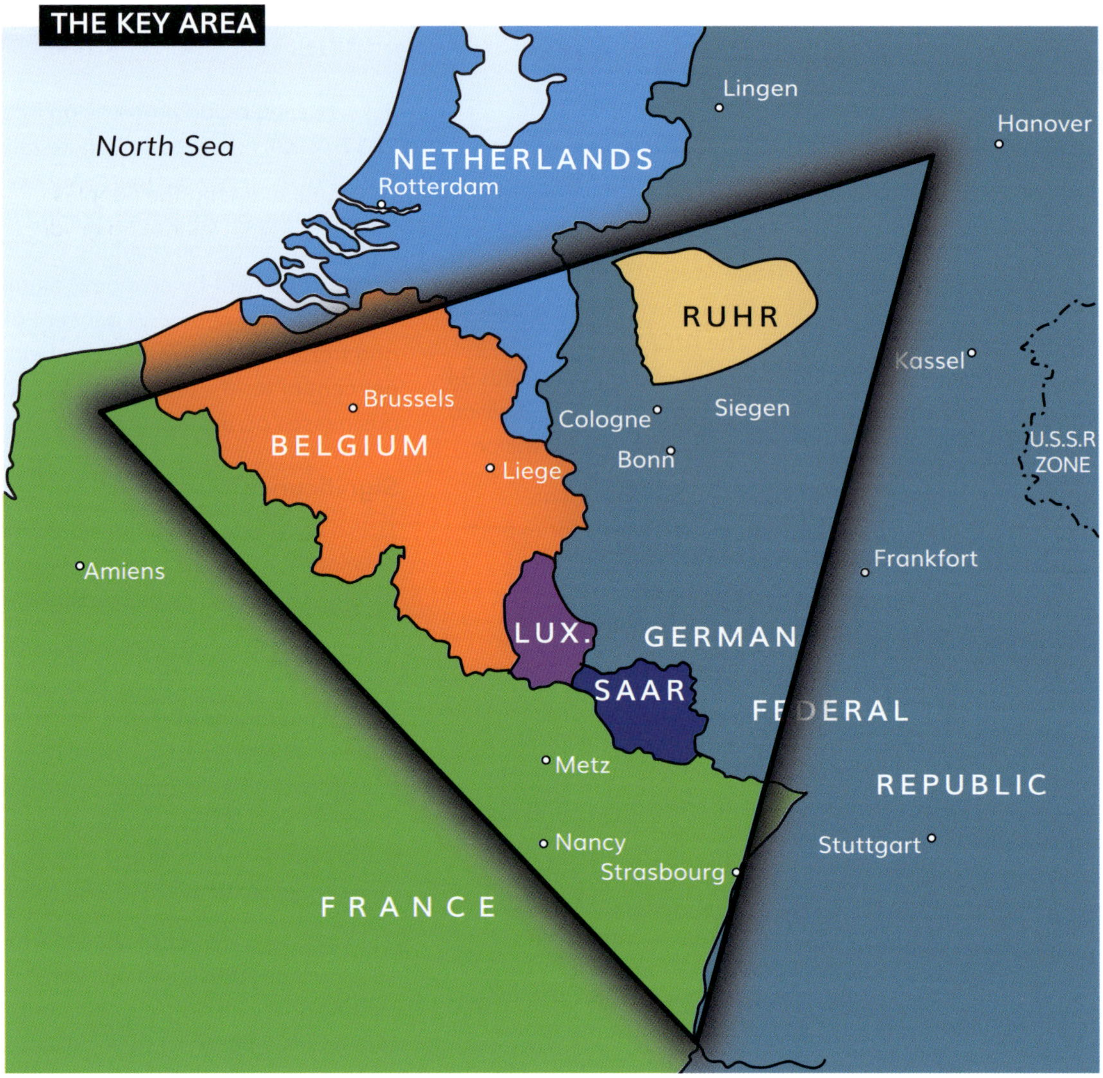

Spec key term

Widening and deepening: A dual process of expanding membership and furthering integration.

integration, whilst plans for the creation of the World Trade Organisation in 1995 saw the intensification of globalised trade.

Since Maastricht, the EU has continued to 'widen', expanding its membership to 28 members (27 since Brexit), and 'deepening' its integration. It has created an Economic and Monetary Union, with a comprehensive single market and a single currency. It has built an 'Area of Freedom, Security and Justice' based on free movement. It has strengthened its supranational powers, replacing the right to a national veto with Qualified Majority Voting in many, but not all, policy areas. Increasingly, it represents its member states in international relations. It is the most deeply integrated organisation of states in the world, and a global actor that, when it is able to act collectively, can rival the world's largest and most powerful states: the United States and China.

Stalled integration

In 2004, EU member states agreed to a constitutional treaty. It would replace the patchwork of previous treaties with a single codified document, improve democracy and make the EU a single legal entity, able to sign agreements on behalf of its members. However, the idea of an EU constitution was controversial with voters who favoured their national identities, and the constitutional treaty was rejected by referendums in France and the Netherlands. It was then modified and rebadged as the Lisbon Treaty, amending previous treaties rather than replacing them, avoiding the symbolic word 'constitution' whilst keeping the measures.

The Lisbon Treaty was rejected by Irish voters in a 2008 referendum, but after the EU promised Ireland more funding a second referendum passed in 2009. Other governments, noting this, ratified the treaty through parliamentary votes. It was the last major amending treaty of the EU.

Regionalism and the European Union

MILESTONES: KEY TREATIES AND AGREEMENTS OF THE EU

1951 **The Treaty of Paris** set up the European Coal and Steel Community (ECSC), formed in 1952 by France, Germany, Italy, Belgium, the Netherlands and Luxembourg.

1957 **The Treaty of Rome** set out a federalist dream of 'ever closer union among the peoples of Europe'. It established the European Economic Community (EEC), which initiated a gradual creation of a customs union and common market. It also established EURATOM, to promote peaceful uses of atomic energy.

1967 **The Brussels Treaty** created the **European Community (EC)** by merging the ECSC, EEC and Euratom under a single set of supranational institutions.

1986 **The Single European** Act began work on the single market. It introduced Qualified Majority Voting (see page X), removing some national veto powers. It allowed the Parliament to suggest legislative amendments for the first time.

1992 **The Maastricht Treaty** established the European Union. It completed the single market, creating a framework for Economic and Monetary Union (EMU). It also created common policies for foreign policy, justice and home affairs. It gave the Parliament equal **co-decision** powers with the Council of the EU in some areas.

1997 **The Amsterdam Treaty** paved the way for eastward expansion of the EU by extending QMV, further reducing the right of national veto. It included the Schengen Agreement, creating a border-free zone across most of the EU.

2001 **The Treaty of Nice** further extended QMV, adjusting voting weighting to account for population size.

2009 **The Treaty of Lisbon** was signed in 2007 and came into force in 2009. It created a president of the European Council and codified the right of states to leave the EU. It introduced democratic reforms, allowing national parliaments to challenge EU law and making co-decision between the Council of the EU and Parliament the standard legislative process. It also allowed the EU to sign international agreements on behalf of states and enhanced its external representation.

> **Spec key term**
>
> **Federalism:** A system of government where power is divided by a constitution between a central authority and regional entities. Neither is subordinate to the other, which distinguishes federalism, as seen in the United States, from devolution, as seen in the UK.

> **Definition**
>
> **Pooled sovereignty:** Is a system in which multiple states decide to collectively make decisions, therefore 'pooling' their individual sovereign powers. They may agree to allow a central authority to make decisions on their behalf and will agree to be bound by collective decisions.

Comparative Theories: Realist and liberal views on pooling sovereignty

Realist	Liberal
Realists argue that states will always prioritise and protect their own sovereignty. States view sovereignty as autonomous control over territory and resources. Any transfer of sovereignty to another body would reduce this autonomy, making them more vulnerable. In an anarchic state system, other states cannot be trusted. They therefore reject the idea of pooling sovereignty. States lose more than they benefit from doing so. Instead, the only way to deal with global challenges is to establish their own strong defences.	Liberals argue that states protect their sovereignty too. States view sovereignty more broadly, as control and influence which can be shared. **Pooling sovereignty**, or sharing power, with states that have similar values involves exchanging some autonomy for collective influence. Institutions can help to build trust. State autonomy has already been eroded by global challenges such as climate change, terrorism and powerful multinational corporations (see **Chapter 3**), so states benefit more from than they lose from pooling their sovereignty.

The question of sovereignty

In the twenty-first century, controversy has centred on the impact of EU supranationalism on state sovereignty. The EU's steadily increasing powers have been seen as beneficial **'pooled sovereignty'** by liberal pro-European politicians and criticised as 'creeping federalism' by 'Eurosceptic' politicians. This view has been especially strong in the UK, eventually leading to 'Brexit': the withdrawal of the UK from the EU in 2020 after almost five decades of membership. The debate on whether the EU resembles a federal state or not is addressed on pp. 320–322.

Political integration

Shared values and objectives

The EU's values and objectives are outlined in the Lisbon Treaty (see Table 9.5). The values underpin its economic, political, social and security objectives.

The EU was awarded the Nobel Peace Prize in 2012 for its success in maintaining peace between its members over the 60 years since the ECSC began. It has built on this success with global objectives to promote global peace, security, prosperity, human rights and sustainable development. It fulfils these by promoting peaceful conflict resolution, mediating in disputes between neighbouring states, by providing a model of multilateral cooperation in IGOs and in its external security and humanitarian work, discussed later in this chapter. It has become what some scholars describe as a 'normative power' in global politics.

However, this normative power has been undermined at times by disunity, particularly from Hungary and Poland over democracy and the rule of law. Whilst EU institutions can impose fines and freeze payments to members for violating its values, stronger action such as suspending voting rights requires member state unanimity, and the EU does not have a mechanism to expel a state.

The powers of the EU and its member states

The European Union is a unique political system that blends elements of supranationalism, intergovernmentalism and national sovereignty. The EU treaties specify the powers of the EU and its member states (see Tables 9.6 and 9.7). The EU's powers or 'competences' are determined by three principles:

- Consent: The EU's authority is given to it through treaties, signed by all member states.

Table 9.5 The EU's Values and Objectives, Adapted from the Lisbon Treaty

Values	Internal objectives	Global objectives
Human dignity Freedom Democracy Equality Human rights Rule of law	Promote peace and EU values. Create an area of freedom, security and justice within external borders. Protect and improve the environment. Promote sustainable development, scientific and technological progress. Combat discrimination, promote equality and protect human rights. Enhance economic, social and territorial cohesion and solidarity among EU countries, respecting cultural and linguistic diversity. Achieve economic and monetary union: a single market and currency.	Promote the EU's values and interests in the wider world. Contribute to global peace and security, with strict observance of international law. - Contribute to: - Sustainable development. - Poverty eradication. - Protection of human rights. - Solidarity and mutual respect among peoples. - Free and fair trade.

Table 9.6 The EU and Member States' Areas of Competence

EU competence	Type of decision-making authority	Examples
Exclusive competences	**Supranational:** the EU has power over states.	Customs union Trade agreements
Shared competences (most common)	**Hybrid of supranational and national:** the EU sets rules and targets, member states create and implement policies.	Single market Environment Home affairs and justice International development
Supporting competences	**National:** the EU has no power to pass laws but can help states.	Health Education
Special competences	**Intergovernmental:** The EU coordinates collective actions that require unanimous consent from members, who retain the power of veto.	Common Foreign and Security Policy Some economic policies e.g. budgets, taxation

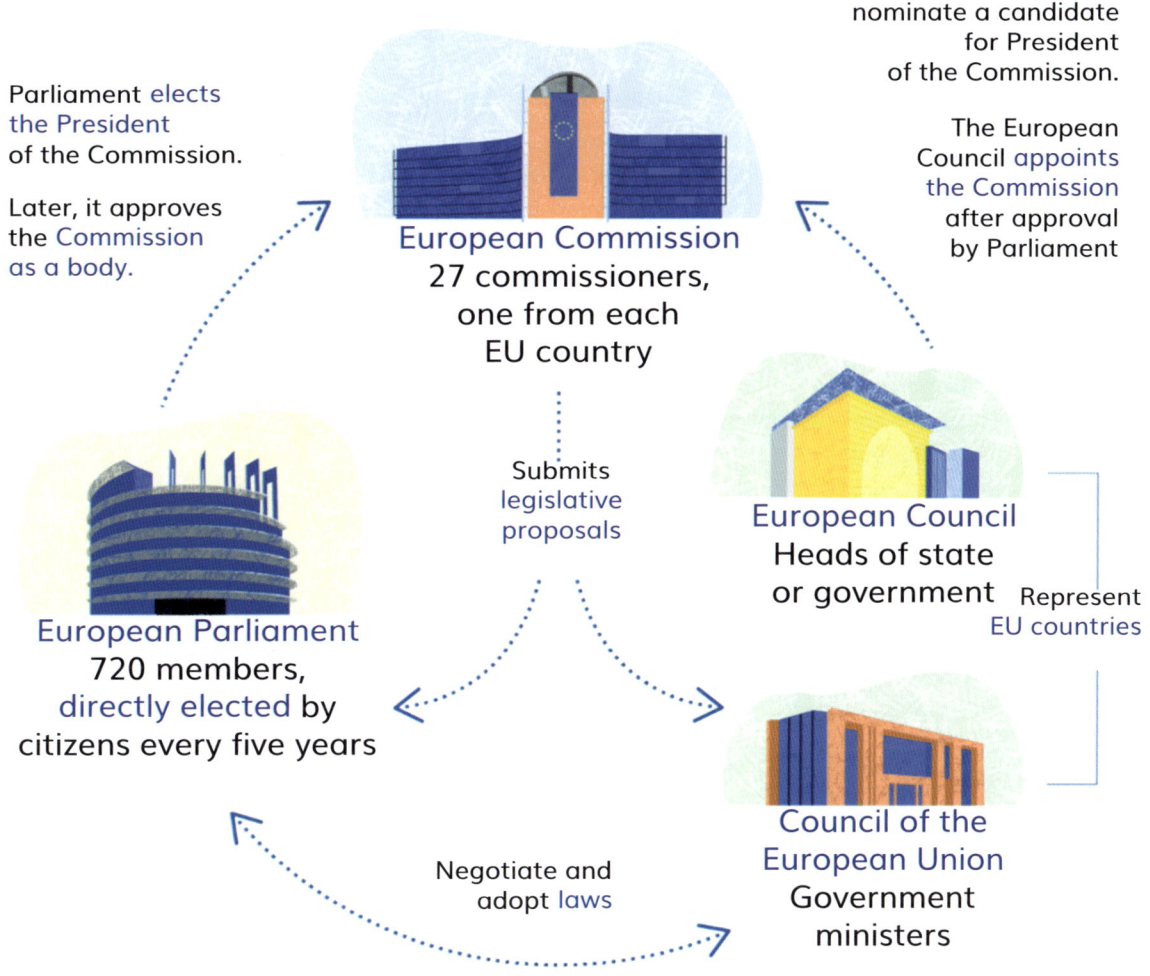

Figure 9.2 How do the Institutions of the European Union work together?

Source: European Parliament

CASE STUDY: SUPRANATIONAL AUTHORITY OVER APPLE'S TAX DEAL

Photo 9.3 **The European Court of Justice's ruling forced Apple to pay $13 billion to the Irish treasury.**

Source: iStock.com/PhillDanze

Context

The dispute between the EU and Ireland over Apple originated in 2014 when the European Commission launched an investigation into Apple's tax arrangements in Ireland. The Commission accused Ireland of providing preferential treatment to Apple through special tax deals. Such favourable treatment could be seen as illegal state aid under EU rules, as it would give Apple an unfair advantage over other companies. Ireland, it is worth emphasising, was happy with the very low tax rate Apple was paying.

European Commission ruling

In 2016, the European Commission issued a landmark ruling that Ireland's tax concessions to Apple constituted state aid, which was illegal under the Treaty on the Functioning of the EU (Treaty of Rome). They ordered Apple to pay a record-breaking €13 billion ($14.9 billion) in back-dated taxes to the Irish government, despite the government arguing that it did not want the money. Both Apple and Ireland vehemently disagreed with the decision. Apple argued that it followed applicable laws and paid all required taxes. The company claimed the vast majority of its profits were generated in the United States and were subject to US taxation. Apple also said that the European Commission's approach set a dangerous precedent that could undermine the international tax system and harm economic growth. Ireland, on the other hand, insisted it had not given special treatment to Apple and had not violated EU rules. The Irish government feared that the case could discourage foreign investment and harm its reputation as a business-friendly destination. Both Apple and the Irish government appealed to the EU's General Court.

European General Court (EGC) ruling

In 2020, the EGC ruled that the Commission had not shown that Apple had received tax advantages from Ireland. The Commission appealed to the European Court of Justice (ECJ) for a final judgment, saying that the EGC had made legal errors in its decision.

European Court of Justice (ECJ) final ruling

In September 2024, the ECJ annulled the earlier EGC ruling, confirming the European Commission findings that Ireland had granted Apple unlawful aid and was required to recover the funds. The ECJ ordered the $13 billion to be paid to the Irish treasury.

Significance

This case illustrates the supranational power of the European Commission and the ECJ in holding Ireland, a sovereign state, to account for not following EU rules as laid out in the Treaty on the Functioning of the EU (TFEU). The first EGC appeal ruling did not contradict the Commission's authority over Ireland but only disputed the standard of evidence. The supranational authority over tax rules and the power to enforce compliance remained clear throughout the case.

Table 9.7 The EU Institutions and Their Powers

Name	Membership	Powers/role	Intergovernmental or supranational authority
European Council	Leaders of the member states, who appoint a full-time Council president.	The European Council provides strategic leadership for the EU and negotiates treaties, meeting four times a year.	**Mostly intergovernmental** Aims for consensus. Retains vetoes on membership, treaties and foreign policy.
Council of the EU	Ministers from member states, grouped into policy area committees. The presidency rotates twice a year.	A legislative body which represents national governments. It amends and approves legislation in 'co-decision' with the Parliament. It can ask the Commission to propose legislation.	**Increasingly supranational** due to Qualified Majority Voting (QMV) in most areas, with states bound by majority decisions. Some **intergovernmentalism**, with national vetoes on sensitive policy areas.
European Commission	The president is nominated by the European Council and approved by Parliament. 27 Commissioners are nominated by member states.	The Commission proposes legislation, implements policies and is the guardian of the EU's treaties. It is executive and civil service combined. It has 32,000 employees.	**Supranational:** Commissioners do not represent member states' interests. The Commission implements EU law which overrides national laws (see case study on Apple's tax deal).
European Parliament	705 Members of the European Parliament (MEPs), directly elected by EU citizens every 5 years.	A legislature with co-decision powers with the Council of the EU. It can reject the EU budget and dismiss the Commission. It cannot propose legislation.	**Supranational:** MEPs represent citizens of the EU, rather than national governments, so they sit in cross-EU political groups, not in national groups.
European Court of Justice (ECJ)	There are twenty-seven Judges, one from each member state.	The ECJ interprets and adjudicates on disputes over EU law and treaties. As EU law has primacy over national laws, the court can overrule domestic laws.	**Supranational:** Judges are expected to remain impartial rather than representing national interests. The ECJ can impose fines for non-compliance with EU law.
European Central Bank (ECB)	The president of the ECB is appointed by the European Council.	The ECB is responsible for monetary policy in Eurozone states: it uses interest rates to manage inflation and the value of the euro.	**Supranational:** it controls monetary policy. It is advised but not directed by an informal 'Eurogroup' of finance ministers from Eurozone states.

> **Definition**
>
> **Qualified Majority Voting:** A compromise between consensus and simple majority voting. For a decision to pass, 55 per cent of member states (15 out of 27 in 2025), representing 65 per cent of the EU population, must vote in favour. This weighting accounts for population differences and prevents any single state from vetoing a decision.

- Proportionality: the EU cannot go beyond the powers given in the treaties.
- Subsidiarity: in areas of shared competence, the EU can only intervene if it can act more effectively than individual states can.

Table 9.7 outlines the membership, role and intergovernmental or supranational powers of the EU institutions. Figure 9.2 shows how these institutions work together.

Key features of the EU's hybrid powers

The European Council's intergovernmental strategic leadership

Although most EU institutions are supranational (see Table 9.3), the intergovernmental European Council is the EU's highest authority. It provides strategic leadership to the European Commission. It agrees treaties that give the EU power to make laws, but it does not itself make laws. It requires unanimity on foreign policy, treaty amendments and new members. This gives each state the right of veto, preserving national sovereignty on sensitive issues. However, it tries to achieve consensus where possible and occasionally agrees opt-outs to treaties if consensus fails — for example, the UK opted out of the euro and the Schengen free travel area. Once agreed, a treaty must be upheld otherwise, as a last resort, a state's voting rights could be suspended if all other members agree. However, this is a very high bar to action. By 2025, Hungary had been violating the rule of law and undermining the EU's values internationally for more than a decade, but the European Council had not yet agreed to condemn its actions or suspend its voting rights.

The increasingly supranational EU legislative process

Having evolved over time, the EU's ordinary legislative procedure was confirmed by the Lisbon Treaty. It requires co-decision between the supranational Parliament and the Council of the EU. This Council has intergovernmental elements because its ministers represent their national governments and defend their national interests. They have the right of veto on foreign policy, the EU budget and taxation. However, the larger the membership, the more likely a decision is to be blocked, so, when the EU expanded, member states removed the right of veto from all the EU's other areas of competence, replacing it with **Qualified Majority Voting** (QMV), in which a state can be outvoted. Once legislation is passed, it becomes binding EU law. These features make the EU legislative process more supranational than intergovernmental.

International relations

Although international trade agreements are controlled by the Commission, states have their own foreign policies and retain the right of veto over any collective international action. They do coordinate their actions within the EU's Common Foreign and Security Policy (CFSP) (see **Case Study: Intergovernmentalism and Supranationalism in the EU's External Relations**).

> **Exam Tip:**
> Students often become confused about why institutions are supranational or intergovernmental. Unlike the UN General Assembly, where majority votes on resolutions remain intergovernmental because states are not bound by them; the EU's legislative process is mostly supranational — not only because it uses QMV, but because an outvoted state must comply with the law made by majority vote, or face penalties.

Economic integration

Economic and monetary union

Economic integration took four decades (this process is summarised in Figure 9.3).

Customs Union: The EU has exclusive powers over the customs union, with a single set of external trade barriers such as tariffs on agricultural products and a 'carbon tax'. It also has many non-tariff barriers, such as environmental, safety and food hygiene standards (see Figure 9.4).

Single Market: Since 1993, the EU has a single market, with complete freedom of movement of goods, capital, services and labour (the 'four freedoms'). This is a 'shared competence': the EU provides overall regulation, but member states implement their own policies within this framework.

Monetary Union followed the single market. The shared currency, the Euro, was introduced in 1999. Initially, there were eleven '**Eurozone**' states, which expanded to twenty by 2023. Denmark opted out, while Sweden, Poland, Hungary, Czechia, Bulgaria and Romania are required to join at some point. The Eurozone is therefore a sub-group of states within the larger European Union.

Regionalism and the European Union **315**

The Eurozone's monetary union is overseen by the European Central Bank, which uses interest rates to manage price inflation. The Covid-19 pandemic, combined with an energy supply crisis resulting from the Ukraine war, led to global inflation in 2022–23. The European Central Bank (ECB) raised interest rates to 4 per cent by June 2023, up from 0 per cent in 2019, to manage the situation.

> **Definition**
>
> **Eurozone:** The EU member states (2025) that use the euro (€) as their official currency, forming a shared monetary union.

Figure 9.3 **The process of economic integration in the EU.**

Customs Union for coal and steel
- European Coal and Steel Community, 1952
- Removed trade barriers on coal and steel, established the principle of supranational authority

Free Trade Area leading to Customs Union
- European Economic Community: a-trade area, with plans for a customs union and common market with free movement of goods, capital, services, labour

Customs Union and Common Market
- European Communities, 1968
- Set a single external set of tariffs on imports from non-EEC countries

Single Market
- European Union, 1993
- Common market: free movement of goods, capital, services, labour
- Removed all non-tariff barriers e.g. regulatory differences

Economic and Monetary Union
- euro and European Central Bank, 1999
- Twenty states joined the Eurozone by 2023

Figure 9.4 **The EU's customs union and single market.**

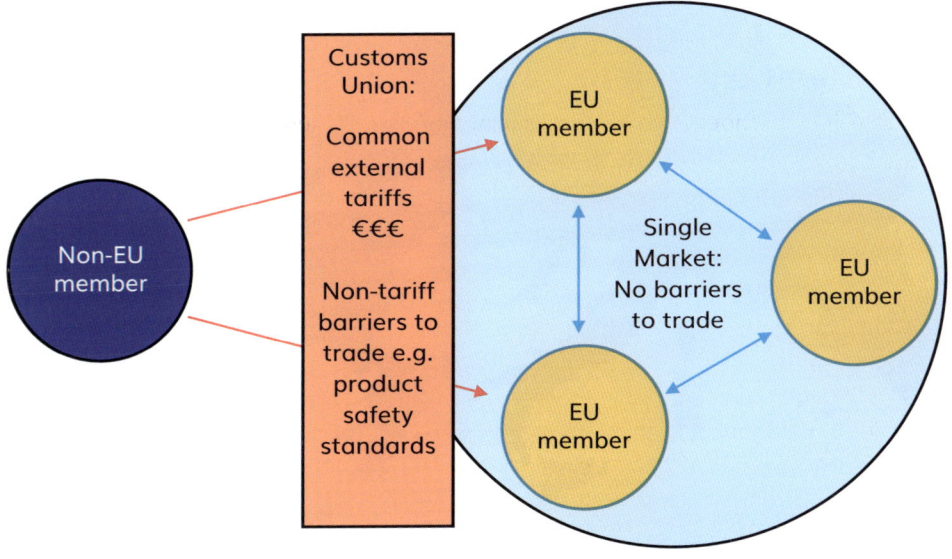

Security integration

EU powers over internal security: the Area of Freedom, Security and Justice (AFSJ)

The EU and its member states have 'shared competence' over the Area of Freedom, Security and Justice. This means that national governments can only legislate where the EU has not done so. Since the Lisbon Treaty, most EU law in this area is proposed by the Commission and passed through Qualified Majority Voting in the Council of the EU, in co-decision with the European Parliament, but national governments retain control of some policies such as law enforcement. Ireland and Denmark negotiated opt-outs from the AFSJ. Areas where the EU legislates include:

Freedom of movement: The Schengen Agreement was incorporated into EU law under the Amsterdam Treaty in 1997. It created a border-free zone inside a shared external border. You can travel from Lisbon in Portugal to Tallinn in Estonia without once being stopped at a border or having your passport checked – a distance of 2,600 miles (see Map 9.3). Apart from Ireland, which opted to keep its common travel area with the UK, and Cyprus, which has ongoing border issues with Turkish-controlled Northern Cyprus, all EU states have joined the Schengen Area. Non-EU states Iceland and Norway have also joined.

External borders: A migration crisis in 2015 saw an unprecedented influx of more than a million asylum seekers from Africa, the Middle East and parts of Asia. Thousands of people died trying to cross the

Map 9.3 The Schengen Area in 2025

Mediterranean. Since then, the European Border and Coast Guard Agency (Frontex) has taken on a greater role in supporting states by coordinating border security. It took seven years, from 2017 to 2024, for the EU institutions to legislate a Migration and Asylum Pact.

Security and justice: Europol investigates cross-border crimes. The European Arrest Warrant (EAW) has replaced extradition agreements across the EU. EAWs have facilitated the arrest of terrorists, such as a failed 7/7/2005 London bomber in Italy, and a terrorist involved in the 2015 Paris attacks in Belgium. Most other aspects of criminal justice are under national control, although the EU is seeking to harmonise them where possible.

Intergovernmental control of external security: the Common Security and Defence Policy

The Common Security and Defence Policy is part of the larger Common Foreign and Security Policy (see **Case Study: Intergovernmentalism and Supranationalism in the EU's External Relations**). It aims to strengthen international security through military and civilian humanitarian and peacebuilding missions. A recent example is the EUNAVFOR ASPIDES naval mission, launched in 2024 to maintain

Comparative Analysis: Supranational and intergovernmental features of EU decision-making

Feature	Supranational authority	Intergovernmental and national authority
EU Leadership	The Council is represented internationally by its full-time president, and by the High Representative for Foreign Affairs and Security Policy.	The intergovernmental European Council requires unanimity for foreign policy, treaty amendments and new members, preserving national sovereignty. It aims for consensus.
EU Lawmaking	The European Commission proposes EU laws. The European Parliament and Council pass laws through co-decision. Qualified Majority Voting (QMV) has mostly replaced veto power. EU legislation binds states.	Ministers in the Council of the EU represent national governments and defend national interests. Veto power preserves some national sovereignty. Although they do work collectively, national governments retain vetoes over common foreign and security policy, the EU budget and taxation.
Areas of competence and the principle of subsidiarity	The EU's exclusive areas of competence include the customs union and international trade. In the Eurozone, the ECB controls monetary policy. In 'shared competences', EU law takes precedence over state laws. These include agriculture and fisheries, environment, immigration and international development.	The principle of subsidiarity ensures that the EU intervenes only when necessary. Parliaments can challenge EU laws if subsidiarity is violated. States control their own education, healthcare, defence and national security, with the EU supporting collaboration if states want it.
EU Law Enforcement	The Commission can use 'infringement procedures' against states that violate the law. If these fail, the ECJ can issue legally binding judgments (e.g. Ireland's tax arrangements) and fines for non-compliance (e.g. Poland was fined €320 million for violating judicial independence and €100 billion in EU funding was frozen).	States negotiated and consented to the treaties that gave the EU its enforcement powers. Whilst the ECJ can issue fines, it is difficult for the EU to force states to uphold its values. It does not have a mechanism for expelling a member, and it is difficult to achieve unanimity to suspend voting rights

security in the strategic Red Sea shipping route. This protects commercial ships from missile and drone attacks by Iranian-backed Houthi rebels in Yemen. The intergovernmental European Council makes strategic decisions about where and how to act, the EU coordinates collective operations and member states volunteer to provide military resources on a case-by-case basis.

There is no EU 'standing army': this is done through NATO and individually by non-NATO states. However, in 2017, the EU launched Permanent Structured Cooperation (PESCO), to encourage states to pool military resources and expertise, enhancing interoperability – the ability to work together on operations, including for NATO. In 2025, EU members agreed a 'ReArm Europe' strategy, which allocates €800 billion of investment to help members strengthen their defence systems and support collaboration between them.

Federalism and the EU

Federalism is a system of government where power is constitutionally divided between a central federal authority and a set of provincial states. Neither have supreme authority – in fact, the term 'states' here is confusing, as they are not fully sovereign. Neither can unilaterally change the constitution without joint approval. This distinguishes federalism – as in the United States – from devolution – as in the UK.

Federal constitutions tend to be codified rather than evolving to meet changing needs. They allocate powers that require national coordination, such as foreign policy, to the federal authority. Other powers are allocated to states, with no opt-outs, although states can vary their implementation. Some powers are shared (see Table 9.8).

In contrast, a **confederation** is an association of sovereign states where authority remains with individual governments. Decision-making in a confederation is intergovernmental, requiring unanimity. Member states can opt out of policies leave or reclaim their powers. Confederations of sovereign states are rare and often temporary. A contemporary example is the Alliance of Sahel States, formed by Mali, Niger and Burkino Faso in September 2023.

Table 9.8 Typical Allocation of Main Powers in a Federal System

	Federal	Shared	States
Economic	Federal fiscal policy International trade Internal market Monetary policy International development	Environment	State fiscal policy Education, health, welfare
Political	Foreign policy Immigration	Constitution	State legislation
Security	Defence Federal law enforcement	Crisis management Inter-state crime	State law enforcement

KEY DEBATE: IS THE EU FEDERAL?

1. Economic and monetary union

✅ The EU has a single market, which has removed all trade barriers, including tariffs, quotas and regulations, allowing trade to flow freely in the same way as a federal state's internal national market.

✅ The Eurozone works like a federal monetary system does, with the European Central Bank (ECB) controlling interest rates, similar to the Federal Reserve in the United States.

❌ Apart from overarching EU rules, control of taxation rates and public spending budgets remains national, unlike in the United States, where taxation is shared between federal and state authorities. The EU budget is tiny in relation to national budgets. This looks more like a confederation of sovereign states rather than a federation.

- ❌ While the ECB manages monetary policy for twenty Eurozone states, Denmark negotiated a permanent opt-out from the euro. Of the six remaining states, only Bulgaria was close to joining in 2025. The others have delayed joining for decades. A federal system would not allow its states to opt out of using the national currency.

2. EU laws and treaties

- ✅ The European Commission acts like a federal executive in its areas of competence, proposing and implementing laws such as competition rules and environmental regulations.
- ✅ Regulations apply directly across all member states and directives require states to align their national laws with EU standards. The European Court of Justice (ECJ) can enforce EU law by fining states.
- ❌ Unlike a federal system where a central government can impose federal law without state consent, EU law is collectively amended and agreed to by sovereign states, who retain the right to veto some policies.
- ❌ Unlike federal governments, the EU allows opt-outs from treaties meaning not all states follow uniform rules. The UK and Ireland opted out of Schengen, and the UK and Denmark opted out of the euro. This flexibility mirrors a confederal system, where states can participate in some areas but not others. A confederation also allows states to leave, as the UK did, but a federation does not.

3. Area of freedom security and justice

- ✅ The Schengen Agreement removed national control over internal borders whilst creating a shared external border, similar to a federal state.
- ✅ The EU has strengthened Europol, created a European Arrest Warrant and has increasingly standardised law enforcement for serious cross-border crimes such as terrorism, cybercrime and human trafficking. These features look quite federal.
- ❌ Despite the use of QMV it took seven years for the EU to draft, propose and pass the Migration and Asylum Pact (2024). Only half of EU states submitted their national implementation plans by the December 2024 deadline. A federal government could have swiftly imposed centralised border control measures on its states.
- ❌ Despite increased cooperation, EU members still control national police forces and criminal laws. Unlike in the United States, where federal agencies enforce national law, the EU relies on individual states for law enforcement.

International relations

- ✅ The EU Commission negotiates trade, development and climate agreements as a single entity, whilst the European Council President, High Representative for Foreign and Security Policy and European External Action Service (EEAS) represent the EU in international forums, as federal state officials would.
- ✅ Under the Common Foreign and Security Policy, the EU can take collective action, such as imposing sanctions or sending humanitarian missions around the world, as a federal state might.
- ❌ The Common Foreign and Security Policy (CFSP) only encourages member states to coordinate their foreign policy rather than acting entirely independently. Member states retain national veto power over foreign policy.
- ❌ Member states maintain their own foreign offices and diplomatic services, and have different diplomatic positions on Israel, Palestine and Russia. These features show that foreign policy is under their control, which it would not be in a federation.

Key Debate Summary: Is the EU federal?

Theme	For	Against
Economic and monetary union	✓ Single market removes trade barriers; ECB sets Eurozone interest rates	✗ National control over tax/spending; some states have not adopted the euro
EU laws and treaties	✓ Commission enforces EU laws; ECJ ensures compliance across all states	✗ States can veto laws; opt-outs sometimes allowed
Area of Freedom, Security and Justice	✓ Schengen removes borders; Europol and arrest warrants increase cooperation	✗ Some states reluctant to legislate and implement migration regulations. National control over policing and criminal law
International relations	✓ EU negotiates trade and sanctions collectively; unified global representation	✗ Foreign policy requires consensus; member states keep separate diplomacy

Exam Tip:

Students often struggle with this debate. In fact, the EU has both federal and confederal features, so, arguably it could be called 'quasi-federal' or 'quasi-confederal'. Consider which is more dominant rather than rejecting one entirely. Consider how powers are divided in the economic, political, security and foreign policy areas, the EU's strategic leadership and its supranational and intergovernmental legislative process.

The process of 'widening' the EU

The EU has expanded seven times, with only one country withdrawing from the organisation.

1952 – 6 members: Belgium, France, West Germany, Italy, Luxembourg and the Netherlands founded the European Coal and Steel Community.

These states were already culturally and economically interconnected with developed economies.

1973 – 9 members: Denmark, Ireland and the UK joined the European Communities

The UK's previous application to join had been vetoed in 1963 by France, which was suspicious of the UK's 'special relationship' with the United States. The UK was accepted in 1973 alongside Denmark and Ireland, hoping to catch up with the EC's strong economic growth.

1981 – 10 members: Greece joins the EC

The Greek economy was weak and mainly agricultural, making economic integration risky. Greece's accession was a political decision to help strengthen its democracy after its military government collapsed in 1974.

1986 – 12 members: Portugal and Spain join the EC

Portugal and Spain were agricultural economies too, and both recently collapsed dictatorships. The motivations and the risks were similar.

1995 – 15 members: Austria, Finland and Sweden join the EU

These three states, having maintained neutrality during the Cold War, decided to join the EEC when the Soviet Union collapsed in 1991. They raised the average GDP per capita of the bloc.

2004 – 25 members: the Eastern expansion adds ten members to the EU

After almost a decade of transition, eight former Eastern Bloc states (Czech Republic, now Czechia Estonia, Hungary, Latvia, Lithuania, Poland, Slovakia and Slovenia) adopted democracy and capitalist economies, and along with the island states of Cyprus and Malta expanded the EU to 25 members.

However, the new members were significantly poorer and culturally quite different too. Existing members were concerned about the potential impacts of mass migration from the east.

2007 – 27 members: Bulgaria and Romania

Two even larger, even poorer states joined, reigniting migration concerns. Free movement was delayed until 2014.

2013 – 28 members: Croatia

Croatia had applied to join in 2003, followed by Macedonia in 2004, Montenegro in 2008, Albania and Serbia in 2009. Croatia became a member within a decade. However, the others were not so lucky. Greece vetoed Macedonia's application in 2008 over its name, which Greece claimed as part of its own national identity.

Crises and 'enlargement fatigue'

Enthusiasm for further enlargement waned as a succession of crises threatened EU unity. From 2010 to 2015, the Eurozone was hit by a debt crisis in the Mediterranean states. Already financially weakened, Greece and Italy struggled in 2015 with overwhelming numbers of people arriving by sea to seek asylum. Germany accepted a million asylum seekers, prompting mass migration across the EU, but other states were reluctant and several reinstated their borders. The Commission threatened resettlement quotas.

Türkiye had applied for membership in 1987, but by 2016, its government was eroding democracy and the rule of law, challenging EU interests in Libya and Syria and refusing to close its EU border to refugees, and its EU application was suspended. Hard-right governments challenged democracy and the rule of law in Poland and Hungary.

With the EU preoccupied with its own problems, Bosnia and Herzegovina applied to join in 2016. However, although the EU provided support for the rule of law, some existing members considered Balkan applicant states to be too poor and too unstable, with porous borders that posed significant risks to European security. Their accession processes slowed.

Macedonia changed its name to North Macedonia to placate Greece, but soon found its application vetoed again in 2020 by Bulgaria over a constitutional dispute.

2020 – 27 members: the UK leaves the EU

Following the 2016 referendum (see Photo 9.5), the UK left the EU in 2020. As the EU's second-largest economy and a significant power in world affairs, the loss of the UK has impacted the economic and political significance of the EU, but equally, the loss of an awkward and powerful member focused most of the remaining state leaders on trying to restore unity rather than expanding.

2022 – Ukraine, Moldova, Georgia and Kosovo apply to join

In response to Russian aggression, the EU agreed to fast-track the applications of Ukraine and Moldova and accepted applications from Georgia, and from Kosovo, despite it not being recognised by several member states. Formal negotiations were launched for North Macedonia and Albania. Progress towards accession slowed in Serbia, whose loyalties were divided between Europe and Russia, and in Bosnia, which was still struggling with political instability after its 1990s conflict. There have been concerns over the rule of law in both states.

2024 – Georgia was granted candidate status but then leant towards Russia

Georgia was granted EU candidate status in December 2023, but the electorate's allegiance is increasingly divided between the EU and Russia. In late 2024, there were widespread protests challenging the legitimacy of its parliamentary elections and the inauguration of a pro-Russian president. The governing Georgian Dream party suspended Georgia's EU application until 2028. Protests spread. It then passed laws to criminalise protesters and restrict foreign media. Undermining democratic norms in this way would prevent Georgia from meeting the EU's 'Copenhagen Criteria' for accession.

By 2025, Montenegro and Albania were closest to achieving accession.

Photo 9.4 Boris Johnson, former UK prime minister, campaigning for Brexit in 2016. The Brexit campaign's messaging focused on how much money Britain would save if it no longer contributed funds to the EU.

Source: Christopher Furlong/Getty Images News via Getty Images

Comparative Analysis: Arguments for and against enlarging the EU

Area of concern	In favour of enlargement	Against enlargement
Economic	**Internal trade benefits:** free access to larger markets, increasing prosperity, supporting regional stability. **External trade benefits:** The desire to become a larger, more attractive global trading partner, able to negotiate more favourable trade deals.	**Economic divides:** worries about support for poorer countries straining the budgets of wealthier ones **Cultural and political tensions:** provoked by economic migration from poorer to wealthier states.
Cultural	A desire to bring European nations with similar cultures together, with opportunities for cultural exchange – particularly for young people.	Culturally, differing values between Western and Eastern European states have caused friction, particularly on migration and minority rights.
Political	**Ideological:** a desire to promote liberal values of free markets, democracy, human rights and the rule of law, promoting regional stability. **Strategic:** strengthening the EU's political influence in a multipolar world.	**Political cohesion:** questions over declining standards of democracy and the rule of law in both candidate and existing member states. **Institutional strain:** questions about whether decision-making can function effectively with more members and greater cultural and political diversity.
Security	The desire to become a more significant global actor and protect itself from transnational terrorism and Russian expansionism.	Fears of expanding the external border into politically unstable neighbouring states with porous borders, allowing irregular migration, terrorism and organised crime to flourish.

Is the EU a significant global actor?

As the most highly integrated regional organisation in the world, with some characteristics that resemble a federal state, the EU has the potential to rival the United States and China. However, its strength varies across the domains of economic, structural, soft and military power. Ultimately, whether it can be viewed as a significant **global actor** depends on whether it can maintain a united position in international relations.

> **Definition**
>
> **Global actor:** entity that participates or acts in international relations.

★ CASE STUDY: INTERGOVERNMENTALISM AND SUPRANATIONALISM IN THE EU'S EXTERNAL RELATIONS

Context

The Maastricht Treaty in 1993 established an intergovernmental Common Foreign and Security Policy (CFSP). The Lisbon Treaty in 2009 included several measures to strengthen the EU's collective external identity. It gave the EU the power to sign international agreements on behalf of its members. It set up the diplomatic European External Action Service (EEAS), which works in 145 states around the world. It created a full-time European Council President – a role which had previously rotated between member state leaders twice a year; and merged the post of the Council's High Representative of the Union for Foreign Affairs and Security Policy (HR) with the post of Vice-President of the European Commission (VP).

This HR/VP is a senior Commissioner and a member of the Councils. In essence, they are the EU's foreign secretary, working across the intergovernmental and supranational institutions to implement the CFSP and lead the EEAS. They attend international forums on behalf of the EU. However, the CFSP's overall strategy remains fundamentally intergovernmental: the HR/VP cannot override a national veto on foreign and security matters.

Other external relations, such as trade, climate and development, are subject to supranational authority. The Commission has exclusive powers to negotiate trade agreements, and its president represents the EU at international meetings. International agreements are proposed by the Commission and agreed by the Parliament and the Council of the EU using Qualified Majority Voting, meaning that all states are bound by the collective decision.

Significance

The EU has become a formidable trade negotiator, as the UK discovered when negotiating its Trade and Cooperation Agreement after Brexit. It has also emerged as a global leader in climate negotiations and is the largest provider of overseas development aid in the world, with ongoing partnership agreements with the African Union and ASEAN. It has authorised many peacekeeping and peacebuilding missions. In 2025, there were naval missions in the Red Sea and around the Horn of Africa, military training in Mali, Niger and Ukraine, peacekeeping forces in Bosnia and the Sahel, ceasefire monitoring in Georgia and Armenia, border security missions in Libya and Moldova, civilian law enforcement in Kosovo, Somalia and more. It has imposed collective sanctions on Russia since 2014.

However, EU member states do sometimes differ on foreign policy, weakening its external influence. Members have been unable to find a strong collective position on the Israeli-Palestine conflict and failed to agree an arms embargo on Saudi Arabia. Hungary blocked declarations criticising Chinese repression of human rights and democracy in Hong Kong in 2020–21, and has regularly diluted and delayed sanctions on Russia. Furthermore, despite its humanitarian forces and a significant boost to defence funding in 2025, the EU does not have a standing military force capable of defensive action. The collective defence of Europe remains under NATO control. The EU is a significant global actor, but it is not consistently so.

KEY DEBATE: IS THE EU A SIGNIFICANT GLOBAL ACTOR?

Economic power

The EU has significant economic power with a large consumer market that attracts investment and external policies to strengthen the economic security of its member states.

- ✓ Its single market includes 447 million consumers. EU states are categorised as high-income states by the World Bank. This attracts foreign direct investment and gives the EU Commission a strong position in trade negotiations.
- ✓ Since 2021, the EU has strengthened its economic security in an increasingly uncertain world with its Next Generation COVID recovery plan, EU Chips Act, 'de-risking China' strategy and the ReArm Europe plan.

However, its economy is smaller than the United States and internal economic divides present risks:

- ✗ In 2024, the EU's nominal GDP was around $17 trillion, compared to the US' approximately $28 trillion.
- ✗ Further EU expansion to Ukraine and the Balkans will require continuing financial support from existing members – rather than significantly increasing the bloc's economic strength, it could weaken it.

Structural power

The EU holds structural power within IGOs:

- ✓ Economic: It is a permanent member of the G7 and G20 and acts on behalf of members at the WTO. Its experience in developing institutions and coordinating economic policies has helped it to influence G20 discussions on reforming the IMF, World Bank and WTO.
- ✓ Other forums: As a UN observer, the EU can speak in the UNGA. It has also achieved collective strength as a global leader in climate negotiations. In 2022, it established a 47-member European Political Community with its neighbours, reinforcing European strategic unity against Russia and Belarus.

Nevertheless, a power imbalance remains, and it can struggle to maintain a collective voice:

- ✗ France holds permanent UNSC membership, whilst Germany, France and Italy are individual members at the G20 and G7. They can pursue their own interests in these forums, weakening the EU as a collective voice.
- ✗ The EU's intergovernmental Common Foreign and Security Policy meant that it struggled to agree on the strength of sanctions against Russia, failed to condemn Chinese repression in Hong Kong in 2020–21 and has not united on the Israel–Gaza conflict.

Soft power

The EU exercises considerable soft power, which is central to its identity as a global actor:

- ✓ Its economic strength, liberal values and political stability make the EU attractive to migrants, particularly to asylum seekers fleeing persecution.
- ✓ The EU projects its values externally and is described as a 'normative power'. In 2023, it mediated in the dispute between Armenia and Azerbaijan. Its humanitarian missions uphold human rights and the rule of law. Massive cuts to US overseas aid in 2025 leave the EU and its members as the largest provider of development aid (100 billion euros in 2023).

However, the EU's soft power is both limited and disputed:

- ✗ A decade of high immigration has resulted in anti-immigrant governments in Hungary, Poland, Denmark, Italy and more, who disagree with Germany on migration. It took seven years to agree the 2024 Migration and Asylum Pact. Disunity impacts soft power.
- ✗ EU humanitarianism is not always welcome. France abandoned its eight-year peacekeeping mission in the Sahel region in 2022 after military governments in Mali, Burkina Faso, Niger and Chad rejected its influence as continued colonialism.

Military power
The EU cooperates on security and has recently strengthened collaborative efforts:
- ✓ Permanent Structured Cooperation (PESCO) was launched in 2017 to encourage states to pool military resources and expertise and enhance interoperability – the ability to work together on operations, e.g. EUNAVFOR ASPIDES to protect shipping in the Red Sea and around the Arabian Peninsula from Houthi attacks.
- ✓ With questions over the reliability of US support for Europe in NATO, in 2025, ReArm Europe boosted EU states' defence spending by €800 billion from 2025 to 2030, and a security partnership was agreed with the UK.

Despite these efforts, the EU is not a significant global military actor.
- ✗ Its Common Foreign and Security Policy (CFSP) requires consensus among member states, which can delay, weaken and sometimes block collective action.
- ✗ NATO provides collective defence in Europe, and the EU lacks a standing army to defend itself. ReArm Europe does not replace NATO.

Key Debate Summary: Is the EU a significant global actor?

	For	Against
Economic	✓ Large consumer market, high-income states, strong trade negotiation position	✗ Economy is smaller than the United States, internal economic divides
Structural	✓ Permanent member of G7 and G20, influence in global economic discussions	✗ Power imbalance, individual interests of member states
Soft	✓ Liberal values, political stability, mediates disputes, humanitarian missions	✗ Anti-immigrant governments, disunity on migration, rejected influence in some regions
Military	✓ Cooperates on security, strengthened collaborative efforts	✗ CFSP requires consensus, NATO provides collective defence, no standing army

Chapter Link
This debate links closely to the question of state power in **Chapter 3: Power and Developments**. Economic and military power are both forms of hard power, although provision of humanitarian aid can also strengthen soft power. Diplomacy in IGOs combines structural and soft power, and threats of hard power.

KEY DEBATE: DOES REGIONALISM UNDERMINE STATE SOVEREIGNTY?

1. Economic powers
Regional organisations undermine sovereignty in economic decision-making:
- ✓ Free trade agreements always involve some loss of sovereignty as states make concessions on trade barriers, for example, Mexico's agricultural sector has suffered from its NAFTA/USMCA membership.
- ✓ The EU overrides state sovereignty by negotiating trade agreements on behalf of its members.

Regional organisations enhance their members' economic power, strengthening 'de facto' sovereignty:

- ✗ The loss of sovereignty in a trade deal is usually compensated for by greater trading opportunities – Mexico's economy has grown from participating in NAFTA/USMCA.
- ✗ ASEAN and the EU's member states benefit from pooling sovereignty for stronger external trade negotiating power. ASEAN members negotiated its external Regional Comprehensive Economic Partnership (RCEP) collectively, preserving more state sovereignty than the EU does.

2. Supranational legislative powers

Regional organisations can override legislative authority of their members, reducing 'de jure' sovereignty:

- ✓ The African Union has a peer review process and can suspend governments that have taken power unconstitutionally, which overrides their sovereignty to govern themselves.
- ✓ The EU's legislative process has become mostly supranational with QMV and co-decision procedures. It requires member states to align their laws with EU directives and regulations. The European Court of Justice can enforce the EU's legislative authority as it did with Apple's tax deal with Ireland and fines imposed on Poland.

Regional organisations strengthen legitimacy and protect 'de jure' sovereignty:

- ✗ The African Union's powers aim to uphold democratic governance among members, strengthening their political stability and their legitimacy, strengthening both internal and external sovereignty.
- ✗ EU states conferred legislative authority on the EU in order to pool their sovereignty on areas that they wanted to deal with collectively. They provide strategic leadership, each retains a national veto on treaty amendments, and they retain national sovereignty on fundamental matters such as national security and taxation. They have the option to leave the union as the UK did.

3. Foreign policy powers

Regional organisations constrain autonomous international action:

- ✓ The USMCA's joint trade requirements, such as the rule that 75 per cent of each car must be produced within the USMCA region to qualify for tariff-free access, limit its members' options for independent trade deals.
- ✓ EU member states are sometimes constrained by the Common Foreign and Security Policy (CFSP), which aims for common positions but can force states to compromise on their own geopolitical goals, for example Hungary only reluctantly agreed to impose sanctions on Russia, which it does not see as a threat, unlike other EU states.

Regional organisations enhance international influence by pooling sovereignty.

- ✗ The African Union enhances its members' global influence as a member of the G20 and by coordinating a collective voice at the UN. ASEAN also works to achieve regional unity in negotiations with China and the United States, and the Arab League has maintained a common position on Israel, strengthening the Arab voice in the region.
- ✗ The EU often speaks with a unified voice on matters such as climate change and human rights. This allows member states, especially smaller ones, to exert diplomatic influence beyond what they could achieve unilaterally.

4. Security powers

Regional organisations lack defence capabilities, limiting de facto sovereignty, or have the power to actively intervene, undermining sovereignty.

- ✓ The African Union's Peace and Security Council has the power to intervene in a state where it believes that crimes against humanity are being carried out – whether this is being done by the state or a non-state actor. Whilst this is morally justifiable, it does undermine the sovereignty of that state.
- ✓ The EU lacks a standing army, limiting its global significance as a military actor. However, its Area of Freedom, Security and Justice is an area where EU legislation can override its members' national legislation, for example on border security.

Definition

De facto sovereignty: Refers to the actual, practical control and exercise of power over a territory, regardless of legal recognition.

De jure sovereignty: Refers to the legal right to exercise supreme authority over a territory and its people, recognised by law.

Exam Tip: Distinguishing between autonomy and pooled sovereignty, between de jure and de facto sovereignty, and between internal and external sovereignty can help to understand the different ways that regional organisations can both undermine and strengthen sovereignty.

Regionalism and the European Union

Pooling security enhances 'de facto' internal and external sovereignty.
- ❌ The African Union's peacekeeping missions in conflict zones, such as in Somalia, improve security and stability for member states, whilst ASEAN fosters regional security cooperation through its intergovernmental defence ministers' meetings and collective disaster relief efforts.
- ❌ The EU's Permanent Structured Cooperation (PESCO) and ReArm Europe plan promote collaboration and interoperability, boosting defence spending and strengthening cybersecurity and counterterrorism.

Key Debate Summary: Does regionalism undermine state sovereignty?

	Regional Organisations Undermine Sovereignty	Regional Organisations Strengthen Sovereignty
Economic Powers	The EU and some trade deals undermine state sovereignty in economic decision-making.	Regional organisations enhance their members' economic power, strengthening 'de facto' sovereignty.
Supranational Legislative Powers	The EU Commission and QMV legislative process can override the legislative authority of EU members, reducing 'de jure' sovereignty.	Regional organisations can strengthen the legitimacy of state governments by requiring democracy and good governance. States can leave if their legislative authority is undermined.
Foreign Policy Powers	The EU has some – but limited – influence on its members' foreign policies.	Regional organisations enhance the international influence of their members by speaking with a collective voice.
Security Powers	Regional organisations lack defence capabilities, limiting de facto sovereignty. The AU has the power to actively intervene, undermining sovereignty.	Pooling resources on security enhances 'de facto' internal and external sovereignty of member states.

> **Chapter Link**
> Intergovernmental regional governance, like global governance, does not significantly undermine state sovereignty (see **Chapter 2: The State and Globalisation and Chapter 4: Political Global Governance**). However, the EU's supranational decision-making and institutions undermine state sovereignty to a greater extent.

KEY DEBATE: HAVE REGIONAL ORGANISATIONS IMPACTED POSITIVELY ON POVERTY, CONFLICT, HUMAN RIGHTS AND THE ENVIRONMENT?

Poverty
Regional organisations reduce poverty by promoting economic cooperation and development.
- ✅ The EU supports poorer member states through its structural and cohesion funds, distributing almost €400 billion from 2021 to 2027.
- ✅ The EU Global Gateway Initiative, launched in 2021, is a values-based alternative to China's Belt and Road Initiative: €300 billion for infrastructure, digital, climate and energy projects in Africa, funded by 'Team Europe': the EU and its members.
- ✅ ASEAN has expanded access to quality education for marginalised communities in remote areas. Since Covid-19, it has supported access to healthcare and vaccinations.
- ✅ USMCA has supported Mexican manufacturing workers' incomes, particularly in the automotive industry.

The benefits of economic cooperation are uneven, leaving some members behind in poverty.

- ✖ The Eurozone crisis left Greece with unemployment above 20 per cent, creating a 'brain drain' of skilled professionals to wealthier states. The EU/IMF bailout enforced austerity measures until 2018, weakening its economy for several years.
- ✖ The African Union lacks funding to address the scale of development needed in poorer states, which struggle with food and water insecurity and conflict.
- ✖ Within ASEAN, huge wealth disparities make it hard for Laos and Cambodia to compete with the advanced economies of Singapore and Malaysia.
- ✖ USMCA has been less effective at tackling rural poverty in Mexico.

Conflict

Regional organisations enhance security and reduce conflict through collective action.

- ✔ The EU was awarded the Nobel Peace Prize in 2012 for maintaining peace among its members. Its Permanent Structured Cooperation (PESCO), launched in 2017, has improved defence collaboration among member states.
- ✔ The AU has a Peace and Security Council with intervention powers and an African Standby Force. It has sent peacekeepers to numerous conflicts, including Burundi (AMIB) and Somalia (AMISOM). It suspended Sudan after a military coup in 2019 and sent envoys to mediate during Sudan's civil war.
- ✔ ASEAN established its Regional Forum in 1994 to support dialogue on security challenges. It warned the United States and China over the risks of conflict in the Taiwan Strait.

Regional organisations often fail to prevent or resolve conflicts.

- ✖ The EU relied on the United States to lead NATO interventions in the 1990s Balkan wars.
- ✖ The AU relies heavily on external funding for peacekeeping, limiting its ability to respond to global power interventions: e.g. Russia in the Sahel, and the UAE in Sudan.
- ✖ Due to its members' differing collective interests, ASEAN has failed to act collectively to challenge China's expansionism in the South China Sea.

   The Arab League failed to resolve conflicts in Syria, Libya and Yemen.

Human rights

Regional organisations promote human rights and intervene when necessary.

- ✔ The EU has a legally binding Charter of Fundamental Rights. It provides humanitarian missions, and its members support the International Criminal Court.
- ✔ The African Union's Peace and Security Council intervenes in crimes against humanity, such as the African Union Mission in Sudan (AMIS) in 2004 in Darfur.
- ✔ ASEAN has created an Intergovernmental Commission on Human Rights to promote initiatives, for example anti-trafficking measures.

Regional organisations often lack the authority or willingness to enforce human rights.

- ✖ The EU has failed to address some violations of its charter, e.g. LGBTQ+ rights in Hungary. In 2025, Hungary decided to leave the ICC when it hosted Israeli Prime Minister Netanyahu, ignoring an ICC arrest warrant.
- ✖ The AU PSC lacked the resources and political will to stop genocide in Sudan from 2023.

   ASEAN's emphasis on non-interference hindered its ability to address the genocide of the Rohingya in Myanmar.
- ✖ Apart from suspending Syria and Libya for attacking their civilians, the Arab League has not challenged human rights violations among its members, despite adopting the Arab Charter on Human Rights in 2004.

The Environment
Regional organisations contribute to environmental protection.

- ✅ Since 2021, the European Green Deal supports the European Climate Law with renewable energy investment and the Carbon Border Adjustment Mechanism, aiming for net-zero emissions by 2050.
- ✅ ASEAN made a regional agreement on cross-border haze pollution from forest fires. USMCA dropped an Investor-State Dispute Settlement (ISDS) procedure between the United States and Canada, removing the power for corporations to challenge environmental regulations.

Environmental efforts often lack sufficient ambition or unity.

- ❌ Poland opposed stricter EU carbon emission regulations due to economic concerns.
- ❌ There are significant problems with deforestation and logging in ASEAN.
- ❌ USMCA kept ISDS for oil, gas and energy between the United States and Mexico, so corporate lawsuits could still prevent Mexico from strengthening environmental protections.

Key Debate Summary: Have regional organisations impacted positively on poverty, conflict, human rights and the environment?

	Positive Impacts	Negative Impacts
Poverty	✓ Regional organisations reduce poverty by promoting economic cooperation and development, especially the EU and ASEAN	✗ The benefits of economic cooperation are uneven, leaving some members behind in poverty, particularly in ASEAN, the AU and the USMCA
Conflict	✓ Regional organisations enhance security and reduce conflict through collective action, particularly the EU and AU	✗ Regional organisations sometimes fail to prevent or resolve conflicts, particularly the Arab League
Human Rights	✓ Regional organisations promote human rights, and they intervene when necessary, particularly the EU and the AU	✗ Regional organisations often lack the authority or willingness to enforce human rights, particularly ASEAN and the Arab League, and sometimes the AU and the EU
Environment	✓ Regional organisations contribute to environmental protection – particularly the EU	✗ Environmental efforts often lack sufficient ambition or unity, particularly ASEAN and the USMCA

Chapter Summary

- Regionalism supports collaboration among neighbouring states to enhance economic, security and political stability.

- Old regionalism was mostly driven by Cold War bipolarity and security concerns. New regionalism is more complex and varied, responding to globalisation by protecting its members' interests in some ways and by integrating them into the wider global economy, promoting wider global partnerships and collective action in IGOs.

- Regionalism can constrain state sovereignty, but more often it enhances it by strengthening collective influence and creating economic growth and stability.

- The EU's integration is both broad and deep, encompassing shared values, intergovernmental and supranational institutions and lawmaking, the Area of Freedom Justice and Security, Economic and Monetary Union (the single market and Eurozone) and coordinated foreign and security policies. It has grown from 6 to 28, now 27 member states, with further expansion plans. Disunity is a concern.

- The EU has some federal characteristics, including legislative power and monetary union, but more closely resembles a confederation of sovereign states in other ways.

- The EU is a globally significant actor in many ways, including its economic and soft power. It has some strong structural powers but has limited military influence.

- The EU has had substantial impacts on poverty reduction, human rights promotion and environmental sustainability. The impacts of ASEAN and the Arab League on conflict and human rights are limited by their emphasis on state sovereignty and political divisions, whilst the impacts of the African Union on poverty, conflict and human rights are limited by resource constraints and political divisions. NAFTA/USMCA is the narrowest of the organisations, with some impacts on poverty in Mexico.

Exam Style Questions

- Examine the different ways in which political and economic factors have led to regionalism. (12)
- Examine the similarities between the African Union and the European Union. (12)
- Examine the intergovernmental and supranational features of the European Union. (12)
- Examine the differences between the Arab League and the African Union. (12)
- Evaluate the view that regionalism promotes globalisation. (30)
- Evaluate the view that regionalism strengthens the sovereignty of its members. (30)
- Evaluate the view that the European Union is a significant global actor. (30)
- Evaluate the view that the EU has become a federal state, similar to the United States. (30)

Further Resources

The Council on Foreign Relations is a US-based non-partisan foreign policy education publisher which provides accessible and useful articles on regional organisations:

https://www.cfr.org/backgrounder/arab-league. 'The Arab League'.

https://www.cfr.org/backgrounder/naftas-economic-impact. 'NAFTA and the USMCA: Weighing the Impact of North American Trade'.

https://www.cfr.org/expert-brief/trump-and-future-usmca. 'Trump and the Future of the USMCA'.

https://www.cfr.org/backgrounder/role-peacekeeping-africa. 'The Role of Peacekeeping in Africa: An explanation of how the African Union, UN and EU work together on peacekeeping'.

https://www.cfr.org/backgrounder/what-asean. 'What Is ASEAN?'

https://www.cfr.org/backgrounder/how-does-european-union-work. 'How Does the European Union Work?'.

https://www.youtube.com/watch?v=O37yJBFRrfg. 'The European Union Explained'.

https://education.cfr.org/learn/reading/european-union-worlds-biggest-sovereignty-experiment. 'The European Union: The World's Biggest Sovereignty Experiment'.

https://www.forbes.com/sites/mikeosullivan/2022/09/17/could-europe-become-a-geopolitical-superpower/?sh=dbf076b3f034. 'Could Europe Become a Geopolitical Superpower?' A brief discussion of the EU's potential superpower status, written in 2022.

Visit https://bloomsbury.pub/essentials-of-global-politics to access additional materials to support teaching and learning.

10 EXAM FOCUS

Introduction

This chapter aims to guide you through Component Three (Global Politics) of your exam, demonstrating how to approach its three different question types while effectively meeting the Assessment Objectives (AOs) and Levels-Based Mark Schemes (LBMS).

The chapter first provides an initial overview of some of the essential aspects of Component Three: the exam paper, the three AOs, the idea of 'synopticity', the requirement for 'balanced' answers and how to approach the three different question types. The chapter will use real student extracts to help illustrate the do's and don'ts of the Global Politics paper. Finally, at the end of the chapter, these skills are brought together in complete question answers.

The exam

The Global Politics content of the course is examined in a single exam, Component Three.

Table 10.1 Breakdown of Component Three

Component Three Length: 2 Hours Total Marks Available: 84 Marks
Section A: » ONE question from a choice of TWO » Total marks available – 12 » Approximate time in the exam – 15 minutes
Section B: » ONE question from a choice of ONE – this is your **compulsory** Comparative Theory question » Total marks available – 12 » Approximate time in the exam – 15 minutes
Section C: » TWO questions from a choice of THREE » Total marks available – 60 » Approximate time in the exam – 90 minutes (45 minutes per question)

Component Three is split into three Sections: A, B and C. Table 10.1 provides a breakdown of the total marks available in each section and an approximate guide for how much time you should spend on each of the Sections.

One of the key challenges of the A Level Politics exams is time management. The two-hour paper is a key reason why many students feel anxious about the exam, because they are concerned they will not complete it within the time limit. We will return to this issue throughout this chapter when we look at the different types of question structures – we will give you specific advice for how to manage this difficult aspect of the exam, which will build your confidence! Good preparation supports time management. The idiom 'proper planning prevents poor performance' is worth repeating to yourself.

The types of questions

Component 3 has three question types:

- Section A – comparative politics question – 12 marks
- Section B – comparative theory question – 12 marks
- Section C – essay questions – 30 marks each

It is important to note that in both Section A and B **ONLY** AO1 and AO2 are being assessed, and each AO accounts for 6 marks out of the total 12 marks available. Whereas in Section C questions, **ALL** of the 3 AOs are assessed and each accounts for 10 marks of the 30 marks available.

> See page 336 for further information about the AOs and how to incorporate them into your answers.

Section A: Comparative Politics questions

In Section A, Comparative Politics questions always begin with the question stem 'Examine ... ' The Cambridge Dictionary defines examine as 'to look at or consider a person or thing carefully and in detail in order to discover something about them'. In other words, the question asks you to consider and explore aspects of global politics in-depth. These questions will always ask you to examine **two** aspects of global politics. These two aspects of global politics will be selected from the following material:

- Political **institutions**, e.g. states, IGOs, RGOs, civil society actors, etc.
- Political **processes**, e.g. globalisation, regionalism, power relations, etc.
- Political **concepts**, e.g. power, sovereignty, hegemon, etc.
- Political **theories**, e.g. deep or shallow-green ecology, hyperglobalism, transformationalist or sceptics, realist and liberal views on globalisation, etc.
- Political **issues** including human rights, the environment, poverty and conflict.

In relation to these aspects of global politics, you will be asked a range of comparative questions. These questions **normally** focus on their similarities, differences, strengths, weaknesses or effectiveness. For example, in the 2024 Component Three exam, one Comparative Politics question was, 'Examine the weaknesses of both the IMF and the World Bank'. Here, the question asks students to look at **weaknesses** of two different political institutions. We will explore exactly how you can approach these types of questions later in the chapter.

Comparative Politics questions are marked out of 12, which are allocated as follows: AO1 – 6 marks, AO2 – 6 marks.

Section B: Comparative Theory question

Section B is the Comparative Theory question. This section focuses on the international relations theories of realism and liberalism, including their views on the anarchical society and society of states theory. You have only **one choice of question** and therefore must answer it. The Comparative Theory question in Section B will always begin with the stem 'Analyse' (*we discuss the meaning of analyse in relation to AO2 on p. 337*). It will also be focused on 'differences' between the two theories over a specific issue, including their views on the anarchical society and society of states theory. For example,

Exam Tip: The vast amount of material for A Level Politics can feel overwhelming, but these are our strategies to help you:

1. Aim to learn **enough material** from each topic to enable you to answer a question on it in the depth you would like.

2. Review the **comparative analysis** and **key debates** throughout this book paying attention to the themes identified.

3. **Practise** writing questions in **timed conditions.** You can use the questions included in this textbook as a starting point.

4. Keep abreast of the latest **developments in the news** so that you can include at least one very recent example to showcase your knowledge and understanding of global politics.

Exam Tip: Section A will not ask a question about realist and liberal theories unless it relates to their views of globalisation.

in the 2025 Component Three exam, the Section B compulsory question was, 'Analyse the differences between the realist and liberal views of the inevitability of war'. Here, the question asks you to look at the differences concerning the 'inevitability of war'.

Similar to Section A questions, Comparative Theory questions are also marked out of 12, which are allocated as follows: AO1 – 6 marks, AO2 – 6 marks.

Section C: Essay questions

Section C essays are breadth questions which require you to cover a range of topics across the course in your answers. The essay questions in Section C will always begin with the stem 'Evaluate the view that … ' (*we discuss the meaning of evaluate in relation to AO3 on p. 337*). This question will be followed with a statement for you to consider, for example in the Component Three exam in 2020, the question was 'Evaluate the view that global governance is more concerned with economic issues rather than human rights issues'. Here, the question is expressing a clear point of view, and it is your task to consider both sides of the argument (*i.e. either economic or human rights global governance is more established than the other*) and consistently argue throughout the essay that one side of the argument is stronger than the other before making a substantiated or justified conclusion.

Whilst Section C questions can (*and often do*) appear to be based upon single areas of the specification, they sometimes do cover different topics from the specification. Irrespective of the breadth of the question, it is the students who recognise the connections between the different topics that often achieve the higher levels in these essays. For example, in the 2024 Component Three exam, one essay question was, 'Evaluate the view that states find the use of hard power to be more effective than soft power'. Whilst this question is based within the 'Power and Developments' topic, students could consider the impact that being members of IGOs or RGOs have on state power across different issue areas, such as Environmental or Economic Global Governance, therefore drawing upon a broad range of topics from the course.

Essay questions are marked out of 30, which are allocated as follows: AO1 – 10 marks, AO2 – 10 marks, AO3 – 10 marks.

Introduction to the Assessment Objectives (AOs)

This section provides a brief introduction to the AOs. Later in the chapter, we will explore ways to incorporate them into answers and look at good (and not so good) examples of them used in practice.

AO1

> 'Demonstrate knowledge and understanding of political institutions, processes, concepts, theories and issues.'

As with Components One and Two, students often feel most comfortable with AO1, which covers their 'knowledge and understanding' of topics. This is unsurprising since lessons often begin with the acquisition of AO1 knowledge and understanding rather than the skills required for AO2 and AO3.

AO1 knowledge and understanding forms the basis of the chapters throughout this book. It is important because without knowledge and understanding, it is not possible to achieve high marks in AO2 and AO3. These skills depend on a solid background knowledge of the subject (AO1) to support the arguments you make. That said, it is possible to achieve **some** marks in AO2 and AO3 with weaker knowledge. This should reassure you if you feel like you cannot access a particular 12 or 30-mark question on the exam paper. This is because with even limited knowledge, you can still acquire some marks (*especially if you follow the advice in this chapter!*)

AO2

> 'Analyse aspects of politics and political information, including in relation to parallels, connections, similarities and differences.'

AO2 requires you to **analyse** aspects of global politics. But what does analysis look like in practice? The Cambridge Dictionary states it includes the 'detailed examination' or 'the process of examining' something. Looking at the levels-based mark scheme, AO2 consists of two parts. First, it requires you to break down your arguments into logical chains of reasoning. Second, it asks you to identify the parallels, connections, similarities and differences between different institutions, processes, concepts, theories and issues. We explore these two parts further on pages 341–344 of this chapter.

AO3

> 'Evaluate aspects of politics and political information, including to construct arguments, make substantiated judgements and draw conclusions.'

AO3 relates to evaluation. Dictionary definitions outline that it requires you to 'judge the importance or value of something' or to 'make judgements about them, for example how good or bad they are'. Since AO3 is only relevant to Section C questions, it is only necessary to use it in the 30-mark essays. It requires you to reach **judgements** about global politics. In order to make convincing judgements, you will need to show knowledge and understanding (AO1) and be able to examine and compare information (AO2) in order to reach a judgement about which side of the argument is stronger (AO3).

Synopticity in global politics

Synopticity refers to being able to make connections across a range of material, in other words, how one aspect of global politics affects another or the similarities and differences between two aspects of global politics. This allows you to highlight your broader understanding of how institutions, processes, concepts, theories and issues in global politics are related to one another. In order to access the higher levels on the mark scheme, you will be expected to show this type of synopticity across topics in your answers.

Synopticity in Component 3 is **only assessed** in your Section B compulsory question. In these questions, you are required to make a synoptic link to Component 1 – Core Ideas. This means selecting relevant AO1 knowledge from the core ideas of conservatism, liberalism or socialism. If you do not include a clear synoptic link, you will be capped at L3 in your answer. This means you will not be able to score above 9 out of the 12 available marks, irrespective of how strong your AO1 and AO2 are.

Breadth of questions

Building on the idea of synopticity, this chapter also emphasises connectivity within Component Three, or showing a breadth of knowledge and understanding. This means that students are able to make connections and links across different topics studied within global politics. It helps for you to visualise your Global Politics topics as a whole body of knowledge as opposed to individual discernible topics. For example, you may discuss the success of different areas of global governance, such as economic or political, in relation to the power of states. In this sense, the success of global governance institutions is often dependent on the support of the most powerful states in the system. Here, you would be using knowledge from three different topics, including Power and Developments, and Global Governance: Political and Economic.

Often, essay questions will cover more than one area of the course, but where they do not, the ability to show these connections is a strong differentiator between student answers. Students who score high

Component III: Global Politics

> **Exam Tip:**
> Stronger answers will often incorporate the ideas of realism and liberalism into their answers. Whilst this is not a requirement of Section A and C essays (*unless otherwise stated in the question*), it can help differentiate between stronger and weaker answers and will help you to score additional marks in AO1 and AO2.

marks, especially in Section C essays, are often able to show these links, and by doing so, they increase their chances of attaining high levels across all three AOs.

In Component Three, the topics covered are the state and globalisation, power and developments, regionalism and the European Union, global governance (political and economic), and global governance (human rights and the environment). Both Section A and C questions may well incorporate aspects of any two (or more) of these topics. See Table 10.2 for examples.

In order to prepare effectively for the exams, students and teachers should try to make up their own questions by combining different aspects of the topics. There are also different revision activities you could try to help you make the connections between topics (see Table 10.3).

Showing balance in your answers

It is important that your answers **show balance** – achieving balance looks different depending on the question type. In a Section A and B question, balance refers to giving both aspects of the question roughly equal treatment. In a Section C question, balance means you should give both sides of the argument roughly equal treatment. The instruction on the question paper says 'You must consider this view and the alternative to this view in a balanced way'. However, showing balance does not mean your judgement should sit on the fence; see the section below for more information about AO3.

So, what does balance mean? While it is not necessary to ensure you have an even word count of arguments in favour compared to arguments against in your answer, it is also important to ensure that both sides of the argument have been fairly considered. So, a 60:40 split is probably fine, but anything significantly less than that may not be considered balanced.

The consequence of not having balance across your answers is that they will probably not reach above Level 2 on the mark scheme. For a Section A and B question, this would cap your marks at 6 out of 12 marks. For a Section C question, this would cap your marks at 12 out of 30.

> **Exam Tip:**
> If a question asks you about three aspects of global politics and you demonstrate strong AO1 knowledge about only two of these aspects, you could be capped at Level 2. This is because your answer would lack balance because it has not looked at the third aspect identified in the question. Only answer a question if you can cover all parts of it!

Table 10.2 Example Cross-Topic Questions

Example Section A Questions (12 Marks)	Example Section C Questions (30 Marks)
• Examine the differences between the United Nations General Assembly and the International Criminal Court • Examine the distinctions between globalisation and global governance • Examine the strengths of civil society actors and international organisations	• Evaluate the view that the effectiveness of global governance depends upon the polarity of the international system • Evaluate the view that the UN is powerless to tackle global challenges because it has limited hard power • Evaluate the view that the European Union is better able to tackle global challenges than the sovereign state

Table 10.3 Revision Tips

- Make a **poster** with cross-topic institutions, processes, concepts and theories and issues, and draw connecting lines between them explaining the links
- Record a **podcast** of the 'story' of Global Politics – you could do this chronologically or using different themes such as 'evolving cooperation', 'the struggle for human rights' for example
- Make a **card game**. On individual pieces of card, write the names of all the different institutions, processes, concepts, theories and issues covered in your Global Politics Course. Draw two cards at a time, and score a point for each different link you identify between them

Assessment objectives in detail

We introduced the AOs at the beginning of this chapter, but now we are going to look at them in more detail.

AO1 in detail

> Demonstrate knowledge and understanding of political institutions, processes, concepts, theories and issues'

AO1 marks are awarded for demonstrating 'knowledge and understanding'. AO1 is demonstrated by showing the examiner what you know that is relevant to a question. AO1 can be shown in a number of different ways, and it helps to think about AO1 as relating to your knowledge and understanding of:

- Institutions
- Processes
- Concepts
- Theories
- Issues

When thinking about your answer to a question, you first start with AO1. The key is to carefully select the knowledge you think will best help you to answer the question. A key concern of students is how much knowledge they should include. To answer this, look at Table 10.4.

The table below identifies the levels-based mark scheme in relation to AO1. You should notice that in the lower levels, only some of your selected knowledge might be relevant and accurate. As you move toward the higher levels, your knowledge must become increasingly accurate and carefully selected so it is relevant to the question. Given the time constraints in the exam, it is not possible to include all the knowledge you have in relation to a question. Therefore, accessing the higher levels hinges on effective knowledge selection – an often underrated skill for AO1, yet one explicitly recognised in the mark scheme.

Students tend to find it easier to talk about political institutions and issues, but more challenging to talk about processes, concepts and theories, since these are far more abstract. Therefore, it is a good idea to familiarise yourself with the key concepts identified on the specification – which are signposted in green boxes throughout this textbook. Not only does strong conceptual knowledge help improve your AO1 score, it also provides a lens through which to analyse and evaluate issues in global politics,

Table 10.4 LBMS for AO1

Level	Level Descriptor
Level 1	'Demonstrates **superficial** knowledge and understanding ... with **limited underpinning** of analysis and evaluation'
Level 2	'Demonstrates **some accurate** knowledge and understanding ... **some** of which are **selected appropriately** in order to underpin analysis and evaluation'
Level 3	'Demonstrates **mostly accurate** knowledge and understanding ... **many** of which are **selected appropriately** in order to underpin analysis and evaluation'
Level 4	'Demonstrates **accurate** knowledge and understanding ... which are **carefully selected** in order to underpin analysis and evaluation'
Section C Questions Only Level 5	'Demonstrates **thorough and in-depth** knowledge and understanding ... which are **effectively selected** in order to underpin analysis and evaluation'

therefore also helping you to achieve marks in AO2 and AO3 (see X for further information). It is important to remember that concepts in global politics are almost always contested – i.e. their meaning is not universally agreed. This means there are different interpretations or ways of looking at concepts. If you recognise this in your answers, you are showing depth of knowledge.

STUDENT EXTRACT – 'Evaluate the view that state sovereignty is now irrelevant in global politics?' (30) – Looking at AO1

EXTRACT 1

Some argue that state sovereignty is becoming irrelevant, particularly its external aspect, due to economic globalisation. The massive, uncontrolled flow of goods, services and money across borders makes it difficult for states to maintain independent economic policies. For example, a global financial crisis, like the one in 2008, showed how quickly external economic shocks can affect national economies, forcing states to accept international aid with conditions from bodies like the IMF, thus limiting their freedom to act externally. However, while external economic pressures are undeniable, states retain significant internal sovereignty over their economic structures. Governments still decide their national budgets, tax rates and whether to open their markets to foreign investment. The recent US-China trade war saw both nations assert their internal sovereign right to impose tariffs, demonstrating that states, especially powerful ones, maintain the ultimate authority to regulate their domestic economy, even if it creates international friction.

> Here the student is showing accurate knowledge about specific types of globalisation and state sovereignty.

> Great use of the Global Financial Crisis to develop the AO1. It could be improved by giving a specific example of a state that received aid with conditions attached.

> Good cross-topic knowledge of how this issue affects powerful states differently.

Some people think that state sovereignty is not as important anymore because of globalisation. This means that trade, money and information move very easily between countries. For example, if there's a big economic problem in one country, like a financial crisis, it can quickly spread and affect many other states. This shows that states cannot fully control their own economies like they used to, and they often have to get help from international groups. However, states still have a lot of control over their money and what happens inside their country. They can decide how much tax to collect or what rules to make for their own businesses. So, while globalisation makes things complicated, states still try to be in charge of their economy.

> Throughout their whole answer, this student has been vague about concepts and examples, which reduces the effectiveness of their AO1.

AO1 knowledge can also include examples which, when used well, can lift ordinary AO1 to really good AO1. Some students underuse their examples, often making a cursory remark about a specific example without showing enough specific knowledge about it or linking it to analysis and evaluation. For example, in extract two above, the student uses no specific examples.

Again, it is common for students (and teachers) to become overly concerned about using the most recent examples. Whilst some recent examples (i.e. within the previous 12 months) can help distinguish stronger and weaker answers, it is not always necessary to use these in order to access the top levels. There are some topics where it is not possible to write an answer without using older examples. For example, it is not possible to analyse and evaluate humanitarian intervention without reference to interventions carried out in the 1990s (examples which are now 2–3 decades old!) The key is to use well-selected and relevant examples to showcase your knowledge on a particular topic.

Many high-achieving students get lost in the detail of AO1 to the detriment of deploying AO2 and AO3. They consequently achieve lower marks than their AO1 would merit. It is important for students to remember that AO1 is only worth 38 per cent of Component Three: it is worth 6 marks in 12-mark questions and 10 marks in 30-mark questions. Knowing when you have included enough knowledge is a key skill in itself. The examiner more than anything else is checking that the knowledge you **have used** is relevant, specific and well-selected to suit the question being asked.

STUDENT EXTRACT – 'Evaluate the view that humanitarian intervention is no longer relevant in global politics' (30) – looking at AO1 examples.

It can be argued that humanitarian intervention is becoming less relevant in global politics, largely due to powerful states prioritising their national interests. This aligns with realist thinking, where states act for their own security, not altruism. For example, President Donald Trump's 'America First' policy reduced US commitment to overseas interventions unless directly beneficial to its national interests. Similarly, the UK cut its development aid from 0.7 per cent to 0.5 per cent, reflecting a shift towards domestic spending over international humanitarian efforts. This trend suggests declining political will for costly interventions purely to 'save strangers'. While human rights abuses are condemned, direct action is increasingly avoided unless a state's own strategic interests are clearly at stake, showing humanitarian intervention's diminishing relevance.

> Throughout this extract, the student is showing specific knowledge of real-world examples. It could be improved by linking it more specifically to the issue of why humanitarian intervention itself is becoming less relevant.

AO2 in detail

> 'Analyse aspects of politics and political information, including in relation to parallels, connections, similarities and differences.'

AO2 marks are awarded for being able to 'analyse aspects of politics'. It can be broken down into two parts:
- Breaking down arguments into logical chains of reasoning
- Identifying the parallels, connections, similarities and differences within political information

The first aspect of AO2 is 'breaking down arguments into logical chains of reasoning'. Out of the two parts of AO2, this is often the part which is underdeveloped in student exam responses and usually separates strong and weak student answers. Essentially, this means that once you have identified an argument in relation to a question, you are able to show how you have reached this argument step-by-step with evidence.

It helps to compare this skill to a GCSE Mathematics exam, where you achieve marks by showing your 'working out'. In this respect, by taking apart your argument, you are showing your working out.

It also helps to imagine you are in a Court presenting an argument to both the Judge and Jury. You would not simply say, 'This person is guilty of committing the murder because they were found near the body of the victim with a gun'. This is not enough evidence to convict the person of murder and is only circumstantial. Instead, you could add additional knowledge (AO1) and spell out the following logical chains of reasoning after the initial argument to develop your analysis (AO2):
- This is because the person's fingerprints were on the gun, which was used in the murder, suggesting they were the last person to hold the gun.
- Furthermore, the person had gunshot residue on their right hand, suggesting they had fired the gun.

Applying this to a global politics context, we could break down the following argument – 'A key strength of the Group of 20 is that it includes the majority of the world's major economic powers'. We could add the following logical chains of reasoning to improve its AO2:

- This is because it includes the twenty most powerful economies, which represent approximately 85 per cent of global GDP, including the United States and China, which are the two largest global economies.
- Because it represents the majority of the world's wealth, it means the decisions it makes will have far-reaching implications on the global economy through the immediate effect on its own members and non-member states, who themselves are influenced by their relationships with the member states themselves.
- We see this impact in response to the Global Financial Crisis in 2008, where the G20 rapidly coordinated a global response to avoid a return to protectionism. This included pledging over $1 trillion in additional reserves to the IMF and multilateral development banks, committing to fiscal stimulus measures and agreeing a framework for strengthening financial regulation and supervision.

When it comes to making logical chains of reasoning, some students simply give lots of AO1 information, but then fail to use it to develop AO2. So how can AO1 information be credited with both AO1 and AO2 marks? This comes down to the **language** a student uses in their answer. By using analytical language, an essay can signpost to the examiner that they are in fact using both AO1 and AO2.

STUDENT EXTRACT – Examine the differences between cultural and economic globalisation (12) – looking at how to develop examples

Economic globalisation is criticised for making societies more unequal and promoting excessive consumerism. For example, lots of people around the world own Apple iPhones. While it can boost overall wealth, the benefits do not spread fairly, with rich countries and big companies gaining most, often harming poorer states.

> The student has identified a relevant example to highlight consumerism, however, only uses it as AO1 knowledge and understanding. If they had explained what this suggests about consumerism, it would also count as AO2 analysis.

STUDENT EXTRACT – Analyse the different explanations which realism and liberalism provide for recent developments in global politics since 2000 concerning the state and globalisation (12) – looking at the use of examples

Realists would argue that Russia's invasion of Ukraine in 2022 is an example of an offensive realist foreign policy. This is because using conflict to acquire territory can be useful for a state to maximise its power and secure its survival. States are concerned about maximising their power in relation to other states because they prioritise relative gains. Here, Russia is trying to increase its power in relation to both Ukraine and its allies in NATO and the European Union, by weakening them through the invasion. Ukraine is weakened because it does not govern within its borders, and the war is costly in lives and resources. For NATO and the EU, their military and economic support to Ukraine is weakening their military and economic power.

> This student successfully integrates their example of Russia's invasion of Ukraine (AO1) into their analysis (AO2).

The second aspect of AO2 is where students show parallels, connections, similarities and differences between global politics information. Many students find this the more accessible aspect of AO2. However, this skill is deployed with varying effectiveness by students in the exam. You can signpost that you are doing this to the examiner through your use of language (see Table 10.5).

AO2 requires students to show parallels, connections, similarities and differences.

Throughout this book, we have paired our explanations in the comparative analysis tables and our arguments in the key debates. This allows us to make direct comparisons and to argue and counter argue points that are precisely opposed to each other. We suggest that you take a similar approach in your essays, as this is a straightforward way to achieve AO2 marks.

So, for example, in a 12 mark question you would compare the two institutions, processes, concepts, theories or issues in the question in each paragraph you write, rather than writing one paragraph on each.

In section C questions, you could match up each argument with a corresponding counter-argument, rather than proposing all your counter arguments followed by all your counter-arguments.

If, in an exam situation, you cannot identify paired arguments, don't worry. This is simply one means of achieving AO2 marks. There are other ways to introduce comparison that can also achieve high marks.

When the examiner marks your answers, they will select the appropriate level on the levels-based mark scheme that your use of AO2 best meets. See Table 10.6 for the differentiators across AO2.

> **Definition**
>
> **Paired argument:** Two aspects of global politics are compared across a related theme.
>
> **Unpaired argument:** Two aspects of global politics are compared, which bear no relation to one another.

Exam Tip: It is important to note that the mark scheme does not require students to 'pair' arguments. Students can also use 'unpaired' arguments and still achieve high marks. What is important is that arguments are compared.

Table 10.5 Examples of paired and unpaired arguments on ecologism (see chapter 7: Environmental Global Governance)

Unpaired Argument	Paired Argument
Deep-green ecologists believe our environmental problems (like pollution or deforestation) are not separate issues. Instead, they see them as a direct result of anthropocentrism and the capitalist economy that is built on it. They think these deeply rooted ideas and systems are the real cause of the crisis. Shallow-green ecologists propose sustainable development to tackle climate change. They support small adjustments to current systems – making them greener and more efficient – can work. Their goal is to maintain economic growth and human well-being through regulations, technology and incentives, without major societal overhauls.	Deep-green ecologists champion ecocentrism, valuing the natural world – all its parts – as inherently equal to humans. They see humanity as part of nature, not its superior. Shallow-green ecologists, in comparison, primarily follow anthropocentrism, placing human value above nature. They value the environment mainly for its use to people – as a resource or service provider.
Why is this an **unpaired** argument? This is unpaired because the statement about deep-green ecology is looking at what its **overall argument** is, whereas the statement about shallow-green ecology is looking at the **solutions** proposed by it.	Why is this a **paired** argument? This is paired because both statements are directly looking at the philosophical underpinnings of each theory – ecologism versus anthropocentrism.

Table 10.6 LBMS for AO2

Level	Level Descriptor
Level 1	'**Limited** comparative analysis … with **partial**, logical chains of reasoning … which makes **simplistic connections** between ideas and concepts'
Level 2	'**Some emerging** comparative analysis … with **some focused**, logical chains of reasoning … which make **some relevant connections** between ideas and concepts'
Level 3	'**Mostly focused** comparative analysis … with **focused**, logical chains of reasoning … which make **mostly relevant** connections between ideas and concepts'
Level 4	'**Consistent** comparative analysis … with **coherent**, logical chains of reasoning … which make **relevant** connections between ideas and concepts'
Section C Questions Only Level 5	'**Perceptive** comparative analysis … with **sustained**, logical chains of reasoning … which make **cohesive and convincing** connections between ideas and concepts'

AO3 in detail

> '*Evaluate aspects of politics and political information, including to construct arguments, make substantiated judgements and draw conclusions.*'

AO3 requires students to evaluate global politics. Evaluation requires pupils to make judgements about global politics and reach substantiated conclusions. As already outlined, marks are only awarded for AO3 in Section C questions.

Using the levels-based mark scheme in Table 10.7, it helps to view AO3 as three parts:

1. Has the answer identified relevant arguments in relation to the question?
2. Has the student reached judgements and conclusions?
3. Are judgements and conclusions substantiated?

Table 10.7 LBMS for AO3

Level	Level Descriptor
Level 1	'Makes **superficial** evaluation … constructing **simple** arguments and judgements, many which are **descriptive** and lead to **limited unsubstantiated** conclusions'
Level 2	'Constructs **some relevant** evaluation … constructing **occasionally effective** arguments and judgements, **some** are **partially substantiated** and lead to **generic** conclusions **without much justification**'
Level 3	'Constructs **generally relevant** evaluation … constructing **generally effective** arguments and judgements, **many** of which are **substantiated** and lead to **some focused** conclusions that are **sometimes justified**'
Level 4	'Constructs **mostly relevant** evaluation of aspects … constructing **mostly effective** arguments and judgements, which are **mostly substantiated** and lead to **mostly focused, justified conclusions**'
Section C Questions Only Level 5	'Constructs fully **relevant evaluation** … constructing **fully effective substantiated** arguments and judgements, which are **consistently substantiated** and lead to fully focused and justified' conclusions

Exam Tip: Judgements refer to interim judgements about specific themes or factors. Conclusions bring together judgements to reach an overall argument.

Relevant arguments

The first part concerns whether the student has constructed an argument. This means that the essay identifies a number of arguments in relation to the question. For example, let's look at the Section C question 'Evaluate the View that the EU is not a Global Actor' (30). The following sentence is an argument relating to the question, 'The European Union does act as a global actor in respect of its economic policies'. The following sentence is not an argument: 'The European Union has its own economic policies'. This is because it does not make any reference to the question, so it is not an argument because it is not related to the question.

Judgements and conclusions

The second part of AO3 concerns the question of whether a student has made judgements and conclusions. This means that, having considered both sides of the argument, you come down on one side of it. To achieve the highest marks here, you should have judgements and conclusions that run through the answer from its beginning to its end:

✓ Overall argument is outlined in the introduction

✓ Overall argument is revisited and justified in interim conclusions

✓ Overall argument is reaffirmed and justified in the final conclusion

We will revisit this again later in this chapter, where we look at the structure of Section C essays. However, the point cannot be overstated. The essay should clearly state in the introduction whether it supports the statement in the question, and the answer to this will be a clear 'yes' or 'no'. Your answers could use the following sentence starter: 'This essay will argue that it does/does not (*delete as appropriate*) support the statement that [insert question]'. Additionally, at the end of each analytical paragraph, there should be an interim judgement. Here, the essay should weigh up the two arguments outlined in the paragraph and outline your conclusion in relation to the question. Finally, the essay should reach an overall conclusion, where it brings together each of the interim judgements to support its overall argument. Importantly, each judgement should be consistent: do not change your mind halfway through!

If an essay contains all three of the aspects in the tick boxes, it is likely that it will reach a Level 3 in AO3, which is the equivalent of 5–6 marks out of the 10 available marks. Therefore, you should be able to access the majority of the marks available in AO3. To achieve higher than L3 in AO3 requires you to make substantiated judgements.

Substantiated judgements

The final part of AO3 concerns the use of 'substantiated judgements'. This is the hardest part of AO3, and to successfully achieve this (in addition to the above aforementioned points), would mean the essay is likely to achieve a Level 4 or 5 in AO3. Again, it helps to liken it to a GCSE Mathematics exam, whereby you need to show your 'working out' in order to achieve the maximum marks available. In other words, strong AO3 needs to show your 'working out'. In other words, what are the merits to each side of the argument and why is your chosen (winning) side more convincing. A L5 answer will clearly show the criteria by which it has reached its judgement. An examiner might not personally agree with the judgement, but will be convinced by it on the basis of the information provided in the essay.

Before moving on, it is important that we say something about the question of nuance within AO3. Students AO3 marks can be achieved by an essay with a clear line of argument. This means that it consistently supports one side of the debate rather than switching sides mid-essay or attempting to 'sit on the fence' by accepting both sides. However, this does not mean that you have to strongly champion one view whilst completely discounting the merits of the opposing view. A debate can be won by a narrow margin as well as by a huge margin, and it may be that on some issues the winner is clear, but on others it is not so clear. Therefore, students can differentiate their answers by referring to the strengths or limitations of specific arguments in favour of or against a statement. For example, a student may decide that global governance is more successful at addressing climate change than human rights, but of the three arguments in favour of the proposition, one of these holds the most weight.

The language you use can signpost to the examiner that you are using AO3 skills, and some examples of this language are outlined in Table 10.8.

Component III: Global Politics

Table 10.8 Signposting AO3

> **AO3 Language**
> - In sum …
> - It is argued …
> - In conclusion …
> - Convincingly …
> - A strong argument is …
> - The most important argument is …
> - Overwhelmingly …
> - The overarching implication is …

STUDENT EXTRACT – 'Evaluate the view that the ICJ is the most effective institution within the United Nations' (30) – AO3 in introductions

> The ICJ is not the most effective institution of the United Nations, with some of its other institutions being more effective, in particular the Security Council and the General Assembly. The essay will examine the effectiveness of the key UN institutions by looking at their power, composition and ability to achieve their aims, concluding without doubt that the ICJ is not the most effective institution of the UN.

The student begins the essay with their overall judgement, which takes a clear position on the view in the question.

The student outlines the issues that will be discussed in relation to the different organs of the UN. This shows the scope and structure of the essay, which conveys a clear and well-organised line of argument.

STUDENT EXTRACT – 'Evaluate the view that cultural globalisation has led to a multipolar system' (30) – looking at AO3 in interim judgements

Extract One:
> In sum, it is clear that cultural globalisation has not led to a multipolar system. This is because the United States clearly dominates when it comes to global brands.

Here the student outlines a brief but clear argument, but it should be substantiated by explaining why cultural globalisation has not led to multipolarity. The student could do this by explaining why cultural globalisation has not led to a multipolar system.

Extract Two:
> Overall, despite the fact that the United States has a clear influence on cultural globalisation through the immense number of American films and media, cultural globalisation is increasingly leading us toward a multipolar system. This is because there are now a large number of other states making a huge impact on film and media, not least Korea with its huge influence through K-Drama and K-Pop. All things considered, it can therefore be claimed that cultural globalisation has led to a multipolar system.

This interim judgement is substantiated. It considers both sides of the argument, balancing one view against the other before reaching a clear judgement.

STUDENT EXTRACT – 'Evaluate the view that humanitarian intervention is no longer relevant in Global Politics' (30) – looking at AO3 in conclusions.

Extract One:
In conclusion, despite there being a need for humanitarian intervention, the actual carrying out of humanitarian intervention has become irrelevant in practice. In recent times, political circumstances have changed due to the conflict of interest between powerful states that do not agree on whether humanitarian intervention should take place. Therefore, humanitarian intervention is no longer relevant.

> This student clearly outlines an overall conclusion to the question. However, it is not substantiated because it does not weigh up the merits of both sides of the argument before justifying why its own argument is the stronger one.

Extract Two:
Conclusively, it can be argued that humanitarian intervention is no longer relevant in Global Politics. Whilst there is still lip service paid to 'human rights' protections in the statements of states, treaties and UNSC and GA resolutions, they do not go beyond this, with there being no support for a single further humanitarian intervention following NATO's intervention in Libya in 2011. Indeed, the fact that the international system is now multipolar means that there is no longer a consensus among the great powers for humanitarian intervention, and no state is willing to act alone in its pursuit. Combined with the increased emphasis on national interests and a rise in anti-globalisation, we can clearly see that humanitarian intervention is no longer relevant in Global Politics.

> This student identifies a clear winning argument. It weighs up both sides of the argument and justifies their overall conclusion that humanitarian intervention is no longer relevant.

Exam Tip: the examiner should know your overall conclusion before they reach it. This is because it should be clear from the introduction and interim judgements which side of the argument you support.

Levels-based mark schemes

The levels-based mark schemes are used by examiners to mark student answers. We have already identified what the levels look like for each of the three AOs. In Section A and B questions, only AO1 and AO2 are assessed, and each is worth 6 out of the 12 available marks. In Section C questions, all three AOs are assessed, and each is worth a total of 10 marks out of the 30 available marks.

When an examiner reads your answers, they are trying to determine which Level best describes your use of each of the applicable AOs. Once they have identified which Level represents the best fit, they will determine whether your use of the AO is low, middle or high within the Level. To reach an overall mark, the examiner will apply a 'best fit' approach. This is easier to do when an answer is consistent across the AOs, for example, a 30-mark essay may reach L4 in each AO and therefore its overall mark will be within L4. However, in practice, it is often the case that an essay will reach different Levels across each of the AOs. For example, a 30-mark essay may achieve the following:

AO1 = L4 (high)

AO2 = L4 (middle)

AO3 = L2 (high)

This answer is going to be a Level 3 answer overall.

A summary of the levels is shown in Table 10.9.

All of this has implications for how many arguments you should use in your exam answers across the three Sections of the Global Politics exam. If writing 3 arguments means sacrificing on the AOs because of time limitations, then you are better off writing 2 arguments and ensuring you access the higher levels across the AOs.

Table 10.9 Identifying Levels for AOs

	AO1 (Knowledge and Understanding)	AO2 (Analysis)	AO3 (Evaluation)
L1	Superficial	Limited	Superficial, simple, descriptive, limited, unsubstantiated
L2	Some accurate	Emerging	Some relevant, some are partially substantiated, generic, without much justification
L3	Mostly accurate	Mostly focused	Generally relevant, many substantiated, some focused
L4	Accurate	Consistent	Mostly relevant, mostly effective, mostly substantiated
L5 30-mark essays only	Accurate, carefully selected	Perceptive, cohesive, convincing	Fully relevant, consistently substantiated, fully focused and justified

Section A questions

What types of questions can be asked in the Section A part of your exam?

Given the size of the specification, it is not possible to construct an exhaustive list of all the possible institutions, processes, concepts, theories or issues which could appear as questions in Section A. Therefore, it is not possible to plan for every possible question in the same way as is possible for Section B questions.

There is also no requirement for the exam to choose institutions, processes, concepts, theories or issues from within a single topic. However, the papers thus far would seem to suggest that these **do** tend to come from within individual topics.

The questions often focus on

- Similarities/differences
- Strengths/weaknesses
- Effectiveness (allowing you to look at **both** strengths and weaknesses, but importantly not reaching a judgement!)

For example, in 2024, one of the Section A questions was, 'Examine the weaknesses of both the IMF and the World Bank'.

Structure of Section A answers

You do not need to write an introduction or conclusion for your Section A answer. You are better off getting straight to the point with your first argument, given the time limitations. A conclusion is unnecessary because there are no AO3 marks available for this question and would therefore receive no additional marks.

> **Exam Tip:**
> There are still large numbers of students who continue to write an introduction and a conclusion, and they achieve no marks for these. This is all the more frustrating for examiners when the student has clearly struggled to write enough within the time constraints.

There are three ways of structuring Section A questions, which vary in level of challenge.

In the following structures (1) and (2) refer to the two institutions, processes, concepts, theories or issues you are writing about.

> **Option 1 (Less Challenge):**
>
> **Paragraph One** – Arguments about institution, process, concept, theory or issue (1) with supporting examples.
>
> **Paragraph Two** – Arguments about institution, process, concept, theory or issue (2) with supporting examples.
>
> **Paragraph Three (Optional)** – Arguments about institution, process, concept, theory or issue (3) with supporting examples.

This structure enables you to write about both aspects of the question and therefore highlights some AO1 knowledge and understanding. It also allows you to access some AO2 marks because there should be evidence of logical chains of reasoning. However, both its AO1 and AO2 marks are limited. Its AO1 marks are limited because by not identifying similarities/differences/parallels it suggests weaker AO1 knowledge and understanding. Its AO2 marks are limited because it is unable to identify similarities/differences/parallels apart from the obvious that the two aspects of the question are different.

> **Option 2 (Moderate Challenge):**
>
> **Paragraph One** – Arguments which are UNPAIRED about institution, process, concept, theory or issue (1 and 2) with supporting examples.
>
> **Paragraph Two** – Arguments which are UNPAIRED about institution, process, concept, theory or issue (1 and 2) with supporting examples.
>
> **Paragraph Three (Optional)** – Arguments which are UNPAIRED about institution, process, concept, theory or issue (1 and 2) with supporting examples.

This structure allows you to demonstrate better AO2 skills than in Option 1 because it directly identifies some similarities/differences between the aspects of the question. It also shows better AO1 knowledge and understanding because you are able to discern between pieces of information about each of the aspects of the question.

> **Option 3 (More Challenge):**
>
> **Paragraph One** – Arguments which are PAIRED about institution, process, concept, theory or issue (1 and 2) with supporting examples.
>
> **Paragraph Two** – Arguments which are PAIRED about institution, process, concept, theory or issue (1 and 2) with supporting examples.
>
> **Paragraph Three (Optional)** – Arguments which are PAIRED about institution, process, concept, theory or issue (1 and 2) with supporting examples.

Exam Tip: Many students want to know whether they should write 2 or 3 arguments in their Section A, B and C essays. The mark scheme does not specify a minimum requirement of arguments and you should use the number of arguments you can comfortably apply the three AOs to. If writing a third argument would come at the detriment of these skills, it would be unwise to do so.

Option 3 shows a high degree of skill. In your AO1, you are able to show strong knowledge and understanding of the aspects of the question by identifying common themes of analysis between them. This also boosts AO2 marks because the answer is clearly showing differences and similarities across a common theme.

So, how do you identify clear themes of points of similarity and difference? It is possible to identify a number of themes that are common across many of the topics covered within the specification; these are helpful for structuring Section A essays using the Option 3 structure (*see above*). It also offers a useful way to revise key institutions, processes, concepts, theories and issues according to pre-selected themes. Throughout this textbook, clear themes are identified in the comparative analysis tables in each chapter.

Chapter 8 provides some common themes that can be used in Global Governance questions.

How many paragraphs should I write for a 12 mark question?

There is no simple answer to this question – it depends on the length and quality of your paragraphs. The examiner will base your overall mark on which level you reach in AO1 and AO2.

Section B question

Section B is the only compulsory question in your A Level Politics exam. It is a Comparative Theory question which draws upon the Global Politics theories of realism and liberalism. For example, in November 2021, the Section B question was 'Analyse the divisions that exist between realists and liberals over the impact of both international organisations and the significance of states'. This means the questions are restricted to the differences between realism and liberalism across the following areas identified on the Pearson Edexcel Politics specification:

- States
- The Balance of Power
- Sovereignty
- Inevitability of War/Likelihood of Conflict
- The Security Dilemma
- Complex Interdependence
- Possibility of Harmony and Balance
- Global Governance
- International Anarchy
- Impact and Growth of International Organisations
- Human Nature
- Power
- Order and Security
- Examples of how each theory explains developments in Global Politics since 2000.

In addition, you could be asked a question about anarchical society and society of states theory. As already explained in Chapter 2, these are not two separate theories, but refer to the same theory. Therefore, it is important to note that for this question, you are expected to know the following information:

- The key claims of anarchical society theory (also called society of states theory)
- The similarities and differences between this and both realism and liberalism

In Chapter 1, there is a suggested approach to structuring an answer to a question based on anarchical society and society of states theory.

Exam Tip: In Chapter 2, variants of all of the above essays have been planned as key debates. Crucially, whilst it may look as if there are lots of possibilities for questions, the material you would use for each is largely the same. It is therefore a matter of how you use the material in relation to the question.

Synopticity

Critically, Section B involves a synoptic link. This means that you must make a reference to either of the core ideas of conservatism, liberalism or socialism. This can come from their core principles, ideas about the state, society, human nature or the economy, or their key thinkers. The synoptic link allows Section B answers which are strong in AO1 and AO2 to reach level 4 on the mark scheme. Answers are capped at level 3 if they do not include a synoptic link, meaning they can access a maximum of 9 out of the 12 available marks. Including a synoptic link alone is insufficient to access level 4 because the AO1 and AO2 must also meet the level descriptors for level 4.

The question paper reminds you to make a synoptic link by stating that 'In your answer you must discuss any relevant core political ideas'. The synoptic link does not need to be long or complex – a sentence is sufficient. However, you must clearly signpost it and must make sure it is **specific**. In other words, by relating a specific core principle, idea or thinker to the specific realist or liberal argument it relates to. It is good practice to signpost your synoptic link to the examiner by underlining it.

Table 10.11 Synoptic Links

Core Idea	Synoptic Link	Link to Realism/Liberalism
Conservatism	Conservatives believe in human imperfection. They argue that human nature is intellectually, morally and psychologically imperfect.	This aligns with realism's pessimistic views of human nature.
Conservatism	Traditional conservatives recognise the importance of authority in society. Thomas Hobbes based his view that life in the state of nature is 'nasty brutish and short' based upon his view that a strong state was needed to control the impulses of humans.	This aligns with realism's view that existence under international anarchy is dangerous and precarious.
Liberalism	Liberals have an optimistic view of human nature, stressing they are rational and capable of moral behaviour. John Locke believed that life in the state of nature was relatively peaceful because human beings developed natural laws.	This aligns with liberal views that human nature is rational and moral.

> **Exam Tip:** Do not spend a long time applying synoptic links to question B answers. There are no additional marks available for the length or complexity of your synoptic link. The synoptic link is simply a ticket to enable you to access L4 should your AO1 and AO2 be strong enough.

Table 10.11 identifies a number of synoptic links which you could learn and apply in Section B answers. It deliberately identifies the key liberal and realist arguments which can be applied to the majority of Section B questions. It is best to learn a couple of these so you can directly write them into your answers.

Section C question

Section C is worth the most marks in your Component Three exam – it is worth 60 out of the 84 available marks. In this section, you complete 2 x 30-mark essays from a choice of 3. The essays will always ask you to 'evaluate the view that' before presenting a judgement. For example, in 2024, a Section C question was 'Evaluate the view that the advantages of globalisation outweigh the disadvantages' (30). The instruction on the exam paper says that 'You must consider this view and the alternative to this view in a balanced way'. In other words, you must present both areas of agreement and disagreement with the question in your answers. If your essay is not balanced, it will be capped at Level 2 (maximum 12 marks). Section C assesses all three AOs, and in each 30-mark question, each AO is worth a total of 10 marks.

Important – Some exam papers in the early years of this specification used the question stem 'Evaluate the extent to which'. This is no longer used. Instead, the question will say 'Evaluate the view that'. This is an important change of emphasis as it means you do not need to state the extent to which you agree with the proposition as required by an 'extent' question. Instead, you simply need to state whether you agree or do not agree with the view.

> **Exam Tip:**
> You must remember to include real-world examples in your Section B answers to illustrate the claims of realists and liberals. Often, strong theoretical answers can lose marks because they do not include any examples.

Core Idea	Synoptic Link	Link to Realism/Liberalism
Liberalism	Classical liberals support the idea of the free-market economy.	This aligns with liberalism and its views on the importance of free trade to promote complex interdependence between states.
Socialism	Emphasise the importance of cooperation. Humans can work collectively to achieve mutual benefits. Marx and Engels were critical of capitalism because it fostered alienation and competition rather than flourishing through cooperation.	This aligns with liberal views on the importance of cooperation because of the prioritisation of absolute gains for all.
Socialism	Emphasises the existence of common humanity and fraternity.	Views about the importance of shared norms and values, such as universal human rights, also align with socialist views about common humanity.

Structuring 30-mark essay answers

Here are three possible ways of structuring an answer to a 30 mark Section C essay question. It should be noted that, whilst we have suggested three arguments on each side of the debate in each option, this is just a guide, not a requirement. Some students might be able to write more, others less. The length and depth of the paragraphs might also vary.

> **Option 1 (Less Challenge):**
> Introduction (with overall argument stated)
> For the view (argument 1, 2, 3)
> Against the view (argument 1, 2, 3)
> Conclusion

The option 1 structure enables students to write about both sides of the argument, thereby demonstrating some AO1 knowledge and understanding. It also allows access to AO2 analysis, as there should be evidence of logical chains of reasoning within the for and against paragraphs. However, both AO1 and AO2 marks could be limited because the structure does not identify similarities or differences or parallels beyond the obvious point that there are two different approaches to the statement in the question. From an AO3 perspective, although the introduction and conclusion provide an overall judgement, the absence of interim judgements throughout the essay makes it more difficult to reach higher levels. Furthermore, AO3 credit depends on whether sufficient time is spent weighing the merits of each side of the argument before reaching a substantiated conclusion.

Option 2 (Moderate Challenge):
Introduction (with overall argument stated)
Argument For View (1)
Argument Against View (1)
Argument For View (2)
Argument Against View (2)
Argument For View (3)
Argument Against View (3)
Conclusion

The option 2 structure uses paired arguments, which can help to highlight the directly opposing points in the two sides of the debate. This approach can help students to access AO2 marks for comparison. However, similarly to Option 1, the option 2 structure does not include interim judgements after each pair of arguments. To achieve good AO3 marks, it is likely that the student would need to carefully weigh the merits of each pair of arguments in the final conclusion. This is a risky strategy, particularly when working under time pressure. It also makes it more difficult to achieve a clear 'line of argument' throughout the essay.

Option 3 (More Challenge):
Introduction (with overall argument stated)
Argument For View (1)
Argument Against View (1)
Interim Judgement 1
Argument For View (2)
Argument Against View (2)
Interim Judgement 2
Argument For View (3)
Argument Against View (3)
Interim Judgement 3
Conclusion

The option 3 structure solves the problems posed by options 1 and 2. Pairing the arguments shows analytical skills for AO2, and making an interim judgement on each pair can help to maintain a clear line of argument throughout the essay for AO3. Doing this throughout the essay rather than just at the end is also a less risky strategy for gaining the third of the marks that are allocated to AO3.

> **Exam Tip:**
> Students should understand that marks are awarded for a clear and well-substantiated argument with accurate knowledge, and effective skills of analysis and evaluation, not for a specific structure. There are other ways to structure an essay that can achieve good marks, if done well. However, in our view, option 3 demonstrates good practice. It can also help students to remember to apply these skills systematically when writing under pressure.

Component III: Global Politics

Exam Tip: Do not waste time (and words) in your introduction by outlining the individual arguments you will explore in the body of your essay. It adds nothing to your overall marks.

Introductions and conclusions

Introductions play an important role in Section C essays.

→ Provide the context.
- A sentence or two outlining the context of the question or how it has arisen can show the examiner that you know your stuff! For example, in the question 'Evaluate the view that globalisation is in decline' (30), the following sentences would help provide the context: 'The reelection of Donald Trump in 2024 on his platform of anti-globalisation and state-first policies mean it is important to question the view that globalisation is in decline'.

→ Define any key terms.
- It showcases your AO1 knowledge if you are able to offer a brief explanation of the concept explored in the question.
- In some cases, the question does not outline a concept, but outlines a term such as 'effectiveness'. In this case, you would briefly outline how you will measure this term in your essay.

→ Outline your overall conclusion.
- It is essential that you outline your overall conclusion clearly.
- Use the wording of the question to make sure you are focused on what is being asked.
- You can underline this to show the examiner you are using AO3!

STUDENT EXTRACT – Evaluate the view that the United Nations is less powerful than nation-states (30) – looking at introductions

The inability of the UN to bring Russia's invasion of Ukraine to an end raises important questions about the power of the UN in relation to nation states. This essay will argue that the UN is less powerful than nation states.

> This is an effective introduction. It identifies why this is an important question, showing the examiner their awareness of recent developments (AO1). It also states the line of argument which will be taken throughout the essay (AO3).

STUDENT EXTRACT – Evaluate the view that the current international system is multipolar (30) – looking at introductions

There is great debate about whether the current international system is multipolar. Some argue that the current system is multipolar, whereas others argue it is unipolar, dominated by a US hegemony. On the one hand, multipolarity refers to a system where three or more states hold roughly equal amounts of military, economic and political power. On the other hand, unipolarity refers to a system where there is one single dominant power. This question will be answered by looking at polarity across military, economic and structural power. It will be argued that the current international system is now multipolar.

> This introduction is far too long. There is no need to use the expressions 'some argue' and 'others argue' as it does not add anything to the marks.

> There is also no need to define the key terms or outline the themes which will be explored in the essay.

> It is good that this introduction outlines the direction of the argument (AO3).

Conclusions are an extremely important part of your essay and are often the most poorly written part of student essays or left out altogether because of time constraints. A good conclusion should do the following:

- Outline your overall argument.
- Summarise the key aspects of the side of the argument you do not agree with.
- Summarise the key aspects of the side of the argument you do agree with.
- Justify why your argument is stronger and repeat your overall argument.

Exam Focus

Your overall conclusion is where you should be bringing together the interim judgements you have made throughout your essay. It might be that one interim judgement is stronger than the others; if so, tell the examiner and explain why. This shows a higher level of skill in AO3.

STUDENT EXTRACT – Evaluate the view that globalisation resolves contemporary issues in global politics (30) – looking at conclusions

In conclusion, while proponents often highlight globalisation's potential to foster interdependence, thereby reducing conflict, spur economic growth to alleviate poverty, and facilitate collective action on environmental challenges, a comprehensive evaluation reveals a more complex and often detrimental reality. Despite the promise of a more integrated world, globalisation frequently exacerbates existing divisions. It can fuel intra-state and inter-state tensions through economic inequality and resource competition, deepening the roots of conflict. Moreover, while some benefit, globalisation's largely unregulated capitalist drive often intensifies poverty for many, concentrating wealth and undermining local economies. Critically, it has also accelerated environmental degradation, prioritising profit and unchecked consumption over planetary health. Therefore, it is clear that far from resolving contemporary issues, globalisation's inherent characteristics and uneven application often compound them.

> This is a well-written conclusion. It outlines the key points from the opposing argument before outlining why they are inaccurate.

> The language this pupil uses is very assertive, meaning that it is more convincing, a key requirement for a level 5 answer.

> It clearly identifies an overall conclusion to the question.

Exam Tip: Allow enough time to write your conclusion. Never leave it out, as the numbers of marks you lose in AO3 will be higher than the number of marks you lose in AO1 and 2 for rushing an analytical paragraph. If you struggle to write three comparative paragraphs, stick to two!

Putting it all together

We have now looked at the elements which make up good answers for Sections A, B and C questions. Now we will bring all of these together to show what a good answer looks like in each of the sections. Throughout this section, the answers will be annotated to show you where the answers are being awarded marks.

Section A

Sample Essay 1 – Examine the criticisms of the United Nations Framework Convention on Climate Change and the Intergovernmental Panel on Climate Change (12)

Both the UNFCCC and IPCC are criticised for not driving fast enough change. The UNFCCC is often criticised for its slow pace and limited effectiveness in actually cutting global greenhouse gas emissions. Despite decades of international conferences and agreements, like the Kyoto Protocol and the Paris Agreement, emissions have continued to rise, showing a failure to achieve significant progress. This is often blamed on political disagreements and states prioritising national interests over global climate action. In comparison, the IPCC, while respected for its scientific rigour, faces criticism for the slow, consensus-driven nature of its report-writing process. Because all governments must approve the 'Summary for Policymakers', some argue that its findings can be watered down or lag behind the most recent, alarming scientific data, thus not conveying the full urgency of the climate crisis.

Another key criticism of the UNFCCC revolves around issues of equity and responsibility, particularly the historical divide between developed and developing states. There have been ongoing disagreements over who should bear the greatest burden for emissions reductions and financial support for climate action, such as funding for the Green Climate Fund. Critics argue that the UNFCCC has struggled to move past these old divisions, even as new economic powers like China and India have emerged. In contrast, the IPCC is criticised not for its scientific findings, but for its inherent inability to directly address these political and financial fairness issues. As a purely scientific body, its role is to assess climate science, not to resolve disputes over historical responsibility or dictate how financial burdens should be shared. This means the IPCC can highlight the problem, but it cannot bridge the political and economic gaps that often paralyse UNFCCC negotiations, leaving a disconnect between scientific urgency and global political will.

Finally, the UNFCCC is often criticised for being too weak due to its respect for state sovereignty. Agreements like the Paris Agreement rely on Nationally Determined Contributions (NDCs), where each country sets its own targets. This allows states to protect their independence but means the UNFCCC cannot force ambitious action, potentially leading to insufficient global efforts. For example, some countries' NDCs are not strong enough to meet the 1.5°C warming limit. In comparison, the IPCC, despite its scientific mandate, sometimes faces accusations of overstepping into policy advice, which can be seen as a threat to state sovereignty, leading to criticism from some governments who perceive its summaries as politically biased rather than purely objective. This can undermine its credibility with certain state actors who then dismiss its scientific warnings, highlighting a challenge where the IPCC's influence can be limited by political pushback against perceived interference in sovereign policy-making.

Annotations:

- This is great AO2 – the student is identifying a point of similarity between the two institutions.
- It is fine to use abbreviations.
- Including the years of these events would strengthen the AO1 knowledge.
- A better answer would provide statistics here in support of the statement.
- An example of the length of time it took to write a specific report would strengthen the AO1 here.

Exam Focus

This is a well-written Section A answer. It does a number of things well:
- ✓ It identifies three paired points (AO2).
- ✓ It develops logical chains of reasoning (AO2).
- ✓ It includes a range of AO1 knowledge which are enhanced by the use of some examples.
- ✓ Examples are effectively integrated into AO2.

However, it would benefit from the following improvements:
- ✗ The AO1 examples need to be more specific.

Sample Essay 2 – Examine the differences and similarities between the European Union and the African Union (12)

Both (1) the EU and AU share the goals of regional cooperation and development, aiming to bring their member states closer together for their collective benefit. Both organisations were established with the broad aim of enhancing unity and promoting the political and economic development of their respective continents. For instance, the EU, originally formed as the European Coal and Steel Community in 1952, evolved to become a highly integrated political-economic bloc, fostering deep ties among its members through milestones like the Treaty of Maastricht in 1992. It also established a monetary union in 1992, which created a single currency, the Euro. Similarly, the African Union (AU) was created in 2002 to strengthen African unity and advance development across the continent. Furthermore, both the EU and AU play significant roles in addressing regional challenges and promoting shared values within their regions. The EU has taken on roles in reducing poverty, resolving conflicts, promoting human rights and protecting the environment within its neighbouring regions, as evidenced by its development aid to the Western Balkans and its diplomatic efforts in the Israeli-Palestinian conflict. Similarly, the AU has adopted some features from the EU's model in its efforts to enhance unity and development, becoming a major peacekeeping force on the African continent to manage and resolve conflicts, such as its African Union Mission in Somalia (AMISOM), deployed since 2007.

Key differences also exist between the EU and the AU, particularly in their level of integration and the authority they hold over member states. The EU is widely considered the most integrated political-economic regional bloc in the world, possessing significant supranational authority where EU laws can directly apply to member states and sometimes override national laws, especially within its single market. For example, since the establishment of the single market in 1993, countries like Germany and France must adhere to EU regulations on product standards, trade and competition, directly impacting their national economies. In contrast, the African Union, while aiming for unity, operates on an intergovernmental basis and places a greater emphasis on protecting its members' national sovereignty, often decision making on the basis of unanimity. This intergovernmental nature was highlighted during the Covid-19 pandemic, where national governments largely dictated their own response measures, despite AU guidance.

> Using the word 'both' throughout this paragraph helps signpost that the student is talking about similarities.

Another key difference lies in their primary areas of global influence. The EU has become the world's largest provider of humanitarian and development aid, using its significant economic power to support developing nations and influence global standards, committing €70.1 billion in official development assistance in 2023. The AU, whilst working towards economic integration with its continental free trade area, is a major peacekeeping force, but only on the African continent, deploying troops to conflict zones like Somalia under the AMISOM mission.

This is a well-written Section A answer. It does a number of things well:
- ✓ It identifies three paired points (AO2).
- ✓ It develops logical chains of reasoning (AO2).
- ✓ It includes a range of AO1 knowledge which are enhanced by the use of some detailed, well-integrated examples.

However, it would benefit from the following improvements:
- ✗ Avoid repetition of examples, e.g. AMISOM.

Section B

Sample Essay 1 – Analyse the differences between realism and liberalism concerning the significance of the state and international organisations (12)

Realism and Liberalism hold very different views on the significance of the state in global politics. Realists believe that states are the most important actors because there is no world government to control them, meaning global politics is anarchical. States must look out for themselves to survive, leading them to be suspicious of others and always seeking power. For example, Russia's invasion of Ukraine in 2022 is seen by realists as a powerful state acting in its own self-interest to boost its security and power, showing the dominance of states. In contrast, Liberals also see states as important but argue they are not the only key players. Liberals believe that many other actors, like IGOs and NGOs, are also important. For example, organisations like the EU have a major impact on the laws and policies of its member states, showing that states can pool their sovereignty and cooperate with one another.

Realists generally see IOs as having limited real power. They argue that states are too focused on their own survival and self-interest to be truly bound by international rules or organisations. For realists, IOs are mainly just tools that powerful states might use to get what they want, rather than being independent forces for good. The frequent deadlocks in the UNSC, where powerful states like Russia or China can use their veto power to block resolutions, illustrate this realist view of IOs being constrained by state power. However, Liberals take a much more optimistic view, arguing that IOs are very important for promoting cooperation and peace. They believe IOs help create areas of 'global governance', which sets rules and norms that guide state behaviour. Liberals think that through IOs, states can build trust, solve shared problems and reduce the likelihood of conflict. For instance, WHO efforts to coordinate a global response to pandemics like Covid-19 show how international organisations can bring states together to tackle common threats.

This answer does a number of things well:
- ✓ It identifies two points of contrast between realists and liberals – looking at the state and IOs (AO2) – the question title provides a structure by identifying two aspects.
- ✓ It develops some logical chains of reasoning (AO2).
- ✓ It includes some AO1 knowledge which is enhanced by the use of some examples.

However, it would benefit from the following improvements:
- ✗ There is no synoptic link in this answer. Its discussion of liberal views on the state is from the liberal IR perspective, not liberal ideas.
- ✗ Its AO1 is not developed. Use more specific concepts such as the security dilemma, relative gains or complex interdependence to score higher marks in AO1.

Sample Essay 2 – Analyse the differences between realism and liberalism concerning the security dilemma and complex interdependence (12)

Realists and liberals disagree on the concept of complex interdependence. Liberals emphasise that states are deeply connected through many different ties, not just military ones. They use the Kantian Triangle to demonstrate how complex interdependence is created. First, interdependence is promoted through global trade. Economic globalisation has meant that there is now a single global economy. Global trade is now worth over $30 trillion, showing how integrated states are. TNCs also have globalised supply chains, for example Apple designs its iPhones in the US, manufactures them in Asia and sources its materials from all over the world. Second, international organisations help to promote trust between states. They reduce the transaction costs of achieving shared goals, and states can build shared expectations about the behaviour of others. International law has also helped regulate the use of force, with war being outlawed except in self-defence or as agreed by a UNSC mandate. Finally, the democratic peace theory shows how democratic states do not fight wars against other democratic states, showing how shared values can promote interdependence. The deep interdependence the Kantian Triangle promotes means that going to war would harm everyone's interests, making conflict less likely. For instance, global supply chains, where a disruption in one country, such as the Evergreen Crisis in the Suez Canal, which disrupted global trade enormously, demonstrate how economic ties can discourage conflict. Realists, however, generally downplay complex interdependence. While they recognise that states can establish alliances with other states, they argue these are temporary at best. This is because under international anarchy, survival is always the ultimate goal of states. Thomas Hobbes shows how life without a dominant power is 'nasty brutish and short' and realists use this to explain why life under international anarchy (the international state of nature) is so dangerous. The Prisoner's Dilemma shows how the most rational choice for states in international agreements is to defect. This is why Donald Trump was so suspicious of the Iran Nuclear Deal in 2015 and ultimately withdrew US support upon becoming president. Russia's invasion of Ukraine in 2022, despite strong economic links with European countries, is an example realists use to show that security concerns can quickly outweigh interdependence.

Realism and liberalism also disagree about the security dilemma. Realists believe that because international anarchy means there is a self-help system, and states rely on their own efforts to survive. When one state builds up its military power, other states feel threatened and build up their own militaries, too, creating a never-ending cycle of fear and arms races. This can eventually lead to war. Mearsheimer argues that this is a 'tragedy' because for defensive realist states, all they had wanted to maximise was their security. However, the ambiguity of modern weapons — i.e. whether they are defensive or offensive — means that states must naturally assume the worst. For example, the Cold War arms race between the United States and the Soviet Union perfectly illustrates this, as each side's military build-up made the other feel less secure. In contrast, Liberals accept that the security dilemma exists but believe it can be reduced through cooperation. They argue that building trust through international organisations and international trade can avoid constant military build-ups. Arms control agreements, such as the NPT, show states trying to manage this dilemma through reaching mutual agreements, which liberals see as proof that cooperation is possible. States can also cooperate because they support absolute gains, meaning that they will not see the acquisition of power by other states as threatening, but instead as a tool to promote their collective security. For example, NATO member states are required to spend 2 per cent of their GDP on their military, and this does not cause fear in other members.

This is a very good answer, especially given the time constraints of the exam. It is what we could reasonably expect an A Level Student to achieve in timed conditions.

- ✓ It identifies two points of contrast between realists and liberals – looking at the security dilemma and complex interdependence.
- ✓ It develops some logical chains of reasoning (AO2).
- ✓ It includes well-selected AO1 knowledge, which is enhanced by the use of well-integrated examples.
- ✓ It includes a synoptic link which allows it to access level 4 (because the AO1 and AO2 are also level 4).

However, it would benefit from the following improvements:

- ✗ The use of the Cold War to illustrate the security dilemma is dated. The pupil should have used contemporary security dilemmas.

Section C

Sample Essay 1 – Evaluate the view that the advantages of globalisation outweigh the disadvantages (30)

Globalisation, defined by the increasing interconnectedness and interdependence of the world through the rapid movement of goods, capital, people, and information, undeniably presents both significant advantages and severe disadvantages. While proponents highlight its potential for economic growth and cultural exchange, a closer evaluation suggests that its benefits are often unevenly distributed and frequently overshadowed by serious drawbacks. Therefore, despite some clear positives, the disadvantages of globalisation – particularly its role in exacerbating inequality and threatening national sovereignty – ultimately do not outweigh its perceived advantages.

One key argument for globalisation's advantages centres on its capacity to foster economic growth and material prosperity worldwide through increased trade and capital flows. By allowing countries to specialise in goods and services where they have a comparative advantage efficiently, globalisation can lead to lower consumer prices and increased overall wealth. For instance, the expansion of global supply chains, exemplified by technology giants like Apple outsourcing manufacturing to Foxconn factories in China, has integrated developing economies into the global market. This has undeniably created millions of jobs and lifted many out of extreme poverty, as seen in China's remarkable economic growth post-joining the WTO. The sheer volume of global trade, which surged to over $30 trillion in 2024, demonstrates an unprecedented level of economic integration and efficiency. Liberals would argue that this helps promote peace in global politics and is a clear advantage of globalisation. However, this economic narrative is severely undermined by globalisation's profound disadvantages in terms of exacerbating inequality and exploitation. The wealth generated is disproportionately concentrated at the top, widening the gap between rich and poor nations, and often within societies themselves. Oxfam has recently said that the top 1 per cent of the global population own the same as 99 per cent, showing how unequal the distribution of wealth is in the global economy. Many developing countries become locked into low-value, labour-intensive industries, their workers exploited by transnational corporations (TNCs) seeking the cheapest labour. For example, the devastating 2013 Rana Plaza factory collapse in Bangladesh, which killed over 1,100 workers, starkly highlighted the dangerous conditions and minimal pay endured by those at the bottom of global supply chains. We also see this currently with Shein, where a recent Channel 4 documentary showed how their workers work in excess of 75-hour weeks and earn as little as £0.03 per item. Furthermore, economic shocks can spread globally with devastating speed; the 2008 global financial crisis, originating in the US, swiftly plunged economies worldwide into recession, demonstrating how a crisis in one highly globalised market can have catastrophic international ripple effects. Realists criticise this interdependence, saying it leads to mutual vulnerabilities and prevents states from being able to achieve their overall goal of survival under international anarchy. Therefore, whilst globalisation can generate immense wealth, its tendency to exacerbate profound economic inequality and vulnerability means its supposed advantages are often deeply problematic and harmful for vast segments of the global population.

> *The student refers to realist and liberal views, which whilst not expected in 30-mark essays, does award additional AO1 and AO2 marks.*

> *The interim judgement is clearly justified (AO3).*

Furthermore, proponents of globalisation emphasise its advantages in promoting cultural exchange, international cooperation and shared understanding, suggesting a more tolerant and interconnected world. The internet and social media platforms, like TikTok or X, facilitate rapid communication and the instant spread of ideas, music, and traditions across diverse cultures, theoretically fostering a global village where differences are celebrated. Glocalisation strategies used by TNCs also show how globalisation can support local cultures. For example, as seen by Nike's 'hyper-local' advertising strategies and McDonald's use of local menus. Globalisation also arguably necessitates stronger international institutions, encouraging states to cooperate on shared transnational challenges that no single state can solve alone, such as climate change or pandemics. The global scientific collaboration during the COVID-19 pandemic, leading to rapid vaccine development, serves as a testament to this cooperative potential. However, these perceived advantages are frequently countered by significant disadvantages related to cultural homogenisation and the erosion of national sovereignty. The spread of dominant Western culture, often driven by powerful TNCs and media outlets like Hollywood and McDonald's, can lead to the marginalisation or even extinction of unique local traditions, languages, and industries, creating a homogenous 'McWorld' rather than genuine cultural diversity. More critically, globalisation challenges the sovereignty of states, limiting their ability to exercise autonomous control. International agreements, the immense power of TNCs, and the demands of global financial markets can severely constrain national policy choices. For example, the need to attract foreign investment or adhere to strict WTO regulations on trade liberalisation can compel states to deregulate industries or privatise public services, even when this conflicts with domestic goals. While some argue that states willingly pool sovereignty in bodies like the EU for collective benefits (e.g., the single market), weaker states frequently face imposed conditionalities from International Financial Institutions like the IMF when seeking bailout loans, forcing politically unpopular austerity measures that can devastate local populations, as vividly seen during Greece's severe debt crisis in the 2010s. This loss of genuine policy autonomy means the supposed advantages of cooperation often come at the expense of national self-determination and cultural distinctiveness, undermining a state's capacity to genuinely represent and protect its citizens' interests.

> *This paragraph is not as well-written as the former paragraph. The argument is less obviously 'paired' with the pupil using a combination of cultural and political globalisation knowledge, without expressly using these concepts.*

> *The examples here are also less specific. That said, there is some good conceptual knowledge (AO1) with references to cultural homogenisation and glocalisation.*

> *The interim judgement is again well-developed; however, because the argument in this paragraph is less focused, the judgement is less convincing (AO3).*

In conclusion, while globalisation offers undeniable avenues for increased economic efficiency and opportunities for cultural diffusion, an evaluation reveals that its substantial disadvantages ultimately outweigh these advantages. The process has demonstrably exacerbated global inequalities, concentrating wealth in the hands of a few while perpetuating the exploitation and vulnerability of many, particularly in the Global South. Moreover, the influence of global economic forces and powerful non-state actors severely erodes the sovereignty of nation states, limiting their capacity to autonomously pursue their own development paths and protect their citizens' interests. Although globalisation facilitates some international cooperation, this frequently occurs on terms dictated by dominant global actors, further entrenching existing power hierarchies. Therefore, until its benefits are more equitably distributed and the fundamental rights of states to self-determination and cultural integrity are genuinely protected, it cannot be argued that globalisation's advantages outweigh its disadvantages; indeed, for countless individuals and nations, it presents more profound threats than tangible opportunities.

> This is an excellent conclusion – it identifies the merits of both sides of the argument before reaching a justified and substantiated overall conclusion. This helps convince the examiner of their argument.

This essay is a nice example of how adopting a two-paragraph approach can help students to consolidate higher levels across all of the AOs, ultimately helping the student to achieve a higher overall mark.

Sample Essay 2 – Evaluate the view that hard power is now redundant in global politics.

The view that hard power, meaning military force and economic coercion, is now completely useless in global politics is inaccurate. Despite the rise of new challenges and forms of influence, hard power remains a crucial and often decisive tool for states. One strong argument for hard power's continued importance is its fundamental role in state survival and deterrence. Under international anarchy, states ultimately rely on their own military strength to protect their borders and interests. The ability to use or threaten force can stop other states from attacking. For instance, Russia's full-scale invasion of Ukraine in 2022 clearly shows that military force is still used to achieve major goals like territorial gain and undermining a rival. Ukraine's ability to resist relies heavily on its own military forces and the substantial military aid it receives from allies. However, some argue that hard power is becoming redundant because large-scale wars between major powers are now seen as unthinkable due to the devastating nature of nuclear weapons, which creates a 'mutually assured destruction' (MAD) scenario. Also, against non-state threats like terrorism, traditional military might can be less effective, as seen in the United States' long struggle in Afghanistan against the Taliban, where overwhelming military power did not lead to a clear victory. Despite these points, military power remains the final guarantee of a state's security and sovereignty, making it far from redundant in protecting a nation's core existence.

> This is a good introduction. It is concise and outlines the line of argument that will be taken throughout the essay.

> Using 'a strong argument' or 'a weak argument' helps you to effectively integrate AO3 throughout your essay.

> This argument is correct, but it needs further development to ensure it is a 'logical chain of reasoning'.

> This is not good practice – avoid saying 'some argue' as it looks as if you are not confident in your assertions.

> This concept needs explaining – do not expect the examiner to 'read-in' what you are trying to say.

> This is a clear judgement, but it has not been justified.

Furthermore, hard power is not just about all-out war; it is still vital for coercive diplomacy and protecting national interests abroad. States use the threat of force, or limited military actions, to make others comply or to protect their citizens and economic assets. For example, major naval deployments, like those by the United States in the South China Sea, are used to assert maritime claims or protect vital shipping lanes, showing military presence as a form of influence. More recently, events such as Israel's bombing of targets in Iran in June 2025 would demonstrate a state's continued willingness to use military force directly to achieve specific security objectives, regardless of international condemnation. This shows hard power being actively employed to manage tensions or prevent perceived threats.

[Annotation: Good use of a contemporary example.]

However, those who argue for hard power's redundancy point to the increasing importance of soft power, which uses cultural influence, economic attraction and diplomacy to persuade rather than force. They highlight how economic sanctions are often preferred to military action, as seen with the European Union's widespread use of economic sanctions against Russia to try and influence its behaviour without direct military confrontation. While soft power is definitely growing in importance, hard power remains a critical, and often decisive, tool for states to achieve their strategic goals and protect their vital interests when diplomacy alone fails.

[Annotation: This is NOT an example of soft power – students often wrongly attribute economic sanctions to soft power. They are hard power because they are coercive.]

[Annotation: This paragraph lacks balance because it is focused predominantly on hard power.]

Lastly, hard power continues to adapt to emerging challenges, even if its usefulness is limited in certain areas. For example, in the new domain of cyber warfare, states are developing advanced offensive and defensive cyber capabilities, which are a form of hard power in the digital world. Countries are building dedicated cyber units to protect their infrastructure and to potentially disrupt adversaries. However, hard power is indeed less useful for tackling very broad and complex global problems like pandemics or climate change, where international cooperation, scientific research, and diplomatic solutions (soft power) are much more relevant. For instance, military responses played a very small role in containing the Covid-19 pandemic, which required a global effort from scientists, health organisations and governments working together. So, while hard power finds new forms and uses, its effectiveness is clearly limited in addressing non-traditional threats that require broader, non-military solutions.

[Annotation: This is a very good example (AO1).]

[Annotation: This paragraph is much stronger as it identifies a paired argument and develops logical chains of reasoning (AO2) with well-selected examples (AO1).]

In conclusion, the view that hard power is now redundant in global politics is not accurate. It continues to be actively used by states to protect their national interests and project influence. Therefore, despite its limitations in certain contexts and the rising prominence of other forms of power, hard power maintains its essential and enduring role in shaping global politics.

[Annotation: This conclusion is very short and does not tackle both sides of the argument effectively (AO3).]

[Annotation: However, it does take a clear line of argument which is followed through from the introduction and through interim judgements.]

Final thought

On our companion website, **https://bloomsbury.pub/essentials-of-global-politics**, you will find a lot of helpful advice on how to prepare for your exam, but before we end the chapter, remember this ...

The most important piece of advice is worth repeating: answer the question set, NOT the one you wish it would be. Make sure you take the time to select the questions you are best prepared to answer!

Make sure you manage your time in the exam: one superbly written essay cannot earn enough marks to substitute for the marks lost by not completing the paper.

Finally, the route to performing to the best of your ability is proper preparation ... This means, using the resources at hand to help you when you find a topic difficult (for example this textbook, companion website and your teacher or classmates) and giving yourself sufficient time to revise; do not leave it till the last minute. Tackle topics you find difficult when you are taught them, not when it comes to revision time.

From all of the contributors to this textbook, we wish you the best of luck!

Index

absolute gains 15, 17
absolute poverty 63, 154
access points 271
accountability 271, 272, 280
AfCFTA (African Continental Free Trade Area) 307
Afghanistan 88, 212
African Union (AU) 206, 233, 295, 296, 299, 305–6, 326, 328
Alliance of Small Island States (AOSIS) 226, 250, 254
alliances 6, 7
altruism 9, 13
Americanisation 50, 54, 300
anarchical society 5–9, 26–9, 266
Annan, Kofi 129
annexation 76, 78–9
anthropocentrism 231
anti-industrialism 232
Apple 312
Arab League (AL) 294, 299, 302–3, 326
Arab Spring 102
Area of Freedom, Security and Justice (AFSJ) 316–18, 319
Argentina and the IMF 164
arms sales 12, 220
ASEAN (Association of Southeast Asian Nations) 233, 295, 296, 298, 299, 301, 303–4, 326, 327, 328
Asian Financial Crisis 77, 163, 183
Asian Infrastructure Investment Bank (AIIB) 89, 268
Assessment Objectives (AOs) 334–5, 337–45
austerity 47
authoritarianism 19, 39, 62, 80
autocratic states 60, 96
autonomous political communities 39
Azerbaijan 226, 248

balance in your answers, showing 336
balance of power 5, 6, 8, 94
bandwagoning 6, 8, 121
B-Corps 233, 235
Begum, Shamima 194
Berg, Peter 232
Billiard Ball Model 5–9
bipolarity 6, 87, 91–2
Boko Haram 51
bond markets 153, 154
bonds 46

borders
    China-India border dispute 14
    and the definition of a state 39
    EU (European Union) 316–17
    US-Canada 18
Bosnia 139, 212, 213
Bosnia and Herzegovina vs Serbia and Montenegro (initiated 1993) 196–7
Brandt Reports 160
breadth of questions 335–6
Bretton Woods Project 181
Bretton Woods system 44, 88, 150–1, 158
Brexit 31, 67, 79, 310, 322
BRICS - Brazil, Russia, India, China and South Africa 93
Brundtland Report 1987, 228
Bull, Hedley 26–7, 190, 266

C40 Cities Climate Leadership Group 233
Cambodia 201
cancel culture 47, 49
capitalism 43, 53–4, 88 see also neoliberalism
carbon markets 231
Chagos islands 113, 126–7
Chatham House 286, 288
China
    autocratic states 96, 101
    China-India border dispute 14
    economic power 88
    foreign investment 269
    global governance 269
    globalisation 43, 60, 62
    hard power 82
    hegemonic power 88–9
    human rights 221
    sharp power 81
    soft power 13, 80
    superpowers 85
    US-China trade dispute 172
circular economy 228
citizenship 39, 194
city authorities 233
civil society
    climate change 228
    economic global governance 152, 181–2
    environment 235
    evaluating 271–2, 274–7

    human rights 210
    liberalism 18
    political global governance 129
civil wars 119–20
'Clash of civilisations' 67
classical liberalism 157
classical realism 9, 10, 13
climate change
    environmental global governance 226–7, 230
    globalisation 51, 52
    liberalism 19
    UN (United Nations) 113, 136–7
    World Bank 165
climate finance 253–4, 255, 256
Climate Vulnerable Forum 250, 254
Club of Rome 228, 248
CO_2 emissions 69, 226, 231
Cobden, Richard 19
cobweb model 15
Cold War 6, 7, 92, 117–18, 138, 143
collective security 7, 296
commodity fetishism 54
common but differentiated responsibilities (CBDR) 239
common markets 296, 298
Common Security and Defence Policy (EU) 317, 319, 326
comparative advantage 157
comparative questions 278–9
complex interdependence 15–16, 19, 263
conditional sovereignty 190
confederations 318
conflict
    autocratic states 99
    democracy 97
    failed states 99
    NATO (North Atlantic Treaty Organisation) 144
    non-democratic states 98
    prevention 109
    realism and liberalism comparative analysis 20–1
    regionalism 328
    rogue states 100
    semi-democratic states 98
    UN (United Nations) 132, 135
consultative status 272
Convention on the Prevention and Punishment of the Crime of Genocide 195
conventions 192, 195

convergence theory 65
cooperation 5, 7, 8–9, 16, 17
COP (Conference of the Parties) 166, 226, 233, 241–6, 250, 254, 280
Copenhagen Accord 2009 242–3, 250
cosmopolitanism 27
Côte d'Ivoire 214
Council of Europe 208, 209
counter-terrorism 144
Covenant on Civil and Political Rights 194
Covenant on Economic, Social and Cultural Rights 194
Covid-19, 31, 44, 64, 67, 268
Crimea 78–9
crimes against humanity 41, 61, 199–200, 204, 326, 328
crimes of aggression 204
crisis response 165
cultural globalisation 62
cultural homogenisation 49, 53–4
cultural hybridisation 49, 50
cultural power 77, 79
cultural relativism 190
culture and globalisation 42, 45–6, 53–4
customs unions 296, 300, 314
cyberwarfare 83

de facto sovereignty 326
de jure sovereignty 326
death penalty 219
debt cancellation 166, 174, 182, 267
decentralised governance 232
decolonisation 158
deep ecology 231–2
defensive neorealism 12
deglobalisation 41, 42, 53
democracy 16, 18–19, 68, 95
Democratic Peace Theory 18–19, 68, 100
dependency theory 65, 158–9
development 65, 152, 154–61
diplomatic power see soft power
disarmament movements 275
dispute resolution 18
Doha 'Development Round' 171, 183, 282
doughnut economics 229, 230

East Timor 200, 214
EBA (Everything But Arms) 297, 298
ecocentrism 231
ecocide 273, 276
ecological ceiling 229
ecologism 231–2
economic global governance 148–86, 284–6
economic globalisation 42, 43–4, 61
economic integration 314–15
economic power 13, 42, 43–4, 88, 324

economic regionalism 296–7, 300
economic sanctions 19, 76–7, 82
economic soft power 77
ecosystems 69, 226, 231
egotism 6
elections 81
emerging powers 84, 86
'End of History' 89, 92, 101
energy prices 154, 230
English language 54
English School 26, 190
enlightened self-interests 13
environment 224–59
    autocratic states 99
    civil society 276
    democracy 95
    ecocide 273
    failed states 99
    global governance 54–5, 224–59, 279–82
    globalisation 66, 69, 70, 268
    non-democratic states 98
    regionalism 329
    rogue states 100
    semi-democratic states 98
Environmental, Social and Governance (ESG) policies 233, 235
equity 272
EU (European Union)
    Brexit 31, 67, 79–80, 310, 322
    democracy 101
    enlargement 321–2
    environment 232
    'good governance' 267
    regionalism 292–331
    soft power 79, 300
EUNAVFOR ASPIDES 317–18
European Arrest Warrants (EAW) 317
European Central Bank 313, 315
European Commission 312, 313
European Court of Human Rights (ECtHR) 55, 195, 208–9
European Court of Justice 209, 312, 313
European integration 306
European Migrant Crisis 48
European Parliament 311, 313, 314
Eurozone 314, 315
Eurozone sovereign debt crisis 179, 183, 321
Ever Given crisis 44, 45
exam (Component Three) 332–4
exam style questions
    comparative theories 33
    economic global governance 185
    environment 258
    global governance 289
    human rights global governance 222
    political global governance 145
    power and development 103
    regionalism 330
    state and globalisation 71

Extinction Rebellion (XR) 235
Extraordinary Chambers in the Courts of Cambodia (ECCC) 201, 202

failed states 96–7
fair trade 160
far right 68
federalism 309, 310, 318–20
finance and banking 44–5
financial power 81
fiscal policy 153
food insecurity 169
foreign direct investment (FDI) 65
fossil fuel divestment 235
free markets 153
free riders 141, 227, 228
free trade 19, 296
freedom of movement 316
Fridays for Future (FFF) 234, 272
Friedman, Thomas L. 68
Friends of the Earth 235
Frontex 317
Fukuyama, Francis 89, 92, 101

G7/G8 17, 151, 152, 172–4
G20 17, 152, 174–7, 295–6
Gambia vs Myanmar (initiated 2019) 198
game theory 7
GATT (General Agreement on Trade and Tariffs) 151
Gaza 62, 112, 121, 198, 205, 302
GDP per capita 88, 93
Geneva Convention 196, 210
genocide 195–7, 200, 204, 276
Gini coefficients 155
Glasgow Climate Pact 2021, 244
global brands 49, 50, 54
global commons 52, 227, 229
Global Financial Crisis (2008) 30, 44, 183
global governance 13, 19, 56, 84, 89, 106–46, 266–7
global monocultures 49
global social movements 267
Global South 123, 160, 161, 169, 174, 183, 268–9
Global Stocktake 243, 245
global warming 69, 226 see also climate change
Global Witness 272, 274, 276
globalisation
    contemporary global issues 59–70
    definition 41–2
    drivers 42
    economic globalisation 43–5
    global governance 267
    harmony and balance 19
    hegemonic power 89
    impact 56–9
    and regionalism 299–301

sceptics 58
theories 57–9
types of 43–59
glocalisation 50–1, 54
Gold Standard 151
'Golden Arches Theory of Conflict Prevention' 68
'good governance' 152, 266
government, systems of 92
Great Power Politics 84
green capitalism 231
'Green New Deal' 231
greenhouse gas emissions 69, 226, 239–57
Greenpeace 235
greenwashing 235
Guantanamo Bay 219
Gulf Wars 84, 119
Guterres, Antonio 129, 133
Gymshark 46

Haiti 212, 213
hard power 6, 9, 22, 76–7, 82–4
Hardin, Garrett 227
harmony and balance 15, 18, 19
Heavily Indebted Poor Countries Initiative (HIPC) 166, 182
hegemonic power 6, 10, 11, 85, 88–9, 264
Hegemonic Stability Theory 94
Herz, John H. 12
High Ambition Coalition (HAC) 250
Himalayan border 14
Hobbes, Thomas 10, 26, 211, 263
human development approach to poverty 155–6
Human Development Index 156
human nature 13, 21–2
human rights 188–223
    autocratic states 99
    cosmopolitanism 27
    definition 190
    democracy 97
    failed states 99
    global governance 188–223, 284–6
    Global Witness 274
    globalisation 55, 68
    liberalism 13
    monitoring 276
    non-democratic states 99
    realism 4
    regionalism 328
    rogue states 100
    semi-democratic states 98
    UN (United Nations) 110, 135–6, 279
Human Rights Watch (HRW) 210, 277
humanitarianism
    ecocide 273
    global governance 267
    globalisation 52, 55
    humanitarian intervention 211–17
    NATO (North Atlantic Treaty Organisation) 140, 144
    political global governance 121, 122
Huntington, Samuel 49, 67
hyperglobalisers 58

identity politics 49
IGOs (intergovernmental organisations)
    evaluating 270–1
    globalisation 42
    human rights 190, 284–6
    liberalism 15, 16
    lobbying 276
    political globalisation 51–2, 61–2
    and state sovereignty 263
Ikenberry, John 94
IMF (International Monetary Fund)
    compared to World Bank 167
    economic global governance 151, 152, 161–3
    globalisation 44
    growth and stability 154
    power 77, 84, 89
immigration policies 219
import substitution industrialisation 159
inclusivity 270
India
    Coca-Cola 66
    cultural power 77
    emerging powers 86
    Kashmir 19
Indigenous communities 68
inequality 63–5, 154–61, 252, 255–7
inflation 153
interdependence 15–16, 19, 61, 67, 77, 263
Intergovernmental Panel on Climate Change (IPCC) 226, 230, 235–8, 243–4
intergovernmentalism 52, 294, 295, 313, 314, 317–18, 323
international anarchy 5–6, 9, 10–11, 26, 264
International Bank for Reconstruction and Development (IBRD) 151, 163–4
International Campaign for the ICC 210
International Court of Justice (ICJ) 18, 55, 109, 113, 125–7, 195, 196–9, 209–10, 269
International Criminal Court (ICC) 55, 82, 110, 117, 192, 195, 204–7, 209–10
International Criminal Tribunal for Rwanda (ICTR) 200
International Development Association (IDA) 163–4
international law
    anarchical society 27
    customary international law 125, 191
    globalisation 55
    hard power 82
    harmony and balance 16, 18
    human rights 191–210
    significant treaties 195
    state sovereignty 39
    UN (United Nations) 109
international organisations
    globalisation 44
    informal 16–17
    liberalism 13, 16–17
    realism 4, 7
    society of states theory 27
    and the UN 109
international society of states 27
international system 5–9
International Tribunal for the Former Yugoslavia (ICTY) 200, 202
international tribunals 199–203
Interpol 17
invisible hand of the market 157
Iran 80
Iran Nuclear Deal 7, 8, 11
Iraq War 18, 82, 88, 92, 212
ISIS 51, 61, 67
isolationist policies 268
Israel 8, 62, 114, 115, 197–9, 205, 220

Jubilee Debt Campaign 181, 273, 275
judgements and conclusions 343
judicial precedent 195
jurisdiction 271

Kaldor, Mary 67
Kantian Triangle of Peace 16
Kashmir 19
Keohane, Robert 15
Kim Soo-hyun 47
Klein, Naomi 54
Kosovo 139–40, 212, 213
Kyoto Protocol 1997 241–2, 247, 251, 272

League of Nations 108
Least Developed Countries (LDC) 226, 250, 254
Lebanon 201
legitimacy 271
levels-based mark schemes 345–6
liberal democracy 89, 92, 101–2
liberalism see also neoliberalism
    comparative analysis 20–5
    different types of states 100
    economic global governance 178–9
    environment 249
    globalisation 56–7, 265
    good governance 266
    human rights 190–1, 193

judicial precedent 197
main ideas 13–19
polarity 94
pooled sovereignty 309
post-2000 developments in global politics 29–32
and the society of states 27–9
sustainable development 229
use of UN veto 122
Libya 214
Like-Minded Developing States (LMDC) 250
Lisbon Treaty 308, 310, 314, 316, 323
lithium 66
lobbying 210, 233, 272
localism 232
Locke, John 27, 211, 263
Loss and Damage Fund 244, 245, 247, 253–4

Maastricht Treaty 295, 307, 323
Machiavelli, Niccoló 10
Make Poverty History 181, 273, 275
Mali 214
mass atrocity crimes 41
McDonaldization 50
Mearsheimer, John 6, 12
media 46–8, 272
MERCOSUR 298
microfinance 64
migration 48–9, 267, 317, 319
military power
    hard power 6, 11, 76
    increasing military power 12
    regionalism 318, 325, 326
    structural power 82
    unipolar systems 88
    United States 88
Millennium Development Goals 136, 154, 267, 275, 282
mining 66
misinformation 81
modernisation theory of development 157–8
Montevideo Convention 1933 4, 38
Montreal Protocol 236, 237
Morgenthau, Hans 10, 191
multidimensional peacekeeping 118
multidimensional poverty 156–7
multilateralism 121, 171, 249, 268, 285
multinational corporations (MNCs) 159, 272
multipolarity 6, 10, 92, 94, 113, 118–19, 269
mutual coercion 227, 228
mutually assured destruction (MAD) 6, 10, 91
Myanmar 198

Naess, Arne 231
NAFTA (North American Free Trade Agreement) 296, 297, 301, 304, 326
nation states 39
national interests 6
nationalism 49, 268
Nationally Determined Contributions (NDCs) 244–5, 283
nations 39
NATO (North Atlantic Treaty Organisation) 6, 7, 76, 137–44, 318
natural law 27
neoclassical development theory 158
neocolonialism 65, 158, 160, 182
neoliberalism 43, 158
neo-Marxism 158
neorealism (structural realism) 9, 10, 12, 178–9
net zero emissions 230, 231, 245
Netflix 48, 49, 54
New International Economic Order (NIEO) 160
new regionalism 295, 307
'New Wars' thesis 67
NGOs (non-governmental organisations)
    definition 18
    environment 70, 235
    impact 272
    liberalism 13, 16
    realism 4
non-democratic states 18–19, 95–6
Non-Proliferation Treaty 18, 27
non-state actors
    economic global governance 181–2
    environment 233–40
    evaluating 271–2
    human rights 209–10
    liberalism 13, 15
    realism 4
non-violent resolution 135
North Korea 26, 82, 83
North-South divide 160, 161
nuclear weapons 6, 11, 18, 91, 275
Nuremberg trials 199
Nye, Joseph 15, 77, 80

obesity crisis 66
Occupy movement 275, 277
offensive neorealism 11–12
oil 151, 248
old regionalism 295
Organisation of Petroleum Exporting States (OPEC) 250
Oxfam International 182
ozone layer 237

Palestine 38, 113, 114, 115, 197, 205, 220, 302
Paris Agreement 2015, 230, 243–4, 247, 251, 268, 282
Pax Americana 87
payoff matrices 9
peace
    and democracy 18
    EU (European Union) 296, 310
    humanitarian interventions 215
    liberalism 15, 16
    peacebuilding 133, 215
    peacekeeping versus peace enforcement 117–19
    and trade 19
    UN (United Nations) 109, 113, 132–3, 134, 135–7, 139, 143–4, 215
PESCO (Permanent Structured Cooperation) 318, 325
polarity 6, 84–94
political entities 38
political globalisation 44, 51–3, 61, 62
political integration 310–14
political regionalism 295–6, 298, 299, 301
pollution 69
pooled sovereignty 309, 310
Pope 77
populism 54, 89, 101–2, 301
post-2000 developments in global politics 29–32
post-conflict societies 201
Post-Washington Consensus 151
poverty
    autocratic states 99
    civil society 275
    democracy 97
    and development 154–61
    economic global governance 152, 180
    failed states 100
    global governance 281–2
    globalisation 63–5
    measuring poverty and inequality 155–7
    non-democratic states 98
    regionalism 327
    rogue states 100
    semi-democratic states 98
    UN (United Nations) 136–7
    World Bank 165, 166
Poverty Reduction Strategy Papers (PRSPs) 152, 182
power 76–84
    as capabilities 22
    maximisation 11–12
    power politics 6
    realism and liberalism comparative analysis 22–3
    state-centric theory 4

Prisoner's Dilemma 7–8, 12, 17
protectionism 159
protest 18, 89, 235, 267
proxy wars 92, 121, 295
purchasing power parity (PPP) 155
Putin, Vladimir 8, 10, 77, 81, 205

Quad (Quadilateral Security Dialogue) 169, 296
Qualified Majority Voting 314, 316, 319

ratification of treaties 192
Raworth, Kate 229, 230
realism
    classical realism 9, 10, 13
    comparative analysis 20–5
    different types of states 100
    economic global governance 178–9
    environment 249
    globalisation 56–7, 265
    human rights 190–1, 193
    judicial precedent 197
    main ideas 4–13
    neorealism 9, 10, 13
    polarity 94
    pooled sovereignty 309
    post-2000 developments in global politics 29–32
    and the society of states 28–9
    sustainable development 229
    use of UN veto 122
ReArm Europe 318, 327
Red Cross 210
regional blocs 294
regional organisations
    definition 18
    liberalism 15, 16
        political globalisation 51–2
        realism 4, 7
regionalism 292–331
relative gains 7
renewable energy 69, 70, 232, 233
Ricardo, David 157
right to develop 254, 255
right-wing extremism 51, 68, 301
Rio 'Earth Summit' 130, 225, 239–41, 267, 272
robust peacekeeping 118
rogue states 80, 83, 97
Rohingya Muslims 127, 198, 328
Rome Statute 191, 192, 196, 204, 205, 276–7
Rostow, Walter 157
rule of law 51, 52, 55
rules of conduct between states 27
Russia
    annexation 76, 78–9, 82
    economic sanctions 77, 82
    International Criminal Court 205
    invasion of Ukraine 5, 7, 10, 41, 67
    liberalism versus realism 32
    NATO (North Atlantic Treaty Organisation) 140–1
    realism 5, 7, 10
    Shanghai Cooperation Organisation (SCO) 8
    sharp power 80–1
Rwanda 200, 203, 212, 213, 280

Sahel 134–5
sample essays 354–62
sanctions 19, 76, 77, 82
Saudi Arabia 97, 220
Schengen Agreement 316, 319
scrutiny 272
Section A questions 346–8
Section B questions 348–9
Section C questions 349–53
security communities 18
security dilemma 12–13, 18
security integration 316–18
security maximisation 12
security paradox 13
security regionalism 296, 298, 299
self-determination 39
self-help 5, 6, 8, 10, 13
semi-democratic states 95, 98
Sen, Amartya 155
separatism 39
September 11th 2000 (9/11) Terrorist Attack on the US 30
'shadow of the future' 17
shallow ecology 231–2
Shanghai Cooperation Organisation (SCO) 6, 8, 296
sharp power 80, 81
Sierra Leone 201, 214
single markets 267, 295–6, 314, 324
smart power 80
Smith, Adam 157
social media 46–7, 54, 67, 68, 81, 234
society of states theory 26–9
socio-cultural regionalism 300
soft power 77–80
    definition 18
    ethical foreign policy 18
    EU (European Union) 324
    realism 13
    unipolar systems 89
Somalia 211, 213
South Africa vs Israel (initiated 2024) 198–9
sovereign debt 153
sovereignty
    definition 5
    and globalisation 60–3
    internal versus external 39–40
    nation state and state sovereignty 38–41

realism 4–5, 10
society of states theory 28
sovereignty as responsibility 41
state sovereignty 39–40, 263, 324–7
Soviet Union 6, 43
Special Court for Sierra Leone (SCSL) 201, 202
Special Panels for Serious Crimes (East Timor) (SPSC) 200
Special Tribunal for Lebanon (STL) 201
spillover 307
Srebrenica 139, 212, 280
state of nature 27
state sovereignty 39–40, 263, 325–7
state-centric theory 4
states
    classification of states within global politics 84–6
    definition 4, 38
    globalisation 36–72
    and international organisations 269–71
    liberalism 15
    realism 4–13
    realism and liberalism comparative analysis 24–5
steady-state economy 229, 232
Stop Ecocide 235, 272, 276
strong sustainability 232
Structural Adjustment Programme (SAP) 158, 163, 182
structural power 81, 84–5, 89, 324
structural realism see neorealism
subsidiarity 314
substantiated judgements 343
Sudan 5, 121
Suez Canal 45, 119
superpowers 84, 85, 87, 92
supply chains 45, 46
supranationalism
    global governance 263, 276, 294, 295
    globalisation 52, 62
    regionalism 312, 314, 317–18, 323, 326
sustainability 70, 153, 155, 180, 297
sustainable development 228–30, 231
Sustainable Development Goals 112, 129, 130, 136–7, 155, 228–30, 268
synopticity 335
Syria vs Egypt 220

tariffs 13, 43, 53, 151, 157, 295, 297–8
technology
    globalisation 42, 46–7
    hard power 83
terrorism 52, 61, 62, 67
think tanks 235
Thucydides 10
Thunberg, Greta 234
tourism 62

Tokyo tribunals 199
trade
    barriers 43, 297–8, 307
    economic global governance 152, 179, 183
    economic regionalism 296–7
    economic sanctions 77
    globalisation 42, 43, 44
    liberalisation 19
    liberalism 16, 17, 19
    realism 13
    United States 53
    World Trade Organisation (WTO) 17
tragedy of the commons 227
transformationalists 58
transnational corporations (TNCs) 43, 45, 46, 49, 60, 66, 70
transnational issues 19, 51, 52
travel 48–9
Treaty of Westphalia 27, 39
'Trickle Down Economics' 65
Truth Social 68
Türkiye 8, 95, 321

Ukraine 5, 7, 10, 32, 78–9, 140, 205
UN (United Nations)
    aims and roles 109–10
    Charter 39–40, 108, 192–3
    climate change 226
    constitution of 16
    Covenant on Civil and Political Rights 194
    Covenant on Economic, Social and Cultural Rights 194
    Declaration on Human Rights 68, 193–5, 210
    Development Programme (UNDP) 156
    ECOSOC 109, 110, 128–9, 131, 152, 272
    environment 136–7, 235–40
    Environment Assembly 136–7
    Framework Convention on Climate Change (UNFCCC) 228, 233, 238–41, 246–9, 250, 279, 280, 282
    General Assembly 109, 110–12, 115
    global governance 267
    Human Rights Commission (UNHRC) 210
    human rights versus environment 279–81
    Intergovernmental Panel on Climate Change (IPCC) 226, 230, 236–8, 243–4
    International Court of Justice (ICJ) 18, 55, 109, 113, 125–7, 195, 196–9, 209–10, 269
    liberalism 15, 17
    Millennium Development Goals 136–7, 154, 267, 275, 282
    non-member observer states 38
    origins 108
    peacebuilding 270
    Peacebuilding Commission 117, 133, 270
    peacekeeping 109, 113, 132–3, 134, 135–7, 139, 143–4, 215
    political globalisation 51–2
    Responsibility to Protect 41, 68, 211, 212, 215, 267
    Secretariat 109, 129
    Security Council 15, 18, 39, 52, 62, 109, 111, 113–24, 142, 205, 212, 269
    Special Tribunals 195, 199–203
    state recognition 38, 39, 111
    structure 109
    Sustainable Development Goals 112, 129, 130, 136–7, 155, 228–30, 268
    Trusteeship Council 109
    veto 116, 117–18, 120–2, 143
underdevelopment 158, 159
unilateralism 121
unipolar systems 6, 84–87
United States
    anti-globalism 49
    Cold War 6
    death penalty 219
    decline of global political influence 91
    deglobalisation 53
    economic power 88
    environment 66
    global governance 84, 267
    Guantanamo Bay 219
    hard power 82
    hegemonic power 85, 88–90
    humanitarianism 211, 269
    and the ICC 207
    Iran Nuclear Deal 11
    military power 76–7, 88
    NATO (North Atlantic Treaty Organisation) 6, 141
    smart power 80
    soft power 13, 89
    superpowers 85
    US-China trade dispute 172
USMCA (United States–Mexico–Canada Agreement) 296, 297, 300, 304–5, 326, 327

Venezuela 205

Wallerstein, Immanuel 159–60
Waltz, Kenneth 10, 12
war see also conflict
    human nature 9
    inevitability of 9–13
    liberalism 13, 15
    war crimes 197, 199, 200, 204
War on Terror 212
Washington Consensus 151, 158, 182
waste 69, 228
'Western' politics 53–4, 62, 102, 206
workers
    exploitation 65, 68
    protection of 297
World Bank
    compared to IMF 167
    economic global governance 152, 163–8
    food insecurity 169
    globalisation 44
    impact 272
    measuring poverty and inequality 155, 157
    poverty measures 63, 64
    soft power 77
    structural power 84
world government 19, 26–7, 264
World Social Forum 275, 277
World Systems Theory 159–60, 161
World Trade Organisation (WTO)
    economic global governance 152, 168–72
    global governance 267
    globalisation 42, 44, 52
    growth and stability 154
    liberalism 17, 19
    origins of 151
World Trade Report 183

Zambia 168
zero-sum power 6, 13, 249, 269
Zimbabwe 66